How To Think Like a Programmer

How To Think Like a Programmer: Program Design Solutions for the Bewildered

Paul Vickers

COURSE TECHNOLOGY
CENGAGE Learning™

Australia • Brazil • Japan • Korea • Mexico • Singapore • Spain • United Kingdom • United States

COURSE TECHNOLOGY
CENGAGE Learning™

How To Think Like a Programmer: Program Design Solutions for the Bewildered, First Edition

Paul Vickers

For product information and technology assistance, contact **emea.info@cengage.com**.

For permission to use material from this text or product, and for permission queries, email **emea.permissions@cengage.com**.

British Library Cataloguing-in-Publication Data
A catalogue record for this book is available from the British Library.

ISBN: 978-1-40807-954-6

Cengage Learning EMEA
Cheriton House, North Way, Andover, Hampshire, SP10 5BE United Kingdom

Cengage Learning products are represented in Canada by Nelson Education Ltd.

For your lifelong learning solutions, visit **www.cengage.co.uk**

Printed in the UK by Lightning Source
1 2 3 4 5 6 7 8 9 10 – 13

Purchase your next print book, e-book or e-chapter at **www.cengagebrain.com**

For Gina, a truly remarkable woman and a blessing beyond measure

Contents

13 Dynamic Data Structures 357

Preface

> Nothing is more important than to see the sources of invention which are, in my opinion, more interesting than the inventions themselves.
>
> *H. Gottfried Leibnitz (1646–1716)*

It is a fact of modern technology that what appears fantastical and wondrous today will, in a very short time indeed seem vulgar and commonplace. However, it is reassuring that in the discipline of computing the fundamental principles remain unchanged regardless of the technology used to implement them. Thus it is with computer programming. Whether we are talking about the punched-card systems of the 1970s or the interactive graphical user interface compilers of today (another technology that will doubtless seem quaint in a few years), the underlying concepts of data, data types and structures, sequence, iteration, selection, and abstraction remain stable. One can argue that the sophistication of modern technology has removed us from the heart of the computer to such a degree that programming skill is now harder to acquire than previously.

And so to the subject matter of this book. No matter what tools and technologies have been made available to assist the programmer in his task (including first course texts), the fact remains that too often the student of programming remains utterly bewildered and unable to complete his apprenticeship. The purpose of this book is to present the concepts and practices of computer programming in ways that will enable the bewildered novice to grasp just what is required. Using real-world examples and example algorithms (rather than the more traditional technical explanations followed by worked examples), I hope that upon completion of this study the reader will have picked up the essence of the discipline and will even feel the joy that comes with successfully constructing a machine (for that is what a program is) that correctly carries out its makers intentions and instructions. Programming really is fun but only if you are not bewildered.

So, this is a book about computer programming. But it is mostly a book on problem solving. Without the ability to do the latter, the former is very difficult indeed (if not impossible). Unfortunately, introductory programming books and university courses often ignore this fact. As far back as 1971 Gerald Weinberg complained that instead of *"trying to teach principles, ... schools seem devoted to teaching how to program in a single ... language. The objective seems to be to get the student writing some kind of program as soon as possible ... at the expense of limiting the future growth of the programmer"* (Weinberg, 1971). Many beginners come away from programming courses thinking that they're no good at programming and then look for ways in which to avoid all further contact with the subject (even to the extent of changing their university course!). As someone who enjoys programming I find this very sad, especially given that it is my belief that the bewildered student's perception is misplaced. I do not think it is programming they cannot do, rather, they have simply not learned basic principles of problem solving. Without this one will always struggle with writing a computer program because writing a program requires one to understand how to solve problems. I have seen too many pained faces in programming laboratories as the bewildered struggle to write a relatively straightforward program. When questioned they say that they do not know which bit of programming language code to use. Further questioning reveals the real difficulty: too often they simply do not understand the problem they are trying to solve. Hence their attempts to describe a solution to the problem in programming language code (for that is all a program is, a formalized, structured description of a solution to a problem) take them nowhere. Because they only encounter their difficulty when they try to write the solution as a program, the bewildered learner concludes that programming is hard and that he or she cannot do it. But until you have learned to solve problems, you cannot really judge whether or not you can program a computer.

The ancient Greeks developed a systematic approach to solving mathematical problems. Pappus, a mathematician who lived in Alexandria in the early part of the fourth century wrote about this method, although it goes back even earlier to the likes of Euclid (around 300 B.C.). The underlying principle is that of *heuristic* (what Leibnitz called the art of invention) which is a way of discovering solutions to problems when we do not have complete certainty that we are making the right decisions. Some people unkindly call heuristic the process of trial and error. I would like to think that while it certainly involves lots of trial and some error, it is at least based upon reasonable or educated guesswork. In 1945 the Hungarian mathematician George Pólya wrote a marvellous book called *How to Solve It* (Pólya, 1990) in which he brought together the HEURISTIC principles of Euclid and Pappus, Descartes, and Leibnitz to help with the solving of mathematical problems. In a nutshell, Pólya's method offers four basic steps: understand the problem, make a plan for solving the problem, carry out the plan, and reflect upon the solution. For nearly sixty years Pólya has helped students of mathematics to prove theorems and find answers. Unfortunately, computing educators have been slow to realize that Pólya also offers the bewildered programmer a ray of hope. Most introductory text books dive straight into writing program code (usually with an example program that displays "Hello World!" on the screen) and mix problem solving with coding. A few have realized Pólya's approach applies well to programming problems. Geoff Dromey applied it to traditional problems in computer science (Dromey, 1982). Simon Thompson applied it to functional programming problems (Thompson, 1997), and Michael Jackson observed that Pólya's principles apply to software development generally (Jackson, 1995).

So, this book attempts to separate problem solving from code writing. I hope that by bringing Pólya's framework to the task of learning to program the learner will begin to see how to think about tackling programming problems: writing program code and the discipline of program design can only be undertaken once the problem has been well understood.

Finally, throughout the book at points where in the past I have found learners to have particular difficulty you will find some frequently-asked questions (FAQ) typical of the kind asked of me by bewildered students. To encourage a dynamic learning community the book's website (at http://www.cengage.co.uk/vickers) contains a section where readers can submit their own FAQs seeking answers to issues that still cause puzzlement. I would like to encourage readers to submit their own FAQs and I will then provide answers to these on the website as appropriate.

Structure of the Book

The view taken in this book is that there are three areas of essential study, each with its own set of basic principles to be learned:

1. **The real-world domain**: this is concerned with problem understanding and problem solving.
2. **Systematizing the solution**: this is really a process of formalizing and checking our solutions, and hence leads into program design.
3. **The computer domain**: this is concerned with programming language syntax, programming concepts and techniques, and data structures. In other words, how to put our solutions into the computer.

The book is divided into two parts: *The Real-World Domain: Problem Solving and Systematizing the Solution* and *The Computer Domain: Data, Data Structures, and Program Design Solutions*.

There are debates every year in university departments over what should be taught first, design or syntax. In this book I take the pragmatic view that problem solving should really come first as this feeds naturally into design which then feeds into the issues surrounding implementation using the chosen syntax (programming language).

To lessen the difficulty of doing 1 and 2 above without reference to a programming language I have adopted the use of pseudo-code (structured English that is used to represent programming concepts) as a bridge to allow algorithm design without the messiness of an actual programming language.

In Part I, *The Real-World Domain: Problem Solving and Systematizing the Solution*, we deal with the essence of problem solving. We are not concerned here with how to get the computer to do things. We are interested only in making sure we understand the various aspects of real-world problems and then looking at how to get answers to those problems. Chapter 1 serves as an introduction to the book. Chapter 2 introduces the discipline of problem solving and shows how it is a necessary skill for would-be computer programmers. Chapter 3 offers a number of different ways of viewing and understanding problems and introduces the pseudo-code notation. In Chapter 4, we deal with simple real-world problems and, in Chapter 5, we move on to more-complicated examples. In both Chapters 4 and 5, we solve problems and then reflect on our solutions. We then look at how those solutions could be expressed in such as way as to allow them to be used by other people to get answers to those problems and others of the same type. We call this aspect *systematizing* the solution and it is essentially the process of building *algorithms*. Chapter 6 takes the concepts and structures of the first five chapters and expands them to give a wider algorithmic vocabulary by looking at some lower-level control abstractions (iteration and selection types) and the notion of data typing. Chapter 7 introduces some of the high-level techniques and terminology necessary for beginning to think about problems in an object-oriented manner. Chapter 8 completes Part I by providing an introduction to program design techniques and notations.

To solve the problems in Part I we will have explored the ideas of *operations, algorithms, data,* and *variables.* Part II, *The Computer Domain: Data, Data Structures, and Program Design Solutions*, looks at how we use these aspects of problem solving to write algorithms in a formalized way that are much closer to real computer programs that can be executed on a computer. Chapter 9 takes the concept of data introduced in Chapters 5 and 6 provides a more formalized view showing how different data types are manipulated and stored inside a computer's memory. Chapter 10 introduces the concept of sub-programming (functions and procedures) and shows how this can improve program structure. Chapter 11 gives a very quick overview of some of the issues surrounding how to get data into and out of a program. Chapters 12 and 13 show how complex structures of data can be maintained and manipulated within the program, with Chapter 13 providing a full set of algorithms for dealing with some common dynamic data structures. Chapter 14 takes the basic concepts of Object Oriented Programming first introduced in Chapter 7 and puts a bit of meat on the bones by looking at the fundamental Object Oriented principles of encapsulation, inheritance, and polymorphism in more detail. Chapter 15 offers some ideas about how to translate our pseudo-code algorithms into real programming language code. Examples are given in the Processing language which is a simplified dialect of the industry-standard Java language. Finally, Chapter 16 completes the main text and gives some guidance on how to go about testing programs and removing any errors (both syntactic and semantic) from them.

With the exception of Chapters 7 and 14 (and the Processing code in Chapter 15), all the solutions to the problems are of a procedural (imperative) nature. It is my opinion that, even when using an object-oriented language as a first language, the programmer still needs to be able to write procedural code. I would go as far as to say that procedural programming is a foundational skill upon which object-oriented techniques can be built; after all, many class methods in Java still need to be coded procedurally.

I am not a fan of large programming texts as I get the impression that cramming every detail of the language into the book is seen somehow as evidence of high quality and good value. It is almost as if the authors feel they are cheating their readers if they do not present every aspect of the programming language in question. Learning to program is sometimes compared with learning a foreign language. Weinberg went as far as to describe programming as a *"communication between two alien species"* (Weinberg, 1971). When learning a foreign language, primer texts do not cover every aspect of the language, every permutation of tense–mood arrangements. Rather, they focus on getting the beginner up to a level of competence in the essential aspects, such as an understanding of word order, a grasp of the present tense, and a small but workable vocabulary. Thus, I have deliberately kept this book as short as possible. In this book I have tried to present some general principles and ways of thinking that can be applied programming problems in the large and translated to whatever language the reader is eventually required to code the algorithms in.

Above all, enjoy!

Paul Vickers

Stocksfield, Northumberland

October 2008

Acknowledgments

First of all I would like to thank all the students over the best part of the last twenty years who have shared their bewilderment with me. People who are bright and otherwise successful in their studies have struggled to grasp the basics of what lies at the core of computer science courses because of the common mistake of confusing programming with programming languages. I hope that by focusing on the fundamental skill of problem solving within an algorithmic context this book goes some way to removing the bewilderment and helping future students to think like programmers.

Thanks go also to my colleagues past and present whose opinions and insights have helped to mould my ideas. Special thanks must go to John Pardoe, Melv King, and Stu Wade who taught me how to program in the first place.

A big thank-you to the editorial and production team at Cengage Learning who have provided a model for author-publisher relationships. Special mentions must go to: Gaynor Redvers-Mutton who picked up the project and ran with it, and through patience and clever cajoling got me to deliver it on time – masterfully done! To Matthew Lane, who dealt with my frequent and pedantic queries with good grace. To Alissa Chappell for her support in aspects of technical production. And to the anonymous reviewers of the manuscript whose support for the project and incisive comments have improved the book – any faults that remain are entirely my own.

The last-minute rush to complete the manuscript on time required a lot of late-night sessions. I must thank my [XX] Black Label clan mates for helping to keep me alert by playing online team matches with me in Insomniac Games' (an appropriate name for the company given the circumstances) *Resistance: Fall of Man* during short breaks at all hours of the night.

Finally, I must thank Gina, Caitlin, Carys, and Zachary who have tolerated too many evenings and weekends with me locked in my study. Gina: thanks for holding the fort and also for redrawing my scruffy diagrams.

The Real-World Domain: Problem Solving and Systematizing the Solution

Part I deals with the essence of problem solving. We are not concerned here with how to get the computer to do things. We are interested only in making sure we understand the various aspects of real-world problems and then looking at how to get answers to those problems. Chapter 2 introduces the discipline of problem solving and shows how it is a necessary skill for would-be computer programmers. Chapter 3 offers a number of different ways of viewing and understanding problems and introduces the pseudo-code notation. In Chapter 4, we deal with simple real-world problems and, in Chapter 5, we move on to more complicated examples. In both Chapters 4 and 5, we solve problems and then reflect on our solutions. We then look at how those solutions could be expressed in such as way as to allow them to be used by other people to get answers to those problems and others of the same type. We call this aspect *systematizing* the solution and it is essentially the process of building *algorithms.* Chapter 6 takes the concepts and structures of the first five chapters and expands them to give a wider algorithmic vocabulary by looking at some lower-level control abstractions (iteration and selection types) and the notion of data typing. Chapter 7 introduces some of the high-level techniques and terminology necessary for beginning to think about problems in an object-oriented manner. Chapter 8 completes Part I by providing an introduction to program design techniques and notations.

Introduction: Starting to Think Like a Programmer

Learning Objectives

- Understand how to use the book and its special features
- Understand how programs are structured recipes (algorithms) to calculate/compute the answer to a given problem
- See how using abstraction is necessary for solving problems
- Understand the difference between solving problems and writing computer programming language code

This chapter serves two purposes. First, it describes for whom the book is intended, how the book is structured, and how to use it. Secondly, you will learn what a computer program is, why programmers write programs, and what they use to write those programs. You will discover the difference between writing program code and solving problems and you will learn why good programmers are, primarily, good problem solvers.

1.1   Who Is This Book For?

This book has two main audiences. The first audience is those who are taking an introductory programming or computer science course in which the first four to six weeks are spent developing the skills necessary to think like a programmer (algorithmically) and the course follows a more traditional programming language text.[1] The second audience is the "bewildered" programmer. If you can identify yourself in one or more of the following descriptions, then this book is also intended for you:

- You have just started to learn a programming language at a university or college. You are only a little way into the course, but already you are starting to feel lost and panicky and may even be falling behind.

- You have tried to learn programming and have come away feeling that it is terribly difficult. You have either fallen at the first hurdle or have finished an introductory course, but in either case you are left feeling bewildered with a sense that you never really understood it. If someone were to ask you which aspects of the subject you were having particular difficulty with, you would reply "all of it".

- You have not learned any programming before, but it is a mandatory part of your university or college degree (which may not even be in Computer Science or Engineering). You feel anxious about it.

- You are taking, or are about to take, an introductory programming course. You have had a look at the set textbook and even the first few chapters seem too advanced for you.

- You are a secondary/high school student and you need an introductory book to get you started with the basics.

- You are a mature reader. You are not necessarily on a formal course of study (though you may be) and you would like to find out what computer programming is about. Perhaps you have had a look at some other books and they all seem too advanced, too technical (even the introductory ones). You do not think you are a dummy or even an idiot, but you would like to see if you can get a foothold on what appears to be an interesting subject.

If you have identified yourself in the above list then continue reading. If you have not, continue reading anyway so that you can recommend this book to people you know who need to read it (and who can then stop bugging you for help!).

1.2   Routes and Entry Points

I am aware that readers will approach this book with different needs and varying levels of prior knowledge and experience, so it may not be appropriate for all to read the book all the way through in a linear fashion. The book is quite long and so has a number of possible routes through it depending on the reader's needs. Below are some recommended routes through the book. You should start by choosing the route description that most closely fits your own situation.

---

[1] If this book is being used at pre college/university level then it might be used over an entire term or semester.

Of course, you can always deviate from the route if you want to read more (or less), or you find that the route is not for you after all. Each route has a sequence of Core reading followed by some Elective reading. The Core plan covers the aims of the Route whilst the Elective offers optional reading that will enhance the Route.

Route 1: The Grand Tour

This route is for the complete novice who has no prior experience and wants to learn the principles of computer programming without the complications of working in a real programming language. You have not been bewildered by prior experience, but think that programming is probably quite hard and that it probably will bewilder you.

Core: Chapter 1 → Chapter 2 → Chapter 3 → Chapter 4 → Chapter 5 → Chapter 6 → Chapter 8 → Chapter 9 → Chapter 10 → Chapter 11 → Chapter 12 → Chapter 13 → Chapter 16

Elective: Reflections, Chapters 7, 14, 15

Route 2: An Overview for the Bewildered

If you have tried studying programming and have been left truly bewildered by all the technical details of programming languages, or if you want to learn about programming for the first time but do not want to go too far into the technical details yet, then you can get a good overview and grounding by reading Part I.

Core: Chapter 1 → Chapter 2 → Chapter 3 → Chapter 4 → Chapter 5 → Chapter 6 → Chapter 8

Elective: Chapter 7 and (optionally) Chapter 14

Route 3: Problem Solving

This route is for those who already know the basics of constructing computer programs but who feel the need for a refresher in problem solving.

Core: Read in depth Chapter 1 → Chapter 2 → Chapter 3 → Chapter 4 → Chapter 5 then scan Chapters 6, 8, 9, 10, 11, 12, 13, and 16 which show structured thinking applied to common programming concepts.

Elective: If you need to work in an object-oriented language then also read Chapters 7, 14, and 15.

Route 4: Introduction to Data Types, Data Structures, and Programming Structures

This route is suitable if you have already gone through the overview (Route 2) or are confident in your problem-solving abilities and you now want an introduction to the more technical aspects of programming without delving into a particular language.

Core: *Chapter 9* → *Chapter 10* → *Chapter 11* → *Chapter 12* → *Chapter 13*

Elective: *Chapter 14* → *Chapter 15*

1.3   Conventions and Learning Aids Used in This Book

This book uses a number of techniques that have been designed to help you get the most out of its content. These are explained below.

Think Spots

The Think Spot is a point in the text where a question (or a number of questions) is raised for you to think about. To get the most benefit you should take a little time to think about the questions rather than just reading them and moving straight on. The famous Kodak Picture Spot signs at Disney World are sited at places where a great photograph can be taken; similarly, the Think Spot is located at points where you will really benefit from some reflective thinking and so develop the bigger picture.

In-text Exercises

Throughout the book you will see a picture of a pencil in the margins alongside some text in a shaded box denoting a short exercise:

This is a short exercise.

As these exercises are intended to help you understand a particular concept, you should not really proceed beyond an exercise until you have had a reasonable attempt at solving it. The exercises are like the Think Spots inasmuch as you need to stop and think, but unlike the Think Spots, you also need to physically do something such as sketching a solution, walking through a problem, or discussing something with a friend.

If an in-text exercise looks like this with a key in the margin, then a solution is also available in Appendix C. Just go to the In-text exercises section for the corresponding chapter in Appendix C and then look for the number that appears next to the key.

This is a short exercise with a solution available in Appendix C.

Key Terms and Important Points

Key terms   ▶ Key terms and important points appear in the margin next to the paragraph or section in which they are introduced or defined. Together with the index this feature should make it easier for you to find what you are looking for.

Brian Wildebeest FAQ

Meet Mr B. Wildebeest. Brian is a wildebeest (also known as a 'gnu' and pronounced 'will-dur-beest') and usually he is happy.

However, sometimes Brian is a bewildered wildebeest at which times he looks like this:

Throughout the book you will see pictures of Brian looking bewildered in the margin. He appears at points where beginning programmers often have trouble understanding the point being made. Further down the page (or possibly on the next page) after seeing Brian you will find a box like this:

I don't understand why you said . . .

This is a common misunderstanding which arises from . . .

In the box is a question Brian the bewildered programmer is asking about the material next to which his picture appeared. Brian's queries are the kinds of frequently-asked questions (FAQ) I have been asked over the years by beginning programmers. The answer to the FAQ usually appears in the box below the question, though sometimes you are required to try to answer Brian's FAQ yourself.

The book's accompanying website (at www.cengage.co.uk/vickers) contains a section where readers can submit their own FAQs seeking answers to issues that still cause puzzlement. I would like to encourage readers to submit their own FAQs and I will then provide answers to these on the website as appropriate.

End-of-chapter Exercises

Each chapter has exercises at the end. The exercises are designed to help you reflect on what has been covered in that chapter. Any time you cannot complete an exercise suggests that you would benefit from going over the material again. Some exercises may be based on a single section (identified by the heading number), others may require ideas from several sections, and a few bring together the whole chapter. Solutions to selected exercises are given in Appendix C.

Projects

After the normal end-of-chapter exercises you will find some longer project-style exercises. These longer exercises are themed and will give you practice in incrementally building larger and larger solutions to more complex problems. The initial themes are introduced in the exercises at the end of this chapter and are then developed with each subsequent chapter. In these projects, you will be working toward developing complete programs that make use of most of the programming techniques discussed in this book. The projects cover a range of different problem scenarios, such as constructing a vending machine algorithm, decoding hazchem signs, working with Roman numerals and dates, playing with sentences that use all the letters of the alphabet, and working with ISBNs for an online bookstore.

Layout

All programming language code, pseudo-code (Chapter 3), examples of text that would appear on a computer screen or in a file on the computer's hard disc (or removable diskette), and examples of text that would be entered into a computer via the keyboard will appear in `this monospaced typewriter-style font`.

Reflections

Sometimes you will see a word or phrase set in SMALL CAPITAL LETTERS. Such words and phrases are the titles of short reflective opinion pieces that appear in the Reflections chapter (immediately following Chapter 16). These *Reflections* are designed to introduce some more complicated ideas that the interested reader can use to deepen their understanding of some of the problems and issues faced by programmers today.

1.4 Why Do We Write Programs and What *Are* They?

People write programs for a number of reasons. Authors like to use computers to help with the jobs of typing in and laying out text, checking their spelling, and so forth. Scientists and mathematicians use computers to calculate the answers to complex problems. Musicians and composers use the signal processing capabilities of computers to manipulate sound. In all cases, before the computer can carry out these tasks we must first tell it how to perform them. We do this by first solving the problem of deciding how the task can be carried out, and then expressing that solution in a form that can be turned into something the computer can interpret. The first stage (deciding how the task can be carried out) is the really important part as without doing this well we cannot progress to feeding the information into the computer.

Many beginners approach computer programming with a sense of awe, as if a computer program is some mystical artefact that only those initiated into the secret and black arts of computer science can produce. It is true that some programs are phenomenally complex comprising tens of millions of lines of programming language code.[2] But, at its heart a computer program is nothing more than a sequence of instructions to tell a machine (the computer) to do something specific.[3] The word processor I used to write this book is a program running on my home computer. When I use an ATM (cash machine) I am interacting with a program that decides whether there is enough money in my account to meet my withdrawal request. When I select a hot wash to get my cotton shirts really clean I am telling my washing machine to use the program (set of instructions) that will draw and heat enough water, release the detergent at the right time, rinse with cool water, and so on.

If you think about it, a computer program is in many ways just like a recipe. If you have ever cooked a meal then you will recall having to carry out particular tasks in a certain order. Even something as simple as making buttered toast or muffins requires that you spread the butter *after* the bread/muffin has come out of the toaster. You successfully make buttered toast or muffins (and keep your toaster in good working order) when you carry out the steps in the right order.

If you have never done so, find a cookery book and look at some of the recipes. You will see all the things you have to do in order to prepare various meals.

A good recipe is one that clearly sets out all that you have to do and when, that gives precise quantities for the ingredients, and that tells you what temperature to use in the oven and for how long to cook the dish. If the instructions are well set out then it should be possible for anyone to follow them and produce the desired result.

A musical score is a bit like a program too. Over hundreds of years musicians and composers have developed formalized languages of notation that allow musical instructions to be communicated on paper. A music score indicates all the notes to be played including their durations and volumes. Sections of the score can be marked for repetition including alternate endings to repeated phrases. Other marks tell the musician to speed up, slow down, pause, play louder, play more softly, etc. As long as a musician knows how to read and interpret a score then he or she can play music written by somebody else. The score in Figure 1.1 is presented in Western musical notation and shows a simple piece of piano music. It has a repeated section and alternative endings for the repeated section.

1.5 Teaching Approach

What is needed by the novice programmer before all else is an understanding of the processes involved in examining and analyzing problems, in understanding the component parts of a problem, and in understanding what is

---

[2] It has been estimated that some of today's very large computer systems are the most complex artefacts ever built.

[3] Actually, the program may itself be considered a machine, only one built from logic rather than metal and plastic. For a clear and concise discussion of the program as machine, see *Software Requirements and Specifications* (Jackson, 1995).

FIGURE 1.1   **A simple musical score: In this piece of music the first two bars are played through three times. The first two times they are followed by the music in Bar 3, and by the fourth bar after the third play through. The dots before the third bar line indicate that the previous section is to be repeated. The brackets with numbers indicate what should be played and how many times.**

required. You, the learner, then need to be able to solve the problem and check your solution for mistakes, inconsistencies, and limitations. Then you must be able to write down your plan for solving the problem in such a way that your solution can be repeatedly applied to the problem even when some of its values are altered.[4] Once this ability is acquired then, and only then, should you concern yourself with the details of programming languages. There is little use trying to write programs in programming language code if you do not first know how to solve the underlying problem, or worse, even understand the problem you have been asked to write a program to solve.

The philosophy behind this book is that before we can write programs on a computer we must first learn to think like a programmer. This can be approached in three stages:

1. Problem understanding and problem solving
2. Writing solutions in a structured form (algorithms)
3. Writing algorithms in a programming language

The book is divided into two parts. In Part I the focus is on learning how to think about and solve problems (Stages 1 and 2). The types of problems to be solved in Part I are real-world tasks with which you are probably already familiar (such as making a pot of coffee, working out how many cans of paint are needed to decorate a room, etc.). These problems will contain the main elements found in programming problems. Once you understand how to solve these types of problems then you can turn, with more confidence, to the task of writing real programs. In Part II you will learn how to take these problem-solving skills and use them to write algorithms in a formalized way that are much closer to real computer programs (moving into Stage 3).

---

[4] For example, imagine if the problem were to calculate the monthly payments on a loan. Your solution should work for all the possible values of loan amount, loan duration, interest rate, and so on, and not just for the example numbers given in the problem specification.

The three-stage approach of the book mirrors the approach taken in writing a program. Before starting to think about writing any programming code, we must first focus on the problem statement, that is, on the *real-world domain*. First we must *understand* the problem and then we try *solving* it. Once we think we have solved it, we *systematize* our solution by writing it out in a more formal way as a series of steps that can be followed by another person.

Only after we have understood the problem and, through careful reflection, checking, and evaluation, have convinced ourselves (as far as we are able) that our solution is correct *and* as easy as possible for someone else to understand, do we then go into the *computer domain* and write our solution as a computer program. We can then enter the program into a computer and test that it works.

Algorithms

Algorithm is a common word in programming circles. An algorithm is a rule, or a finite set of steps, for solving a mathematical problem. In computing it means a set of procedures for solving a problem or computing a result. The word *algorithm* is a derivation of Al-Khwarizmi (native of Khwarizm), the name given to the ninth-century mathematician Abu Ja'far Mohammed ben Musa who came from Khwarizm (modern day Khiva in the south of Uzbekistan). Thus, this book is about learning how to understand problems and design algorithms that are solutions to those problems.

Abstraction: Taking a Higher View

One thing all programmers do, whether they realize it or not, is use something called ABSTRACTION. Abstraction happens when we view something in general terms without focusing on its concrete details. For example, if you talk about driving in your car, the word *car* is really an abstraction for the specific

FIGURE 1.2   **Abu Ja'far Mohammed, aka Al-Khwarizmi after whom the algorithm is named**

individual car you drive. Your car will be different from my car. Even two cars of the same make, model, year, and specification are still different from each other inasmuch as they are both *individuals. Person* is an abstraction, as are *man, woman, child, boy, girl*, and so on. We all use abstraction in our everyday lives; indeed, without it we would not be able to function for it enables us to ignore all the fine details that would otherwise overwhelm us. The money in my pocket (how much, what currency, how many coins, what year were they minted, how many notes, their serial numbers), the people in the shop (how many men, women, boys, girls, what are their names, nationalities, ethnic groups, ages, heights, educational qualifications, first languages, etc.), and the stars in the sky are all abstract ways of managing an otherwise unmanageable amount of information.

Programmers use abstraction as a way of simplifying and managing detail. However, unlike most of our everyday abstractions, programmers do not actually ignore the detail, instead they *defer* its consideration. At some point the detail will need to be considered. Part of being a programmer is learning how to juggle abstractions, ignoring the fine detail when it is appropriate to do so.

This book follows the practice of dealing with **control abstraction** and **data abstraction** separately. The algorithms you will learn to build in this book **control** and manipulate **data** in order to produce desired results. When you withdraw money from your bank you are performing control (the sequence of actions necessary to withdraw the money) to manipulate data (the amount of money in your account, the date it was withdrawn, and so forth). Regarding data, this book takes a highly abstract view treating all the data in the problems it presents simply as values. Our control abstractions take a fairly general form in the beginning but as the book progresses the level of abstraction is lowered as we consider more specialized ways of performing actions.

Heuristic

This book takes a HEURISTIC approach to solving problems and expressing those solutions as algorithms. Having solved the problem and produced a corresponding algorithm, the programmer would then translate the algorithm into programming language code (a lower level of abstraction). When presented with an algorithm in a computer programming language such as Java or BASIC, the computer can carry out the instructions in the algorithm many millions of times faster (and more reliably and accurately) than any person could.

Most books jump right away into the specific requirements of a given programming language and the learner will, through no fault of his or her own, associate the art of programming with writing instructions in a programming language. But using a programming language is one of the final steps in the process of writing a program. This book focuses on teaching you to concentrate on the most important stages: understanding the problem at hand and solving it algorithmically.

Too many beginning programmers blend problem solving with coding and treat them as one activity and then (reasonably) see programming as hard. Problem solving requires thinking about the problem at a high level of abstraction while

FIGURE 1.3   **Abstraction in the programming process**

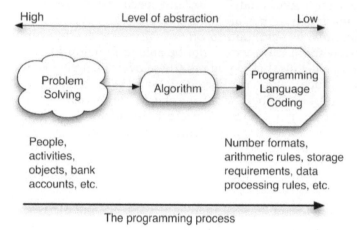

The programming process

writing programming language code requires a very low level of abstraction. Inevitably, the learner starts trying to apply the very low level of abstractions in their thinking about the problem. In fact, if problem solving and coding are separated we discover that the coding aspects are reasonably straightforward while it is really problem solving where the difficulty lies.

One skill you will develop as a programmer is being able to think in terms of high-level abstractions (understanding and thinking about the problem at hand) and in terms of low-level abstractions (individual data items, their format, and their status) simultaneously. However, having witnessed the confusion that can arise when a beginner is asked to do this from the very beginning, I decided in this book to make a clear separation between the high-level problem-solving skills and the low-level language-coding skills. Once you have become comfortable in approaching problems and producing algorithmic solutions, it is then time to think about translating the algorithms into a programming language. Eventually, after learning how to solve problems and then how to translate algorithms into programming language code you will find yourself able to mix the low-level abstractions with the high-level ones and the boundary between problem solving and writing in the chosen programming language will become more fluid.

Getting the Most from This Book

To get the most out of the book (and especially the exercises) you will find it helpful to get a willing friend or relative who can try out your solutions. If your friend can follow your instructions without seeking clarification from you and, using your instructions, can successfully complete the task or calculate the right answers, then you have begun to grasp problem solving and solution description. What you will have done is solve the general problem and create a set of steps and instructions that, when followed exactly, will allow you (or anybody else using the instructions) to solve any specific problem of the same type. In fact, the instructions are the solution to the problem and anyone using them no longer has to solve the problem, they simply have to follow some steps to calculate (or compute) the required answer.

1.6 Structure of the Book

The book is set out in the following way. In Chapter 2 we will look at what is meant by problem solving and how learning to solve problems will help us to become computer programmers. We will learn how to apply a structured strategy for problem solving. This strategy has steps dealing with understanding and describing the problem, planning how to solve it, and testing the solution.

Chapter 3 introduces different ways to think about problems and provides a form of structured English called *pseudo-code* that we will use to write down our algorithms (solutions to problems).

Chapters 4 and 5 are concerned with a few real-world problems that are used to develop skills in problem analysis and solution. The complexity of the problems gradually increases during the course of the two chapters to allow the introduction of basic programming concepts and techniques that you need in order to be able to think like a programmer, to solve problems, and to write down systematic solutions.

Chapter 6 takes our basic problem-solving skills and adds some more special-ized vocabulary with which we will develop a repertoire of standard structures for implementing solutions to common programming problems.

Chapter 7 takes a small excursion into a different way of approaching programming and problem solving. Today object-oriented programming is very common and this chapter introduces some of the very basic concepts of this approach and shows how we can begin to think in object-oriented terms.

Solving the problem is the process of deriving a correct set of instructions that would enable us (or our friend) to calculate the right answer every time. By writing the instructions down in such a way that they are unambiguous and can be easily followed by anybody reading them, you have created an effective solution. If your solution does not involve unnecessary steps and is easily followed, then you have a good solution. A bad solution would be one that is hard to follow or is clumsy, or both (though this is a general rule that does not always apply – sometimes speed of execution is more important than elegance or comprehensibility). Therefore, in Chapter 8 we will look at some of the techniques available to you for designing good programs that are, after all, just solutions to problems.

Into the Computer Domain

In Part II (Chapters 9–16) we will move closer to the computer by looking at some of the common ways programs load, save, organize, and structure their data. Chapter 9 takes the concept of data introduced in Chapters 5 and 6 and provides a more formalized view showing how different data types are manipulated and stored inside a computer's memory. Chapter 10 introduces the concept of sub-programming (functions and procedures) and shows how this can improve program structure. Chapter 11 gives a very quick overview of some of the issues surrounding how to get data into and out of a program. Chapters 12 and 13 show how complex structures of data can be maintained and manipulated within the program, with Chapter 13 providing a full set of algorithms for dealing with some common dynamic data structures. Chapter 14 takes the basic concepts of object- oriented programming first introduced in Chapter 7 and puts a bit of meat on the bones by looking at the fundamental object-oriented principles of encapsulation, inheritance, and polymorphism in more detail. Chapter 15 offers some ideas about how to translate our pseudo-code algorithms into real programming language code. Examples are given in the Processing language which is a simplified dialect of the industry-standard Java language. Finally, Chapter 16 gives some guidance on how to go about testing your programs and removing any errors (both syntactic and semantic) from them.

Pseudo-code: An Algorithmic Language

As you probably have observed, people tend to use natural language (especially spoken language) imprecisely and meanings are often ambiguous.[5] Imagine the friend you have chosen to follow the instructions you will be writing down as you work through this book is unspeakably stupid and speaks only one language that has about thirty words in it. He is unable to interpret vague or woolly instructions and will reject any instructions that do not conform to the exact grammatical rules of his own, small language. Furthermore, he will slavishly obey everything you say to the letter. Imagine how careful you would have to be to write down your solution exactly right so that your friend could understand it and carry out your wishes. That is precisely how it is with a computer that cannot think for itself. For this reason, although this part of the book does not deal with an actual programming language, it does use a form of structured English (called *pseudo-code*) for expressing solutions to problems. The pseudo-code used in this book is first introduced in Chapter 3. Learning to use pseudo-code provides a solid foundation for making the move to a computer programming language later on.

---

[5] Take the following anonymous book dedication: "to my parents, George Pólya and God." What does that mean? Surely the author is not claiming that God is one of his parents? The sentence is syntactically (grammatically) correct though its meaning can be misunderstood. The addition of an extra comma makes things much clearer: "to my parents, George Pólya, and God." Most people are taught not to put a comma after the element that precedes the "and" in a list, yet in this case adding the *serial comma* really helps to make the author's meaning crystal clear. You may be interested to know that the serial comma is also known as the Oxford comma as it is a stylistic practice of the Oxford University Press (OUP). The OUP uses it precisely because it removes ambiguity from lists. Most people do not use it, but I do. If you look closely you will see that it is used throughout this book. You hadn't noticed? Shame on you, programmers need to have an eye for detail you know.

1.7 Coding Versus Problem Solving

We can say that a recipe is a solution to the problem of preparing a meal. Likewise, a computer program is a description of a solution to a computational or logic problem that is carried out by a computer rather than a person. The problem may be to work out the amount of tax we owe or to calculate the average mark of a university student. The problem may even be something as general as allowing a person to enter text, amend it, move it around, apply various formatting to it, save it, and print it out (just what a word processor does). However, in all these cases the program is the series of steps that, if followed, will lead to the desired outcome (assuming the program was correctly written). However, notice that the program does not actually solve the problem at hand,[6] rather it *calculates* (or computes) the *answer* to the problem. That is, it calculates the correct tax or it correctly stores the text entered by the user of the word processor. The solution to the problem is provided by **you**, the programmer. It is you who solves the problem by deciding the correct series of instructions that, when followed, result in the desired outcome. The process of solving the problem is really the essence of computer programming. Many people are fooled into thinking that writing programming language code is what defines programming. Not so. Writing the code is merely the stage of expressing the solution to the problem in a way that it can be communicated to the computer. Once we have the solution, correctly expressing it in the chosen programming language does take skill and experience, but to be able to write the program code we must first solve the problem. Moreover, before we can solve the problem we must first understand it. It is one thing to try to write the program code for a problem we understand but have not completely solved yet (though this is still bad practice); it is quite another thing to try to write the code for a problem we do not even understand. Explaining tasks to a person and to a computer is essentially the same; the difference is the required level of precision, or un-ambiguity (abstraction), in the language used.

1.8 Chapter Summary

In addition to learning how this book is organized and the various ways it can be read, we also discussed what computer programs are, why we write them, and how good problem-solving skills are essential for successful programming. The programming process can be thought of as a three-stage activity: in the first two stages, we work on understanding and solving the underlying problem. When that is accomplished we proceed to Stage 3, which is translating the problem solution into programming language code ready for compilation and execution on the computer.

Many beginners go astray because they start at Stage 3, that is, they read the problem definition and immediately try writing programming code. This is a major cause of bewilderment, hence the emphasis in this book is on doing

---

[6] Certain problems in mathematics and engineering excepted.

Stages 1 and 2 properly. Before moving on to discussing the nature of problem solving in the next chapter, try the exercises below to make sure you have grasped the ideas presented in this chapter.

1.9   Exercises

1. What is an algorithm?

2. What is a program? Try giving an answer in no more than thirty words. Do you know someone who is very poor at understanding technology (usually they cannot program their video recorder or set the stations on their car radio)? If so, how would you explain to him or her what a computer program is?

3. Describe your wallet using three different levels of abstraction: low (as many details as you can think of), medium (the main points), and high (identifying characteristics only).

4. *Put on my shoes* is a highly abstract description of a common task. To describe the task at a lower level of abstraction requires some details to be known. Jot down some of the main pieces of information that are needed to be able to describe step-by-step the process of putting on a pair of shoes.

5. Learning to write Java/C/Visual Basic/programming language of your choice is not the same thing as learning to program. Why not?

6. What were the causes of the First World War?

1.10   Projects

Below are the four themed projects that will be used to develop your programming skills throughout the rest of the book. After each set of end-of-chapter exercises you will find additional exercises related to one or more of these projects. As you progress through the book you will find yourself extending your solutions until you have outline algorithms for complete programs. Your task for this chapter is to read through the project descriptions and familiarize yourself with their contents. Try to identify what problems might exist.

StockSnackz Vending Machine

The University of Stocksfield has installed a StockSnackz brand vending machine in its staff common room for the benefit of the faculty. The University places a high value on its staff so the machine dispenses free snacks including chocolate, muesli bars, apples, popcorn, and cheese puffs. Drawing upon your own experiences of using vending machines, think about the problems associated with maintaining the StockSnackz machine: How will the user select an item? Which items should be dispensed? What happens when the machine runs out of an item? What information does the machine owner need to know about the number of dispensed snacks? If the snacks were not free, how is money taken and change given?

Stocksfield Fire Service: Hazchem Signs

Attached to the back of trucks transporting chemicals in many countries you will find a hazchem sign (Figure 1.4).The three-character code at the top is the EAC, or Emergency Action Code, which tells firefighters how to deal with a chemical spillage and fire.

FIGURE 1.4   **Hazchem sign**

The first character of the EAC is a number identifying the method to be used for fighting any fire. The second character is a letter identifying the safety precautions to be taken by firefighters, whether a violent or explosive reaction is possible, and whether to dilute or contain any spill. The third character is either blank or an E indicating the existence of a public safety hazard. The four-digit code is the United Nations substance identification number that is used to find out the exact name of the chemical. The hazard warning diamond gives specific information about the nature of the hazard. Table 1.1 shows how to decode the EAC.

What patterns can you see in Table 1.1? How might these patterns help in solving problems related to the decoding of an Emergency Action Code?

Puzzle World: Roman Numerals and Chronograms

We express numbers in base 10 using digits derived from a Hindu-Arabic system. Arithmetic is straightforward in this system. However, consider the Roman Empire that had an altogether different numbering system. In the Roman system, numbers are represented by combinations of the primitives given in Table 1.2 below. The number 51 is written as LI, the number 1,500 is written as MD, and so on. Further, the numbers 4, 9, 40, 90, 400, and 900 are written as IV, IX, XL, XC, CD, and CM respectively. Thus, 14 is XIV, 99 is XCIX, etc. (What is common to the numbers 9, 40, 90, and 900?) In this system, the year 1999 would be written as MCMXCIX and the year 2007 as MMVII.

As you can imagine, arithmetic is not so simple using such numbers. For example, consider the simple sum 1,999 + 2,007 using Roman numerals:

$$MCMCXIX + MMVII = ?$$

Table 1.1   **Emergency Action Code: required firefighting methods and precautions**

1	Coarse spray	3	Foam
2	Fine spray	4	Dry agent

P	V	LTS(CPC)	Dilute spillage
R			
S	V	BA & fire kit	
T			
W	V	LTS(CPC)	Contain spillage
X			
Y	V	BA & fire kit	
Z			
E		Public safety hazard	

Key

V = Can be violently or explosively reactive

BA = Breathing apparatus

LTS = Liquid-tight Suit/Chemical Protection Suit and BA required

DILUTE = Spillage may be washed away when greatly diluted with large quantities of water.

CONTAIN = Spillage must not enter water courses or drains.

DRY AGENT = Water must not be allowed to contact substance.

Table 1.2   **The basic Roman numerals**

Roman Numeral	Decimal Equivalent
I	1
V	5
X	10
L	50
C	100
D	500
M	1000

The answer is MMMMVI. Why do we need to know about Roman numerals today? The media industry still uses them. TV shows have the year of production expressed in Roman numerals, as do some movies, books, and so on. The pages in the front matter of books (before the first chapter) are numbered using Roman numerals with Arabic digits being reserved for the main body (look at the page numbers for the preface in this book).

Imagine you are writing software for a media production company that needs a reliable way of dealing with translation of dates into Roman numerals. What sorts of problems might you face in converting between decimal numbers and Roman numerals?

Pangrams: Holoalphabetic Sentences

Pangrams are holoalphabetic, that is words or sentences that contain every letter in the alphabet. Here is a famous one used by computers to show how text looks in different fonts: *The quick brown fox jumps over the lazy dog.* Pangrams are useful in digital typography because they demonstrate all the letters in a font within a more meaningful context than just writing the alphabet – the interactions between the letters are also easier to see.

The "perfect" pangram is *isogrammatic,* that is, it uses each letter only once. It is extremely hard to produce meaningful isogrammatic pangrams in English. For example, here is one that uses only 26 letters:

Quartz glyph job vex'd cwm finks.

It is not terribly meaningful even if they are all real words. Most pangrams are not isogrammatic, so the next goal is to make them as close to being isogrammatic as possible. Here are some more pangrams with their letter count shown in parentheses.

Pack my box with five dozen liquor jugs (32, *e, i,* and *o* repeated).
Waltz, bad nymph, for quick jigs vex (28, only *a* and *i* repeated – not as meaningful though).
Six plump boys guzzled cheap raw vodka quite joyfully (46).
Sympathizing would fix Quaker objectives (36).
Quick waxy bugs jump the frozen veldt (31).
Brick quiz whangs jumpy veldt fox (27).

Think about what problems exist in constructing a pangram and in determining whether a sentence is a pangram. If it is, determine if it is isogrammatic.

Online Bookstore: ISBNs

The International Standard Book Number (ISBN) is a unique 10- or 13-digit number used to identify books. The system was invented in 1966 (then simply called SBN – Standard Book Numbering) by W.H. Smith (the UK bookseller and stationer) and was adopted as an international standard (ISO 2108) in 1970. From January 2007, ISBNs have 13 rather than 10 digits.

FIGURE 1.5   **Anatomy of the International Standard Book Number (ISBN)**

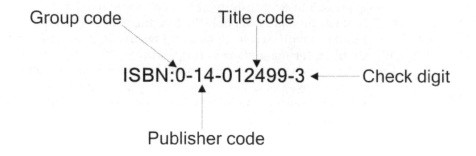

The number comprises four parts:

1. The country of origin or language code (called the group code)
2. The publisher's code
3. A number for the book title
4. A check digit

The different parts can have different lengths and usually are printed with hyphens separating the blocks (the hyphens are not part of the number). The check digit is introduced to ensure that the previous nine digits have been correctly transcribed. It can be a digit (0–9) or the character 'X' (representing the value 10 – it is not necessary yet to understand how the check digit is calculated).

Until January 2007 all ISBNs were 10 digits. A new 13-digit format was introduced in January 2007 (known as ISBN-13 or "Bookland EAN"). All 10-digit ISBNs can be converted to ISBN-13 by adding a prefix of 978 and recalculating the check digit. The 10-digit ISBN 0-14-012499-3 becomes 978-0-14-012499-6 and 0-003-22371-X becomes 978-0-003-22371-2. In the following chapters, you will find exercises focusing on three specific problems related to ISBNs:

1. Validating an ISBN (checking it is correct)
2. Converting a 10-digit ISBN to ISBN-13 format
3. Displaying a raw ISBN such as 0140124993 with the correct hyphenation; Table 1.3 shows correct hyphenations for a few ISBNs.

---

[7] The book in question is Karma Ura and Karma Galay (eds), *Gross National Happiness and Development: Proceedings of the First International Seminar on Operationalization of Gross National Happiness,* The Centre for Bhutan Studies, Thimphu, Bhutan, 2004. However, you won't find it on Amazon. The group code is 99936 which is used for books published in the Kingdom of Bhutan.

Table 1.3 **Hyphenating an ISBN**

Raw ISBN	Hyphenated ISBN	Book Title
0140124993	0-14-012499-3	How to Solve It
999361419X	99936-14-19-X	Gross National Happiness and Development[7]
8466605037	84-666-0503-7	Los Simpson ¡Por Siempre!

Thinking of the three ISBN-related problems stated above, what sub-problems can you identify? That is, what things would you have to do to be able to solve the three problems for any ISBN?

2 A Strategy for Solving Problems

The sooner you start coding your program the longer it is going to take.

H. F. Ledgard (1975)

Learning Objectives

- Understand what problems are and that they have several possible solutions
- Identify different types of problem
- Apply a strategy to help understand, solve, and evaluate the solution to a problem

This chapter is about problems and some of the many ways of going about solving them. It begins by considering the meaning of the word *problem* and then discusses some of the difficulties we have with solving problems. Section 2.4 presents a strategy for solving problems. This strategy is the cornerstone of the book, for it is the tool that you will use to solve the various problems presented in the remaining chapters. The rest of the chapter shows you how to apply the strategy to real problems (Section 2.5).

2.1 Introduction

There is a great temptation among people starting to learn programming to use the computer far too early. Often they will quickly read over the task set by their teacher and then go to the computer and start typing in programming language code in a trial-and-error fashion in the hope that this will at some point result in a program that produces the right answers. Occasionally this works, but the resultant program is usually very badly constructed and hard to understand. More often, the student comes away from the experience feeling bewildered, feeling that programming is *very difficult.*

This is a natural temptation. When we buy a new gadget, how many of us really read the instructions before trying it out? We are used to learning through trial and error. While you may manage to make good use of a vacuum cleaner without reading its instructions, the same approach rarely works well with programming. Someone once said, "Hours spent using a new software program saves minutes reading the manual." With programming, it is vital to spend the majority of our time thinking about the problem and designing a solution to it. One of the very last stages of programming is actually turning on the computer, typing in, and running the program. When I began teaching programming to college students, this discipline was easier to instill because powerful personal computers and feature-rich program development environments were not commonly available. We used screen editors on terminals connected to a main-frame computer. Access to the terminals was restricted owing to their cost, so students had limited time in which to type in, compile, and test their programs. Programmers brought up on batch card readers would say they had it easy – at least they had direct access to the compiler while they waited overnight for the computer operators to compile their programs. Back then, you simply had to spend time poring over your code trying to ensure it was correct before approaching the computer because you had few other options. These days, the excellent integrated program development environments running on modern desktop machines provide too much temptation for the tentative novice pro-grammer to resist. The belief is that the compiler will somehow help them to get their code right and that if a few half-understood lines of code are typed in, given enough attempts at compilation and execution, success is bound to follow. However, unless you have a good grasp of the problem you are trying to solve, and a good attempt at an outline solution to it, this try-it-and-see approach usually leads to many errors and even more frustration! In the sections that follow, we will focus on the core skill that a programmer needs: learning to solve problems.

2.2 What Is a Problem?

There is an old story that illustrates a number of points about problem solving. Three students, one of physics, one of engineering, and one of business, were asked by a university professor how they would use a barometer to determine the height of a tall building. The physics student said he would find the atmos-pheric pressure at the top and the bottom of the building and, using a known formula, would convert the difference between the readings into the height.

The engineering student said that she would drop the barometer from the top of the building, time its descent to the ground, and thus calculate the height. The business student said he would offer the barometer to the building's caretaker as a gift in return for telling him the height.

What does this teach us about problem solving? Simply that most problems can be solved in a number of ways and it is not always clear which way is better. The problems that we solve in introductory programming courses are usually reasonably well defined in that the end or objective (also known as the program requirements) is often specified quite clearly, though this is not always the case. However, the ways of solving the problem vary. We want to choose the best way according to some list of recognized criteria. Our goal as professionals is to provide high-quality software solutions. We want to use a method of proceeding from problem specification to high-quality software solution in a reasonable manner.

2.3 The Problem with Problem Solving

We must be aware that no matter how systematic our approach, many problems will still contain aspects that simply require a lot of thinking and even some intuitive leaps. Take a crossword puzzle for instance. There are two principal types of crossword puzzles: those offering definitions of words that you have to find (e.g., "difficult question; something hard to understand – seven letters"),[1] and those that offer a cryptic puzzle that contains clues to the answer (e.g., "person startled by the parabolic spaceship perhaps? – nine letters").[2] The definition-type crossword puzzles are straightforward to solve: you just need a broad vocabulary and a good memory. Cryptic crosswords do not only require a good vocabulary, they also need an understanding of the different hints that cryptic clues contain and an ability to think laterally.

A problem-solving strategy provides a framework within which you are more likely to arrive at a good solution. Unfortunately, no programming method allows you to derive the correct solution merely by following a few simple rules; all programming problems require you to think for yourself.

Problem Domain Versus Programming Language Domain

When we move from solving problems in the real world to expressing those solutions in a form that a computer can process, we discover a second class of problem introduced by computer programming languages. For example, take the following problem of calculation. Suppose a certain car has a fuel tank with a capacity of 60 litres and an average fuel consumption of 14 km/l. How far can the car travel on one tank of fuel, and how many litres are needed to travel 650 km?

---

[1] What is the answer? Why, "problem," of course!

[2] OK, so that is just a nonsense clue that was made up, but surely you have seen similar clues. The famous crossword puzzle in *The Times* of London is an example of the cryptic genre.

Work out the answers for yourself now.

This is a straightforward problem in arithmetic. We could make it slightly trickier: Assuming you start with a full tank, how many times must you refuel to travel 2000 km? Trickier still is to find how many *miles* you can travel on 10 *gallons* of fuel using the same car. The last two are each refinements of the first problem. How can we solve such problems? How can we write an algorithm to solve the problem? Can you then write an algorithm that provides a general solution to all problems of this type where the car's fuel tank capacity and fuel consumption can vary?[3]

Let us say we have solved the first problem by discovering that the range of the car equals its fuel capacity multiplied by its fuel consumption and that the amount of fuel required for a journey is the distance divided by the car's fuel consumption. We may be feeling confident that all that remains is the simple matter of translating the solution into our chosen programming language. In principle, this stage is straightforward but we will often discover that the language introduces subproblems. Using a calculator we find that the range of our car is 840 km (60 × 14) and that the amount of fuel needed to travel 650 km is $650 \div 14 = 46.428571$ litres. Now two questions arise: should the range (840 km) be displayed as a whole number, and how many digits should be used to display the fuel needed? What if the fuel consumption of the car were 14.6 km/l and its tank capacity 60.3 l? In this case, its range would be 880.38 km and the amount of fuel needed to travel 650 km would be 44.520547 l. Now the range is also a fractional number. Should we round everything up to the nearest whole number? Or should we display everything to two decimal places? Or three decimal places? The answers to these questions are important because you will discover that programming languages treat different kinds of numeric values in different ways and that displaying numbers in different formats can be a tricky business. Some programming languages make it very easy to display fractional numbers to a specified number of decimal places while others make it less straightforward. The point is that we need to be aware that the translation of a solution into programming language code can raise a further set of difficulties that should be treated as problems in their own right. We must distinguish between those subproblems that belong to the problem itself and those that belong to the programming language syntax (or our incomplete knowledge and/or misunderstanding of it). For example, discovering that the distance travelled must be divided by the fuel consumption to find the fuel needed for a journey belongs in the domain of the problem itself while displaying the answer to two decimal places is a problem in the domain of the programming language. In this part of the book, we will predominantly be dealing with problems of the former type.

---

[3] Also, what do we mean by a gallon? In the United Kingdom, a gallon is 160 fluid ounces, there being eight pints in a gallon and 20 ounces in a pint. However, in the United States there are only 16 ounces in a pint, so a gallon there contains only 128 fluid ounces.
That means that a UK (imperial) gallon is (on these terms) 1.25 times the size of a US gallon, or a US gallon is 80% of the size of an imperial one. And then we learn that the US fluid ounce is 1.04 imperial fluid ounces, so 1 imperial gallon is really 1.20 US gallons. Sigh.

2.4 A Strategy for Problem Solving

In *How to Solve It*, GEORGE PÓLYA wrote, "*It is foolish to answer a question that you do not understand*" (Pólya, 1990). While this sounds like a self-evident truth, time after time I have witnessed confused beginners sitting at their computers chewing their pens in frustration because they cannot get their program to work. When faced with a programming problem, many novices begin by looking over the requirements to find out what they have to do. After some head scratching, accompanied by a general feeling of unease or bewilderment, they head for the computer, fire up the compiler, and start writing down some code in the hope that they will eventually hit upon a sequence of instructions that will solve the problem. The main difficulty here is that they are mixing the final language of the

▶ Description vs. solution

problem description (the programming language code) with the task of *problem solving*. It is very much like trying to tell a friend how to bake a cake before you know how to do it yourself. In all likelihood, you will give your friend many false starts, contradictory instructions, tell him or her to do things in the wrong order, and generally end up with a big mess and wasted ingredients.

The Stages of Problem Solving

To make progress in programming you *must* begin by making sure you understand the problem – you need a strategy for solving problems. The first decision we will make in our strategy is to separate the task of solving the problem from the task of writing down the solution. Pólya (1990) proposed a strategy for solving mathematical problems that runs roughly as follows:

1. Understand the problem
2. Devise a plan to solve the problem
3. Carry out the plan
4. Look back (check the result and reflect upon it)

This is a good foundation for a programming strategy, and we shall adopt it with a couple of additions. Part of learning to think like a programmer involves reflecting upon what you have done. By describing what you have learned from each programming task, you begin to develop a repertoire of experience and knowledge about problems that will help you to solve similar or related problems in the future. While thinking about what you have learned is certainly useful,

▶ Write it down

writing it down is even more so for two reasons. First, once an idea is written down it can be retrieved later (otherwise, you may forget it). The second reason is that writing something down requires thinking very clearly about it. Before we can express something in writing, we must first have a good understanding of it. Often I will think I have understood something but it is not until I try writing down my explanation that I discover my understanding was not as clear as I thought. We will add a step to our strategy that deals with describing what we have learned:

1. Understand the problem
2. Devise a plan to solve the problem
3. Carry out the plan

4. Look back (check the result and reflect upon it)

5. Describe what we have learned from the process

Finally, as good programmers we should always assume that at some time in the future another programmer will need to pick up our programs and modify them. The act of changing a program after it has been finished is called SOFTWARE MAINTENANCE and it is estimated to consume anywhere between 70% and 90% of the total cost of a software system. That is, more money is spent on changing a program after it has been released for use than is spent on developing it in the first place. One obvious reason for carrying out maintenance is to remove errors that were not spotted during its development. Another reason is to update the software to increase its capabilities or to make it compatible with a newer version of an operating system. Whatever the reason, it is quite likely that a program written by one programmer will be maintained by a different person. As professionals, we must strive to ensure that our program is as easy to understand as possible so that the maintenance programmer does not have to waste a lot of time trying to figure out what we have done. So, as well as writing clearly laid-out and well-structured programs, we also need to provide good DOCUMENTATION that explains them. Documentation can be *internal* (comments within the program code to explain certain points) and *external* (general statements about the whole program, including design documents, requirements specifications, and so on). Therefore, we shall add a final stage to our problem-solving strategy that deals with explaining our results and documenting the program. Our outline framework for problem solving now looks like this:

▶ Software maintenance

1. Understand the problem
2. Devise a plan to solve the problem (plan an attack)
3. Carry out the plan/attack
4. Assess the result (i.e., look back – check the result and reflect upon it)
5. Describe what we have learned from the process
6. Explain our results (and document our program)

The complete strategy is given at the end of this chapter (after the exercises and projects) as Table 2.2. The following sections explain each element of the strategy.

Understanding the Problem (Step 1)

The first task is to understand the problem. Some problems will be very easy to understand, others harder. We must become familiar with the language of the problem, read it several times, and become aware of its principal parts. Sometimes rephrasing the problem or describing it with a different representation from the original can be useful. For example, drawing a picture or a diagram may shed light on what is required. In Chapter 3, we will look at using alternative representations to help us in describing problems and solutions.

When you have familiarized yourself with the problem, you can start digging out the details. What do we know for sure, and what is unknown? Look at the different parts of the problem and consider them individually. Then think about how they relate to each other. What effect would a change in one aspect have on the other parts and on the problem as a whole? For instance, going back to our earlier car example, we can say that we know the car's fuel capacity (60 litres) and we know its average fuel consumption (14 km/l). The *unknown* is the car's range as that is what the problem statement asks us to find out. Changes in either the fuel capacity or fuel consumption will affect the car's range so we see that the three values are related.

Devising and Carrying Out the Plan (Steps 2 and 3)

For Steps 2 and 3 we can use analogy, that is, we can draw upon our repertoire of similar problems that we have met in the past. If the current problem resembles a problem you have seen before, write down how it is similar and, just as important, write down how it differs. It is vital to record the differences also, for ignoring them may lead you to make unjustified ASSUMPTIONS about the current problem.

For those aspects that are similar, can you use the same solution techniques that you used in the past problems? Many programming problems fall into well-understood patterns that can be reused. All that is required is to adapt one of the standard solutions to the particular circumstances of your problem. As you continue you will learn that a great many programming problems are variations on a smaller number of previously solved problems.

Standard ▶
solutions

What do the following real-world problems have in common?

1. Put together a self-assembly wardrobe.
2. Hang a new door in the kitchen.
3. Fix a small bookshelf to the bedroom wall.
4. Put a new hard drive inside the computer.

One answer is that they may all require you to use a screwdriver. What other answers did you come up with?

Devise a Plan

All but the most trivial programming tasks will usually comprise a number of smaller subproblems. Even simple programs typically require you to solve the related problems of

- providing your program with the data it needs (input);
- processing the data; and
- displaying the results or saving them to a file (output).

Exploring the second subproblem (processing the data) will likely yield a further set of subproblems. Each subproblem should be treated as a problem in its own right with its own structure and its own principal parts.[4]

---

[4] Michael Jackson deals with just this subject in his excellent book, *Problem Frames: Analyzing and Structuring Software Development Problems* (Jackson, 2001).

Try partitioning (separating out) the problem of getting up in the morning into a few simpler subproblems (or tasks).

Some subproblems may be easier to solve than others. Begin with them; their solution may give you clues to the remaining problems. If a particular problem is too difficult to solve immediately, can you extend the principle of analogy and solve a simpler version of it or a related problem? Doing so may just give you the inspiration you need.

In understanding the problem, I recommend making a drawing, or a sketch, or an alternative description of the problem. One technique I have observed to be very effective is to retell the problem in your own words to another person. Often, I have had a puzzled student approach me with a problem and the moment he or she explained it to me the penny dropped and the student answered his or her own question without me speaking a word. If you cannot find someone else, explain the problem to the wall, your teddy bear, or a mirror. Do not worry about feeling foolish – after all, there is nobody around to laugh or you would have used them instead.

Left over? ▶   Whenever I take apart a piece of machinery or an appliance in an attempt to fix it, I am always relieved when, having reassembled it, there are no parts left over. Sometimes, though, our problems have parts left over, pieces of information that we have overlooked or have not used. Check that you have not overlooked something. Is there a piece of information that did not seem important? If so, revisit it and see if it will help after all.

Although we should keep consideration of programming language details separate from understanding and solving the problem, this is not always possible. Michael Jackson (2001) gives the following advice:

> *When you structure a problem you can't avoid moving some way towards its solution – that is, towards talking about the computer and its software. . . . There is nothing wrong with that, provided that you don't neglect the problem world, and don't give a description of the computer and its software when you should be giving a description of the world. You always need to know clearly which one you are talking about. (p. 15)*

Carrying Out the Attack

Once you think you have a firm grasp on the solution, write down the sequence of actions necessary to solve the problem. Even if you have not worked everything out yet writing down the overall sequence of actions will help. The first question you can ask yourself is whether the ordering of the actions is correct. Does the order rely on certain conditions to be true? Have these conditions come from the problem statement or are they ASSUMPTIONS you have made? Is it possible to verify the assumptions?

Write down the sequence in which the various actions associated with getting up in the morning should be carried out.

If you are finding it too complicated to understand a problem, try removing some of the details to see if the simplification gives you a clearer understanding (though you must remember to deal with the details later on!).

Once you have a sequence of actions, check whether they all need to be carried out in all circumstances. Perhaps some of the actions only need to be carried out when certain conditions are met. For example, the sequence of actions involved in leaving the house and walking to the bus stop might involve putting up the umbrella. Unless you like permanent shade, you would probably only put up your umbrella if it is raining hard enough. So, although the solution to the problem of leaving the house and catching a bus contains the raise-umbrella action, whether or not the action is carried out depends on the circumstances that apply at the time; one day you may put up the umbrella, the next you may not.

Is it sufficient to carry out each action once only, or do some actions need to be repeated? For instance when mowing the lawn, whether or not I need to empty my lawn mower's grass box more than once depends on three things: the capacity of the grass box, the size of the garden, and the length of the grass. For my garden and my current mower two of these things are constant (lawn size and box capacity) but the length of the grass will be different each time I cut it.

Thinking back to getting up in the morning, are there any optional or conditional tasks involved in getting up in the morning?

Here is a tip that works well across Steps 1, 2, and 3. If you are having trouble understanding the problem, working out your plan, or carrying out your plan, then use the following technique. I have used it extensively and found to be an invaluable aid to problem solving: sleep on it. I often find that the answer to a problem that seemed intractable presents itself naturally if left alone for a while. As a student I used the following strategy for completing programming assignments: on the first day read through the assignment brief and take in the main points, then put it away. A couple of days later take out the brief and read it through again, but this time make some notes. Summarize the problem requirements, and then put it away. Two days later try designing an initial solution. Refine it a few times then put it away. Continuing in this way worked well for me most of the time. The trick was not to spend too long at any one time on the problem. There comes a point where no matter how long you stare at a problem you just cannot get the answer. It is best to put it away and come back to it fresh another day; often you will find that when you pick it up again the answer you were searching for comes more easily. Contrast this with the traditional student approach of leaving the assignment until the day before it is due and then working through the night to complete it. That is not a good strategy for programming because you are not leaving yourself enough reflection and background processing time. It is amazing what problems your brain can work through if you stop bothering it and leave it alone to get on with the job.

◄ Sleep on it

Assessing the Results (Step 4)

When you have a solution that seems to be right then try it out. Ideally, you should get someone else to try out your solution. The problem with testing your own solutions is that you are likely to be blind to your own logical errors. You will intend a certain course of action and will interpret your instructions as meaning what you intended. But when you give your instructions to someone else they may just find instructions that mean something quite different from what you intended. It is the differences between what we intend, and how we actually express our intentions that result in bugs (defects) in our programs. Having a friend walk through your solution is a great way of ensuring that you learn to be more precise and unambiguous in your writing down of solutions. Did your friend manage to complete the task using your instructions? Did they manage to complete the task without asking for help or clarification? Did they misinterpret any of the instructions? If so, did they *really* misinterpret them or were they correct and you were wrong in the way you wrote the instruction? If you and your friend used the solution, did you both get the same answers? If not, who was wrong, and why? If you did get the same results, were they the correct ones?

Get your friend to evaluate/criticize your steps for getting up in the morning that you wrote down earlier.

Did your solution give the right outcome or the correct results? If so, well done, but are you sure it is correct? If you change some of the values and conditions, do you still get the correct answers? If you did get the right answers, did any parts of the solution seem cumbersome? With hindsight, is there a better way of doing things?

If you got the wrong answers, do you know why? Trace through your solution step-by-step to see if you can find where it is going wrong.

This step of assessing the result is very important as it will highlight errors in the solution and areas that could be improved. You should repeat Steps 2, 3, and 4 until you are as confident as you can reasonably be that your solution is the best one you can achieve. Only then should you move on.

Describing What We Have Learned (Step 5)

Having gone through several cycles of devising a plan, carrying out the plan, and assessing the results, you should have a list of things you have learned. These lessons will form part of your problem-solving and programming repertoire of experience. When you first begin programming you will find that you have errors in your solutions that you just cannot get rid of. You approach your teacher, or another experienced programmer, and they spot in less than thirty seconds the fault that you have just spent several hours looking for. There is a temptation to feel foolish and to ascribe great intelligence to the person who spotted the error so quickly. However flattering that is, it is more likely that the experienced programmer just has a bigger repertoire of programming errors than you and has learned to recognize common symptoms. Programming teachers seem especially good at this, but only because they have used that programming task (or a variant) lots of times with lots of classes of many students. The first time they helped a student track down the error it may have taken them quite a few minutes. But each time after that they were able to spot the problem in just a few seconds. Writing down the lessons you learned from solving the problem will help you in fixing the lessons in your memory and will thus add to your programming repertoire. Where you encountered errors in your solution, making a note not just of the particular error, but also its symptoms is highly recommended; you never know when you might encounter the same symptom in the future. If you do not write it down you will probably forget it.

Documenting the Solution (Step 6)

Documenting solutions is a very important but much overlooked task. Once a problem has been solved and the solution handed in for grading there is a strong temptation to simply move on to the next piece of work. There are several reasons why documentation is so important. We noted earlier how SOFTWARE MAINTENANCE (changes made to programs after they have been completed) rather than new software development accounts for most programming activity. Watts Humphrey notes that the person best able to correct errors in a program is the person who wrote it in the first place (Humphrey, 1997). But the reality of the software industry is that people change jobs, get promotions, leave the company, etc., so it is not always possible for the original developer to carry out the maintenance. It is vital, therefore, that programmers learn the discipline of writing good, clear, and useful documentation that will help future programmers to read, understand, and maintain their programs (problem solutions). Even when you know you are going to maintain the program think about this: are you really sure that in six months you will still be able to understand the complex sequence of instructions that took you a week to construct? You see, you may understand your solution now but that is because you have spent a lot of time working with it. But it is likely that you will not understand it quite so well in the future. Now, if you could have trouble understanding your own solution in just a few months time, how do you think another programmer will approach it?

There are several types of documentation that programmers can produce. For now, we shall concentrate on explaining our solutions. Each solution should be preceded by a short statement of its purpose. For example, "this is a recipe for making bread," or "the following instructions will enable you to convert a temperature in degrees Fahrenheit to its equivalent in degrees Celsius." Then, look at the main body of your solution and list all the conditions that need to be true before the solution can be successfully applied. For example, a recipe for making bread will require that you have access to the necessary ingredients, a water supply, the right utensils, and a working oven with a temperature control. This sounds like the blindingly obvious, but it is a good discipline to get into because it will serve you well when you come to writing some real programs.

Look for ▶
assumptions
and
preconditions

A major cause of defects in programs is that the programmer has made ASSUMPTIONS that just are not true. They may seem to be very reasonable assumptions that are consistent with the problem statement, but they are assumptions nonetheless. Assumptions must be challenged to ensure that they are well-founded.

Documenting the conditions that must be met before your solution can be applied (sometimes known as preconditions) will help you to find some of your hidden assumptions. There is no point asking your friend to follow your bread-making recipe if the oven's electricity supply is not turned on – the oven will be cold and the dough will not bake. Your friend may have enough initiative to realize that the oven must first be turned on at the power socket before it can be used, but a computer does not have any initiative. If your program tells it to set the oven temperature and then put in the dough, that is exactly what it will do. If the electricity is not switched on, and you did not tell the computer to switch the electricity on, then it will not get switched on!

In documenting your solution you may find that you need to revisit Steps 2, 3, and 4 again to amend the instructions in the light of any assumptions you have found. This is good practice and it shows a commitment to getting things right.

2.5 Applying the Strategy

How can this strategy work in practice? That is what the rest of the book is about and we shall look at a number of problems together with solutions developed using this strategy. The complete strategy is provided as Table 2.2 at the end of this chapter, and again at the back of the book as a handy reference. Of course, we are doing this with the intention of eventually writing some computer programs, so we must take care that our solutions can eventually be translated into programming language code. Therefore, we will study how to *systematize* our solutions. That is, your solutions will be written down in a structured and consistent way using semi-formal language. Do not be frightened by this. We introduced ideas like this in Chapter 1 when we discussed musical scores and recipes. Remember, a good recipe is a set of straightforward and unambiguous instructions which, if repeated will lead to more or less the same results each time. The aim of the rest of the book is to get you to the point where you can analyze a problem, work out a solution, and write down the solution as a series of instructions in such a way that you could pass these instructions to the person sitting next to you and they could then use them to calculate the answer to the problem *without needing to clarify any matters with you.*

2.6 Chapter Summary

In this chapter we have looked at what it means to have a problem to solve and how problems can be broken down into smaller constituent parts. Understanding and solving problems lies at the heart of successful computer programming and so a strategy for solving problems was then introduced.

2.7 Exercises

The following exercises describe a problem situation. For each problem apply the *How To Think Like A Programmer (HTTLAP)* strategy (Table 2.2 at the end of this chapter) and devise a sequence of steps that will meet the requirements of the task. Be careful to look for hidden assumptions. To help, you can ask yourself, "If I specify it that way, will it still work in all cases?" Hint: In the example above we questioned whether it is possible to bathe after getting dressed. Pay close attention to Steps 4 and 5 "Assess the result" and "Describe what we have learned." Does your solution work well? What other valid ways are there to arrive at a correct outcome? What did any errors in your solution teach you a) about your understanding of the problem and b) about the problem-solving process? Solutions to a selection of the exercises can be found in Appendix C.

1. Suppose a certain car has a fuel tank with a capacity of 60 litres and an average fuel consumption of 14 km/l. How many times must you fill the tank to travel 2,000 km? How many miles can you travel on 10 gallons of fuel using the same car? You can answer this using imperial gallons (8 imperial pints, where 1 pint = 20 imperial fluid ounces) or US gallons (8 US pints, where 1 pint = 16 US fluid ounces). 1 US fluid ounce = 1.0408423 imperial fluid ounces. Thus, 1 litre = 0.219969157 imperial gallons = 0.264172051 US gallons. Or, 1 imperial gallon = 4.54609 litres, and 1 US gallon = 3.785411784 litres. 1 mile = 1.609344 km.

2. Getting dressed in the morning (that is, just the tasks associated with getting dressed; do not include getting up, washing, etc.).

3. Using an electric filter machine (also called a percolator) to make a pot of coffee and pour a cup.

4. Filling a car with fuel.

5. Making a cheese and onion omelette.

6. Travelling from home to work/college.

7. Completing a piece of homework/college assignment.

8. A wedding ceremony. Note, this is very culturally dependent, so my solution may not resemble yours at all!

9. Choosing what to study at university.

10. Hanging a picture on the wall.

2.8 Projects

StockSnackz Vending Machine

A StockSnackz vending machine is being installed in the staff common room at the University of Stocksfield for the free use of the faculty. The machine has 10 numbered buttons. Pushing Button 1 dispenses a milk chocolate bar, Button 2 a muesli bar, Button 3 a pack of cheese puffs, Button 4 an apple, Button 5 a pack of popcorn, while pushing Button 6 displays on the machine's small screen a summary of how many of each item have been dispensed. Pushing Buttons 0, 7, 8, or 9 has no effect.

Using the *HTTLAP* strategy write down the series of steps needed to install the new machine, fill it with supplies, and let people obtain snacks from it over the course of the first day. You may assume that the machine can store unlimited supplies of each item. At the end of the day, the dean of faculty will want to know how many snacks have been dispensed. For now, treat the problem of lots of people obtaining lots of snacks over the course of a day as a single abstract activity "Dispense snacks."

Stocksfield Fire Service

The Stocksfield Fire Service has asked you to write a program for identifying the precautions to take when dealing with chemical spillages. The program is to be installed on palm-top computers used by the fire fighters who will tap in the Emergence Action Code and be told what to do by the computer. For example, if they tapped in the code 2WE they would receive the instructions:

```
FIRE FIGHTING
~~~~~~~~~~~
Use Fine Spray.


PRECAUTIONS
~~~~~~~~~
Substance is prone to violent or explosive reaction.
Wear liquid-tight suit/chemical protection clothing.
Contain the spillage.


PUBLIC SAFETY
~~~~~~~~~~~
Public safety hazard: Warn people to stay indoors with doors &
windows shut.
```

Use *HTTLAP* to write down the overall series of steps needed to translate each character of the three-character EAC.

Puzzle World: Roman Numerals and Chronograms

There are rules governing how Roman numerals can be written (though these rules are not universally applied). Look at the Roman numbers in Table 2.1 below and see how far you can get in inferring the rules. Use the questions in *HTTLAP* to structure your thinking.

Without any other information, what steps might you perform in the process of converting a decimal number to Roman numerals? Or a Roman number to decimal? Outline the overall stages of the process now.

Table 2.1   **Conversions of Some Numbers in Roman Numerals**

Roman Number	Decimal Equivalent
III	3
IV	4
CIX	109
LVIII	58
XCIX	99 (why not IC?)
D	500
M	1000
MCMC	Invalid

Pangrams: Holoalphabetic Sentences

Consider how you would go about systematically determining whether a sentence is a pangram. You might want to use a bag of Scrabble tiles as an aid. Write down the basic sequence of actions you would take. As before, make use of the *HTTLAP* questions to guide you.

Online Bookstore: ISBNs

To begin our investigation of ISBNs, think about how you would approach the problem of adding hyphens to an unformatted ISBN. Doing this makes them easier to read and so would make an Internet bookshop more user-friendly. Go back to the Projects section in Chapter 1 and look again at Figure 1.5 and Table 1.3. What patterns you can spot in the way the numbers are hyphenated? Write down the sequence of actions necessary to write out the various parts of the ISBN with hyphens in between.

2.9   "How To Think Like A Programmer"

On the next two pages you will find a summary of our problem solving strategy given as Table 2.2 "How To Think Like A Programmer". Use it for the exercises in the coming chapters to help you arrive at solutions. The table is based upon Pólya's original list of questions and suggestions in *How to Solve It* (Pólya, 1990).

Table 2.2   ***How To Think Like A Programmer (HTTLAP)***

---

1. Understanding the problem

You have to understand the problem. Do not go to the next stage until you have done this.	What are you being asked to do? What is required? Try restating the problem? Can the problem be better expressed by drawing a diagram or a picture? By using mathematical notation? By building a model out of wood, paper, or card?
	What is the *unknown*? Is finding the unknown part of the problem statement? Write down what you **do know** about the problem. Have you made any assumptions? If so, what can/should you do about it?
Sleep on the problem and come back to it fresh.	What are the principal parts of the problem? Are there several parts to the problem?

2. Devising a plan to solve the problem

Start thinking about the information you have and what the solution is required to do.	Have you solved this problem before (perhaps with different values/quantities)? Is this problem *similar* to one you have met before? If so, can you use any knowledge from that problem here? Does the solution to that problem apply to this one in any way?
	Are some parts of the problem more easily solved than others? If the problem is too hard, can you solve a simpler version of it, or a related problem?
	Does restating the problem (perhaps telling it in your own words to someone else) help you to get a grip on it? Try describing the problem in a different *language* (e.g., diagrammatically, pictorially, using mathematics, building a physical model or representation).

Stop bothering your brain and sleep on the problem.

Did you make use of all the information in the problem statement? Can you satisfy all the conditions of the problem? Have you left anything out?

3. Carrying out the plan

Write down your solution. Pay attention to things done in order (sequence), things done conditionally (selection) and things done repeatedly (iteration).

Write down the basic sequence of actions necessary to solve the general problem. This may involve hiding some of the detail in order to get the overall sequence correct. Is your ordering of actions correct? Does the order rely on certain things to be true? If so, do you know these things from the problem statement? Or have you made any assumptions? If you have made assumptions then how will you verify that they are correct?

If you cannot see a way to solving the whole problem can you see any parts of the problem that you can solve? If the problem is too complicated, try removing some of the conditions/constraints and seeing if that gives you a way in.

Go back to your sequence of actions. Should all actions be carried out in *every* circumstance? Should some actions (or groups/blocks of actions) only be carried out when certain conditions are met?

Go back to your sequence of actions. Is carrying out each action once only sufficient to give the desired outcome? If not, do you have actions (or groups/blocks of actions) that must therefore be *repeated*?

Sleep on it again.

Go back once more. Do any of your actions/blocks of actions belong *inside* others? For example, do you have a block of actions that must be repeated, but only when some condition is met?

4. Assessing the result

Examine the results obtained when using your solution.

Use your solution to meet the requirements of the problem. Did you get the right answer or the correct outcome? If not, why not? Where did your solution go wrong? If you think you did get the right answer, how can you be sure? Did any parts of the solution seem cumbersome or not very sensible? Can you make those parts simpler, quicker, or clearer?

Get someone else to use or follow your solution.

Give your solution to someone else and ask them to use it to complete the task. Were your instructions clear enough for them? Did they have to ask for help or clarification? Did they misinterpret your instructions? If so, why?

Did they get the same answer as when you did it? If not, whose answer was correct?

5. Describing what you have learned

Make a record of your achievements and the difficulties you encountered.

What did you learn from this exercise? What do you know now that you did not know before you started?

What particular difficulties did you encounter? Were there any aspects of the problem that caused you particular difficulty? If so, do you think you would know how to tackle them if you met something similar in the future?

Compare your finished solution with your first attempt. What do the differences teach you?

6. Documenting the solution

Explain your solution. Make sure that it can be understood.

Are there any aspects of your solution that are hard to understand? Is this because they are badly written, or simply because the solution is just complicated? If you were to pick up your solution in five years time do you think any bits would be hard to understand?

3 Description Languages and Representations

Learning Objectives

- Understand the different languages and representations that can be used to visualize, understand, and solve problems
- Analyze a variety of real-world problems and choose appropriate ways of representing their principal parts
- Write solutions to problems in a semi-formal structured English (pseudo-code)

This chapter begins with some of the notations and languages you can use for representing problems in Section 3.1 and concludes with Section 3.2 introducing a semi-formal language (known as *pseudo-code*) that you will use for writing down your problem solutions.

3.1   Description Languages and Representations

The strategy introduced in the last chapter advises restating the problem to gain understanding. This section looks at some common forms of representation that you can use to describe problems and design solutions.

Natural Language

Natural language is just that, natural. It is our main form of communication and it comes so naturally to most of us that we use words to describe and explain most things. Actually, that is not quite true. While we may think we predominantly use words, psychologists tell us that non-verbal communication makes up a very large part of human communication. Much of the information content of our conversations and other interactions comes from the way we stress and inflect words and the ways we change our expression and move parts of our body.

Errors of the Third Kind

We know that natural language can also be imprecise and ambiguous. Computers are neither of these things and to program them we need to be very clear in our thinking and our expression. Furthermore, in order to write good solutions our understanding of the problem needs to be clear and precise otherwise we might very well solve the wrong problem. When I was a student I was taught about *errors of the third kind*. An error of the third kind is, for example, a computer program that is extremely well written, easily maintained, efficient, quick, and accurate, but which does not do what the customer asked for. It does not matter how good your coding skills are if you do not first get a clear and correct understanding of the problem you are trying to solve. As Samuel Johnson (1709–84) wrote: *"A cucumber should be well sliced, and dressed with pepper and vinegar, and then thrown out, as good for nothing."* If you hate cucumber, preparing one for your salad is an error of the third kind.

Diagrams, Pictures, and Visual Thinking

While natural language is invaluable often we need to use other forms of representation that will give us clearer insights. St Francis of Assisi (1181–1226) told the Friars Minor to *"preach the gospel and, if necessary, use words."* We must be prepared to use other ways of describing problems.

Consider the following problem. I have a canvas bag in which there are five red jelly beans and a single blue jelly bean. If I put my hand into the bag, *without looking in*, what is the likelihood that I will pull out a red bean? And what is the likelihood that I will get the blue one? How do you visualize this problem? Do you keep a mental list that there are five red beans and a single blue bean? Perhaps you do because this is quite a simple problem (there are six beans in all, one of which is blue). Therefore, I have a one in six chance of getting the blue one, and five chances in six of getting a red one. For very small or simple problems words can be quite sufficient to give us a good enough grasp. But try solving this example that I have adapted from one used by James Adams in *Conceptual Blockbusting* (Adams, 2001, p. 4):

> One morning at eight o'clock you set off in your car to visit a friend who lives some distance away. You encounter the odd traffic delay and your driving speed varies as the speed limits on the different stretches of road change. It is a long drive so you stop twice to refresh yourself and to eat and drink something. You arrive at 6.00 p.m. and decide to stay overnight. The next morning you set off again at 8.00 a.m. You take the same route back, but encounter heavy traffic in different places. Because one traffic jam was so large you only stop once for refreshments. Still, you arrive back home at six o'clock. Question: Is there a point on the road that you pass at exactly the same time of day on the outward and return journeys?

How did you get on with that? What was your answer? Perhaps your intuition told you that there is no such point because of all the variations in speed? If so, your intuition is quite wrong for there is a point you pass at the same time of day on the way out and the way back. But how do you show that? If you tried to use natural language (verbal reasoning) then you have probably still not solved the problem. I solved the problem by drawing a picture:

FIGURE 3.1   **Journey to a friend**

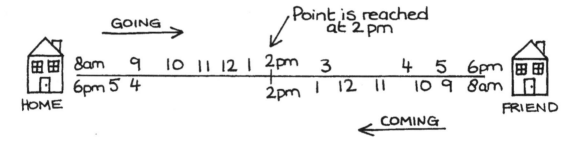

My picture is a simplified graph plotting distance travelled against time. The row of numbers above the line is the times of the outward journey marked out as hours. The gaps between the times vary to represent the changing speeds. The lower line is the return journey. This rough sketch shows that these two journeys cross the same point at around 2 p.m. This worked for me because I often reach for a pen and paper to draw a problem. Figure 3.2 shows a slightly different way of looking at the problem. This time the friend's house is at the top, home at the bottom. Time is marked along the *x* axis and the distance travelled as the two lines. Fast progress is a steep line; stopping for a rest makes the line flat. Again we can see the two routes crossing at around 2 p.m.

FIGURE 3.2   **Another visualization of my journey to a friend**

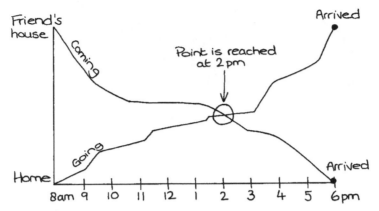

For those who can think visually the solution is even simpler if a quick change is made in the way the puzzle is phrased. Instead of thinking of two journeys on two different days and looking for a point, just imagine you and your friend each setting out from your homes at eight in the morning. Will you meet along the road? Of course you will, so the problem is solved and there is no need for a diagram or graphs and rulers. Notice what was done with the visual reasoning? We did not solve the puzzle exactly as written – instead we used the advice in Step 2 of our problem solving strategy and solved a simplified or related problem. In my case I drew a diagram, but the mental visualization works even better. The point is that sometimes a picture says much more than even two thousand words if the two thousand words do not help you get to the answer.

I am confused: you seem to be saying that we do not need to use diagrams at all.

No. I am saying that there is generally more than one way to solve a problem. Some ways of thinking about a problem lead more easily to a solution than others, but not everybody is always able to use every way of thinking about a problem. I often use pictures to help me understand problems, hence my first solution to the problem involved a sketch, but the second solution shows that reframing the problem can also help sometimes. The lesson is to use whatever technique helps you the most, and often you will need to try more than one technique.

Chessboard and Dominoes

Try to solve this old puzzle:[1] Take a chessboard and 32 dominoes. Each domino fits over two (non-diagonally) adjacent squares on the chessboard. It is easy to cover the chessboard with the dominoes (Figure 3.3). Now cut two opposite corners from the chessboard, leaving 62 squares and then remove one domino. Can you still cover the chessboard?

---

[1] Thanks to my colleague Paul Brna for introducing me to this puzzle.

FIGURE 3.3   **Covering the chessboard with 32 dominoes**

What was your answer? If you tried a mental image because that technique worked so well for the last problem then you may have decided the answer is *yes*, you can cover the remaining squares. Alas, you cannot! There are some pieces of evidence that serve to misdirect the unwary. We began with 64 squares on the board, and 32 dominoes each of which covers two squares. The number of squares is twice the number of dominoes. So, if we remove two squares and one domino we still have twice the number of squares as dominoes, so it seems that we can still cover the board. The mistake here is that we have overlooked some of the details. The problem solving strategy advises us to look for any bits left over after we have devised a plan of attack. Our solution only took into account the number of squares, the number of dominoes, and the ratio of the two. We have formed an abstract, or less-detailed, view of the problem. ABSTRACTION can be a very useful tool; indeed, the strategy advises solving a simpler problem if the original proves too challenging at first. But we must not forget to revisit the problem to see if the abstraction, or simplification, has had an adverse affect. This can be a feature of abstraction – sometimes we must use abstraction to remove detail but with it goes a consequent loss of information that we must be aware of if we want to avoid making more incorrect ASSUMPTIONS.

So what details have we overlooked? Chessboards have 32 white and 32 black squares arranged alternately. A domino, therefore, covers one white and one black square. If you look at a chessboard you will observe that one pair of corner squares is black, the other pair white. So, if you remove two corners you have removed two squares of the same colour. This means that we cannot cover the board any more, as Figure 3.4 shows.

FIGURE 3.4   **31 dominoes cannot cover a chessboard with two corners removed**

If you are puzzled, try restating the problem. Instead of a chessboard, let's imagine we have 32 men and 32 women who want to get married. Instead of dominoes we now have 32 marriage certificates which can only be used to marry one man to one woman. All the marriage certificates can be used because we have 32 eligible couples. Now, let's remove two men (white squares). Now can we use up all the marriage certificates? No, because we have 30 men and 32 women.

You must be careful to make sure you either make use of all the information in the problem, or, if you leave some out, that it does not affect the solution. By all means simplify, but do not forget to check for bits left over once you have put it all together again. Part of the difficulty with this puzzle is that you start out forming a mental image – you visualize a chessboard – but then some numbers are given and that can trap you into thinking of the problem purely arithmetically. If you had carried on with the mental image of the chessboard and tried laying out the dominoes in your mind's eye you might have got the answer. Restating the problem made for an easier solution (and no mental gymnastics holding all those dominoes in place in your mind). Of course, you could have drawn out a chessboard, cut out some paper dominoes and experimented, but this would take longer.

Ant and Sugar

You might be thinking that everything can be understood with a diagram, but that is not so; if your reasoning is faulty your picture will not help you. Here is an example of where drawing a perfectly good diagram led me astray. Try it yourself:

> There is a large square room whose walls are 24 feet long. The ceiling is eight feet high. On the floor in a corner is a bowl of sugar. In the opposite corner by the ceiling is an ant. What is the shortest path the ant can take to get to the sugar? Adapted from an example given in Adams (2001).

Where to start with this one? Does restating the problem verbally help? I do not think so as this appears to be an arithmetic problem. It helps to pick a description language that is suited to the characteristics of the problem. Start by drawing a diagram.

FIGURE 3.5   **Diagram of room with positions of ant and sugar marked**

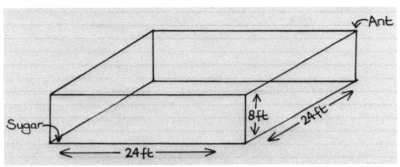

Figure 3.5 shows a three-dimensional sketch of the room together with the positions of the ant and the sugar. I have added the room's dimensions because this information is given in the problem statement. From the diagram can you see the shortest walking route to the sugar? The problem seems easy to visualize but there is still room for error.

Think about it carefully and then trace the shortest walking route from the ant to the sugar.

How did you do? Below are two candidate answers to the problem for you to consider. One of them is correct.

FIGURE 3.6   **Candidate solution #1**

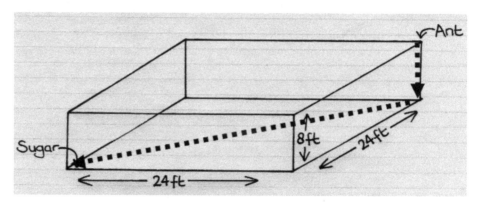

FIGURE 3.7   **Candidate solution #2**

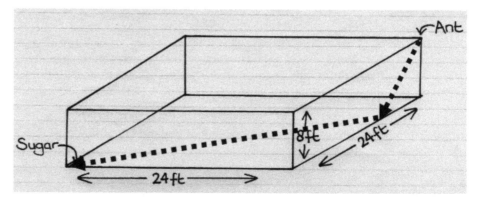

Did seeing both possible solutions cause you to change your mind? Which one is correct? When I first tried this problem I gave candidate #1 as my answer: straight down to the floor and diagonally across the floor: it was nice and simple and quite easy to calculate. The walk down to the floor is eight feet, for that is the height of the room. The diagonal can be calculated using Pythagoras' theorem

Think Spot

(the square on the hypotenuse of a right-angled triangle equals the sum of the squares of the two opposite sides). We know the lengths of the two opposite sides as they are the length and width of the room (twenty-four feet each). The diagonal is the hypotenuse. Let us call the diagonal d, the length l, and the width w giving:

$$d = \sqrt{l^2 + w^2}$$

which evaluates to:

$$d = \sqrt{576 + 576} = 33.941 ft$$

Does this answer look right? I must admit, this answer puzzled me as Pythagorean-type problems are usually presented in books so that you end up with a 3–4–5 triangle (i.e. the hypotenuse = 5, and the two other sides 3 and 4, as $3^2 + 4^2 = 5^2$). The solution I arrived at with decimal places felt wrong. The reason my answer seemed strange is because my shortest path was wrong – the second candidate is the correct one (Figure 3.7). This path requires the ant to walk diagonally down the wall and then across the floor to the corner. That I did not get this answer is because my diagram was not the best one for the problem. My difficulty was that I tend to see things literally. The problem talked of a room, so I drew a three-dimensional model of the room. From that I made an incorrect assumption about the quickest route and hence calculated the wrong answer. Like the earlier journey problem, this puzzle is much more easily understood if it is restated slightly. The journey-to-a-friend answer was obvious when we changed the scenario slightly to simplify the problem; we kept the essential details the same but simply moved the two opposite journeys to the same day. The ant's quickest path is much easier to see if we fold the room out flat and draw it in two dimensions:

 Think Spot

FIGURE 3.8   **Plan view of room**

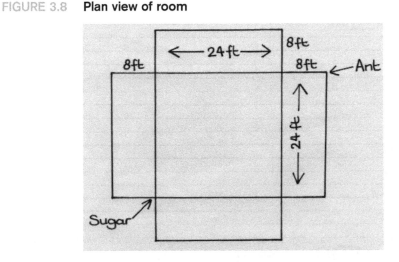

Try marking the shortest path from the ant to the sugar on this new representation of the problem. The answer is given in Figure 3.9 but think carefully and check your answer before you look.

Did you get the right answer? Calculating the length of the path is now very simple, again requiring Pythagoras' theorem. The base of the triangle is 32 ft (24 ft + 8 ft) and the height is 24 ft. Looking for the 3–4–5 pattern we can see that 32 ft is 4 × 8 ft and the height is 3 × 8 ft. Therefore, the hypotenuse (the length of the path) must be 5 × 8 ft = 40 ft.[2]

Of course, reducing the room to two dimensions takes away some of the detail and the dotted line indicating the shortest path could be interpreted two ways. It could be the line along the wall and the floor that the ant takes which is what we have used it for. But if you did not know anything of the problem and looked at the diagram from cold, you might just as well visualize the path as the straight line through the air from the top corner to the opposite bottom corner. It all depends on the context, and everyone using the diagram needs to be aware of just what the context is and what everything means. If you cannot see this interpretation then think about it some more. It may help to make (or imagine) a cardboard model of the room with a piece of elastic stretched between the two corners. Unfold the model of the room until it is flat (as in the diagram above). What does the elastic do? If you coat the elastic with ink and then unfold the model, what mark does the elastic leave on the card? You should find that it leaves a line that maps exactly onto the dotted line shown in Figure 3.9. If you fold the model back up into a box you will see that the ink trail now looks just like the path shown in Figure 3.7. Simplifying the model, or taking a more *abstract* view means the two different paths now look identical. That is ABSTRACTION again and you need to be careful.

FIGURE 3.9   **Plan view with path marked**

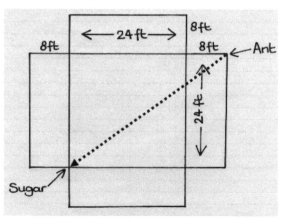

---

[2] If you want to do this the long way, then $path^2 = 32^2 + 24^2 = 1024 + 576 = 1600$. Now take the square root of 1600 to give the answer: 40.

How many problems is the ant-and-sugar puzzle composed of? It decomposed into two subproblems: the first was to identify the shortest path and the second was to calculate the length of that path. Whether the first or second subproblem is more difficult to solve depends on the way your mind works and your knowledge of Pythagoras'. I had trouble visualizing the path but found the application of Pythagoras' theorem simple. Therefore I made an error of the third kind. That is, I correctly solved the wrong problem, and so came up with a correctly-calculated but wrong answer. Maybe you could identify the path easily but had forgotten (or had never learned) Pythagoras' theorem. Without that knowledge it is much more difficult to calculate the length of the path. The advantage of this position is that you have correctly *solved* the problem of finding the path. All that remains is discovering how the answer can be *calculated* and this can be achieved by looking in a geometry text book or asking someone who is more knowledgeable in mathematics than you.

> **Errors of the third kind**

What does this problem have to do with programming? Suppose that you have been employed by a thrifty electrician who likes to use as little cable as possible when wiring rooms. He often needs to run a cable from the bottom corner of a room up to the opposite top corner. The cable can go underneath the floorboards and the electrician will chase a conduit into the plaster to take the cable up the wall. He wants you to write a program for his hand-held computer that will allow him to enter the height, length, and width of any room and which will calculate the shortest length of cable needed. We have already solved the problem of calculating the answer, so all that remains is to turn that solution into a repeatable routine (a recipe) that can, in turn, be translated into programming language code. That is the subject of the next two chapters, so we will leave the ant to get on with finding the sugar.

Think Spot

Mathematics

Unfortunately, many students today are afraid of mathematics. This is increasingly common among computer science students which is a shame because an appreciation of some basic and discrete mathematics (which includes theory and logic) would make the underlying principles of computer programming much more transparent. However, it is a fact that apart from courses on which it is a central part of the curriculum, mathematics is largely ignored. You will have observed that some of the problems in this chapter have had arithmetic at their core. Of course, you do not need to be a mathematician to be able to do basic arithmetic and algebra. Applying Pythagoras' theorem does not make you a mathematician, simply someone who can do a bit of algebra. The level of mathematical skill required for the problems in this book is less than that needed for the mathematics that is taught to sixteen-year-olds in schools, so do not worry. This section is not going to deal with serious mathematics. Rather, I just want you to be aware that algebra (and the occasional bit of geometry) can give you a clearer understanding of certain problems.

Here is a puzzle of the kind found in intelligence tests: The hard drive in Nick's computer has twice the capacity of Alf's. Between them their computers have 240 gigabytes of hard-drive storage. What is the capacity of each hard drive?

Verbal reasoning is not going to help much here, but an algebraic representation is quite useful. Let x stand for Nick's hard drive and y for Alf's. We can state the following:

(1) $x + y = 240$

(2) $x = 2y$

That is, in (1) we know that the size of both drives together is 240 GB and in (2) that drive x is twice the size of drive y. As x is the same value as $2y$, then we can substitute this term for x in the first equation to give:

(3) $2y + y = 240$, or $3y = 240$

If we divide both sides by 3 we get

(4) $y = \dfrac{240}{3} = 80$

Therefore, Alf's hard drive is 80 GB. Nick's is twice the size, so it must be 160 GB (80 + 160 = 240). Problem solved. The trick was to realize that the language the problem was written in was not the best language for working toward further understanding. Do not be afraid to turn to algebra as it is a very good description tool for certain problems.

Why won't verbal reasoning be any use here?

I said it would not help much because it does not provide a manageable way to describe the problems in terms that make it easy to solve. If you are not convinced, try using verbal reasoning to represent the following problem in your head:

If my computer is worth two-thirds of the value of my computer plus two-thirds of the value of my camera plus two-thirds of the value of my radio plus two-thirds of the value of my coffee machine, and my camera is worth two-thirds of the camera plus two-thirds of the radio plus two-thirds of the coffee machine, and my radio is worth two-thirds of the radio plus two-thirds of the coffee machine, how many coffee machines is my computer worth?

Physical Models

Physical models can be very useful and are used by many professionals in their problem solving. Architects build physical models of buildings. Engineers make models and working prototypes to show how their machines will work. Physical models give you a view that natural language cannot. They give you a clear idea of the boundaries of the thing to be built. Physical models provide an all-round three-dimensional view which blueprints cannot. Blueprints, on the other hand, can be rolled up and carried easily as well as showing precise and detailed measurements. Computer programs are not physical – they are intangible webs woven from logic, so how can a physical model help with writing programs? Consider the ant-and-sugar problem. I suggested visualizing a physical model of the room with a bit of elastic stretched between the corners.

To write this ▶ program you will need a matchbox, a rubber band, a small knife, and some ink . . .

Now I want you to actually make the model. You do not need to get the dimensions to scale; the inside of a matchbox will suffice. Make a small hole in a bottom corner and a small notch in the opposite upper corner. Take a rubber band and cut it so that it forms a single thread. Make a knot near one end and thread it through the hole so that the knot rests against the outside of the box. Pull the band reasonably tight, put it through the notch in the upper corner and make another knot so that you now have the band forming the diagonal between the two corners. Coat the band with some ink and, holding the upper corner end of the band firmly, fold out the end of the matchbox flat so that the rubber band rests taut against the base of the box (much like Figure 3.9). Now fold the end of the box back up again. If all has gone well you should now have a trail of ink marking out the shortest walking route between the two corners (like Figure 3.7).

This physical model gives a very clear visualization of the problem. Depending on how you manipulate the model you can have both the three-dimensional and two-dimensional views of Figure 3.7 and Figure 3.9. The model should put to rest any confusion between the ant's route and that taken by a fly.

If a physical model helps you to visualize or understand a problem better, then use it. I have used physical models in lectures to illustrate basic programming concepts; sometimes acting out the steps a computer program follows can make it much easier to understand what it is doing. Not understanding how programs actually execute inside the computer is a common cause of frustration among novices who have an incorrect mental model of the program. Because they think the program is operating differently from the way they understand means they cannot discover why it does not produce the answers they want.

3.2 Pseudo-code – A Language for Solution Description

Once the problem has been described and understood we must solve it and then write down our solution. Often the solution is best phrased in a different language from the one used to describe it. For example, you may remember from school the solution for calculating the two roots of a quadratic equation as "minus *b* plus or minus the square root of *b* squared minus four *ac* over two *a*." Is that only "*b* squared minus four *ac* divided by two *a*" or is everything divided by 2*a*? The algebraic description makes things clear:

$$\frac{-b \pm \sqrt{b^2 - 4ac}}{2a}$$

Everything is divided by 2*a*. If you can remember your algebra you will be able, for different values of *a*, *b*, and *c*, to calculate the positive and negative roots using the above formula. However, while algebra may be the best language for describing some algebraic problems, text for some problems, and pictures for other types of problem, the computer will understand none of them. These different forms of representation are purely to help us with understanding and solving problems. To tell a computer how to calculate the answers we must tell it the solution in the way *it* understands, hence the need for programming language systems. Because this part of the book focuses on problem solving and solution description it does not deal with a specific programming language. However, that does not mean we can ignore the problem of translating our solution descriptions (be they mathematical, visual, physical, or textual) into the formal notation of a programming language. We still need a formalized and structured way of writing down our solutions.

James Adams (2001) observed that solving problems is a habit, that is, we do it every day, most of the day. The difficulty with programming is that we have to articulate our solutions in a precise and unambiguous way – and this we are not used to doing. You may be quite good at solving problems, but are you good at explaining your solutions to others?

Try explaining to someone how to get to your house or the post office from wherever you are right now. Did you do well? Did they look confused? How do you capture and set out all the rules of your decision making? How many of your rules are ambiguous or incompletely stated?

Much of our problem solving is unconscious or subconscious. Adams continues: *"the natural response to a problem seems to be to try to get rid of it by finding an answer – often taking the first answer that occurs and pursuing it because of one's reluctance to spend the time and mental effort needed to conjure up a richer storehouse of alternatives from which to choose"* (Adams, 2001 p. 9).

While you could probably achieve a measure of success simply by writing your instructions in natural language, this is not the way we shall go. We know how natural language can be ambiguous; indeed, many lawyers make a very good living trying to ensure that contracts and legal codes are precise and free from ambiguity. The richness of language also means that we use many different words and expressions to convey just one idea. For example, say I am training my child to do household chores, and I want her to start emptying the kitchen bin. I could say "empty the bin when it is full." Or, I could say "if the bin is full then empty it." Or even, "should the bin run out of room then you must empty it." Part of being a good programmer is learning to think precisely, to say exactly what you mean and to mean exactly what you say. We must develop this skill because the computer has no ability to question our instructions. It cannot decide that an instruction is ambiguous and ask "are you sure you meant that?" It will follow your instructions *exactly* even if your instructions are wrong.

To help develop skills of clear and precise expression we will use something called *pseudo-code* (also called structured English or even Program Design Language) for writing down the solutions to problems. It is called pseudo-code because it is not real programming language code but something that looks a bit like it. Pseudo-code is a halfway house between loose natural language and logically precise programming languages. It is a mixture of natural language words and expressions and formal keywords and constructs that have specific meanings. Pseudo-code is a description language that many programmers use to express their ideas in a structured way but without the complexities of a real programming language. Here is an example of a pseudo-code description of the process of getting up in the morning:

```
    Task number          Task, or action

1. Switch off alarm;

2. Get out of bed;                    Semicolon denotes end of actions

3. Shower/wash face, brush teeth, etc.;

4. Get dressed ;
```

What does writing some instructions in this way achieve? By using the semi-colon as a separator we can easily see that there are four distinct actions. By numbering and putting each action on a separate line the sequence of actions is also very clear.[3] The idea of sequence is very important in programming as things must be done in the right order to get the right results. Sometimes the sequence of tasks does not matter. For example, it is not vital that we switch off the alarm before getting out of bed and we could just as easily swap the ordering of the first two actions. Or can we? What if the alarm clock is on the other side of the room from our bed and we cannot reach it without getting up? In this case, it is very important in which order we write the instructions as they could not be followed otherwise. Knowing the correct sequence of actions requires us not just to understand the problem of getting up in the morning, but also to know something of the context in which this problem is situated. James Adams notes that it can be *"difficult to see a problem from the viewpoint of all the interests and parties involved,"* but that *"consideration of such view-points . . . leads to a 'better' solution to the problem"* (Adams, 2001 p. 33). To write a correct set of instructions we have to know something of the relationships between the principal parts of the problem – we must know, for instance, where the alarm is in relation to the bed.

Problem ▶
frames

Looking at the problem to understand its boundaries and its context is called *framing*. When you buy a picture to hang on your wall you need a frame to hold it. The frame has to be of the correct size and of an appropriate material and colour. When we frame a problem we are describing, classifying, and relating it to other problems we have already met. Knowing if it is similar to a problem we have met before will bring to mind some relevant questions to ask and some techniques to help us solve it. We saw examples of this earlier when we considered description languages. Some problems were more easily visualized by drawing a diagram than by attempting to reason them out verbally.[4]

---

[3] As you become proficient in its use you will find you do not always need to number your pseudo-code statements. However, for the purposes of instruction I have used numbers in this book as they make it much easier to talk about individual statements. Feel free to use or not use statement numbering as you wish in your own work.

[4] Michael Jackson wrote a book on the subject of framing problems (Jackson, 2001) which you are advised to read once you have completed your programming courses.

There are a million other things we could consider too, such as the size of the room, whether the alarm has a remote control or not and so on. How do I know when to stop?

This is not an easy question to answer. The short answer is that you will learn with experience how much detail is needed, and that you know you have not been thorough enough if your solution doesn't work. A more detailed answer involves thinking about ABSTRACTION (see earlier) and ASSUMPTIONS.

Returning to getting up in the morning, we can see other orderings are more obvious: We need to get out of bed before we can wash or shower, and it is clearly not possible to wash or shower after we have got dressed. Or is it? Certainly, taking a shower fully clothed would be silly, but if I only want to wash my face then I can do that dressed or undressed. Often, by examining the orderings of sequences we recognize that what seemed like an obvious and immutable sequence of actions is much more complex than we had first thought. In the above example, we can resolve the question of the ordering of the four actions by including some conditions. For instance, we could ask whether the clock is reachable from the bed and if it is, switch off the alarm then get out of bed, otherwise get out of bed and then switch off the alarm. By phrasing the instructions in this way our solution is more general and applies to many more arrangements of bedroom furniture. (We will deal with the issue of conditional statements in Chapter 4.)

You may be thinking that this is becoming very pedantic now, after all, what does programming have to do with whether the alarm clock is on the other side of the room? When we specified turning off the alarm before getting out of bed we made an ASSUMPTION. When programmers start making assumptions about the way things are or the way things should be then there is a chance that their programs will not perform as the customer expected. If this means your word processor occasionally inserts a spurious character or two into your documents (likê thìs) you may not be too worried. But consider something more serious. The European Space Agency's Ariane 5 rocket exploded 39 seconds into its maiden flight due to an ASSUMPTION made by the developers of its guidance software.

So as not to bombard you with too many details too soon, we will develop our pseudo-code as we progress through the book. You can find the complete details of the pseudo-code notation in Appendix A. There is no accepted standard for pseudo-code (sometimes also called *program design language*), indeed, there are many different styles. What tends to happen is that programmers use the constructs of their chosen programming language in their pseudo-code. This makes the process of translating from pseudo-code to programming language more straightforward. Because this book does not focus on a single language, I have tried to use as general a notation as possible. You will find, therefore, that the words of the pseudo-code do not necessarily match up with the words used by your programming language.

3.3 Chapter Summary

In this chapter we looked at tools for describing problems, namely words, diagrams and pictures, mathematics, and physical models. We started to use a semi-formal language notation (pseudo-code) for expressing solutions to problems. This pseudo-code will form the basis of our algorithm designs and will, once its various features have been introduced over the course of the book, provide a suitable notation that can be translated into real programming languages for implementation on a computer.

3.4 Exercises

For the following exercises use the *HTTLAP* strategy and apply any visual thinking, diagrams, or algebra techniques that you find helpful. Solutions to a selection of the exercises can be found in Appendix C.

1. Nick's computer has three times the memory of Lynne's and Alf's computers put together. Shadi's PC has twice as much memory as Chris's. Nick's computer has one-and-a-half times the memory of Shadi's. Between them, Alf and Shadi's computers have as much memory as Lynne's plus twice the memory of Chris's. Shadi, Chris, Nick, Alf, and Lynne's PCs have 2,800 megabytes of memory between them. How much memory does each computer have?

2. The fly–sugar problem. This exercise is a variation of the ant–sugar problem. A room measures 3.2 m long, 2.4 m wide and 3 m high. A fly sits in one of the upper corners looking at a bowl of sugar in the lower corner diagonally opposite. Assuming the fly can, indeed, fly, calculate the shortest route to the sugar. This is easiest if you use a combination of algebra and diagrams as it is a problem in geometry.

3. Chessboards have alternate black and white squares, and the square in the top left corner is always white. Imagine you are making a chessboard but for some peculiar reason you have decided to paint each square in a random order. Without continually counting "white, black, white, black . . ." from the top left corner each time or looking at pictures of a chessboard each time, consider how else you could determine whether any given square should be black or white.[5]

4. A farmer keeps sheep and chickens. In the farmyard there are 68 animals with a total of 270 legs. Assuming every chicken has exactly 2 legs and each sheep exactly 4 legs, how many chickens and sheep are there in the farmyard? The farmer changes the number of sheep and chickens such that there are now 75 animals but still 270 legs. How many of each animal does the farmer own now?

5. When you pay cash for something, good cashiers give you your change using the fewest coins possible. Using the *HTTLAP* strategy, write an algorithm that works out the ideal change to give for any amount between 1 and 99 pence/cents. If you are working with euros or British pounds then the coins available to you are 1, 2, 5, 10, 20, and 50 (cents or pence). If working with US dollars, then the available coins are 1, 5, 10, and 25 (I am ignoring the rare and unpopular half-dollar and one-dollar coins). Here are some examples:

    ■   To give 67 pence in change requires $1 \times 50p + 1 \times 10p + 1 \times 5p + 1 \times 2p$.

    ■   To give 43 euro cents in change requires $2 \times 20c + 1 \times 2c + 1 \times 1c$.

    ■   To give 63 US cents in change requires $2 \times 25¢ + 1 \times 10¢ + 3 \times 1¢$.

---

[5] Hint: If you number the rows and columns such that the top row is R1 (Row 1) and the leftmost column is C1 (Column 1), what do you notice about the row and column values of any white square?

If you want to use a different currency simply substitute your chosen coins.[6]

The following exercises all appeared in Chapter 2. For each, rewrite your solution using the *HTTLAP* pseudo-code notation.

6. Getting dressed in the morning (that is, just the tasks associated with getting dressed; do not include getting up, washing, etc.).

7. Using an electric filter machine (also called a percolator) to make a pot of coffee and pour a cup.

8. Filling a car with fuel.

9. Making a cheese and onion omelette.

10. Travelling from home to work/college.

11. Completing a piece of homework/college assignment.

12. A wedding ceremony. Note, this is very culturally dependent, so my solution may not resemble yours at all!

13. Choosing what to study at a university.

14. Hanging a picture on the wall.

3.5 Projects

StockSnackz Vending Machine

Take your existing solution from Chapter 2 and write it using pseudo-code. Does drawing a diagram of the vending machine and its principal components help?

Stocksfield Fire Service

Take your existing solution from Chapter 2 and write it using pseudo-code.

Puzzle World: Roman Numerals and Chronograms

Take your existing solution from Chapter 2 and write it using pseudo-code.

Pangrams: Holoalphabetic Sentences

Take your existing solution from Chapter 2 and write it using pseudo-code.

Online Bookstore: ISBNs

Take your existing solution from Chapter 2 and write it using pseudo-code.

---

[6] Hint: To solve this problem you will need to think about the remainders, or left over, after division has taken place.

4 Problems of Choices and Repeated Actions

Devising and writing a program is a problem-solving process. To develop a software system, you must understand the problem, work out a solution strategy, and then translate it into a program.

I. Somerville (2001)

Learning Objectives

- Recognize the role of sequence, choice (selection), and repetition (iteration) in solving problems
- Apply the problem solving strategy to real-world problems involving alternative courses of action and repeated courses of action
- Understand the importance of the role assumptions and abstraction play in problem solving
- Understand the importance of reflecting upon what has been learned during a problem solving activity and how proper documentation is necessary

In this chapter we will start applying our strategy to some problems that occur in the real world. Chapter 3 ended with some exercises for you to try. If you have not tried most of them, then please go back and do so before continuing with this chapter. You will benefit much more from this chapter once you have attempted to solve those initial problems. If you did attempt the exercises, did you come up with one solution for each of them, or did you come up with a few different solutions, all of which seemed to be valid? Why did you get more than one answer? If you did not, please go back and think over the exercises to see if your solution would cover all possible situations in which you might need to solve those problems.

You will learn in this chapter about different types of problem that we encounter in programming tasks. You will learn the three basic high-level control abstractions – *sequence* (ordered sequences of actions), *iteration* (repeated actions), and *selection* (alternative courses of action) – which are the building blocks of algorithmic solutions. You will learn also the importance of evaluating your solutions as you go to make sure they are correct.

4.1 Making Coffee

Using Exercise 7 from Chapter 3 as a starting point we will now explore real-world problems in more detail. Exercise 7 was about making coffee. Perhaps you first came up with a solution like this:

Solution 4.1 Make coffee:

1. Put water and coffee in machine ;
2. Turn on machine ;
3. Pour coffee into mug ;

On the surface this solution seems fine. Can you find any problems with it? Did you use the *HTTLAP* strategy (Table 2.2)? Perhaps you thought it was too simple a problem to waste your time using the strategy? Below is an example of applying the *HTTLAP* strategy to this problem. We will write down the process in a question-and-answer format taking the questions from the strategy. Questions taken directly from the *HTTLAP* strategy in Table 2.2 are shown in **bold type**. Questions that were triggered in my mind as a result are shown in *italics*. First, take a look at Figure 4.1 which shows a simple coffee machine.

? Think Spot

FIGURE 4.1   **My coffee machine**

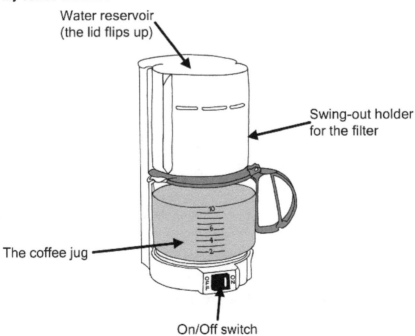

Understanding the Problem

Q. What are you being asked to do?

A. I need to make a pot of coffee and pour a cup.

Q. **What is required?**

A. A cup of coffee.

Q. **Is that all that is required?**

A. I think that before I can get a cup of coffee I need the machine's jug to have enough coffee to pour into the cup.

Q. **What is the unknown?**

A. How much coffee to make. I need to pour a cup, but also I have to make a pot. How much is a pot? Does it mean a whole pot, or just enough coffee to fill one cup?

Q. **Can the problem be better expressed by drawing a diagram or a picture?**

A. I do not know. Looking at Figure 4.1, I can see the jug probably holds more coffee than the cup.

Q. **What are the principal parts of the problem?**

A. 1) Make a pot of coffee. 2) Pour a cup. Or, looking at it another way: 1) The filter machine, 2) the cup, 3) the coffee, 4) some water, 5) the cup of coffee – is there just coffee in it, or milk and sugar as well?

Q. **Are there several parts to the problem?**

A. I guess so. Making the coffee is a separate problem from pouring it. Making the coffee is not a single action either – I need to get the water, measure some coffee, etc.

Q. **Have you made any assumptions?**

A. Well, I have assumed that the jug holds more than one cupful of coffee. That is not always the case – you can buy single-cup filter machines.

Q. **What can you do about the assumptions?**

A. I could ask the person who wants me to make the coffee what size coffee machine to use.

I think I have got a good understanding of the problem and the issues it raises. Remember, you can always come back to Step 1 later on, so let's continue to Step 2.

Devising a Plan to Solve the Problem

Q. **Have you solved this problem before/is it similar to one you have solved before?**

A. In the context of this book, the answer must be *no*.

Q. **Are some parts of the problem more easily solved than others?**

A. Yes. Pouring the coffee is easy. Adding the water and the coffee grounds requires some thought as to *how much* to add. After pouring the coffee I do not know if anything else is needed (e.g., milk and sugar).

Q. Does restating the problem help? Try restating it in a different language.

A. I do not think that applies here. It is not a weird logical problem, or one that requires a puzzle to be solved. The picture of the coffee machine does clarify the main parts of the problem.

Q. Did you make use of all the information in the problem statement?

A. Yes, I think so. In fact, the statement seems to be incomplete as I do not know how much coffee to make or whether milk and sugar are needed.

Q. Can you satisfy all the conditions of the problem?

A. If I make some assumptions, yes. Without any further information, I have to define what is meant by "pot of coffee" (how much is in a pot) and what constitutes pouring a cup – is it *just* pouring out the coffee, or is it also adding milk or sugar?

Q. Have you left anything out?

A. No, I do not think so; I seem to have gleaned all the information I can from the statement.
Let's now move on to Step 3.

Carrying Out the Plan

According to *HTTLAP* here, we have to "write down the basic sequence of actions necessary to solve the general problem." We should do this using the pseudo-code notation introduced in the last chapter. So, now consider the solution I came up with:

Solution 4.2 Make coffee:

```
 1.  Put water in coffee machine ;
 2.  Open the coffee holder ;              An underlined action is
 3.  Put filter paper in machine ;    ←    based on an assumption
 4.  Measure coffee for one cup ;          that needs resolving
 5.  Put coffee into filter paper ;
 6.  Shut the coffee holder ;
 7.  Turn on machine ;
 8.  Wait for coffee to filter through ;
 9.  Pour coffee into mug ;
10.  Turn off machine ;
```

In Step 3 of *HTTLAP* we are asked:

Is your ordering of actions correct? Does the order rely on certain things to be true? If so, do you know these things from the problem statement? Or have you made any assumptions? If you have made assumptions then how will you verify that they are correct?

We shall address these questions now. Why did I have 10 steps in my sequence? Because the principal actions of making the coffee and pouring it out are insufficient to explain how to solve the problem – a sequence of actions is needed to make the pot of coffee itself. Why separate putting in the water and the coffee into two actions? Because they *are* separate actions. That covers the first step, but what of the others? Recall *HTTLAP* says not just to write down a sequence of actions but also to examine the solution carefully to look for hidden assumptions and other action orderings that would work too.

In working for understanding and planning the attack (Steps 1 and 2), we observed that while we know we need to pour one cup, a question remained over how much coffee to make. There is insufficient information, so I have made an ASSUMPTION that I should only make enough coffee for one cup. Is this assumption valid? Possibly, but I cannot be sure; in this instance I would try to get more information. I should ask the person who wants me to make the coffee how much coffee they want. They might have themselves assumed that I will make a whole pot and that after they have finished the cup I have poured, they intend to go and pour themselves another. For now I have simply made the assumption that only one cup is required, so Task #4 specifies how much coffee to put in the machine. Notice I have underlined this action as a note to myself that there is an assumption here that needs resolving.

Actually, there is at least one more assumption associated with this task. Try to identify it before continuing.

In fact, I have assumed that already I have coffee in a suitable form for putting in the machine. A filter machine uses ground coffee. What if we do not have ground coffee but only some whole roasted beans? In that case I would need to grind up enough beans for one cup of coffee first. Is this being pedantic? Yes, but it illustrates the point that what might seem like an obvious answer often masks a number of assumptions that may or may not be correct.

What assumption underlies Task #3? Some coffee machines have built-in filters that are taken out and washed. Others need a paper filter. I have assumed that this machine takes paper filters (see Task #5).

By now you may have found another assumption that I appear to have missed. Task #1 talks of putting in water, but how much? This is linked to Task #4, and we see that my solution has an assumption that I have not accounted for yet which I should correct. I do not think there are any other assumptions buried in this solution so we can look at the other tasks.[1] Task #6 has to be done if the machine is to work properly – my coffee machine needs the coffee holder to be shut otherwise the water will go straight into the pot bypassing the coffee altogether. Task #7 should be obvious – turning on my machine starts the water-pumping mechanism. Did you have something like Task #8 in your solution? It is quite an important task. Task #9 was in the problem specification. Task #10 wasn't, but as I assumed I only needed to make enough coffee for one cup then

---

[1] If you have really got your eye on the ball then you may have come up with an additional assumption – is the coffee machine plugged in and the electricity outlet switched on? If so, pat yourself on the head and carry on. If not, do not worry because I forgot it too – someone with more common sense than me pointed it out.

it makes sense to turn the machine off – I do not want the hot plate keeping an empty jug warm. Notice how my earlier assumption percolates through the whole solution (pun intended)?

If I were going to make more than one cup of coffee, when should the machine be switched off, for it certainly needs turning off at some point? I could try something like this:

```
10. When jug empty turn off machine ;
```

Both Task #8 and the rephrased Task #10 imply that a decision must be made.

4.2 Making Choices

Step 3 in *HTTLAP* asks whether all actions should be carried out in every circumstance, or should some actions/groups of actions be carried out only when certain conditions are met? It is very common for solutions to problems to include some decision making. Consider the extended coffee-making problem:

> *Using an electric filter machine (also called a percolator) make a pot of coffee and pour a cup for a guest. Add sugar and cream/milk as required.*

Now the problem contains some instructions that require some decisions to be made, that is, whether to add sugar and milk to the coffee.

> Using Solution 4.2 above as a starting point, write out a new solution to include this extra requirement.

What has changed from the original problem? What is meant by the new requirement to "add sugar and cream/milk as necessary"? We need to return to Steps 1 and 2 of *HTTLAP* and make sure we understand the problem well before trying to solve it.

Q. What are you being asked to do?

A. In addition to what is already known about the problem I need also to add milk and sugar as necessary.

Q. What is required?

A. Possibly some milk and possibly some sugar.

Q. What is the unknown?

A. Whether to add the milk and sugar and, if so, how much to add.

Q. Can the problem be better expressed by drawing a diagram or a picture?

A. No.

Q. What are the principal parts of the problem?

A. 1) the milk, 2) the sugar, 3) the lightening and sweetening requirements of the drinker.

Q. Are there several parts to the problem?

A. Yes, adding the milk is a separate decision from adding the sugar. Before either can be added we need to find out whether it is wanted.

Q. Have you made any assumptions?

A. Not yet.

I am confident I have a good understanding of the problem and what is required. The questions in Step 2 do not seem to add anything to my understanding of this problem: I have made use of all the information and I have not made any assumptions (that I am aware of) so we can consider the following solution as a starting point:

Solution 4.3 Make coffee:

```
1.  Put water in coffee machine ;
2.  Open the coffee holder ;
3.  Put filter paper in machine ;
4.  Measure coffee for one cup ;
5.  Put coffee into filter paper ;
6.  Shut the coffee holder ;
7.  Turn on machine ;
8.  Wait for coffee to filter through ;
9.  Add sugar ;
10. Add milk/cream ;
11. Pour coffee into mug ;
12. Stir coffee ;
13. Turn off machine ;
```

(Note, the underlined tasks are based on the assumptions made earlier in Solution 4.2.) Notice I have added a task to stir the coffee – this ensures an even distribution of the milk and sugar throughout the drink.[2] Is the solution correct? It works for someone who takes white coffee with sugar, but not if your guest wants their coffee a different way. At the point of making the coffee we make a decision and we must put that decision making into the solution description. This can be done by extending the pseudo-code to include a special *construct* that expresses *conditional actions*, that is, actions or tasks that are performed only when a specified condition is met. Solution 4.4 below uses the new construct "IF":

IF – a selection ▶
construct

Solution 4.4 Make coffee

```
1.  Put water in coffee machine ;
2.  Open the coffee holder ;
3.  Put filter paper in machine ;
```

---

[2] If you are wondering why I have added the milk and sugar to the cup before pouring the coffee, well that is my coffee-making tip to you: the sugar dissolves almost immediately if it is put into the cup before the coffee. This means minimal stirring is needed and it avoids the coffee drinker's plague of finding that the last swig of coffee contains a mouth-puckering avalanche of undissolved sugar. I do not take sugar anymore, but I remember what it was like. My guests always compliment me on my coffee.

4. <u>Measure coffee for one cup ;</u>
5. Put coffee into filter paper ;
6. Shut the coffee holder ;
7. Turn on machine ;
8. Wait for coffee to filter through ;
9. IF (sugar required)
      9.1. Add sugar ;
   ENDIF
10. IF (white coffee required)
      10.1. Add milk/cream ;
   ENDIF
11. Pour coffee into mug ;
12. Stir coffee ;
13. Turn off machine ;

Huh?

In your first solution you didn't deal with people who don't want milk or sugar, but my solution did try to consider this. Was I wrong to deal with it this early? Do you always need so many versions of a solution? Don't you sometimes get the right answer straight off?

It was certainly not wrong to think about milk and sugar from the outset, and of course, you do sometimes get the full solution first time round. However, when starting out I think it is helpful to spend a lot of time working on the separate components of a problem. In this case we dealt with the overall structure and then considered the finer points such as milk and sugar requirements. Also, I want to introduce the pseudo-code for dealing with choice and repetition in a timely manner.

The flowchart in Figure 4.2 shows diagrammatically how the IF construct works. Flowcharts can be helpful for explaining certain programming concepts and they are considered in more detail in Chapter 8.

FIGURE 4.2   **Control flow diagram for the IF construct**

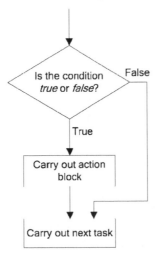

Actions, or tasks, are shown as rectangles. The arrows show what task comes next. Decision points are shown by diamonds. The pseudo-code word "IF" asks a question, the answer to which can be either *true* or *false*. (The statements "it is true that sugar is required" and "it is not true/it is false that sugar is required" should make the meaning of *true* and *false* clear.) If the answer is true then the task following the IF is carried out otherwise it is not. Parentheses in the pseudo-code () enclose the question which is called the *condition*. The action or sequence of actions to be obeyed (known as the action *block*) when the condition is satisfied (i.e., *true*) is written below the IF, indented by three spaces, and terminated by the keyword ENDIF. The indentation shows actions that are subordinate to others; in other words, one action belongs to, or is contained within, another. We will return to this idea later. The ENDIF shows clearly what actions belong to the IF, that is, what actions are carried out only when the condition is met. Consider Cases 1 and 2 below:

Case 1

```
IF (condition)
   Action 1 ;
   Action 2 ;
ENDIF
```

Case 2

```
IF (condition)
   Action 1 ;
ENDIF
Action 2 ;
```

The placement of ENDIF tells us that in Case 1 both Action #1 and Action #2 are carried out when the condition is met. In Case 2, only Action #1 is obeyed when the condition is met, while Action #2, being outside the action block, comes after the IF and so is obeyed regardless of the condition. Look back at Solution 4.4. Do you see that because Task #11 comes outside the action blocks of the two IFs that the coffee will always be poured while milk and sugar will only be added if the relevant conditions are met? Furthermore, each time we carry out this solution the outcome could be different. If the first guest wants black unsweetened coffee then the two conditions are not met and no milk or sugar is added. The next person may want white unsweetened coffee – no problem. Likewise, the person who wants sugary black or sugary white coffee can also be accommodated. It looks like this is a good general solution. The tasks are written in such a way that whatever combinations of milk and sugar requirements arise we have an algorithm we can follow that will give the desired result. Well, nearly. There remains still a subproblem: what if our guest wants two spoonfuls of sugar? D'oh!

Before continuing you should attempt the following exercises that will ensure you understand how the IF construct works (solutions in Appendix C).

Before you leave home in the morning you check to see whether it is raining; if it is you take an umbrella with you. Write an **IF...ENDIF** construct that shows this decision-making process.

Write an **IF...ENDIF** construct that adds a 10% tip to a restaurant bill and compliments the chef if the service was of a high standard. After the **ENDIF** add a statement to pay the bill. Convince yourself that the tip is only added when good service is received.

4.3 Making It Again: Repeated Actions

While Solution 4.4 is good it does not allow for situations where more than one spoonful of sugar is required. How could we solve the problem of adding enough sugar? We could first ask our guest if sugar is required and then add a spoonful. Then we could ask if more is required and add another spoonful. For a guest who wants two sugars, the action sequence would look like this:

Solution 4.5 More than one sugar:

```
IF (sugar required)
    Add spoonful of sugar ;
ENDIF
IF (more sugar required)
    Add spoonful of sugar ;
ENDIF
```

The trouble here is that the solution works only if we decide to ration guests to two spoonfuls each. Of course, we could add another IF to allow for three spoonfuls, but it is not a very elegant solution as it requires us to ask our guest three times if he wants sugar even if the answer to the first question was *no*. Even then it does not cater for those who want four or even more sugars. The good thing about Solution 4.4 was that it worked for all the combinations of milk and single spoonful of sugar. We would like to achieve the same general-purpose type of solution for the question of how many sugars to add. Looking at Solution 4.5 do you notice anything special? What about the fact that the action "Add spoonful of sugar" has been repeated? Think about how you would go about this for real. You probably would not ask your guest if sugar is required and then keep on asking and adding more until they say no. Rather, you would ask how many sugars are wanted and then repeatedly add a spoonful until the request is satisfied; if no sugar is required we simply add no sugar.[3] To express actions that are repeated we add the **WHILE** construct to the pseudo-code.

WHILE – an iteration construct

---

[3] In programming terms we might say that we carry out the action "Add a spoonful of sugar" zero times. That may sound weird (doing something zero times) but it is an important concept and one which will be revisited in Chapter 6.

FIGURE 4.3 **Layout of the WHILE construct**

```
WHILE (condition is true)
    Action 1 ;
ENDWHILE
```

Or with multiple actions:

```
WHILE (condition is true)
    Action 1 ;
    Action 2 ;
    ...
    Action n ;
ENDWHILE
```

Is condition true or false?　False

True

Carry out action block

Next task

The first example in Figure 4.3 shows a WHILE construct whose action block contains a single task. The second example has an action block with multiple tasks. The layout should be fairly clear as it resembles the IF construct. Recall that the IF means "if the specified condition is true (satisfied) then carry out the tasks in the subsequent action block." In contrast, the WHILE says "while the specified condition is true carry out the tasks in the action block." The difference is that the action block is repeatedly obeyed while, or as long as, the condition is true (this is known as a *loop* because we keep *looping* around the action block). Thinking of our coffee problem we could say "while (or, as long as) sugar is still required, perform the task of adding a spoonful of sugar." Of course, we must make sure there is some way for the condition to eventually become false otherwise we will be stuck forever repeatedly carrying out the tasks in the action block.

Write a **WHILE** loop to handle adding sugar to the coffee (use the notation from Figure 4.3). Remember to close the action block with an **ENDWHILE**.

Here is my solution based on what we have learned so far. I have included the tasks that come before and after the sugar-adding to provide context:

Solution 4.6 More sugar required using WHILE

```
 8.  Wait for coffee to filter through ;
 9.  WHILE (sugar required)
         9.1  Add spoonful of sugar ;
     ENDWHILE
10.  IF (white coffee required)
         10.1 Add milk/cream ;
     ENDIF
11.  Pour coffee into mug ;
```

On the surface Solution 4.6 seems to do the trick: there is a mechanism for dealing with the repeated action "Add spoonful of sugar" and milk is only added once if required. But consider what this means for a moment. Taking the milk question first, how do you get the information necessary to decide whether the condition "white coffee required" has been satisfied? You would ask your guest whether they want milk. Look at Task #10 which we can treat as asking a question, the answer to which tells us whether to carry out the conditional task "Add milk/cream." We ask the question once (Task #10) and then, depending on the answer, either carry out Task #10.1 or not. Now look at the WHILE construct which repeatedly adds spoonfuls of sugar. Like the IF, the WHILE needs to ask a question in order to decide whether to carry out the tasks in the action block. If the answer to the question is *true* then the action block is carried out. After obeying the tasks in the action block the construct *loops* back to ask the question again (as you can see from the flowchart in Figure 4.3). This cycle repeats until the condition in the question becomes false at which point we step through to the next task following the WHILE (Task #10 in the case of Solution 4.6).

The question is, each time we come back to the WHILE's condition how do we decide whether enough sugar has been added yet? If we treat the WHILE the way we treated the IF we could simply ask our guest if they want any sugar. If so, we add a spoonful and then loop back and ask the question again. However, this is inelegant as you would not really keep going back to interrogate your guest after every spoonful of sugar. Rather, you would ask the guest first how many sugars are required. Armed with the answer we can go the kitchen to get on with the task without needing to trouble the guest further. If we have a particularly poor memory we could write down the number of sugars required on a piece of paper. Then, when we come to Task #9 a simple bit of arithmetic tells us whether sugar is needed. Supposing our guest asked for one sugar, let's see how to carry out Task #9. The coffee has filtered through (Task #8) and so we arrive at the WHILE loop with the condition (sugar required). Our guest asked for one spoonful and we have not added any yet, so the condition is *true* – sugar is required. We add a spoonful of sugar (Task #9.1) and then loop back to the WHILE. The condition is now *false* (the guest wanted one spoonful and that is what we have put in) so we proceed to Task #10. If two sugars were wanted, then we would loop round twice before the condition becomes false. What if our guest did not want any sugar at all? The first time we reach the WHILE its condition is already false because number of spoonfuls required and the number of spoonfuls we have put into the coffee are already equal (both zero). You should be able to see that what we are doing is keeping a count in our heads of the number of spoonfuls of sugar added to the coffee. When that number reaches the required value then no more sugar is required. We can represent this process explicitly in pseudo-code thus:

```
Find out how many sugars required ;
WHILE (sugars added not equal to number required)
    Add spoonful of sugar ;
    Add 1 to number of sugars added ;
ENDWHILE
```

We will return to keeping track of numbers in the next chapter when we deal with working storage.

In the above **WHILE** loop, why is there a statement to add 1 to the number of sugars added?

To recap, here is the full solution to the coffee-making problem so far:

Solution 4.7 Coffee making

```
 1.   Put water in coffee machine ;
 2.   Open coffee holder ;
 3.   Put filter paper in machine ;
 4.   Measure coffee for one cup ;
 5.   Put coffee into filter paper ;
 6.   Shut the coffee holder ;
 7.   Turn on machine ;
 8.   Wait for coffee to filter through ;
 9.   Find out how many sugars required ;
10.   WHILE (sugars added not equal to number required)
           10.1   Add spoonful of sugar ;
           10.2   Add 1 to number of sugars added ;
       ENDWHILE
11.   IF (white coffee required)
           11.1   Add milk/cream ;
       ENDIF
12.   Pour coffee into mug ;
13.   Stir coffee ;
14.   Turn off machine ;
```

How does it look? Does it work? The last part of *HTTLAP* Step 3 says:

> *Go back to your sequence of actions. Should all actions be carried out in every circumstance? Should some actions (or groups/blocks of actions) only be carried out when certain conditions are met?*
>
> *Go back to your sequence of actions. Is carrying out each action once only sufficient to give the desired outcome? If not, do you have actions (or groups/blocks of actions) that must therefore be repeated?*
>
> *Go back once more. Do any of your actions/blocks of actions belong inside others? For example, do you have a block of actions that must be repeated, but only when some condition is met?*

Taking the first question we have seen that not all the actions should be carried out in every circumstance, hence the IF construct to deal with adding milk and the WHILE construct to cope with adding sugars: milk and sugar must only be added when they are wanted by the drinker.

The second question helps to refine the solution by differentiating between the cases where we need an IF construct and a WHILE construct. To carry out an action (or group of actions) once when a certain condition is met, we use the IF construct (as we did when adding milk). Adding the milk once is sufficient to satisfy the whitening requirements of coffee-making,[4] but adding sugar once may not be enough. We see that we have an action (add spoonful of sugar) that must be repeated while (as long as) a certain condition remains true (sugar required), hence the use of the `WHILE` construct.

The third question tries to ensure that we have put every action in the right place. Updating the count of the number of sugars added (see Task #10.2 in Solution 4.7 above) belongs inside the loop as it needs to be done each time a spoonful of sugar is added. Having carried out the plan, that is, written down a solution to the problem, we can progress to Step 4 of *HTTLAP*.

Assess the Result

In Step 4 of *HTTLAP* we examine the results obtained using our solution. There are two principal reasons for this. First, we need to make sure the solution produces the correct results. Secondly, we should make sure that it produced the results in a sensible and efficient manner. The solution should be clear to follow, as easy to carry out as possible, and not be unwieldy. An example of an unwieldy solution would be the sugar-adding routine in Solution 4.5. Examination of Solution 4.5 revealed a repeated action that was better expressed using a `WHILE` loop. We then examined the `WHILE` and discussed how its condition is tested. In this case, the condition was "sugar required," meaning we keep on adding sugar while more is needed. The question arose as to how to get the information to test the condition. It did not seem sensible to keep on asking our guest how many sugars he wanted, so we solved that problem by asking once (Task #9, Solution 4.7) and then comparing that value with the number of spoonfuls added so far. The next task is to add the milk. How do we  know whether to add milk? We ask our guest. Think about this for a moment. Remember, we are supposed to test these solutions and see if any parts can be made simpler, quicker, or clearer. Is there any opportunity for that here? Ideally you should get someone else to take the solution away and follow its instructions. Let's trace through Solution 4.7 as if we were doing it for real. The first eight actions are:

```
1.   Put water in coffee machine ;
2.   Open coffee holder ;
3.   Put filter paper in machine ;
4.   Measure coffee for one cup ;
5.   Put coffee into filter paper ;
6.   Shut the coffee holder ;
7.   Turn on machine ;
8.   Wait for coffee to filter through ;
```

These tasks deal with setting up the machine, putting in the water and coffee, and getting it going. They seem reasonable and it is hard to see how changing the order of any of the tasks would lead to a better solution.

---

[4] Alright, so I am assuming that everybody who takes milk takes the same amount. Experience tells me that this is clearly not the case. Some people just want a spot of milk while others go as far as wanting half coffee, half milk. If you think about it, this is a very interesting problem in its own right.

Convince yourself of this by writing down a few different orderings of the eight actions above. Are any tasks dependent on other tasks happening first?

Task #9 from Solution 4.7 says:

```
9.   Find out how many sugars required ;
```

This task requires some interaction with our guest, and armed with the answer we can then proceed to Task #10:

```
10.  WHILE (sugars added not equal to number required)
        10.1  Add spoonful of sugar ;
        10.2  Add 1 to number of sugars added ;
     ENDWHILE
```

Assume that our guest asked for two spoonfuls of sugar. The condition asks whether the number of sugars added is equal to the number required. If not then we carry out the tasks in the WHILE's action block. Table 4.1 below gives a trace of the sugar-adding loop. Each row represents one execution of the WHILE. The first column shows the number of sugars asked for by the guest. Column 2 shows how many sugars have been added **at the point of testing the condition**, that is, before the action block is obeyed. The third column shows the state of the condition given the values in Columns 1 and 2. The final column shows what tasks we carry out as a result of the value of the condition in Column 3.

Table 4.1 **Tracing through the** WHILE

Sugars Required	Sugars Added	Condition True/False	Actions Taken
2	0	True	#10.1 – Add spoonful of sugar #10.2 – Add 1 to number of sugars added (now 1)
2	1	True	#10.1 – Add spoonful of sugar #10.2 – Add 1 to number of sugars added (now 2)
2	2	False	Leave the **WHILE** and proceed to task #11

The first time Task #10 is encountered we see that two sugars are required and we have not yet added any. The condition is true (the number of sugars required is **not** equal to the number of spoonfuls added so far) and we proceed to Task #10.1 (adding a sugar) and Task #10.2 (increasing the count of the number of sugars added so far, i.e., one).[5] We loop back to the top of the WHILE and test

---

[5] We have assumed that the value of the number of sugars added begins at zero. This is not a reasonable assumption for some programming languages – see the reflection on INITIALIZATION OF VARIABLES. Do not worry about it yet, though – we have got coffee to make.

the condition again. This time we have added one sugar, but that is not equal to the number required; the condition is true and we carry out Tasks #10.1 and #10.2 again. Once more we go back to the top of the WHILE. Now the number of sugars added and the number required are the same (both two) so the condition is now false and we end the WHILE and proceed to Task #11.

```
11.  IF (white coffee required)
         11.1  Add milk/cream ;
     ENDIF
```

Task #11 is about adding milk (or cream) to the coffee.[6] How do we test the condition? We ask our guest. If he says *yes* we add the milk, otherwise we do not. Either way we then proceed to:

```
12.  Pour coffee into mug ;
```

```
13.  Stir coffee ;
```

14. <u>Turn off machine ;</u>

These tasks are fairly clear. Look at Task #11. Recall that we are inspecting the solution to see if it is cumbersome or could be made simpler, quicker, or clearer. Think about the way we interact with our guest. First we get the machine going (Tasks #1–#8). Next, we ask whether sugar is required. Armed with that knowledge we go to the kitchen and add any sugar. Then we go back and ask whether milk is required and then return to the kitchen again to add any milk and then pour the coffee. This is cumbersome. Perhaps it would be better if we added another information gathering task so that we can get the milk and sugar requirements in one go? This would give the task sequence in Solution 4.8 below. The new task is #10 "Find out whether milk required." For the person making the coffee this seems like a more sensible arrangement of the tasks. It is better because gathering the information requires effort – in this case it means travelling from the kitchen to the living room. By putting Tasks #9 and #10 next to each other we have minimized the effort.

As Action #11.1 comes after Action #11, won't it always be carried out regardless of whether milk is wanted? I thought actions that followed each other sequentially were executed sequentially.

This is a common misunderstanding. It is true that #11.1 follows #11, but the key is in the use of the IF construct. Recall that the actions between the IF and ENDIF keywords are only executed when the condition next to the IF keyword is true. If the condition is not true, i.e., no milk is wanted, then Action #11.1 will not be obeyed. Of course, if the action block had more than one statement (e.g., #11.2 and #11.3 as well) then these would be executed in the order written when the condition is true.

---

[6] I am aware that I have left in an unresolved choice until now; that is, the choice between milk and cream. Actually, I do not mean there to be a choice: if you are in Europe then you would likely be offered milk, whereas in the United States it is typically called cream. For the purposes of this example let's say they are the same thing.

Solution 4.8 The final coffee making routine?

```
1.   Put water in coffee machine ;
2.   Open coffee holder ;
3.   Put filter paper in machine ;
4.   Measure coffee for one cup ;
5.   Put coffee into filter paper ;
6.   Shut the coffee holder ;
7.   Turn on machine ;
8.   Wait for coffee to filter through ;
9.   Find out how many sugars required ;
10.  Find out whether milk required ;
11.  WHILE (sugars added not equal to number required)
          11.1  Add spoonful of sugar ;
          11.2  Add 1 to number of sugars added ;
     ENDWHILE
12.  IF (white coffee required)
          12.1  Add milk/cream ;
     ENDIF
13.  Pour coffee into mug ;
14.  Stir coffee ;
15.  Turn off machine ;
```

Ideally, you should give your coffee-making solution to someone else to work through. Make sure you explain to them how to obey the **IF** and **WHILE** constructs.

There is always a danger when evaluating your own work that you will miss an error. You have probably experienced this when completing written work. You can read a page of your own work over and over and never spot a glaring mistake; only when someone else proofreads it for you does the error get noticed. If you gave your solution to someone else, did they get the same result as you? If not, do you know why? Was it because you (or your friend) did not follow the instructions correctly, or is there an error in the instructions?

Think Spot

If your friend interpreted an instruction differently from the way you intended, it can be useful to get a third person to give their opinion. If they both see it differently from you then perhaps your understanding of how to phrase things is the problem. This is an important programming issue because all software defects are the result of a difference between the programmer's intentions and the way they are expressed in the programming language code. Remember, the computer is incapable of misinterpreting your program; it is your understanding of what you have written that is wrong. There is no such thing as COMPUTER ERROR, only programming error. Computers only produce wrong results because their programs are in error. The only real computer error is if the electronic components break down, the hard drive crashes, etc. The rest are all defects introduced by programmers. If the solution worked, and we cannot find any way to improve we can proceed to Step 5 of *HTTLAP*.

There is no such thing as computer error, only programmer error ▶

Describing What We Have Learned

In Step 5 we make a record of our achievements and list any difficulties we encountered. Here is my dialogue with *HTTLAP*:

Q. What did you learn from this exercise?

A. What seemed like a really straightforward task (describing the process of making coffee) turned out to have some unexpected twists. Also, I became aware of how many assumptions I made: there are aspects to the problem that cannot be addressed without further dialogue with the problem owner.

Q. What do you know now that you did not before you started?

A. There are lots of ways of arranging task orders. Some of them led to the same result but were harder to carry out (e.g., the difference between asking the milk and sugar requirements in the same place (Solution 4.8) and separating the two tasks (Solution 4.7). It is important to consider how straightforward the instructions are to carry out.

Q. What particular difficulties did you encounter? Were there any aspects of the problem that caused you particular difficulty? If so, do you think you would know how to tackle them if you met something similar in the future?

A. I think the trickiest bit was dealing with the milk and sugar requirements. Knowing how to handle repeated actions and conditional actions is useful and I think I will be able to use this idea again. The adding sugars loop could be applied to activities like making tea or even in cooking meals; recipes call for quantities of ingredients to be added. It could even apply to feeding a parking meter: you have to keep putting coins in until there is enough money to cover your parking period.

The last piece of advice in Step 5 of *HTTLAP* is to compare the finished solution with your first attempt and say what the differences teach you. Here is the first solution that we wrote down after following the first three steps of *HTTLAP*:

```
1.   Put water in coffee machine ;
2.   Open the coffee holder ;
3.   Put filter paper in machine ;
4.   Measure coffee for one cup ;
5.   Put coffee into filter paper ;
6.   Shut the coffee holder ;
7.   Turn on machine ;
8.   Wait for coffee to filter through ;
9.   Pour coffee into mug ;
10.  Turn off machine ;
```

And here's the final solution:

```
1.   Put water in coffee machine ;
2.   Open coffee holder ;
3.   Put filter paper in machine ;
4.   Measure coffee for one cup ;
5.   Put coffee into filter paper ;
6.   Shut the coffee holder ;
7.   Turn on machine ;
8.   Wait for coffee to filter through ;
9.   Find out how many sugars required ;
10.  Find out whether milk required ;
11.  WHILE (sugars added not equal to number required)
         11.1   Add spoonful of sugar ;
         11.2   Add 1 to number of sugars added ;
     ENDWHILE
12.  IF (white coffee required)
         12.1   Add milk/cream ;
     ENDIF
13.  Pour coffee into mug ;
14.  Stir coffee ;
15.  Turn off machine ;
```

Think Spot

What are the differences? The first eight tasks are the same at which point the two solutions diverge (apart from pouring the coffee and turning off the machine). The milk and sugar requirement was not part of the original algorithm and was introduced later on. Even so, compare the original solution involving the new requirement (Solution 4.3) with the final one. Solution 4.3 only had two simple milk and sugar actions (#9 and #10): add sugar and add milk/cream. Thinking about these two tasks revealed two subproblems, one involving a simple choice (whether to add milk or not) and the other involving a repeated action. It became clear that trying to describe exactly what to do in order to add milk and the right amount of sugar is more complicated that it first appeared. Perhaps the instructions are a little more detailed than we would normally make them for a person: saying something like "add as many sugars as the guest wants" should be sufficient. But if you wanted to learn to manage staff in a coffee shop you would not be reading this book. Remember, a computer does not possess intelligence and needs every task to be spelled out in minute detail. This detailed description of making coffee is half the way between instructing a person who can think for himself and use prior knowledge and experience to interpret instructions, and writing a program for a machine that has the intelligence of a piece of rock. And just like a rock, a computer will not be affected in the slightest by you shouting at it just because it is not doing what you want it to.

This technique of comparing the initial draft solution with the finished one is one I have used when teaching novice programmers. It can be particularly instructive to see just how different the finished product can be from the first attempt. It works best when you say *why* the differences are there rather than just identifying them. If you can explain why you have included certain aspects in your solution then it is more likely that you understand it. Often, the first attempt at a solution is made before good understanding of the underlying problem has been gained. This is why the *HTTLAP* strategy is so important because it forces you to address your understanding. It is the half-baked first solution with which many novices proceed that causes so much bewilderment. The reflection and dialogue in Steps 1–3 should reduce confusion and lead to better solutions. It is alright to produce a poor first solution as long as you treat it as the starting point of an iterative process of seeking understanding. By getting into the discipline now of critically evaluating your solutions **before** you try implementing them on a computer you will save yourself much confusion later on. Turning a solution into programming language code is challenging enough without being saddled with a poor solution as well.

Documenting the Solution

The final step in *HTTLAP* is to write the documentation. Actually, you should be documenting as you go along. If you leave all the documentation until the end then it is unlikely you will complete it or even do it at all. In fact, we have completed some of the documentation already. Look back at the dialogues with the *HTTLAP* questions. The answers to those questions help to explain why the solution is designed the way it is. Furthermore, a well set out solution is itself part of the documentation. That is, an easy to understand instruction is self-documenting. For all but the simplest of problems and solutions, it is unlikely that you can avoid writing at least some extra documentation. Many computer programs last for years undergoing continual amendment and improvement

 (known as SOFTWARE MAINTENANCE). Is it likely that an undocumented solution will be easy to understand in, say, five years time after the memory of its construction has faded? Now that we have what we think is a working solution, we must go through it and ensure that it is as clearly explained as possible. *HTTLAP* has one more set of questions to help achieve this.

Q. Are there any aspects of your solution that are hard to understand?

 A. That is a hard question to answer. The IF and WHILE could be hard for someone who is not familiar with the idea of expressing choices that way. Let's agree that we do not need to worry about explaining how IFs and WHILEs work in principle as we can explain the pseudo-code language to our friend before we give him any solutions to try out. Putting aside the details of how the constructs work, are there any other aspects of the solution that are hard to understand? One way to approach this question is to think about parts of the solution that were hard to produce. If deriving the solution was not obvious to you, then its expression may not be easy to understand for someone who has not invested the same time as you in working through the intricacies of the problem. For example, take the two questions we ask our guest in Tasks #9 and #10 (Solution 4.8). Why are they there, and why are they in the place they are? Why is Task #10 not closer to the IF that uses its answer? Because it is less cumbersome to get the answers to both questions in one go

rather than run back and forth between the guest and the kitchen. We could document our solution with a comment to that effect.

Q. **If they are hard to understand, is it because they are badly written, or simply because the solution is just complicated? If you were to pick up your solution in five years time do you think any bits would be hard to understand?**

A. The thing about documentation is that it is not for the benefit of our friend who is to carry out the instructions. The computer that executes a program does not read the manual. The documentation is for the benefit of the person who will have to maintain the solution later on in order to correct any defects or add extra bits to cope with new requirements (such as the request to add milk and sugar). You do not want this person to have to work through the entire problem-solving process again just to understand your solution. The documentation should help that person to understand what your solution does and why it is structured the way it is. That will make it much easier for them to change it. And here's the clincher: that person could be you.

How, then, should we document solutions? It is common practice to write two kinds of documentation. The first kind is text that describes the solution, making mention of the information that is needed to be able to carry out the task, and what is produced at the end. The second type is commentary documentation, short explanations placed within the solution to amplify or clarify particular aspects. Solution 4.9 below shows Solution 4.8 with added documentation.

The first part of Solution 4.9 is the general textual documentation. It is not very long or detailed as this is a fairly simple problem. Interspersed throughout the solution you will notice lines beginning with "//." These are commentary lines and have the "//" to distinguish them from the actual tasks. Thus "// Set up coffee machine" is a comment to tell the reader that the tasks following it are to do with setting up the machine. With these comments we have broken the solution tasks into smaller groups each of which deals with a discrete part of the coffee-making problem.

Looking at the documentation, especially the comments that separate sections of the pseudo-code, can you take an abstract view of the algorithm and restate it as a small number of higher-level parts? Hint: for example, what do Tasks #13 and #14 have in common?

Solution 4.9 Documented coffee-making solution

Instructions for making coffee

```
These instructions will allow you to make a cup of coffee for a guest
using a filter machine. To complete the task you will need to find
out the sugar and milk requirements of your guest.
```

```
// *****************************************
// Instructions for making coffee
// Written by Paul Vickers, June 2007
// *****************************************
```

// Set up coffee machine

1. Put water in coffee machine ;
2. Open coffee holder ;
3. <u>Put filter paper in machine ;</u>
4. <u>Measure coffee for one cup ;</u>
5. Put coffee into filter paper ;
6. Shut the coffee holder ;
7. Turn on machine ;
8. Wait for coffee to filter through ;

// Add sugar and milk as necessary

9. Find out how many sugars required ;
10. Find out whether milk required ;
11. WHILE (sugars added not equal to number required)
      11.1   Add spoonful of sugar ;
      11.2   Add 1 to number of sugars added ;
   ENDWHILE
12. IF (white coffee required)
      12.1   Add milk/cream ;
   ENDIF

// Pour and serve coffee

13. Pour coffee into mug ;
14. Stir coffee ;

// Shut the machine down

15. Turn off machine ;

// End of instructions

An abstract view of the solution reveals that it comprises three principal parts:

1. Setting things up – loading the machine, turning it on, etc.
2. Dealing with a cup of coffee – adding milk and sugar, pouring and stirring the coffee.
3. Shutting things down – turning off the machine.

As you become more familiar with programming you will start to recognize this as a general pattern. In programming terms it would be phrased as:

1. Initialization
2. Processing
3. Finalization

You will commonly find yourself writing algorithms that have these three main components. It will not always be easy to neatly divide an algorithm up into such sections, but you should see elements of this pattern in much of what you do.

4.4 Chapter Summary

In this chapter we have taken the real-world problem of making coffee and have followed the *HTTLAP* strategy to produce a workable solution that is generally applicable to a range of coffee requirements. *HTTLAP* helped us to gain a detailed understanding of the problem and to reflect on our attempts at solving the problem. The solution is still based on a few underlying assumptions that need resolving. It is also limited in that it can only be used to make a single cup of coffee. Of course, it would not take much work to amend it so that we could first find out how many cups of coffee are required and then proceed accordingly. In fact, this is exactly what we will do in the next chapter. Strictly speaking, if we were intending to turn our solution into a computer program then there is still a little more work to do, and the condition for the WHILE needs to be refined. But we will deal with the issues behind this in Chapter 6 where we will look at forming loop conditions and will explore three different loop constructs.

4.5 Exercises

1. In what circumstances would you use the IF and WHILE constructs? How are they different?

2. Examine the following algorithm fragment:

    ```
    put on hat ;
    IF (weather is sunny)
       put on sunglasses ;
    ENDIF
    put on shoes ;
    ```

    What items of clothing will be put on a) when it is raining and b) when it is sunny?

3. Examine the following algorithm fragment:

    ```
    Go to shop ;
    buy milk ;
    IF (today is Saturday)
       buy weekly newspaper ;
    buy peanuts ;
    ENDIF
    buy bread ;
    ```

    What items will be purchased a) on Thursday, b) on Saturday?

4. Consider the following algorithm fragment:

    ```
    1.   Eat breakfast ;
    2.   Wash breakfast dishes ;
    3.   WHILE (not finished breakfast) ;
              3.1 Read a story in morning paper ;
              3.2 Take next bite of breakfast ;
         ENDWHILE
    ```

    How many stories in the morning paper will the person get to read?

5. In the *Stocksfield Diner* customers can choose whether or not to have their hamburgers plain or with any combination of cheese, lettuce, and tomatoes. Write three IF constructs that add items as required by the customer.

6. Use the *HTTLAP* strategy to design an algorithm to represent filling a bath. The taps should be turned off altogether when the bath is full. When the bath is half full check the water temperature and if it is not warm enough adjust it by turning the cold tap down a quarter turn.

7. The Department of Horticulture at the University of Stocksfield is testing a new fertilizer. They are interested in how long the fertilizer may be kept before its effectiveness is lost. They have done some calculations that indicate the fertilizer loses 6% of its potency every month. Using *HTTLAP*, design an algorithm that finds how many months it takes before the fertilizer has lost more than 50% of its effective power after which is must be thrown away. The first four months of potency figures would look like this:

    ```
    Month 1, potency 100%
    Month 2, potency 94%
    Month 3, potency 88.36%
    Month 4, potency 83.0584%
    ```

    The algorithm should produce summary messages for each month as above stopping after the potency has gone below 50%.
    Note, you are removing 6% of the fertilizer's remaining potency each month, not its original potency. That is why after month 3 the potency is 88.36% and not 88%.

8. For the following scenarios write down a basic sequence of actions (no selections or iterations needed) and then try to partition the actions to see if the sequence fits the Initialization, Processing, and Finalization algorithm pattern:

    a) Getting up and ready in the morning

    b) Cooking a meal

    c) Writing an essay or school report

    For the problems below follow the stages of *HTTLAP* to produce a set of instructions for carrying out the task (including any necessary selections and iterations). Do not try to cut corners and, wherever possible, get a friend to try out your solutions as you would be amazed at what issues this will raise. **Do not** neglect the documentation step.

9. Mow a lawn. Start with the simplest form of the problem and then introduce some of the real issues that you would face when mowing the lawn such as, height of cut, what happens when the grass box gets full, the role of the weather, and so on.

10. You are a judge in the new hit reality TV show *Earth's Next Top Professor*, in which a number of university professors all compete in a series of weekly tasks to be crowned Earth's Top Professor and win a job teaching in the Department of Applied Studies at the world renowned University of Stocksfield. In order to decide which professor must leave the show each week you score each candidate according to four characteristics:

    ■ Teaching ability, from 1–10

    ■ Sense of humor, from 1–10

    ■ Subject knowledge, from 1–10

    ■ Good looks, from 1–10

Using the *HTTLAP* strategy design an algorithm that asks a judge for the name of one of the candidates followed by the score the judge is awarding for each of the four characteristics. There is a constraint: the total points value must not exceed 20 points. If the judge awards more than 20 points then a score of 5 is assigned to each characteristic.

Now extend your solution so that the judge is asked for scores for each of the remaining professors.

Now extend your solution so that each of the three judges on the show is asked for their scores for each of the remaining professors.

11. Make a single cheese and onion omelette to feed up to three people. The number of people will vary each time. A one-person portion needs two eggs, a pinch of salt and pepper, a small amount of milk (say 3 fl. oz/100 ml), 1/4 of a small onion, 2 oz (about 60 g) of cheese, and a pat of butter (or margarine if you prefer). The milk, eggs, onion, cheese, and butter need to be mixed prior to cooking in a large frying pan. Make sure the pan is not too hot when you add the mixture. Cook until the surface of the omelette is just starting to firm up. Serve and garnish with parsley and grated parmesan cheese if desired.

12. Decorate your bedroom with new wallpaper.

A Harder Exercise for the More Ambitious

13. What difficulties would you have if the requirements of Exercise 5 were changed so that a customer **cannot** have a plain hamburger but has a choice of **either** cheese **or** lettuce and tomatoes – that is, hamburger with cheese **or** hamburger with lettuce **and** tomatoes? What facility does the IF construct seem to be lacking?

4.6   Projects

StockSnackz Vending Machine

We dealt with our vending machine dispensing snacks throughout the day by a single highly abstract action "Dispense snacks." Now we have the constructs available to deal with optional and repeated actions we can extend the solution. Using pseudo-code notation, add any iterations and selections necessary to your solution from Chapter 3 to show many individual items being dispensed. You might want to start with the subproblem of dispensing the correct snack that corresponds to the button that was pressed. After that, move on to solving the problem of allowing this to happen repeatedly.

Stocksfield Fire Service

Using pseudo-code notation, add any selections and iterations necessary to your solution from Chapter 3 to the problem of decoding the hazchem Emergency Action Code.

Puzzle World: Roman Numerals and Chronograms

Go back to the problem of translating Roman numbers into decimal that you looked at in Chapter 3. You should be aware that just as English words can be misspelled, so can Roman numeral strings be malformed. For example, the

Roman numeral string MCMC is malformed as it contradicts the syntax of the system. Before we can translate a Roman number into decimal we must first determine whether the Roman number is valid. If it is, then we can translate it into decimal. The rules for forming valid Roman numeral strings are:[7]

1. Smaller numerals follow larger numerals (see Rule 3 below). Summing the values of the numerals gives the value of the number.

2. The numerals I, X, C, and M (1, 10, 100, 1000 – all powers of 10) may be repeated up to three times in a row. No other numerals may be repeated.

3. Sometimes, a smaller numeral may precede a larger one (as in IV). These cases form compound numerals which are evaluated by subtracting the value of the smaller numeral from the larger one. To form a compound numeral **all** the following conditions must be met:

    a) The smaller numeral must be a power of ten (1, 10, 100, 1000).

    b) The smaller numeral must be either one-fifth or one-tenth the value of the larger one.

    c) The smaller numeral must either be the first numeral in the number, or follow a numeral of at least ten times its value.

    d) If the compound numeral is followed by another numeral, that numeral must be smaller than the one that comes first in the compound numeral (i.e., you can have XCI but not IXI).

Work through the *HTTLAP* strategy to draft an outline solution to the problem of validating a Roman number.

Pangrams: Holoalphabetic Sentences

Using iteration and selection constructs (WHILE and IF) update the sequence of actions you produced in Chapter 3 for determining whether a sentence is a pangram.

Online Bookstore: ISBNs

The check digit in an ISBN is calculated by a *Modulus 11* technique using the *weights* 10 to 2. This means that each of the first nine digits is multiplied by a number in a sequence from 10 to 2. If you add these products together and then add the value of the check digit, this total sum should be divisible by 11 without leaving a remainder. If it does give a remainder then the check digit does not match the rest of the number and we know the ISBN has been copied down incorrectly. The check digit is calculated in the following manner:

Multiply the first nine digits by 10, 9, 8, 7, . . ., 2 respectively and add the results. Divide this sum by 11 and take the remainder. Finally, subtract this remainder from 11 to give the check digit. If the value is 10 the check digit

---

[7] Rules taken from Edward R. Hobbs' *Compvter Romanvs* resource at http://www.naturalmath.com/tool2.html.

becomes "X." For example, we can validate the ISBN 0-14-012499-3 as follows:

$$\text{Check digit} = \frac{(0 \times 10) + (1 \times 9) + (4 \times 8) + (0 \times 7) + (1 \times 6) + (2 \times 5) + (4 \times 4) + (9 \times 3) + (9 \times 2)}{11}$$

$$= 118 \div 11$$

$$= 10, \text{ remainder } 8$$

So, the check digit $= 11 - 8 = 3$. As this is the same as the last number in 0-14-012499-3 we know that 0-14-012499-3 is a valid ISBN.

Using *HTTLAP*, write down the basic sequence of actions necessary to calculate the check digit for any ten-digit ISBN (assume the ISBN will be in a raw format without hyphens). Once you have identified the sequence, look to see if you can identify any repeated actions which could be better expressed using an iteration.

Calculating and Keeping Track of Things

If you cannot describe what you are doing as a process, you do not know what you are doing.

W. Edwards Deming (1900–1993)

I'VE BEEN ASKED TO REDUCE HEADCOUNT.

TO BE FAIR ABOUT IT I CREATED A SCIENTIFIC ALGORITHM TO DECIDE WHO GOES.

I THOUGHT YOU WERE FIRING THE PEOPLE WITH THE HIGHEST SALARIES.

OKAY, MAYBE "ALGORITHM" IS AN OVERSTATEMENT.

Learning Objectives

- Understand the role of working storage in algorithms
- Identify the variables (data items) needed in a problem solution (algorithm)
- Estimate likely ranges of values for variables
- Apply the problem solving strategy to real-world problems involving variables and nested action blocks

We ended the last chapter with a solution to a coffee-making problem. As we delved deeper into the details of parts of the task we began to see the need to keep track of certain pieces of information. For instance, we kept a running tally of the number of sugars we had put into the coffee to ensure that the correct number was added. Keeping track of things is a key feature of algorithms and this chapter explores this further.

In Section 5.1 you will be introduced to the notion of *working storage* and how the need to write down and record values (known as *variables*) as you go is central to programming. Section 5.2 shows how these variables can be manipulated using arithmetic to solve programming problems. We then see how this knowledge enables us to talk about high-level data abstractions. As with the previous chapter, the problem solving strategy introduced in Chapter 2 is applied throughout.

5.1 Problems Involving Working Storage

Solution 4.6 described how to add the right number of sugars to a cup of coffee. However, as we noted there was not sufficient information in the instructions to be able to work out when the condition "sugar required" was actually met. We further realized that the way we can tell whether sufficient sugar has been added is to first find out how many are needed and then to keep a count of how many spoons we have added. This led to Solution 4.7 in which these two aspects (finding out how much sugar is wanted and keeping count) were made explicit. This may have seemed laborious and long-winded because anyone with any common sense would have understood what we meant. But that is precisely the problem: Computers do not have any common sense and cannot *understand* anything. Instead of writing your coffee-making solution for an adult, imagine you are writing it for a small child who has never done anything quite like it before. You would be quite happy to spell out in detail the steps required. Likewise, a computer needs the most precise instructions possible. In order to add the correct number of sugars we explained how to keep track of two items of information which were needed to test whether the sugar requirements of our guest had been met.

Most problems for which we write programs need the computer to do the equivalent of keeping things in its head (such as running totals). The last coffee-making problem in Chapter 4 got close to this with the repeated adding of sugar. We can see this more clearly if we think more about the coffee problem. So far we have only considered the actions and decisions necessary to make the coffee itself. We did not think about where to pour it (we took the existence of a mug for granted).

FIGURE 5.1   **Drink choices of some guests**

We began by making coffee for one person, so naturally we would fetch one cup or mug. The number of mugs is related to the number of people wanting coffee. Imagine you have some friends over for the evening and you ask them if they want a drink. You ask who's for tea, who's for coffee, who's for water, who's for a soft drink, and so on. For those taking tea or coffee you ask whether milk or sugar is required. Some people are very good at this and can keep track of everything while others write a list (Figure 5.1). Whichever way you do it you make a record of all the facts you need to be able to go into the kitchen and prepare the drinks. Having made a note of how many coffees, teas, etc. are wanted you can now get out the correct numbers of mugs, cups, and glasses without having to interrupt the task to make further enquiries.

To simplify matters, think only about the coffee drinkers. What do we need to know to complete the task? First we must find out how many want coffee, and whether they want milk or sugar. Suppose five want coffee: three black without sugar, one black with one sugar, and one white with two sugars. We have the information needed to go and make the drinks.

Suppose the next day there are eight guests and this time six people want coffee. Three want it black, three want it with milk, and nobody wants sugar.

What has changed? What aspects of the problem remain constant between the two days?

The number of coffees required has changed as have the milk and sugar requirements. Although the numbers are different, the things they represent (i.e., the number of coffees required, the number of coffees with milk, and the number with sugar) remain the same. That is, we are asking the same questions but each time getting different answers depending on the desires of our guests.

Variables ▶

What we have here are *variables*. In programming a variable is a quantity, or item of information or data, whose value changes each time the program is run, or many times during one execution of the program. A name is given to the item to identify it and then values are assigned to it. You will remember something similar in mathematics lessons in school when you were given questions such as:

In the equation $y = 2x + 3$ calculate the value of y when x has the values 4 and 5.

Both x and y are variables because the values they stand for can change. If x stands for the value 4, then y stands for the value 11 ($y = 2 \times 4 + 3 = 8 + 3 = 11$) and when x stands for the value 5 then y stands for the value 13.

Huh?

Is a variable in programming the same as a variable in algebra?

It is very similar. In algebra we use letters like x and y to stand for values that can change. The difference is that we cannot assign values to variables in algebra – they are only used to stand for unknown values. You will see below that variable *assignment* is a fundamental feature of the sort of programming this book is looking at.

Think Spot

What are the variables in the coffee-making problem? What are the values that you need to keep track of to solve the problem and which may change each time you make coffee? Approach the problem by following *HTTLAP*. Here is the problem to solve:

Using an electric filter machine (also called a percolator), make coffee for up to six guests. Add milk and sugar as required.

Work through *HTTLAP* Step 1 (understanding the plan) to make sure you really do understand what this new problem means. You might find it helpful to write down a dialogue like the one in Section 4.1. Pay particular attention to the question about assumptions. Aim to spend 15 to 20 minutes on this exercise. (You could make yourself a coffee and think about it properly.)

Was the problem harder to understand than the previous one? Here is my own dialogue with *HTTLAP*.

Understanding the Problem

Q. **What are you being asked to do?**

A. Make coffee for up to six people.

Q. **What is required?**

A. Between zero and six cups of coffee. Each cup may or may not need milk and/or sugar to be added.

Q. **What is the unknown?**

A. How much coffee to make. I need anything up to six cups (and that could be none). I do not know the capacity of the pot. Is it large enough to hold six cups of coffee? I also do not know how much milk or sugar is needed.

Q. **Can the problem be better expressed by drawing a diagram or a picture?**

A. Maybe. Here is a picture of the main parts of the problem.

FIGURE 5.2   **Pictorial representation of the coffee making problem**

Q. **What are the principal parts of the problem?**

A. 1) Make a pot of coffee. 2) Pour several cups. 3) Each cup may or may not need milk or sugar. Or, looking at it another way: 1) The filter machine, 2) the cups, 3) the coffee, 4) some water, 5) the cups of coffee – just coffee, or milk and sugar as well?

What if no coffee is wanted? Is this what you mean by zero cups being required? Why even make a pot at all? How do I *not* make coffee, the solution already seems to assume we will always need to make some?

This is an interesting point. Look back at one of the earlier coffee making solutions and see how you could adapt it to allow for this possibility. *Hint: there is some kind of condition involved.* In fact, this problem is dealt with in a few pages' time – if the problem is too difficult for you at the moment you may choose to wait to see how to deal with it.

Q. Are there several parts to the problem?

A. I guess so. Making the coffee is a separate problem from pouring it. Each cup of coffee is an individual problem as I need to decide whether to add milk or sugar. Making the coffee is not a single action either – I need to get the water, measure some coffee, etc.

Q. Have you made any assumptions?

A. No, not yet. But I could assume that the pot holds enough coffee for six cups. But I guess that the problem could just as easily have asked for twelve cups of coffee, or even twenty. Is it reasonable to assume the pot will always be big enough?

Q. What can you do about the assumptions?

A. Not sure yet.

Did you think about the problem of the pot size too? Having understood the problem as best we can we shall move on to devising a plan to solve the problem in Step 2.

Devising a Plan to Solve the Problem

Q. Have you solved this problem before/is it similar to one you have solved before?

A. Yes, I know how to make coffee for one person.

Q. Are some parts of the problem more easily solved than others?

A. Yes. Pouring the coffee is easy. Adding the water and the coffee grounds requires some thought as to *how much* to add. After pouring the coffee I do not know if anything else is needed (e.g., milk and sugar). Also, I do not know whether my pot of coffee is big enough to make all the coffee required.

Q. If the problem is too hard, can you solve a simpler version of it, or a related problem?

A. Good idea. Let's keep things simple. I think it will be hard enough to try and solve the problem with the assumption that the coffee pot is large enough for the required coffee so I'll solve that problem first. Once I have done that I'll come back and have a look at the more general problem of making coffee for any number of people.

Q. Does restating the problem help? Try restating it in a different language.

A. No.

Q. Did you make use of all the information in the problem statement?

A. Yes, I think so.

Q. Can you satisfy all the conditions of the problem?

A. If I make the assumption that the pot is big enough to make all the coffee.

Q. Have you left anything out?

A. No, I do not think so; I seem to have gleaned all the information I can from the statement.

Time for Step 3:

Carrying Out the Plan

This is where we write down the basic sequence of actions necessary to complete the task. We have already solved a problem like this in Chapter 4 (Solution 4.8) so we can use that solution as the starting point for this one.

Solution 5.1 Making coffee for six people – first draft

```
1.  Put water in coffee machine ;
2.  Open coffee holder
3.  Put filter paper in machine ;
4.  Measure coffee ;
5.  Put coffee into filter paper ;
6.  Shut the coffee holder ;
7.  Turn on machine ;
8.  Wait for coffee to filter through ;
9.  Find out how many sugars required ;
10. Find out whether milk required ;
11. WHILE (sugars added not equal to number required)
        11.1  Add spoonful of sugar ;
        11.2  Add 1 to number of sugars added ;
    ENDWHILE
12. IF (white coffee required)
        12.1  Add milk/cream ;
    ENDIF
13. Pour coffee into mug ;
14. Stir coffee ;
15. Turn off machine ;
```

Look over Solution 5.1 above and identify in what ways the algorithm needs to be updated. You do not need to write new statements at this point, just identify the parts of the current problem that this solution does not yet address.

software ▶
reuse

It is clear that some changes are needed because this solution only deals with making one cup of coffee. You may have noticed that I have already removed the one-cup reference from Action #4. By using Solution 4.8 as the basis for this solution, what we have done is to solve a simpler version of the current problem. Actually, we have not even solved a simpler problem; we have *reused* a solution of a simpler problem. Reuse is an important idea in programming. The philosopher wrote *"there is no new thing under the sun"* (Ecclesiastes 1:9), and, with experience, you will find that you are able to reuse a great many ideas from the algorithms that you write. You will have to change some of the details but you will learn that a technique that works well for one problem will work well for other problems of the same (or similar) type.

Isn't reusing solutions like this simply cheating?

If you were an architect, would not you reuse techniques and tricks you had learned to help with designing new buildings? If you are making use of structures and algorithms you developed previously for a different purpose then this is just an efficient use of time. If you are using algorithms created by other people then there are issues of intellectual property rights to be faced (particularly in countries where algorithms can be patented). You would do well to read a book on ethics for computing professionals which will help you understand this issue more fully.

Of course, you must make sure before you use solutions written by other people that you first have their permission to do so. All algorithms are made up of only three basic building blocks (see Chapters 6 and 8) so the skill of programming is learning the right combinations of these blocks.

In the above dialogues with *HTTLAP* where I identified the principal parts of the problem I decided that making the coffee is a separate (but related) problem from pouring a cup; that is, I have identified *sub*problems. Making the coffee is one task that comprises several actions. Pouring a cup is a separate task that requires decisions to be made and actions to be repeated.

Look at Solution 5.1 and identify these two aspects of the problem. State which group of actions deals with making the coffee and which group describes how to process a single cup.

The problem asks us to make coffee for up to six people. Step 3 of *HTTLAP* asks the question:

Q. Is carrying out each action once only sufficient to give the desired outcome? If not, do you have actions (or groups/blocks of actions) that must therefore be repeated?

As we need to make coffee for up to six people what does that say about Tasks #9 through #14? Clearly, they will need to be repeated for each cup of coffee.

Using a **WHILE** structure try writing the pseudo-code that allows Tasks #9 to #14 be applied to the problem of processing up to six cups of coffee.

Here is a possible solution:

Solution 5.2 Processing more than one cup of coffee

```
1.   WHILE (cups of coffee required)
        1.1   Find out how many sugars required ;
        1.2   Find out whether milk required ;
        1.3   WHILE (sugars added not equal to number required)
                 1.3.1   Add spoonful of sugar ;
                 1.3.2   Add 1 to number of sugars added ;
              ENDWHILE
        1.4   IF (white coffee required)
                 1.4.1   Add milk/cream ;
              ENDIF
        1.5   Pour coffee into mug ;
        1.6   Stir coffee ;
     ENDWHILE
```

As all the tasks (#9 through #14 in Solution 5.1) needed to be carried out once each for each cup of coffee we can make them into the action block of a WHILE. To understand how this works follow it through for six cups of coffee. The first time we encounter the WHILE the condition "cups of coffee required" is true as we still need to pour six cups and we go into the action block. For this current cup of coffee we ask how many sugars are required and whether milk is wanted. Then, the next WHILE (Task #1.3) repeatedly adds spoons of sugar to the cup. Following that, if milk is required we add it. Finally we stir the coffee and go back up to the first WHILE (the outer one). The condition is still true so we carry out the action block once more. And so it goes on repeating until we have poured six cups each with its own milk and sugar requirements. After pouring the sixth cup the condition for the outer WHILE is false (no more coffee is required) so we leave the WHILE and carry on with the next

Construct ▶
nesting

task in the sequence (turning off the machine). Notice how the WHILE and the IF from the original solution are now *inside* another WHILE? That is, the sequence of Actions #9 to #14 is itself repeated within an enclosing WHILE. This enclosing of structures within one another is called *nesting* and it allows us to describe solutions to complex problems.

? Think Spot

Look at Solution 5.2. Is it sufficient to solve the problem of pouring up to six cups of coffee? What about the condition belonging to the outer WHILE (Task #1)? How can we tell when it has been satisfied? Just as we had to keep count of the number of sugars added to a cup, so we need to keep count of the number of cups of coffee we have poured. Using the same technique as last time we can extend Solution 5.2 to include this aspect. The updated version is given below as Solution 5.3; new or changed tasks are shown in bold type.

Solution 5.3 Keeping count of the coffees

```
1.   Find out how many coffees required ;
2.   WHILE (cups poured not equal to cups required)
        2.1   Find out how many sugars required ;
        2.2   Find out whether milk required ;
```

```
2.3  WHILE (sugars added not equal to number required)
        2.3.1  Add spoonful of sugar ;
        2.3.2  Add 1 to number of sugars added ;
     ENDWHILE
2.4  IF (white coffee required)
        2.4.1  Add milk/cream ;
     ENDIF
2.5  Pour coffee into mug ;
2.6  Stir coffee ;
2.7  Add 1 to number of cups poured
ENDWHILE
```

Think Spot

We have introduced two new tasks: #1 to find out how many coffees are wanted and #2.7 to update the number poured so far. The condition on the outer WHILE loop (statement #2) has also been amended to show exactly how to decide when enough cups have been poured. Does this solution let us deal with up to six cups of coffee? If after carrying out Task #1 we find out that nobody wants coffee then we will not even enter the WHILE loop in Task #2 as its condition will immediately be false. Likewise, if Task #1 results in an answer such as 1, 2, or 6, and we follow Task #2 correctly then we will pour one, two, or six coffees, so everything looks fine. In fact, there is a problem.

Think about it now to see if you can spot it – we will deal with it fully later.

Consider the rest of the problem we have been asked to solve. Currently we have a candidate solution for the coffee-pouring part of the problem; the coffee-making aspect still needs attention. Solution 5.1 had the following sequence of actions for this part:

```
1.  Put water in coffee machine ;
2.  Open coffee holder ;
3.  Put filter paper in machine ;
4.  Measure coffee ;
5.  Put coffee into filter paper ;
6.  Shut the coffee holder ;
7.  Turn on machine ;
8.  Wait for coffee to filter through ;
```

The above sequence was written on the assumption that only one cup of coffee was required (that was the problem that was being solved in Chapter 3 from which this solution has been reused), thus Tasks #1 and #4 did not specify exactly how much water and coffee to measure. The current problem calls for us to make an arbitrary quantity of coffee – anything up to six cups. If the number of cups can change then we must be more specific about the meanings of

Tasks #1 and #4. By now you should have a good idea of how to go about solving this subproblem.

> Rewrite the above sequence of actions to accommodate the requirement for a variable number of cups. If you get stuck look back at Solution 5.3 for clues as it solved a similar problem.

Here is my solution to this subproblem:

Solution 5.4 Making the pot of coffee

```
1.  Find out how many cups are required ;
2.  Put water for number of cups required in coffee machine ;
3.  Open coffee holder ;
4.  Put filter paper in machine ;
5.  Measure coffee for number required ;
6.  Put coffee into filter paper ;
7.  Shut the coffee holder ;
8.  Turn on machine ;
9.  Wait for coffee to filter through
```

Carrying out the tasks for adding water and coffee depends on knowing how much coffee to make. Therefore, I have added a new Task #1 to find out how many coffees are needed. The renumbered Tasks #2 and #5 have been reworded to take account of this. Now we can put the two parts of the solution together. You may have noticed that both Solution 5.4 and Solution 5.3 have a Task #1 for finding out how many coffees are required. Clearly we do not need to do this twice, so we will remove the task from the cup-processing solution because Task #1 in Solution 5.4 provides the same information. Putting the two solutions together (and remembering to turn off the machine at the end) we get Solution 5.5 below. Notice that I have started putting in the documentation as this should never be left until the very end.

Solution 5.5 Complete solution for making coffee

```
// Set up coffee machine
1.  Find out how many cups are required ;
2.  Put water for number of cups required in coffee machine ;
3.  Open coffee holder ;
4.  Put filter paper in machine ;
5.  Measure coffee for number required ;
6.  Put coffee into filter paper ;
7.  Shut the coffee holder ;
8.  Turn on machine ;
9.  Wait for coffee to filter through
```

```
// Process the cups of coffee
10. WHILE (cups poured not equal to cups required)
        // Add   sugar and milk as necessary
    10.1  Find out how many sugars required ;
    10.2  Find out whether milk required ;
    10.3  WHILE (sugars added not equal to number required)
              10.3.1  Add spoonful of sugar ;
              10.3.2  Add 1 to number of sugars added ;
          ENDWHILE
    10.4  IF (white coffee required)
              10.4.1  Add milk/cream ;
          ENDIF
    10.5  Pour coffee into mug ;
    10.6  Stir coffee ;
    10.7  Add 1 to number of cups poured
    ENDWHILE
11. Turn off machine ;
```

Assessing the Result

Does this solution work, that is, does it produce the right results? Try it out by giving it to your friend to test.

In the exercise below Solution 5.3 I asked you to try and spot a residual problem with the coffee-brewing aspect of the solution. The difficulty is this: the problem statement asked us to write the actions necessary for making and pouring up to six cups of coffee, adding milk and sugar as necessary. With Solution 5.5 as it stands there is nothing to limit the number of cups we try to make. If Task #1 results in 12 requests for coffee then Tasks #2, #5, and the WHILE loop in Task #10 will accommodate this request. You may say that there is nothing wrong with that because a) the solution still lets us make six cups and b) this version is better because it is even more flexible. That is not the point. The requirement was to produce a solution for making up to six cups. If we provide something that goes against what was asked for then we are not doing our job as programmers properly.[1] This also brings us back to the assumption I made that the pot is big enough to hold six cups of coffee. What if it weren't? Or what if Solution 5.5 were applied to trying to make 30 cups of coffee? In either case we would realize something was wrong when we tried to carry out Task #2 – the water simply would not fit into the machine. The so-called "better" solution is actually worse because it will go wrong when the demands for coffee exceed the capacity of the machine.

---

[1] Such imprecise adherence to specifications is the cause of many defects in programs today. Serious and even life-threatening problems can arise as a result.

 I still don't see what is wrong with Solution 5.5 as it lets us make the number of coffees we need. You say that it places no restriction on the number of cups we could make. How is this a drawback?

There are two issues here. First, the solution does not precisely and exactly meet the stated requirements. This may sound very picky, but requirements are stated for a reason and just because they do not seem sensible to us as programmers does not mean there is not a strong justification for them. Of course, if you are responsible for gathering the program requirements as well then you can ask your client if they really want a six-cup restriction and, perhaps, you will find out that the restriction was a mistake. But in the absence of further information we must assume the requirement is correct. This leads us to the second issue: it may be that the coffee machine cannot fit more than six cups in its pot. You would notice this when you tried to overfill the machine and would likely stop pouring in water before flooding the kitchen counter. However, this implies the person following the algorithm has common sense or intelligence, neither of which is possessed by the computer we are ultimately hoping to write programs for. Not specifying both the upper and lower bounds of iterations (or other values) can lead to catastrophic failure – see the discussion on ASSUMPTIONS for a real-life example.

Thus, we have another problem. How to solve it? Start with the simpler problem first: continue assuming, for the time being, that the machine is big enough to hold six cups of coffee and look at how to limit the solution so that it cannot make more than six cups. We will consider the more general problem of making an unspecified number of cups of coffee later.

Think about the different ways you could prevent Solution 5.5 from being applied to more than six cups of coffee. Any problem always has more than one solution, so spend some time now writing down some possible ways of solving this problem. Here are some hints to get you started:

- Consider rephrasing the condition in the **WHILE** (Task #10)
- Can you restrict carrying out Tasks #2 through #11 in some way?
- How about putting some conditions on Task #1?

There are several ways to solve this problem. Here is a very simple solution:

Solution 5.6 Restricting the number of cups: first attempt

```
1.   Find out how many cups are required ;
2.   IF (six or fewer cups wanted)
         2.1  Put water for cups required in coffee machine ;
         2.2  etc. etc.
     ENDIF
```

 In other words, if asked to make six (or fewer) cups then we follow the existing coffee-making instructions, otherwise we do nothing. It solves the problem but it is rather all-or-nothing. Think about how you would do it in real life. Imagine

there are ten guests in your house and you have enough coffee left in the tin to make six cups. You ask if they want coffee and eight of them respond. What do you do? You would not do it the way I have just suggested above and not let anybody have coffee; rather, you would probably give coffee to the first six who asked and tell the other two that they can have something else to drink. We could express this in pseudo-code as:

Solution 5.7 Restricting the number of cups: second attempt

```
1.   Find out how many cups are required ;
2.   IF (more than six cups wanted)
         2.1   limit cups required to six ;
     ENDIF
3.   Put water for number of cups required in coffee machine ;
4.   etc. etc.
```

What we have done is to allow the number of cups required to have any value up to and including six. If more than six people ask for coffee then we simply say that the number of cups required is six. What if the number of cups required were zero? We have already discussed this question in relation to the part of the solution that deals with pouring the individual cups. We noted that the WHILE loop that controlled that part could cope with a zero cups requirement because the action block would simply be ignored in such a case. However, what of the rest of the solution? As it stands, if nobody asks for coffee the solution still requires us to measure water for zero cups (Task #2 in Solution 5.5), put in the filter paper, measure out no coffee, shut the coffee holder, turn on the machine, wait for no coffee to filter through and then turn off the machine. Something is still not right. We need to prevent Task #2 onwards from being carried out if no coffee is wanted. The partial Solution 5.6 above, while wrong for the more-than-six-cups problem,[2] would actually work for the zero cups problem. Putting it all together should make this clearer:

Solution 5.8 A final solution to making six cups of coffee?

```
1.   Find out how many cups are required ;
2.   IF (more than zero cups wanted)
         2.1.   IF (more than six cups wanted)
                    2.1.1   limit cups required to six ;
                ENDIF

         2.2.   Put water for cups required in coffee machine ;
         2.3.   Open coffee holder ;
         2.4.   Put filter paper in machine ;
         2.5.   Measure coffee for number required ;
         2.6.   Put coffee into filter paper ;
         2.7.   Shut the coffee holder ;
         2.8.   Turn on machine ;
         2.9.   Wait for coffee to filter through ;
```

---

[2] By "wrong" I mean that if more than six cups are requested then nobody gets any coffee whereas a better solution would be to give coffee to the first six people who asked.

```
        // Process the cups of coffee
2.10. WHILE (cups poured not equal to cups required)
        // Add sugar and milk as necessary
            2.10.1.  Find out how many sugars required ;
            2.10.2.  Find out whether milk required ;
            2.10.3.  WHILE (sugars added not equal to required)
                        2.10.3.1.  Add spoonful of sugar ;
                        2.10.3.2.  Add 1 to number of sugars
                                   added ;
                     ENDWHILE
            2.10.4.  IF (white coffee required)
                        2.10.4.1.  Add milk/cream ;
                     ENDIF
            2.10.5.  Pour coffee into mug ;
            2.10.6.  Stir coffee ;
            2.10.7.  Add 1 to number of cups poured
        ENDWHILE
2.11. Turn off machine ;
ENDIF
```

Finding the Variables

Now we must think about the variables of the problem. I asked earlier what values you need to keep track of to solve the problem and which may change each time you make coffee.

Find the variables in the coffee-making solution above. Write down their details in the table below. Give them meaningful *identifiers* (names) as this makes the solution much easier to read and understand. For each variable you identify give a short description that clearly explains what the variable represents. Also, indicate the range of values that the variable might typically represent. There are five variables to find. To get you started I have put in the first one.

Variables for Coffee Making Problem

Identifier (variable's name)	Description	Range of Values
1. coffeesRequired	Holds the number of cups of coffee to be made	0 to 20
2. _____	_____	_____
3. _____	_____	_____
4. _____	_____	_____
5. _____	_____	_____

Think Spot

The easiest variable to find is the one that stands for the number of cups of coffee required. We can call it `coffeesRequired` because that concisely sums up the value that it stands for. What is this variable's purpose? It should store the number of cups of coffee we need to make. Typical values it might take are 3, 4, 8, 10, etc. In the context of making coffee at home it is unlikely ever to go much above 10, but it could. Let's say the range will normally be between 0 and 20. How probable is it that it would be 30, 60, or even 100? Estimating the range of values that a variable is likely to take is important in programming because when it comes to writing the solution in a programming language we will need to specify how much of the computer's memory each variable will take up. Getting this aspect wrong can cause programs to function incorrectly. In the case of the Ariane V rocket, a software malfunction had disastrous consequences (see ASSUMPTIONS). What is important at this stage is to assess the likely *magnitude* of the variable, that is, is it going to be 10 or less, 100 or less, 1000 or less, etc.?

Naming Conventions

Before we continue, consider some naming conventions for variables. In the example above I used the name `coffeesRequired` for the variable to hold the number of cups of coffee. Why not just call it "coffees required" rather than running all the words together without spaces? It comes back to what we will have to do when writing up the program in programming language code. The grammatical rules of programming languages generally say that identifiers (variable names) must not have any spaces in them (for reasons we do not need to explore here). How do you make variable names easily readable without spaces? A convention used some years back was to separate out the words within an identifier by using the underscore "_" character. This would give us `coffees_required`. Sometimes the initial letters of each word are capitalized (`Coffees_Required`), or just the first letter (`Coffees_required`). In recent years a different naming style has found favour in the programming community. In this style underscore characters are not used (except as the first character of some special variable types). Instead, all the words of the identifier are run together, but the initial letter of the second and all subsequent words is capitalized. All other letters remain in lower case, hence `coffeesRequired`. This seems to work quite well and people generally find it easy to read.[3] There are no hard rules, merely conventions. However, be aware that some languages (e.g., C, C++, C#, and Java) are *case sensitive* which means that capital and lower case letters are treated differently. This means that `coffeesRequired` and `CoffeesRequired` are **different** names in C, C++, C#, and Java. As long as you

---

[3] This naming convention is called *camel casing*. I'm not sure why it is called that. The best explanation I have seen is that camelCasing looks something like the humps on a camel. For recommendations on which casing styles to use for which types of program information see Microsoft's guidelines at http://msdn.microsoft.com/library/default.asp?url=/library/en-us/cpgenref/html/cpconcapitalizationstyles.asp.

familiarize yourself with the rules of the programming languages you are working in then you will be alright.

I want to make two more points on style before we return to making the coffee. First, we will not use UPPER CASE LETTERS for variable names.[4] For a start, they do not look very nice and C (and C++, C#, and Java) programmers have largely adopted a convention whereby variable names are put in lower case (with initial capitals) with upper case names being reserved for other types of program information. The second point to make is that while single letter identifiers are common in algebra and mathematics, they are not generally considered good practice in programming. This is because variable names such as a, b, and c tell the reader nothing about what the variable stands for. Using identifiers like numberOfCups makes it much easier to remember what the variable represents and how it should be used. Some programmers use single letter variables for temporary values, but for now I would simply advise their avoidance.

Returning to the coffee problem, Table 5.1 has my version of the completed variable table:

Table 5.1   **Variable Definitions for the Coffee-making Problem**

Variables for Coffee Making Problem		
Identifier (variable's name)	Description	Range of values
1. coffeesRequired	Holds the number of cups of coffee to be made	0 to 20
2. milkRequired	Holds the milk preference for one drinker	{Yes, No}
3. sugarRequired	Holds the sugar requirements for one drinker	0, 1, 2, 3
4. coffeesPoured	Holds the number of cups poured so far	0 to 20
5. sugarsAdded	Holds the number of sugars added so far	0, 1, 2, 3

The four other variables I have listed are milkRequired, sugarsRequired, coffeesPoured, and sugarsAdded. milkRequired is to store whether or not a person wants milk/cream in their coffee. If you ask someone if they want milk/cream and disallow vague answers like "just a spot please" or "yes, lots" they will answer "yes" or "no." Therefore, there are only two possible answers, and so in the "Range of Values" column I have enclosed the two values with braces "{ }" to show that this is the full set of possible values. Contrast this with coffeesRequired. Although its indicated range is 0 to 20, it is possible (albeit unlikely) that it could be higher

---

[4] Except, of course, for the COBOL language in which everything is written in upper case characters.

still. Therefore, as 0 to 20 is only an indicative range and does not express the complete set of values that `coffeesRequired` could theoretically represent we have not enclosed it by braces. Also, notice that the values represented by `milkRequired` are not numeric but the yes/no answers to a question. You will see in Chapter 6 it is important in many programming languages to distinguish between different *types* of data. In this case we are noting that some variables are numeric while others (e.g., `milkRequired`) represent another kind of data that stands for the answers to yes/no or true/false-type questions.[5] The variable `sugarsRequired` stands for the number of spoons of sugar wanted by an individual drinker, so for each person its value could be different.

Why has `milkRequired` not been used to represent the number of cups of coffee in which we need to put milk? Why has `sugarsRequired` been chosen to represent the sugar requirements for an individual drinker rather than the total number of spoons needed for all the cups put together? If you cannot see the answer think about what the alternative would be.

In the case of `sugarsRequired` its value would be 1 (the total number of sugars required by all those who want coffee in Figure 5.1). Now can you see the difficulty? If not, consider `milkRequired`. We cannot use this variable to represent the total milk requirements as the answer is "No" for Dave and "Yes" for Annie – what is the sum of "no" + "yes"? Granted, we could use a numeric variable instead and have `milkRequired` represent the number of cups of coffee in which milk is needed, but what is lost in following such an approach?

The reason these variables stand for the requirements of an individual coffee drinker is that it is individual cups of coffee that we deal with. You do not make a pot of coffee, add milk and sugar to the pot, and then pour the contents into several mugs. Rather, you make a pot and then *for each cup* you add milk and sugar as required. If `sugarsRequired` represented the total number of sugars required how would we know how many to put into each cup? You can see that each time we pour a cup of coffee the values of `milkRequired` and `sugarsRequired` could be different; their values *vary* over the course of making coffee for our guests.

There are two variables remaining: `coffeesPoured` and `sugarsAdded`. Recall that the problem requires us not just to know how many coffees to make and how many sugars to add, but also to keep track of how many coffees we have poured and how many spoons of sugar have been added to each cup. This information is necessary in deciding whether or not to stop pouring coffee and adding sugar. The variables `coffeesPoured` and `sugarsAdded` keep track of this information. `coffeesPoured` has the same value range as `coffeesRequired` and `sugarsAdded` has the same range as `sugarsRequired`.

---

[5] `milkRequired` represents a special type known as Boolean data, named after George Boole (1815–1864). Boole devised a system of algebra (Boolean algebra) in which elements can have one of two possible values (True and False). Operations on the elements are logical (AND, OR, NOT, etc.) rather than arithmetic (+, −, ×, ÷, etc.).

Think Spot

Now that we have identified the variables, it is worth looking back at Solution 5.8. Task #2.10.3.2 adds 1 to sugarsAdded and Task #2.10.7 adds 1 to coffeesPoured. Think about what this means. Each time you add a spoonful of sugar you add 1 to the variable sugarsAdded in order to keep track of where you are up to; after dealing with each cup of coffee you add 1 to coffeesPoured. Suppose six coffees are required. After pouring one cup and adding two sugars we go back to the WHILE in Task #2.10 and decide whether to continue. The number of cups poured does not yet equal the number required so we go back into the loop and deal with another cup of coffee. Suppose when we reach Task #2.10.1 that the next guest also asks for two sugars. The WHILE that follows (#2.10.3) adds sugars as long the number of sugars added is not equal to the number required. But the variable sugarsAdded still holds the value 2 from the last time we added sugars. In real life we would start counting afresh with each new cup, so we must do the same in the algorithm. Thus, we need a task to set sugarsAdded back to zero each time we start a new cup of coffee. Also, the variable coffeesPoured strictly needs initializing to zero before Task #2.10. See Solution 5.9 below in which I have added these two initialization instructions. Notice also that I have enclosed the variables' identifiers in boxes. The box makes it clear that a variable is being talked about. You should also notice that wherever the value that the variable stands for is mentioned I have replaced it with the variable identifier in a box. For example, in Solution 5.8 Task #1 reads "Find out how many cups are required" while in Solution 5.9 it reads "Find out how many cupsRequired."

Solution 5.9 Coffee making solution with variable initialization

```
1.   Find out how many cupsRequired ;
2.   IF (more than zero cupsRequired)
        2.1.   IF (more than six cups wanted)
                  2.1.1.   limit cupsRequired to six ;
               ENDIF
        2.2.   Put water for cups required in coffee machine ;
        2.3.   Open coffee holder ;
        2.4.   Put filter paper in machine ;
        2.5.   Measure coffee for number required ;
        2.6.   Put coffee into filter paper ;
        2.7.   Shut the coffee holder ;
        2.8.   Turn on machine ;
        2.9.   Wait for coffee to filter through ;
        // Prepare the cups of coffee
        2.10.  Initialize number of cupsPoured to zero ;
        2.11.  WHILE (cupsPoured not equal to cupsRequired)
                  // Add  sugar and milk as necessary
                  2.11.1.   Initialize sugarsAdded to zero ;
                  2.11.2.   Find out how many sugarsRequired ;
                  2.11.3.   Find out whether milkRequired ;
```

```
                         2.11.4.  WHILE ( sugarsAdded  not equal to
                                   sugarsRequired )
                                       2.11.4.1.  Add spoonful of sugar ;
                                       2.11.4.2.  Add 1 to number of
                                                   sugarsAdded  ;
                                  ENDWHILE
                         2.11.5.  IF (white coffee required)
                                       2.11.5.1.  Add milk/cream ;
                                  ENDIF
                         2.11.6.  Pour coffee into mug ;
                         2.11.7.  Stir coffee ;
                         2.11.8.  Add 1 to number of  cupsPoured
                    ENDWHILE
              2.12.  Turn off machine ;
         ENDIF
```

5.2 Problems Involving Arithmetic

Now you are wired on caffeine,[6] we will leave the coffee machine alone for a while and consider a different problem that involves a little more arithmetic than counting spoons of sugar (though not much more).

Paul's Premier Parcels (PPP) is a delivery company. Each morning the parcels to be delivered for that day are lined up on a conveyor belt in the warehouse by the warehouse staff. The belt takes the parcels to the loading bay where a van waits. The loading crew weigh each parcel to see if it will fit on the van. If so, they put the parcel on the van and wait for the next parcel to arrive. As soon as a parcel arrives that would take the van over its maximum payload the van door is closed, the van is sent off on its rounds and another empty van is brought up. The van is not kept waiting to see if any lighter parcels that will fit show up. This activity continues until all the parcels have been loaded onto vans. Happily, there are always enough vans for the waiting parcels. PPP wants to install a weighing machine on the conveyor belt linked to a computer so that the process of weighing parcels can be speeded up. Each van has the same maximum payload of 750 kg, and PPP only accepts parcels up to 120 kg in weight. After all the parcels have been loaded the company's managing director wants to know how many vans were needed that day and what was the heaviest payload that was sent out.

Following the *HTTLAP* strategy, understand the problem and devise a plan to solve it.

Where do we begin with this? The thing you absolutely **do not do** yet is write down the solution; you must first make sure the problem is well understood. Starting with Step 1 "understanding the problem," work through the questions in

[6] Grief! We have assumed nobody has asked for decaffeinated coffee. How would you deal with that?

the *HTTLAP* strategy to make sure you understand what is required. If you cannot understand the problem then it is best to discover this now so that you can do something about it. You do not have to use the structured Q&A dialogue that I have used previously, but make sure you do write down the answers rather than just making mental notes. Mental notes have a way of not being particularly well formed (as well as slipping away). It is when you try to write something down that you realize how well you understand it. Here is my dialogue with *HTTLAP*.

Understanding the Problem

Q. **What are you being asked to do?**

A. Load vans with parcels.

Q. **What is required?**

A. Parcels need to be loaded onto vans until the vans are full. Each van has a maximum capacity (750 kg) and there are no parcels heavier than 120 kg. To decide whether a parcel will fit on a van it is weighed. To report on how many vans were used and which one had the heaviest cargo.

Q. **What is the unknown?**

A. The number of vans and parcels. I also need to know how to decide whether a parcel will fit. It has something to do with weighing it, and the van's capacity clearly features in the decision. The manager wants to know how many vans are needed and which one had the heaviest load, so I need to find out this information too.

Q. **Can the problem be better expressed by drawing a diagram or a picture?**

FIGURE 5.3   **A van with some parcels**

Q. **What are the principal parts of the problem?**

A. The parcels, their weights, the vans, the maximum payload, a single van load of parcels.

Q. Are there several parts to the problem?

A. Yes. Each van needs to be loaded. This involves weighing parcels and calculating whether they will fit. There is also a problem involving reporting back to the manager.

Q. Have you made any assumptions?

A. It wasn't spelled out in the problem description, but I am assuming that the physical size of the parcels does not matter. Only the weights of the parcels was mentioned, so is it safe to assume that as long as the van can take the weight of a parcel that there will always be the physical room to accommodate it?

Q. What can you do about the assumptions?

A. I should really go back to PPP and get an answer. Here is the question I put to PPP:

"I am working on your van-loading problem and you have not said whether or not the physical size of the parcels is a factor. That is, is it possible that even though the weight of a parcel can be accommodated that it will be too large to fit into the available space?"

And here is their answer:

"Good question. It has never happened before as we tend to deliver mostly consumer electricals which never get too big. Assume it's OK."

Once the problem has been understood we can proceed to devising a plan to solve it.

Devising a Plan to Solve the Problem

Q. Have you solved this problem before/is it similar to one you have solved before?

A. Not exactly, but the structure of the problem bears some resemblance to the last coffee making problem. There the problem involved a repeating structure to process individual cups of coffee, and within that was another loop to add sugars. This problem clearly involves some repeated actions to load parcels onto a van, and it is possible that more than one van will be involved, so the shape of the problem looks to be quite similar. Borrowing the outline structure of the coffee solution may save some time here.

Q. Are some parts of the problem more easily solved than others?

A. Counting the vans sent out is easy. Deciding whether a parcel will fit sounds more difficult, though I do not know until I try it. I also wonder how to tell which van had the heaviest payload.

Q. If the problem is too hard, can you solve a simpler version of it, or a related problem?

A. I think I'll try solving the problem of loading an individual van before tackling the rest of the problem.

Q. Does restating the problem help? Try restating it in a different language.

A. No.

Q. Did you make use of all the information in the problem statement?

A. Yes, I think so.

Q. Can you satisfy all the conditions of the problem?

A. Yes.

Q. Have you left anything out?

A. No, I do not think so.

Carrying Out the Plan

Write down the basic sequence of actions to solve the problem of loading a single van. For now, hide the detail of dealing with multiple vans and concentrate on a single van.

What are the actions and decisions involved? Perhaps as a rough sketch you first came up with something like Figure 5.4.

FIGURE 5.4   **Loading a van**

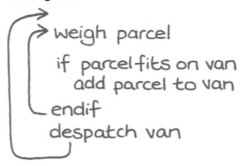

Figure 5.4 reveals some of the structure of the problem. Each parcel needs to be weighed to see if it will fit on a van. If it does, then it is put on the van. I have drawn a line back up to "weigh parcel" to indicate that this is a repeated action (there is more than one parcel). At some point a parcel will not fit so the van can be despatched to make its deliveries. I have drawn another line to indicate that we will likely need more than one van to carry all the parcels, though we are ignoring that complication for now. Although this is not a fully worked out solution it helps me to see the things that need to be done and to recognize that some actions must be repeated. There are some unanswered questions though, such as how do we know if a parcel fits on the van, and are the actions in the right order?

At this point many beginners have difficulty in writing down the solution. They can find it very hard to move from the conceptual understanding of the problem to being able to express the solution in a clear, precise, well-structured, and unambiguous manner. If you are experiencing this right now, do not worry. It is not that you are stupid, but that you are not used to thinking in this way. Take a step back and think about how we would approach the problem if we were one of the parcel loaders in the warehouse.

You have been tasked with the job of loading parcels on to vans. How do you do it? Consider this for a minute or two. Walk through the process in your mind. Imagine yourself standing at the loading bay taking parcels off the conveyor belt. There is an empty van standing in front of you, and you have just weighed the first parcel. What do you do next, and why? When do you stop loading parcels and tell the van to drive off? When you have a clear picture of the process in your mind, write it down.

I visualized the problem by imagining parcels of different weights coming down a conveyor belt (see Figure 5.5 below).

FIGURE 5.5   **Parcels on the conveyor belt**

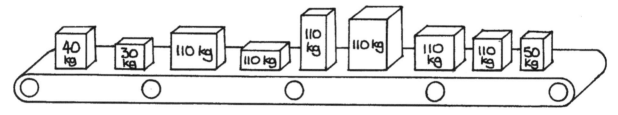

Say the first parcel weighed 40 kg (Figure 5.5). The van is empty, and can carry a total payload of 750 kg, so this parcel will fit. I load the parcel and fetch the next one. This one weighs 30 kg. Will it fit? Yes. Why? Because there is room on the van. How do I know? The van can take 750 kg and it is currently holding 40 kg, which means that there is room for another 710 kg. This parcel is only 30 kg, which will take the van's load up to 70 kg, which is well below 750 kg. The next parcel weighs 110 kg. Adding it to the van will take its payload up to 180 kg, so I know there is room for it, so on it goes. The next five parcels also weigh 110 kg each taking the van's load up to 730 kg. The next parcel weighs 50 kg. That would take the van over its maximum weight so I cannot load it on this van. Therefore, I despatch the van, noting that it went out with a 730-kg load. I bring on the next van, and start the process again with the 50-kg parcel. I have written this down as a sequence of actions in Solution 5.10 below. At this stage I am only thinking of the overall sequence and have not addressed any selections or iterations that may be present.

Solution 5.10 Loading a van

```
1.   Weigh first parcel (40 Kilos) ;
2.   Check that parcel will fit (yes) ;
3.   Load parcel on van ;
4.   Weigh next parcel (30 kg) ;
5.   Check that parcel will fit (yes) ;
6.   Load parcel on van ;
7.   Weigh next parcel (110 kg) ;
8.   Check that parcel will fit (yes) ;
9.   Load parcel on van ;
10.  Weigh next parcel (110 kg) ;
11.  Check that parcel will fit (yes) ;
12.  Load parcel on van ;
13.  Weigh next parcel (110 kg) ;
14.  Check that parcel will fit (yes) ;
15.  Load parcel on van ;
16.  Weigh next parcel (110 kg) ;
17.  Check that parcel will fit (yes) ;
18.  Load parcel on van ;
19.  Weigh next parcel (110 kg) ;
20.  Check that parcel will fit (yes) ;
21.  Load parcel on van ;
22.  Weigh next parcel (110 kg) ;
23.  Check that parcel will fit (yes) ;
24.  Load parcel on van ;
25.  Weigh next parcel (50 kg) ;
26.  Check that parcel will fit (no) ;
27.  Despatch van ;
28.  Make note of van's payload ;
```

Think Spot

That is quite a long list, but notice that after weighing the first parcel (Task #1) there is a repeated sequence of actions: Check the parcel will fit, load it on the van, weigh the next parcel. In other words, as long as parcels will fit on the van keep loading and weighing parcels. When a parcel will not fit on the van, stop the process and despatch the van. *HTTLAP* Step 3 asks whether we have any actions or blocks of actions that must be repeated. Clearly we do, and we saw in the coffee making problem how to express the repetition formally with a WHILE structure. The WHILE causes a block of actions to be followed while (as long as) some condition is met. What is the condition here? We said above that as long as there is room on the van we should keep loading and weighing parcels. We can express this using a WHILE structure.

Solution 5.11 Loading a van with a WHILE

```
1.   Weigh first parcel ;
2.   WHILE (room on van)
        2.1.   Load parcel on van ;
        2.2.   Weigh next parcel ;
     ENDWHILE
```

```
3.   Despatch van ;
4.   Make note of van's payload ;
```

Why has the "check parcel will fit on van" action been removed?

Because this check is done by the **WHILE**. The **WHILE** says "while parcels will fit on the van, load it and fetch the next parcel". The condition belonging to the **WHILE** determines whether to carry on loading the van or not. We know we must stop loading when we get a parcel that will not fit, so the condition can be expressed to make this clear....

 Think Spot

Looking at Task #2, how do we know if there is room on the van? We solved this problem above when we visualized the process. There is room for a parcel if the weight of the parcel when added to the current load on the van does not take the total van payload over its maximum limit, that is, the parcel's weight + the van's payload is less than or equal to the van's capacity. In the example above, when the van's load was 730 kg the next parcel weighed 50 kg. This gives us the question "is 50 + 730 less than or equal to 750?" The answer is no because 50 + 730 = 780, so we stop loading the van. We could write this out as:

```
WHILE (van payload + parcel's weight less than or equal to capacity)
```

We can use this to refine the solution thus:

Solution 5.12 Adding the condition to the WHILE

```
1.   Weigh first parcel ;
2.   WHILE (payload + parcel weight less than or equal to capacity)
        2.1.   Load parcel on van ;
        2.2.   Weigh next parcel ;
     ENDWHILE
3.   Despatch van ;
4.   Make note of van's payload ;
```

Is this solution sufficient to allow a computer (an idiot) to correctly load a van?

Because we are used to keeping track of things in our heads automatically, you may not have spotted the problem with Solution 5.12. The WHILE loop asks whether the van's current payload plus the current parcel weight is within the van's capacity. How do we know what the van's current payload is? In the visualization above we kept a running total updating the payload by adding the weight of each loaded parcel. If keeping a running total is required to solve the problem, we must write it down. For an empty van the payload will start at zero, so an instruction to initialize the current van's payload is needed. Each time we load a parcel we need an instruction to add that parcel's weight to the payload. That way the condition in the WHILE can be properly tested:

Solution 5.13 Updating of payload

```
1.   Initialize payload to zero ;
2.   Weigh first parcel ;
3.   WHILE (payload + parcel weight less than or equal to capacity)
         3.1.   Load parcel on van ;
         3.2.   Add parcel weight to payload ;
         3.3.   Weigh next parcel ;
     ENDWHILE
4.   Despatch van ;
```

Why has the task "Make note of van's payload" been removed?

Now we can consider what variables are to be used.

Identify and write down the variables needed for Solution 5.13. Remember to write down their names, an explanation of their purpose, and an indicative range of possible values.

Table 5.2 lists the variables I have identified.

Table 5.2   **Variables for Solution 5.13**

Variables for Van Loading Problem		
Identifier (variable's name)	Description	Range of Values
1. parcelWeight	Stores the weight of one parcel	{1 to 120}
2. payload	Stores the weight of the total load on the van	{0 to **capacity**}
3. capacity	Stores the maximum payload of a van	750

parcelWeight is used to hold the weight of a single parcel. We have been told by the company that they do not accept parcels heavier than 120 kg, so the possible range of values is between 1 and 120 kg. We have also been told that no parcel will ever exceed 120 kg,[7] so I have used braces {} to indicate that this is the

---

[7] I have assumed that any weights should be rounded off to the next highest kilogram to avoid parcels of, say 900 g or 400 g, being treated as 0 kg in weight. A better solution, perhaps, would be to deal in grams rather than kilograms. The maximum weight of a parcel would then be 120,000 g, and the capacity of a van 750,000 g and it gets around the problem of dealing with fractions of a kilogram.

range of all possible values for this variable. However, be aware that the requirements of the problem could change in the future to allow heavier parcels so this restriction may need to be revisited. payload is used to hold the weight of the total load carried in a van and its value can range from zero (an empty van) up to the maximum capacity (in this case, 750 kg). I have used capacity in the definition of payload's range of values because capacity holds the maximum value of payload's range. Using these identifiers I have rewritten Solution 5.13 as Solution 5.14 below to show where the variables are used.

Solution 5.14 Van loading with variables added

```
1.   Initialize payload to zero ;
2.   Get first parcelWeight ;
3.   WHILE (payload + parcelWeight less than or equal to capacity)
          3.1.   Load parcel on van ;
          3.2.   Add parcelWeight to payload ;
          3.3.   Get next parcelWeight ;
     ENDWHILE
4.   Despatch van ;
```

Assessing the Result

Having produced a solution to the problem of loading a van we should assess it to see if it is correct and that we understand it. One thing to notice is how similar the solution to loading a van is to the solution of adding sugar to a cup of coffee (Solution 4.8). After a while you should start to recognize common problem structures that can be solved with a common solution design.[8] Does the solution work for the problem of loading a single van with parcels? You can simulate the situation by cutting out pieces of paper each with a different weight written on it to represent the parcels (a physical model of Figure 5.5). An envelope or a box can stand for a van. Finally, you could draw a table with the names of the variables as column headings as in Figure 5.6.

Work through the instructions in Solution 5.14 updating the table of variables as you go.

Figure 5.6 shows the table filled in for the first two parcels from Figure 5.5. Each time you take a parcel, ask whether the condition in the WHILE is true. If so, put the parcel (paper) in the van (envelope), and write down the new value of the van's payload. Take the next parcel and go back to the WHILE. Keep going as long as parcels will fit. Once you have worked through the solution shuffle the parcels up and try again to see if the solution still works. Once you are happy with it, give it to your friend, explain the problem and see if they can follow the solution to produce the correct results (a properly loaded van).

---

[8] Both Solution 4.8 and Solution 5.14 use a special structure called a *read-ahead loop*. This (along with other loop constructs) is dealt with in Chapter 6.

FIGURE 5.6   **Table of values for van-loading simulation**

capacity	parcelWeight	payload
750		0
750	40	40
750	30	70

Loading More Than One Van

When devising a plan to solve the problem, I said I would start with the simpler problem of loading a single van. It is time to finish the job and solve the problem of loading all the parcels onto (possibly) multiple vans. How does the problem look now that we have solved the subproblem of loading a single van? The problem statement asked us to load all the day's parcels onto vans and to bring on a new van as soon as a parcel came along that would put the current van over its maximum payload. Furthermore, the manager wants to know how many vans were sent out and which one had the heaviest load.

It is clear that the manager is interested in vans – loading them, counting them, and finding out which is the heavier. We have solved the problem of loading a single van, so now we must look at loading more than one, counting them, and recording their weights. At this point you may like to go back to the coffee-making Solution 5.9 to see how that solution was structured. Does Solution 5.9 give you any clues as to how you might go about dealing with this problem? Questions from *HTTLAP* should help you clarify your thinking.

Q. What are the principal parts of the problem? What is the unknown?

The principal parts of the problem seem to be parcels and vans; we want to know how many vans were used and what their weights are. The unknown each time is how many parcels there are and, consequently, how many vans will be needed. The main ingredient of the problem appears to be the parcel; we must keep fetching and loading vans as long as we have parcels that need delivering.

Devising a Plan to Solve the Problem

We could visualize the overall problem structure thus:

```
WHILE (parcels to be delivered)
Load parcels on to vans, keeping count of the number and weight of
vans used ;
ENDWHILE
Report on number of vans sent out ;
Report on heaviest payload ;
```

That is, load the vans as long as there are parcels to be sent out, tell the manager how many vans were sent, and tell the manager the weight of the heaviest van. We have already solved the problem of how to load an individual van, so we just need to keep repeating this van loading as long as there are still parcels to load.

> Write down an outline solution to the problem using the above structure and Solution 5.14. Remember, if you are finding it difficult to start, think about a similar problem you have already solved (Solution 5.9).

How did you get on? Perhaps you have something similar to Solution 5.15.

Solution 5.15 Loading multiple vans – first attempt

```
1.   WHILE (conveyor not empty)
         1.1.   Initialize payload to zero ;
         1.2.   Get first parcelWeight ;
         1.3.   WHILE (payload + parcelWeight less than or equal to
                capacity)
                   1.3.1.   Load parcel on van ;
                   1.3.2.   Add parcelWeight to payload ;
                   1.3.3.   Get next parcelWeight ;
                ENDWHILE
         1.4.   Despatch van ;
     ENDWHILE
2.   Report numberOfVans used ;
3.   Report heaviestVan sent
```

It is not a complete solution and, as we will see in a moment, it has some serious defects. But do you see how the overall structure of the solution fits the problem? The outer WHILE (Task #1) says to keep going as long as there are parcels on the conveyor belt. What do we do when we have got the parcels? We load them onto vans. How do we load them onto vans? We know how to do that – take an empty van and put on parcels until it can take no more then despatch it (Tasks #1.3 to #1.4). But what happens next? The van-loading part ends with Task #1.4 (despatching the van) but then comes the ENDWHILE to close the action block for the first WHILE. We test the first WHILE condition again, that is, we see if there are still parcels on the conveyor belt. If so, we need to bring on and load another van, so we go back into the loop. And so on. Or is it? Can you see how this nested structure allows us to use the solution for loading a single van over and over again until there are no more parcels? Only when there are no more parcels to load do we go on to do Tasks #2 and #3 (reporting back to the manager).

 Think Spot

Assessing the Result

I said that Solution 5.15 has some deficiencies. See if you can identify what the defects are. If you need a hint think about:

■   The variables numberOfVans and heaviestVan. How will they get their values?

- The condition for the WHILE in Task #1.3: what happens when loading a van if the conveyor belt is empty?

- The position of Task #1.2 and Task #1.3.3. Task #1.3.3 gets a new parcel. If it will not fit on the van then the van is despatched and the WHILE in Task #1 is begun again which causes Task #1.2 to be obeyed again. What is the implication of this?

Think about these issues for a little while and do not read any further until you have an answer or are completely mystified.

Take the question of Tasks #2 and #3 first. I have introduced new variables to hold the number of vans despatched and the weight of the heaviest van. How should numberOfVans be given a value, that is, how is its value calculated? Each time a van is despatched the number of vans used should go up by 1. So, a simple counting mechanism is needed, but where?

> Identify the point in Solution 5.15 at which numberOfVans should be increased by 1. Also, consider whether it needs an initial (starting) value.

Adding a new Task #1.5 "Add 1 to numberOfVans ;" deals with the problem of keeping count of the vans. Each time a van is sent out the counter is increased by 1. In addition, numberOfVans needs to start at zero so that after the first van is despatched its value changes to 1. Therefore, a new instruction is needed before Task #1 to set numberOfVans to zero.

Consider now how to keep track of the heaviest van. It is not as simple a job as keeping count of numbers of vans, so we would do well to treat it as a problem in its own right and use the advice from *HTTLAP*. First then, is to understand the problem.

Q. What is required?

A. We need to record the largest payload that was sent out.

How would you tell which van had the heaviest payload? What would you do? There are several ways we could go about this. We know the weight of a van's load when we despatch it because we store this information in the variable payload. One solution would be to write down each van's payload as it goes out and at the end read down the list to see which one is the larger. Of course, this means storing a number of payload values. If we sent out fifty vans we would need space to write down fifty payload values. In addition, when it comes to writing this solution up as a real computer program we would have to set aside memory in the computer to handle all these values. It is not especially hard to do[9]

---

[9] We do not know in advance how many vans there will be, so we need a way of storing a variable number of values. If we knew the number could never exceed a certain value we could use a programming object called an array. If we do not know the maximum number of van journeys then we would need something more flexible such as a linked list or a vector (Java). These concepts are dealt with in Part II.

but there is a cleaner way that needs only the variables already identified in Solution 5.15. A principle I was taught when I first learned programming was the KISS! Rule. KISS! Stands for Keep It Simple, Stupid! and the point is that complex programs are hard to understand (and thus to maintain) while simple programs are simple to understand. We should always strive to keep our solutions as simple and as uncluttered as possible. That makes them easier to understand, and hence makes it more likely that we will find any defects quicker (and probably make fewer mistakes in the first place). Sometimes this means writing code that is not as computationally efficient as it might be, but unless shaving a few microseconds off the execution time is critical the extra comprehensibility of the code is worth the price.[10]

Try yourself to work out what this cleaner solution is. How could you keep track of the heaviest van load without recording the weight of every van? Each time you send a van out you could ask whether it is the heaviest one. You cannot tell until you have dealt with all the vans, but you *can* decide whether it is the heaviest van you have seen *so far*. All you have to do is keep asking of each van whether it is the heaviest one so far. If it is, you write down its weight. If the next van is even heavier then you cross out the earlier value and write in the new one, and so on. When you have sent out all the vans you will have a figure that holds the weight of the heaviest van despatched. Solution 5.15 already has a variable to hold this value: heaviestVan. What is the sequence of actions necessary to find the heaviest van? After carrying out Task #1.4 in Solution 5.15 we know the weight of the current van. How can we tell if it is the heaviest van so far? Think about this yourself now.

If we compare its weight with the heaviest value we wrote down last time we found a heavy van we can tell if this one is heavier. Write down a solution to this problem now.

Because this solution requires asking a question about the weight of a van you should have spotted that we need to use an IF structure. It should look something like this:

Solution 5.16 Finding the heaviest van

```
IF ( payload more than heaviestVan )
    Assign value of payload to heaviestVan ;
ENDIF
```

Solution 5.16 uses the condition in the IF to see whether the weight of the current van is heavier than that of the heaviest van found so far. If it is, then the condition is true so the action block is carried out and the value of heaviestVan is overwritten by the current value of payload. This can be inserted into

---

[10] Of course, processor-intensive applications such as digital signal processing or complex mathematics may just require the most efficient code possible. In those situations the programmer needs to ensure that the hard-to-understand-but-efficient code is **really** well documented with thorough explanations of how it works.

Solution 5.15 after Task #1.4. Is that enough to solve the problem? Not quite. After loading the first van we try to compare its payload with heaviestVan, but what are we comparing it to? There have not been any vans loaded and despatched yet, so heaviestVan will not have a value. This means heaviestVan must be initialized to something before we start loading the vans.

> Decide what value **heaviestVan** should be initialized to.

A van is the heaviest one so far if its payload is *more than* the value of heaviestVan. After filling up the first van it will obviously be the heaviest one so far as no other vans have been loaded. Suppose the first parcel weighed 1 kg and the second one weighed 750 kg. The second would overload the van so its total payload would be 1 kg. For it to be the heaviest van, its payload of 1 kg must be more than the starting value of heaviestVan. Thus, we can initialize heaviestVan with any value less than 1. Would zero be an appropriate initial value? Where should the initialization instruction go?

The initialization needs to be done before any vans are loaded and the van loading starts with the WHILE in Task #1. Therefore, the initialization of heaviestVan should be the first task in the solution.

Fixing the WHILE Loop

Earlier I asked you to consider the condition for the WHILE in Task #1.3 (Solution 5.15) – what happens when the conveyor belt becomes empty during the loading of a van? Of course, the conveyor belt must become empty sometime otherwise there would be an infinite number of parcels. The condition for Task #1.3's WHILE is currently only concerned with whether a van is full. If we interpreted the condition literally (which a computer would) we will get into trouble because at some point we will run out of parcels at which point parcelWeight cannot be updated with a new value. Therefore, we need to extend the condition in Task #1.3 to deal with this situation. The outer WHILE (Task #1) has a condition that will be false when the conveyor belt is empty which causes the loop to terminate. We need to add this condition to the one in Task #1.3. We can make a compound (multi-part) condition thus:

WHILE (payload + parcelWeight less than or equal to capacity) AND (conveyor not empty)

Compound ▶
conditions

The keyword "AND" has been used to join two conditions. This means that **both** the conditions must be true if the action block of the WHILE is to be carried out. When either one of them turns false (when a parcel will not fit or we run out of parcels) then the loop will terminate. When a parcel arrives that will not fit we stop the loop and despatch the van. Or, if we are loading a van when the last parcel arrives the loop will also terminate.

There is one final defect in Solution 5.15. I said earlier that there is a problem with the placement of Task #1.2. Task #1.3.3 gets a new parcel. If it will not fit on the van then the van is despatched and the WHILE in Task #1 is begun again which causes Task #1.2 to be obeyed again. What is the implication of this? It means that when Task #1.3.3 fetches a parcel that will not fit on the van we effectively lose that parcel because when we enter the loop again we carry out Task #1.2 which fetches another parcel. Thus, we are not dealing with the parcel that would not fit before getting the next one to start the van-loading process over again. If you cannot grasp this, then trace through the solution with the envelopes and parcels technique from before (Figure 5.6). How can we solve this problem? Think about the purpose of Task #1.2. It is to get the first parcel, that is, the parcel that is needed to start the whole van-loading sequence going. If you think about it there is only one **first** parcel; it is the first one on the conveyor belt at the start of the day. As we only need to fetch the first parcel once all we need to do is move Task #1.2 immediately before the WHILE in Task #1. That way we have the first parcel and go into the loops. After despatching the first van and going back into the loops again we still have hold of the parcel that was fetched with Task #1.3.3. Try it out to see for yourself.

Assigning Values

We are almost ready to write out the revised solution but first I want to introduce a new pseudo-code notation. Up till now we have been writing things like "initialize payload to zero" and "assign value of payload to heaviestVan." It is time to introduce a more formal symbol that represents giving a value to something. It is called the *assignment symbol* and it looks like this:

$$\boxed{\text{heaviestVan}} \leftarrow \text{zero} ;$$

Assignment ▶ symbol

The "←" symbol is an instruction to assign the value of the thing on its right to the variable on its left. If we had a piece of paper with a column heading for each variable (as in Figure 5.6) then the instruction would mean we write down a new value for the variable on the left-hand side of the ←. Strictly speaking, what we should do is erase the current value of the variable and replace it by the new one, for that is what the assignment symbol means: it is an instruction to overwrite the value of the variable on its left with the value on its right. The right-hand side could be a simple value like "zero", "2", "20", etc., or it could be the name of a variable, or it could even be an arithmetic expression, such as "2 + 3" or even "payload + parcelWeight." When a variable appears on the right of the "←" symbol, then the value it stands for is used. So, the task

$$\boxed{\text{payload}} \leftarrow \boxed{\text{payload}} + \boxed{\text{parcelWeight}} ;$$

is an instruction to add the value of parcelWeight to payload. You can read it as "the value of payload becomes the current value of payload plus parcelWeight." That is, the value of the expression on the right hand side of the "←" is calculated and is written into the variable on the left. Below is the complete solution to the van-loading problem which uses this new assignment symbol.

Solution 5.17 Complete van-loading solution

1. $\boxed{\text{capacity}} \leftarrow 750 ;$
2. $\boxed{\text{numberOfVans}} \leftarrow \text{zero} ;$
3. $\boxed{\text{heaviestVan}} \leftarrow \text{zero} ;$
4. Get first $\boxed{\text{parcelWeight}} ;$

```
5.   WHILE (conveyor not empty)
       5.1.   payload ← zero ;
       5.2.   WHILE (payload + parcelWeight less than or equal to
              capacity ) AND (conveyor NOT empty)
                  5.2.1.   Load parcel on van ;
                  5.2.2.   payload ← payload + parcelWeight ;
                  5.2.3.   Get next parcelWeight ;
              ENDWHILE
       5.3.   Despatch van ;
       5.4.   numberOfVans ← numberOfVans + 1 ;
       5.5.   IF ( payload more than heaviestVan )
                  5.5.1.   heaviestVan ← payload ;
              ENDIF
     ENDWHILE
6.   Report numberOfVans used ;
7.   Report heaviestVan sent ;
```

If you examine Solution 5.17 you will notice that Tasks #1 to #4 deal with initialization: they set the starting values for the variables that need them and fetch the first parcel weight. Notice an extra task to assign a value to **capacity** (Task #1). This is done so that the comparison in Task #5.2 can be made; if **capacity** is not given a value then how will we know whether the van's current load has exceeded that capacity? Task #1 is a simple assignment that moves the value 750 into **capacity**. Task #5.2.2 updates **payload** by adding its current value to that of **parcelWeight** and moving the result back into **payload** overwriting what was there before. Using the same technique, Task #5.4 adds 1 to **numberOfVans**. Task #5.5.1 copies the value of **payload** into **heaviestVan**.

Assessing the Result

Having produced a solution we must again assess it.

Use the envelopes and paper parcels technique with the set of parcel weights in Table 5.3 to simulate the loading process by following the algorithm in Solution 5.17. At the end of it you should be able to report the number of vans sent out and the weight of the heaviest payload.

Table 5.3   **Sample Parcel Weights**

Parcel Weights for Van-loading Simulation
50, 90, 120, 110, 40,
30, 85, 85, 110, 100,
100, 100, 100, 120, 90,
50, 85, 120, 40

If you followed the solution properly you should have used three vans and found the heaviest payload to be 745 kg (the second van load).

It is useful at this stage to make a note of any limitations in the solution. A limitation is not the same thing as a defect. A defect stops the solution from meeting its requirements. A limitation is simply an acknowledgement of the boundaries of the solution. That means that we can specify under what conditions it should work and, in what situations it will not work. This is very useful to know because if the situation changes (e.g., the parcel size increases) then we can more easily see what aspects of the solution need to be changed.

One limitation is that the solution is written under the assumption that no parcel will ever weigh more than the capacity of a van. There is no reason why this assumption should remain true for ever. It is possible that a number of smaller vans with much smaller capacities could be added to the fleet. In this case the solution would need to be amended so that the capacity of each van is recorded before it is loaded.

Another limitation is that no attempt is made to optimize the parcel loading. As soon as a parcel is encountered that will not fit on a van the van is despatched. A more efficient (and environmentally friendly) approach would be to try and organize the parcels into batches each of which is as close to the van capacity as possible. But this is a different problem and not the one we were asked to solve.

There is one more observation to make about the solution and it is to do with the conditions that test whether the conveyor belt is empty. You may have wondered how the solution works when the last package is fetched off the belt. For instance, take the situation where there is only one parcel on the belt. Task #4 fetches this parcel and then the condition in Task #5 asks whether the belt is empty. If not, the loop will be entered and the parcel is loaded onto the van. Strictly speaking, after we have lifted the parcel then the belt is indeed empty which would mean that the last parcel on the belt is never delivered. I have deliberately left the solution as it is because the way this problem is solved is dependent on which programming language this algorithm is eventually translated into. If the parcel weights were stored on a computer file and a program were written in C to read these weights, then the C instruction that would correspond to Task #5 would not result in the belt/file being deemed to be empty. This is because computer files have a special marker at the end after all the data and it is not until this special marker is read by the program that the file would be judged to be empty. So, the translation of this solution to the computer domain may require some changes, depending on the language being used. For instance, Task #5 could be implemented by a test to look ahead to see if the belt is empty, and if not, the parcel is fetched.

Describing What We Have Learned

It is important to reflect on the lessons learned during the problem solving process, so let's think about what this problem has taught us. Again, *HTTLAP* has some guiding questions.

Q. **What did you learn from this exercise? What do you know now that you didn't know before you started?**

A. I have extended my knowledge of ways to use WHILEs and IFs to control decision making. For example, knowing when to stop loading a van is based on the result of some arithmetic. I'm beginning to see how arithmetic is an important part of solving problems. Also, I have developed my understanding of variables and how they can be assigned values.

Q. **Were there any aspects of the problem that caused particular difficulty? If so, do you think you would know how to tackle them if you met something similar in the future?**

A. Finding the heaviest van was a challenge. But this technique could easily be applied to problems such as finding the lightest van, or an employee with the most commendations, etc. There was a nasty problem with losing parcels in between the loops. The solution that worked for a single van didn't work when applied to multiple vans; I had to move the instruction to get the first parcel weight. This was a hard defect to spot and it was easiest to find during a dry run. It shows me that what seems to be right on paper often turns out not to work when the strict interpretation used by a computer is applied. Common sense would have made a real person not lose track of the parcels, but a computer can only do exactly what it is told.

You will have learned other lessons from this exercise so take some time to reflect upon them now and write them down.

Documenting the Solution

The final stage in *HTTLAP* is to document the solution. We should produce an annotated solution like we did at the end of Chapter 4. But first we need to document all the variables in the solution. The last time we did this we only had three variables (Table 5.2).

Complete that table now by adding in the remaining variables.

The solution is given as Table 5.4 below.

Table 5.4 **Variables for Van-loading Solution**

Variables for Van Loading Problem		
Identifier (variable's name)	Description	Range of Values
1. `parcelWeight`	Stores the weight of one parcel	{1 to 120}
2. `payload`	Stores the weight of the total load on the van	{0 to `capacity`}
3. `capacity`	Stores the maximum payload of a van	750
4. `numberOfVans`	Stores the number of vans used to deliver the parcels	0 to 20
5. `heaviestVan`	Holds the value of the heaviest payload	{0 to `capacity`}

Table 5.4 has two more variables than Table 5.2: `numberOfVans` and `heaviestVan`. Because we do not know the maximum number of vans that could be sent out (the size of the fleet was never specified, and anyway it could change as vans are bought and sold) I have provided an indicative range of 0 to 20. The range starts at zero because it is entirely possible that on a given day there could be no parcels to deliver and so no vans would be sent out. `heaviestVan` has the same range of values as `payload` because it is used to hold a copy of a `payload` value. We can now produce a documented solution which is given below as Solution 5.18.

Solution 5.18 Annotated van-loading solution

Instructions for loading vans with parcels
These instructions will allow you to load an unspecified number of parcels onto an unspecified number of vans. The load capacity of a single van is 750 kg and no parcel will weigh more than 120 kg. Parcels are taken off the conveyor belt and loaded onto vans. A van is judged to be full when a parcel is encountered that would take it over its maximum payload. At this point the van is despatched and an empty one brought up. A report is required at the end detailing the number of vans used and the weight of the heaviest payload.

```
// ********************************************
// Instructions for loading vans
// Written by Paul Vickers, June 2007
// ********************************************
// Initialize variables
1.   capacity ← 750 ;
2.   numberOfVans ← zero ;
3.   heaviestVan ← zero ;
4.   Get first parcelWeight ;
5.   WHILE (conveyor not empty)
         // Process vans
     5.1.   payload ← zero ;
     5.2.   WHILE (payload + parcelWeight less than or equal to
            capacity) AND (conveyor NOT empty)
                // Load a single van
            5.2.1.   Load parcel on van ;
            5.2.2.   payload ← payload + parcelWeight ;
            5.2.3.   Get next parcelWeight ;
         ENDWHILE
     5.3.   Despatch van ;
     5.4.   numberOfVans ← numberOfVans + 1 ;
         // Check whether this is the heaviest van
     5.5.   IF ( payload more than heaviestVan )
            5.5.1.   heaviestVan ← payload ;
         ENDIF
     ENDWHILE
```

6.   Report ⬚numberOfVans⬚ used ;

7.   Report ⬚heaviestVan⬚ sent ;

5.3 Chapter Summary

In this chapter we looked at some more complicated problems that required the use of arithmetic and keeping track of values. This led us to seeing the need for *variables* and we discussed how to decide on the variables needed for a given problem and how to indicate their range of possible likely values. These concepts were applied to a problem of loading and despatching vans which needed nested WHILE loops in the solution.

5.4 Exercises

1. What values do the following assignment statements place in the variable result?

a) ⬚result⬚ ← 3 + 4 ;

b) ⬚result⬚ ← ⬚result⬚ + 7 ;

c) ⬚result⬚ ← ⬚result⬚ ;

d) ⬚result⬚ ← ⬚result⬚ – 7 ;

2. A fairly common programming task is to swap the values of two variables. Because a variable can only hold one value at a time, a common solution is to introduce a temporary variable. For example, assume variable a has the value 7 and variable b the value 4. The following algorithm swaps their values via the intermediate variable temp:

1. ⬚temp⬚ ← ⬚a⬚ ;

2. ⬚a⬚ ← ⬚b⬚ ;

3. ⬚b⬚ ← ⬚temp⬚ ;

All well and good, but suppose you didn't want to use temp? Can you find a way to swap the values using only a and b in the solution?

3. Professor Henry Higgins wants to attend a conference in Lincoln, Nebraska in the United States. The conference is being held in June and Professor Higgins wants to know what sort of clothing to take. Coming from northern Europe where temperatures are measured in degrees Celsius, Professor Higgins is unfamiliar with the Fahrenheit scale used in the United States. Therefore, he wants you to design an algorithm that will first convert a temperature in °F to its equivalent in °C, and then recommend clothing based on the result. If the temperature in Lincoln in June is 24 °C or above then Professor Higgins should take summer clothes; if it's less than 24 °C but above 15 °C then spring clothes are in order, otherwise winter clothes should be taken. There is a simple formula to convert from Fahrenheit to Celsius: $c = (F - 32) \times \frac{5}{9}$. Thus, a temperature of $98\,°F = (98 - 32) \times \frac{5}{9} = 33.67$ Celsius. Try your algorithm out with the following Fahrenheit temperatures: 57, 65, 72, 76, and 85.

4. Using the *HTTLAP* strategy design an algorithm that uses repeated subtraction to find out how many times one number divides another. For example, 20 divides 5 four times, 36 divides 7 five times (with a remainder of 1).[11]

5. We are used to seeing times in the form hh:mm:ss. If a marathon race begins at 10:00:00 and the winner finishes at 14:07:41 we can see that the winning time was 4 hours, 7 minutes and 41 seconds. Design an algorithm that takes the start and finishing times of a runner and displays the time it took them to complete the race. If your solution worked using the start time of 10:00:00, does it still work for a start time of, say, 10:59:57?

6. It is usual, when working with times, to convert real-world timings into a figure in seconds as this makes comparisons between two times much simpler. Given that there are 3600 seconds in an hour, write an algorithm that takes the start and finish times of a marathon runner in the form hh:mm:ss, converts them to a time in seconds, subtracts the start seconds from the finish seconds to give an elapsed time, and then converts this elapsed time in seconds back into a real world time of the form hh:mm:ss for display. For example, say I started a marathon at 09:05:45 and finished at 13:01:06, my start time would be $09 \times 3600 + 05 \times 60 + 45 = 32,400 + 300 + 45 = 32,745$ seconds. My finish time would be $46,800 + 60 + 06 = 46,866$ seconds. My race time would then be $46,866 - 32,745 = 14,121$ seconds. This comes to 03:55:21. The real problem here is how did I get 03:55:21 from 14,121? The solution is related to the change-giving problem from Chapter 3.

7. In the solutions to the coffee making problem we have been careful to give precise instructions for how to add the required number of sugars to each cup. If you look closely you may spot that we have not been as careful as we might have been with the rest of the solution. I am referring specifically to the instruction "measure coffee for number required" (Solution 5.8). If you think about it you should realize that this action too needs more detailed instructions. How exactly do you measure the right amount of coffee? How many spoons (or scoops) of coffee do you need? Assume a standard measure of one dessert spoon for each cup of coffee required. Rewrite the task to make the instructions precise. Describe any variables that you need to add to the variable list.

8. I said that it would be hard enough to try and solve the problem on the assumption that the coffee pot is large enough for the required coffee and that I would come back to the more general problem of making coffee for any number of people. You are to tackle that problem now. The capacity of the coffee pot is eight cups. Try to extend the coffee making solution you produced for Exercise 7 to deal with the requirement of being able to make more than eight cups of coffee.[12]

---

[11] Hint: $20 - 5 = 15$ giving 1 subtraction. $15 - 5 = 10$, giving a second subtraction. $10 - 5 = 5$, giving a third subtraction, and $5 - 5 = 0$ giving a fourth subtraction. Hence, 20 divides 5 four times as 4 (the number of subtractions) $\times 5 = 20$.

[12] Hint: If you are having trouble getting started, look at Solution 5.9. The **WHILE** in Task #2.10 pours a number of coffees from one pot. If ten cups are wanted, then you will have to make two pots of coffee. If more than sixteen cups are needed then you will have to make more than two pots of coffee.

9.   *Paul's Premier Parcels* was so pleased with your work that they want you to extend your van-loading solution to incorporate some extra requirements. In addition to the existing reports the manager wants to know the weight of the lightest payload that was sent out. He also wants to know the average payload of all the despatched vans. Using *HTTLAP* draw up solutions to these additional problems and try to incorporate them into Solution 5.18. Think about what extra variables may be needed and how they should be initialized and their values calculated. An average of a set of values is calculated by dividing the sum of all the values by the number of values in the set. Thus, the average of 120, 130, and 140 is $\dfrac{120 + 130 + 140}{3} = 130$.

10.   In 2006, FIFA (the world governing body for international soccer) revised the way teams are allocated points for international soccer matches as shown in Table 5.5. Thus in a normal match the winning team gets 3 points with the losers getting zero. If a match is won through a penalty shootout the winning team only gets 2 points and the losers get 1 point. Both teams get 1 point each for a draw.

Table 5.5   **FIFA Points Allocations**

Result	Points
Win	3
Draw	1
Lose	0
Win (with penalty shootout)	2
Lose (with penalty shootout)	1

Design an algorithm that analyzes the result of a match and awards points to the two teams accordingly. For example, given the following score line:

    England 2: Brazil 0, Penalties: No

England would be awarded 3 points and Brazil 0 points. For this match:

    Netherlands 5: Portugal 4, Penalties: Yes

The Netherlands would get 2 points and Portugal 1 point.
Now extend your solution to deal with an unspecified number of matches. The algorithm should stop calculating points when a score line appears that has a negative goal score for either team. Teams may play more than one match, so each team's points tally will need to be updated as necessary. At the end, the team with the highest points tally should be declared top of the world rankings.

11.   Vance Legstrong, a world-class Stocksfield-based cyclist has asked the Department of Mechanical Engineering at the University of Stocksfield to help him out with the selection of gear wheels on his new bicycle. Vance wants to know, for each of 10 gears on his bicycle how many times he must make one full turn of the pedals in order to travel 1 km. A bicycle's gear ratio is given as the ratio between the number of teeth on the chain wheel (the one the pedals are connected to) and the number of teeth on the gear wheel (the one attached to the rear wheel). The rear wheel has ten gear wheels all with

a different number of teeth. The chain wheel has 36 teeth and the gear wheels have teeth as given in Table 5.6.

Table 5.6 **Number of Teeth on Bicycle Gear Wheels**

Gear Wheel	Number of Teeth
1	36
2	34
3	32
4	30
5	28
6	26
7	24
8	22
9	20
10	18

Thus, the ratio of gear 1 is 1 as the chain wheel ÷ gear wheel = 36/36. The ratio of gear 5 is 1.2857, and so on. The diameter of the wheels on Vance's bicycle is 27 inches

a) Design an algorithm to calculate the gear ratios of all ten gears.

b) Extend your solution to tell Vance how many pedal turns are needed to travel 1 km in each gear. You may assume that no freewheeling is allowed. Think about how far the bicycle will travel for each full turn of the pedals.

A sketch of the principal components may be useful. You may like to tackle some of subproblems separately.[13]

5.5 Projects

StockSnackz Vending Machine

Up till now we assumed the vending machine had unlimited supplies. It is time to put away such childish notions. Therefore, extend your solution so that the machine now shows a "sold out" message if it has run out of a selected item.

---

[13] Hint: One of the subproblems is finding out how far one turn of the pedals will move the bicycle. In gear 1, turning the pedals one full turn will rotate the rear wheel one full turn as the gear ratio is 1:1, thus the bicycle will travel 27 inches; In gear 5, the rear wheel will make 1.2857 full turns. Another subproblem is finding out how many times the pedal has to turn to move 1 km: how many inches are there in 1 km? You can start off by knowing that 1 inch = 2.54 cm and there are 100 cm in 1 m and 1000 m in 1 km.

For testing purposes set the initial stock levels to 5 of each item (otherwise it will take your friend a long time to work through the algorithm!).

Previously if the buttons 0, 7, 8, 9 were pressed the machine simply did nothing. Now it is time to design a more typical response. The machine should behave as before when buttons 1–6 are pressed but should now show an "Invalid choice" message if the buttons 0, 7, 8, 9 are pressed. For both problems remember to write down all the variables (together with their ranges of values) that are needed.

Stocksfield Fire Service

Look at the algorithm you created in Chapter 4 for the hazchem problem. Identify and write down all the variables you think you may need for this solution. Remember to also indicate the typical ranges of values that each variable can take.

Puzzle World: Roman Numerals and Chronograms

Look at the algorithm you created in Chapter 4 for the Roman numerals validation and translation problems. Identify and write down all the variables you think you may need for your solutions. Remember to also indicate the typical ranges of values that each variable can take.

Pangrams: Holoalphabetic Sentences

Look at the algorithm you created in Chapter 4 for the pangram problem. Identify and write down all the variables you think you may need for this solution. Remember to also indicate the typical ranges of values that each variable can take.

Online Bookstore: ISBNs

Identify likely variables and their ranges of values for:

a) the ISBN hyphenation problem
b) the ISBN validation problem

Write your solution to the ISBN validation problem using an iteration to work through the nine main digits of the ISBN.

Extending Our Vocabulary: Data and Control Abstractions

Learning Objectives

- Understand the ways in which different kinds (types) of data affect the way solutions to problems are designed
- Recognize appropriate operations that can be carried out on different data types
- Identify different ways of carrying out selection and iteration and understand how different specialized control constructs can be used appropriately
- Understand the difference between simple and compound selections, and how complex conditions can be expressed to control the selections
- Understand the difference between determinate and indeterminate iterations and how complex conditions can be expressed to control the iterations
    - Determinate: count-controlled iteration
    - Indeterminate: zero-or-more and at-least-once iterations
- Analyze real-world problems to identify the appropriate selection and iteration constructs to use

In this chapter we will revisit the basic programming ideas of data, sequence, iteration, and selection and look at some of the different ways they can be expressed. From this we will build up a repertoire of standard structures for implementing solutions to common problems.[1]

We came across the idea of sequence, iteration, and selection constructs a few times in previous chapters. These constructs are very important concepts as they are the three fundamental building blocks from which all programs are built.[2] If you examine all the solutions

---

[1] You may come across the term *design patterns* which are standard ways of approaching common problems. There is a bit more to design patterns than that, but they have become very popular in software engineering as they provide tried-and-tested approaches that can be tailored to fit individual circumstances. They are used especially in object-oriented programming projects. If you want to know more, take a look at Shalloway and Trott's (2001) book on the subject.

[2] Well, nearly all. There is a technique called parallel programming in which courses of action that are executed simultaneously (in parallel) on multiple processors are specified. Multi-threading (something you will come across on a C++ or Java course) is a similar concept to parallel programming. Happily, you do not need to know anything about parallel programs to understand this book.

from the previous chapters you can see that they are all just different combinations of sequential actions, repeated actions, and alternate courses of action. When you think about it in these terms, programming is really very simple as there are only three building blocks. Of course, there are only a few notes in a musical scale, but putting them together well to make pleasing music is a valuable skill. One of the marks of a programmer is understanding how to arrange actions in sequences, iterations, and selections to best arrive at the desired outcome. Therefore, in this chapter you will learn about sequential statement blocks (Section 6.2) and the different types of selection (Section 6.3) and iteration (Section 6.4) constructs available in most programming languages. But first, we will take a look at data.

6.1 Data Abstractions

In Chapter 5 we looked at identifying the different variables in a problem and estimating the likely ranges of values they could take. At this point, it is instructive to pause and to see how doing this enables us to begin constructing lower-level abstractions of the data. We have talked much about data. For example, we might talk about bank account data such as the account number, the balance, the account holder's name, and so on. But what exactly is "data"? Data is actually a plural noun (the singular being "datum" from the Latin, meaning "given"), but which is commonly treated as a singular noun. Thus, in texts on programming you will see phrases such as "the data *are* stored in a file" and "the data *is* read into the program." Linguists would, perhaps, prefer us to use the plural, but I think the damage is now done and the singular use so widespread that we can use either. Dictionaries will define data as a set of facts from which other facts can be inferred. For example, given the bank account data "opening balance," "total credits," and "total debits," it is possible to calculate another datum (data item): "closing balance."

In books on computing and information systems, data is commonly defined as unorganized facts. Information is then defined as organized facts, or data with meaning attached. This is a simplistic view and not altogether helpful, for many programs access data files in which the data are highly organized and structured. A more helpful stance is taken by Checkland and Holwell (1997) who define data as facts about the real world that can be verified and checked. In problem solving we then select certain items of data for our attention and organize them in such a way as is helpful for gaining insight into the problem and thus producing a solution.[3] In programming terms, data are usually taken to mean the various items, values, facts, etc. that the program manipulates in order to execute the solution to the problem. For example, in the coffee-making problem we identified the following data (see Table 5.1):

- The number of coffees to be made
- The milk preference of a drinker

---

[3] Checkland and Holwell (1997) call such selected data *capta*. They define information as capta (selected data) that has been enriched by having meaningful attributes attached to it. Information that is itself organized into structures is then called *knowledge*.

- The sugar requirements of a drinker
- The number of cups poured so far
- The number of sugars added to a cup so far

Having identified the required data, carrying out the coffee making task simply required us to write down the value of these data on a notepad, or to store them in our head. Notepads and short-term memory are useful for people solving simple problems and computers use an electronic equivalent.

Humans are very good at simplifying complexity and working at high levels of abstraction. For instance, you may not ever have been consciously aware of it when reading your bank statements, but you are able to decode different types of data (such as transaction amount, transaction date, payee name, and so on) with ease. Look at Figure 6.1, which shows a bank statement for Henry and Eliza Higgins.

FIGURE 6.1 **Sample bank statement**

First Bank of **Stocksfield** Current Account

Date	Details		Withdrawn	Paid in	Balance
1 Jan 2004	BROUGHT FORWARD				1,025.49
3 Jan 2004	Cheque	101	35.00		990.49
10 Jan 2004	ATM Stocksfield		100.00		890.49
25 Jan 2004	Direct Debit	Mastercard	359.99		530.50
27 Jan 2004	Credit no. 101	000002		59.00	589.50
31 Jan 2004	CARRIED FORWARD				589.50

101

Account number 12345678
Branch code   00-00-00

Professor Henry and Mrs Eliza Higgins

The statement contains a number of different kinds of data. The name of the bank is printed at the top together with the account type. These are both textual items. The transaction dates are a mixture of text and numbers. The transaction details also contain text with some numbers in it. The "withdrawn," "paid in," and "balance" columns contain numbers in a currency format. The oval in the bottom left corner has the statement page number which, unlike the currency figures, is a whole number. The account holders' names are clearly textual as are the labels "Account number" and "Branch code." The account number itself is an eight digit number, and the branch code has a "two-digit, hyphen, two-digit, hyphen, two-digit" format.

I am sure that when you looked at Figure 6.1 you did not think about the statement in this kind of detail. You probably just read the statement as a summary of banking transactions. You did not need to know that the currency figures were numeric values with precision to two decimal places, that the names of the account holders are written using a mixture of upper and lower case letters, and so on. Because of this you may never have been aware that data comes in different kinds. But think back to when you started to learn arithmetic. Perhaps at first you were taught to do simple sums using whole numbers, such as 3 + 5, 11 + 7, and so on. Subtractions were also simple, and the teacher made sure that the problems always gave a positive answer because five-year-olds find negative numbers a difficult concept to grasp. Perhaps multiplication came next followed by division. Again, problems of division were simplified so as to yield a whole result: fractional numbers come later on in the curriculum. So, a very young child would be able to solve 18 ÷ 9, but not 17 ÷ 9. Why is 17 ÷ 9 so much harder than 18 ÷ 9? Because it involves knowing about fractional numbers, decimal points, numbers between 0 and 1, and so on. That is, 18 ÷ 9 resides in the domain of whole numbers whereas 17 ÷ 9 though composed of whole numbers does not give a whole-number result. Perhaps you first learned to solve problems of this kind by saying that the answer is 1 with a remainder, or leftover, of 8.

When thinking about the problem initially it is fine to consider the data at the high level of abstraction where they are just values. However, eventually our solutions must be translated into programming language code ready for execution by a computer. Unfortunately, computers store different kinds of values in different ways. Each programming language supplies its own set of data abstractions which specify what kinds of values a data item can take, the range of those values, and the actions that can be performed using those values. When you have completed this part of the book and start to learn how to translate your algorithms into a specific programming language you will need to be aware of the different ways the language treats different kinds of data. Because this book is not concerned with detail at that level we do not need to go that far, but it is helpful to begin classifying data into lower-level abstractions than we have been working with up till now.

Consider, for example, the number 7. What can we do with that number? We can add it to another number, subtract it from another number, multiply it, divide it, or even raise it to a power. When we define a data item in terms of the range of values it can take and the different operations that can be performed upon it we have described what a programmer would call an ABSTRACT DATA TYPE or ADT. An ADT describing whole numbers might look like Table 6.1.

Table 6.1   **ADT for Whole Numbers**

Whole Numbers	
Range	$0 \ldots \infty$
Operations	$+, -, \times, \div$

It is a **data type** because it differentiates between different kinds of values and the operations that can be performed on those values. For example, it makes sense to do

+, −, ×, ÷ on numbers but not on words. For example, what does "Henry" ÷ "Higgins" mean if we take the "÷" symbol to stand for numeric division?

It is **abstract** because we are not concerned (at this point) with how the values are stored inside a computer nor with how the operations are performed. That is, we are interested in knowing that the "×" is an operation that multiplies two values but we are not interested in the details of the algorithm that expresses the solution to the problem of how, exactly, to multiply any two numbers.

Programmers must be aware of the different kinds of data they are dealing with for just as 18 ÷ 9 and 17 ÷ 9 require slightly different approaches, so a computer uses different mechanisms for storing different kinds of data. This is why in Chapter 5 I also asked you to estimate the range of values that could be taken by the variables in a problem (see Table 5.1 on page 101). We need to know what kind and what size of value a variable will take in order to be able to correctly instruct the computer to store and manipulate it.

▶ Data types
In programming, the classification of data according to its kind is called *typing*. Each data item in a program must belong to a particular data type. Some programming languages (Ada,[4] for example) are *strongly typed* with very strict rules governing how data of different types can be mixed and manipulated. Other languages, such as early versions of BASIC, are more *loosely typed* and the manipulation rules are less strict. Languages like C, C++, and Java are more strongly typed than BASIC but are less strongly typed than Ada. Whatever the strength of the typing, programming languages have in common that data must be declared to be of a particular type.

Typing is not a sadistic whim of programming language designers to make life awkward for beginners. When you specify a variable as belonging to a particular type you are also implicitly stating what range of values the variable can take and what operations can be performed on those values. For example, we could take a simple view of our bank statement as comprising either numbers or text. If we say that a transaction's value is a decimal numeric type then we know we would expect to be able to perform addition, subtraction, multiplication, division, and other arithmetic operations on that value. We also know that a decimal number can only be formed from the digits 0 to 9 and a single (but optional) decimal point character.[5] If an entry that was supposed to be a number appeared as "hello" we would know something was wrong. Likewise, treating a value as text means that we would expect values to be made up of combinations of letters and other characters. So, on our bank statement, "Credit no. 101" is text,[6] as are "Account number" and "Professor Henry and Mrs Eliza Higgins." Furthermore, we would not expect to be able to add, subtract, and multiply text values in the way that we can with numbers. For instance, what does "XX" + "YY" mean?

---

[4] Named after the nineteenth-century niece of Lord Byron, Lady Ada Lovelace, who is credited with being the world's first computer programmer.

[5] In many European countries the comma is used as the decimal placeholder with the full stop/period being used to separate thousands. Thus the value 1,499.50 (one thousand four hundred and ninety-nine point five) would be written in France as 1.499,50 for example.

[6] Actually, it is probably a combination of the text "Credit no." and the numeric value 101.

Think Spot

What answers did you come up with? I guess the answer could be "ZZ" or "XXYY." How about "YYXX"? Here is a more subtle problem. What does "A" + "B" mean? If "A" and "B" are text, then the answer could be "AB," or "C," or "BA," etc. But what if "A" and "B" are hexadecimal numbers? In that case "A" + "B" should give 15 in hexadecimal.[7] It is important to know what type of data we are dealing with so that it can be correctly interpreted and only valid operations applied to it. The enclosure of A and B by speech marks may have led you to think that that they were text values rather than hexadecimal digits, but that is only an ASSUMPTION. The typing rules of a programming language will specify what operations are allowed, and how those operations are carried out. In some languages, when applied to text, the "+" operator stands for concatenation (appending one piece of text to another). So, "XX" + "YY" would give "XXYY." The point to note here is that the "+" operator has different meanings for different types of data.[8] Specifying a type tells the computer how to interpret what is required. Strongly-typed languages are very strict and will often not allow data of one type to be combined with data of another type. For example, in a very strongly-typed language, an expression like 15 + "X" may not be permissible as the expression mixes a numeric value with a textual value. However, some loosely-typed languages may allow just such an expression in which case the computer would convert both data items to some common type to allow the operation to be carried out.[9] For example, in the above expression, a loosely-typed language may first convert the "X" to a numeric representation, say 24, as that is X's position in the alphabet. There are other possible conversions that could be done, and as a programmer you need to be aware of how the language you are using stores data types. There is an everyday situation that is analogous to data typing. Cars that run on unleaded fuel have specially shaped filler caps that will only accept unleaded-fuel

Strongly-typed ▶ nozzles. This is to prevent leaded fuel or diesel being pumped in and ruining the
fuel tanks! engine. This is an example of strong typing as the tank design prevents fuel of an incompatible type being placed into the tank.

There are many different types offered by the various programming languages. Furthermore, many languages allow you to define your own types as needed. Thus it is impossible in a book that does not focus on a particular language to cover everything that could be said about data types. Therefore, for our purposes all we need to be aware of is that data do belong to different types. When considering the data in our problems it is useful to think in terms of ABSTRACT DATA TYPES, that is, the range of values data of that type can take and the corresponding operations that we might reasonably perform upon that data.

Now we turn our attention to the algorithmic building blocks of sequence, iteration, and selection.

---

[7] A = 10 in decimal, B = 11, so 10 + 11 = 21 decimal, or 15 in hexadecimal. 15, of course, means $1 \times 16 + 5$.

[8] We call this an *overloaded* operator in programming for it has multiple meanings depending on its context of use.

[9] The popular web scripting language JavaScript is notoriously flexible with data types and can catch the unwary programmer out (especially those used to strong typing).

6.2   Sequence

The sequence is the simplest of the three programming building blocks, as easy as A, B, C. Think of three actions, say "get up," "get dressed," and "eat breakfast," label the three actions "A," "B," and "C," and write them out in the order you would do them, and you have a sequence:

A. Get up

B. Get dressed

C. Eat breakfast

That is all a sequence is, a set of actions, tasks, or instructions that are carried out in the order in which they're written. You will recall from the *HTTLAP* strategy that writing out a sequence of actions is the first step in writing down the solution to a problem.

6.3   More Selections

In Chapter 4 we looked at how to solve problems involving choices and introduced the selection construct IF. The IF allows us to choose whether or not to carry out an action block depending on the value of a condition. At this point you might want to refresh your memory and have another look over Chapter 4.

Simple and Extended Selections

Often tasks or courses of actions only need to be carried out when certain conditions are met. We call this process *selection* because we are telling the algorithm to select between alternative courses of action. All the problems in Chapters 4 and 5 involved making choices and could be solved using an IF that only had one choice to make. That is, we either carried out the action block or we did not. The IF is controlled by a *relational expression.* For example, the coffee making solutions had sections resembling the following:

Relational ▶
expressions

```
IF (milk required)
    Add milk ;
ENDIF
```

In this example when the condition "milk required" is satisfied then milk is added. When the condition is not satisfied then no milk is added. We can rephrase this more formally as selecting between a course of action and the *null* action.[10]

---

[10] Null is a word that is used much in computing and programming. It means to be void, empty, lacking existence, amounting to nothing. Thus, a null action is one that does nothing at all. A null variable is one that has no value.

You said the selection's null action is carried out. I cannot see any activity labelled "null" in the algorithm. Where is it?

Null means something that is absent or non-existent. Thus, you will not find a null statement – it simply refers to the action that is taken when the condition in the IF gives a false result, i.e., nothing at all.

Extended Selections

However, there are times when the choice is not between an action and the null action but between two positive but alternative courses of action. Take, for example, the case of withdrawing money from a cash machine (ATM). After inserting your card you key in your PIN/security code and choose an option to withdraw cash. If you have enough money in your account (or you are within your credit limit) then the machine should dispense the cash. We could express this in pseudo-code as:

```
IF (funds available)
    Dispense cash ;
ENDIF
```

What if your request for cash would exceed your limits? In this case the ATM should decline your request and display a message such as "Sorry, but you have insufficient funds." The simple IF construct is not able to deal with this situation because its alternative to dispensing cash is the null (non-existent) action, so we would have to resort to something clumsy like this:

```
IF (funds available)
    Dispense cash ;
ENDIF
IF (insufficient funds available)
    Display message of apology ;
ENDIF
```

The above solution does not match how we would phrase such a selection in real life. If you were telling a bank clerk how to handle cash requests you would say something like: "If there are sufficient funds then give the customer the requested cash *otherwise* apologize and explain that their request cannot be satisfied." The key to this is the word "otherwise" which sets out an alternative course of action to be followed if the first action cannot be performed. We can extend our pseudo-code to allow this by adding a new keyword "ELSE" (for some reason, ELSE is used rather than OTHERWISE in most programming languages).

```
IF (condition)
    Action 1 ;
ELSE
    Action 2 ;
ENDIF
```

The "ELSE" enables us to replace the null action with a real action to be carried out when the condition belonging to the IF is false. Here is the cash withdrawal solution rewritten using our new IF...ELSE construct:

```
IF (funds available)
    Dispense cash ;
ELSE
    Display message of apology ;
ENDIF
Return card ;
```

You can read this as "IF there are funds available then dispense the cash ELSE (otherwise) display the message of apology, and afterwards return the customer's card." The important thing to note is that only one of the two actions blocks is carried out: **either** the dispense cash task **or** the apology task, but not both. If the funds are available the cash is dispensed, the apology task is skipped, and the customer's bank card is then returned. If there are insufficient funds then the dispense cash action is skipped and the apology message is displayed instead, followed again by returning the customer's card.

The reason we would use the IF...ELSE rather than two IFs one after the other is because both action blocks are dependent on the same condition. In the example above where we had two IFs, one to dispense money if funds were available and another to display an apology if funds were not available, we can see that both actions (dispensing cash and displaying an apology) are conditional upon the funds available. Furthermore, the apology is displayed when the opposite condition to the first IF is met. That is, we have two conditions: "funds available" and "funds not available" which are simply opposites. Using two IF constructs leads to a clumsy solution in which we not only have to write out the condition that must be satisfied for money to be dispensed but also to write out the condition to be met when an apology is displayed. We make use of the fact that the apology condition is simply the opposite of the cash dispensing condition by using the IF...ELSE construct.

Write an **IF...ELSE** statement that chooses between wearing sandals or shoes depending on whether it is raining.

Multi-part Selections

The IF...ELSE construct also allows us to solve more complicated problems than the simple either-or example above. Let's go back to the van-loading problem from Chapter 5. The company was so pleased with our work that they have asked us to extend the solution. The van drivers have been complaining that some small parcels were much heavier than they looked and some large ones were lighter than expected. This led to a spate of back injuries when lifting parcels off the vans and the drivers are getting concerned. The management has decided to label each parcel with a sticker. Now, as they are loaded onto the vans at the depot parcels will be categorized as light, medium, or heavy. A light parcel is anything up to 5 kg. Parcels over 5 kg but less than 10 kg are classed as medium-weight and anything weighing 10 kg and over is classified as heavy. We could write a solution to this problem using three separate IF statements as in Solution 6.1 below.

Solution 6.1 Clumsy multiple selection

```
IF (parcelWeight up to (and including) 5 kilos)
    Add 'light' sticker ;
ENDIF
IF (parcelWeight more than 5 and less than 10 kilos)
    Add 'medium' sticker ;
ENDIF
IF (parcelWeight 10 kilos or over)
    Add 'heavy' sticker ;
ENDIF
Load parcel on van ;
```

Think Spot

Solution 6.1 solves the problem but it is not a very good solution. Using a sequence of individual IFs makes it appear that the three selections are separate and unrelated, that is, all three actions could be followed if all three conditions are met. However, we know that the three conditions are mutually exclusive – if any one of them is true the other two must be false.

Do not move on until you understand how the three conditions are mutually exclusive, that is, only one can be true at a time. You can show this by drawing a truth table:

parcelWeight	Condition		
	parcelWeight up to (and including) 5 kilos	parcelWeight more than 5 and less than 10 kilos	parcelWeight 10 kilos or over
4 kg	True	False	False
5 kg			
9 kg			
10 kg			
11 kg			

For each value in the parcel weight column fill in the true or false value for each of the three conditions. How many conditions are true for each parcel weight? The first row has already been filled in for you. A solution is given in Appendix C.

Therefore, the solution is not making full use of what we know about the problem. The IF...ELSE allows us to select between two related courses of action. The problem here is similar except there are three courses of action rather than two. We can represent this situation by extending the IF...ELSE to allow more than two choices.

Rewrite the three separate selections above using a single three-way IF . . . ELSE structure now. Once you have tried to do that, compare your answer with Solution 6.2 below.

Solution 6.2 Using IF...ELSE to add stickers

```
IF (parcelWeight up to 5 kilos)
    Add 'light' sticker ;
ELSE IF (parcelWeight less than 10 kilos)
    Add 'medium' sticker ;
ELSE
    Add 'heavy' sticker ;
ENDIF
Load parcel on van ;
```

Rather than ending the selection after the first ELSE we have added another IF...ELSE structure. You can read this as saying "if it is a light parcel then add a light sticker, otherwise if it is a medium-weight parcel add a medium sticker otherwise add a heavy sticker." The condition for the first IF should be easy to understand. A light parcel is one that weighs 5 kg or less, so the condition is straightforward. When we examine the second condition after the "ELSE IF" it is different from the second condition in Solution 6.1. Solution 6.1 had the condition "parcelWeight more than 5 kg and less than 10 kg" while Solution 6.2 just has "parcelWeight less than 10 kg." Why do you think this is?

A medium parcel is one that weighs more than 5 kg but less than 10 kg, so surely Solution 6.2 is wrong as it only tests to see whether the parcel is less than 10 kg? Wouldn't a parcel of 4 kg therefore be classed as medium weight because it is less than 10?

Think about what the ELSE means. How does it affect the condition? In English we might say "otherwise" rather than ELSE. What does "otherwise" mean?

Solution 6.2 is correct because the conditions are linked by the ELSE keyword. Recall that the IF...ELSE construct says that if the first condition is false then carry out the alternative action. Look at Solution 6.2 to see how this rule is applied. The first IF asks whether the parcel is 5 kg or less in weight. If it is, then a "light" sticker is added, the rest of the selection is skipped, and the next action in the sequence (the one after the ENDIF) is carried out which, in this case, is "Load parcel on van." If the parcel is not 5 kg or less then we follow the ELSE path, which, in this case, has its own condition "parcelWeight less than 10 kg." Why doesn't this condition say "parcelWeight more than 5 kg and less than 10 kg"? Consider how we got to this point. We are only testing this condition because the first one "parcelWeight up to 5 kg" was false, that is, we found a parcel that weighed more than 5 kg. If we already know that it weighs more than 5 kg, to determine whether the parcel is medium weight all we need to do is find out whether it is also less than 10 kg. For example, take a parcel that weighs 7 kg. The first condition will be false because the parcel is not up to five kilos in weight. So we move to the ELSE that

has its own IF construct which asks whether the parcel is less than 10 kg. It is, so we have correctly identified a medium-weight parcel.

What happens when the parcel is 10 kg or heavier? This time the second condition would also be false so the next ELSE is followed. At this point we know that we are not dealing with a light- or a medium-weight parcel so, by definition, it must be a heavy one. Therefore, there is no need to test its weight again and we can go ahead with putting on a "heavy" sticker. A mistake many beginners make is to put an "IF (condition)" after the final ELSE in a multi-path selection. If the preceding conditions have been correctly formed, then by the time the final ELSE is reached there should be no need to make another test as all other possibilities for action have been exhausted. In the parcel weighing problem, if a parcel is not light and it is not medium weight then it **must** be a heavy parcel (look back at the truth table you completed earlier).

Writing Selection Conditions

When considering the parcels it is becoming unwieldy to write all the IF conditions in longhand. Table 6.2 lists a set of symbols we will use from now on when making comparisons between different values. These symbols are known formally as **relational operators**.

Table 6.2 **The Relational Operators**

Operator	Pseudo-code
Less than	$<$
Less than or equal to	$\leq$
Equals (equality)	$=$
Greater than or equal to	$\geq$
Greater than	$>$
Not equal to (inequality)	$\neq$

The relational operators allow us to express real-world conditions in our programs. For example, in many countries you must be at least 18 years old to vote in elections. An algorithm that processes requests to register for the vote might have a section like this:

```
IF (age ≥ 18)
    Statements for issuing a voting card ;
ELSE
    Display 'Sorry, too young' message ;
ENDIF
```

This is much easier to write (and easier to read) than the longhand equivalent:

```
IF (age is greater than or equal to 18)
    Statements for issuing a voting card ;
ELSE
    Display 'Sorry, too young' message ;
ENDIF
```

Now that we are armed with the relational operators we can learn to write selections with properly formed conditional expressions. Take the problem of assigning a grade to a piece of homework. In the University of Stocksfield, grades are calculated on the basis of the percentage mark awarded for pieces of work according to the Table 6.3:

Table 6.3   **Grade Calculation**

Percentage Mark	Corresponding Grade	Condition
80% or above	A	(mark ≥ 80)
70% to 79%	B	(mark ≥ 70) AND (mark ≤ 79)
60% to 69%	C	(mark ≥ 60) AND (mark ≤ 69)
50% to 59%	D	(mark ≥ 50) AND (mark ≤ 59)
40% to 49%	**E**	(mark ≥ 40) AND (mark ≤ 49)
Less than 40%	**F**	(mark < 40)
Both E and F are fail grades		

The selection for assigning an "A" grade is quite simple: the mark is 80% or above. We could write this in pseudo-code as follows:

```
IF (mark ≥ 80)
    grade ← 'A' ;
ENDIF
```

Think Spot How would you extend this selection to include the "B" to "F" grades? You could write independent IF statements:

```
IF (mark ≥ 80)
    grade ← 'A' ;
ENDIF
IF (mark ≥ 70) AND (mark ≤ 79)
    grade ← 'B' ;
ENDIF
IF (mark ≥ 60) AND (mark ≤ 69)
    grade ← 'C' ;
ENDIF
IF (mark ≥ 50) AND (mark ≤ 59)
    grade ← 'D' ;
ENDIF
IF (mark ≥ 40) AND (mark ≤ 49)
    grade ← 'E' ;
ENDIF
IF (mark < 40)
    grade ← 'F' ;
ENDIF
```

But, as we saw above, this is a clumsy solution because the different IFs repeat the tests that have gone before.

Write the above **IF** statements as an extended **IF...ELSE** selection.

If you are finding this exercise a bit tricky, think about each of the grade calculations as a separate problem, but a problem that is related to the one before. What does each previous grade test tell you about the value of the mark? Try thinking of it this way: if the mark is not 80 or above and so does not deserve a grade "A," then what do we now know about the mark's value?

If you managed the above exercise, or you have spent more than fifteen minutes sweating over the answer, look at my solution below.

Solution 6.3 Extended IF...ELSE for calculating a grade

```
IF (mark ≥ 80)
    grade ← 'A' ;
ELSE IF (mark ≥ 70)
    grade ← 'B' ;
ELSE IF (mark ≥ 60)
    grade ← 'C' ;
ELSE IF (mark ≥ 50)
    grade ← 'D' ;
ELSE IF (mark ≥ 40)
    grade ← 'E' ;
ELSE
    grade ← 'F' ;
ENDIF
```

Look carefully at Solution 6.3 and compare it with your own. Was yours the same? If you had >69 instead of ≥70 that is alright because they're logically equivalent. Did you have the ELSE at the end for the "F" grade, or did you include another IF? Why did I not have a final IF? Let's walk through the solution from the top.

Huh?

I don't understand why you said >69 is logically equivalent to ≥70.

Is 70 bigger than 69? Yes. Is 70 greater-than-or-equal-to 70? Yes, it is equal to 70. So, 70 is both greater than 69 and it is greater-than-or-equal-to 70. So, the relational expressions >69 and ≥70 evaluate to the same result for any given value.

The first IF asks whether the mark is greater than or equal to 80. If it is, a grade "A" is awarded. That bit shouldn't be baffling you. But how about the first ELSE part? It includes an IF to see whether the mark merits a "B" grade instead. At this point you may have written:

```
ELSE IF (mark ≥ 70) AND (mark ≤ 79)
```

If you did, you were correct to use an ELSE, but not correct to include the second relational expression after the AND. Why not? Think about what we already know about the value of mark. The first IF asked whether it was greater than or equal to 80. If it was then an "A" grade was awarded and the algorithm would then skip to the next statement following the entire IF...ELSE structure. But if the first selection's condition yielded false what does that tell us? It tells us that the mark is **not** greater than or equal to 80 which means it **must** be less than 80. Therefore, because we know it is less than 80, to decide if a "B" grade is warranted we now only have to ask whether the mark is at least 70; if we already know the mark is less than 80 then it is silly to repeat that test. Notice how the remaining IFs all take account of what went before. If the mark is not 70 or above then it must be 69 or below, which means we can award a "C" grade if it is still 60 or above, and so on until we get to the final ELSE.

Why does the final **ELSE** not have its own **IF**?

The answer to the above exercise is that by the time we get to this part we know that the mark must be less than 40. As it is less than 40 we know it deserves an "F" grade. Putting another IF there means that that condition could itself yield false, which means that there is yet another grade option. But if the mark is not a grade "A," "B," "C," "D," or "E" then what else can it be other than an "F"? There is no other choice, so we do not need another test on the last ELSE.

If this is at all unclear then take some time now to review Solution 6.3. Try working some data through the algorithm and work through each of the tests by hand to see how the IF...ELSE selection works. Also, convince yourself that taking account of the results of previous selections will only work with an IF...ELSE structure; writing a sequence of separate IF statements with the same conditional expressions as Solution 6.3 would not work.

Sometimes we will have a number of different values of the variable for which we want to take the same course of action, but those values do not lie in a neat range (like they did in the grade calculations above). For example, consider the old rhyme for deciding how many days there are in a month:

Thirty days hath September, April, June, and November.

All the rest have thirty-one,

Except February alone which has twenty-eight days clear,

And twenty-nine in each leap year.

That is, months 4, 6, 9, and 11 all have thirty days, month 2 has twenty-eight or twenty-nine days, depending on whether it is a leap year, and all the other months (1, 3, 5, 7, 8, 10, and 12) have thirty-one days. Figure 6.2 below shows a selection to assign the appropriate value to a variable daysInMonth according to the value held in the variable month.

FIGURE 6.2   **IF...ELSE for days in month calculation**

```
IF (month = 4) OR (month = 6) OR (month = 9) OR (month = 11)
    daysInMonth ← 30 ;
ELSE IF (month = 2)
    Actions to deal with February ;
ELSE
    daysInMonth ← 31 ;
ENDIF
```

Notice how the different months with common actions have been linked using the word OR. There is one problem remaining: how to deal with February.

How should February be processed? How many days should there be in February? Taking February alone, write an **IF...ELSE** construct that assigns the correct value to **month** depending on whether the current year is a leap year.

Here is my solution to the February problem:

Solution 6.4 Dealing with February

```
IF (isLeapYear)
    daysInMonth ← 29 ;
ELSE
    daysInMonth ← 28 ;
ENDIF
```

For the IF condition you might have written something like "IF current year is a leap year" which is fine: I have just used a variable name isLeapYear as shorthand for this.

Finally, add the February solution to the overall solution from Figure 6.2.

Solution 6.5 shows the overall solution to the problem.

Solution 6.5 Complete days in month solution

```
IF (month = 4) OR (month = 6) OR (month = 9) OR (month = 11)
    daysInMonth ← 30 ;
ELSE IF (month = 2)
    IF (isLeapYear)
        daysInMonth ← 29 ;
    ELSE
        daysInMonth ← 28 ;
    ENDIF
ELSE
    daysInMonth ← 31 ;
ENDIF
```

? Think Spot

I have shaded the IF...ELSE that deals with February simply to make clear that this part of the algorithm is nested within the second IF – you should convince yourself that this nested IF...ELSE is only carried out if month is equal to 2.

6.4　Iteration

The third of our basic programming building blocks is the loop, or iteration. Recall that iteration constructs let us write sections of code that are repeatedly executed.

Determinate Iterations

Iterations can be classified as being either *determinate or indeterminate*. A determinate iteration is one in which the number of times the action block is to be repeated is known in advance or can be calculated at the time the loop is executed. For example, an algorithm that reports the average rainfall for each month of the year would probably use a determinate loop. That is because there are twelve months in the year so we know we must carry out the instructions to display the rainfall for a single month twelve times. That is an example of knowing the number of iterations in advance. A program that calculates the number of leap years between two years chosen by the user would also use a determinate loop. Although the number of iterations is not known in advance, it can be calculated at the time the loop is executed. For example, there is a six-year range between 1999 and 2004 inclusive (1999, 2000, 2001, 2002, 2003, and 2004) but only a three-year range between 2004 and 2006. The number of years that need to be tested for being leap years is not known when we write the algorithm, but the loop is bounded by the chosen start and end years meaning the number of times the loop needs to execute its action block can be calculated.

We have seen an example of a determinate loop in the coffee-making problem. The number of times the instructions for adding sugar to a cup of coffee could be calculated for each cup (see Solution 5.9 on page 103). Here are the instructions for adding sugar which I have taken from Solution 5.9 and renumbered (as well as using the assignment symbol):

Solution 6.6 Determinate loop for adding sugar

```
1.   sugarsAdded  ← zero ;
2.   Find out how many sugarsRequired ;
3.   WHILE ( sugarsAdded < sugarsRequired )
         3.1   Add spoonful of sugar ;
         3.2   sugarsAdded  ← sugarsAdded + 1 ;
     ENDWHILE
```

Look carefully at Solution 6.6 above. Apart from adding the assignment symbols I have also rewritten the condition for the WHILE: Solution 5.9 originally said "sugarsAdded not equal to sugarsRequired." We will get to why I have done that in a moment. First:

Explain why this is a determinate loop.

Notice the structure of the determinate loop. Because it is known how many times the loop must iterate, a *counter* is needed to keep track. In Solution 6.6, the

Determinate ▶
and count-
controlled
loops are
names for the
same thing

counter is the variable `sugarsAdded`. In a determinate iteration the counter must be initialized to its starting value prior to the loop (Task #1). The counter must then have an increment added to it (or subtracted from it if the loop is counting down through a range) and this is done in Task #3.2. This step is very important because it allows the loop to terminate by eventually causing the condition to become false. The use of a loop counter has led to this type of iteration also being known as a *count-controlled loop*. The common structure, then, of a determinate (or count-controlled) loop looks like this:

```
Initialize counter to starting value ;
WHILE (counter less than finishing value)
    Actions for loop body ;
    Add increment to counter ;
ENDWHILE
```

Of course, there are variations (for example, if the loop is counting down, rather than up, then the condition would be "counter > finishing value") but the overall structure is the same. In fact, this type of loop usually has a special construct dedicated to it which we will look at a little later on.

Think Spot

Why have I changed the condition from "not equal to" to "less than"? It is a subtle point but it makes the program more correct. For the sake of argument, suppose I accidentally wrote Task #3.2 as

3.2 $\boxed{\text{sugarsAdded}}$ ← $\boxed{\text{sugarsAdded}}$ + 10 ;

That is, because of a simple typing error when writing the statement I am adding 10 rather than 1 each time a sugar is added. Programmers are no more immune to typos than anyone else and it is very easy to make a mistake of this kind. The mistake has been made and we have not spotted it in our checking. Even a dry run of the solution fails to spot the error because we do not see the "10." Our brains are very good at making us see what we expect to see; we expect to see a "1" because that is what we intended to write, so that is what we see. The error remains and gets incorporated into the eventual computer program. What happens? Say two sugars are required.

Trace through the **WHILE** loop now adding the two sugars and state at what point the loop terminates.

Tracing through the loop we encounter the WHILE for the first time and the original condition asks whether the number of sugars added is not equal to the number required. At this point we have added zero spoons of sugars so the condition is true. We enter the action block, add a spoonful of sugar and then carry out the defective task #3.2 and add 10 to `sugarsAdded`. When we go back to the WHILE to test the condition again, this time `sugarsAdded` has the value 10 and `sugarsRequired` the value 2. Is the condition true or false? It is still true, of course, for 10 is not equal to 2. The action block is carried out again and now sugarsAdded equals 20. The condition is still true so the action block is executed once more. And again. And again. And again. The algorithm is now stuck in an infinite loop because the condition can never become false as the ever increasing sugarsAdded will never be equal to 2. The loop **never terminates**.

If we change the condition to that shown in Solution 6.6 something different will happen. The first time into the loop sugarsAdded (0) is less than sugarsRequired (2) so the action block is carried out and 10 is added to sugarsAdded. The next time the condition is tested it becomes false because 10 is not less than 2 and so the loop terminates. The wrong number of sugars has been added to the coffee, but the algorithm at least finishes, and the fact that the coffee has the wrong number of sugars might suggest to us that the loop is in error. We need to get into the habit of defining conditions in terms of the absolute minimum required for them to be true. In this case, we only want to add sugars as long as the number added is less than the required value. As soon as the number added equals (or exceeds) the number required then we know we can stop.

Indeterminate Iterations

Indeterminate loops are those in which the number of iterations is unknown in advance and cannot be calculated. We have already seen a loop of this type in the van-loading problem. The first loop in Solution 5.18 said

    WHILE (conveyor not empty)

And the second said

    WHILE (⌈payload⌉ + ⌈parcelWeight⌉ less than or equal to ⌈capacity⌉) AND
        (conveyor NOT empty)

In the first WHILE the number of iterations is not known by those loading the vans. They are simply required to keep loading and despatching vans as long as there are parcels on the conveyor belt. Unlike the sugar-adding solution where the number of sugars required is known before entering the loop, here the number of parcels is an unknown quantity. Of course, it would be possible to find out this information by going round to the warehouse and counting all the parcels waiting to go onto the conveyor belt. But there is no need for that as it is not necessary to know the number of parcels in advance – knowing it will not help us to load the vans any better. Anyway, what if after counting the parcels and walking back to the loading bay the company received delivery of another batch of parcels?

Likewise, the second WHILE is indeterminate on two counts. First, it needs to stop when the parcels run out (an unknown quantity), and secondly, we cannot know in advance how many parcels will go on each van unless we weigh them all first and do the sums before bringing on a van. Again, there is little to be gained from doing this and we are quite happy weighing and loading individual parcels, stopping as soon as one will not fit, despatching the van, and bringing up the next one to carry on the process until we run out of parcels.

An order processing program for an online retailer might use an indeterminate/indeterminate loop of the form

    WHILE (orders to process)

```
        Fetch details of order ;
        Calculate order value ;
        Calculate shipping costs ;
        Print invoice ;
    ENDWHILE
```

The number of orders will likely change between runs of the algorithm and there is nothing to be gained from knowing in advance how many times to repeat the invoice printing routine. This is quite unlike the sugar problem where it is absolutely essential to know how many times to execute the sugar-adding action. The alternative would be to specify an indeterminate loop and then, after adding each spoonful of sugar, to ask our guest if more sugar is still required. Think about this now to check that you can see why this would be an unwieldy and unnatural way of approaching the task.

The indeterminate loop used in the van-loading solution has the general form:

```
Get first item ;
WHILE (continuation condition)
    Process item ;
    Get next item ;
ENDWHILE
```

This structure is commonly known as the *read-ahead loop* as the first item to be processed in the loop's action block is fetched ahead of the iteration construct (before the WHILE). The task to fetch the next item to process then comes at the end of the action block after all the instructions that deal with the previous item. We would typically use the read-ahead technique when the values of the items being processed are needed for testing the iteration condition. For example, in the van-loading problem we must know a parcel's weight before we can decide whether it will fit on the van. Therefore, before the loop condition can be tested for the first time we must already know the weight of a parcel. Contrast this with the *read-and-process* structure:

```
WHILE (continuation condition)
    Get item ;
    Process item ;
ENDWHILE
```

The difference between the read-ahead and the read-and-process loops is subtle. Read-ahead is used when information about the items to be processed is needed in order to test the loop's controlling condition. In situations where we do not need to know anything about the items in advance we can use the read-and-process structure. In this scheme the WHILE's condition is tested and if the condition gives a true result then the action body is entered. The first task inside the action block is to fetch an item to process. The remainder of the action block contains tasks to deal with the item.

The nature of the WHILE construct means that a loop's action block is carried out zero or more times (there was an example of this in Solution 6.6). That is, if the WHILE's condition gives a false result the first time it is tested then the loop's body will not be entered and so the loop is said to have iterated zero times. For this reason the WHILE is known as a zero-or-more iteration. Sometimes we need

? Think Spot

"Read-ahead" ▶ technique

"Read-and- ▶ process"

zero-or-more ▶ iteration

to write loops that execute at least once. For example, an ATM asks you for your PIN before dispensing any cash.[11] Usually an ATM gives you three chances to enter the correct PIN after which it keeps your card. The point is that the loop that keeps asking you for your PIN must iterate at least once. An at-least-once iteration can be built using a WHILE but it requires careful initialization of variables to ensure that the condition is true the first time round.

Another common situation is where we know (or can calculate) in advance the number of times a loop must iterate. Such loops typically have a counter (or *sentinel*) variable to keep track of how many times it has iterated, hence they are often called count-controlled loops. We saw above how to build count-controlled loops with the WHILE in which a counter variable is used to keep track of the number of iterations and which causes the loop to terminate when the counter reaches a defined maximum limit. At-least-once and count-controlled loops are such common features in programs that most programming languages provide specialized iteration constructs to deal with them. Below we shall look at two such constructs using our pseudo-code.

Count-controlled Iterations

Consider the following count-controlled loop built with the WHILE construct. The iteration prompts the user to enter the average rainfall for each month of the year and calculates the running total rainfall for the year:

```
totalRainfall ← 0 ;
month ← 1 ; // Give counter a starting value
WHILE (month ≤ 12) // Specify upper limit for counter
    Display 'Please enter the month's rainfall' ;
    Get monthRainfall ;
    totalRainfall ← totalRainfall + monthRainfall ;
    month ← month + 1 ; // Increment added to counter
ENDWHILE
```

The chief problem with writing count-controlled loops using a WHILE is that it is easy to forget to increase the value of the counter at the end of the loop meaning that the iteration will never terminate. Sometimes programmers also forget to initialize the counter before the loop. Like most programming languages, the *HTTLAP*

The FOR loop ▶

FIGURE 6.3   **The FOR loop for count-controlled iterations**

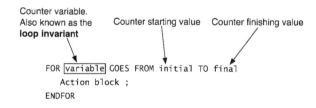

Counter variable.
Also known as the
loop invariant   Counter starting value   Counter finishing value

```
FOR variable GOES FROM initial TO final
    Action block ;
ENDFOR
```

---

[11] PIN? The number you use at cash machines. Why didn't I write "PIN number"? Because PIN stands for Personal Identification Number, and you wouldn't say "Personal Identification Number number" would you?

pseudo-code offers an iteration construct specifically designed for writing count-controlled loops. It is called the FOR loop and Figure 6.3 shows an annotated example:

A count-controlled loop must have a counter variable (known as the *loop invariant*) to keep track of the number of iterations. The loop invariant is so called because it is usually forbidden by programming language rules for any statement within the iteration's action block to change (vary) its value. Initial and final values for the counter are specified in the first line of the loop. By subtracting one from the other the number of iterations can be calculated. The general form of the FOR loop is shown in Figure 6.3. Its starting value is provided by the expression after the keyword FROM and its final value is given by the expression after the keyword TO. The mechanics of the loop are quite simple. Upon entry the counter will be given the value provided by initial. As long as that value is less than or equal to final then the action block is executed. After the last statement in the action block has been performed the counter is **automatically** increased by 1 and its value is again compared to final. At the point that the counter's value exceeds that of final the loop terminates.

FIGURE 6.4   **FOR loop with simple initial and final values**

```
FOR month GOES FROM 1 TO 12
    Display 'Please enter the month's rainfall' ;
    Get monthRainfall ;
    totalRainfall ← totalRainfall + monthRainfall ;
ENDFOR
```

To see how this works in practice examine Figure 6.4 which shows the rainfall solution from above rewritten using a FOR loop.

Reading the first line of Figure 6.4 should make clear what is happening. The counter variable month starts the loop with the value 1. The loop body is then executed. After the statement for adding the month's rainfall to the annual total is carried out the FOR loop *automatically* adds 1 to month making its value 2. This is less than or equal to the final value (12) so the loop body executes again. Work through it by hand and you will discover that month takes the values 1, 2, 3, 4, 5, 6, 7, 8, 9, 10, 11, 12 in succession. When it has the value 12 the loop body is executed once more after which month's value is increased to 13. This is now greater than the final value of 12 and the loop terminates.

There are two things to note. First, month does not need an initial value *prior* to entering the loop as the FOR assigns the value of the expression after GOES FROM to the loop counter. Secondly we do not need to remember to add 1 to the loop counter because this too is taken care of by the FOR construct. Thus, the two principal disadvantages of using a WHILE for count-controlled loops have been overcome by the FOR.

In Figure 6.4, the initial and final values were the values of simple variables. However, you can also use expressions to specify the starting and finishing values of the loop counter. For example, see Figure 6.5 below in which the variable age provides the initial value while the final value comes from an arithmetic expres-

FIGURE 6.5   **FOR loop with calculated initial and final values**

```
FOR year GOES FROM age TO age + 10
    Action block ;
ENDFOR
```

sion. Assume that year and age have already been declared and that age has been given a value prior to the FOR.

If the value of age were 38 then the loop would iterate eleven times with the counter variable year taking the values 38 to 48 inclusive. If age were 21, then the loop would still iterate eleven times, but this time the counter would take the values 21 through to 31. In either case, although we do not necessarily know at the time of writing the algorithm what the value of age will be, when the algorithm is executed, the number of iterations can still be calculated.

I don't understand why you said in the above example that the loop iterates eleven times when the counter goes from 38 to 48. Thirty-eight plus 10 equals 48, so why do you say eleven times?

Thirty-eight plus 10 does indeed give 48. But if you write down the numbers 38 through 48 inclusive you will find you have written eleven numbers.

We could also write something like the following to display every letter of the alphabet:

```
FOR letter GOES FROM 'A' TO 'Z'
    Display letter ;
    // Other actions that deal with upper-case letters ;
ENDFOR
```

FOR loops should be used when you need a loop that can most easily be controlled by a counter variable. Most programming languages provide a version of the FOR loop, but the exact details and layout vary.

The above **FOR** loop counts through all the uppercase letter characters from A to Z. How would we write the loop so that it works *backward* through the letters? Try it now. Hint: rather than thinking of the loop automatically *adding* to the counter, imagine it *changing* the counter's value to the next appropriate value.

All the FOR loops we have considered so far have counted upward through a range of values. The quick exercise above asked you to write a loop that works downward or backward through a range. Here is my solution:

Solution 6.7 FOR loop that counts backwards

```
FOR year GOES FROM 'Z' TO 'A'
    Action block ;
ENDFOR
```

All you need to do is make the initial value larger than the finishing value and the loop will subtract one from the counter each time around.

At-least-once Indeterminate Loops

We know that the WHILE is a zero-or-more iteration. When you need a loop that will iterate at least once then you should use a DO...WHILE construct. Figure 6.6 shows the layout of the DO...WHILE loop in the *HTTLAP* pseudo-code. Apart from the different keyword, the main difference from the plain WHILE loop is that the condition that terminates the loop is tested after the action block in the DO...WHILE whereas in the WHILE it is tested *before* the action block is executed. This means that before the DO...WHILE can test to see whether the loop should

FIGURE 6.6   **DO ... WHILE: an at-least-once indeterminate iteration**

Keyword DO denotes start of loop

```
DO
    Action block ;
WHILE (conditional expression) ;
```

Action block is iterated through while (as long
as) the conditional expression remains true

terminate it must first execute the action block. This positioning of the condition means that the DO...WHILE must execute its action block at least once,

FIGURE 6.7   **DO ... WHILE loop for getting a PIN**

```
DO
    Display 'Please enter your PIN' ;
    Get PIN ;
WHILE (PIN ≠ storedPIN) ;
```

hence it is an at-least-once iteration construct.

Again, to see how we might use this construct in practice look at Figure 6.7 which shows a DO...WHILE loop for getting a PIN from an ATM user.

Can you see how the loop works? The program encounters the keyword DO and then proceeds to execute the action block that follows. Immediately after the action block is the keyword WHILE followed by a condition. If this condition gives a true result the loop will iterate back through the action block again. This process carries on until the condition becomes false. This is just like the plain WHILE loop except that the condition is tested at the end of the action block rather than before. So, if the first time through the user does not enter a PIN that matches the one that has been stored on file (i.e., they have entered the wrong PIN) then the condition is true, that is, the PIN entered does not equal storedPIN. As the condition is true the loop will iterate again. It will keep doing this until the condition becomes false (that is, the PINs are equal). We cannot predict at the time we enter the loop how many goes it will take the user to enter the correct PIN, so we can see that this is an indeterminate loop. There is a problem with this example though: it may never finish. When writing loops of this kind it may be necessary to put in some extra logic to terminate the loop if a specified maximum number of iterations is reached. In the case of an ATM you are typically allowed three attempts to enter your PIN correctly before the machine seizes your card.

6.5 Applications of the WHILE and DO...WHILE Loops

 Think Spot

Below we shall consider typical applications of WHILE and DO...WHILE loops using *sentinels* which are used to solve many of the typical problems programmers face.

Sentinel-controlled Loops

A sentinel guards a camp or looks for approaching danger and gives warning. In the movie series *The Matrix*, the sentinel robots kept watch for signs of the human uprising. In programming terms a sentinel is a variable that is monitored for a particular value. A sentinel-controlled loop iterates while the value of the sentinel variable is not equal to a terminating value. Consider the following problem:

> *It is required to calculate the average age of a class of children. The program should be able to calculate the average for any number of children (including zero). Children's ages will be entered one at a time. When there are no more ages to enter the user will indicate this by entering an age value of 0. Once all the ages have been entered the algorithm will display the average age of the group.*

I could show you right away how this is solved using a sentinel-controlled loop, but it would help you more to work it through from first principles using the *HTTLAP* strategy.

Understanding the Problem

Q. What are we being asked to do?

A. We need to calculate and display the average age of a class of children.

Q. What is required? Try restating the problem.

FIGURE 6.8   **Some groups of children and their average ages**

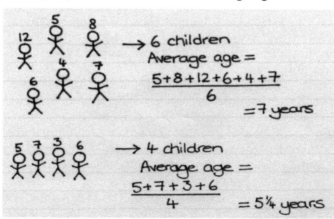

A. A collection of children's ages and an age of zero to tell the algorithm we have finished entering age values are required. So, the algorithm must ask for the user to enter ages and must stop accepting ages once an age of zero has been entered. Following that it must calculate and display the average age of those entered by the user. Here is a sketch of the problem situation:

Q. **What is the unknown? Have you made any assumptions?**

A. For a given set of ages there are two unknowns: the average age, and the total age of all the children. Also, as the size of the groups can vary, the number of children is also unknown. There is one more thing. In my sketch of the problem the first group has an average age of 7 (a whole number) while the second group has an average age of 5.25 years (a fractional value). The problem statement did not specify whether the average should be calculated or reported as a whole number or as a decimal fraction. Without any opportunity to find out I shall assume that a decimal fraction is required.

Q. **What are the principal parts of the problem?**

Table 6.4   **Variables for the Average Age Problem**

Identifier	Description	Range of Values
1. `age`	Holds the age of an individual child (a zero is used as an end marker)	0 to 17
2. `numberOfAges`	Holds the number of individual ages entered Needed for calculation of average	0 to ...?
3. `totalAge`	Total of all ages added together	0 to ...?
4. `averageAge`	The average of the ages	0.0 to ...?

A. The principal parts would seem to be the problem data (a set of ages, the total age of the group, the number of ages in the group, and the group's average age), getting the ages into the program, and calculating and displaying the average. Table 6.4 shows the variables we are likely to need in the solution to this problem.

Devising a Plan to Solve the Problem

Q. **Have you solved this problem before?**

A. Perhaps. Exercise 3 in Chapter 5 required us to calculate the average payload of a delivery van. If you did that exercise then you have solved a problem similar to this one before.

Q. **Are any parts of the problem more easily solved than others?**

A. Calculating the average is easier than getting the numbers in. Getting the numbers will need some iteration while calculating the average is simple arithmetic.

Q. Can you satisfy all the conditions of the problem? Has anything been left out?

A. We must be careful when calculating the average that the user has actually entered some age values. If the number of ages entered is zero, then we must not attempt to calculate the average as we will be trying to divide by zero which cannot be done.

Carrying Out the Plan

Q. Write down the general sequence of actions necessary to solve the general problem.

A. Solution 6.8 below shows my outline solution to the problem.

Solution 6.8 Calculating the average age: outline solution

```
1.   Get the ages from the user ;
2.   Calculate and display the average age ;
```

Q. Should all actions be carried out in every circumstance?

A. No. I already identified that the average should only be calculated when the user has entered at least one age.

Q. Should some actions be repeated?

A. Action #1 involves iteration as we must allow the user to repeatedly enter age values.

Having identified the need for a selection and an iteration I need to refine my solution:

Solution 6.9 Calculating the average age: expanded outline solution

```
1.   Get first age from user ;
2.   WHILE (ages to process)
     // Process age
     // Get next age
     ENDWHILE
3.   IF (more than zero ages entered)
          3.1.   Calculate average age ;
          3.2.   Display average age ;
     ENDIF
```

Is the above solution sufficient? No – the body of the loop needs to be completed as does the condition and body for the IF in Action #3. This section is supposed to be about sentinel-controlled loops, so let's quickly complete writing Action #3 and get back to focusing on the loop.

Solution 6.10 Age average calculation

```
1.   Get first age from user ;
2.   WHILE (ages to process)
```

```
// Process age
// Get next age
ENDWHILE
```
3.   IF (|numberOfAges| > 0)

      3.1 |averageAge| ← |totalAge| ÷ |numberOfAges| ;

      3.2   Display |averageAge| ;

    ENDIF

Let us focus on constructing the loop for Action #2. The first question to ask is why have I chosen a WHILE construct rather than a DO...WHILE? Simply because it is possible to enter a zero as the first age. As zero is the value that is used to terminate the loop we have a zero-or-more iteration. Being an at-least-once iteration the DO...WHILE loop would cause the program to treat the zero entered by the user as an actual age value. There is a way round this which we shall look at later on, but for now we will stick with the WHILE as that is the natural zero-or-more iteration.

The read-ahead ▶
technique
revisited

In this problem we need the WHILE to terminate when the age entered by the user has a value of zero. This means that we must get the user to enter an age value prior to the start of the loop so that its value can be tested in the WHILE's condition. Recall from above that this is known as a read-ahead loop as the value tested in the loop condition is fetched immediately ahead of the loop. As we shall see below when we look at end-of-file-controlled loops, some situations call for a read-and-process structure rather than a read-ahead technique.

Action #1 can be expanded into two actions: one to prompt the user to enter an age and another to put that value into the **age** variable. The WHILE loop needs to terminate when the age entered by the user is zero, so the conditional expression needs to be **age ≠ 0** – that is, age not-equal-to zero. Within the body of the loop we need to do three things: first add the age entered to the running total; second we must add 1 to the variable **numberOfAges** which keeps count of the number of ages entered by the user; and third we need to get another age value from the user. Thus we get Solution 6.11 below:

Solution 6.11 Calculating the average age: completed WHILE loop

1.   Display 'Please enter an age (zero to finish)';

2.   Get value of |age| ;

3.   WHILE (|age| ≠ 0)

      3.1. |totalAge| ← |totalAge| + |age| ;

      3.2. |numberOfAges| ← |numberOfAges| + 1 ;

      3.3.   Display 'Please enter an age (zero to finish)';

      3.4.   Get value of |age| ;

    ENDWHILE

4.   IF (|numberOfAges| > 0)

      4.1. |averageAge| ← |totalAge| ÷ |numberOfAges| ;

      4.2.   Display |averageAge| ;

    ENDIF

There is one more thing to do – we should complete our solution with the necessary variable initializations.

Solution 6.12 Average age calculation: with variable initializations

```
1.   numberOfAges ← 0 ; // Initialize numberOfAges to zero
2.   totalAge ← 0 ;   // Initialize totalAge to zero
3.   Display 'Please enter an age (zero to finish)';
4.   Get value of age ;
5.   WHILE (age ≠ 0)
         5.1.   totalAge ← totalAge + age ;
         5.2.   numberOfAges ← numberOfAges + 1 ;
         5.3.   Display 'Please enter an age (zero to finish)';
         5.4.   Get value of age ;
     ENDWHILE
6.   IF (numberOfAges > 0)
         6.1.   averageAge ← totalAge ÷ numberOfAges ;
         6.2.   Display averageAge ;
     ENDIF
```

Have a look now at the WHILE loop (Action #5) in Solution 6.12. This is an example of a *sentinel-controlled loop*. Notice how the variable **age** is used here. The loop terminates when the **age** variable gets a value of zero. For this reason, **age** is called the *sentinel* for the loop – the variable is like a guard that monitors the incoming data and causes an alert to go out when a particular value is observed (in this case, zero). Of course, no alerts really happen, and the variable does not actually monitor anything, but thinking of the variable as a sentinel is a useful metaphor. Many programming terms are metaphors because grounding concepts in real-world objects and activities can aid understanding.

6.6   Chapter Summary

In this chapter you learned how to construct sequences, iterations, and selections to fit a range of common programming problems. You learned about counter-controlled (FOR) loops and sentinel-controlled (WHILE and DO...WHILE) loops, simple (IF) and extended (IF...ELSE) selections.

6.7   Exercises

1. There are two things wrong with the following IF...ELSE statement. What are they?

```
IF (mark ≥ 40)
   Display 'You have passed.' ;
ELSE IF (mark ≤ 40)
   Display 'You have failed.' ;
ENDIF
```

2. When should you use a FOR loop rather than a WHILE or DO...WHILE loop? When should you use a DO...WHILE rather than a WHILE or FOR loop?

3. As any loop written using a FOR or a DO...WHILE can also be constructed using the basic WHILE construct, what is the benefit of using the FOR and DO...WHILE?

4. State the difference between a determinate and an indeterminate loop.

5. In Stocksfield High School, all the children's work is marked out of 5. An A grade is awarded for work scoring between 4 and 5. A score of at least 3 would get a B grade, and a C is given for a score of at least 2. Any other score gets an F (fail). For example, scores of 4.0, 4.8, and 5 would get grade A, 3.2 and 3.9 would get a B, 2.9 a C and 1.9 an F. Write an IF...ELSE construct that assigns the appropriate grade to the variable studentGrade depending on the value of the variable studentMark.

6. Stocksfield High School has just changed its grading system. Now an A grade is given for marks between 4 and 5, a B for marks of at least 3.5, a C for marks of at least 3.0, a new pass grade D for marks of at least 2.0, and an F for every mark lower than 2.0. Amend your solution to Exercise 5 to account for this change.

7. Write your solution to Exercise 6 using a sequence of IF statements without ELSE parts. What do you have to do to the condition of each IF statement in order to ensure they work properly?

8. Extend your solution to Exercise 5 to assign, calculate and display the student grades for a class of twenty students.[12]

9. Using *HTTLAP* design an algorithm for a guessing game. The algorithm should choose a number between 1 and 10 and the player has three tries in which to guess the number. If the player guesses correctly, the response "Correct!" should be given. When an incorrect guess is made, the response should be "Hot!" if the guess was one away from the actual number, "Warm..." when the guess is two away, and "COLD!" when the guess is three or more away. Make sure your loop finishes if the player guesses correctly in less than three turns.

Table 6.5 Driver Details and Insurance Premiums

Name	Age	Sex	Car Value	Speeding Ticket?	Premium
Nick	60	M	15,000	No	450.00
Chris	24	M	24,000	No	799.20
Lynne	23	F	8,000	No	240.00
Alf	17	M	35,000	Yes	1,415.50
Shadi	23	M	15,000	No	499.50
Becky	18	F	12,000	Yes	631.60

---

[12] Hint: You will need an iteration construct. Is the loop determinate or indeterminate?

10. *Honest Brian's Insurance* sells car insurance policies. The company is owned by Brian who is a cautious type and so hikes the premiums for young male drivers (who are statistically much more likely to make a claim). The basic premium charge is 3% of the value of the vehicle. This figure is raised by 11% for male drivers under 25 years of age, and by 6% for female drivers under the age of 21. A further £/$/€ 250 is added to the premium of any driver who has had any kind of speeding ticket. Design an algorithm to calculate the insurance premiums for the drivers in Table 6.5 (which also shows the premium your algorithm should generate).

Table 6.6 **Wind Speeds in the Beaufort Scale**

Beaufort Scale	Wind Speed (miles per hour)	Description
0	<1	Calm
1	1–3	Light air
2	4–7	Light breeze
3	8–12	Gentle breeze
4	13–18	Moderate breeze
5	19–24	Fresh breeze
6	25–31	Strong breeze
7	32–38	Near gale
8	39–46	Gale
9	47–64	Strong gale
10	55–63	Storm
11	64–72	Violent storm
12	≥73	Hurricane

Table 6.7 **Internet Bookstore Postage Charges**

Weight	Postage Rate	Handling Fee per Book
Up to 200 g	1.75	0.25
Up to 400 g	2.50	0.40
Up to 1000 g	4.00	0.45
Over 1000 g	6.00	0.5

11. The Beaufort scale is used to classify wind speeds. Use Table 6.6 to design an algorithm that declares a variable windSpeed, assigns that variable a value representing the wind speed in miles-per-hour (use zero for values < 1) and then displays the corresponding

Beaufort number and description. For example, if `windSpeed` had the value 20 the algorithm would display

`Beaufort scale:5, Fresh breeze.`

12. You have been asked by an online bookstore to design an algorithm that calculates postage costs. Postage is calculated by adding a fixed weight-based charge to a handling fee for each book in the order. Table 6.7 shows how the charge is calculated.

For example, an order for one book weighing 180 g would cost 1.75 + 0.25 = 2.00 to deliver. An order weighing 1500 g total with three books in it would cost 6.00 + 0.5 × 3 = 7.50 to deliver. Using *HTTLAP*, design an algorithm that calculates the postage charge for book orders. The parcel weight and number of books in the order should be provided by

Table 6.8   **Stocksfield High School e-mail Addresses**

Teachers	e-mail	Pupils	e-mail
Henry Higgins	`h.higgins@ ...`	Emily Harris	`emily.harris@ ...`
Alfred P. Doolittle	`a.p.doolittle@ ...`	Sarah Jane Smith	`sarah.smith@ ...`
Jennifer P.D. Quick	`j.p.quick@ ...`	John Dobby	`john.dobby@ ...`

the user. The algorithm should calculate postage costs for an unspecified number of orders, terminating when the parcel weight given by the user is a negative number.

13. Stocksfield High School gives e-mail addresses to all its pupils in the form:

`givenName.familyName@stocksfieldhigh.ac.uk`

Teachers are given email addresses of the form:

`firstInitial.secondInitial.familyName@stocksfieldhigh.ac.uk`

where the second initial may not be present.
Table 6.8 shows some example teacher and pupil names and the corresponding e-mail addresses.

   Design an algorithm that declares a variable `emailAddress`, assigns to the variable a value provided by the user, and displays the family name of the owner of that e-mail address and whether they are a pupil or a teacher. For example, if the user typed in

`emily.harris@stocksfieldhigh.ac.uk`

the algorithm would display

`Harris:Pupil.`

If the user typed

`a.p.doolittle@stocksfieldhigh.ac.uk`

The algorithm would display

`Doolittle:Teacher.`

Note: The algorithm should be able to handle any valid Stocksfield High e-mail address, not just the ones listed in Table 6.8.

14. Design an algorithm that declares an integer variable timesTable, gets a value for this variable, and displays the times table up to 15 × *n*. For example, if timesTable had the value 12, then the following output would be displayed:

```
 1 × 12 =  12
 2 × 12 =  24
 3 × 12 =  36
 4 × 12 =  48
 5 × 12 =  60
 6 × 12 =  72
 7 × 12 =  84
 8 × 12 =  96
 9 × 12 = 108
10 × 12 = 120
11 × 12 = 132
12 × 12 = 144
13 × 12 = 156
14 × 12 = 168
15 × 12 = 180
```

6.8 Projects

StockSnackz Vending Machine

Now that you have been introduced to the IF...ELSE construct, revise your previous vending machine solution to deal more elegantly with the problem of dispensing the chosen snack. Using IF...ELSE will also make the problem of dealing with buttons 0, 7, 8, and 9 much simpler.

Now that a proper selection construct has been used it is time to make the vending machine much more interesting. The University of Stocksfield is losing too much money through greedy staff stocking up on free snacks. With the exception of the sales summary (Button 6) all items must now be paid for and cost 10 pence each. If a user presses a button for a snack before sufficient money has been inserted an "insufficient funds" message should be displayed. If the user has deposited sufficient money for an item then the machine will dispense the chosen snack. Assume no change is given. Extend your solution to reflect these new requirements.

Now extend your solution so that if the user has deposited more than 10 pence the machine gives any required change after dispensing the chosen item. You may assume that the machine always has sufficient stock of each denomination of coin to be able to make exact change. The machine accepts (and gives back) the following denominations of coins: 1, 2, 5, 10, 20, 50 pence. Change should be dispensed using the fewest coins possible. Note, you have already solved the change-giving problem (see the exercises for Chapter 3) so see if that solution can be reused (perhaps with some amendments) here. There is a mathematical operator called *modulo* which gives the remainder after division. It often has the symbol %, but our pseudo-code uses MOD. It works like this: $20 \div 7 = 2$: 7 goes into 20 twice. 20 MOD 7 = 6 : the left over after dividing 20 by 7 is 6. You will find this useful for working out how to give change.

In the United Kingdom and countries using the euro currency, another two denominations of coin are available. The United Kingdom has £1 and £2 coins and the Euro Zone similarly has €1 and €2 coins. Extend your solution to cater for these larger denomination coins. If your machine works on US dollars and you would like to accept the rarer half-dollar and one-dollar coins, by all means go ahead.

Stocksfield Fire Service

In this chapter you learned about alternative iteration and selection constructs. Examine your EAC algorithm and replace IF statements with IF...ELSE constructs wherever possible. What benefits does this bring?

Puzzle World: Roman Numerals and Chronograms

Examine your solutions to the Roman number problems and decide whether you need to use any of the alternative iteration and selection constructs. Update your algorithms accordingly.

Pangrams: Holoalphabetic Sentences

The pangram algorithm needs to be amended so that it allows the test to be run on any number of sentences. The algorithm should keep testing sentences until the user decides to finish. Rewrite your solution to incorporate this feature. What iteration constructs could be used? How will you solve the problem of deciding whether the user wants to continue? Explain why you used your chosen solution strategy. What other loop constructs could you have used? How would that affect the way the algorithm behaves? What other ways could you have tested to see if the user wants to finish? What are the principal advantages and disadvantages of your solution and these alternative solutions?

Online Bookstore: ISBNs

The ISBN validation problem is best suited to using a count-controlled loop for the part which deals with multiplying the nine digits of the number with their respective weights. Update your solution replacing the WHILE construct with an appropriately phrased FOR loop.

You are now in a position to tackle the hyphenation problem. For correct presentation, the ten digits of an ISBN should be divided into four parts separated by hyphens:

■ Part 1: The country or group of countries identifier
■ Part 2: The publisher identifier
■ Part 3: The title identifier
■ Part 4: The check digit

Table 6.9   **Hyphenation for Group "0" ISBNs**

Group Identifier "0" Publisher Code Ranges	If Publisher Ranges are Between	Insert Hyphens After		
00——————————-19	00–19	1st digit	3rd digit	9th digit
200————————699	20–69	"	4th "	"
7000——————-8499	70–84	"	5th "	"
85000————-89999	85–89	"	6th "	"
900000———-949999	90–94	"	7th "	"
9500000——-9999999	95–99	"	8th "	"

Table 6.10   **Hyphenation for Group "1" ISBNs**

Group Identifier "1" Publisher Code Ranges	If Publisher Ranges are Between	Insert Hyphens After		
00——————————09	00–09	1st digit	3rd digit	9th digit
100————————399	10–39	"	4th "	"
4000——————-5499	40–54	"	5th "	"
55000————-86979	5500–8697	"	6th "	"
869800———-998999	8698–9989	"	7th "	"
9990000——-9999999	9990–9999	"	8th "	"

To keep matters as simple as possible we will only deal with hyphenating ISBNs that have a group/country code of 0 or 1 (the English language groups). The positions of the hyphens are determined by the publisher codes. To hyphenate correctly, knowledge of the prefix ranges for each

---

[13] Hint: You can see that the publisher code takes between two and seven digits. Every ISBN with group identifier of 0 or 1 has a hyphen after the first digit (the group code) and after the ninth digit (i.e., immediately before the check digit). The third hyphen is inserted after the publisher code. For an ISBN in group 0 you can tell from the first two digits of the publisher code how long the rest of the code is. For example, looking at the table above we see that publisher codes beginning with digits in the range 20..69 are three digits in length, while those beginning 95..99 are seven digits long.

[14] Another hint: You need to manipulate the ISBN digit-by-digit. We have not covered how to access individual characters, so when it comes to that aspect use informal *HTTLAP* pseudo-code.

country or group of countries is needed. The publisher code ranges in the English group (US, UK, Canada, Australia, New Zealand, etc.) are given in Table 6.9.

Using Table 6.9 develop an algorithm for displaying with correctly placed hyphens any ISBN that starts with digit 0.[13, 14]

For an extra challenge, allow ISBNs with a group code of 1 to be hyphenated. The rules for this group are slightly different than for group "0" and are given in Table 6.10.

This problem is slightly trickier than the group 0 hyphenation because you are not always just testing the first two digits of the publisher code. Use your solution to the group 0 hyphenation problem as a starting point and then work through the *HTTLAP* strategy to help you arrive at a solution to this problem.

7 Object Orientation: Taking a Different View

Learning Objectives

- Recognize the difference between procedural and object-oriented problem solving
- Analyze real-world problems to identify the object classes, properties, and methods needed to solve a problem in an object-oriented manner

In this chapter we consider another way of approaching algorithmic problem solving in which the solution is structured around objects which are collections of related data items and their associated actions. Using objects as the basis for algorithms is a very popular programming technique but it is very easy to do badly unless some particular rules are followed very carefully. Because of the very introductory nature of this chapter it is beyond the scope of this book to consider those rules (which can be very subtle) in depth so we will focus instead on the bigger picture which will give you a foundation should you need to learn an object-oriented programming language (such as Java, Eiffel, C++, C#) at a later date.

7.1 The Procedural Paradigm

Up till now we have been designing algorithms by considering what actions need to be performed and what data (variables, data items) are needed to support those actions. We have constructed our algorithms using control abstractions (IF, FOR, WHILE, and DO ... WHILE statements) for the building blocks of sequence, iteration, and selection and data abstractions (numbers and text) for dealing with the values handled in the algorithms. We have been following what is called the *procedural paradigm* for programming. A paradigm is a generally accepted way of doing things within a particular discipline. Programming has a number of different paradigms or ways of viewing problems and expressing solutions to them.

Computers from the 1950s until the present day have been built according to a fundamental design called the VON NEUMANN architecture. In such computers the central processing unit (or CPU – the main part of the computer's processor chip) carries out in sequence instructions that manipulate values stored in the computer's memory. Early programming languages were designed to mimic the operation of a VON NEUMANN machine: the languages had variables to represent values in the computer's memory, instructions were executed sequentially, and assignment statements were used to manipulate the values of the variables. Such languages belong to the procedural (also known as imperative) paradigm. However, this is not the only way that computation can be carried out and different programming paradigms arose to facilitate different ways of solving problems. Besides procedural programming the other main paradigm in use today is *object-oriented programming*, supported by languages such as Smalltalk, Java, Delphi, C#, C++, and Visual Basic.NET. Because even the object-oriented languages use procedural structures inside their objects the approach of this book has been procedural and the *HTTLAP* pseudo-code has followed the procedural model. Of course, today's programmers must be conversant in the object-oriented way of doing things, so in this chapter we will give an overview of the object-oriented way of looking at the world. This serves two purposes. First, you should learn that many of the problem solving skills you have been developing are equally applicable in this object-oriented paradigm. Secondly, this chapter will prepare the ground so that should you need to learn an object-oriented language such as Java or C# in the future, the concepts will not be alien to you.

7.2 Objects and Classes, Properties and Methods

In the procedural approach solutions are constructed by considering the data belonging to the problem and then designing algorithms that manipulate (process) that data to achieve the desired outcome. For example, in the coffee-making problem we identified the following data items:

- The number of coffees to be made
- The milk preference of a drinker
- The sugar requirements of a drinker
- The number of cups poured so far
- The number of sugars added to a cup so far

We then used our understanding of the problem and its data to design an algorithm that correctly manipulated those data items so as to make and pour the required number of cups of coffee each with its own milk and sugar combinations. A computer program is then created by translating the algorithm into programming language code.

Consider the problem of opening and operating an account with an online digital music download service. We might identify key operations such as "open account," "credit account," "spend money," "download track," "query the balance," "query download history," "close account," and so on. We might also identify key data such as account number, amount deposited, amount spent, current balance, customer name, customer address, country in which the account is held, date account was opened, date account was closed, and so on. In our procedural way of thinking we would design a set of algorithms to solve the problem of carrying out these operations and the algorithms would use the variables we identified to store the necessary values.

We can see that some of the data values are associated directly with the music store account, while others are associated with the customer who holds the account. The customer (name, address) pays money into the account while the account receives money from the customer. The account has a balance which the customer may request. The customer may view a history of all recent downloads. Receipts for track downloads are e-mailed to the customer. When discussing the problem sometimes we talk about individual data items, but other times we talk in a more abstract way about the entities/objects/things to which those items belong, such as "my iTunes account," "Customer No. 35478," and so on. In 1967 Alan Kay coined the term Object-Oriented Programming to refer to programming that is focused upon these objects and the actions they perform.

Where procedural algorithms (the kind we have been writing up until now) focus upon data and the operations needed to manipulate that data, an object-oriented solution focuses on the behaviour of *objects*. An object is a mechanism for gathering together into a single package a set of related data items and operations that provide views of the state of those data.

For example, a music downloading system written in a procedural way would have variables to hold customer account details and various algorithms to allow account transactions to be recorded. In an object-oriented approach the account variables and their associated algorithms would be gathered together and stored inside an object. The principle is that data and the operations that manipulate the data are kept together separate from other data and operations. Access to the data is tightly controlled which, in theory, makes it much harder for one part of a program to cause problems in another part.

Consider Figure 7.1, which shows a receipt sent by Brian's Digital Downloads to its customer Professor Henry Higgins. Make sure you do the following exercise before moving on.

Look at the statement and identify the information that pertains to Professor Higgins' account.

FIGURE 7.1   **Receipt from Brian's Digital Downloads (aka BriTunes)**

From: Brian's Digital Downloads
Subject: **Receipt #19298398**
Date: 8 May 2007 14:00:01
To: Henry Higgins

Receipt

Invoiced To:
Prof. Henry Higgins
27a Wimpole Street
London, W1G 8GP

Item	Artist	Title	Price
B1010	Plastic Bertrand	Ça plane pour moi	0.99

Account: 52747   Total: 0.99
Paid by Credit Card •••• •••• •••• 9876
Thanks for shopping with us. Please visit again.

You might have decided that the account number, name of account holder, and the registered credit card are all associated with the account. We might also consider that the receipt number, transaction details, and Professor Higgins' address also belong to the account, but it could be argued that the receipt number and transaction details belong to a transaction and the address belongs to a customer (Professor Higgins). The account, transaction, and customer are all associated with each other, but could be considered to be separate entities. Each transaction itself has an item number (identifying the track downloaded), the name of the artist, the title of the track, and the price paid. All these details relate to the account with the number 52747 belonging to Professor Higgins.

So, we see data belonging to a customer account, data belonging to the customer, and data belonging to a transaction. While an account, a customer, and a transaction are associated, they are not the same thing: a customer possesses characteristics that an account and a transaction do not. Thus, by taking an abstract view we can treat these sets of data as part of a larger entity. In the case of Figure 7.1 we might say these entities are Account #52747, Customer Professor Henry Higgins, and the Transaction for item B1010 (we might also decide Item is something of interest too).

Classes

Because the BriTunes music store will have many accounts, customers, and transactions, we would say that Henry Higgins' account is simply an instance of a more general BriTunes Account class. Higgins himself is an instance of another class of entity called Customer, and so on. There will be many individual accounts each with its own specific details, many customers each with their own name and address, and many transactions. In the object-oriented world we call these different groups of entities **classes**. A class is simply a name given to a kind of object, defining the range of properties and activities associated with that object.

We already use classes in the everyday world. Take the number 7. Seven belongs to the class of numbers known as NATURAL NUMBERS. In mathematics, the natural numbers are all the positive integers from 1 to infinity.[1] Natural numbers have certain properties, the most obvious, perhaps, being that they are whole numbers and possess no fractional parts. They also have certain actions associated with them that may be used to manipulate them. For instance, we know we can add, subtract, multiply, and divide them, we can raise them to a power, and so on. In object-oriented parlance we might define a class called `NaturalNumbers`. Any object belonging to that class would then only be able to take values between 1 and infinity. The class would also provide actions such as +, −, ×, ÷ which could be used to change the property of a natural number object. Does this look familiar? It should, because we have already seen something like this in the form of abstract data types in Chapter 6. We said that an abstract data type, or ADT, is a way of defining the range of permissible values for a data item belonging to that type together with the set of operations that can be performed upon those values. In fact, classes are closely related to ADTs. An ADT defines a set of values together with operations that may be used with those values. A class defines a set of operations that may be used to provide a view onto its properties. At a simplistic level ADTs and object classes look the same.[2]

Classes appear similar to ADTs ▶

FIGURE 7.2 **Classes are templates for creating objects**

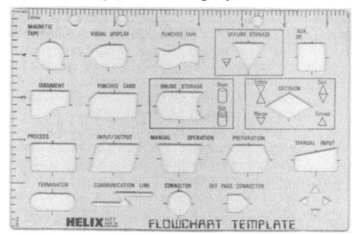

A class, then, is a template for creating objects of a given type. Figure 7.2 is a picture of my old student flowcharting template (circa 1985). Each of the cut outs is a template for drawing an instance of the cut out type. For example, the rectangular cut out labelled "Process" (second from bottom on the left) is used for drawing

---

[1] In Computer Science the natural numbers go from zero to infinity.

[2] At this stage it may be helpful to think of a class as a kind of abstract data type, though they are not the same. The difference between an ADT and an object class is subtle but really quite profound. It is beyond the scope of this book to enter into a discussion of how they are different.

many individual process box objects. The cut out is the template, the object that is drawn with it on the paper is an instance of that template class (see Figure 7.3).

FIGURE 7.3   **Objects drawn with the template**

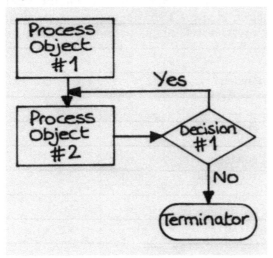

In a banking problem we might have a class called CurrentAccount which we can use to create individual bank account objects such as myAccount, hisAccount, herAccount, and so on.

Because the properties of an account need to be manipulated – balances need to be updated, money needs to be paid in and withdrawn, new statements need to be produced, and so on – a class has a set of behaviours or associated capabilities that define what that class can do, which of its properties may be changed, which may be viewed, and so on. These behaviours are called **methods** as they are the method by which an object manipulates its properties.

To summarize: a **class** brings together a set of data items known as **properties** (also called **members**) and a collection of **methods** which are the algorithms that define how those properties may be manipulated and accessed. An **object** is an individual occurrence or **instance** of the class in which the actual data items for an individual object are stored.

Getting Up in the Morning

To illustrate how we might take an object-oriented view of a problem, let's return to one of the first problems we tackled in Chapter 2, that of getting up in the morning. A rough procedural solution written in pseudo-code might look like this:

Solution 7.1 Procedural approach to getting up in the morning

```
1.   Switch off alarm ;
2.   Get out of bed ;
3.   Shower/wash face, brush teeth, etc. ;
4.   Get dressed ;
```

Of course, the algorithm might differ for you – it's very much geared towards my own routine. In the object-oriented world view we would see our task as building a simulation of the problem situation. That means we need to define classes that represent the principal parts of the problem. Remember that a class defines a set of behaviours that an object (thing) can exhibit and that those behaviours change the properties of the object. Figure 7.4 shows how we might define a `Person` class to represent the person who is waking up, washing, and getting dressed.

FIGURE 7.4   **Class definition for Person**

class Person	
Properties	awake: yes, no ; inBed: yes, no ; needsShower: yes, no ; isDressed: yes, no ;
Methods	WakeUp ; GoToSleep ; GetUp ; GoToBed ; GetWashed ; GetDressed ; GetUndressed ;

We can see that a `Person` object would possess a number of properties. There are data items representing whether the person is awake or asleep, in or out of bed, in need of a shower, and wearing clothes or not. (You might also have decided that a `Person` should have a name.) Notice that for each of these properties I have also followed the practice of earlier chapters and have indicated the range of values they can take. Associated with each of these four properties are methods that change the properties' values: `WakeUp` and `GoToSleep` would change the value of `awake` to "Yes" and "No" respectively. `GetUp` and `GoToBed` would change the value of `inBed`, and `GetDressed` and `GetUndressed` would set `isDressed` to the appropriate value. We can also see that `GetWashed` might be used to change the value of `needsShower` to "No," but what would change it to "Yes"? We might decide that a shower is needed every morning, so we could arrange for `WakeUp` to also set `needsShower` to "Yes" to reflect this state of affairs. Clearly there are different ways we could set this out, but the point to note is that an object possesses properties (data items that describe its current state) and methods that are used to view and change these data items. It is a principle of object orientation that only the methods of the object itself should be allowed to manipulate its properties. Looking back at the getting up algorithm in Solution 7.1 we can see that something is missing: what of the alarm? Why is there no `SwitchOffAlarm` operation in the `Person` class?

In the light of what was said above about an object's operations being used to view and change an object's properties, spend a few moments thinking through why it might not be appropriate to have a `SwitchOffAlarm` operation in the `Person` class.

You said that the methods would change the values of the classes' properties, but I cannot see where this happens.

Indeed. What we have done is taken an abstract view and have treated the methods as if they will automatically do what we need them to. In fact, a method is just an algorithm and at some point we will need to specify the actions that they must perform in order to have the desired effect. For now we will not be doing that and instead will concentrate on the higher-level problem of identifying the classes involved in the problem and of designing an overall algorithm that will get the object of those classes to do what we need. At the end of this chapter you will find some exercises that get you to try designing the algorithms for the individual methods.

The reason why there is no `SwitchOffAlarm` operation in the `Person` class is that the alarm itself could not reasonably be considered to be a property of a `Person`. A popular tenet of OO thinking is that classes should only possess properties that strictly belong to objects of that class. A person might own an alarm clock, but an alarm clock is not part of the make up of a person. If an alarm is not truly one of the attributes of a person, but it plays an important role in our problem, then we decide that it must be an object in its own right.

Following the way we defined a **Person** class above to guide you try writing out a class definition for an **Alarm** object. Think about the essential properties we need to capture for this problem and then consider what methods will be needed to change those properties.

Solution 7.2 below shows my definition for the `Alarm` class.

Solution 7.2 Possible definition for Alarm class

class Alarm	
Properties	ringing: yes, no ; time: 00:00:00 to 23:59:00 ; alarmTime: 00:00:00 to 23:59:00 ; alarmIsSet: on, off ;
Methods	SetTime: hh:mm:ss ; GetTime ; SetAlarmTime: hh:mm ; GetAlarmTime ; SetAlarm ; UnsetAlarm ; StartRinging ; SwitchOff ; (i.e. stop ringing)

Compare your solution to mine. I don't expect your solution to be exactly the same as mine as you were not given any information about the problem situation, so you have had free rein to be inventive. Also, do not treat my solutions as complete or exhaustive – they are merely indicative. In my `Alarm` class I have identified four properties. `ringing` is simply an indicator of whether the alarm is ringing/beeping or not. The alarm will start ringing at the appointed time by the `StartRinging` method. We can stop the alarm ringing with its `SwitchOff` method. The **time** property is used to make sure the alarm's clock is set. We can set the time with `SetTime` and see what time the alarm is set to with `GetTime`. The reason for the colon followed by an "hh:mm:ss" time specification indicates that the `SetTime` method needs information to work with. The statement that tells `Alarm` to run its `SetTime` method must also provide a time value otherwise `SetTime` will not know what time to set the clock to. `alarmTime` is the property used to specify what time the alarm should go off (say, 7 a.m.). The `alarmTime` is set with `SetAlarmTime` (another method that needs a value to be given to it, hence the colon) and can be viewed with `GetAlarmTime`. I have assumed that the alarm time only needs to be set to the nearest minute hence the lack of an "ss" value in the `SetAlarmTime` method. Finally, we do not want our alarm to go off every morning – perhaps you have a lie in at the weekend? So the `Alarm` has a property `alarmIsSet`: if this is "on" then the alarm will go off at the time specified by `alarmTime` and if it is "off" then it will not ring. `SetAlarm` is used to turn this property "on" and `UnsetAlarm` to turn it "off." Note that this is different from `SwitchOff` which is used to stop the alarm ringing when it has gone off.

Huh?

Is it me, or is this all getting quite complicated? The problem of getting up in the morning seemed quite simple until you started talking about objects. Now it seems needlessly complicated.

No, it's not you. Unfortunately, because of the way we need to think about problems in the OO paradigm, before we can begin to structure algorithms that describe the overall solution we need to expend a lot of effort defining the objects, their properties, and their operations. The getting up in the morning problem is a very simple one that is very easy and quick to tackle with procedural thinking. Alas, object orientation is better suited to larger more complex problems. At the moment we are doing the equivalent of using an 18-wheeler to deliver a pizza. If we had to ship 10,000 pizzas from coast to coast, the truck would become a more attractive option, but for local deliveries of a few pizzas we suffer from a problem of large fixed overheads. The difficulty we face is that using a complex problem of the sort that would really benefit from an OO solution would require a lot of even harder concepts to be faced at once. So, we will continue with this smaller problem in the knowledge that the ideas being learned here will seem much more appropriate when applied to a larger problem. For example, how to manage the morning routines of a dormitory of 200 people with an unknown number of alarm clocks, a limited number of showers, and different getting-up and going-to-bed times.

So far we have managed to identify two classes and define their behaviours. What we need now is some way of getting those classes to actually perform their operations. What we must do is to create new objects that belong to these classes and then instruct those objects to carry out their various methods. For the sake of keeping matters as simple as possible what we will do is design an algorithm that wraps all this up together. In object-oriented terms we will be creating a **controller** that handles the creation of the objects needed in the solution and telling those objects what to do. First of all we need to create an individual `Person` object. Remember that classes are only templates. Just as a cookie cutter is not a cookie, it is a template for a cookie and to get a cookie we must press the cutter into the dough, so we must create a `Person` object from the `Person` template. Let's create a `Person` object called `brian` thus:

1. `brian` ← new Person;

Object ▶
instantiation

In object-oriented parlance creating a new object from a class is called **instantiation** as we are creating a new *instance* of a class (just like creating a new cookie using the cookie cutter). This would set up an object variable called `brian` which would have the associated data items `awake`, `inBed`, `needsShower`, `isDressed` and the methods that also belong to all `Person` objects. In our procedural solution to the problem the first action was

```
Switch off alarm ;
```

As the alarm is itself an object we must instantiate it and then tell it to switch itself off. We extend our controller algorithm to give Solution 7.3:

Solution 7.3 First section of the object-oriented controller algorithm

1. `brian` ← new Person;
2. `briansAlarm` ← new Alarm ;
3. tell `briansAlarm` SwitchOff ;

? Think Spot

Before we move any further we should inspect Solution 7.3 to see whether it deals fully with ensuring that `brian` is awake and the alarm is switched off. Let us assume for now that when an object is instantiated all of its properties are assigned sensible initial values. In an object-oriented programming language it is necessary to design methods that are carried out whenever an object is instantiated. Such a method (known as a *constructor*) would set the object's properties to their required starting values. For the purposes of this chapter we shall assume that these initializations are done automatically. Taking a `Person` object first, it has four properties: `awake`, `inBed`, `needsShower`, and `isDressed`. Assume for now that when a `Person` object is instantiated its properties are initialized as follows:

Property	Value
awake	No
inBed	Yes
needsShower	Yes
isDressed	No

Huh?

Why do we tell the alarm to switch itself off? In the real world it would be Brian who turns off the alarm, and you said an OO solution is a simulation of the problem situation. How can an alarm switch itself off?

This is a common difficulty faced by those new to object-oriented thinking. You're right, in the real world Brian would turn off the alarm. However, in the OO world turning off an alarm requires the **Alarm** object to change one of its properties, and properties can only be changed by methods belonging to that object. What we must do is send the **Alarm** object a message asking it to turn itself off. We could, of course, insert a method in a Person object (**TurnOffAlarm**, say) that sends a message to an **Alarm** object asking it to perform its own **SwitchOff** operation. The problem is that the **Person** object then has a method that strictly does not do anything that pertains to a person; recall we said that we should try to store only properties and operations in an object that are essential to the make up of that object. There is a way of establishing a link between two objects to express the real world relationship that Brian has with his alarm (it's called an association class), but that goes beyond the scope of this chapter's brief introduction. For now, we will use a simple controller algorithm to handle all the instructions to request objects to perform their methods.

Looking at Solution 7.3 we see that although Statement #3 switches off the alarm, brian is still asleep. We need to pass brian a message to ask him to wake up:

tell ⬚brian WakeUp ;

The WakeUp method would then set the awake property from its current value of "No" to "Yes." We might reasonably expect brian to wake up before the alarm is switched off, so our algorithm now becomes Solution 7.4:

Solution 7.4 Controller algorithm extended to wake brian up

1.   brian ← new Person;
2.   briansAlarm ← new Alarm ;
3.   tell brian WakeUp ;
4.   tell briansAlarm SwitchOff ;

Now that brian is awake and the alarm switched off we can complete the action sequence by sending the brian object messages to perform the other morning methods, as in Solution 7.5.

Solution 7.5 The complete controller algorithm

1.   brian ← new Person;
2.   briansAlarm ← new Alarm ;
3.   tell brian WakeUp ;
4.   tell briansAlarm SwitchOff ;
5.   tell brian GetUp ;
6.   tell brian GetWashed ;
7.   tell brian GetDressed ;

Think Spot

Take a closer look at Solution 7.5. We noted previously that the brian object's properties had been initialized upon instantiation to a particular set of values which meant that we had to explicitly tell the brian object to wake up. In Statement #4 we tell the briansAlarm object to switch off its ringer. What we haven't addressed in this algorithm (because we have been concerned with the more abstract problem of the overall sequence) is the question of how the alarm knew what time it was in order to start ringing in the first place. We have not dealt with setting the alarm's clock or the time at which it should ring. Usually, when plugged into a power outlet any appliance with a digital clock starts flashing "00:00" to show that its clock needs setting. What time should an Alarm object show when instantiated? We could take the real-world view and specify that its time and alarmTime properties are both set to "00:00:00" upon instantiation. Assume, then, that when an Alarm object is instantiated its properties have the following values:

Property	Value
ringing	No
time	00:00:00
alarmTime	00:000:00
alarmIsSet	No

We could then send the alarm messages to tell it to set itself to the current time and the desired waking-up time with such statements as:

tell ⌐briansAlarm¬ SetTime: '10:08:35' ;

tell ⌐briansAlarm¬ SetAlarmTime: '07:00:00' ;

I have introduced a colon after the operation name to show that the method requires some information for it to carry out its task. SetTime and SetAlarmTime both need time values to be able to update the time and alarmTime properties respectively. I have given the SetTime method the value "10:08:35" to work with because that was the actual time of day at which I wrote that line. We could take a more general-purpose view and write:

tell ⌐briansAlarm¬ SetTime: currentTime ;

where currentTime represents the actual time of day at which the message is passed to the briansAlarm object. This is quite a sensible approach to take because when this algorithm eventually gets translated into programming language code we will find that the programming language we use has some kind of system clock object which can provide the current time.

Extend the controller algorithm in Solution 7.5 to include these messages to the briansAlarm object.

Solution 7.6 Controller algorithm with alarm times set

1. ⌐brian¬ ← new Person;
2. ⌐briansAlarm¬ ← new Alarm ;
3. tell ⌐briansAlarm¬ SetTime: currentTime ;
4. tell ⌐briansAlarm¬ SetAlarmTime: '07:00:00' ;
5. tell ⌐brian¬ WakeUp ;
6. tell ⌐briansAlarm¬ SwitchOff ;
7. tell ⌐brian¬ GetUp ;
8. tell ⌐brian¬ GetWashed ;
9. tell ⌐brian¬ GetDressed ;

Solution 7.6 shows the controller algorithm with the two new statements to set the alarm's clock and wake-up time. One problem still remains. Look at Statements #4 and #5, or rather, look at what happens *between* statements #4 and #5. Statement #4 passes the message to briansAlarm telling it to set itself so that it will start ringing at 7.00 a.m. Statement #5 then proceeds to tell brian to wake up. How do we know when executing Statement #5 that it really is 7.00 a.m. and that briansAlarm is ringing? This is a problem we are not going to tackle in depth here because its solution requires much lower levels of abstraction than this short introduction can provide. Part II of this book goes a little deeper into object-oriented programming and considers issues just like this. For the purposes of this high-level look at objects we can adopt a pragmatic simplification of the problem.

The question is: how do we know when it is time to carry out Statement #5? In the real world we would know it is time to wake up because the alarm starts ringing and we are roused from our sleep – our brain listens out for the alarm clock's ring. In essence, what we need between Statements #4 and #5 is some kind of delaying statement (a loop perhaps?) at which the controller waits until `briansAlarm` starts ringing. Solution 7.7 shows the controller algorithm with such a wait operation.

Solution 7.7 Controller algorithm with wait statement

```
1.  brian ← new Person;
2.  briansAlarm ← new Alarm ;
3.  tell briansAlarm SetTime: currentTime ;
4.  tell briansAlarm SetAlarmTime: '07:00:00' ;
5.  wait until briansAlarm ringing property = 'Yes' ;
6.  tell brian WakeUp ;
7.  tell briansAlarm SwitchOff ;
8.  tell brian GetUp ;
9.  tell brian GetWashed ;
10. tell brian GetDressed ;
```

Getting Values Out

Statement #5 in the new algorithm (Solution 7.7) tells the controller to wait until the `ringing` property of the `briansAlarm` object has the value "Yes." It appears to be accessing an object's property directly which is something we said is not good OOP practice. What we really need is a method that gives us back the value of the `ringing` property. We have already seen examples of methods that need information to be supplied to them in order to carry out their task (e.g. `SetAlarmTime` above). Let us introduce a new method to the alarm class called `RingingStatus:`. Here is its algorithm:

RingingStatus:

```
1.  ← ringing ;
```

The slightly strange notation appears to assign the value of the `ringing` property to nothing at all. Imagine that the assignment statement here is passing the value of `ringing` outside the object and its value will be given to whatever variable is used when the `RingingStatus` method is used. For example, say our controller algorithm has a variable called `answer`. We could assign `answer` a value like this:

```
tell briansAlarm RingingStatus: answer
```

What this means is that the assignment statement in the `RingingStatus` algorithm takes the value of the object's `ringing` property and assigns it to the variable after the colon, in this case, `answer`. `answer` now has the same value as the `ringing` property of the `briansAlarm` object. We can now rewrite our solution with a proper loop to deal with waiting for the alarm to ring. The new version of the controller algorithm is found in Solution 7.8 with the new wait loop shown in bold.

Solution 7.8 Controller algorithm with a wait loop added

```
1.   brian ← new Person;
2.   briansAlarm ← new Alarm ;
3.   tell briansAlarm SetTime: currentTime ;
4.   tell briansAlarm SetAlarmTime: '07:00:00' ;
5.   DO
          5.1.   tell briansAlarm RingingStatus: answer ;
     WHILE (answer ≠ 'Yes') ;
6.   tell brian WakeUp ;
7.   tell briansAlarm SwitchOff ;
8.   tell brian GetUp ;
9.   tell brian GetWashed ;
10.  tell brian GetDressed ;
```

If you examine Solution 7.8 now you will see it comprises two principal parts: Statements #1–#5 set up and initialize the simulation of the real world: object instances are created for Brian and his alarm clock, the alarm clock is set to the right time, its alarm is set to 7.00 a.m., and the simulation is put into a waiting state until the alarm goes off. Statements #6–#10 deal with the actual getting up routine. If you look at Statements #6–#10 as a whole they resemble very closely our original procedural solution to the problem which was:

```
1.   Switch off alarm ;
2.   Get out of bed ;
3.   Wash/shower face, brush teeth, etc. ;
4.   Get dressed ;
```

The two may look superficially similar because object-oriented solutions still use the three building blocks of sequence, iteration, and selection. However, the journey we took to arrive at Solution 7.8 highlights the differences. The first part of Solution 7.8 is needed to set up all the objects that the remainder of the algorithm uses. The details of the updating of values are hidden within the objects themselves. In fact, we have completely ignored the issue of designing the algorithms for the objects' operations. You may be thinking that this was a lot of work to arrive a solution that resembles one we had before. It *was* a lot of work and the reason is that object-oriented solutions have a certain overhead associated with them in terms of defining and setting up all the objects that will perform the solution tasks. For very simple problems such as those we have considered in this chapter, the amount of overhead tends to outweigh the algorithms that get the objects doing the right things in the right order at the right time. However, as problems become more complex, the choice to use an object-oriented approach starts to seem more rational and less like using a sledgehammer to crack open a nut.

7.3 Chapter Summary

This chapter introduced you to some of the very basic principles and terminology of object-oriented programming. We saw how problems are solved by identifying classes of objects which define **properties** and **methods** that individual objects belonging to that class should possess. We saw how object classes are **instantiated** to create an individual **object. Messages** are then passed to the object to instruct it to carry out its methods; an object's methods are the mechanism by which an object's properties are accessed and updated. Finally, we saw how the objects can be coordinated by the use of a **controller** algorithm. There is much more to learn about object-oriented programming which is beyond the scope of this chapter. In Part II of this book the object-oriented approach is considered in more detail with more complex problems in order to cover the remaining core features of object-oriented programming: inheritance, encapsulation, data hiding, and polymorphism.

7.4 Exercises

1. Think of a real-world piece of machinery that you use regularly. It could be a VCR, a games console, even a washing machine. Now view the item as if it were a software object: list its methods (the things it can do) and its properties (the information it needs to do its job -- some of this might be represented on its display screen/light panel if it has one).

2. Design algorithms for each of the methods for the Person class.

3. Design algorithms for each of the methods for the Alarm class.

4. Assume our Person class has another method, BedStatus, that tells us the value of the inBed property. If we had several instances of the Person class, what would the algorithm look like that counts up how many of the Person objects are still in bed?

5. We defined the Person class to contain methods dealing with going to bed as well as getting up in the morning. Extend the controller algorithm in Solution 7.7 to show the brian object going to bed. Also, assume that the controller is being run on a Friday and that on Saturdays Brian sleeps late which requires his alarm to be reset to the later time of 10.00 a.m.

6. We treated the problem of getting dressed as a single action. If we assume that the task involves putting on underwear, socks, trousers, a shirt, and shoes:

    a) Define classes for each of these different clothing types (Underwear, Socks, Trousers, Shirt, Shoes). Think about what properties and methods each clothing class should have.

    b) Instantiate the following objects belonging to the different clothing classes: tanPleats (Trousers), whiteBoxers (Underwear), blackAnkles (Socks), brownBrogues (Shoes), whiteLongSleeve (Shirt).

    c) Extend your solution to pass messages to each of these clothing objects instructing them to be PutOn.

7. Suggest some other methods that could sensibly be included in the Person class and design algorithms for those methods.

7.5 Projects

StockSnackz Vending Machine

Look at the vending machine problem through an object-oriented lens. Suppose we decide that there are three classes involved in a vending machine: the Snacks it dispenses, a Vendor mechanism for dispensing the snacks, and the MoneyHandler that receives coins, ensures sufficient money has been paid, and gives change. The MoneyHandler would also have to tell the Vendor mechanism to release a Snack. Try defining the methods and properties for each of these three classes.

Stocksfield Fire Service

No exercise.

Puzzle World: Roman Numerals and Chronograms

No exercise.

Pangrams: Holoalphabetic Sentences

No exercise.

Online Bookstore: ISBNs

No exercise.

8 Looking Forward to Program Design

The beginning of wisdom for a programmer is to recognize the difference between getting his program to work and getting it right.

M.A. Jackson (1975)

Learning Objectives

- Identify different formalized program design methods and their associated graphical notations
- Understand the difference between bottom-up and top-down approaches and between data structure, data flow and object-oriented methods
- Use different graphical notations to highlight different aspects of a given problem

In the preceding chapters we have spent much time looking at how to understand and solve problems. The goal was always to write down solutions to the problems in a structured manner using a semi-formal language. Although we have not written any programming language code, essentially what we have been doing is designing programs or, more properly, *algorithms*.

Sections 8.3 and 8.4 begin to build the bridge between the problem solving of Chapters 1 to 7 and technical programming issues by introducing you to formalized program design methods and associated diagrammatic notations that can be used.

8.1 Algorithms

The solutions to the coffee-making and van-loading problems are algorithms because they specify the series of steps necessary to arrive at the desired result. Any computer program is an algorithm or a collection of algorithms. Programming is essentially a two-part process: deriving an algorithm to solve the problem/calculate the answer and expressing that algorithm in a form that can be executed by a computer. The first step we call *program design* and the second step we call *coding* for it is the process of writing down the design in programming language code.

It is evident from the work we did in the earlier chapters that it is difficult to separate the task of problem-solving from that of program design. Indeed, by writing down the solutions to the problems in pseudo-code we have effectively designed an algorithm (or program). The reason I called Chapter 2 *A Strategy for Solving Problems* rather than *Introduction to Program Design* is three-fold. First, I wanted to steer clear of any hint of the panic that can arise in the beginner when faced with writing programs. Secondly, there are actually quite a few different formalized approaches to program design and I wanted to defer discussion of those techniques until after working through the process of real-world problem description, comprehension, and solution. Finally, different people solve problems in different ways. By applying rules and strict notational techniques program design methods in some way constrain the problem-solving activity and may even work against a particular individual's unique way of thinking. Therefore, I thought it a good idea not to present a discussion of program design methods until after we had addressed the discipline of solving problems. I hope that in the future your programming activity will be a mixture of free-form problem solving techniques (such as drawing diagrams, building models, etc.) and using formalized design methods to mould that thinking into a form that can be turned into a good computer program.

8.2 *HTTLAP* is not a Program Design Method

The solutions to the problems in the previous chapters were not always easy to determine. Some parts of the problems were fairly easy to solve but others required some hard thinking. We had to be very careful to challenge our assumptions and to ensure that the algorithms we wrote were sensible, easy to understand, and led to the right results. Designing computer programs is hard to do well though the task gets easier with experience. Something else that can make the process of writing programs easier is to use a program design method. A program design method is a set of steps and guidelines that steer you towards solving the problem in hand. Program design methods typically make use of particular notations or diagramming techniques.

You may be thinking that our *HTTLAP* strategy is a program design method. I would argue that it is not because a good method should be aimed at solving problems of a particular kind. The *HTTLAP* strategy is more of a set of principles that sets out to help you to understand problems generally. It guides you through to writing down a solution, but it does not actually tell you *how* particular problems should be solved. Good design methods, on the other hand, have rules that when followed lead you to a solution whose structure fits well with that of the original problem.

Huh?

Haven't you cheated me by not providing such a program design method in Chapter 2?

Not at all. You see, *HTTLAP* has no particular type of problem in mind, and as such is a general set of guidelines. The trouble with general program design methods is their very generality. As M. A. Jackson observed "if a method offers help with every possible problem, you mustn't expect it to help much with any particular problem" (Jackson, 2001, p. xvii). The focus of this book is the basics of understanding and solving problems with a view to implementing those solutions as a computer program. Having understood the problem you can then progress to using an appropriate program design method to assist with the technical translation.

The *HTTLAP* strategy is a framework for helping you to start thinking about problems generally. It offers a checklist of activities that should help you towards developing skills for analyzing and understanding problems. What *HTTLAP* does not do is provide help with specific types of problem; this is what program design methods are for, or rather, what program design methods *should* be for. Unfortunately, there are very few program design methods aimed at specific classes of problem. By this I mean that many methods offer general guidance on how to solve programming problems. Ironically, the weakness of many design methods lies in their focus on developing solutions. While the goal of any programmer is to develop a solution, to do this correctly he must first understand the problem he is trying to solve. Design methods tend to be good at helping you to describe your solution, but not so good at helping you to understand the principal parts of the problem itself. The goal of *HTTLAP* is to lead you towards greater understanding of the problem, its complexities, and ambiguities, and to assist you with identifying and challenging the assumptions (and simplifications) you make in the process. As programmers, we must understand that the real world is infinitely more complex than any computer program we write. A program is a solution to a problem that lies in the real world, but in order to build the program we must be able to simplify the problem to the extent that it can be solved in a finite number of steps. One of the skills a programmer must learn is where to draw the boundary. If you attempt to solve every little detail and complexity related to your problem you may never finish. In the coffee-making problem, we made a few assumptions and drew a boundary around the problem we were trying to solve. Sometimes we make the boundary explicit, other times we do it unconsciously.

For example, the coffee-making solution only works for situations where there already exists a working coffee machine, where there is coffee in the cupboard, the machine is plugged in to a working electricity outlet, and where there is an available water supply. It also assumes that milk, sugar, and clean cups are to hand and that we have sufficient supplies of each to meet the needs of our guests. If any of these conditions is not met then our solution will not work. You may think that is going to absurd lengths, but it is an important principle to note. A programmer must not only understand what his solution will do, but also what the solution will **not** do. What a program will not do is often more interesting that what it will do. When discussing the coffee-making problem with a colleague, his solution upon considering the many complexities of the problem was to telephone the catering department and order coffee for six people. This is a common practice in industry these days and is known as "outsourcing" – paying somebody else to develop the solution for you.[1] However, as the sign on former US President Harry S. Truman's desk said, *the buck stops here* which, for us, means we must learn to develop the solutions.

8.3 Program Design Methods

The purpose of the rest of this chapter is not to provide instruction in the many program design methods that exist. Instead, I want to focus on some of the graphical notations that are used by design methods with a view to showing you how representing a problem (or a solution) in different ways can lead you toward greater understanding of the task. Chapters 2 and 3 looked at some of the ways that real-world problems can be described and modelled, for example using pictures, diagrams, and mathematics. In this chapter, as we move toward considering the computer in which our solutions will eventually reside, we will look at some common representational techniques that are used to describe programs and algorithms. Some of these notations are quite formal and precise allowing ambiguity to be minimized. Others offer a greater degree of vagueness which can sometimes be useful but which can lead to difficulties later on if the unclear aspects are not properly resolved.

Before considering these program design notations, I want first to quickly introduce some of the main approaches to software development. We will not go into these in great detail for that would require a book in its own right. Also, the program design approach to be used is often determined by the language in which you are working or the requirements of a particular college course, and this book is not aimed at solving problems with a particular programming language.[2] If you are using this book as part of a college or university course, you are likely going to be given in-depth training in program design later on and your course will have particular design techniques specified in the syllabus.

Top-down Design: "Dysfunctional Decomposition"

One of the more popular approaches advocated in programming methods and books is TOP-DOWN design, also known as "functional decomposition" or "stepwise refinement." It is popular because it is general and because it makes an appeal to common sense. The premise of TOP-DOWN design is simple: starting with an overall problem

---

[1] Thanks to Rob Davis for that piece of creative thinking. You can tell that Rob used to work in a Business School.

[2] I find this to be an unfortunate state of affairs because it prejudges the solution. The programming language is often picked first and then a design method is chosen that fits with the language rather than one that fits the problem.

statement you decompose it into a set of smaller subproblems. Each subproblem in turn is decomposed into its own smaller subproblems. This process is continued until at the bottom level the subproblems are so small that they can be easily expressed in programming language code. The result is a hierarchy of subproblems (Figure 8.1).

FIGURE 8.1   Top-down hierarchical functional decomposition of a problem

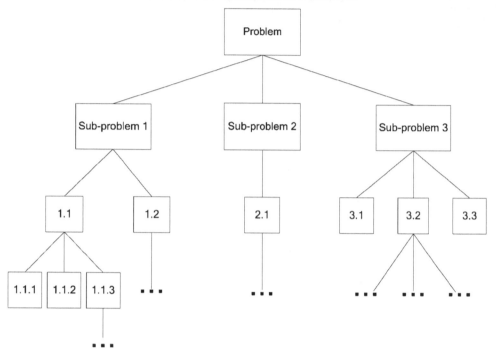

This process of stepwise refinement has psychological appeal as we are led to believe that we are gaining understanding of a problem through breaking it up into simpler subproblems in a kind of divide-and-conquer approach. Indeed, is this not just what *HTTLAP* recommends? Actually, no. In *HTTLAP*, while we are trying to solve the big problem by solving simpler related problems, there was no indication that the set of simpler problems is in any way hierarchically related. Top-down design does not give any advice on *how* to decompose the hierarchy; it merely says that we should keep on decomposing the problems until we arrive at some easily understood level. This division of a problem into separate sub-problems requires that we make the biggest decision (deciding what the first level of decomposition will be) at the start of the process just when we know the least about the problem. To be able to do an effective functional decomposition we must first have already solved the problem in our heads (Jackson, 1983). The top-down design then becomes a description of a problem already solved rather than something that helps to actually solve the problem. There is a more complete discussion of why I do not think top-down is very useful in the Reflections chapter. Because I do not think this method of functional decomposition is helpful I prefer to call it Dysfunctional Decomposition: again, the argument is given in more detail in the Reflections section.

Divide and conquer ▶

Dysfunctional Decomposition ▶

Bottom-up Design

Rather than starting with the problem and breaking it up into smaller and smaller parts, another technique for designing software is to start by considering the small details first. Solutions to the many small problems are worked out and these solutions are then assembled into a hierarchy of functions in a bottom-up manner. Avison and Fitzgerald (1995) claim that it is often difficult to make these separately designed solutions fit together later on as no account has been taken of the overall shape of the problem and its solution.

Data-structure Approaches

Many problems involve the processing of structured data. At their most basic level **all** programs process data, but that is not what I mean. It is often the case that the underlying data can be arranged in structured hierarchies. For example, you might be required to write a program that prints invoices for CD purchases made at an online music store. The invoices are to be arranged sorted by album title within artist name, as in Table 8.1.

Table 8.1   **CD Ordering for an Online Store Invoice**

Artist	Album	Catalog No.	Price
Adams, Bryan	18 'til I Die	5405512	9.99
Adams, Bryan	Reckless	3950132	6.99
Adams, Bryan	Waking up the Neighbors	3971642	8.99
Pink Floyd	Dark Side of the Moon	CDEMD1064	7.99
Pink Floyd	The Wall	CDEMD1071	10.99
Pink Floyd	Wish You Were Here	CDEMD1062	7.99
ZZ Top	Afterburner	K9253422	7.99
ZZ Top	Eliminator	7599237742	5.99
ZZ Top	Tres Hombres	K256603	8.99

A data structure oriented approach can be used to design a solution to the problem. The underlying structure of the data is used as the basis for the program's design. Perhaps the best well-known (and well-regarded) data structure design method is Jackson Structured Programming (JSP) (Jackson, 1975). JSP[3] has stages devoted to analyzing and describing the data structures, transforming these structures into a program design, and finally adding the necessary operations and conditions to allow the design to be translated into the chosen programming language. What JSP did was to simplify the program design process for a certain

---

[3] JSP (see ACRONYM) is also the abbreviation for *Java Server Program* – quite a different thing altogether.

class of problems (those that have underlying data structures). It provided a systematic framework that removed much of the guesswork from program design.

One feature of JSP that is especially good is that you know in advance what type of problems it will help you solve. If your problem is not one of transforming structured data then you know JSP will not help you solve it. Why is this a good thing? Because the method knows its limitations and does not offer you false hope. Furthermore, when you do have a problem that JSP fits then you know JSP will lead you towards a good solution. Jackson extended the approach in 1983 to work with designing complete software systems as opposed to individual programs. The newer method is called JSD, or Jackson System Development (Jackson, 1983). Section 8.4 below covers some of the diagrammatic conventions used by JSP (and JSD). Some commentators have incorrectly asserted that JSP and JSD are TOP-DOWN methods, probably because the tree diagrams they use superficially resemble the hierarchical arrangements of TOP-DOWN designs. JSP and JSD are most assuredly **not** TOP-DOWN methods.

Other data structure methods include Logical Construction of Programs (LCP) and Warnier-Orr Methodology which sometimes goes by the name Data Structure Systems Development (DSSD).

Data-flow Approaches

Methods that describe the flow rather than the structure of information or data are called data flow oriented methods. For instance, in an invoicing system such a method might concentrate on the passing of orders from the customer to the company, the movement of stock around the company, the delivery of goods to the customer, the transfer of money between the customer and the company, the sending of delivery notes and invoices to the customer, and so on. Data flow approaches attempt to describe the movement of information and thereby the processes that transform the information into various forms. For example, we might define a process that receives an order from the customer and which checks the order to ensure it is correct and which then passes the validated order on to another process that calculates the money owed, and so on. Such methods typically use data flow diagrams (DFD) to assist the developer. Unfortunately, data flow methods often give little real help in the form of systematic rules for deciding how a problem should be partitioned into the various subprocesses that carry out the information processing tasks. In the late 1970s (the early days of so-called structured analysis) DFDs were used in a more formal and rule-based manner that gave the programmer some reasonably clear guidelines to follow. However, in recent years much of the formality has been abandoned in an attempt to be less restrictive. A result of this is that rather than becoming more helpful, such approaches in fact give the programmer even less clear guidance and leave more decisions to clever thinking and intuition. Data flow approaches are generally organized around the TOP-DOWN philosophy.

Two of the better-known methods that employ data flow techniques today are SSADM (Structured Systems Analysis and Design Method) and Yourdon Structured Method (YSM). *SSADM: A Practical Approach* (Ashworth & Goodland,

1989) is a student-friendly introduction to SSADM. Yourdon's method is described in *Modern Structured Analysis* (Yourdon, 1988).

Object-oriented Approaches

Programming languages such as C++, Java, and latterly C# have brought into the mainstream object-oriented programming (OOP). Like the structured programming movement of the 1970s, the object-oriented approach gathered force in the 1980s in an attempt to solve the so-called software crisis. Too many software development projects were running vastly over budget and beyond their schedules. Furthermore, many software systems did not work properly and, in extreme cases, were thrown away shortly after installation. Like structured programming before it, OOP was claimed to be the solution to the software crisis because it embodied good practice and reusability. While it is true that many OOP principles are good, the practice did not solve the software crisis.[4] Beware of people who claim that OOP will solve all the ills of the software industry. It may help you to engineer software to a high standard, but if you have solved the wrong problem your efforts will be in vain.

As we saw in Chapter 7 the philosophy of the approach is to build software components that keep the data and the code that processes that data together in a single unit, or object. Because of the focus on engineering individual components, there is an element of bottom-up design in OOP methods. There are quite a few object-oriented design methods and approaches. One that has grown in popularity today is the Rational Unified Process which is based upon the Unified Modelling Language (UML).

8.4 Graphical Notations

We saw in Chapter 3 that different representations can shed light on seemingly intractable problems. By and large, program design methods use diagrammatic notations to assist the programmer. There are many different notations available and the novice can be unsure which one to pick. Often the decision is made for them by a college course that imposes a particular design method. Some say that it does not matter which notation you pick arguing that they all show the same thing and one is as good as another. This is simply untrue: they draw on the same raw material (the principal parts of a problem or program) but they emphasize different aspects. In the following sections we shall look at some of the more common notations to see what they provide and, just as importantly, what they *do not* provide to the programmer. I hope that you will, with practice, begin to see what the different notations are well suited to and thus be able to make informed choices when designing your own programs.

---

[4] This is probably because the design methods still did not help the developers to understand the problems properly. Without a good understanding of the underlying problem even the best tools will not help you to build a good solution.

Flowcharts

FIGURE 8.2   **Basic flowcharting symbols**

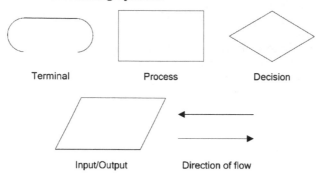

| Terminal | Process | Decision |

| Input/Output | Direction of flow |

A flowchart is a diagrammatic representation of an algorithm. We have seen some already in Chapter 4 where they were used to illustrate the IF and WHILE constructs. The flowchart is one of the earliest diagrammatic techniques for programming and remains popular today.[5] However, it has fallen out of favor in some quarters because it can be hard to update and it is easy to draw really badly structured algorithms in flowchart notation.[6] Figure 8.2 shows five of the symbols from which basic flowcharts can be constructed (there are more symbols which are not shown here).

The terminal symbol is used to show the start and end of an algorithm. The process box shows tasks performed by the algorithm, such as adding numbers. The decision symbol is used to show points at which the algorithm needs to make a decision. Selections and iterations both use the decision symbol. (Think about why this is so.) A decision symbol has two exits: one for when the condition is true and one for when the condition is false.

Huh?

Does this mean that selections and iterations are really the same thing?

Almost. What is the essential difference between them, and what is the essential similarity? A selection performs a single course of action if a condition is met while an iteration repeatedly tests the condition and performs the action. An iteration, then, is a selection that repeats. In programming terms, selections and iterations are both *branching* constructs: they represent points at which program flow leaves the purely sequential ordering. A selection branches to a new location (depending on the value of a condition) from which execution continues. A loop also tests a condition and then branches to a new section of code, but when that section finishes, the program returns back to the branch point.

---

[5] A former colleague once told of when he worked as a maintenance programmer in a certain large organization. Each time the main program needed to be updated the team would gather in the corridor and watch in reverential awe as the scroll on which the flowchart was kept was rolled out along the floor. They then walked up and down inspecting the flowchart looking for the bits that needed amending.

[6] Jackson comments that flowcharts can often be obscure and playfully passes on David Gries's name for them – "flowcharts" (Jackson, 1983, p. 43).

The input/output symbol is used to denote any actions that involve getting information into or out of the algorithm, such as getting parcel weights, reporting results, etc. The flow arrows connect the symbols and show which way the algorithm flows.

Using the symbols from Figure 8.2, I have drawn Figure 8.3 which is a flowchart of the van-loading solution. I tried to make the layout of the flowchart match that of the pseudo-code from Solution 5.18 by keeping the main flow running vertically down the page. However, as becomes apparent in this example, even with relatively small algorithms it is hard to keep the flowchart nicely structured **and** on one page. As you can see I have had to move some of the sections horizontally to allow everything to fit. There are symbols to show that part of a flowchart is on a different page, but for such a small solution I wanted to avoid that. Compare Figure 8.3 with Figure 8.4 in which I have redrawn the flowchart to use more horizontal space. Both flowcharts describe the same algorithm, but their layouts are different. One of the drawbacks of flowcharts is that there are no fixed rules governing their layout. Figure 8.3 and Figure 8.4 are only two possible layouts for this solution – I could draw many more. Because programmers can draw flowcharts differently it is not always easy to read and understand somebody else's charts. Because there are no fixed rules for their layout deciding just how to draw a flowchart can be tricky. Furthermore, if the algorithm needs to be amended, the flowchart may need to be completely redrawn in order for its layout to accommodate the changes. Nowadays, many programmers prefer to use pseudo-code over flowcharts as the layout is much more standardized and easier to read.

The above criticisms notwithstanding, a flowchart can sometimes be just the thing for illustrating a point. The small examples in Chapter 4 are easy to understand and help to explain the logic of the IF and WHILE constructs. If you find flowcharts easy to draw then by all means use them, only be careful that you do not end up constructing poorly structured algorithms with them. You can check this by converting a flowchart to pseudo-code. If the pseudo-code starts looking very messy, or it is hard to translate the flowchart into pseudo-code, it is a sign that your flowchart is not very well laid out.

Tree Diagrams

I have found tree diagrams very useful for describing problems and designing and documenting programs. They're used mostly in the JSP/JSD software design methods. As well as describing the structure of programs you can use tree diagrams to describe the structure of data, problems, and objects in the real world. Jackson tree diagrams have strict rules governing their construction which means that their meaning is precise and unambiguous. There is only one way to arrange the boxes in a tree diagram for any given algorithm (allowing for minor differences in relative spatial positioning) and they are always read from top-to-bottom and left-to-right.

There are three component types in a basic tree diagram: sequence, iteration, and selection. An action (or group of actions) is represented by a box. Sequences of actions are shown by placing the boxes left to right as in Figure 8.5.

FIGURE 8.3   **Flowchart for van-loading**

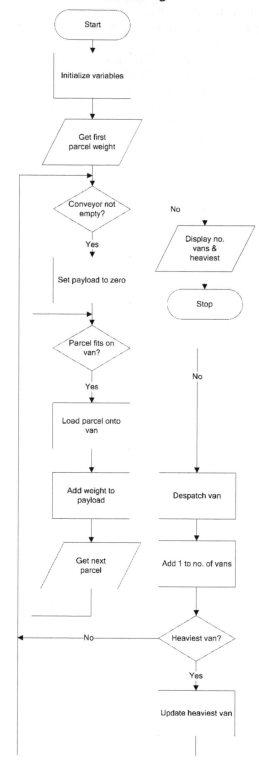

FIGURE 8.4   **Another flowchart for van-loading**

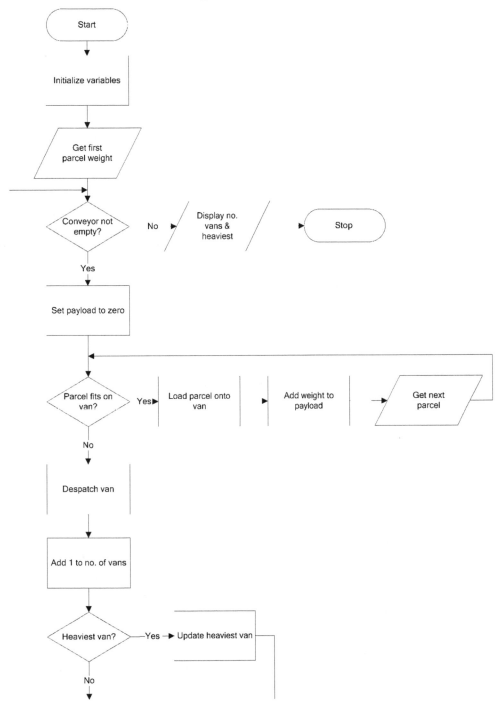

FIGURE 8.5   **Tree diagram for a sequence**

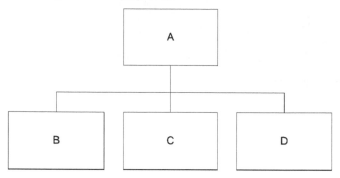

In Figure 8.5 box "A" is a sequence. "B," "C," and "D" are the component actions of the sequence (that is, they comprise the action block of "A"). "A" is not an action itself but a name for the sequence of actions performed by "B," "C," and "D." We could write Figure 8.5 in pseudo-code thus:

// Sequence A

```
Action B ;
Action C ;
Action D ;
```

// End of Sequence A

Selections are represented by Figure 8.6 (a) and (b). In Figure 8.6 the component "A" in both example (a) and example (b) is the selection. Figure 8.6 (a) represents a simple IF construct which would be written in pseudo-code as:

// Selection A

```
IF (condition)
    Action B ;
ENDIF
```

// End Selection A

FIGURE 8.6   **Selection constructs: (a) is a simple selection (b) is a selection with an ELSE path**

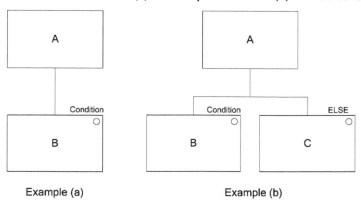

Figure 8.6 (b) gives a compound selection (one with an ELSE path). Its pseudo-code equivalent would be:

```
// Selection A
IF (condition)
    Action B ;
ELSE
    Action C ;
ENDIF
// End Selection A
```

The circle symbol in the top right corners of "B" and "C" of Figure 8.6 denotes the component in which it lies is followed when the condition written above the box is met. Remember the cash machine example from an earlier chapter? We wrote a selection construct that dispensed cash if there were sufficient funds in the account, otherwise an apology was displayed. Figure 8.7 is the tree diagram that corresponds to that selection.

FIGURE 8.7   **Tree diagram for cash withdrawal**

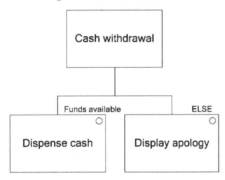

Tree diagrams can also be drawn to show the null action of a simple IF construct (see Section 6.3 in Chapter 6 for a reminder of the null statement). For example, Figure 8.6(a) could be redrawn as Figure 8.8 below. Notice that no ELSE is placed over the null action's box.

FIGURE 8.8   **Selection with *null* action**

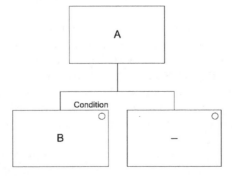

Iterations are shown by putting a star in the corner of the repeated task. Figure 8.9 shows how we could represent the sugar-adding part of our coffee-making problem. The box labelled "WHILE" is the iteration structure, the box "Add Sugar" is the iterated action (denoted by the asterisk in its corner).

FIGURE 8.9   **Tree diagram for iteration**

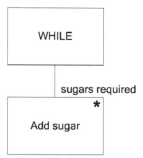

The corresponding pseudo-code for Figure 8.9 would be:

// Adding sugar
```
WHILE (sugars required)
   Add sugar ;
ENDWHILE
```
// End of adding sugar

Using the three components (sequence, iteration, and selection) we can draw tree diagrams for complete problem solutions. Figure 8.10 shows the van-loading solution expressed as a tree diagram. Because tree diagrams have strict rules governing their construction we do not have the difficulty of deciding how best to lay out the solution that we faced with flowcharts.

Compare Figure 8.10 with Solution 5.18 to ensure that you can see how the tree diagram has been derived from the pseudo-code. The vertical sequence of actions in the pseudo-code is reflected in the horizontal sequence of boxes on the tree diagram. The nesting of constructs in the pseudo-code is reflected in the vertical branches of the tree.

Tree diagrams are very good at highlighting the relationships between components. You can easily see what parts belong to what; nested structures are plainly visible and the consequences of following certain selection paths are clear. You can see in Figure 8.10 that processing a parcel is a repeated activity and that it comprises a sequence of three actions. Processing a parcel is done after the van's payload is set to zero and before the van is despatched. Tree diagrams are also known as structure diagrams because they highlight the structure of the solution.

FIGURE 8.10   **Tree diagram for van-loading solution**

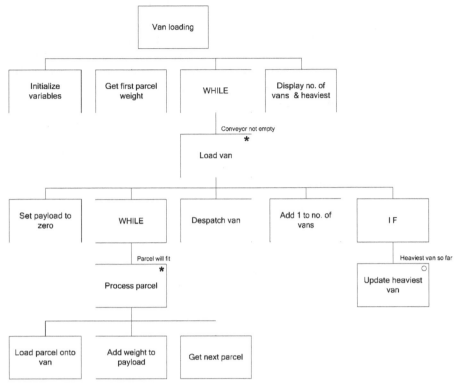

State Transition Diagrams

When it is important to describe a program or an object in terms of the events that happen and the different *states* that those events trigger, it is useful to draw a state transition diagram.[7] Many courses in software engineering and event-driven programming use state transition diagrams (STD) as their preferred diagramming technique. The main focus of the STD is the set of states that a program can be in and the events that cause changes in state. There are several different notational styles used for drawing state transition diagrams, but they share common features. Figure 8.11 shows the basic symbols used in a simple form of state transition diagram.

FIGURE 8.11   **Symbols for basic state transition diagrams**

---

[7] Some people call them finite state machines because they show all the possible, but finite, states that a program (machine) can take. The starting and ending states are clearly visible.

The "start state" (with a double border) is the state in which an algorithm begins. The stop state (with the thick border) is its final resting state and the regular "state" is one of the intermediate states. Events cause a program to move from one state to another, and so these are shown as connecting arrows.[8] For example, consider Figure 8.12 which shows a very simple STD for a library book. If we ignore complications such as loan renewals, books being lost and stolen, and the disposal of books when they get to the end of their useful life, we might consider a library book to have two main states: it is either on the shelf or it is on loan. A book begins its life in the library by being catalogued after which it is placed on the shelf. A book remains on the shelf until it is borrowed at which point it is considered to be on loan.[9] It remains on loan until such time as it is returned when it goes back on the shelf. Figure 8.12 shows these different states and the events that cause transition from one state to the next.

FIGURE 8.12   **Simple state transition diagram for a library book**

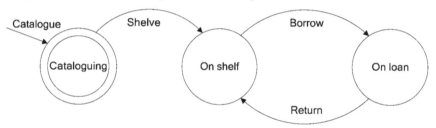

Any state transition diagram can be redrawn as a tree diagram (and vice versa). For example, Figure 8.13 shows the library book redrawn as a tree diagram. Notice how Figure 8.12 and Figure 8.13 give different views onto the same problem. The STD focuses on the resting states in a solution; it brings to the foreground exactly what states are possible to achieve from any other state. It also shows clearly what events can come next. For example, from the "on shelf" state the only possible event that can occur is the "borrow" event. The tree diagram, on the other hand, focuses on the structural relationships of events. Figure 8.13 shows clearly that "borrow" and "return" events come in pairs and that such pairs occur repeatedly throughout the life of a book.

Figure 8.14 shows a more complex STD for someone eating a meal. The meal comprises three courses. The starter is fixed so someone may choose not to have it and to go straight to the main course. There is a choice of a meat or vegetarian dish for the main course and a choice of coffee or cake for dessert. The process begins by sitting down and waiting for the food to arrive. Trace through the

---

[8] Or "graph edges" as a mathematician or a formal computer scientist would know them.

[9] Another complication we are overlooking for now is the fact that a book might very well be off the shelf even though it is not on loan: somebody may simply be reading it in the library.

FIGURE 8.13 **Tree diagram for library book**

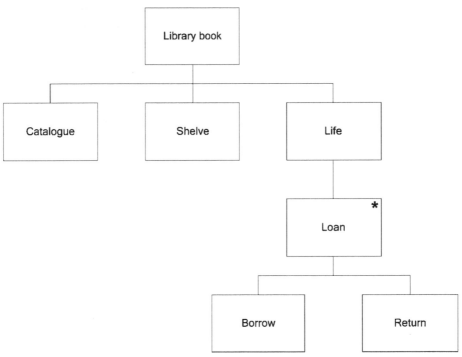

Think Spot diagram by following the different event/state paths. Notice that you can go from waiting straight to either of the main courses, or from waiting to the starter and then to either main course. From each main course you can go to either the cake or the coffee. The "meal finished" state is achieved after dessert (cake or coffee).

FIGURE 8.14 **State transition diagram for a meal**

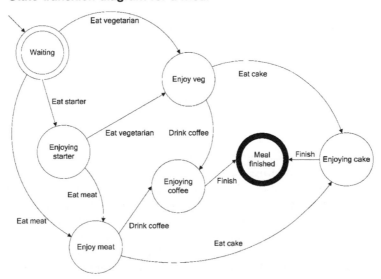

Figure 8.15 shows the corresponding tree diagram for the same meal. Notice how the tree diagram very clearly captures the sequential progression from starter through main course to dessert. The choices belonging to each course are also easy to see.

FIGURE 8.15   **Tree diagram for meal**

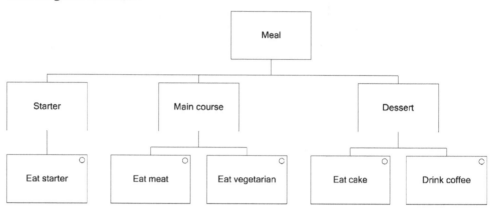

Data Flow Diagrams

Data flow diagrams (DFDs) are a very popular diagramming technique common in many TOP-DOWN design methods and are taught on most systems analysis courses. There are several different styles and notational forms but they have roughly the same ingredients. The main function of a DFD is to show how data flows between the structural units of a program. Figure 8.16 shows the main symbols used in a simple form of DFD notation (the shapes of DFD symbols change according to which notational style is being used, though their meaning is usually the same. (For example, the SSADM method uses boxes rather than circles to denote processes.)

FIGURE 8.16   **Basic symbols for a data flow diagram**

A process is a program or an algorithm. Sources and sinks are people, companies, other programs, etc. that provide or receive data from the processes. A data store is used to store information (a bit like a filing cabinet). The data flow arrow shows the direction in which data flows between the processes, sinks, and data stores. For example, consider Figure 8.17 which shows a data flow diagram depicting the principal components in the coffee making problem.

The "make coffee" process is the algorithm that expresses the solution to the coffee making problem. The guests in the problem are denoted by the box. Guests

FIGURE 8.17   **DFD for coffee making problem**

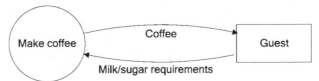

provide the algorithm with their milk and sugar requirements. The algorithm in turn provides the guests with coffee. A DFD does not show task ordering, selections, or iterations like a tree diagram does as its focus is to show what items of data move around the system. Figure 8.17 is a special type of DFD called a

Context ▶
diagram

context diagram. Context diagrams are used to show the top level of a problem, a program, or a system. The program, system, or algorithm is represented by the process circle. The main data flows in and out of the algorithm are shown as are the principal components or objects with which the algorithm interacts.

The next step in methods based on data flow diagrams is to start to functionally decompose the problem in a TOP-DOWN manner. The top-level process of the context diagram is decomposed into subprocesses that correspond to the main functional units. Each subprocess in turn is further decomposed into its own subprocesses. This continues until the various subprocesses can be easily expressed in programming language code. For example, consider Figure 8.18, a context diagram for a company called Stitch in Time. Stitch in Time is a small two-person operation that makes leggings for pregnant women. Knowledge about Stitch in Time came from an interview with the company's two owner-employees.

FIGURE 8.18   **Context diagram for Stitch in Time**

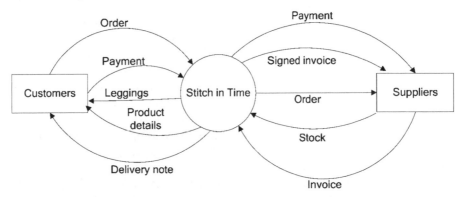

The context diagram shows that the company (represented by the process circle) sends leggings, product details, and delivery notes to its customers from whom it receives orders and payments. Stitch in Time sends orders, payments, and signed invoices to its suppliers who, in turn, send it stock and invoices. The context diagram shows reasonably clearly what interactions the company has with its principal stakeholders.

Think Spot

The next step is to decompose the process in the context diagram into its principal functional areas. Unfortunately, TOP-DOWN methods do not offer much help on how to do this. Think about how you might decompose the main process in Figure 8.18. What factors might you consider in making your decisions? What makes logical sense? If you are stuck, you might, for example, decide that three main subprocesses are needed: one to handle customer orders, one for ordering stock, and one for keeping the accounts.

> Having thought about the problem for a while (at least ten minutes), try drawing a DFD that shows how all the subprocesses you identified are linked by various information flows. This is not a trivial task and requires quite a bit of information about the documents used in the company; as you do not have this information you should make some educated guesses and assumptions at this point.

My own solution is shown below as Figure 8.19. Notice how the DFD in Figure 8.19 shows much more information than the context diagram in Figure 8.18. This is because the context diagram shows the problem solution and the people or objects which provide information to the solution and receive its outputs. The decomposed DFD in Figure 8.19, on the other hand, shows much more of the internal detail of the problem. It shows the information that flows around the company (orders, stock levels, stock requirements, etc.). Knowledge of this information comes from studying the problem situation (perhaps by carrying out interviews), but the decisions about how to decompose the processes themselves are left to the programmer. You might reasonably ask why it is necessary to have three subprocesses rather than two, or even five or six. That is a good question to which I do not have a very good answer other than it seemed like a good idea at the time. That is one of the challenges of TOP-DOWN design – it does not provide any guidance on how to decompose the processes. If you get it wrong you tend to find out when you have already put in a lot of work which means it takes a lot more effort to redesign the solution.

Think Spot

Looking at Figure 8.19 you may also see that the labels on the diagram are not precise. What does "keep accounts" mean? What does "handle customer orders" mean? Come up with a few definitions yourself. The labels on a DFD can be very precise or very ambiguous depending on how well the designer understands the problem. Too often functional decomposition is used to defer awkward or difficult decisions rather than addressing the main issue which is a lack of understanding. While *HTTLAP* is not a design method and does not give precise instructions about how to solve any particular problem you should still find it helpful. This is because its focus is on problem understanding and resolution of difficulties, ambiguities, and assumptions. This is in contrast to many of the TOP-DOWN methods which do not particularly address the question of understanding the problem.

UML – the Unified Modelling Language

Unified Modelling Language, or UML, has become a standard notation for use in object-oriented system development projects. UML provides a set of notations for

FIGURE 8.19   **First level DFD for Stitch in Time**

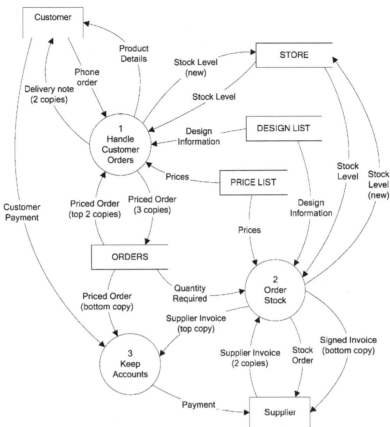

describing different aspects of a system design including object classes, use cases, activity diagrams, sequence diagrams, collaboration diagrams, state diagrams, packages, and implementation diagrams. UML is specifically aimed at object-oriented design and programming languages and is commonly used on many university programming courses. Because of the number of different diagram types in UML and UML's focus on object-oriented design we shall not dwell upon it here.

Summary of Diagramming Techniques

The above notations are all ways of getting different views of a program, a problem, an object, etc. When we discussed solving problems in Chapters 2 and 3 I suggested using a variety of description languages to help you get a proper understanding of the problem. You will recall that some problems were easier to describe with one technique while a different language was needed for other problems. A similar principle holds for program design notations. For example, while tree diagrams and state transition diagrams describe the same things (a tree diagram can be derived from any state transition diagram and vice versa) they each make certain aspects of the problem easy to see while obscuring others.

When picking a program design notation we need to realize that none of them is a universal tool. What I mean by that is that no single design method or design notation is suitable for all problems. A given notation may be excellent for describing certain types of problem, but absolutely hopeless for other types. The state transition diagram/tree diagram comparison showed this very plainly. STDs were good for describing problems where it is important to know about what can come next at any point. Tree diagrams were good for describing problems where the order of events and their structural relationships is most important. Data flow diagrams can be useful for getting a feel for the principal parts of a problem and for showing where the various items of data go. However, DFDs are not very precise and the meanings of process names and data flow names can be quite ambiguous. Flowcharts can be useful for showing the control flow aspects of a problem. The decision points are highlighted and actions sequences are a major feature. However, they do not offer any advantages over tree diagrams which show much the same information. Furthermore, unlike tree diagrams, flowcharts do not have a standard layout and can lead to very poorly structured solutions. That said, they can be helpful for making quick sketches of a problem in an attempt to work for greater understanding.

Therefore, when it comes to program design you need to be very careful of people who recommend a particular design method or diagrammatic notation as being suitable for every type of programming problem. It is great when the method or notation fits well with the structure and characteristics of the problem. But where methods and notations do not offer a good fit then you will continually feel you are fighting with the method rather than working with it. Ralph Waldo Emerson is credited with saying "foolish consistency is the hobgoblin of little minds." As you develop your skills in computer programming, please try also to develop a critical and enquiring mind when it comes to tools and techniques for helping you to design programs.

8.5 Exercises

1. Draw a flowchart for the coffee making solution in Solution 4.9.

2. Draw a tree diagram of the coffee making solution in Solution 4.9.

3. Try drawing flowcharts, tree diagrams, and state transition diagrams for some of the algorithms you have developed in the exercises in previous chapters. Alternatively, use the various algorithm solutions in Appendix C as the basis for your diagrams.

4. Think about buying a book or a CD from an Internet store. Identify what the principal components of the transaction are and then draw a data flow diagram showing how the various data items (including physical objects such as books) flow between the main players in the situation. Do not restrict yourself just to the store and the customer – think about who else might be involved.

5. Find a book on UML in your nearest library. What sort of programming paradigm is it best suited to?

8.6 Projects

StockSnackz Vending Machine

Draw a tree diagram and a flowchart of your solution so far. Examine the two representations and decide which one you found a) easier to draw and b) easier to read.

Stocksfield Fire Service

Draw a tree diagram and a flowchart of your solution so far. Examine the two representations and decide which one you found a) easier to draw and b) easier to read.

Puzzle World: Roman Numerals and Chronograms

Use one of the diagramming techniques covered in this chapter to draw a graphical representation of your algorithm for the Roman numerals problem.

Pangrams: Holoalphabetic Sentences

No exercise.

Online Bookstore: ISBNs

No exercise.

The Computer Domain: Data, Data Structures, and Program Design Solutions

Part II of the book lowers the level of abstraction and moves closer to the machine domain. In the chapters that follow we will take the basic language of problem solving developed in Part I and apply it to problems mainly focused on the storage and manipulation of data. The *HTTLAP* pseudo-code is thus extended and more closely resembles a real programming language. This will help you to start learning to write down your solutions in a form that is very close to an actual programming language. This will help to bridge the gap between the kind of problem solving we tackled in Part I and writing working programs such as are required on any programming course. Because this is not a book about a particular programming language we will continue to write solutions to problems in the *HTTLAP* pseudo-code. However, we will extend the pseudo-code to include many of the features found in modern programming languages. Chapter 9 presents a closer look at data and data types building upon that material covered in Chapter 6. Chapter 10 adds another element to our problem solving vocabulary—the sub-program. Chapter 11 introduces the basic principles of dealing with getting data into and out of a program via files and streams. Chapters 12 and 13 cover some of the main ways of structuring and managing data complete with fully-worked out algorithmic solutions that can be adapted to fit the need. Chapter 14 builds upon Chapter 7's short overview of object-oriented programming by introducing the concepts of encapsulation, polymorphism, and inheritance. Chapter 15 looks at how the pseudo-code algorithms may be translated into a real programming language (in this case the Java-based Processing language) and executed on a computer. Chapter 16 rounds off the numbered chapters with an introduction to testing and debugging strategies.

Finally, and because you may be using this book on a course where you *are* learning a programming language, Appendix A gives the nearest equivalents to the *HTTLAP* pseudo-code features in Processing, C, C++, Java, Pascal, and BASIC; this selection has been chosen so as to cover some of the popular language variants in use today (though there are still bound to be differences for language dialects I have not mentioned – e.g. Delphi, Visual Basic, C#, and J# to name four).

9

Data Types for Computer Programs

Learning Objectives

- Understand how data belong to different types
- Understand how operators can be used to perform tasks on data
- Understand how the Boolean data type can be used to improve selection and iteration conditions

This chapter revisits data. In Chapter 6 we looked at some of the different ways in which we can view data such as text and numbers. This chapter builds on those foundations and shows how different types of data item can be stored and manipulated in the way a real programming language would do it. The principal integer, real number, character, string, and Boolean data types are introduced together with some examples of their typical usage (Section 9.1). Section 9.2 examines the various arithmetic and relational operations that can be performed upon these data types and Section 9.3 looks at some applications of the Boolean data type.

9.1 Data and Data Types

In Chapter 6 we started to think about the ways different kinds of data may be handled. For example, strings of characters may have different operations performed upon them than whole numbers. We learned that the classification of data according to its kind is called *typing* and that each data item in a program must belong to a particular data type. There are many different types offered by the many available programming languages. Furthermore, many languages allow you to define your own types as needed. Thus it is impractical here to cover everything that could be said about data types. Therefore, in the following sections we will look at just five of the main types of data that you are likely to encounter, namely: integers, real numbers, characters, strings, and Boolean data. These five types provide something of a foundation for type-based programming and so the following sections should give you a good start in understanding data types and their different uses.

Literals and Identifiers

In Chapters 4 and 5 we saw the need for variables. They were used to store values that were needed in order to carry out the tasks in a solution. Each variable was given a unique identifier (name) that gave a clue as to the variable's purpose. In programming terms a variable is an area of the computer's memory or working storage. Values are placed into the memory by reference to the variable's identifier. We can visualize a variable as a box (Figure 9.1). On the side of the box is written the variable's *identifier* (the name by which it is known). Inside the box is a piece of paper on which is written (in pencil) the value that the variable currently stands for.

FIGURE 9.1   **Variables as boxes**

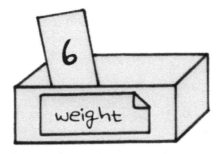

Figure 9.1 shows a variable whose identifier is 'weight' and whose value is 6. When a variable is first defined in a program it has no value. In effect, the piece of paper is blank, as in Figure 9.2.

We saw in Chapter 5 how to use the assignment symbol '←' to give values to variables. The task:

```
weight ← 6 ;
```

leads to weight having the value 6 as in Figure 9.1 above. If we then carried out the following task:

```
weight ← weight + 2 ;
```

FIGURE 9.2   **New variable with no value**

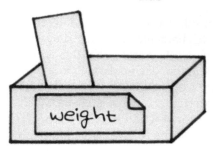

weight's value would be increased by 2. You can visualize this as rubbing out the value that is currently on the paper in the box and writing in a new number, as in Figure 9.3.

FIGURE 9.3   **New value for weight**

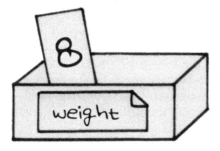

Just about every book on programming will mention *literals*. This term often sounds confusing to the beginning programmer, but it is really very simple to understand. Literals are simply those values in expressions that are not identifiers.[1] Consider the following statements:

1.   `result` ← 32000 + `bonus` ;
2.   `circumference` ← 3.14159 × `diameter` ;
3.   `name` ← 'Henry Higgins' ;
4.   `middleInitial` ← 'Q' ;

In statement #1 `result` is assigned the value of the expression 32000 + bonus. bonus is a variable identifier (we covered this in Chapter 5) and 32000, being a value rather than an identifier, is a numeric literal. 32000 is a value that is not stored in any variable (there is no box for it) and that may not be altered by the program, therefore, it is constant in nature. In statement #2 the value 3.14159 is another numeric literal. 'Henry Higgins' is a string literal in statement #3 and, in

---

[1] Strictly, a literal is a constant value that is made available at run-time by its inclusion in the program text. Run-time is a term which means the point in time at which a program is run or executed on a computer.

statement #4, 'Q' is a character literal. Literal, then, is just the formal term for a value that is hard-wired into the program text and which can only be changed by amending and re-compiling the program.

Before looking at some basic programming data types it is instructive to consider the binary number system which lies at the heart of computing and programming.

The Binary Number System

Regardless of their complexity, all computers manipulate data. Because computers are built up from electronic switches that can be turned on or off, they store data in a binary format. Binary is just a number system and you are already familiar with the decimal number system. In the decimal system we use the digits 0 to 9 to represent any number. Numbers greater than 9 are represented by adding extra digits to the left to represent powers of 10. For example, in decimal, 8 + 8 is written as 16, which is 1 ten and 6 units. 8 × 16 is written as 128, that is, 1 hundred (1×10^2), 2 tens (2×10^1), and 8 units (8×10^0). In the decimal system, each column represents a power of 10: 10^0 for the units, 10^1 for the tens, 10^2 for the hundreds, 10^3 for the thousands, etc. In binary only the digits 0 and 1 are used, and the columns represent powers of 2 rather than powers of 10. Thus 1 + 1 gives the answer 10 in binary which is 1 two and 0 units. 1 + 1 + 1 = 11 (1 two and 1 unit). Eight is written as 1000 (1 eight, 0 fours, 0 twos, and 0 units). So, our decimal expression 8 × 16 = 128 would be written in binary as 1000 × 10000 = 10000000. The columns in binary represent the powers of 2: 2^0, 2^1, 2^2, 2^3, 2^4 (or 1, 2, 4, 8, 16), etc. Table 9.1 shows the binary equivalents of four decimal values (8, 27, 255, and 999).

Table 9.1   **Comparison of Decimal and Binary Values**

Decimal	Binary Equivalent									
	2^9 (512)	2^8 (256)	2^7 (128)	2^6 (64)	2^5 (32)	2^4 (16)	2^3 (8)	2^2 (4)	2^1 (2)	2^0 (1)
8							1	0	0	0
27						1	1	0	1	1
255			1	1	1	1	1	1	1	1
999	1	1	1	1	1	0	0	1	1	1

Why do computers use binary? Because the binary digits 0 and 1 can be represented by the two states of a switch: 'on' and 'off'. Computer memory is organized in banks of switches grouped into multiples of 8. One binary digit (or *bit* – from **bi**nary digi**t**) can store values in the range 0..1. Two bits can store the decimal values 0, 1, 2, and 3 (00, 01, 10, and 11) and 8 bits can hold values between 0 and 255 (00000000 to 11111111). A group of 8 bits is called a *byte*. 1024 bytes is called a *kilobyte* (abbreviated to kB, or just k) and 1024 kilobytes is known as a *megabyte* (abbreviated to MB).[2] You have probably heard of these terms before. If you buy a computer you will be told it has so many hundred megabytes of main memory with a hard drive that can hold hundreds of gigabytes.[3] So, the only data a computer understands is in the binary format, that is, ones and zeroes. Everything we type into a computer is ultimately stored in a binary format. We will not dwell on binary any longer as you can learn about it in much more detail in any computer systems architecture course or book. Knowing that all values are stored in a binary format we can proceed to look at some of the basic data types used in programming languages.

Integers

The most fundamental data type used in computer programs is the *integer.* Integers are whole numbers without any fractional parts.[4] The complete set of integers is thus $\{-\infty, \ldots, -1, 0, 1, \ldots, \infty\}$ (i.e. minus infinity up to infinity). So, numbers like 1, 3, -10, 10,000,000 are all integers. Integers are an *ordinal* type which means that all the members of the type are arranged in a fixed order and can be counted. That is, -1 comes before 0 which in turn comes before 1; 3 comes after 2, and so on. Numbers such as 1.6, 32 $\frac{1}{2}$, 3.14159, and 0.75 are not integers because they are not whole numbers. Integers are easily stored in a computer because they can be converted to an exact binary representation. For example, decimal integer 16 becomes 10000 in binary and 37 becomes 100101. Most programming languages allow you to declare integer data items. Here is how we declare an integer variable in the *HTTLAP* pseudo-code:

◄ Ordinal types

integer:sugarsRequired ;

and sugarsRequired may now only be used to hold integer values.

Declaring More than One Variable of the Same Type

It is very common that you will want to declare several variables, all of the same type. We could, for example, write the following declarations to declare five integer variables:

integer:number1 ;
integer:number2 ;
integer:number3 ;
integer:number4 ;
integer:number5 ;

---

[2] And 1024 MB = 1 GB (gigabyte) with 1024 GB = 1 TB (terabyte).

[3] My very first computer had 32 kB of memory and a 5 $\frac{1}{4}$ inch floppy drive that could store 200 kB of data. My next computer had a huge 1 MB of memory and a hard drive with an unthinkable vastness of 40 MB. The computer on which I am writing this book has 1 GB of memory and two hard drives each with 80 GB capacity. 80 GB is over 2000 times as large as 40 MB!

[4] More formally, we say that the integers comprise all the NATURAL NUMBERS together with their negatives and zero.

This is allowable, but as all the variables are of the same type, we can use a short-hand notation thus:

integer: number1 ,
number2 ,
number3 ,
number4 ,
number5 ;

Or even

integer: number1 , number2 , number3 , number4 , number5 ;

though, from a readability point of view I prefer not to put several variable declarations on one line. The shorthand notation lets us state the type and then list several variables all of that type with the identifiers separated by commas (though the last one still needs the semi-colon). This list-type declaration is common in many programming languages.

Often, programming languages offer different sizes of integer. Typically, a basic integer type is allocated 4 bytes (32 bits) of storage which means an integer variable can hold values in the range −2147483648, . . . , −1, 0, 1, . . . , 2147483647. In earlier chapters we made a point of specifying the likely ranges of values that variables in our algorithms would take. This serves two purposes. First, it allows us to identify the basic type of data (integer, string, etc.) and second it allows us to assess the magnitude of the variable. If a variable is only ever going to take values between zero and 20, then allocating four bytes of storage to it seems excessive. Modern programming languages offer a range of integer types to allow programmers to be more precise in their declarations. A typical set of integer types is given in Table 9.2.

Table 9.2 **The Four *HTTLAP* Integer Types**

Type	Representation	Range of Values
byte	Signed 8-bit	−128 . . . 127
shortint	Signed 16-bit	−32,768 . . . 32,767
integer	Signed 32-bit	−2,147,483,648 . . . 2,147,483,647
longint	Signed 64-bit	−9,223,372,036,854,775,808 . . . +9,223,372,036,854,775,807

For example, we can see that a variable of type **integer** is allocated 32 bits (4 bytes) of memory. The first bit is used as a sign (0 for positive and 1 for negative) which means that 31 bits are left to store the number itself. The largest value that 31 bits can store is 1111111111111111111111111111111, or 2,147,483,647 in decimal. Thus, for the coffee making algorithm we might decide upon the types given in Table 9.3 for the numeric variables we identified in Table 5.1:

Table 9.3   **Data Types for Numeric Variables in Coffee-making Problem**

Identifier	Description	Range of Values	Type
coffeesRequired	Number of cups of coffee to be made	0 to 20	byte (−128…127)
sugarsRequired	Sugar requirements for one drinker	0, 1, 2, 3	byte (−128…127)
coffeesPoured	Number of cups poured	0 to 20	byte (−128…127)
sugarsAdded	Number of sugars added	0, 1, 2, 3	byte (−128…127)

Because all the numeric values are expected to have only small values we decide that they should all be declared as type **byte** as this type has the closest-fitting range of values of all the possible integer types. In fact, many programming languages allow us to define our own types if we think the predefined ones do not meet our needs closely enough. In the coffee making case we might decide to declare a new type that only permits integer values in the range 0 to 25. The advantage of such an approach is that should a value outside that range ever be assigned to a variable of that type, then an error will occur as it would be outside the rules.

We will return to the subject of integers later when we look at the different *operators* that can be used to manipulate them (see Section 9.2).

Real Numbers

If we could only store and manipulate integer numbers, calculating the answer to expressions such as 17 ÷ 9 would lead to some quite complex program code. This is because (as we have already discussed in Chapter 6) 17 ÷ 9 does not give an integer result; when performed on a standard calculator, we get the result −1.888888889 (or similar depending on the calculator's display size). That is because most pocket calculators work in the domain of *real* numbers, that is, numbers that have a fractional part. Real numbers are not *ordinal* because it is not possible, given any real value, to define what value comes next.

Why can real numbers not be ordinal? Surely 3.0 comes after 2.0 and 1.8 comes before 1.9?

Think about it. We know that 4 comes after integer value 3. But what value comes after the real number 3.1? Is it 3.2, or is it 3.11, or 3.101, or 3.1000000000000000000000000001? In fact, between 3.1 and 3.2 there is an infinite number of real values all greater than 3.1 but less than 3.2. Thus we cannot meaningfully assign ordinal positions to real numbers.

Fixed and ▶ floating point numbers   In the everyday world we usually write real numbers in what is called *fixed point* notation, such as 3.14159, 1.99, 98.6, 0.000011574, 1609.34 and so on.[5] The bank statement in Figure 6.1 has examples of fixed-point real numbers in the columns showing monetary values. The number of digits that appear after the decimal point is determined by the level of precision. To represent monetary values we normally work to two decimal places of precision (e.g. £1.99, $29.95, €16.50, etc.). The value of pi is commonly written to five places of precision, that is, 3.14159 (though an infinite number of digits is required to express its exact value – calculations have been performed to determine the value of pi to a trillion decimal places, but no repeating pattern has been found!).

Sometimes, the numbers we work with are so large (e.g. the number of songs downloaded from Apple's iTunes service) or so small (e.g. 0.0000000033356 seconds – the time it takes light to travel one meter) that it becomes difficult to represent them with fixed-point notation. Instead an exponential form is used.[6] For example, the number of atoms in a cube of gold 0.5 cm per side is 7 368 500 000,000,000,000,000. This is a very large number and so scientists and engineers would write it in its exponential form: 7.3685×10^{21} or 7.3685E + 21. In exponential form (also known as scientific notation) the number is written as the base number (called the *mantissa*) multiplied by 10 raised to a power (exponent), i.e. *mantissa* $\times 10^{exponent}$. The exponent specifies how many decimal places are in the number. So, 1000 would be written 1.0×10^3, and 0.009 would be written 9.0×10^{-3}. In programming environments exponential form is typically written as *mantissa*E $\pm$ exponent. So, 1000 would be 1.0E + 03 and 0.009 would be 9.0E − 03. Note, the minus sign in the exponent does not denote a negative number, but negative powers of 10, that is, numbers between 0 and 1. To represent negative numbers in scientific notation we just put a minus sign at the start. So, −0.009 would be −9.0E − 03, −1000 would be −1.0E + 03, and so on.

We would use real-number types when we want to store and manipulate fractional numbers. However, we must remember that real numbers are typically an approximation of an exact value. Just as the value $\frac{1}{3}$ cannot be represented exactly as a decimal number (0.33333 . . .), so many real numbers cannot be represented exactly in a computer. This can cause problems when making decisions based upon the value of a real number. We will not go into those pitfalls here, but you can read about some of them in the optional section 'Programming traps for the unwary' at the end of this chapter following the exercises. To declare a variable to store real numbers we use the `real` type:

real: angle ;

We can then assign it a value:

angle ← 66.5 ;

A typical programming language would use 32 bits to store real numbers. Sometimes, the need arises for really big values, so a 64-bit type is commonly offered

---

[5] 3.14159 is an approximation of the value of pi; 1.99 is the price of an all-you-can-eat breakfast; 98.6 is the normal temperature of the human body in degrees Fahrenheit (37°C); prior to 1956, 0.000011574 was the length of a mean solar second expressed as a proportion of the length of a mean solar day; 1609.34 is the number of meters in a mile.

[6] iTunes served its 1,000,000,000th song download in February, 2006!

too. In *HTTLAP* we call this larger type **doublereal**. Table 9.4 shows the size, range of values, and number of significant digits available to numbers of both types. For most applications we will find the standard **real** type sufficient for storing real numbers.

Table 9.4 **Sizes of *HTTLAP* Real Number Types**

Type	Size	Range of Values	Significant Digits
real	32-bit	$\pm\, 1.40239846E - 45 \ldots \pm 3.40282347E + 38$	7–8
doublereal	64-bit	$\pm\, 4.94065645841246544E - 324 \ldots$ $1.79769313486231570E + 308$	15–16

Characters and Strings

Whilst we can do much with numeric values, we often need to store other kinds of data, particularly textual data (such as the name of a bank account holder). If you have ever typed an email, sent a text message on a mobile phone, or written an essay using a word processor then you have already manipulated our next data type: the *character*.

Characters

You type an email or enter a text message into a mobile phone by keying in one at a time the individual characters that make up the words and punctuation of the message. The characters available are defined in a *character set*. A character set is an ordered collection of the different letters, symbols, punctuation marks, and digits that can be used to store, manipulate, and display textual data. The letters of the alphabet are all characters, as are the digits '0' to '9', punctuation marks, and symbols such as '\$', '#', '+', etc. A way to picture a character is to think of a tile with the character written on its face (just like you have in the game Scrabble). Figure 9.4 shows seven characters represented as tiles. There are a few important features of characters shown in Figure 9.4. First of all, notice that the characters 'A' and 'a' are different. They're both the same letter, but the first one is the upper-case (capital) form and the second one is the lower-case (small) form.[7] This is an important distinction as each character is unique. Just because we understand there to be a particular relationship between 'A' and 'a', between 'D' and 'd' between 'Z' and 'z', etc. does not mean that the computer has the same understanding. As far as the computer is concerned *all* the characters are just pictures on tiles, pictures to which it ascribes no intrinsic meaning. In addition to the letters of the alphabet are digit characters, punctuation marks and other symbols, and even characters from other alphabets.[8]

---

[7] Historical note: the terms upper and lower case refer to the trays of lead type used by printers in the days when typesetting was done by hand. There were two trays, or *cases*, of type arranged one above the other. The upper case contained all the capital letters and the lower case contained the normal letters. Hence upper case and lower case.

[8] In this example you can see the characters א (aleph – the first letter of the Hebrew alphabet) and Ω (omega – the upper case form of the last letter of the Greek alphabet).

FIGURE 9.4   **Examples of character tiles**

You probably wondered what the numbers in the corners of the tiles in Figure 9.4 mean. I said above that a character set is an *ordered* collection of characters. This means that the characters are arranged in sets in a specific order. Think of a character set as a big alphabet. The English alphabet has 26 letters arranged in the order 'A', 'B', 'C' . . . 'Z'. A character set employs the same idea, and assigns each character a unique ordinal number (character code) to identify it which also shows that character's position in the set. The numbers on the tiles in Figure 9.4 are the character codes for two common character sets in use today. The number in the bottom right corner of the tile is the character code in the ASCII character set whilst the top-left number is the code in the Unicode character set.[9] The ASCII codes are given in decimal notation whilst I have put the Unicode numbers in hexadecimal format because Unicode values can go up to 65,535 (FFFF in hexadecimal).

ASCII is a fairly old standard that uses 7-bit (normal) and 8-bit (extended) codes to give 128 and 256 unique character codes for the normal and extended character sets respectively. Each ASCII code represents a unique character. The normal 7-bit code set is used to represent all the English upper- and lower-case letters, the digits '0' to '9', some punctuation marks, and some other special symbols. The extended (8-bit) character set offers a further 128 characters (such as accented letters, letters from some other languages, and some graphic symbols). Table 9.5 shows the characters usually found in the normal and extended ASCII character sets. The unique number for each character (its ASCII code) is found by adding the character's row and column number. For example, the character 'A' is in column 1, row number 64, so its ASCII code is 65. The space character (what you get when you hit the spacebar on a computer keyboard) has ASCII code 32 (row 32 + column 0).

From Table 9.5 you can see that the capital letters 'A' to 'Z' have the ASCII codes 65 through to 90 inclusive. The lower-case letters 'a' to 'z' have the codes 97 to 122. The digits '0' through '9' run from codes 48 to 57.

---

[9] ASCII is pronounced 'askey' and stands for American Standard Code for Information Interchange. The standard ASCII set has 128 character positions.

Table 9.5 **The ASCII Character Sets**

	0	1	2	3	4	5	6	7	8	9	10	11	12	13	14	15
0	NUL	☺	☻	♥	♦	♣	♠	•	◘	TAB	LF	0	♀	♪	♫	☼
16	►	◄	↕	‼	¶	§	▬	↕	↑	↓	→	←	∟	↔	-	▼
32		!	"	#	$	%	&	'	(	)	*	+	,	-	.	/
48	0	1	2	3	4	5	6	7	8	9	:	;	<	=	>	?
64	@	A	B	C	D	E	F	G	H	I	J	K	L	M	N	O
80	P	Q	R	S	T	U	V	W	X	Y	Z	[	\	]	^	_
96	`	a	b	c	d	e	f	g	h	i	j	k	l	m	n	o
112	p	q	r	s	t	u	v	w	x	y	z	{	|	}	~	⌂
128	Ç	ü	é	â	ä	à	å	ç	ê	ë	è	ï	î	ì	Ä	Å
144	É	æ	Æ	ô	ö	ò	û	ù	ÿ	Ö	Ü	ø	£	Ø	×	ƒ
160	á	í	ó	ú	ñ	Ñ	ª	º	¿	©	¬	½	¼	¡	«	»
176	░	▒	▓	│	┤	Á	Â	À	©	╣	║	╗	╝	¢	¥	┐
192	└	┴	┬	├	─	┼	ã	Ã	╚	╔	╩	╦	╠	═	╬	¤
208	ð	Ð	Ê	Ë	È	ı	Í	Î	Ï	┘	┌	█	▄	¦	Ì	▀
224	Ó	ß	Ô	Ò	õ	Õ	µ	þ	Þ	Ú	Û	Ù	ý	Ý	¯	´
240	-	±	‗	¾	¶	§	÷	¸	°	¨	·	¹	³	²	■	

Write down the ASCII codes for the following characters

Character	ASCII code	Character	ASCII code
B		TAB	
V		{	
3		Z	
?		z	

The ordering of character sets is important as it allows standard numeric and alphabetic ordering to be preserved. That is, just as B comes before C in the alphabet (and the telephone book), so character 'B' comes before character 'C' in the ASCII character set. As we shall see later on when we look at *operators* this ordering makes the programmer's life easier as it is then relatively straightforward to sort lists of names and do other tasks that rely on ordered relationships.

Unicode is a character standard developed by the Unicode Consortium. The ASCII set is limited to 256 characters because only one byte is used to store the character codes. Because the Unicode standard uses two bytes 65,536 individual characters can be represented (which is nearly sufficient to store all the world's written languages in one character set). Values from 0 to 65,535 can be written in four hexadecimal digits (0000 to FFFF) and so this is why Unicode character codes are typically written in hexadecimal rather than decimal.

We declare a character variable like this:

character: ⬚button⬚ ;

And we can assign it a value like this:

⬚button⬚ ← 'Y' ;

Notice that the character literal in the assignment statement is enclosed by single quotes; this is because without the quotation marks, Y would be treated as an identifier (you could have a variable called Y).

> Write *HTTLAP* pseudo-code definitions for two character variables **firstInitial** and **secondInitial**. Then write two *HTTLAP* assignment statements to assign the initial letters of your first and last names to the two variables.

Because characters and their code numbers are so intimately related, most programming languages provide commands to manipulate characters either by their literal values or their ordinal values. It is common for a programming language to have a command such as Ord () which gives the ordinal (ASCII) value of the character given inside the parentheses and a function Chr () which gives the character corresponding to the ordinal value inside the parentheses. Assuming the presence of Ord and Chr in the *HTTLAP* pseudo-code we could assign the letter 'A' to a character variable myLetter directly like this:

⬚myLetter⬚ ←'A' ;

or indirectly like this

⬚myLetter⬚ ← Chr (65) ; **// 65 is the ASCII code for 'A'**

Likewise, we could assign the ASCII code of a character to an integer like this:

⬚charNumber⬚ ← Ord ('A') ;

> What does the following statement assign to **myLetter**?
>
> ⬚myLetter⬚ ← Chr (Ord ('B')) ;

Strings

Remember, a character variable can only store a single character, so an assignment such as button ← 'Yes' ; is incorrect as it attempts to assign three characters to the character variable button. How can we deal with whole words and phrases rather than just individual characters? We are used to thinking in terms of words and sentences rather than individual letters, but to a computer a word is simply a collection of letters. The last word of the previous sentence is a *string* of seven characters: 'l', 'e', 't', 't', 'e', 'r', and 's'. Figure 9.5 shows a string of eight characters.

In Figure 9.5 the string has been visualized by showing the eight character tiles threaded onto a piece of string. This allows programmers to manipulate many

FIGURE 9.5   **A string of characters**

characters as if they were a single entity, just as a piece of physical string would hold tiles together in the real world. If a string of characters is a strange concept to you think of a pearl necklace (also commonly called a "string of pearls"). A pearl necklace is treated as a single object: the necklace is picked up, put down, worn around the neck, and so on. But when you pick up the necklace you are also picking up all of the individual pearls. The string not only makes it easier to move the characters around (as, indeed, would a paper BAG, but that is another story) but also allows an ordering to be enforced. That is, the string of characters in Figure 9.5 will always read 'A string' until the tiles are removed and rethreaded in a different order.

We said that strings are ordered collections of characters. Assume that each character's position in a string is given by an integer, where the first character occupies position 0 and the last character occupies position n − 1 where n is the length of the string. Write down what characters occupy positions 0, 1, and 7 in the string shown in Figure 9.5.

What is the position of the last character in the string in Figure 9.5?

In Figure 9.5 the space follows the 'A' in the string. Does the space character come before or after the 'A' in the ASCII character set?

We can declare a `string` variable like this:

    string: name ;

And we could assign it a value like this:

    name ← 'John Doe' ;

Using the *HTTLAP* pseudo-code declare two `string` variables `firstName` and `lastName`. Then write two assignment statements to assign your first name to `firstName` and your family name to `lastName`.

Given the declarations:

    character: firstInitial ;
    string: firstName,
            lastName ; // n.b. two variables of the same type can be
                       // declared with a single type name and then a
                       // list of variables separated by commas.

And the assignments:

    firstInitial ← 'H' ;

```
firstName ← 'Henry' ;
lastName ← 'Higgins' ;
```

What do you think *should* be the value of `firstName` after the following statement?

```
firstName ← firstInitial ;
```

What do you think should be the result of the following statement?

```
firstInitial ← lastName ;
```

The answers to the above two questions very much depend on how strongly typing is treated. If *HTTLAP* represented the class of very-strongly-typed languages, then as `firstName` and `firstInitial` are of different types the assignment statement

```
firstName ← firstInitial ;
```

would strictly not be allowed. However, many programming languages allow cross-type assignments when the operation results in something that is compatible with the type of the variable on the left hand side of the assignment operator. In this case as `firstName` is a string and a string is an ordered collection of characters, we might take the view that the assignment of a character variable to `firstName` should be allowed. After all, we could take the view that a character is simply a one-character string. `firstName` would therefore have the value `'H'` after the assignment. (This is taking the view that a character is simply a string of size 1.) The second assignment statement

```
firstInitial ← lastName ;
```

is more problematic as the character variable `firstInitial` is not large enough to store the contents of the string variable `lastName` and so the assignment would not be allowed. There are two choices here for the programming language designer. Either all such operations could be forbidden resulting in an error (which would also forbid any attempt to assign the value of a one-character string variable to a character variable) or some interpretation could take place and the string could be truncated to a single character (the first one, say) which is then assigned to the character variable. If this approach were adopted then `firstInitial` would have the value `'H'` after the above assignment. This approach would allow tricks like the following:

```
firstName ← 'Henry' ;
lastName ← 'Higgins' ;
firstInitial ← firstName ;
lastInitial ← lastName ;
```

which results in `firstInitial` having the value `'H'` and `lastInitial` having the value `'H'`. However, it could be argued that this is a very dangerous thing to allow because if the programmer is under the false apprehension that `firstInitial` and `lastInitial` have been declared as strings, the results of the above assignments would be confusing! It would be better, perhaps, to forbid such assignments and insist the programmer writes something like the following to get correct assignments to `firstInitial` and `lastInitial`:

```
firstInitial ← firstName [0];
lastInitial ← lastName [0];
```

which would assign the first characters of the strings `firstName` and `lastName` to `firstInitial` and `lastInitial` respectively.

Huh?

I don't understand what the numbers in square brackets mean in the above example.

That's because I have borrowed some notation from Chapter 12 which deals with a type of data structure called the array. Simply put, the square brackets denote a positional value. A string is an ordered collection, so [0] refers to the first character of a given string, [1] to the second character, and so on. This concept will be dealt with more thoroughly in Chapter 12. What is important to understand here is that when you mix variables of different types in assignment statements you need to know what rules your chosen programming language uses to deal with converting data of one type to another. *HTTLAP* pseudo-code is not a real programming language, so the above section deals hypothetically with a few possible interpretations. Chapter 15 shows how the pseudo-code can be translated into the real programming language *Processing* and then run.

Advantages of Data Typing

At first sight it may seem that enforcing strict typing rules just makes life awkward. However, types offer a number of advantages. The automatic identification of type violations by the computer can prevent many serious defects from getting into finished programs (just like the filler cap on the fuel tanks of cars with catalytic converters prevents the wrong type of fuel being put in and ruining the engine). Also, as we shall see when we explore the concepts of sub-programming in Chapter 10, knowing the types of values passed to and from functions, procedures, and object methods makes it harder to make further serious mistakes. Some languages are very strict about mixing data types in expressions whilst others are more tolerant. If the specially shaped filler cap is an analogy of strong typing, then a milk bottle is an analogy of weaker typing: the milk bottle is a container designed for holding milk but it could equally be used to hold water. Very strict typing rules would not allow anything but milk to be put into the bottle. A strongly typed environment may allow other compatible types to be put into the bottle (such as cream, water, or other liquids). In an environment where typing does not exist or is not enforced you could put anything you want into the milk bottle, even sand, marbles, or jelly beans.

Given:

```
real:number ;
string:word ;
number ← 3.14159 ;
```

What value should the following statement place in **word** if there were no type rules?

```
word ← number ÷ 2.5 ;
```

And given
$\boxed{\text{word}} \leftarrow$ 'one thousand' ;
What value should the following statement place in **number** if there were no type rules?

$\boxed{\text{number}} \leftarrow \boxed{\text{word}} + 1$;

For the first question we can calculate $3.14159 \div 2.5$ easily enough (it's 1.256636), but what should go into word? Should it be a string representation of the value, i.e., '1.256636'? Should it be a string made up of ASCII characters 1, 2, 5, 6, 6, 3, and 6 ('☺●♣♠♠♥♠') or something else? What about the second question? What does word + 1 mean when word is 'one thousand'? Should we know that the string means 1000 and so add 1 to it and store 1001.0 in number? Or should it make the new string "one thousand1"? If so, how can the string be stored in the real-type variable number? I hope that these silly examples serve to show the importance of understanding the typing rules of programming languages. Of course, in most languages, statements of the form

$\boxed{\text{number}} \leftarrow \boxed{\text{word}} + 1$;

would be rejected by the compiler before the program even runs, but even when you do not break the typing rules, it is possible to get yourself into trouble through not paying close attention when mixing variables of different but compatible types in one statement.

Data Type boolean

We have looked at types that allow us to store and manipulate numbers, characters, and strings of characters. The above types would cater for all the information on the bank statement in Figure 6.1. But look back now at Table 5.1. Whilst the various integer types could be used for the variables coffeesRequired, sugarsRequired, coffeesPoured, and sugarsAdded, what type should the variable milkRequired be? The possible values that milkRequired can take are 'Yes' and 'No'. We could make it a string variable, or even an integer with zero representing 'No' and one representing 'Yes' but there is another way, and it involves the use of *Boolean* values.

George Boole (1815–64) devised his Boolean algebra in which elements can have one of two possible values – True and False. Operations on the elements are logical (AND, OR, NOT, etc.) rather than arithmetic ($+$, $-$, $\div$, $\times$, etc.). Boolean logic underpins mathematical set theory and much of computer science and programming. Just as integer and real variables store numbers and the results of numeric calculations, so Boolean variables store the values True and False and the results of questions that give true/false (yes/no) type answers. In the coffee making problem, when asking a guest whether milk is required, the answer will be 'yes' or 'no'. Putting it another way we can say the statement 'milk is required' will be either True or it will be False. We can use a Boolean variable milkRequired to represent the statement 'milk is required'. Its value will then be set to True or False depending on our guest's wishes. Here is how to declare a Boolean variable:

boolean: $\boxed{\text{paysTax}}$;

And here is an assignment to the variable paysTax:

$\boxed{\text{paysTax}}$ ← true ;

There is more to be said about Boolean data, but we will deal with this later on in this chapter when we consider the relational and logical operators.

Constant and Variable Data

As well as having a specific type the data in our programs also belongs to one of two basic categories: constant or variable. We have already looked at variable data and have seen how variables can be used to store the values necessary to carry out the aims of the program. Whilst we could use variables to store all the data in a program, often we make reference to values that will not change. For example, a program that does many geometrical calculations will likely need to make use of π (pi) whose value is approximately 3.141592653589793.[10] Like the speed of light, the value of π is a fixed universal constant that does not change.[11] We could use π in a program by declaring a variable:

real: $\boxed{\text{pi}}$;

And assigning it a value:

$\boxed{\text{pi}}$ ← 3.14159 ;

However, having done this there is nothing to stop me writing a statement such as:

$\boxed{\text{pi}}$ ← $\boxed{\text{pi}}$ + 2 ;

Clearly this is not a desirable state of affairs as it changes the value of π within the program. What is needed is a means of declaring constant or unchanging data. Such data items are, not surprisingly, known as *constants*. When constants are declared they are given a value and that value cannot be changed by any part of the program. Attempting to change the value of a constant will typically result in an error message (usually from the compiler which will not permit such code). In our pseudo-code we will declare constants like this:

real: $\boxed{\boxed{\text{pi}}}$ IS 3.14159 ;

The box denotes pi as an identifier that holds a value, but the double border means that it is constant data which cannot be changed by any part of the program. The type denotes what kind of data the constant refers to and the value after the keyword 'IS' denotes the value for which the constant stands. You should read this declaration thus: "pi is a real-type constant that stands for the value 3.14159". The pseudo-code uses the word IS rather than the assignment

---

[10] Just in case you had forgotton, π is the ratio of the circumference of a circle to its diameter. π is also known as *Archimedes constant*. Its name comes from the first letter of the Greek word περιφέρεια which means "periphery".

[11] Unless something weird goes on in black holes or parallel universes, that is. Also, I am aware that some physicists have theorized that the speed of light has not been constant across time, but that is *way* beyond the scope of this book! Also worthy of note is that light can be slowed to a crawl in laboratory conditions. Spooky.

operator ← to reinforce the fact that constant data cannot be assigned values the way variables can. Their value is fixed at their declaration and cannot be changed (that is, they are *immutable*).[12]

Constants can then be used in program statements thus:

> circumference ← pi × diameter ;

The pseudo-code statement above is an instruction to multiply the value of the variable diameter by the value of the constant pi and to assign the result to the variable circumference.

Declare a constant monthsInYear to hold the value 12.

9.2 Operators

Look at an assignment statement in its simplest form:

> diameter ← 3 ;

The above statement assigns the integer literal 3 to the variable diameter. We have seen more complex assignments such as the one above that multiplies the diameter by pi and assigns the result to the circumference variable. That was an example of an *operation*. An operation uses one or more values to perform a task. The task to be performed is defined by the *operator*. The values used by the operator are called the *operands*. Let us have a look at that circumference calculation again. Figure 9.6 shows the arithmetic broken down into its operator and operands. The multiplication is performed by the multiplication operator. Multiplication needs two values, so this operator takes two operands. For this reason it is called a *binary operator*.

Operators and ▶
operands

FIGURE 9.6   **Operators and operands**

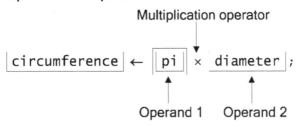

Arithmetic Operators

Table 9.6 gives the set of arithmetic operators available in our pseudo-code. Most arithmetic operators are binary, though + and − can be unary as well (they can take a single operand).

---

[12] In computer science an immutable object is one whose internal state (or value) may not be changed after it has been created. Constants are, therefore, immutable whilst variables are mutable.

Table 9.6   **The Arithmetic Operators in the *HTTLAP* Pseudo-code**

Operator	Meaning	Usage	Result	Binary/unary
∧	Exponentiation	9∧3	729	Binary
×	Multiplication	2 × 3	6	Binary
÷	Division	9 ÷ 3	3	Binary
MOD	Modulus: divides two integer expressions and gives the remainder	11 MOD 3	2	Binary
+	Addition	2 + 3	5	Binary
−	Subtraction	3 − 2	1	Binary
+	Positive: makes the value of its operand positive	+3	+3	Unary
−	Negation: negates the value of its operand	−3	−3	Unary

The exponentiation operator is used to raise one amount to the power of another. For example, 9 cubed is 9^3, that is $9 \times 9 \times 9$ which is 729. So, the pseudo-code 9∧3 means raise 9 to the power of 3. 10∧4 gives 10,000 (that is, 10^4).

Huh?

What do you mean "they can take a single operand"?

Say we had an integer variable **b** whose value was 6. We could write the following assignment statement

$\boxed{a} \leftarrow -\boxed{b}$;

in which the value of **b** is negated by the unary form of the "−" operator and the result stored in **a**. So **a** now has the value −6 and **b** remains unchanged. Similarly,

$\boxed{c} \leftarrow +\boxed{a}$;

would assign the value 6 to **c**, as the "+" operator can also be unary.

Notice that there are two division operators: ÷ and MOD. The ÷ operator works on both integer and real types. If its operands are both integral expressions (whole numbers) then the result will be an integer. If one or both operands are real expressions then the result will be real. This feature trips many an unwary novice so I refer you to the discussion on problems with type conversions in the optional 'Programming traps for the unwary' section at the end of this chapter after the exercises.

MOD gives ▶
the remainder

The MOD operator can be confusing at first. It will only work with integer operands as it gives back the remainder after dividing its two operands. So, 11 ÷ 3 gives a result of 3 (3 goes into 11 three times) whilst 11 MOD 3 gives a result of 2 (3 goes into 11 three times with a remainder of 2).

Operator Precedence

The arithmetic operators can be combined to allow us to write arithmetic expressions such as:

result ← 3 + 4 × 6 ;

> What is the value of **result** after the above statement has been executed?

If you did the calculation from left to right, that is adding the 3 to the 4 to give 7 and then multiplying by the 6, then you would get a result of 42. If you did the multiplication first the answer would be 4 multiplied by 6 which gives 24 to which the 3 is added giving 27. So, there are two ways this expression can be evaluated. How, then, should it be interpreted? If the above statement were translated into any of the popular programming languages then **result** would have the value 27 and not 42. To remove the ambiguity surrounding evaluation order, the operators are assigned a priority, or precedence, level. Precedence rules govern the order of evaluation for the various terms in expressions. Higher-precedence operators are evaluated before those of lower precedence and operators of equal precedence are evaluated left to right. The order of evaluation is:

- Expressions in parentheses are evaluated first;
- exponentiation, then
- any unary operators are evaluated next followed by
- multiplication, division, and modulus;
- addition and subtraction is then evaluated;
- finally, any relational operators (see Table 6.2 in Chapter 6) are evaluated.

A complete list of precedence levels for all the operators available in our *HTTLAP* pseudo-code is given in Table 9.7.[13]

Table 9.7 **Operator Precedence Levels for *HTTLAP* Pseudo-code**

Precedence Level	Operators	Description
1	( )	Parentheses
2	∧	Exponentiation
3	NOT, unary +, unary −	Logical NOT, unary positive, unary negation
4	×, ÷, MOD, AND	Multiplication, division, modulus, logical AND
5	+, −, OR	Addition, subtraction, logical OR
6	=, ≠, <, ≤, >, ≥	Relational operators (equals, not equals, less than, less-than-or-equal-to, greater than, greater-than-or-equal-to)

[13] Please note that although this precedence order is based upon those used by many programming languages you should check your chosen language's reference manual for its actual operator precedence rules before typing in any programs.

To force an expression with addition or subtraction to be evaluated before any multiplication or division we can surround the expression with parentheses. So, the two statements:

$$\boxed{\text{result}} \leftarrow 5 \times 3 + 6 \ ;$$
$$\boxed{\text{result}} \leftarrow 5 \times (3 + 6) \ ;$$

would yield 21 and 45 respectively. In the first statement the 5 is multiplied by the 3 giving 15 which is then added to the 6 to give 21. In the second statement the term in parentheses is evaluated first, giving 9 which is then multiplied by the 5 to give a result of 45.

For the following expressions write down what value is placed into the variable `result`.

1.   result ← 2 × 3 + 4 ;
2.   result ← 2 × (3 + 4) ;
3.   result ← 2 × 3 − 8 ÷ 2 ;
4.   result ← 2 × (3 − 8) ÷ 2 ;
5.   result ← (12 + 8) ÷ 5 × 2 ;
6.   result ← (12 + 8) ÷ (5 × 2) ;
7.   result ← −9 ∧ 2 ;

Think Spot

How did you get on? If you went through the seven questions very quickly then it is possible you made a mistake so go back and check through your answers once more. It is mistakes at this level that contribute to the number of bugs in faulty programs. Misinterpreting the evaluation order of expressions is a common mistake and leads to some hard-to-spot bugs. Table 9.8 gives the answers. Lots of practice is the best cure for uncertainty about how to write and evaluate compound expressions. Therefore, you will find more problems of this kind in the exercises at the end of this chapter.

Table 9.8   Answers to Operator Precedence Quiz

No.	result	Explanation
1.	**10**	Multiplication is done before the addition, so we have 2 multiplied by 3 giving 6 which is added to the 4 to give 10.
2.	**14**	The term in parentheses is evaluated before the multiplication, so we have 3 added to 4 giving 7 which is then multiplied by the 2 to give 14.
3.	**2**	We have a mixture of operators here. The multiplication and division have a higher precedence than the subtraction, so the subtraction will be done last. As multiplication and division have the same precedence level they will be evaluated in order from left to right. We will get 2 multiplied by 3 giving 6, then the 8 is divided by the 2 to give 4. The subtraction is then performed on 6 − 4 which gives the final answer of 2.
4.	**−5**	The problem has the same operators and operands as the last one but this time the subtraction operation has been put inside parentheses meaning it will be

evaluated first. So, the subtraction is now 3−8 which gives −5. Now the multiplication is performed. The first operand is 2 and the second is now −5, so the result of this operation is −10. Finally the division is done using the operands −10 and 2 giving the final result of −5.

5.   **8**   Again we have an expression in parentheses which is evaluated first giving 20. The remaining operators have the same precedence level so they are evaluated left-to-right, so next we perform 20 ÷ 5 giving 4. The 4 is now multiplied by the 2 giving a result of 8.

6.   **2**   Here we have two expressions in parentheses so they are evaluated first in order left-to-right. The first expression gives 20 as in the previous example. The second parenthetical expression multiplies 5 by 2 giving 10. Finally the division is performed on the 20 and the 10 giving a result of 2.

7.   **−81**   A nasty one this. The way the expression is laid out makes it look like we are raising −9 to the power of 2 (i.e. squaring −9). As we know, multiplying a negative by a negative gives a positive, so −9 × −9 would give 81. So why the answer −81? Because exponentiation has a higher precedence than the unary minus operator (see Table 9.8). This means that the $\wedge$ is applied first, giving 9$\wedge$2 which equals 81. Then the unary minus is applied to give −81. If you wanted the square of −9 you would have to write `result` ← `(−9)` $\wedge$ `2`. Fun eh?

Using Relational Operators with Boolean Variables

In addition to the arithmetic operators Table 9.7 showed the precedence level of the relational operators which were introduced in Chapter 6 (see Table 6.2). Recall that the relational operators are used to make comparisons. We made use of relational operators to replace conditions that were written in longhand. For example, we took the following condition:

```
WHILE ((payload + parcelWeight less than or equal to capacity)
       AND (conveyor NOT empty))
```

and used a relational operator to give:

```
WHILE ((payload + parcelWeight ≤ capacity) AND (conveyor NOT
       empty))
```

Where the arithmetic operators yield arithmetic results, the relational operators give Boolean results. That is because they are used to test whether a certain condition is True or False. We could read the WHILE statement above as "While it is true that the payload added to the parcel weight is less than or equal to the capacity and it is true that the conveyor belt is not empty then . . ."

Notice that relational expressions return a value of either True or False. That means that the results of relational expressions can be assigned to Boolean variables which can hold True and False values. Why would you want to do this? Consider a case where the result of some condition needs to be used several times in a program. Rather than writing the code each time the condition needs to be tested, its result could be stored in a Boolean variable which is then used instead. For example, there may be several occasions that a program needs to know whether a person is an adult or not. If we define legal adulthood as being at least 18 years of age, then an adult is someone whose age is greater than or equal to 18 years. We could declare a Boolean variable isAdult and assign it as in Solution 9.1.

Solution 9.1 Assigning a value to isAdult

```
1.  boolean: isAdult ;
2.  IF (age ≥ 18)
        2.1. isAdult ← true ;
    ENDIF
```

Think Spot   There is something not quite right about the above statement. What happens to isAdult if age is less than 18? At the moment there is no way to make isAdult False. Solution 9.2 shows a corrected version:

Solution 9.2 Another attempt at assigning isAdult

```
1.  boolean: isAdult ;
2.  IF (age ≥ 18)
        2.1. isAdult ← true ;
    ELSE
        2.1. isAdult ← false ;
    ENDIF
```

Or even:

Solution 9.3 Yet another go!

```
1.  boolean: isAdult ;
2.  isAdult ← false ;
3.  IF (age ≥ 18)
        3.1. isAdult ← true ;
    ENDIF
```

Actually, Solution 9.2 and Solution 9.3 are long-winded ways of writing the test given in Solution 9.4.

Solution 9.4 The concise and preferred way to assign isAdult

```
isAdult ← (age ≥ 18) ;
```

Think Spot   Examine Solution 9.4 and see if you can understand how it works. Why is it better than the other solutions? Think about how the assignment operator ← works. In an assignment statement the value of the expression on the right of the ← is assigned to the variable on the left. In an integer assignment such as

```
sum ← 3 + 4 ;
```

the expression on the right, 3 + 4, evaluates to the integer result 7 which is then assigned to the variable sum. Because sum is an integer type, the assigned expression is also an integer. The same principle holds when assigning values to Boolean variables. If the result of an integer expression can be assigned to an integer variable, so the result of a Boolean (or conditional) expression can be assigned to a Boolean variable. We can write simple assignments like:

~~isAdult~~ ← true ;

which is analogous to the integer assignment statement

sum ← 3 ;

But we know that integer assignment statements can have expressions with multiple terms in them (sum ← 3 + 4), and the same is true for Boolean assignments. The statement

~~isAdult~~ ← ~~age~~ ≥ 18 ;

can be read just like any other assignment statement. The value of the expression on the right is assigned to the variable on the left. The expression on the right is a relational expression that yields a Boolean result; age will either be greater-than-or-equal to 18 or it will not. The expression thus evaluates to either a Boolean True or False depending on the value of age. This True/False value is then assigned to the variable on the left, isAdult. We can see that when age is 18 or more the expression will have a True value and so isAdult will hold True. When age is less than 18 the expression evaluates to False and so isAdult will be assigned the Boolean value False. This method of assigning Boolean variables ensures that they are always assigned a result. In the earlier solutions we might have forgotten to initialize isAdult to False, or to include the ELSE path, which means that isAdult could have the wrong value, or even remain undefined following its declaration.

Nope, I still don't get how ~~isAdult~~ ← ~~age~~ ≥ 18 ; works. It doesn't make sense!

Consider how the assignment operator works. In its abstract form an assignment statement looks like this:

~~variable~~ ← expression ;

The left hand side of the statement contains a variable identifier to which a value is to be assigned. What value? The value comes from the expression on the right hand side. The expression can be a simple literal value, another identifier (variable or constant) of a compatible type, or a compound expression. Here is an example of each where a value is being assigned to an integer variable number.

```
number ← 3 ;       // A numeric literal is assigned to number
number ← age ;     // The value of integer variable age is assigned
                   // to number
number ← 2 × age ; // Value of compound expression is assigned
                   // to number
```

In all three cases the thing on the left (**number**) takes the value of the expression on the right (3, whatever the value of age is, and twice the value of **age** respectively). What remains the same in all three cases is that the integer variable **number** is being assigned a single integer value which is the result of *evaluating* the expression on the right hand side of the assignment operator ←.

Conceptually, Boolean assignment is exactly the same, only this time the statement is of the form:

`booleanIdentifier` ← `BooleanExpression` ;

Because a Boolean variable can only be assigned a Boolean value (True or False) the expression on the right has to give a Boolean result. Here are three examples of Boolean assignments using a literal, another identifier, and a compound expression:

```
isAdult ← true ; // A Boolean literal is assigned to isAdult
isAdult ← boolValue ; // Value of Boolean variable boolValue is
                      // assigned to isAdult
isAdult ← age ≥ 18 ; // Value of expression is assigned to
                     // isAdult
```

9.3 Selections with Boolean Variables

We have seen the relational operators in selection statements (IF, IF. . .ELSE) to test the values of numeric variables. Sometimes we need to test the values of Boolean variables. Consider the sub-problem from the coffee making problem of whether to add milk to a cup of coffee:

```
IF (milk required)
    Add milk ;
ENDIF
```

What sort of test is 'milk required'? It is not a relational expression in the sense of comparing one numeric value against another. If we write it out in full with a relational operator we would get:

```
IF (milk required = true)
    Add milk ;
ENDIF
```

So, it is a simple test of a value being True or False. This suggests that the condition 'milk required' could be represented by a Boolean variable milkRequired. This variable could be set to True or False depending on the guest's preference and its value can then be tested in the selection. In fact, if you turn back for a moment to Table 5.1 in which we listed the variables needed for the coffee making solution you will notice that the variable milkRequired was specified as taking two possible values: 'Yes' or 'No'. As we saw above we can use Boolean variables to store yes-and-no, true-and-false-type values. We need to declare the variable thus:

boolean: `milkRequired` ;

Then we can assign it a value according to the guest's preference:

`milkRequired` ← guest answered 'Yes' ;

The selection would then be:

```
IF milkRequired
    Add milk ;
ENDIF
```

Note, saying 'IF ($\boxed{\text{milkRequired}}$)' is functionally equivalent to writing 'IF ($\boxed{\text{milkRequired}}$ = true)' and is the preferred way of testing Boolean variables for being true.

> Without using either the equality operator (=) or the inequality operator (≠), rewrite the above **IF** statement to add lemon juice when **milkRequired** is False. (Do not worry about adding milk when it is True – I do not want you to write an **IF . . . ELSE** statement here.)

Using Booleans in Flag-controlled Iterations

In Chapter 6 we saw a few applications of WHILE loops. Now that we have the Boolean data type in our toolbox we can look at another way of controlling iterations. A common loop technique is to use a Boolean variable as a sentinel. Such Boolean sentinels are known as *flags*. Why flag? Flags are raised and lowered on flagpoles. A raised royal standard flying on the flagpole at Buckingham Palace tells Londoners that the monarch is in residence. Thus, a raised flag is like Boolean True whilst a lowered flag is like Boolean False. A flag, then, is a Boolean sentinel whose value determines whether the loop is to continue. Solution 9.5 below shows a flag-controlled DO. . .WHILE loop.

Solution 9.5 A flag-controlled loop

```
1.    integer: number,
2.              square ;
3.    character: response ;
4.    boolean: finished ;
5.    DO
         5.1.   Display 'Enter a number :' ;
         5.2.   Get value of number ;
         5.3.   square ← number × number ;
         5.4.   Display 'Your number squared is ' ;
         5.5.   Display square ;
         5.6.   Display 'Do you want another go? Y/N' ;
         5.7.   Get value of response ;
         5.8.   finished ←(response = 'N') OR (response = 'n') ;
      WHILE (NOT finished);
```

The flag in Solution 9.5 is the Boolean variable **finished**. Read through the algorithm and work out what it does. Statements #1 to #4 are declarations for the variables. Statement #5 is the start of the DO. . .WHILE loop that forms the body of this program. Inside the loop the user is asked to enter a value (statement #5.1) which is stored in the variable **number** (statement #5.2). In #5.3 the number is multiplied by itself and the result stored in **square**. Statement #5.4 displays some explanatory text and is followed by action #5.5 which displays the value of **square**. Actions #5.6 and #5.7 ask the user to say whether or not they want another go and to enter a 'Y' or 'N' character to indicate their response. This character is stored in the variable **response**. It is in statement #5.8 that the flag variable **finished** is set. Recall how Boolean assignment statements work: the value of the expression on the right hand side of the assignment operator ← is assigned to the variable on the left. In this case the expression on the right hand side is a conditional one that yields a result of True if `response` is either 'N' or 'n'. If `response` is neither 'N' nor 'n' then it yields a value of False. This True/False value is thus stored in `finished`. The flag `finished` is then used in the WHILE clause of the loop after statement 5.8. Remember, writing:

```
WHILE NOT finished
```

is equivalent to writing

```
WHILE finished = false ;
```

Using flags can make loop conditions more natural to read. In the above example we know the user has chosen to finish when the response is either an 'N' or an 'n'. We call the condition when an 'N' or an 'n' is entered `finished`. The loop will continue to iterate as long as the flag is not raised (another metaphor). As soon as it is raised (that is, it becomes true) the loop terminates.

Let's look at another example, this time using a WHILE loop. Recall the van loading problem from Chapter 5. The following code is the inner WHILE loop taken from Solution 5.17 and rewritten using the relational operator '≤':

```
5.2   WHILE (payload + parcelWeight ≤ capacity) AND (conveyor NOT
            empty)
         5.2.1 Load parcel on van ;
         5.2.2 payload ← payload + parcelWeight ;
         5.2.3 Get next parcelWeight ;
      ENDWHILE
```

Try rewriting the above loop but this time using a flag variable to control the iteration. If you have trouble, look back at the previous example with the DO. . .WHILE to see how the flag was used there. For this problem you will need to declare a Boolean variable to use as the flag. Consider where the flag needs to be set.

Solution 9.6 shows my answer to this problem.

Solution 9.6 Flag-controlled van-loading loop

```
1.   boolean: roomOnVan ;
     . . .
     // outer WHILE loop, etc.
     . . .
         5.2.   roomOnVan ←(payload + parcelWeight ≤ capacity) AND
                (conveyor NOT empty) ;
         5.3.   WHILE (roomOnVan)
                  5.2.1.   Load parcel on van ;
                  5.2.2.   payload ← payload + parcelWeight ;
                  5.2.3.   Get next parcelWeight ;
                  5.2.4.   roomOnVan ←(payload + parcelWeight ≤ capacity)
                           AND (conveyor NOT empty) ;
                ENDWHILE
```

Notice in Solution 9.6 that the flag `roomOnVan` needs to have its value set in two places: once immediately before the `WHILE` in order that it has a value that can be tested the first time the loop is encountered, and the second time as the last statement in the loop to ensure that its value is updated following the fetching of the next parcel.

What is the advantage of using a flag in this instance? Should I have stuck with the original version? Is there a right way and a wrong way? As you will come to discover, for any given programming problem there will be several (even many) ways that the algorithm describing a solution can be organized and written. Some of those ways will be constrained by the programming language being used, but others will not. In the van loading example, although the `WHILE` itself may be easier to read with the addition of the flag variable, I am not sure that there is an overall advantage. In fact, it could be argued that the flag-controlled solution is worse than the original. The first version had a single occurrence of the relational expression that controlled the termination of the loop. The addition of the flag variable meant that the relational expression needed to be written twice (once for each place that the flag must be set). This is potentially error-prone as the expression may not be copied correctly. Errors in complex relational expressions can be very difficult to find, and so in this case I would prefer the non-flag controlled version as it minimizes the scope for errors of this kind.

Perhaps you are thinking that flags are more trouble than they're worth, but this is not so. Consider the program in Solution 9.7.

Solution 9.7 Program to sum a series of numbers

```
1.    integer: number,
2.             sum ;
3.    boolean: positive ;
4.    sum ← 0 ;
5.    positive ← true ;
6.    Display 'This program will sum a series of positive numbers. ' ;
7.    Display 'Please keep entering positive numbers. ' ;
8.    Display 'Enter a negative number to finish. ' ;
9.    DO
          9.1.   Display 'Enter a number (negative to finish) ' ;
          9.2.   Get value of number ;
          9.3.   sum ← sum + number ;
          9.4.   IF (number < 0)
                     9.4.1.   positive ← false ;
                  ENDIF
      WHILE (positive) ;
10.   Display ('The total of your numbers is') ;
11.   Display (sum) ;
```

Just remember this: all `WHILE` and `DO. . .WHILE` loops must terminate (otherwise your program is in error). In order to terminate the loops test a conditional expression. The value of that expression (True or False) will determine when the loop terminates. If a loop should terminate when a particular value is reached then a sentinel variable is used to watch out for that value. If the sentinel is a Boolean variable then it is called a flag. A flag is just a Boolean sentinel. A sentinel is just a variable that is tested to see if it has yet reached a particular value.

Compound Relational Expressions

Consider the following statement which uses the operators AND and NOT which we first saw back in Chapter 5.

```
1.   WHILE (payload + parcelWeight ≤ capacity) AND (NOT (conveyor
          empty))
     1.1.  // Statement block ;
     ENDWHILE
```

In addition to the relational operator '≤' we have also used two logical operators, AND and NOT to form a compound relational expression. Just as a compound arithmetic expression comprises a number of numeric expressions joined by arithmetic operators (e.g. 3 + (4 × 7)) a compound relational expression is made up of a number of relational expressions joined by *logical operators*. There are three logical operators: AND, OR, and NOT.[14] The logical operators AND and OR are used to connect relational expressions. NOT is used to negate or invert the value of a relational expression (a bit like the '−' sign negates the value that follows it, e.g. −40). Table 9.9 shows these operators[15] together with their formal names and their mathematical symbol equivalents which you will come across in many text books.

Table 9.9   **Logical Operators and their Symbolic Representations**

Operator	Mathematics	
	Name	Symbol
AND	Conjunction	∩ or ∧
OR	Disjunction	∪ or ∨
NOT	Negation	¬

[14] There are other logical operators too, namely NAND, NOR, XOR, and XNOR but we do not need to concern ourselves with them in this book. You might also come across two other operators: if and iff (yes, the two fs are correct – it means 'if and only if'). Their common symbols are → and ↔ respectively. You will use these operators on courses in logic or discrete mathematics, and on some more formal programming and computer science courses. We do not need them for this book, but if you are continuing your computing studies beyond introductory programming then you will need to become familiar with their operation sooner or later. But for the curious there is an entry in the Reflections chapter on LOGICAL OPERATORS AND CONNECTIVES which gives a bit more detail.

[15] In some texts the logical operators are called *logical connectives*, but they're the same thing. I use the word *operator* in this book because as far as we are concerned they behave like operators in that they work on operands and they give a result.

Like the relational operators, the logical operators give a Boolean result. For instance, if both operands of the AND operator are True then the overall result is True otherwise it is False. The OR returns True if either one or both of its operands are true. NOT gives the opposite of its single operand. We can use a *truth table* to illustrate the results that the operators give for all permutations of their operands.

Table 9.10   **Truth Table for AND, OR, and NOT**

Value of p	Value of q	p AND q	p OR q	NOT p	NOT q
False	False	False	False	True	True
False	True	False	True	True	False
True	False	False	True	False	True
True	True	True	True	False	False

p and q are Boolean values (variables, if you like). When connected by the logical operators AND, OR, and NOT, you get the results shown in the four right-most columns.

In Table 9.10 the first two columns list values of two Boolean variables called p and q. Each variable can take either of the values True and False. Therefore, there are four possible combinations of values for these two variables. These combinations are shown in the first and second columns. The third, fourth, fifth, and sixth columns show the result of applying AND, OR, and NOT respectively to the Boolean variables p and q; AND and OR are applied to p and q together, whilst NOT (being a unary operator) is only applied to one expression at a time. Notice, that because NOT gives the inverse value of its operand the last two columns in Table 9.10 are the exact opposites of the first two columns.

AND, OR, and NOT enable us to write sophisticated compound relational expressions. The example on the previous page had two relational expressions: 1) $\boxed{payload}$ + $\boxed{parcelWeight}$ ≤ $\boxed{capacity}$ and 2) NOT(conveyor empty). They were joined with the operator AND. Table 9.11 gives the truth table for this compound expression. For space reasons the table uses p to stand for payload + parcelWeight ≤ capacity and q to stand for conveyor empty. A separate column shows the effect of adding the operator NOT to q, that is, conveyor empty. The Boolean values in italics are the ones that are the operands for the AND.

Table 9.11   **Truth Table for Compound Expression**

Conditional Expressions		Applying the Operators	
p	q	NOTq	p AND NOT q
False	False	True	False
False	True	False	False
True	False	True	True
True	True	False	False

Looking at Table 9.11 we can see that the compound expression only yields true in one case: when p is true and q is false. That is, when the payload added to the parcel weight is less than or equal to the capacity of the van and when the conveyor is not empty. All other permutations give a False result and would thus cause the WHILE loop to terminate. Of course, this is just what we want because van loading *should* stop when a parcel will not fit or when there are no more parcels to load (conveyor empty). One must be very careful when forming compound relational expressions because it is very easy to get them wrong. Whilst novices have the most trouble with this, even expert programmers make errors in building compound relational expressions.

Consider a program that calculates the average mark achieved by a class of students in a test. The program can work with any size of class. The teacher enters the mark for each student together with the student's surname. Entering a surname of 'ZZZZZ' and a mark of zero signals the end of the data after which the average mark should be calculated. Solution 9.8 below shows how we might try to construct the WHILE loop that accepts student marks and keeps track of the running total.

Examine the compound condition for the **WHILE** loop (statement #8) and use whatever method you need to determine whether it is correct. Remember, the loop should continue accepting names and marks until the teacher enters a name of '**ZZZZZ**' and a mark of 0.

Solution 9.8 Possible WHILE loop for processing marks

```
1.   string:[name] ;
2.   integer:[mark],
3.          [total] ;
4.          [numberOfMarks] ;
5.   [total] ← 0 ;
6.   [numberOfMarks] ← 0 ;
7.   Get ([name] and [mark] from user) ;
8.   WHILE (name ≠ 'ZZZZZ') AND (mark ≠ 0)
         8.1.  [total] ← [total] + [mark] ;
         8.2.  [numberOfMarks] ← [numberOfMarks] + 1 ;
         8.3.  Get (next [name] and [mark] from user) ;
     ENDWHILE
```

At first sight the condition in statement #8 sounds right: "continue accepting marks while the name is not 'ZZZZZ' and the mark is not zero". Unfortunately, the loop is wrong and will terminate as soon as a mark of zero is entered (even when the name is not 'ZZZZZ'. A truth table will show this nicely.

Complete the truth table below. In the table expression **name** ≠ '**ZZZZ**' is represented by *p* and **mark** ≠ **0** by *q*. Four pairs of values are provided for **name** and **mark**. Fill in the values for *p*, *q*, *p* **AND** *q*, and in the 'Continue the loop?' column write 'Yes' if the loop should continue or 'No' if it should terminate. I have filled in the first row already.

Variables		Conditions			Continue the loop?
name	mark	p	q	p AND q	
SMITH	89	True	True	True	Yes
ZZZZZ	0				
HIGGINS	0				
ZZZZZ	54				

If you worked it out correctly, your answer should match Table 9.12 below.

Table 9.12 **Truth Table for the Incorrect WHILE Loop in Solution 9.8**

Variables		Conditions			Continue the loop?
name	mark	p	q	p AND q	
SMITH	89	True	True	True	Yes
ZZZZZ	0	False	False	False	No
HIGGINS	0	True	False	False	No
ZZZZZ	54	False	True	False	No

It is worth spending a bit of time exploring just what is happening in Table 9.12. In the first case name is 'SMITH' and mark is 89. The first condition, p, says name ≠ 'ZZZZZ'. So, when name is 'SMITH', then p is true; that is, it is true to say that name is not equal to 'ZZZZZ'. Likewise, q is true because mark *is* not equal to 0. As both p and q are True then p AND q is true, so the loop continues.

The next case is the one we expected to terminate the loop as name is 'ZZZZZ' and mark is 0. p is false because it is not true to say that 'ZZZZZ' is not equal to 'ZZZZZ' (they *are* equal). q is likewise false. Thus p AND q yields false and the loop will terminate as expected.

In the third case (name of 'HIGGINS' and mark of 0) p is again true but q is now false because the condition is mark ≠ 0. This time mark *is* 0 so it is false to say that mark is not equal to zero. This makes the compound condition false because AND requires both of its operands to be true for it to give a true result. This causes the loop to terminate before we intended. Thus a valid case (it is possible for someone to score zero) causes an error in the program. The fourth case similarly causes a premature end to the loop, but this case is less likely to occur – I have never met anyone whose name is 'ZZZZZ'. The problem here is that we have used an expression that sounds right in English but which is logically incorrect. We want to terminate the loop when a name of 'ZZZZZ' and a mark of 0 is entered. We expressed this as WHILE (name ≠ 'ZZZZZ') AND (mark ≠ 0) DO. On the surface it sounds right but, as we have seen, it is not. The correct condition for the WHILE loop in this case is given in Solution 9.9.

Solution 9.9 Correct WHILE loop for processing marks

```
1.   string:│name│ ;
2.   integer:│mark│,
3.            │total│,
4.            │numberOfMarks│ ;
5.   │total│ ← 0 ;
6.   │numberOfMarks│ ← 0 ;
7.   Get (│name│ and │mark│ from user) ;
8.   WHILE (name ≠ 'ZZZZZ') OR (mark ≠ 0)
        8.1.   │total│ ← │total│ + │mark│ ;
        8.2.   │numberOfMarks│ ← │numberOfMarks│ + 1 ;
        8.2.   Get (next │name│ and │mark│ from user) ;
     ENDWHILE
```

Notice how the AND has been replaced by OR. The correctness of this can be demonstrated by another truth table. Because OR gives a True result when either or both of its operands are True we can see from Table 9.13 that the loop now will only terminate when name is 'ZZZZZ' and mark is 0 which is the desired behaviour (though it is still unlikely that a mark of 54 for a student named 'ZZZZZ' would ever be entered!).

Table 9.13   Truth Table for the Correct WHILE Loop in Solution 9.9

Variables		Conditions			
name	mark	p	q	p OR q	Continue the loop?
SMITH	89	True	True	True	Yes
HIGGINS	0	True	False	True	Yes
ZZZZZ	54	False	True	True	Yes
ZZZZZ	0	False	False	False	No

Continuing ▶
condition

Terminating ▶
condition

However, the solution with the OR does not come naturally to us. Here is a tip for forming compound WHILE loop conditions. In the example above we tried to write the condition that will be true each time the loop iterates. We may call this the *continuing condition*. Another way to tackle the problem is to write down the condition that will be true when the loop terminates (the *terminating condition*), then negate this condition and use the negated version in the WHILE loop.

Do this now for the student mark program above. Write down the condition that will be true when the WHILE loop terminates, that is, write down the *terminating condition*.

The correct answer is:

$$(\boxed{name} = 'ZZZZZ') \text{ AND } (\boxed{mark} = 0)$$

that is, the loop should terminate when name is 'ZZZZZ' and mark is 0; when the teacher types in 'ZZZZZ' and 0 the loop will stop. If this condition will stop the loop then any other values of name and mark will cause it to continue. Negating the condition gives us the *continuing condition*:

NOT ((name = 'ZZZZZ') AND (mark = 0))

Notice that the NOT has been applied to the whole compound condition through the use of the extra set of parentheses. We can now use this condition in the WHILE statement to give:

```
1.   WHILE NOT((name = 'ZZZZZ') AND (mark = 0))
       1.1.  // Statement block
     ENDWHILE
```

Although this looks different from the condition in Solution 9.9 it is functionally (or rather, logically) equivalent. Another truth table will demonstrate that. This time p stands for name = 'ZZZZZ' and q for mark = 0.

Table 9.14   **Truth Table for the New WHILE Condition**

Variables		Conditions				
name	mark	p	q	p AND q	NOT (p AND q)	Continue the loop?
SMITH	89	False	False	False	True	Yes
HIGGINS	0	False	True	False	True	Yes
ZZZZZ	54	True	False	False	True	Yes
ZZZZZ	0	True	True	True	False	No

We can see that the new condition results in exactly the same outcome as that in Solution 9.9. In other words

WHILE (name ≠ 'ZZZZZ') OR (mark ≠ 0)

and

WHILE NOT ((name = 'ZZZZZ') AND (mark = 0))

mean the same thing. The first WHILE can be read as "while the continuing condition is still True do . . ." and the second as "while the terminating condition is not True do . . .". Personally, I find it easier and safer when building a compound condition to control a WHILE loop to write down the terminating condition and negate it. Over the years I have seen many a beginning programmer's loop fail through a malformed controlling condition because they have not learned this useful trick. If you really want to write the continuing condition then you can still do it by applying one of De Morgan's laws to the terminating condition.

De Morgan's Laws

De Morgan was a nineteenth century mathematician and logician who came up with the following handy "laws" (note, the symbol $\equiv$ means "logically equivalent to"):

1. NOT $(p$ AND $q) \equiv$ (NOT p) OR (NOT q)
2. NOT $(p$ OR $q) \equiv$ (NOT p) AND (NOT q)

These laws can be easily demonstrated with truth tables. Table 9.15 shows the truth table for the first of De Morgan's laws. The bold columns represent the two expressions in the law. The other columns are intermediate stages in the logic.

Table 9.15 **Truth Table for De Morgan's Law #1**

De Morgan's Law #1: NOT $(p$ AND $q) \equiv$ (NOT p) OR (NOT q)

p	q	p AND q	NOT (p AND q)	NOT (p)	NOT (q)	(NOT p) OR (NOT q)
True	True	True	**False**	False	False	**False**
True	False	False	**True**	False	True	**True**
False	True	False	**True**	True	False	**True**
False	False	False	**True**	True	True	**True**

We can see from Table 9.15 that the two expressions in De Morgan's first law are, indeed, equivalent. In fact, you will see that they are also identical to the two versions of the WHILE loop we discovered above. Here is the truth table for the second law.

Table 9.16 **Truth Table for De Morgan's Law #2**

De Morgan's Law #2: NOT $(p$ OR $q) \equiv$ (NOT p) AND (NOT q)

p	q	p OR q	NOT (p OR q)	NOT (p)	NOT (q)	(NOT p) AND (NOT q)
True	True	True	**False**	False	False	**False**
True	False	True	**False**	False	True	**False**
False	True	True	**False**	True	False	**False**
False	False	False	**True**	True	True	**True**

So, having written the WHILE loop using the negation of the terminating condition:

```
WHILE NOT ((name = 'ZZZZZ') AND (mark = 0))
```

We can, if we wish, transform it using De Morgan's Law #1 into

```
WHILE ((NOT (name = 'ZZZZZ')) OR (NOT (mark = 0)))
```

But we know that NOT (name = 'ZZZZZ') can be written as name $\neq$ 'ZZZZZ' so using the more familiar $\neq$ operator we get

```
WHILE (name ≠ 'ZZZZZ') OR (mark ≠ 0)
```

Table 9.17   **The Logical Opposites for the Relational Operators**

Operator	Logical Opposite	Opposite Symbol	Comment
$=$	NOT equals	$\neq$	Speaks for itself!
$<$	NOT less than	$\geq$	If x is not less than y then x must be either equal to or greater than y.
$\leq$	NOT less than or equal to	$>$	For x not to be less than or equal to y it must be greater than y.
$>$	NOT greater than	$\leq$	If x is not greater than y then x must be either equal to or less than y.
$\geq$	NOT greater than or equal to	$<$	For x not to be greater than or equal to y it must be less than y.
$\neq$	NOT unequal to	$=$	For x not to be unequal to y it must be equal to y.

Applying De Morgan's laws to the above example was quite easy to do as NOT name = 'ZZZZZ' could be more concisely written as name $\neq$ 'ZZZZZ'. NOT effectively means "the logical opposite of".[16] The logical opposite of "equal to" is "not equal to" which we normally write as $\neq$. Table 9.17 shows the logical operators and their corresponding logical opposite.

Applying De Morgan's laws can result in a lot of NOTs appearing in your algorithms! Using Table 9.17 will help you remove many of these NOTs which can clutter up your program by using the logical opposite symbols instead. In fact, simplifying compound relational expressions is a good idea as it helps to keep your programs more readable. Table 9.18 below gives some logical equivalences in addition to De Morgan's laws that you can use to tidy up your programs.

Table 9.18   **Some Logical Equivalences**

Expression	Logical Equivalent	Comment
NOT NOT (p)	p	The double negative!
(p OR q) AND r	p OR (q AND r)	This is a distributive axiom. It is like saying $(3 + 4) - 5 = 3 + (4 - 5)$
(p AND q) OR (p AND r)	p AND (q OR r)	Another distributive axiom. Example: ((name = 'ZZZZZ') AND (mark = 0) OR (name = 'ZZZZZ') AND (mark = 100)) $\equiv$ (name = 'ZZZZZ') AND ((mark = 0) OR (mark = 100))

---

[16] In a coin toss **NOT** heads is tails and **NOT** tails is heads. That is, if the toss is not heads then it is tails and if it is not tails then it is heads.

9.4 Chapter Summary

In this chapter you learned about data and its various types (such as integers, real numbers, characters and strings, Boolean values, constant data, and variable data) and how to manipulate data using *operators*. In the second half of the chapter you learned about some of the pitfalls that you will encounter when using data in programs and how to avoid some of the more common traps.

9.5 Exercises

1. What is the difference between a literal and a variable?

2. Could values such as 5.5, 3.142, 1090.1 be assigned to the following variable?

    integer:`intNumber` ;

3. Why are real numbers not ordinal?

4. What are the largest positive values that can be stored in the following variables?

    integer:`number` ;
    shortint:`number2` ;
    byte:`number3` ;
    longint:`number4` ;

5. What is the difference between the integer value 4 and the character '4'?

6. What is the character type used for?

7. Declare a string variable myName and assign your name to it.

8. Given the following declaration and assignment statements:

    boolean:`onVacation` ;
    `onVaction` ← true ;

    How can the following IF statement be improved?

    IF (`onVacation` = true)
       Display ('No milk today, thankyou') ;
    ENDIF

9. Given the declaration:

    integer:`membersOfFamily` IS 5 ;

    What is wrong with the following statement?

    `membersOfFamily` ← `membersOfFamily` + 1 ;

10. Given the declaration:

    integer:`result` ;

For each of the following statements state what value will be assigned to result.

1. result ← 3 + 4 × 7 ;
2. result ← 4 × 7 + 3 ;
3. result ← (4 × 7) + 3 ;
4. result ← 4 × (7 + 3) ;
5. result ← 4 × 7 + 3 × 8 ;
6. result ← 4 × (7 + 3) × 8 ;
7. result ← 4 × 7 ÷ 2 × 3 ÷ 21 ;
8. result ← 4 × 7 ÷ 2 × 3∧3 ÷ 21 ;

11. Given the declaration:

    boolean:bigger ;

For each of the following statements state what value will be assigned to bigger.

1. bigger ← 3 > 4 ;
2. bigger ← 3 × 2 > 4 ;
3. bigger ← 'a' > 'Z' ;
4. bigger ← 3 × 4 = 2 × 6 ;

12. Anyone resident in the UK and who is a citizen of the UK, the Republic of Ireland or of a Commonwealth country and is aged 18 or over on the date of a parliamentary election is eligible to vote, unless they are a member of the House of Lords, imprisoned for a criminal offense, mentally incapable of making a reasoned judgement, or have been convicted of corrupt or illegal practises in connection with an election within the previous five years. Declare variables to represent the components of this problem. Then write an assignment statement that uses these variables in a relational expression to assign the value true or false as appropriate to the Boolean variable eligibleToVote which will store an individual's eligibility to vote. Finally, draw a table showing different values of the variables and the Boolean value that would be assigned to eligibleToVote as a result.[17]

13. Think about this problem of representation. Why do you think it is that real numbers are often only stored as an approximation of their true value?[18] Can you think of ways that exact real numbers could be represented? For example, the fraction $\frac{1}{3}$ leads to an approximation when represented in the decimal number system (0.333333333 . . .), whilst the fraction $\frac{1}{10}$ can be represented exactly in decimal (0.1) but not in binary.

14. Design an algorithm that will convert any lower case letter to its upper case equivalent. Use a character variable theLetter to hold the letter. For example, if theLetter was assigned

---

[17] Hint: You might want to start by solving a simpler version of the problem first and then building up the solution to include all the component parts. For example, you could start out by solving the simpler problem saying anyone who is resident in the UK and aged 18 or over is eligible to vote.

[18] Hint: Think about how numbers are stored internally by the computer.

the value 'e' the algorithm would assign it a new value of 'E'. Before converting the lower-case letter, first ensure it really is a lower-case letter and not some other character.[19]

9.6 Projects

StockSnackz Vending Machine

Amend your solution to take into account any necessary data types introduced in this chapter. Consider carefully the data types needed to handle the monetary values.

Stocksfield Fire Service

Write your solution to the EAC decoding problem as an algorithm using the more formalized *HTTLAP* pseudo-code introduced in this chapter. Make sure you declare all your variables with appropriate data types. You need to think carefully about what you are going to use to store the EAC. The easiest method to get you started is to store each of the three characters of the EAC in separate character variables.

Puzzle World: Roman Numerals and Chronograms

Use strings and formal pseudo-code to rewrite the Roman number validator algorithm.

Chronograms (also called eteostichons) are sentences in which certain letters, when rearranged, stand for a date and the sentence itself is about the subject to which the date refers. All letters that are also Roman numerals (I, V, X, L, C, D, M) are used to form the date. Sometimes the sentence is written such that the Roman numeral letters already give a well-formed Roman number. For example, in the sentence:

My Day Closed Is In Immortality

if we ignore the lower-case letters we get the number MDCIII which equals 1603. The sentence commemorates the death of Queen Elizabeth the First of England in 1603. More commonly, the Roman numbers are not well formed and the date is obtained by adding the values of all the Roman numerals in the sentence, as in:

LorD haVe MerCI Vpon Vs. (V used as a U, mercy spelt with an 'i')

This is a chronogram about the Great Fire of London in 1666. The date is given by

$$L + D + V + M + C + I + V + V = 50 + 500 + 5 + 1000 + 100 + 1 + 5 + 5 = 1666.$$

Outline the basic algorithm for finding and displaying in decimal the date "hidden" in a chronogram. To begin, assume that only upper-case letters are used for roman numerals ($I = 1$, but i is a letter). Also, assume that the Roman numerals

---

[19] Hint: Think about the ordinal values of the characters. Some arithmetic is involved. Use the Chr and Ord commands mentioned in this chapter.

do not have to form a valid string of numerals and that the hidden date is obtained simply by summing the values of all roman numerals found (as in the "Lord have mercy upon us" example above).

For an extra challenge, extend this solution to accept only chronograms that have a well-formed Roman number in them. Thus "My Day Closed Is In Immortality" would give the valid date MDCIII, whilst "LorD haVe MerCI Vpon Vs" would not give us a result as LDVMCIVV is not a well-formed number (1666 should be written as MDCLXVI).

Pangrams: Holoalphabetic Sentences

Update the variable list for your pangram solution by assigning proper *HTTLAP* types. Rewrite your algorithm using the more formal *HTTLAP* pseudo-code, assignment statements, Boolean expressions in IF and WHILE conditions, and so forth.

Online Bookstore: ISBNs

The ISBN validation problem is best solved using an iteration construct. Write your solution as an algorithm using the more formalized *HTTLAP* pseudo-code introduced in this chapter. Make sure you declare all your variables with appropriate data types. You need to think carefully about what you are going to use to store the whole raw 10-digit ISBN: you need to deal with each digit individually and the final digit may be an 'X'.

9.7 Optional Section: Programming Traps for the Unwary

We have covered the basics now of data and data types, operators and expressions, and manipulating compound relational expressions. This optional section looks at some of the traps that beginning programmers (and even some experienced ones) fall into when working with numeric data. Some of the explanations get a bit technical so you may prefer to skip this section until you have gained a bit more experience and confidence. If you do skip this section, keep it in mind as it may have the explanation of odd program behaviour. If you have numeric variables that do not seem to be behaving properly or that take on unexplained strange values it could be because you have fallen into one of the traps outlined below.

Problems with Integers: the Number's Too Big

When working with small (16-bit or smaller) integer types a trap that beginning programmers (and even experts from time to time) fall into is inadvertently *overflowing* a value. Consider, for a moment, a hypothetical integer data type which only has space for three digits. The range of values we could store in such a type would thus be 0 . . . 999. What happens if we have a value of 999 and we try to add 1 to it? This results in an attempt to store a four-digit value (1000) in a three-digit space. We can imagine the digit '1' being pushed off the end leaving a value of 000 (see Figure 9.7).

FIGURE 9.7 **Integer overflow**

Something similar happens in programming when an integer type is holding the largest value it can store and an attempt is made to increase its value. As most current programming languages use 32-bit integers (maximum value = 2,147 483,647) this is less common today than when 16-bit integers were more common (maximum value = 32,767). However, it can still happen and if you find integer values suddenly changing from a large positive value to a large negative value you have probably just witnessed *overflow* taking place. When filling a bath if you forget to turn the taps off, when the bath is full the excess water that won't fit will overflow onto the floor. When you try to fit too big a number into an integer something similar takes place. Let's use a 16-bit integer as an example. Most integer types let you store negative as well as positive values by using the left-most bit as a sign. A 0 in the left-most bit means a positive number whilst a 1 means a negative number. Using this system the binary representation of the value +32,767 in a 16-bit integer would look like Figure 9.8.

FIGURE 9.8 **A full 16-bit integer**

Sign bit 0 indicates a positive number. Value is +32,767.

Attempting to add 1 to this value results in all the 1s turning to zero with a 1 carrying over into the left most bit resulting in the situation shown in Figure 9.9. This is exactly the same principle used when working in decimal where 9 + 1 = 10. Nine is the largest decimal digit, so the sum results in a carry.

FIGURE 9.9 **After the overflow**

Sign bit now '1' indicating a negative number. Value is now –32,768.

Simply by adding 1 the integer has gone from +32,767 to −32,768. The reason the number has turned negative is down to the way computers represent negative values.

Overflow is less common in languages like Java that use 32-bit integers. However, the principle still remains, except that in signed 32-bit integer systems we would need to reach a value of 2,147,483,647 (over 2 billion) before hitting a possible overflow state.

Here is a related problem that can cause bewilderment in beginners. Let's say we are designing an algorithm to calculate an employee's final salary by adding a performance bonus to a basic pay level. We learn from our problem analysis that an employee's basic salary can never be above 35,000 and that bonuses have a maximum value of 2000. Therefore, we decide to use the 16-bit shortint type for the basicSalary and the bonus variables. Aware of the possibility of overflow we realize the final salary can take a value (37,000) larger than a shortint can store and so declare the variable finalSalary as a 32-bit integer-type variable. Confident that we are on the right track we write the algorithm in Solution 6.7 below:

Solution 9.10 Algorithm for salary problem

```
shortint: basicSalary ,
          bonus  ;
integer: finalSalary  ;
basicSalary  ← 32000  ;
bonus  ← 2000  ;
finalSalary  ← basicSalary  + bonus  ;
```

Because finalSalary is an integer and can therefore store any value in the range −2,147,483,648 to 2,147,483,647 we might expect this solution to get round the problem of overflow. Unfortunately the problem remains, and finalSalary will have the value −31,536. Can you think why? The sum 32,000 + 2000 gives a result far smaller than the maximum limit of the integer type, so what is going on? The problem lies in the expression basicSalary + bonus. Although finalSalary has been declared as an integer, basicSalary and bonus are both shortints. As both parts of the expression basicSalary + bonus are of type shortint, the result will also be a shortint. A shortint can store a maximum positive value of 32,767, so again we get an overflow. It is this overflowed shortint result that is then assigned to finalSalary. If the expression basicSalary + bonus had an integer in it then the whole expression would evaluate to an integer rather than a shortint.

We could get round the problem by making basicSalary or bonus an integer rather than a shortint, but that defeats the purpose of using a type that is appropriate to the size of the variable. Another solution would be to copy bonus into a temporary integer variable:

```
integer: intBonus  ← bonus  ;
```

but this also seems unsatisfactory and clumsy. A common way of getting round the problem is to *cast* one of the shortint values into an integer on the fly. Type casting is a technique where you convert an expression from one type into another without having to store it in a variable. Casting is very common in object-oriented programming. You could do it like this:

```
finalSalary ← (integer) basicSalary  + bonus  ;
```

which for the purposes of the expression makes basicSalary look like an integer rather than a shortint. Note that casting does not change the variable or expression it is applied to, it just makes that variable or expression appear to be a different type.

Problems with Real Numbers

Real numbers can cause the unwitting programmer many problems. This is due to the way real numbers are stored in a computer. You have already come across problems with real numbers in the real world. In the decimal system is it not possible to represent the fraction $\frac{1}{3}$ exactly. We can write $\frac{1}{3}$ as 0.3333 or even 0.333333333333 but they are only approximations as we need an infinite number of decimal places. The floating point system used in digital computers likewise has certain values that it cannot represent exactly. This leads to a number of problems when handling real numbers in programs. The first of these is called representational error.

Representational Error

Writing $\frac{1}{3}$ in decimal notation causes a *representational error.* Representation errors occur because a finite number of bits is used to store a real number. Real numbers, therefore, are approximations of their actual value. Program 9.1 is a short Processing (see Chapter 15) program that results in a representational error.

Program 9.1

Processing program demonstrating representational error

```
float r = 1.0, r2 = 0.0;
r2 = r2 + 0.1 + 0.1 + 0.1 + 0.1 + 0.1 +
     0.1 + 0.1 + 0.1 + 0.1 + 0.1 ;
println ("Test 1") ;
println ("r is " + r + " and r2 is " + r2) ;
println ("r equals r2 is " + (r == r2)) ;
r2 = 0.1 + 0.9 ;
println ("Test 2") ;
println ("r is " + r + " and r2 is " + r2) ;
println ("r equals r2 is " + (r == r2)) ;
```

You do not need to know the Processing language to follow this program. Two real number variables r and r2 (Processing, like Java calls its real type float) are declared and assigned the values 1.0 and 0.0 respectively. Then ten lots of 0.1 are added to r2 with the intention of it eventually accumulating the value 1.0. The next three statements display the results of these assignments. The values of r and r2 are displayed on the screen followed by the Boolean result of the conditional expression r == r2. (In Processing '==' is the operator for testing equality, the '=' is the assignment operator.) Then r2 is assigned the result of the expression 0.1 + 0.9 and the results are displayed again. In both cases r2 is nominally assigned the value 1.0. However, as the screen shot in Figure 9.10 shows, the output of the program (see the bottom window) indicates that 1.0 is not necessarily the same as 1.0! In fact, the result of adding ten 0.1s to r2 results in it having a value of 1.0000001 rather than 1.0.

This emphasizes the point that you should treat real numbers with caution and comparing two real numbers to see if they are equal can lead to all sorts of problems.

FIGURE 9.10 **Evidence of Representational error**

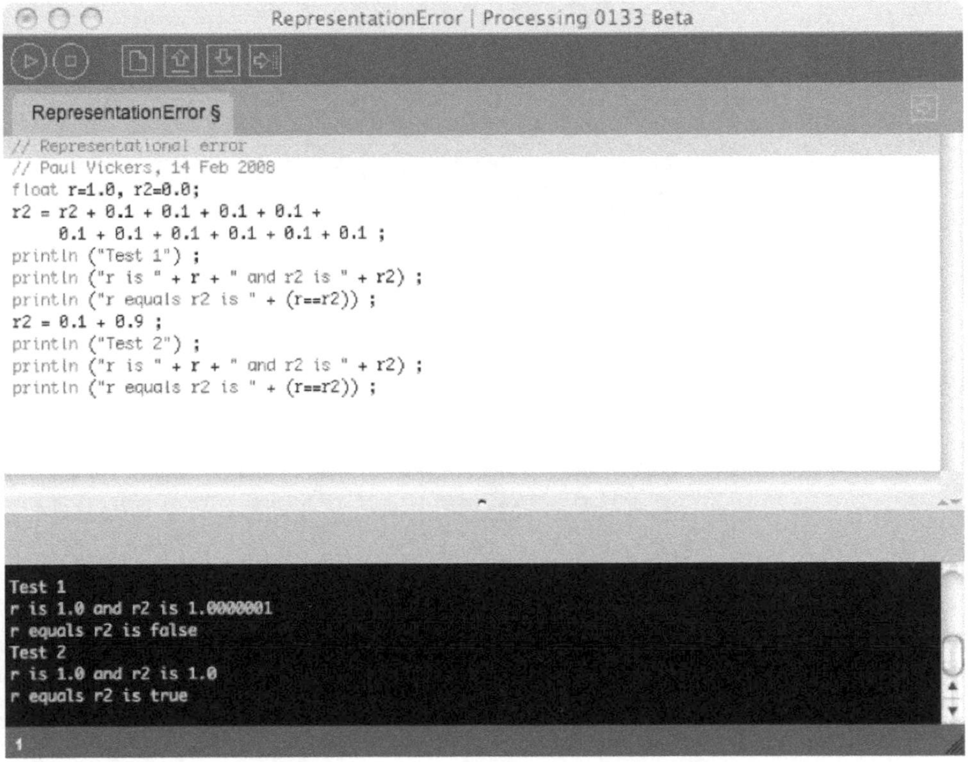

Cancellation Error

Another issue with real numbers is *cancellation error*. When two numbers of very different magnitudes are added the smaller number may be cancelled out (have its effect masked) by the larger number. Program 9.2 is a small Processing program (see Chapter 15) that adds a variable y with a value of 10000.0 to a variable x whose value is 0.00012134 and stores the result in a variable z. The final statement displays the values of x, y, and z. We might expect the output would show '0.00011234 + 10000.0 = 10000.00012134'.

Program 9.2

Processing program demonstrating cancellation error

```
float x = 0.00012134f,
      y = 10000.0f,
      z = x + y ;
println (x + ' ' + ' ' + y + ' = ' + z) ;
```

The actual output obtained is shown below in Figure 9.11. There are two things to note. First, Processing has defaulted to displaying x in scientific notation (1.2134E − 4) rather than in fixed-point notation. But far more important is the value of z which shows as 10000.0, the same as y. The fact that y is so many times larger than x has caused the Processing floating point representation system to exhibit masking where the value of x is cancelled out by y.

FIGURE 9.11   **Evidence of Cancellation error**

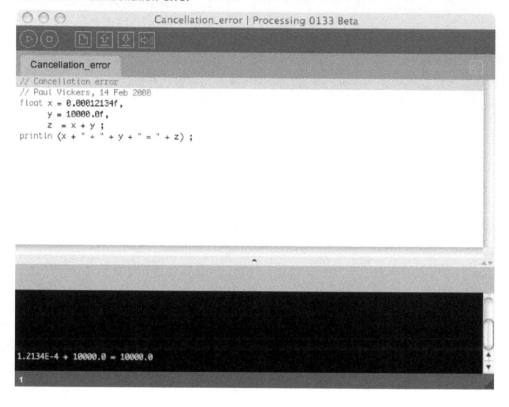

Mixing Types

Given the following pseudo-code declaration:

real: realNumber ;

What do you think the value of **realNumber** will be after the following statement?

realNumber ← 7 ÷ 4 ;

If you answered 1 and a bit, 1 ³⁄₄, or 1.75 then you are incorrect. If you perform this action in a real programming language **realNumber** will be assigned the value 1.0. The reason for this is that the expression 7 ÷ 4 is an integer expression as both the operands are **integers**. Therefore, the result will be an **integer**, and an **integer** is a whole number, so 4 goes into 7 one time. The result of 1 will be assigned to **realNumber** which will store it as 1.0. The point here is that you need to be very careful when mixing types in expressions and assignments as you may not always get the results you expect.

Given the following declarations and assignments:

integer: intNumber1 ,
       intNumber2 ;
real: realNumber2 ;

```
integer:|intResult| ;
real:|realResult| ;
|intNumber1| ← 17 ;
|intNumber2| ← 9 ;
|realNumber2| ← 9.0 ;
```

Work out the effects of the following four statements:

1. |intResult| ← |intNumber1| ÷ |intNumber2| ;
2. |realResult| ← |intNumber1| ÷ |intNumber2| ;
3. |intResult| ← |intNumber1| ÷ |realNumber2| ;
4. |realResult| ← |intNumber1| ÷ |realNumber2| ;

Here are my answers to the above exercises.

1. intResult takes the value 1 as both operands of the ÷ operator are integers, so integer arithmetic is done and 9 goes into 17 one whole time.

2. realResult takes the value 1.0. Again, both operands are integers, so the result of the expression is an integer which is 1 as before. As this integer is being assigned to a real variable, it will be stored as 1.0.

3. This statement should fail. In a real programming language the compiler would object to it. This is because one of the operands is a real value (realNumber2) which makes the expression give a real result, and a real value cannot be assigned to an integer variable.

4. realResult takes the value 1.8888888 . . . because the expression gives a real result which is then assigned to the real variable realResult.

Real Overflow and Underflow

Real numbers can also suffer from a version of overflow and underflow. We know that working at the limits of the value range allowed by the integer types can cause integer variables to suddenly take on an unexpectedly large positive or negative value. Similarly, multiplying two very large real numbers can give a result that is too big to store resulting in overflow. Likewise, if two very small numbers are multiplied and the result is too small to represent then a value of zero may be recorded thus giving underflow. The way overflow and underflow is handled varies between languages.

Representing Exact Real Numbers

In the everyday world some real numbers represent exact values. For example, a sandwich might cost £1.99, $1.99, or €1.99. Here, 1.99 is an exact quantity as it also means 199 pence (£1.99) or 199 cents ($1.99 & €1.99). However, counting in pence (or cents) is unwieldy so we generally express monetary values as an amount in pounds, dollars, euros, pesos, and so on where the fractional part stands for the pence, cents, centavos, and so on. Such values, though possessing fractional parts, still represent exact values as they can all be converted to an integer representation (that is, $1.47 is the same monetary value as 147 cents). Exact real numbers are common in financial environments. Strangely, many programming languages do not provide a data type for storing such values and programmers have to use real numbers (or integers if representational problems are to be avoided). However, newer languages have started to offer support for this data type. C#, for example, provides the `decimal` type for representing exact fractional values.[20]

Many real numbers, however, do not represent exact quantities. Take the value of pi (π) which is the ratio of the circumference of a circle to its diameter. π is approximately equal to 3 (its value as given in the Bible — see 1 Kings 7:23).[21] To get a feel for π's overall size 3 is a good enough estimate. But for problems in geometry at school we were taught to use a more precise value, typically 3.142. Of course, 3.142 is only a rounding up of 3.1416 which, in turn, is a rounding up of 3.14159. As you might already know, 3.14159 is itself only a rounding up of a yet more precise value and, in fact, π has an infinite number of digits. Recent efforts have calculated π's value to around a billion digits, but that is only the tip of the iceberg. Even monetary values are not always exact. Say I buy a new computer for £999.99. In the UK I would have to pay sales tax of 17.5 percent which brings the total to £1174.98825. Obviously, I cannot pay that exact amount so it would likely be rounded up to £1174.99 which is now an approximation of the actual amount to two places of precision.

The upshot of this is that it is not a good idea to test real numbers for equality. For example, although 9.99 $\times$ 3 evaluates to 29.97 algebraically, writing program code to test whether 9.99 $\times$ 3 equals 29.97 may, or may not evaluate to Boolean true depending on the computer system and programming language being used. This is because 9.99 is a real number which is stored only as an approximation in the computer's memory. One way round this problem is to convert the numbers to an integer representation before the calculation. Another way is to make use of exact real number data types (such as C#'s `decimal` type) but this is only satisfactory in certain circumstances.

D'oh! More Arithmetic Problems

The last two sections dealt with problems that are specific to integer and real data. There are a few more general arithmetic problems that trip up the bewildered programmer regardless of the numeric type being used. These problem areas lead to errors that are *extremely easy* to make but which can be *extremely hard* to find. When you do eventually track them down it is common to have a Homer

---

[20] C# (pronounced C Sharp) is a C-based object-oriented language developed by Microsoft primarily to allow programmers to write applications for the Microsoft .NET framework.

[21] The bible is sometimes criticized for getting the value of pi wrong. 1 Kings 7:23 reads: *"And he made a molten sea, ten cubits from the one brim to the other: it was round all about, and his height was five cubits: and a line of thirty cubits did compass it round about."* I discovered an interesting fact when looking at the Arcytech website (http://www.arcytech.org/java/pi/facts.html). The word for "compass" here is סביב based on the root סבב. All Hebrew words have a numeric value. The numeric equivalent of סביב is 111 compared with 106 for סבב. The ratio of these two numbers is 1.047169811... When multiplied by 3 this gives 3.141509434... which is not a bad approximation of pi.

Simpson moment of exclamation (hence the title of this heading). The first problem area for many novices is operator precedence and parenthesis placement. Having read through the section on operators in this chapter it is unlikely that you would be surprised that the statement

$\boxed{\text{result}}$ ← 3 + 4 × 5 ;

assigns the value 23 to result. You know by now that multiplication has a higher precedence than addition, so the 4 × 5 is evaluated first and its result (20) is added to the 3 to give 23. If we wanted to do the addition first we would have to write

$\boxed{\text{result}}$ ← (3 + 4) × 5 ;

as expressions in parentheses have a higher precedence than the other operators. However, whilst most novices are aware of them the precedence rules still catch them out from time to time (recall −9 ∧ 3).

Equation 9.1 gives the formula for calculating the annual repayment of a mortgage where R is the annual repayment, P is the loan principal (the amount borrowed), r is the interest rate as a percentage, and n is the term of the loan in years.

$$R = \frac{P.r(1 + \frac{r}{100})^n}{100\left[(1 + \frac{r}{100})^n - 1\right]}$$

Which of the following statements (could be more than one) are correct pseudo-code representations of Equation 9.1?

1. R ← P × r × 1 + r ÷ 100 ∧n ÷ 100 × 1 + r ÷ 100 ∧ n − 1 ;
2. R ← P × r × (1 + r ÷ 100)∧n ÷ 100 × (1 + r ÷ 100)∧ n − 1 ;
3. R ← P × r × (1 + r ÷ 100)∧n ÷ 100 × ((1 + r ÷ 100)∧ n − 1) ;
4. R ← (P × r × (1 + r ÷ 100)∧n) ÷ (100 × (1 + r ÷ 100)∧ n − 1) ;
5. R ← P × r × (1 + r ÷ 100)∧n ÷ (100 × ((1 + r ÷ 100)∧ n − 1)) ;
6. R ← (P × r × (1 + r ÷ 100)∧n) ÷ (100 × ((1 + r ÷ 100)∧ n − 1)) ;
7. R ← (P × r) × (1 + r ÷ 100)∧n) ÷ (100 × ((1 + r ÷ 100)∧ n − 1)) ;
8. R ← (P × r × (1 + r ÷ 100)∧n)) ÷ (100 × ((1 + r ÷ 100)∧ n − 1)) ;
9. R ← (P × r) × (1 + r ÷ 100)∧n) ÷ ((100 × ((1 + r ÷ 100)∧ n−1))) ;

See what I mean about precedence? Statements 5, 6, 7, 8, and 9 will all give the correct result whilst statements 1, 2, 3, and 4 will not. It is all a question of precedence and parentheses. Equation 9.1 itself has brackets in it to show the order in which its terms should be calculated. But a one-to-one translation from Equation 9.1 to the pseudo-code (statement 3) is not sufficient. Statement 3 has exactly the same number of parentheses as Equation 9.1 has brackets but it is still wrong because the division line in Equation 9.1 says that the result of the expression above it should be divided by the result of the expression below it. Unfortunately for us the precedence rules mean that $P \times r \times (1 + r \div 100) \wedge n$ is divided by 100 and the result of that is then multiplied by the remaining terms. To correctly interpret Equation 9.1 we need to surround the expression $100 \times ((1 + r \div 100) \wedge n - 1)$ with parentheses to ensure the division is done last of all. Statement 5 is the first correct translation being the solution with the minimum number of parentheses needed to correctly interpret Equation 9.1. Statement 6 surrounds the top half of the formula in Equation 9.1 by parentheses too, but this is not actually necessary because operator precedence means the correct answer is obtained without the parentheses. The remaining correct statements all have various combinations of parentheses, many of which are, strictly, unnecessary.

Paul's Three Laws of Parentheses

When are parentheses unnecessary? There is no definitive answer to this, so here are Paul's three laws of parentheses (with apologies to the memory of Isaac Asimov):

Rule #1. Avoid parentheses, except where this violates rule #2.

Rule #2. Use the minimum number of parentheses necessary to ensure desired order of operator execution, except where rule #3 applies.

Rule #3. Logically unnecessary parentheses may be added where it is felt they *add* to the readability of a statement, assist with comprehension, or help to spell out exactly what processing order is intended by the programmer.

10

Sub-programming and Baking Cakes: Procedures and Functions

Learning Objectives

- Understand how programs can be broken up into smaller functional units known as sub-programs
- Learn the difference between command procedures and expression procedures (functions) and when to use each kind of sub-program
- Understand how sub-programs send and receive data through the use of value and reference parameters

In this chapter we turn our attention to a very important aspect of programming: the sub-program. Sub-programs (variously known as procedures, functions, methods, and sub-routines) make it possible to write very large and complex software systems. Without sub-programs software development would be much more time-consuming, programs would be far longer, and more errors would result. Sub-programming also increases the scope for code REUSABILITY which has become increasingly important since the rise in popularity of object-oriented languages.

You will learn about *procedures* (Section 10.2), *functions* (Section 10.4), and their associated *parameters* and *arguments* (Section 10.3). You will learn how to write and call (execute) procedures and functions using two different mechanisms: call-by-value and call-by-reference (also Section 10.3).

10.1 What Is Sub-programming?

What is sub-programming? A firm that wins a large construction project often does not have all the skills and resources to be able to deliver the project on its own. It is common practice for firms to sub-contract some of the work out to other companies. A specialist concrete-pouring firm may be brought in to lay the foundations, while a roofing company takes care of the other end of the building. The point is that while the main company has the overall responsibility for the construction project, it subcontracts (delegates, farms out) certain tasks to other companies or agents that it knows can get the job done. The subcontractors are entities in their own right, but in the context of the project, they can be viewed as sub-units of the main company. As far as the customer is concerned there is only one company working on the project. The customer only pays the main contractor and only deals with the project manager from the main company.

A somewhat similar situation exists in programming. Rather than write a program as one long algorithm software developers identify parts of the program design that perform discrete tasks and which can be treated as algorithms in their own right. Because these algorithms have a stated purpose with defined start and end points they resemble programs themselves. But their function is to serve the purpose of the program to which they belong so they are called sub-programs. For example, in the van loading solution we could describe the inner `WHILE` loop as a sub-program the sole purpose of which is to load an individual van with parcels. By using the techniques of sub-programming we could take this section of code out and turn it into a sub-program that is then invoked by the main program (much as the main company invokes the services of the foundation-pouring company in the construction project).

The most common reason for using sub-programs is to define useful actions that need to be invoked at several places throughout a program (or even by many programs). Consider the following piece of algebra that calculates the positive and negative roots of a quadratic function:

Equation 10.1

$$x_{1,2} = \frac{-b \pm \sqrt{b^2 - 4ac}}{2a} \tag{10.1}$$

If you remember your high school mathematics lessons you know how to read Equation 10.1. The symbol $\sqrt{}$ is mathematical shorthand for 'square root'. But what does 'square root' mean? Is square root a fixed value? No – its value depends on the number to which it refers. For example, $\sqrt{16}$ is 4 (because $4 \times 4 = 16$) whilst $\sqrt{225}$ is 15. Calculating a square root is a non-trivial task involving some interesting algebra. But square roots are so common that tables have been published listing the square roots of various values. Pocket calculators can calculate a square root for you at the push of a button. The problem of calculating a square root has been solved and the solution provided to us as a button on the calculator or as a value in a book of tables. In Equation 10.1 we can think of $\sqrt{}$ as a sub-program that does part of the work of calculating the roots of a quadratic equation. Every time we want the square root of a value or expression we put in the $\sqrt{}$ symbol.

FIGURE 10.1   **Calculator with square root key**

The same principle applies to programming. We can identify tasks that need to be done in several places in the program and separate those tasks into sub-programs. Up until now we have not directly encountered any sub-programs in the pseudo-code solutions, but they have been hinted at. If you look back at the pseudo-code solutions in earlier chapters you will notice that the word `Display` is used a lot. What does this mean? It means that at the points where it appears we want something to be displayed on the screen. But how does the text appear on the screen? This is actually a good problem in its own right. We must identify the area of the computer's memory that relates to the monitor screen. Then we must take each character in turn and send it to the correct register in the CPU (central processing unit) advancing the cursor position along the screen as we go and, if necessary, moving to the start of a new line when there is no more room on the current one. If every time a programmer wished to display a word on the screen it was required to write mountains of program code to accomplish it very little useful work would get done. Displaying text on a computer's screen is so common that all programming languages provide sub-programs that deal with this task for us. If you like, there is a sub-contractor whose sole purpose is to display on the screen whatever you ask it.

Bob the Baker

To help illustrate the concepts in the following sections we will consider a shop selling breads and cakes. The shop is called "*Bob the Baker*" and is run by Bob Bakerman.

When he first started Bob sold only speciality breads that he baked himself. As the business grew Bob started getting requests to make cakes. Not having much experience of making cakes himself Bob hired Barbara, a qualified master pastry chef, to take care of making the cakes and pastries. Barbara works in a different part of the kitchen and likes to listen to motivational talks all day long on her iPod which means she cannot hear Bob when he speaks. Consequently, Bob and Barbara have developed a working relationship whereby each time Bob wants a batch of cakes made he writes down his request on a piece of paper which he pins to Barbara's notice board. We will use Bob and Barbara to help explain the concepts that follow.

Types of Sub-program

There are three basic types of sub-program in common use today:

1. Command procedures (also known simply as *procedures*).
2. Expression procedures (also known simply as *functions*).
3. Methods (the name given to the particular kind of command and expression procedures used in object-oriented languages).

Command and expression procedures are used to assemble blocks of related actions that can be accessed (invoked) from other parts of a program. Command procedures are sub-programs to which you can delegate tasks, such as displaying text on the monitor screen. Procedures are used just like simple statements. For example, look at Example 10.1 which shows the procedure Display being invoked in a FOR loop.

Example 10.1 Algorithm using the Display procedure

```
1.  integer: number  ;
2.  FOR number GOES FROM 2 TO 12
        2.1.  Display (number, ' squared is ', number × number ↵) ;
    ENDFOR
```

Statement #1 in Example 10.1 declares an integer variable called number. The FOR loop in statement #2 iterates 11 times. Each time round the loop, statement #2.1 invokes the procedure Display to write on the screen the current value of number and its square (that is, number × number). The ↵ symbol just before the closing parenthesis in statement #2.1 indicates that after displaying number and its square the screen should move down a line. In effect, we want the program to hit a virtual "Enter" key after writing out the text. If we missed out the ↵ then all 11 bits of text would appear on one line. Notice how everything that we wanted Display to write on the screen was placed inside a pair of parentheses ()? Parentheses are used in programming languages to tell a sub-program what values it should process.

Parameters ▶ and arguments

These values are called *arguments*, or *parameters*, and we will look at them in detail later on. For now, just accept that the things inside the parentheses in statement #2.1 are passed to the Display procedure so that it can write them onto the screen. We have actually seen arguments before. In Chapter 7 we passed messages to an object's methods like this:

```
tell briansAlarm SetTime: '10:08:35' ;
```

The time value '10:08:35' is effectively an argument that was passed to the SetTime method.

The output that Example 10.1 would produce (assuming it was a real programming language) is given as Figure 10.2.

FIGURE 10.2   **Screen output for Display**

```
2 squared is 4
3 squared is 9
4 squared is 16
5 squared is 25
6 squared is 36
7 squared is 49
8 squared is 64
9 squared is 81
10 squared is 100
11 squared is 121
12 squared is 144
```

A function is much like a procedure in that it also carries out actions. The difference is that a function always gives back (returns) a result. For example, we might have a square root function called SqrRoot that you supply with a value or expression. The function will take the value supplied to it, carry out the actions necessary to calculate the square root of that value, and then give back the answer.

Methods ▶ As we saw in Chapter 7 object-oriented languages use special types of sub-programs called *methods*. 'Method' is really just the object-oriented term for a function or procedure (though there is a bit more to it than that as we shall see in Chapter 14). In addition, most languages allow sub-programs to be written and compiled in separate files allowing them to be used by more than one program. We will now use the *HTTLAP* pseudo-code to show how procedures and functions can be written. The techniques we will look at can be very easily translated to real programming languages.

10.2 Procedures

A procedure is a name given to a block of statements that perform a specific task. Tennent (1981) called them *command procedures* as they are modules of code that carry out tasks and are issued like commands from within the main program body. The idea is analogous to a boss issuing commands to employees. In the bakery, while Bob makes his bread he wants Barbara to bake him a cake. Barbara is listening to her motivational messages, so Bob writes a bake-a-cake instruction (or command) on a piece of paper and puts it on Barbara's notice board. Barbara reads the notice and bakes a cake. If Bob is the main program body, then Barbara (the pastry chef) is a command procedure. Bob issues commands to Barbara and Barbara carries them out.[1]

Here is the pseudo-code notation for a simple command procedure:

```
PROCEDURE identifier
    Statements ;
ENDPROCEDURE
```

Using the above as a model, we could define a procedure `Hello` that displays a salutation and another procedure, `Goodbye`, that displays a farewell message:

```
1.   PROCEDURE Hello
        1.1.   Display ('***************'↵) ;
        1.2.   Display (' Welcome !!!! *'↵) ;
        1.3.   Display ('***************'↵) ;
     ENDPROCEDURE
2.   PROCEDURE Goodbye
        2.1.   Display ('***************'↵) ;
        2.2.   Display (' So long, and *'↵) ;
        2.3.   Display ('    come again *'↵) ;
        2.4.   Display ('***************'↵) ;
     ENDPROCEDURE
```

We can then use these procedures in our programs, as in Program 10.1 below.

```
1.   PROGRAM Simple Command Procedures
// Here are the procedure definitions
2.   PROCEDURE Hello
        2.1.   Display ('***************'↵) ;
        2.2.   Display (' Welcome !!!! *'↵) ;
        2.3.   Display ('***************'↵) ;
     ENDPROCEDURE
3.   PROCEDURE Goodbye
        3.1.   Display ('***************'↵) ;
        3.2.   Display (' So long, and *'↵) ;
        3.3.   Display ('    come again *'↵) ;
        3.4.   Display ('***************'↵) ;
     ENDPROCEDURE
```

Program 10.1

Program using simple command procedures

---

[1] The analogy breaks down slightly as Bob would still be able to carry on with his work while Barbara carries out his commands. If the bakery worked just like the world of sequential programs, then Bob would have to stop what he was doing until Barbara was finished, and Barbara would not be able to do any work until Bob issued her another command. Modern languages like Java and C# allow programmers to specify sections of code that will run concurrently (a technique known as multi-threading), but for the most part, and especially on introductory programming courses, the main program will normally have to wait until the procedure has finished its work.

```
// Here is the main program block
4.   integer: number ,
5.            square ;
6.  Hello ; // Call the Hello procedure
7.  number ← 13 ;
8.  square ← number × number ;
9.  Display ( square ↵) ;
10. Goodbye ; // Call the Goodbye procedure
// End of program
```

If the program in Program 10.1 displayed its output on the computer screen, it would look something like Figure 10.3:

FIGURE 10.3   **Simple command procedures output**

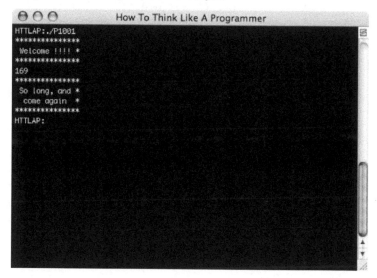

> Sub-program statements are only executed when the sub-program is invoked

The procedures are defined in statement blocks 2 and 3 in Program 10.1, but they are only called into action in statements #6 and #10 respectively in the main program block. This is a key point to learn: the statements in a sub-program are only executed when the sub-program is invoked. Sub-programs are outside the main program statement block and so are not invoked automatically.

10.3 Arguments and Parameters

The simplest type of procedure carries out a predefined task without variation each time it is called (or *invoked*). If Bob's shop only sold one type and size of cake Bob could get Barbara to make a cake with the simple command: "Please bake a cake". Sometimes programming problems are simple enough that procedures that run the same way each time they are called can be written, but it is much more common that the procedure will need to vary its activity in some way each time it is called. Bob's bakery would not do well if it only sold one type and size of cake, so Bob would need to qualify his instructions with details that will tell Barbara exactly what sort of cake to bake, what size it should be, and even how many to bake. If he wanted three cakes, then without adding qualifications to his command Bob would have issue the command three times. Of course, we could write a loop to save writing the command three times, but would it not be better if we could just tell Barbara once to bake a batch of cakes with a specific qualification indicating how many? For example, Bob might say:

"Please bake three small chocolate sponge cakes", or
"Please bake one large lemon drizzle cake".

In both cases Barbara is being commanded to bake cakes, but in each case the command is qualified with specific details – "three", "small", "chocolate sponge" and "one", "large", "lemon drizzle". In programming we call these qualifiers *arguments* or *parameters*. An argument is an item of data attached to a procedure call that gives the procedure specific instructions. A parameter is the name by which a sub-program calls the corresponding argument. Bob might have had some instruction slips printed up that look something like Figure 10.4.

FIGURE 10.4   **Bob's cake instruction slips**

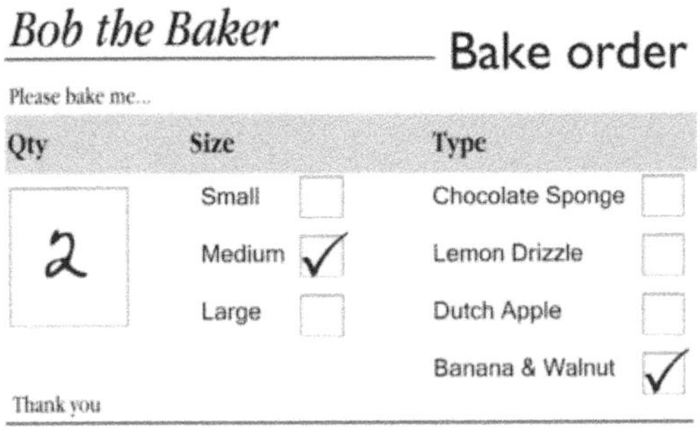

Figure 10.4 is a completed slip that instructs Barbara to bake two medium-sized banana-and-walnut cakes. The instruction slip is the call to the "bake cake" procedure and the three boxes are the argument values that tell Barbara what type of cake to bake, what size, and how many. We may invoke a procedure in pseudo-code like this:

```
BakeCake (2, 'medium', 'banana & walnut') ;
```

where BakeCake is the name of the procedure and the bracketed values are the arguments. This tells the procedure BakeCake to execute its algorithm using the values of its three parameters to specify how many, what size, and what type of cake to bake.

Here is the pseudo-code notation for writing a procedure:

```
PROCEDURE identifier (type:parameter1,...,)
    Statements ;
ENDPROCEDURE
```

Naming Conventions

It is common practice to use "Pascal casing" when naming functions and procedures.[2] In Pascal casing the initial letter of each word in an identifier is written

---

[2] It is called *Pascal casing* because it is a style that was popularized by Pascal programmers.

in upper case, hence BakeCake. Notice that this is very similar to the camel casing used for variable names. The only difference is that the first letter of a variable is left as lower case whilst for procedures and functions it is upper case. The reason for this is that it is now easy to tell when reading a program whether an identifier belongs to a variable or a procedure/function.

Formal and Actual Parameters

When talking about parameters it is important to distinguish between a sub-program's formal parameters and its actual parameters. A *formal parameter* is the name (identifier) a sub-program uses to stand for the value that is passed to it. An *actual parameter* is the value actually passed to the sub-program. Consider Program 10.2 below:

```
1.   PROGRAM Baking cakes
// Procedure definitions
2.   PROCEDURE BakeCake (integer:quantity,
                         string:size,
                         string:type)
     2.1.   integer:counter ;
     2.2.   FOR counter GOES FROM 1 TO quantity
            2.1.1.   Statements to bake a cake . . . ;
            ENDFOR
     ENDPROCEDURE
// Here is the main program block
3.   BakeCake (2, 'medium', 'banana & walnut') ; // Call the
     procedure
// End of program
```

Program 10.2

Using the Bakecake procedure

The procedure definition in Program 10.2 shows that BakeCake expects to receive three parameters: quantity (an integer), size (a string), and type (also a string). The identifiers quantity, size, and type are the names of the procedure's formal parameters. That is, they are the names by which the statements inside BakeCake will know the values passed to the procedure. Statement #3 in Program 10.2 invokes the BakeCake procedure with three *actual parameters*: 2, 'medium', and 'banana & walnut'. These are the actual values passed to the procedure. Invoking the procedure with these parameters will cause the *formal parameters* quantity, size, and type to take the values 2, 'medium' and 'banana & walnut' respectively. It is more common to simply call the formal parameters 'parameters' and the actual parameters 'arguments'.

Huh?

Why don't the actions in procedure BakeCake get performed until statement #3? I thought actions were obeyed in the order they appear.

Up until this point you would be correct in thinking that. What is different now is that BakeCake is a set of actions that have been wrapped up and defined as a sub-program. The sub-program is declared in statement block #2, but until something explicitly asks it to execute it will not. Statement #3 is the task that actually calls for BakeCake to execute its actions.

When a sub-program is invoked the actual parameters are paired off one-for-one with the formal parameters. In most programming languages there is a rule that any sub-program invocation must provide one actual parameter for each of the sub-program's formal parameters. Furthermore, the actual parameters must be of the same type as the corresponding formal parameters. Going back to the bakery analogy, we can visualize this process by imagining Barbara writing the quantity, size, and type requirements onto a blackboard when she receives an instruction slip from Bob (see Figure 10.5).

FIGURE 10.5   **Parameter passing**
Each of the actual parameters on Bob's command slip is copied into the corresponding column on Barbara's blackboard.

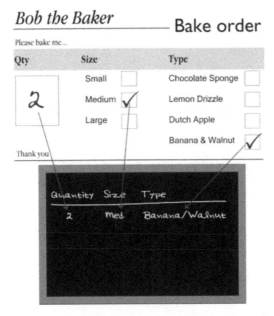

It is important to realize that the formal and actual parameters are distinct and separate items. In the default mode (as illustrated in Program 10.2) changes to the values of the formal parameters are not reflected in corresponding changes to the actual parameters. If Barbara decided to change the value of the `type` parameter from 'banana & walnut' to 'B&W' this would have no effect on the command slip passed to her by Bob – it would still say 'banana & walnut'. The `Display` procedure is of this type; it takes a number of actual parameters that are displayed on the screen and the values of those parameters are not affected in anyway by the behaviour of the procedure. We would not want a `Display` procedure that took a string variable `myName` which contained the value 'Paul', displayed 'Paul' on the screen but then changed the value of `myName` to 'John'. The thing about parameters of this kind is that the values of the actual parameters are *copied* into the memory locations of the formal parameters when a sub-program is invoked. Any subsequent changes to the formal parameters have no effect on the values of the actual parameters.[3] Consider Program 10.3 below.

---

[3] Actually, there is a way of changing the parameter values and we will see how later, on page 283.

Program 10.3

Formal and
actual
parameters

```
1.   PROGRAM Parameter madness
// Procedure definitions
2.   PROCEDURE AddNumber (integer: number , integer: amount )
     2.1.  number ← number + amount ;
     ENDPROCEDURE
// Here is the main program block
3.   integer: myNumber ;
4.   myNumber ← 10 ;
5.   AddNumber ( myNumber , 5) ; // Call the procedure
6.   Display ( myNumber ) ;
//End of program
```

From what you have just learned about the relationship between formal and actual parameters, for Program 10.3 state:

1. What value is taken by the formal parameter **number** in procedure **AddNumber** when statement #5 is executed.

2. What value is taken by the formal parameter **amount** in procedure **AddNumber** when statement #5 is executed.

3. The value assigned to **number** in statement #2.1

4. The value that is displayed on the screen by statement #6.

The answers to the above exercises are given in Table 10.1 below.

Table 10.1   **Answers to In-text Exercise**

Question	Answer	Reason
1	10	Statement #5 calls the AddNumber procedure with two actual parameters, myNumber and 5. The first actual parameter's value is 10 (statement #4) and this is copied into AddNumber's first formal parameter, number.
2	5	The second actual parameter in statement #5 is the integer literal 5. this is matched with the second of AddNumber's formal parameters, amount.
3	15	number ← number + amount is thus number ← 10 + 5 which evaluates to 15.
4	10	number belongs to the procedure AddNumber and is completely separate from myNumber. The only relationship is in statement #5 where myNumber's value is **copied** to number. Changing number's value in statement #2.1 has **no effect** on myNumber's value.

So, in Program 10.3, statement #4 assigns a value of 10 to the program variable myNumber. Statement #5 invokes the procedure AddNumber which takes two integer parameters. The actual parameters in this example are the variable myNumber (whose value is 10) and the integer literal 5. The procedure adds the value of the second parameter to the first. In statement #6 the value of myNumber is displayed on the screen.

If you decided that the program displays the value 10 on the screen you are correct. If you thought the answer was 15 then you have missed the point about the relationship between formal and actual parameters. Recall that the values of the actual parameters are *copied* into the formal parameters and any subsequent operations on the formal parameters do not affect the actual parameters. As the actual parameters can be literal values (as opposed to values stored in identifiers) this is a good thing; it would not make sense to call the procedure BakeCake with the actual parameters 5, 'medium' and 'banana & walnut' and have the procedure attempt to change the value of 'medium'. 'medium' is a string literal and so is not allocated any storage in the computer's memory.[4]

 Think Spot

Call by Value

Sub-programs, such as Display, that require parameters but which do not change the values of their arguments (the actual parameters) are, perhaps, the most common type of parameterized sub-program; sometimes, though, it is desirable to write a sub-program that changes the values of its parameters. Imagine that Bob wants to give Barbara a 4 percent raise in salary. Bob's cousin Ben handles the bakery's finances. To do this, Ben would need to know Barbara's salary and the size of the raise. All salary details are stored in a file to which both Ben and Bob have access. Furthermore, as it is a raise rather than a bonus, the value of Barbara's salary needs to be changed by Ben and the new value written back to the file so that Bob can continue to pay Barbara at the higher rate. Bob might send Ben a note asking him to add a percentage increment to Barbara's salary:

Bob the Baker ———————————————— Payroll

Please increase Barbara's salary by 4 %

Thank you ————————————————————

Ben would then look up Barbara's salary in the file, work out what a 4 percent increase should be, add it to the salary and write the new value back to the file. This is analogous to a sub-program that takes two parameters and which

---

[4] Literals and identifiers are discussed in Chapter 9.

changes the value of one of them. We might try expressing this sub-program in pseudo-code thus:[5]

```
1.   PROGRAM Changing parameter values - incorrect version
// Procedure definition
2.   PROCEDURE RaiseSalary (integer: salary ,
                                    integer: sizeOfRaise )
     2.1.   integer: raiseAmount ;
     2.2.   raiseAmount ← salary × sizeOfRaise ÷ 100 ;
     2.3.   salary ← salary + raiseAmount ;
     ENDPROCEDURE
// Here is the main program block
3.   integer: barbarasSalary ;
4.   barbarasSalary ← 20000 ;.
5.   RaiseSalary ( barbarasSalary , 4) ; // Call the procedure
6.   Display ( barbarasSalary ) ;
// End of program
```

Program 10.4

Incorrect
salary raising
program

Program 10.4 has a sub-program called RaiseSalary which takes two formal parameters, salary and raiseAmount (which is the increase required expressed as a percentage). RaiseSalary calculates the value of the increase and adds it to the value of salary. But we saw above that when a sub-program is invoked the values of its actual parameters are copied to the formal parameters and so changes to the formal parameters do not affect the actual parameters. Program 10.4 does not work the way we want as it leaves the value of barbarasSalary unchanged. What we need is a way of telling the sub-program to work directly on barbarasSalary. This is accomplished by passing a *reference* parameter rather than a *value* parameter. To understand what this means a quick revision of identifiers is needed. Recall that when an identifier is declared in a program (such as barbarasSalary in statement #3 of Program 10.4) a section of the computer's memory is set aside to hold the identifier's value. In Chapter 9 we used the analogy of a box for visualizing variables. Using that idea, Figure 10.6 shows the variable barbarasSalary.

The box represents the memory in which the variable barbarasSalary is stored. The label on the side of the box is the variable's identifier and the slip of paper inside shows the current value stored in barbarasSalary. When we write a statement like

oldSalary ← barbarasSalary ;

the computer will look up the value in the memory location reserved for barbarasSalary and assign the value it finds there to the memory location

---

[5] If you can't understand how the calculation in Program 10.4 works, here's an example. Let's say we want to raise 20,000 by 4 percent. A simple way to do this is: $20,000 + \dfrac{20,000 \times 4}{100}$. Another way, but which involves real numbers is $20,000 \times 1.04$.

FIGURE 10.6   **Visualizing barbarasSalary**

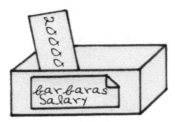

reserved for the variable oldSalary. When identifiers are used in this way we are referencing them by their value. In fact, this is something of a sleight of hand that the computer performs on our behalf. The variable's identifier is just a name given to a location in memory; that is, an identifier can be considered to be the variable's *address*. Every location in the computer's memory has an address. The computer needs these addresses in order to find data and move them about. If you want to send a letter to your bank you must put its address on the envelope otherwise the post office will not know where to deliver it. The address on the envelope is not the bank itself or even the building the bank is in: the address is a device that tells the post office *where to find* the bank. Put a different address on the envelope and you will get a different building with different contents. Thus we may think of the bank's building as our box (the computer's memory location). The address on the envelope is the identifier, and the contents of the bank building (inside the box) are the *value*. A different address means a different building with different contents (value). When we use identifiers in program statements we are really dealing with addresses – the identifier is the address of the variable in which we are interested. When the computer sees a statement like

$$\boxed{\texttt{oldSalary}} \leftarrow \boxed{\texttt{barbarasSalary}} \; ;$$

it looks up the value stored in the memory location represented by the identifier barbarasSalary and copies it into the memory location represented by the identifier oldSalary. Because this process is hidden from us we tend to associate an identifier with its value and think they are just different names for the same thing. Not so: the identifier tells the computer where to find the value we want. The assignment statement above can be more correctly read as: "assign the value stored in the location known as barbarasSalary to the location known as oldSalary." An identifier, then, is simply a name given to an address in the computer's memory. It is a bit like referring to a house by its name rather than its street number. What implications does this have for us when writing sub-programs? Recall statement #5 in Program 10.4:

> An identifier ▶
> is a shorthand
> name given
> to a location in
> the computer's
> memory.

5. RaiseSalary ($\boxed{\texttt{barbarasSalary}}$, 4) ;

What is passed to the sub-program RaiseSalary? The second argument is easy: it is the literal value 4. The first argument is an identifier. When the computer encounters an identifier it looks up the value held in the memory location belonging to that identifier and substitutes the identifier for its value. So, the *value* of barbarasSalary is passed to the sub-program RaiseSalary. This process is illustrated in Figure 10.7.

Think Spot

FIGURE 10.7   **Passing parameters by value**

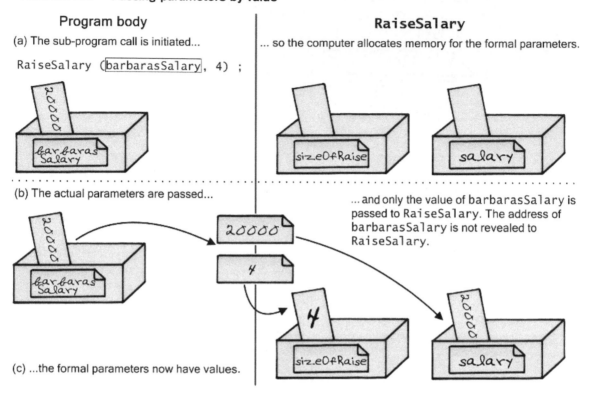

Program body

(a) The sub-program call is initiated...

RaiseSalary (barbarasSalary, 4) ;

RaiseSalary

... so the computer allocates memory for the formal parameters.

(b) The actual parameters are passed...

...and only the value of barbarasSalary is passed to RaiseSalary. The address of barbarasSalary is not revealed to RaiseSalary.

(c) ...the formal parameters now have values.

When the sub-program is called, the computer allocates memory for the formal parameters. The formal parameters only exist during the execution of the sub-program (just as the variables of a program only exist in memory while the program is running). Each time the sub-program is invoked its formal parameters (and any other identifiers it declares) will be allocated memory, the sub-program will do its work, and finally, all the formal parameters and other identifiers belonging to the sub-program are destroyed when the sub-program completes its algorithm. In Figure 10.7 the call to the sub-program causes the formal parameters salary and sizeOfRaise to be allocated memory. The integer literal 4 is copied into sizeOfRaise and the *value* of barbarasSalary (20,000) is copied into salary. Notice the statement that invokes RaiseSalary uses the identifier barbarasSalary. Remember, that when identifiers are used in this way the computer retrieves only their value. The sub-program call is effectively saying, "get a copy of the value stored in barbarasSalary and pass it to RaiseSalary". Thus, Figure 10.7(b) shows a slip of paper with the value of barbarasSalary being passed across. The consequence of this is that when RaiseSalary performs operations on its own formal parameter salary these operations have no effect on barbarasSalary because only the *value* of barbarasSalary was passed across. For this reason, this technique is known as **call by value**.

Call by value ▶

To recap: a *formal* value parameter is like a variable that belongs to the sub-program which gets its initial value from the corresponding *actual* parameter (or argument) when the sub-program is invoked; any changes to a formal value parameter do not affect the value of the argument/actual parameter.

Table 10.2   **Values of Program and Sub-program Identifiers during Execution of Program 10.4**

Program Statements	Program Identifiers barbarasSalary	Sub-program Identifiers salary	sizeOfRaise	raiseAmount
3. **integer**: barbarasSalary ;	undefined	N/A	N/A	N/A
4. barbarasSalary ← 20000 ;	20000	N/A	N/A	N/A
5. RaiseSalary (barbarasSalary, 4) ;	20000	20000	4	N/A
Sub-program Statements				
2.1 **integer**:raiseAmount ;	20000	20000	4	undefined
2.2 raiseAmount ← salary × sizeOfRaise ÷ 100 ;	20000	20000	4	800
2.3 salary ← salary + raiseAmount ;	20000	20800	4	800
Program Statements				
6. Display (barbarasSalary) ;	20000	N/A	N/A	N/A

Call by Reference

What we wanted was to make the sub-program RaiseSalary **update** the value of barbarasSalary. As it stands, it can only calculate what the new salary should be; it loses that value when it has finished (its identifiers are destroyed when it exits). The solution is to use **call by reference**. In a call by reference, a *reference* parameter is used rather than a *value* parameter.[6] Rather than sending the value of a variable we pass a reference to the variable, that is, we make the variable's address visible to the sub-program by prefixing the parameter's name with the keyword REFERENCE in the call to the sub-program. So, instead of passing the value 20000 to RaiseSalary we pass the address in which the value 20000 is stored; that is, we tell RaiseSalary *where to find* the value of barbarasSalary. By passing the address of barbarasSalary the sub-program then has direct access to the memory location that holds barbarasSalary. Knowing the variable's address it can visit that location directly and make changes to the value it finds there. Figure 10.8 shows how a reference to barbarasSalary is passed. For the sake of illustration a hypothetical address value has been used for barbarasSalary in Figure 10.8. Computer memory addresses are usually given in hexadecimal (base 16) format

[6] We will deal with pointer and reference variables more fully in Chapter 13. The Reflections chapter also has a short discussion on POINTERS VS REFERENCES.

(see Section 6.2 and Section 13.1), so we have given barbarasSalary a hypothetical address of $F020 for the sake of illustration.

FIGURE 10.8   **Calling RaiseSalary by reference**

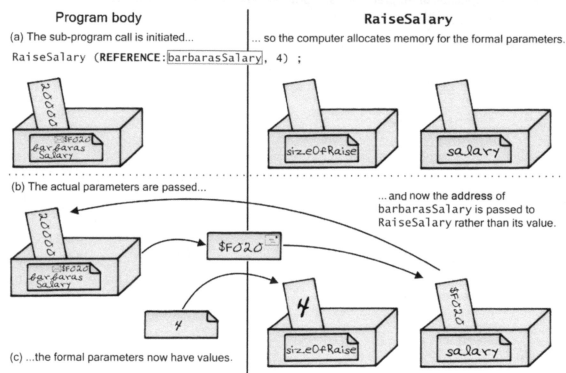

Program body

(a) The sub-program call is initiated...

RaiseSalary (**REFERENCE:** barbarasSalary, 4) ;

RaiseSalary

... so the computer allocates memory for the formal parameters.

(b) The actual parameters are passed...

...and now the **address** of barbarasSalary is passed to RaiseSalary rather than its value.

(c) ...the formal parameters now have values.

Figure 10.8 shows that the formal parameter salary holds not the value of barbarasSalary but its address. Because salary is a reference parameter, any operations on the formal parameter salary will actually be performed on barbarasSalary. In effect, salary has become an alias for barbarasSalary. Thus, the statement

salary ← salary + raiseAmount ;

adds the value of raiseAmount to barbarasSalary. The statement assigns the value to salary, but salary is a reference to barbarasSalary so the operation is directed to the area of memory that holds barbarasSalary. Table 10.3 shows the relationship between salary and barbarasSalary. Think of salary as pointing to barbarasSalary. Whenever an operation uses salary, salary points (redirects) the operation to barbarasSalary.

To implement reference parameter passing we use the keyword REFERENCE in the sub-program's formal parameter list and in every invocation of the sub-program. REFERENCE distinguishes an identifier from a value type. Program 10.5 below shows the correct version of the salary program; the changes from Program 10.4 are in statements #2 and #5.

Huh?

You said "any operations on salary will actually be performed on `barbarasSalary`." I don't understand this as previously you said that `salary` and `barbarasSalary` were completely separate; this seems to suggest that they are the same thing.

`salary` and `barbarasSalary` are separate. They are individual identifiers declared in different parts of the program. In the first call-by-value example both identifiers held integer values and were stored in different memory locations (addresses). In the call-by-reference situation, the declaration of `salary` is changed so that rather than being a normal integer identifier, it holds, instead, the address of another integer identifier. `salary` is like an alias – it is a separate identifier, but it refers to the same location in memory as the actual parameter it is matched with (`barbarasSalary` in this case). Program 10.5 shows this more explicitly.

```
1.   PROGRAM Changing parameter values - Correct version
// Procedure definition
2.   PROCEDURE RaiseSalary (REFERENCE:integer:salary,
                               integer:sizeOfRaise)
     2.1.    integer:raiseAmount ;
     2.2.    raiseAmount ← salary × sizeOfRaise ÷ 100;
     2.3.    salary ← salary + raiseAmount ;
   ENDPROCEDURE
// Here is the main program block
3.   integer:barbarasSalary ;
4.   barbarasSalary ← 200000 ;
5.   RaiseSalary (REFERENCE:barbarasSalary, 4) ; // Call the
                                                  //procedure
6.   Display (barbarasSalary) ;
// End of program
```

Program 10.5
Correct version
of the salary
raising program

Table 10.3 below shows the values of the identifiers after the execution of each statement in Program 10.5. Notice how the formal parameter `salary` no longer has a regular value but, instead, holds the address of `barbarasSalary`.

You may be wondering at this point why the program does not just refer to `barbarasSalary` directly in the `RaiseSalary` sub-program. It is generally not good practice to do this. First of all, it restricts `RaiseSalary` to only being able to update Barbara's salary. (What if Bob wanted his own salary raised?) One of the main reasons for using sub-programs is that parameters enable the same block of code to work with different values and different variables. Secondly, if `barbarasSalary` were declared in another sub-program, then it would likely be outside the scope of `RaiseSalary` which would then not be able to see it. By using `barbarasSalary` directly in the body of `RaiseSalary` we are creating a situation in which the block that declares `barbarasSalary` and `RaiseSalary` are *strongly coupled*. It is a rule of thumb in software engineering that such strong COUPLING is to be avoided wherever possible for it makes programs less flexible and more prone to error and failure. It is a general aim of programmers that subprograms should, as much as is possible, be functionally independent and only perform a single task (or related group of tasks). Coupling sub-programs through

Table 10.3　**Values of Program and Sub-program Identifiers during Execution of Program 10.5.** The arrows show that salary holds a reference to barbarasSalary.

Program Statements	Program Identifiers barbarasSalary	Sub-program Identifiers Salary	sizeOfRaise	raiseAmount
3. `integer:`barbarasSalary ;	undefined	N/A	N/A	N/A
4. barbarasSalary ← 20000 ;	20000	N/A	N/A	N/A
5. RaiseSalary (REFERENCE: barbarasSalary, 4) ;	20000 ←———●	F020	4	N/A
Sub-program Statements				
2.1 `integer:`raiseAmount ;	20000 ←———●	F020	4	undefined
2.2 raiseAmount ← salary × sizeOfRaise ÷ 100 ;	20000 ←———●	F020	4	800
2.3 salary ← salary				
6. + raiseAmount ;	20800 ←———●	F020	4	800
Program Statements				
Display (barbarasSalary) ;	20800	N/A	N/A	N/A

the use of shared variables makes them harder to separate and, thus, less independent. The way to maintain functional independence whilst avoiding strong coupling is to use parameters. Parameters create a looser coupling that allows sub-programs to be used much more flexibly as their data requirements are fully satisfied through their parameters. Because RaiseSalary does not know about or rely upon any identifiers but its own we could, conceivably, reuse it in another program that also does salary calculations. Reference parameters allow us to couple a sub-program to another data item but in a safer and more easily controlled way.

To recap: A reference parameter is needed when a sub-program must change the value of that parameter. The actual parameter in a sub-program invocation must, therefore, be a reference to a variable. The formal reference parameter represents the actual variable during the execution of the sub-program, thus any changes to the value of the formal reference parameter are made to the actual parameter.

10.4　Functions – Expression Procedures

Expression procedures, or functions, are the other common type of sub-program. Like command procedures they are used to perform specific tasks and typically take one or more arguments. What, then, is the difference between functions and procedures, and why do we need functions? If a command procedure is a command, then a function, or *expression procedure* is an expression. In programming terms an expression is something that has a value, so a function is a sub-program that has a value (or, more properly, a sub-program that *returns* a value). Consider Equation (10.2):

Equation 10.2
$$a = \sqrt{16}$$
(10.2)

Equation (10.2) says that *a* is equal to the square root of 16. Think of square root as a function that takes a single argument (in this case, the value 16) and which *gives back* or, in programming terminology, *returns*, a result. We say that $\sqrt{16}$ equals 4. That is, the value of $\sqrt{16}$ is 4, or $\sqrt{16}$ is an expression whose value is 4. But to get the value 4 some calculation has to be done. The details of the calculation are hidden from us, much like the processing carried out by a procedure is not visible from the place it is invoked. Let's say that our pseudo-code has a built-in sub-program called SquareRoot that returns the square root of its single parameter. We might invoke the function thus:

a ← SquareRoot (16) ;

The pseudo-code above says: assign the value of SquareRoot (16) to a. We already know that the assignment operator ← assigns the value of the *expression* on its right to the variable on its left. Recall that an expression is either a simple value (e.g. 16) or a combination of operators and operands that evaluates to a single value (e.g. 4×4). This means that SquareRoot (16) is an expression, that is, it has a value (4, in this case). If we know that SquareRoot is a function (a sub-program) then we can see that, like procedures, functions carry out specific tasks, but in addition, they give back a result – the function is thus like an expression as it possesses a value. To show how the invocations of functions and procedures are different, consider the following pseudo-code in which the BakeCake and SquareRoot sub-programs are invoked:

1.   BakeCake (2, 'medium', 'banana & walnut') ;
2.   a ← SquareRoot (16) ;

In statement #1 the *procedure* BakeCake is called as a *command*, whilst in statement #2 the *function* SquareRoot is invoked as an *expression*. Because functions are themselves expressions their result needs to be dealt with explicitly otherwise it would be lost. Consider the following **incorrect** statements:

1.   a ← BakeCake (2, 'medium', 'banana & walnut') ;
2.   SquareRoot (16) ;

Statement #1 attempts to assign a procedure call to the variable a. Because BakeCake is a procedure and hence does not have a value, this instruction makes no sense. In statement #2, the function SquareRoot is called without dealing with its return value. Just as you would not want to write the following as a program statement:

6 + 4 − 3 ;

because an expression on its own is not very useful, so invoking a function without dealing with its return value is of little use.[7] Invoking a function is like Bob saying to Barbara "make a cake *and* report back to me how it went". Not only would Barbara make the cake but she would *return* a how-it-went message.

Declaring Functions and their Return Values

Because a function is a sub-program, it is structured in much the same way. Here is the pseudo-code notation for a function that takes one or more parameters:

```
FUNCTION identifier (type:parameter1,...,)RETURNS type
    Statements ;
    RETURN expression ;
ENDFUNCTION
```

There are three differences between the function and procedure definitions. First, functions are declared using the keyword FUNCTION. Secondly, after the parameter list comes the keyword RETURNS followed by a data type; this defines what type of data value the function will return back to the code that invoked it. Finally, there should always be a statement of the form RETURN *expression*. This is the statement that tells the function what value to return when it closes. The expression can be a single value or a compound expression of literals, identifiers, and operators. The only constraint is that its final value must be the same type (or a compatible type) as the function's return value. Program 10.6 shows how to declare and use a function called **Cube** which takes a single integer parameter and returns the cube of the parameter.

```
1.    PROGRAM Cubing a number
// Function definitions
2.    FUNCTION Cube (integer:number) RETURNS integer
        2.1.   RETURN number × number × number ;
      ENDFUNCTION
// Here is the main program block
3.    integer:myNumber,
4.           myNumberCubed ;
```

Program 10.6

Declaring and using a function

---

[7] There are exceptions to this rule. In the C-based languages, which includes Processing, all sub-programs are written as functions. Command procedures are achieved by declaring a void return type for the function. However, in Processing, all functions can be invoked as command procedures with the result that the return value is ignored. The reason for this is that many functions return a value that indicates whether an error occurred during the function's execution. For instance, a function that reads a value from the keyboard might return a value of zero if it was successful, or −1 if it was unsuccessful. In many cases these *success flags* can be ignored and the function can be invoked as a command procedure. But sometimes programmers want to know whether a function met with any errors in which case the function's return value is explicitly dealt with. It is beyond the scope of this book to delve into this topic in any more detail as the rules vary from language to language.

```
5.   myNumber ← 3 ;
6.   myNumberCubed ← Cube (myNumber) ; // Call the function
7.   Display (myNumberCubed) ;
//End of program
```

Statement #2 is the header for the function Cube. Cube takes a single integer value parameter called number and it returns an integer. As cubing a value is quite simple involving multiplying the value by itself twice, the body of the function has a single statement that returns the result of number × number × number.

The main program block begins at statement #3. Statement #5 assigns the value 3 to myNumber which is then passed as the actual parameter to the function Cube in statement #6. The result of Cube is assigned to myNumberCubed in statement #6. What is the value of Cube (myNumber)? It is whatever is passed by the function's RETURN statement, so in this case it would be 27 (as 3 × 3 × 3 = 27).

Function Calls by Reference

The above example showed a function called by value. Just like procedures, functions can also take reference parameters. Sometimes a function is needed that returns two values (e.g. the real and imaginary parts of a complex number in engineering applications). As programming languages only allow functions to have a single return value we use reference parameters to give other values back. To illustrate this consider a function that is required to convert a length in centimeters into inches. It will use two formal parameters: centimeters and inches and will return a boolean value. The function should use centimeters as a value parameter and inches as a reference parameter: inches will be used to pass back the length conversion. The function's return value will be boolean as this is to be used as success flag: a value of true means the function was able to perform the conversion. The function and the main program block that invokes it are given as Program 10.7 below.

```
1.   PROGRAM Length conversion
// Function definitions
2.   FUNCTION Convert (integer:centimeters,
                    REFERENCE:real:inches) RETURNS boolean
      2.1.   real:inchesPerCM IS 0.393700787 ;
      2.2.   IF (centimeters ≥ 0)
                 2.2.1.   inches ← centimeters × inchesPerCM ;
                 2.2.2.   RETURN True ;
      2.3.   ELSE
                 2.3.1.   RETURN False ;
             ENDIF
      ENDFUNCTION
// Here is the main program block
3.   integer:cm ;
4.   real:ins ;
5.   boolean:success ;
6.   cm ← 254 ;
```

Program 10.7

Function with reference parameter

```
7.   success ← Convert (cm, REFERENCE:ins) ;
8.   IF success
        8.1. Display (ins) ;
9.   ELSE
        9.1.  Display ('Centimeters value cannot be negative') ;
     ENDIF
//End of program
```

Think Spot

Spend a few minutes reading through Program 10.7 to see if you can understand what happens. The function is called Convert and it has two formal parameters and returns a Boolean result. The first parameter, centimeters, is a value parameter which provides Convert with the value that is to be translated into inches. The second parameter, inches, is a reference parameter which means the function can change the value of the identifier that is used as the actual parameter. It is this parameter that will be used to send back the inches equivalent of the value held in centimeters. The reason we have not chosen to send back the inches value in the function's return is that this function returns a Boolean flag which indicates whether or not it was able to perform the length conversion. If you examine the function's statement block you will see that it only calculates the inches equivalent of centimeters when the value of centimeters is at least zero. If centimeters is greater than or equal to zero then the conversion is done, the result assigned to inches and the Boolean value true is returned. If centimeters is less than zero then no calculation is done, inches is left unchanged, and the Boolean value false is returned. This means that the value of the second actual parameter will only be changed by the function if the value of the first parameter is positive. If it is, and a successful length conversion is carried out then the function returns true otherwise it returns false. This 'success flag' is used by the main program to decide what to do with the function call. The call to the function is in statement #7. The result of the function is assigned to the Boolean variable success. If success holds the value true after the function has been called, then we know that ins holds a value that represents the length of cm in inches. So, the IF construct in statement #8 tests to see whether success is true.[8] If it is, then the value of ins is displayed. If success is false then we know the function was not able to successfully convert the length and so the program displays an error message. This use of Boolean values to represent the outcome of a function and reference parameters to deal with the passing of values out of the function is a common practice amongst programmers.[9]

Input, Output, and Input–output Parameters

In the above examples we have seen parameters used in different ways for getting data into and out of a sub-program. Value parameters can be classed as *input*

---

[8] Perhaps you have realized that we can do away with statement #7 altogether by rewriting statement #8 as IF (Convert (cm, REFERENCE:ins)).

[9] Some programmers (probably brought up on C, which does not have a proper Boolean data type) often write functions that return integers where a value less than zero denotes false and a value of zero or greater denotes true.

parameters as their values cannot be changed by the sub-program and so their purpose is to provide the sub-program with data it needs to do its work. Reference parameters that are used only to carry data out of a sub-program (e.g. `inches` in Program 10.7) are called *output parameters*. Reference parameters that provide the sub-program with both input data and a means for passing values back out again we may call *input–output parameters*. An example of an input–output parameter was `salary` in Program 10.4. The input value of `salary` was used to calculate the pay rise after which it was used to carry an increased salary amount back out of the sub-program.

Functions Without Parameters

If procedures can be declared that take no parameters, can the same be done for functions? The answer is yes, but the need for such functions is rare. Think about it: the purpose of a function is to return a value and that value is normally calculated from one or more parameters. If there are no parameters then the return value is independent of the code that invoked the function.[10] An example of a parameterless function could be one that returns a random number; every time the function is invoked a different random number is returned. Object methods that allow the values of an object's properties to be inspected (see Chapters 7 and 14) are actually parameterless functions, so they do have a use in object-oriented programming. In the kind of procedural programming this book mainly deals with, parameterless functions are quite rare and you will generally find yourself using functions that take one or more parameters.

Methods

We saw in Chapter 7 that when using object-oriented languages we talk less about procedures and functions and instead use the term *method*. Methods are sub-programs that belong to object classes. They are still functions/procedures, but in object-oriented programming we call them methods instead. Methods are dealt with more fully in Chapter 14.

10.5 Chapter Summary

In the above sections we have looked at sub-programs that come in a variety of flavours. There are two types of sub-program:

- command procedures (procedures) and
- expression procedures (functions).

Sub-programs can take zero or more parameters which may themselves be value parameters or reference parameters. Table 10.4 below summarizes this classification and gives an example of each type.

---

[10] Or, the need for parameters has been bypassed by referring to program data directly. We have already commented that such strong COUPLING is generally to be avoided.

Table 10.4   **Combinations of Command Procedures, Expression Procedures, and Parameters**

Types of Sub-program	Invocation Mode	Example Usage
Procedures that take no parameters	Parameterless	`DisplayMenu () ;`
Procedures that do not change the values of any of their parameters	Call by value	`Display ('Hello World!') ;`
Procedures that change the values of one, or more, of their parameters	Call by reference	AddBonus (**REFERENCE:** mySalary , bonusAmount) ;
Functions that take no parameters but which return a single result	Parameterless	a ← RandomNumber () ;
Functions that return a result but which do not change the values of any of their parameters	Call by value	a ← SquareRoot (16) ;
Functions that return a result and which change the values of one, or more, of their parameters	Call by reference	success ← CMsToInches (25, **REFERENCE:**lengthInInches) ;

There is quite a lot to take in on sub-programs. It would be a good idea to read through this section again. If any aspects still seem unclear, go back to the full discussion and follow the examples through again until the ideas make sense.

10.6   Exercises

1. What is the difference between a function (expression procedure) and a procedure (command procedure)?

2. A function is required that takes a single parameter representing a temperature in degrees Fahrenheit and returns the Celsius equivalent. What is missing from the following solution? If the omission is corrected, are there some statements that can be removed?

```
FUNCTION FahrenheitToCelsius (real: Fahrenheit) RETURNS real
    real: celsius ;
    celsius ← (Fahrenheit - 32) ÷ 1.8 ;
ENDFUNCTION
```

3. Design a function that takes two integer parameters and returns the larger of the two. What will it do when both arguments have the same value?

4. Write a function that takes four parameters: day, month, year (all integers), and UKFormat (a Boolean). The function should combine the three date parameters into a single string which it should then return. The UKFormat parameter is used to determined how the string is put together. If UKFormat is true then the return string will be in the form dd/mm/yy otherwise it should be in the form mm/dd/yy. For example, if the four arguments were 1, 12, 1984, true (December 1, 1984) then the returned string would be '1/12/1984'. If UKFormat were false, then it would return '12/1/1984'.

5. Design a function that takes a single string parameter and returns the number of space characters in the string as an integer.

6. Amend Solution 5.9 by adding two procedures AddSugar and AddMilk. Then replace the statements in the algorithm that deal with adding milk and sugar with calls to the new procedures.

7. Design a procedure called Swap that swaps the values of its two integer reference parameters, and then write a line of pseudo-code that invokes the procedure. What would happen if value parameters were used instead of reference parameters?

8. Write a function IsEven that determines whether its single value integer parameter is even or odd. If the parameter is even the function should return a Boolean value true otherwise it should return Boolean false.

9. In the exercises for Chapter 9 you were asked to write an algorithm to convert a lower-case letter into an uppercase one. Assume *HTTLAP* has two functions Ord and Chr with the following headers:

   ```
   FUNCTION Ord (character:aCharacter) RETURNS integer
   FUNCTION Chr (integer:ordinalValue) RETURNS character
   ```

   Ord accepts a single character value in its parameter and returns the ordinal value (ASCII code) of that character. Chr accepts an ASCII value in its integer parameter and returns the corresponding character.

   Make use of Ord and Chr to write your own function ToUpper to convert lower-case letters to upper case. The function should take a single character parameter and return a character which is the upper-case equivalent of the parameter. If the character in the parameter is not a lower-case character then the function should simply give that character back as its return value. For example

   ```
   myLetter ← ToUpper ('e') ;
   ```

   would place the character 'E' in myLetter whilst

   ```
   myLetter ← ToUpper ('Z') ;
   ```

   would place 'Z' in myLetter and

   ```
   myLetter ← ToUpper ('3') ;
   ```

   would place '3' in myLetter.

10. Take the van loading solution from Chapter 5 (Solution 5.18) and move the contents of the inner WHILE loop to a sub-program. Decide whether the sub-program should be a procedure or a function and also determine what parameters (if any) it needs.

10.7 Projects

StockSnackz Vending Machine

Examine your algorithms for the vending machine and look for opportunities to make them easier to follow or to reduce redundancy by introducing sub-programs.

Stocksfield Fire Service

Take your algorithm for decoding an EAC and turn it into a function that decodes the EAC and displays messages, returning a Boolean value of true if none of the three characters of the EAC was invalid otherwise returning false.

Puzzle World: Roman Numerals and Chronograms

Four sub-programs are now required for the Roman numeral problems: one to translate decimal numbers into Roman numerals, one to translate Roman numbers into decimal numbers, one to validate Roman number strings (to be used in conjunction with the second sub-program), and one to process chronograms.

Using your solutions from earlier chapters as a basis, write four sub-programs to meet the following requirements.

1. A function that accepts an integer value as its parameter and returns a string that contains the Roman numeral equivalent.

2. A function that accepts a Roman numeral string as a parameter and returns a Boolean value indicating whether the number is well formed or not.

3. A function that accepts a Roman numeral string as an input parameter and which returns an integer. This function should use the validation function to determine whether the Roman number is well formed. If it is, then it returns the integer equivalent. If not, it should return a negative integer (-1, say) to indicate that the Roman number provided to it as a parameter was not well formed and so could not be converted.

4. A function to process chronograms. The function should have three parameters: an input string parameter used to hold the chronogrammatic sentence, a string output parameter that will be used to pass back out the Roman numeral string hidden in the chronogram and an integer output parameter used to pass back the decimal translation of the Roman number. The function will also return a Boolean value. A return value of true is used to indicate that the Roman number in the chronogram was well-formed, and a false value to indicate the number was not well formed. If the number is well-formed then the function can invoke the translator function to convert it to an integer, otherwise it will have to do a simple summing of all the Roman numeral digits found in the chronogram.

Pangrams: Holoalphabetic Sentences

Use your pangram solution as the basis for a procedure that takes a string as an input parameter and places the word 'Yes' or 'No' in an output string parameter to show whether the candidate string is a pangram or not.

Now change your procedure into a function so that instead of giving the test result via a parameter, the result is returned in the normal manner associated with functions. Choose whether you are going to return a Boolean value, an integer value (0 for false and 1 for true), a character value (perhaps 'Y' or 'N') or a string value ('Yes' or 'No'). Discuss the relative merits and disadvantages of the different return types for this problem.

Online Bookstore: ISBNs

Develop your ISBN solutions as sub-programs:

1. Turn the hyphenation algorithm into a procedure that takes a single ISBN as an input parameter and displays it correctly hyphenated on the screen. For an extra challenge, extend the procedure to use an output parameter (also a string) into which the hyphenated version of the ISBN in the input parameter is placed.

2. Develop your ISBN validation algorithm as a function. The function will take a single ISBN as an input parameter and which returns a Boolean value indicating whether the ISBN is valid or not. Extend the function to add a second parameter into which the calculated check digit for the given ISBN is placed.

Streams and Files, Input and Output

Learning Objectives

- Learn the basic concepts of files and streams and understand their differences
- Understand how files and streams are used to get data into and out of a program
- Appreciate some of the issues of dealing with files and streams in real programming languages
- Learn how to deal with non-existent files

Programs that can calculate the answers to arithmetic problems are all well and good, but in most cases their answers need to be seen. A payroll program needs to print payslips. An ATM/cash machine needs to display information on the screen to allow the customer to choose from the available options. In addition, many programs will require the user (the person operating the program) to supply it with values that it needs to do its job. For instance, before the ATM can dispense any cash it needs the customer to type in the required amount. It can then decide whether there are sufficient funds in the account and dispense the cash or display a message explaining why cash cannot be given.

This short chapter is all about getting data into and out of programs (Section 11.1). You will learn how this can be done using *streams* (Section 11.2) and *files* (Section 11.3) and will see how the computer keyboard and monitor display are both special kinds of stream.

11.1 Input and Output

The data that we enter into a program are called its *input* whilst the things the program displays and prints onto paper are called the *output*. Programs typically accept input, process it, and then produce output accordingly. In this chapter we will look at the basic ways in which programs obtain their input and produce output.

There are three main destinations for the computer's output: the monitor screen, a printer, and folders on a disk drive.[1] A word-processing program uses all three: it displays the contents of documents on the screen and allows them to be edited. When requested the word processor will send those documents to the printer and will allow you to save them onto a disk so that they can be worked upon at another time. We have already seen a sub-program that produces output on the monitor screen: the `Display` procedure.

There is an old technique to assist with the design of programs called the IPO chart. IPO stands for input–process–output and takes the classical view of a program as something that receives input data, processes it in some way, and passes the results as output. This is a highly abstracted view of software, but it is helpful to bear in mind from time to time. The word-processor program receives key strokes and mouse clicks and produces formatted text that can be printed out or stored in the computer's filing system. An online music store program will take lots of inputs related to what tracks can be downloaded, their prices, discount codes, gift vouchers, refunds, the amount of credit available to a customer, and so on and will process that data to produce outputs in the form of email invoices, funds transfers, file downloads, and so forth. This abstraction is often drawn as a flow chart like the one in Figure 11.1.

FIGURE 11.1   **Input–process–output diagram**

Up till now we have only really considered data in terms of its types and how to process it. Useful computer programs generally allow data to be stored permanently in files and documents. In this chapter we will look at the basics of getting data into and out of programs. This involves looking at data *streams* and the different ways streams can be routed to allow keyboards, mice, computer files, monitor screens, and other input–output mechanisms to connect with our programs.

---

[1] Yes, you can send data across a network too, but in principle this is very similar to sending data to a folder.

11.2 Streams

It may have become apparent by now that many computing terms are grounded in real world objects, events, and processes. In the physical world a stream is a small, naturally occurring, moving channel of water. Water flows from the source of the stream (typically a spring) down to its destination (usually a larger river or a lake or pond). The thing about a stream is that water goes in at one end and comes out at the other (ignoring rain and snow for the moment). What is more, the water that goes into the top of the stream first comes out first at the bottom. Acoustics engineers will talk of auditory streams, that is, distinct channels of sounds coming from identifiable sonic sources. In my study at home where I am writing this section there are several auditory streams: there is the music coming from the hi-fi system; the (very) quiet whirr of my computer's fan; the sound of the rest of the family watching TV in the den; the clicking of keys as I type text into the word processor. All these streams are readily distinguishable and contin-ually "flowing". In the programming world a stream is a sequence of data that goes from a source to a destination. The data all flow in the same direction and the data items all come out of the stream in the same order that they were put in. A data stream can be visualized as a drainpipe. Figure 11.2 shows the stream of values 1, 2, 3, 4 . . . going one by one into the top of the drainpipe. Gravity carries them down and they come out the other end in the same order they went in. This is the simplest type of stream – the sequential data stream.

FIGURE 11.2   **A data stream as a drainpipe**

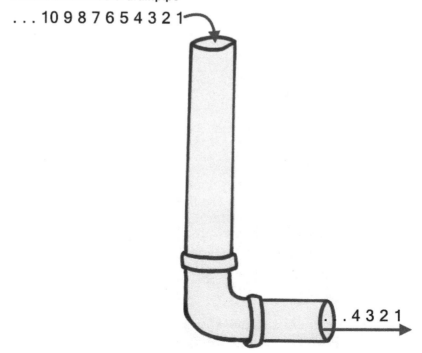

The thing about pipes is that they can be attached to something at either end. If you can imagine a drainpipe with a computer keyboard attached to one end and a computer program attached to the other end then you have a useful picture of how the computer accepts key presses from the user as a stream of data and writes a stream of output data that appears on the monitor screen (see Figure 11.3).

The stream is a fundamental concept in programming and most input and output operations are achieved through manipulating some form of a stream. In many languages the implementation details of the streams are hidden from the programmer, but you will certainly encounter them directly in languages like Java and Processing.

FIGURE 11.3 **A program with input and output streams**

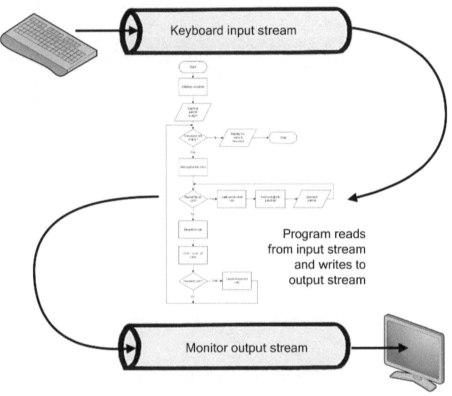

The Monitor Output Stream

The first contact with a stream is usually the "Hello World!" program that appears near the front of just about every computer programming text book. Because this is not like other programming books, "Hello World!" does not come at the front, so here it is in its pseudo-code form.

Program 11.1
The classic "Hello World" program

```
1.  PROGRAM Hello world
2.  Display ('Hello World!') ;
// End of program
```

It is not a very complicated program, having only one executable statement. You know from Chapter 10 that statement #2 is a sub-program call to the Display procedure. Display takes the argument 'Hello World!' and displays it on the monitor screen. Or rather, it would if it was a programming language. To really get this to happen you need to translate Program 11.1 into programming language code. Figure 11.4 shows the output of the program after it has been translated into the Processing language and run.

FIGURE 11.4   **The "Hello World!" program translated into Processing**
The program code is shown in the white "code window" whilst the output from the print statement is shown in the black "output window".

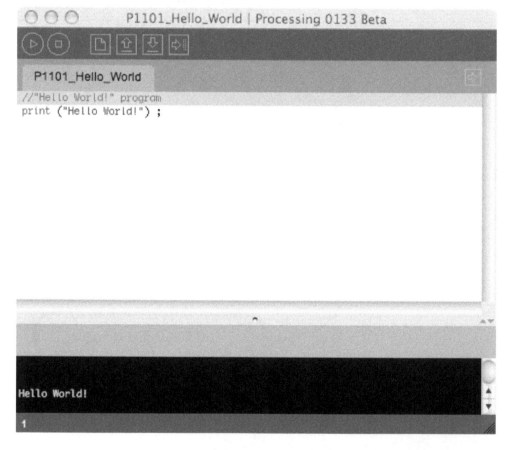

When Display is invoked a connection is made to the stream that is linked to the part of the computer that deals with visual display unit operations. Then the characters in the 'Hello World!' string are sent one by one down the stream and the computer's graphics system processes them in turn and renders them in a form that can be displayed on the attached monitor. Most programming languages have versions of the Display procedure (we have already seen it is called print in Processing) and they are generally used without needing to know that a stream is being manipulated. However, if you dig into the programming language technical manuals you will find references to streams. For example, some language manuals will tell you that the `printf` function (yes, it is a function) writes its parameters to something called *stdout*, which is short for *standard output stream*. By default standard output is the monitor screen on most computer systems. But, because it is a stream, it can be redirected to another output device (that is, the drainpipe can be reconnected to something else).

Usually, display procedures can take any number of parameters which means we could write the following pseudo-code:

1. **integer:**| number | ;
2. | number | ← 3 ;
3. Display ('The number is ', number, ↵, The square of ',| number |,
         ' is ', | number | × | number |, ↵) ;
4. Display ('And the cube is ', | number | × | number | × | number |) ;

Statement #3 is broken over two lines because it will not fit across one line. The output from this algorithm (assuming we had a compiler for *HTTLAP*) would look like Figure 11.5.

FIGURE 11.5   **Example of output using Display**

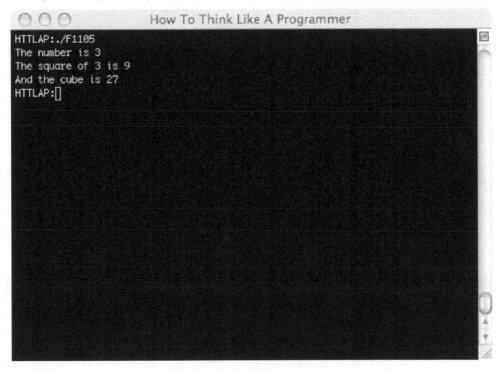

Notice how if you want to send more than one parameter to Display you just separate them by commas. Try and relate Figure 11.5 back to the two invocations of Display. What causes the output to move to the next line? How can two Display statements generate three lines of output? The answer lies in the '↵'

Think Spot

character which indicates that the output should move to the next line at this point.[2] Processing (and Java on which it is based) offers two functions: `print` and `println`, the latter automatically adding a new line instruction to its output, the former keeping the output on the same line. Also, the `print` function can use the special character sequence \n which stands for "newline" and behaves just like the ⏎ symbol in the *HTTLAP* pseudo-code which means a single `print` statement in Processing can yield multi-line output just like the pseudo-code example above. The use of the ⏎ symbol in the *HTTLAP* pseudo-code is really just to act as an *aide mémoire* so that when turning the pseudo-code into real programming language code later on we remember to deal with the line-feed issue.

The Keyboard Input Stream

The computer keyboard is likewise connected to programs via a stream.[3] Characters are sent in the order they are typed into the stream and the program processes them as they come out at the other end. Up till now, every time we have needed to get data from the user we have used statements such as:

    Find out whether milk required;

Or

    Get first parcel weight ;

The *HTTLAP* ▶
Get procedure

Now that we are comfortable with the idea of sub-programs we can make matters more formal and introduce some sub-programs for accepting input to a program. In the *HTTLAP* pseudo-code we shall use the procedure `Get` to accept input from the keyboard. Like `Display`, `Get` can take a variable number of parameters of any type and this allows us to write general input instructions. For example, we could ask the user to type in their age:

1. **integer:** age ;
2. Display ('Please enter your age and then hit ENTER: ') ;
3. Get (keyboard, **REFERENCE:** age) ;

Statement #2 calls the `Display` procedure with a string literal parameter that prompts the user to enter a value. Statement #3 calls the `Get` procedure that

---

[2] This character is called *carriage-return–line-feed* after the two operations that were needed to move the paper up one line on a typewriter. The carriage that held the paper was returned back to its starting position (the beginning of the line) and then it was rotated to feed the paper up one line. These two actions were usually accomplished on manual typewriters by pushing a large lever on the right-hand side of the carriage. On electric typewriters, a key was added to the keyboard with the character ⏎ on it. When word processors and computers came onto the scene, they retained this convention, though sometimes the key is labelled "RETURN" (short for carriage-return–line feed), and now it is often labelled "ENTER" (though the keyboard I am using at the moment still has the old ⏎ character on its "RETURN" key).

[3] In fact, there is also usually something called a buffer between the keyboard and the stream. A buffer is a temporary storage area that a computer uses to manage the transfer of data in and out.

allows the user to type a number on the keyboard. Notice the first argument: **keyboard**. This is a convention we use in the *HTTLAP* pseudo-code to indicate that the Get procedure is to fetch its data from the keyboard input stream. The reason for this is because we could also get data from files on the computer's hard drive (see Section 11.3) so we need to differentiate between the keyboard stream and other streams.[4] Why does Get use a reference parameter rather than a value parameter? Get needs to change the value of its parameter, so it must use a call-by-reference. Get is not restricted to taking a single parameter, so we can also do things like:

1. **integer**: age ;
2. **string**: name ;
3. Display ('Please enter your name and your age and then hit ENTER: ') ;
4. Get (keyboard, **REFERENCE**: name, **REFERENCE**: age) ;
5. Display ('Your name is ', name, ' and your age is ', age) ;

Statement #4 gets values from the keyboard for the two variables name and age.

In the real programming languages you will find the functions and procedures for displaying and fetching data have many more facilities for formatting and selecting data than indicated by the *HTTLAP* Display and Get procedures. But this is pseudo-code and not a real programming language, so Display and Get have been deliberately kept simple. Furthermore, the ways that different programming languages deal with the nuances of input and output vary greatly. Display and Get are sufficient for the purposes of this book as they allow us to indicate that basic screen output and keyboard input are required in the program.

Write pseudo-code to declare an integer **number**, request the user to enter an integer, get the integer from the keyboard, and display that integer multiplied by 2 on the screen.

11.3 Files

Programs that display data on the screen and get data from the keyboard are useful, but provide no persistence of the data. When the program is run again, the data have to be rekeyed, and the output recomputed. There is usually a need to save the results of a program in some more permanent form. For example, a word-processor program must be able to save documents so that they can be retrieved and edited later on. Thus, we need streams that connect the program to the computer's permanent memory (the hard drives, USB memory sticks, DVD-ROM drives, and so on) so that data can be written to and read from storage. To this

---

[4] I have not added a stream name to the Display procedure because in *HTTLAP* Display only writes to the monitor screen. A different procedure will be used for writing data to output file streams.

end, programming languages provide *file streams* and associated functions and pro-cedures to enable data to be written to and read from files in the computer's filing system.

The simplest type of file is a standard text file. A text file is one that can be opened and edited in an ASCII-text editor (such as Notepad on a Microsoft Windows computer, TextEdit on an Apple computer, and Vi on a Unix or Linux machine). Text files contain only ASCII characters and are reasonably straightfor-ward to handle in a program.

We could, in theory, deal with an unlimited number of different files within one program; for example, imagine writing a program that reads the number of characters in every file on your computer's hard drive. Therefore, we need iden-tifiers to specify which file we are interested in. Consider the following statement that declares a file variable in the *HTTLAP* pseudo-code:

`file:`⌑salaryFile⌑ `;`

The new data type, `file`, tells the program that rather than holding a numeric or character value, the variable `salaryFile` will link the program to an actual file on the computer system (it could be on the hard drive, a diskette, a CD-ROM, or even on a networked drive or internet location). Having declared a file variable we need to associate it with an actual file in the computer's filing system. The follow-ing statement links the file variable `salaryFile` to the ASCII text file `salaries.txt`:

⌑salaryFile⌑ ← `'salaries.txt' ;`

In real programming languages, a statement like the above with an unqualified file name (a file name without a directory or folder location) would cause the pro-gram to look in the current folder (usually the one the program itself is located in) for the file. If we wanted to tell the program to look in a specific location, we could write a statement like the following (for a Microsoft Windows system):

⌑salaryFile⌑ ← `'C:\My Documents\bakery files\salaries.txt' ;`

The segment of the string before the file name is called the *path* which is the location of the file in the computer's filing system. For computers with different filing systems (such as the Apple Macintosh or Unix machines) the path format would be different.[5] The point is that most programming languages will allow file names to be simple (just the file name) or full (the file name plus the path). Actually, the above example is bad programming practice because it restricts the program to only being able to use the folder `C:\My Documents\bakery files\`. A better-written program would allow the user to specify the locations of files. We can show this in the *HTTLAP* pseudo-code by declaring a string variable to hold the file path:

`string:`⌑filePath⌑ `;`

giving the path variable a value:

⌑filePath⌑ ← `'C:\My Documents\bakery files\' ;`

---

[5] It would be `'bakery files\salaries.txt'` on my Apple Mac.

and then using `filePath` in the file variable assignment:

> `salaryFile` ← `filePath` + 'salaries.txt' ;

String ▶
concatenation

The above statement uses '+' to concatenate (join) the two strings `filePath` and `'salaries.txt'` to form the single compound string `'C:\My Documents\ bakery files\salaries.txt'`. Of course, really we should also use a string variable to hold the name of the file so that we can change not just the location but also the name of the file that the program uses. Having declared and initialized the file variable, the final stage before being able to use it is to open it. Thinking of an office filing cabinet may help here. Imagine Bob telling his accountant to list all the salaries he pays to his employees. He tells the accountant that the salaries are kept on a piece of paper inside a file labelled "Salaries" in a hanging folder labelled "bakery files" in the third drawer of the filing cabinet (which happens to be labelled "C:"). Though Bob has told the accountant *where* the salaries file is, the accountant still has to open the filing cabinet, select the correct folder, take out the salaries file, and open it to reveal the paper on which the salaries are written. Programming languages vary in the way files are opened, so our *HTTLAP* pseudo-code will use a simple command to represent this step:

> Open (`salaryFile`) ;

Of course, the file must be closed and put away when we have finished with it so that another program can access it (just like you need to put a real file away again in the filing cabinet):

> Close (`salaryFile`) ;

Write pseudo-code to declare a file to hold a set of class test marks, open the file, and then close it again.

Using Files for Input

Having declared, assigned, and opened the file variable we can now use it to tell the `Get` procedure to read data from the file stream associated with the file variable. For example, the statement

> Get (`salaryFile`, **REFERENCE:**`name`, **REFERENCE:**`salary`) ;

tells `Get` to read two values from the `salaryFile` stream and store them in `name` and `salary` respectively. Consider Program 11.2 which gets the salary details of Bob the Baker's employees from a file named `salaries.txt` and displays them on the screen after which it closes the file again.

```
1.  string:name ;
2.  integer:salary ;
3.  file:salaryFile ;
```

```
4.    salaryFile ← 'salaries.txt' ;
5.    Open (salaryFile) ;
6.    WHILE NOT (EndOfFile (salaryFile))
          6.1.  Get (salaryFile, REFERENCE:name, REFERENCE:salary) ;
          6.2.  Display (name, ':', salary ↵) ;
      ENDWHILE
7.    Close (salaryFile) ;
8.    Display ('End of Data') ;
```

Program 11.2

Reading salary details from a file

Statements #1 to #3 declare the `name`, `salary`, and `salaryFile` variables used by the program. Statement #4 associates the file variable with the file `salaries.txt` on the computer's filing system. The file is opened in statement #5. Look at the condition in the `WHILE` loop in statement #6. What do you think `NOT EndOfFile (salaryFile)` means? It means we want the loop body to be executed while (as long as) we have not reached the end of the file: clearly the loop needs to stop once everything on the file has been read. Statements #6.1 and #6.2 read the name and salary data from `salaryFile`. When the last name and salary data have been read from the file then we have reached the end of the file and so the loop can terminate. `EndOfFile` is a function that takes a file variable as its single parameter and returns a Boolean false if the file still has data in it that has not been read yet, and true after the last item of data has been read. Object-oriented languages (such as Processing and Java) utilize an end-of-file property that belongs to the file stream object itself.[6] Whichever way the end-of-file test is implemented in a programming language the basic idea is the same.

How do you know EndOfFile is a function?

`EndOfFile` is a sub-program, specifically a function. We can tell that because it takes parameters and is used as an expression. Here is the statement that called (invoked) it:

```
WHILE NOT (EndOfFile(salaryFile))
```

We can see that it takes a value parameter `salaryFile` which tells us it is a sub-program. The fact that it is used as an expression rather than a command tells us it is a function. The use of the Boolean operator `NOT` also tells us that `EndOfFile`'s return value is a Boolean value.

Sometimes you will not want to process all the data in a file. Let's say Bob just wants to know whether his salary bill is less than 100,000. If we read each salary record from the file and keep a running total we can stop processing the file as soon as the total reaches 100,000 even if the end of the file has not been reached. This would require a compound condition for the `WHILE` loop: one condition to test the running total and another to check for the end of the file in case the total of all the salaries adds up to less than 100,000.

---

[6] In the case of Processing we use the file's `ready` method to determine this. There is an example of its usage in Chapter 15.

What would the condition be? Write it now. Remember, you can think about this in either of two ways: either write down the condition that will be true when the **WHILE** loop terminates and then negate it, or write down the condition that causes the loop to continue.

Here are my two solutions to the problem, both of which are logically equivalent:

WHILE NOT ((total ≥ 100000) OR (EndOfFile (salaryFile)))

and

WHILE ((total < 100000) AND NOT (EndOfFile (salaryFile)))

The first solution takes the condition that is true when the loop terminates and negates it. The loop must terminate either when the total reaches 100,000 or when the end of the file is reached. This gives:

(total ≥ 100000) OR (EndOfFile (salaryFile))

and negating it gives

NOT ((total ≥ 100000) OR (EndOfFile (salaryFile)))

The second solution uses the condition that must be true for the loop to carry on: the total is less than 100,000 and the end of the file has not been reached.

Convince yourself that the two solutions are logically equivalent. Review the section on De Morgan's laws (page 252) if you are stuck.

Using End-of-file Sentinels

In Chapter 8 we discussed sentinel-controlled loops. A sentinel is a variable that is continuously monitored for a particular value. In the example above total was used as a sentinel and when its value reached (or exceeded) 100,000 the loop was terminated. Sometimes we will be asked to process files that mark the end of the data with a dummy record. For example, the salary file might have as its last record a name of 'ZZZZZZZZZZ' and a salary of zero. The name and salary variables themselves then become sentinels and are used in the condition that controls the loop. The loop needs to continue as long as the sentinels have not reached their terminal values, thus:

WHILE (name ≠ 'ZZZZZZZZZZ') OR (salary ≠ 0)

Of course, we can use De Morgan's first law to rearrange the condition to

WHILE NOT ((name = 'ZZZZZZZZZZ') AND (salary = 0))

which shows the WHILE negating the condition that is true when the last record of the file is reached.

The use of end-of-file sentinels requires a read-ahead loop technique, whilst using the true end-of-file condition needs a read-and-process loop structure.

Consider Programs 11.3 and 11.4 which implement the read-ahead and read-and-process structures respectively.

Table 11.1 shows two versions of `salaries.txt`. The first version includes the end markers whilst the second version just has the salary data for Bob's employees without the end markers. The file with the sentinels is processed by Program 11.3.

Program 11.3

Read-ahead processing using end-of-file sentinels

```
1.   string: name ;
2.   integer: salary ;
3.   file: salaryFile ;
4.   salaryFile ← 'salaries.txt' ;
5.   Open ( salaryFile ) ;
6.   Get ( salaryFile , REFERENCE: name , REFERENCE: salary ) ;
7.   WHILE (( name ≠ 'ZZZZZZZZZZ') OR ( salary ≠ 0))
        7.1.  Display ( name , ':', salary ↵) ;
        7.2.  Get ( salaryFile , REFERENCE: name , REFERENCE: salary ) ;
     ENDWHILE
8.   Close ( salaryFile ) ;
9.   Display ('End of Data') ;
```

The file without sentinels is processed by Program 11.4.

Program 11.4

Read-and-process using end-of-file marker

```
1.   string: name ;
2.   integer: salary ;
3.   file: salaryFile ;
4.   salaryFile ← 'salaries.txt' ;
5.   Open ( salaryFile ) ;
6.   WHILE NOT (EndOfFile ( salaryFile ))
        6.1.  Get ( salaryFile , REFERENCE: name , REFERENCE: salary ) ;
        6.2.  Display ( name , ':', salary ↵) ;
     ENDWHILE
7.   Close ( salaryFile ) ;
8.   Display ('End of Data') ;
```

Table 11.1 **Two Versions of salaries.txt**

salaries.txt			
File with Sentinels		File Without Sentinels	
Bob	40000	Bob	40000
Barbara	20000	Barbara	20000
Jim	28000	Jim	28000
ZZZZZZZZZZ	0		

Trace through each of the two programs with their respective versions of the salary file to convince yourself that they both accomplish the same results.

Using Files for Output

As well as reading data from files we also need to be able to write data *to* files. In this book we will take a simplified approach to this topic; this section outlines some of the alternative approaches to file input and output that are found in the real world. As this book is dealing with fundamentals we will not look at the more advanced topics except in outline – better to grasp the basics now and when you are confident, you can explore the richer file input/output facilities offered by your chosen programming language.

In the previous section we opened, read data from, and then closed a simple text file. If we want to save data to a file we can follow a similar series of steps: open the file, write data to it, and close the file. Consider Program 11.5.

```
1.   string: name ;
2.   integer: salary ;
3.   file: salaryFile,
4.          reportFile ;
5.   salaryFile ← 'salaries.txt' ;
6.   reportFile ← 'report.txt' ;
7.   Open (salaryFile) ;
8.   Open (reportFile) ;
9.   WHILE NOT (EndOfFile (salaryFile))
         9.1.   Get (salaryFile, REFERENCE: name, REFERENCE: salary) ;
         9.2.   Display (name, ':', salary ↵) ;
         9.3.   IF (salary > 25000)
                    9.3.1.   Write (reportFile, name, salary, 'High'↵) ;
         9.4.   ELSE
                    9.4.1.   Write (reportFile, name, salary,
                    'Normal'↵) ;
                    ENDIF
         ENDWHILE
10.  Close (salaryFile) ;
11.  Close (reportFile) ;
12.  Display ('End of Data') ;
```

Program 11.5

Writing to a file

Statement #4 declares a second file variable reportFile which we will use as an output file. reportFile is attached to the file report.txt on the computer's hard drive in statement #6 and it is opened in statement #8. So far, this is the same process as for an input file. The selection in statements #9.3 and #9.4 contains the instructions for writing data to reportFile. If the salary that was just read from the input file is greater than 25,000 the salary record is written to reportFile with the string 'High' appended (statement #9.3.1) otherwise the data are written to reportFile with the string 'Normal' appended to the end (statement #9.4.1). There are two things to observe in statements #9.3.1 and #9.4.1. First we have introduced a new procedure, Write, which sends data to an output file rather than to the screen. Secondly, we have used the ↵ character at the end of the Write statements so that the next data to be written to the file will appear on a new line.

? Think Spot Like Get, Write takes as its first parameter the name of a stream that it will write data to. I said above that Write is a procedure. How can you tell from reading Program 11.5 that Write is a procedure and not a function? Remember, functions return values and so are used like expressions. Procedures do not return values and so are used like commands. Write is used as a command in Program 11.5 so we can tell that it is a procedure.

File Input/Output in Real Programming Languages

In the above sections our file access was restricted to the simple reading from and writing to text files. For the purposes of familiarization with the principle of file access this is fine. In the above examples we have used separate text files for reading and writing. The *HTTLAP* pseudo-code assumes that all input files will have their data read once only in strict order starting at the beginning of the file; to read the first record twice would involve opening the file, reading a record, closing the file, then reopening it again. The pseudo-code assumes, for output files, that the file will be empty when it is opened; we have made no provision for adding data to the end of an existing file that already has data in it. However, in the real world of programming languages and programming problems life can get rather more complicated than the preceding sections might lead you to believe. Very often we need to read data from and write data to the same file. Other times we may need to re-read a section of a file, or we might need to overwrite part of a file leaving the rest intact. The level of support offered for file and stream manipulation differs from programming language to programming language, so it is difficult to offer a general guide here.

Binary Files

Most programming languages also have facilities for handling binary files. A binary file cannot be meaningfully edited using a text editor as it contains data in a format specified by the programming language. You can think of a binary file as being a bit like a file that has been compiled by the program: the binary file is only intended to be readable to the program that created it and it will contain many special character codes.[7] You are probably quite familiar with dealing with binary files, though you may not have realized it. Many word processors save documents in a proprietary binary format (though recently there has been a move towards a common format based on the XML standard). This allows all formatting information (such as bold text, different fonts, images, etc.) to be included in the document when it is saved. If word processors could only use ASCII text files they would not be able to offer the powerful document-editing facilities that they do. If you want proof of this, create a document in your favourite word processor and save it using the word processor's default file format. Then try and open the document in a text editor program. For example, Figure 11.6 shows a word processor with an open document. I saved the file using the word processor's default file format as binaryfile.doc.

---

[7] In Processing or Java we would do this using a process known as *serialization*.

FIGURE 11.6   **Viewing a document in a word processor**

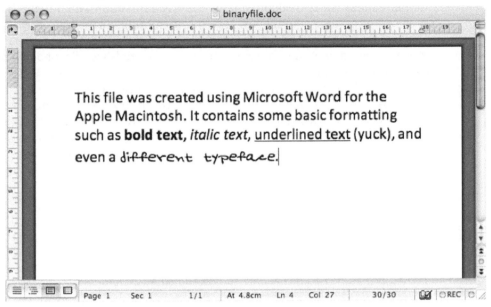

I then used an ASCII text editor to open the word processor file. The result is shown in Figure 11.7.

FIGURE 11.7   **Viewing the word processor binary file in a text editor**

As you can see, while the word processor program window only shows the formatted text, the text editor window shows all the information that is in the binary file. You can make out the raw text, but surrounding it are lots of strange looking characters which are the codes for the word processor's formatting commands. Every time you save a new word processor document, spreadsheet file, or database you are creating a binary file.

Binary file formats generally offer the programmer much more flexibility than text files. Entire records can be read and written in one go whereas, with a text file, each field of each record would have to be written individually. Some languages provide advanced stream handlers for binary files that allow a program to move forwards and backwards through a file repeatedly which offers great flexibility. File handling differs greatly across programming languages so we will not go into any more detail here.

Dealing with Non-existent Files

Because we are writing pseudo-code we have assumed that the input files we want to get data from will already exist. However, it is quite possible for a program to try to access a file name that does not exist; for example, a program could ask a user to enter the name of a file they want to process: if they type the name of a non-existent file it is not the program's fault but the program must be able to deal with this situation. The way this is handled varies from programming language to programming language, but in most of today's newer object-oriented languages it is accomplished by dealing with the *exception* that is thrown by the computer when an error condition arises (see example in Chapter 15). In some versions of Pascal if you tried to open a non-existent file the program would simply terminate with a run-time-error message. While this could be annoying, you at least knew something had gone wrong. Some C compilers, on the other hand, would generate a program that would carry on regardless "pretending" to read data from the non-existent file; depending on the context, it may take the programmer a while to notice that the program was not producing the correct results because no visible error message would occur. In Processing or Java you would write an exception handler that specifically watches out for this problem and deals with it when it arises.

Some languages use a function rather than a procedure to open a file with the function returning an error value if the file was not found. Other languages have their file-opening procedure assign a null value to the file variable if the file does not exist. Some languages do neither and instead require the programmer to write a special *compiler directive* to trap file errors.[8]

---

[8] A compiler directive is a feature specific to the compiler rather than the language itself which allows certain checking features to be turned on and off.

For the purposes of this book we will simply assume that all files are present and available for access.

11.4 Other Stream Types

While introductory programming courses tend to focus on monitor output, keyboard input, and basic file operations, modern programming languages offer a variety of stream types for dealing with richer input and output forms such as files of objects (a binary file format that cannot be read in a text editor) and industry-standard database systems. Because each language deals with streams in a different way and provides a variety of stream-handling objects and sub-programs, it is not instructive to go into further detail in this book. What you should be able to do is take the foundational principles outlined in this chapter and apply them to the extended mechanisms provided by any programming language.

11.5 Chapter Summary

In this chapter you learned how data are put into streams that allow input to and output from a program. Streams are generally non-permanent (the keyboard and the monitor display, for example) but can be diverted to files to allow input from and output to more permanent (persistent) forms of storage.

11.6 Exercises

1. Have a closer look at statements #9.3.1 and #9.4.1 in Program 11.5. Both statements write name and salary to reportFile – the only difference is the string they append to the end of the line. Give two solutions to the file writing section that remove the code duplication.

2. What is wrong with the algorithm fragment below?

   ```
   integer: myNumber ;
   Display ('Please enter an integer value: ') ;
   Get (keyboard, myNumber) ;
   ```

3. In Exercise 14 for Chapter 6 you were asked to write an algorithm to display a multiplication table. Amend your algorithm so that the table is written to a text file instead of the screen. The table to be calculated is stored as a single integer value in a text file table.txt which your program needs to read.

4. The algorithm below is intended to read from a file distances.txt which contains a number of real values representing distances in nautical miles between Stocksfield and a number of other cities. Each line contains a string holding the city name followed by a real value holding the distance to that city. There is no terminating record. Table 11.2 shows the cities and distances in nautical miles that are held in distances.txt as well as showing what the calculated distance in km should be.

The algorithm converts these distances to kilometers (1 nautical mile = 1852 meters) and displays the converted distances on the monitor screen. There are three errors in the algorithm. State what they are and correct them.

```
1.   integer: metersPerNM  IS 1852 ;
2.   string: city  ;
3.   real: distance ,
4.         distanceInKM  ;
5.   file: distancesFile  ;
6.   distancesFile  ← distances.txt' ;
7.   Display ('Distances of cities from Stocksfield (km).↵') ;
8.   Display ('~~~~~~~~~~~~~~~~~~~~~~~~~~~~~~~~~~~~~~~~~~↵') ;
9.   WHILE NOT EndOfFile ( distancesFile )
        9.1.   Get ( distancesFile , city , distance ) ;
        9.2.   distanceInKM  ←  distance  ×  metersPerNM  ;
        9.3.   Display ( city ,  ' = ',  distanceinKM  ,'km'↵) ;
     ENDWHILE
10.  Close ( distancesFile ) ;
```

Hint: there may be errors of omission as well as incorrect statements.

Table 11.2   **Distances from Stocksfield (Long:-1.9167, Lat:54.9333N)**

City	Distance from Stocksfield	
	Nautical Miles	km
Wylam	3.21	5.94
Newcastle	10.75	19.91
Edinburgh	75.02	138.93
Dublin	179.98	333.32
Cardiff	211.07	390.91
London	215.88	399.81
Paris	396.35	734.04
Berlin	561.44	1039.78
Jerusalem	2093.40	3876.98
Ottawa	2755.48	5103.14
Washington DC	3062.38	5671.52
Canberra	9123.53	16896.77
Wellington	9971.13	18466.53

5. Having found and corrected the errors in the previous exercise, now amend the algorithm so that it deals with a differently formatted distances.txt in which a line containing a city name of 'Stocksfield' and a distance of 0.0 marks the end of the data.

11.7 Projects

StockSnackz Vending Machine

Extend your solution so that every time a transaction takes place its details are written to a log file.

Stocksfield Fire Service

Write the results from your EAC decoding function to a text file as well as displaying them on the screen.

Puzzle World: Roman Numerals and Chronograms

Incorporate the functions you designed in Chapter 8 into a program that repeatedly offers the user choices to translate Roman numbers into decimal, decimal numbers into Roman, validate Roman number strings, and find the dates in chronograms. All four choices should be displayed and the appropriate functions invoked when the user selects one of the four options. A fifth option to quit the program should also be displayed, and the program should continue offering the user choices and performing the appropriate tasks until the user selects to quit.

Pangrams: Holoalphabetic Sentences

Using the function you wrote in the last chapter, write a program that prompts the user to enter a sentence and which calls the pangram-tester function to determine whether that sentence is a pangram. This prompt-and-test process should continue as long as the user wants to keep trying sentences.

Online Bookstore: ISBNs

Using the functions you wrote in Chapter 10, design a program that presents the user with two options: to validate an ISBN and to hyphenate an ISBN. The two choices should be displayed and the appropriate function or procedure invoked depending on the choice. For the validation choice the user is then prompted to enter a ten-digit ISBN without any hyphens. For the formatting option, the user is likewise invited to enter a raw ten-digit ISBN. This choice should be repeatedly given until the user indicates they wish to stop (by entering a 9, say). The outcome of each sub-program call, together with the supplied ISBN should also be written to a log file (a text file).

12 Static Data Structures

Learning Objectives

- Learn some of the basic structures (such as arrays and records) used to store multi-value data
- Understand how related data items can be combined and stored in a data structure
- Understand how to declare new data types to define a data structure
- Learn how to use arrays to store multi-dimensional data (e.g. tables)
- Understand the difference between static and dynamic data structures

In earlier chapters you learned about constant and variable data and how to store individual values in single variables. In this chapter you will learn how to group collections of data items into *data structures*. We start off by considering the *string* as a simple data structure (Section 12.1) and then go on to look at data *records* (Section 12.2). In Section 12.3 you will learn the difference between *static* (fixed size) and *dynamic* (changeable size) data structures, and then in Sections 12.4, 12.5, and 12.6 you will learn about the static data structure known as the *array* and some of the ways it can be used in programming problems.

12.1 Introduction

Without data, programs cannot do very much. Recall that programs typically process input data in order to produce output data. The ways in which data are stored and arranged can significantly affect the ways in which the program can process it. Data are organized into *data structures* which can range from the very simple to the very complex. We have already seen one of the simplest data structures there is: the integer variable. The statement

integer: number ;

is an instruction to set aside an area of memory that can hold precisely one integer value. This data structure has various properties and allows a number of different operations to be performed up on it (e.g. arithmetic tasks). We have also seen how to store real numbers and characters. However, we tend not to talk of simple variables like these as data structures. Rather, a data structure is normally considered to be a collection of data items that are related to one another in some way. We have already come across such a data structure in the string data type.

FIGURE 12.1   **A string data structure**

As Figure 12.1 shows, a string is a collection of individual characters that are *tied* together in a set order.[1] The ordering is important because a string's meaning is in the order of its characters. The reason we gather the characters together into a single collection is because it is more convenient to store and move a string as a whole than it is to have to deal with all of its characters individually (hence the picture of the piece of string holding all the characters together). If we did not have a string data structure then we would need to declare individual character variables for each letter in Figure 12.1's string. Furthermore, to give a value to the string we would have to assign a value to each of the characters in turn. While this may be a nuisance think how much more unwieldy it would be when dealing with longer strings such as names, addresses, the names of chemicals, etc. No, the characters of a string are not independent – they are part of a larger whole. Most programming languages provide a string data structure that allows for much easier manipulation of strings. It is more convenient to think of these characters collectively as a single entity (the string) because their meaning is in the string they form rather than as individual characters.

---

[1] This metaphor is not wholly accurate as one might infer that all the characters of a string are located in consecutive memory locations. This is not necessarily the case and will depend on the chosen programming language.

The way strings are stored and accessed in the computer's memory varies between programming languages. However, the general abstract data structure is common. If an integer can be pictured as a piece of paper in a shoebox which is labelled with the integer's identifier and which has a specific address in memory, then we can imagine a string being stored in memory something like Figure 12.2.[2]

FIGURE 12.2   **Visualizing a string in the computer's memory**

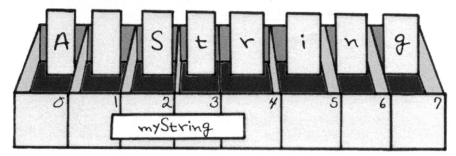

We can visualize a string as a collection of boxes that are fastened to each other. Each box takes up an allocation of the computer's memory and contains a single character. None of the characters has an individual identifier, instead the whole collection has an identifier (myString in Figure 12.2). Like an integer, the string in the variable myString is accessed through its identifier allowing statements like

```
myString  ← 'A string' ; // The string literal 'A string' is
                          // assigned to the string variable
                          // myString
```

Each compartment (or element) in myString is numbered reflecting its position in the string. This numbering is important as it allows direct access to the individual characters that make up the string. We shall see later on when looking at *arrays* how to make use of this feature, for now just keep it in mind. The point to notice about the string is that it is a collection of related data items of the same type (in this case, the data type character).

12.2   Record Structures and Data Types

Very often there is a need to group items of different data types. An example of this would be the patient records a doctor keeps. Each record in the file pertains to a single patient and contains many pieces of different information.

---

[2] This implies that the characters of a string are located in consecutive memory locations. This is not necessarily the case – the compartments in the tray could be distributed all over the computer's memory! How a string is actually stored in the computer depends on the chosen programming language.

A simple patient's record might contain the patient's name (family name and given name), title (Dr, Mr, Mrs, Ms, etc.), date of birth (day, month, and year), address, telephone number, the date they joined the practice, and the date of their last check up. Each item in the record is separate and not necessarily of the same type. For instance, the date of birth could be stored as three integers (day, month, and year) whilst the names would likely be held as strings. Programming languages generally provide mechanisms for storing records, though the terminology differs. Below is the *HTTLAP* pseudo-code for defining a record variable:

```
NEWTYPE RecordTypeIdentifier IS
    RECORD
        type:⌷member1⌷ ;
        type:⌷member2⌷ ;
        ...
    ENDRECORD
RecordTypeIdentifier:⌷identifier⌷ ;
```

A Word on Programmer-defined Data Types

Notice that before we can declare a record variable we first have to define a new *type*. Above we have defined a new RECORD type called RecordTypeIdentifier and declared a variable of that type. We will return to RECORD types shortly. Programming languages generally provide mechanisms for the programmer to define new data types in addition to the built-in integer, real, character, Boolean, and string types. For example, perhaps we have a problem that requires the user to repeatedly type in a number representing a month of the year followed by another figure representing the rainfall that month. The user could enter rainfall details in any month order. Because there are only 12 months in a year we know that the month variable should never have a value outside the range 1..12. We can write code to test the value input by the user and reject any invalid data. But we can further refine our solution by declaring a new integer type that only permits values between 1 and 12, thus:

Sub ranges ▶

```
NEWTYPE MonthType IS 1..12 ;
```

We can then declare a variable of type MonthType which will then only be able to take integer values in the sub-range 1..12.

```
MonthType:⌷month⌷ ;
```

Try defining your own data type for variables that can hold only the digit characters '0' to '9'. Once you have defined the type, declare a variable called **myDigit** of the new type.

Here is my solution:

Solution 12.1 Type definition for digitType

```
NEWTYPE DigitType IS '0'.. '9' ;
DigitType: myDigit  ;
```

Single-value data types like DigitType and MonthType are useful for restricting the range of values a variable can take. But we can also define types that allow data structure variables to be declared. A data structure variable is one that stores a collection of related values rather than a single value. This facility offers great flexibility and allows us, for example, to create the following example of a patient record for a doctor's office:

```
NEWTYPE PatientRecord IS
    RECORD
    string:  title ,
             familyName ,
             givenName  ;
    integer: birthDay ,
             birthMonth ,
             birthYear  ;
    string:  streetAddress ,
             postalTown ,
             postCode ,
             telephone  ;
    integer: joinDay ,
             joinMonth ,
             joinYear ,
             checkupDay ,
             checkupMonth ,
             checkupYear  ;
    ENDRECORD
PatientRecord: patient  ;
```

PatientRecord is a new RECORD type, and the statements between the RECORD...ENDRECORD keywords define what fields the record type possesses. Each field is declared like a variable. Thus the givenName field holds a string while joinDay holds an integer. Having defined the new type it is then used in the declaration of the variable patient that stores a single PatientRecord. A PatientRecord, in turn, holds 16 individual fields. So, patient is a data structure that holds the 16 items of data pertaining to a single person. Records are useful because they allow us to group related data items into a single variable. A single variable to store patient details is preferable to having 16 separate variables. We can visualize a record as in Figure 12.3.

The record variable's identifier is patient which is written on the label attached to the end of the box in Figure 12.3. The box is divided into 16 labelled compartments, one for each of the record's fields. Each compartment has a piece of paper

FIGURE 12.3   **Visualization of a RECORD variable**

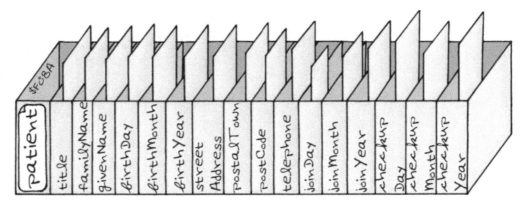

in it that will hold a value. Now the record has been declared we need a way of accessing its fields to assign values to it. This is done is via the *dot selector*. For example, to create a new patient, we could write the following:

```
 1.   patient . title     ← 'Professor' ;
 2.   patient . familyName ← 'Higgins' ;
 3.   patient . givenName  ← 'Henry' ;
 4.   patient . birthDay   ← 15 ;
 5.   patient . birthMonth ← 3 ;
 6.   patient . birthYear  ← 1956 ;
 7.   patient . streetAddress ← '27A Wimpole Street' ;
 8.   patient . postalTown ← 'London' ;
 9.   patient . postCode   ← 'W1G 8GP' ;
10.   patient . telephone  ← 'Whitehall 55' ;
11.   patient . joinDay    ← 29 ;
12.   patient . joinMonth  ← 9 ;
13.   patient . joinYear   ← 1962 ;
14.   patient . checkupDay ← 4 ;
15.   patient . checkupMonth ← 3 ;
16.   patient . checkupYear ← 2004 ;
```

This would lead to our visualization being updated as in Figure 12.4. The fields of the record could then be displayed on the screen:

```
Display ( patient . familyName ) ;
```

If we had a second patient record

PatientRecord: patient2 ;

and we wanted to copy all of the first record's fields to it, we could do it by copying each field in turn, as in

```
patient2 . title ← patient . title ;
```

Dot selector ▶

FIGURE 12.4   **The patient record with populated fields**

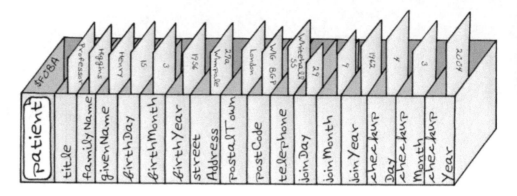

But this could be cumbersome, so, like many programming languages, the *HTTLAP* pseudo-code allows the contents of a record to be copied in their entirety to another record of *the same type*:

$$\boxed{\texttt{patient2}} \leftarrow \boxed{\texttt{patient}} \ ;$$

The above statement copies the contents of each field in `patient` to the corresponding fields in `patient2`.[3]

The record structure allows us to store a single record in one variable in the same way that the integer type allows the storage of a single integer in one variable. The power of the record type is that the fields do not have to be of the same type. The question then arises of how we could store *many* patient records. The answer is to build a data structure of `PatientRecords`. This could be achieved with an array (see Sections 12.4–12.6) or with a linked list (see Chapter 13).

12.3 Dynamic and Static Data Structures

There is a theoretically infinite number of different data structures possible as any assortment of data values could be arranged in any number of ways. However, there are some basic kinds of data structure that programmers use to build larger, more complex structures. The string is typically based on the *array* structure, though in Processing and Java a class is used. An array (also sometimes called a *vector*) is a variable that, instead of reserving a section of memory for a single value, reserves a rectangular collection of memory chunks for holding a collection of data items where each *element* of the array holds a single data item (though that data item could, itself, be a more complex data structure). Most programming languages require all the elements of the array to be of the same

---

[3] In Java (and other object-oriented languages) you have to be careful of assignments like this. If `patient` and `patient2` were declared as objects (class instances) rather than value types, then the assignment would copy a reference to `patient` into `patient2`, that is, both variables would now point to the *same object*. The upshot is that a change to any of the fields in `patient2` would also be a change to `patient`. When working with object types you need to use the class's built-in or inherited copy method to achieve what this example does.

type, though this is not always the case, especially with the newer versions of object-oriented languages.[4]

String ▶ The string is an example of a static data structure. A static data structure is one that has a fixed size beyond which it may not grow. In old languages a string typically could not contain more than 255 characters. Java and Processing are a little more generous, allowing typically 2,147,483,647 characters per string, but this is still a fixed size and cannot grow regardless of how much memory the computer may have.[5] Static data structures have the advantage of being easy to manipulate by the programmer. Their principal limitation is that they can neither expand to provide extra capacity if needed nor can they shrink if their capacity is not being used. A 255-character string variable will take up enough storage to hold 255 characters whether it holds one character, ten characters, or 255 characters. A static data structure is like a garage. Once you have built it you can only fit cars of up to a certain size in it. If you buy a new car that is too big for your garage then you either park it in the rain or knock down the garage and build a larger one. Similarly, if your car is very small your garage will have lots of empty room inside which could have been given over to something more useful (a tool shed, perhaps?).

For this reason programming languages also provide facilities for *dynamic* data structures which can grow and shrink in size using only as much memory as needed. Dynamic data structures are like modern car seat belts that snugly fit large and small people alike (or like those flexible-tape queue management systems you see in banks, airports, and cinemas these days).[6] If you like, a dynamic

FIGURE 12.5 **A static data structure is like a garage . . .**

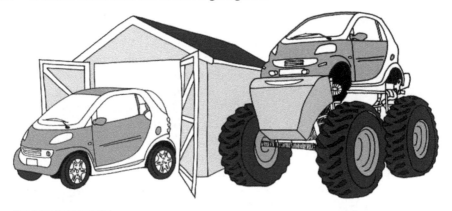

---

[4] In other words, an array in C would be a collection of integers, or floats, or characters, etc., but not a mixed collection. C#, on the other hand, being object-oriented, would allow collections of items descended from the root `Object` ancestor class.

[5] The Java string size is limited to `Integer.MAX_VALUE` which is normally $2^{31}-1$.

[6] Granted, a seat belt has a finite length, but in reality so does a dynamic data structure which is still limited by the total amount of memory the computer can allocate to it. As long as the car user is within the operating limits of the seat belt then the belt will fit them whatever their size. As long as the dynamic data structure does not use up all the memory it can accommodate as many or as few items as required. In fact, dynamic data structures using up too much memory (often through a badly formed insertion loop) are a common cause of frustration amongst programmers as they can lead to difficult-to-spot bugs.

data structure is a garage with expandable walls that can move out and in to accommodate different sized cars snugly. Table 12.1 lists some examples of the various static and dynamic data structures that can be built with most modern programming languages. There is some crossover in some cases as Java offers a vector type that can grow and shrink, and stacks and queues can be implemented using arrays, but the table gives a general flavour and should not be considered exhaustive or final.

Table 12.1   **Static and Dynamic Data Structures**

Static Data Structures	Dynamic Data Structures	
	Simple	Recursive
Array, table, vector, matrix	Linked list, stack, queue	Binary tree, multiway tree, ordered tree, B-tree

In the sections that follow we will look at the basics of implementing static and dynamic data structures. For the static structures, this chapter will concentrate on arrays. For the dynamic structures Chapter 13 will explore the simple list (unsorted and sorted), the stack, and the queue. It is beyond the scope of this book to consider the recursive structures as the bewildered programmer needs to focus energy on mastering the more basic types.

12.4   Arrays as Lists

Arrays are common in the everyday world. A key rack is a good metaphor to use when thinking of arrays. The rack is a single unit that has a number of hooks arrayed across its back panel. Each hook is designed to hold a key (or, perhaps, a bunch of keys). Sometimes the hooks are `labelled` to aid identification of the keys, but this is not always the case. To move all the keys stored in the key rack you simply pick up the entire rack; the rack is a container for the keys.

Another common metaphor for the array is a set of pigeon holes (or a mail rack) as in Figure 12.6. Each pigeon hole is used to hold something (typically mail in an office). The compartments are often `labelled` and arranged in alphabetical order. The mail rack is an *array* of pigeon holes or compartments.

FIGURE 12.6   **An array of pigeon holes**

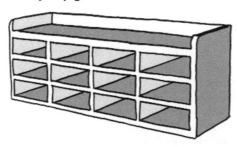

Arrays are very useful in programming. Consider the case where Bob wants to find the average weight of large chocolate cakes baked by Barbara. Assume Barbara has nine cakes and a set of scales. Bob could ask her to tell him the weight of each cake in turn and he would then add this weight to a running total and divide the final total by the number of cakes to give the average weight. Expressed as pseudo-code the algorithm might look something like Program 12.1.

```
1.  PROGRAM Average weight calculation ;
2.  real: weight ,
3.        totalWeight ,
4.        averageWeight ;
5.  integer: counter ;
6.  integer: numberOfCakes IS 9 ; //Constant for no. of cakes
7.  totalWeight ← 0 ;
8.  FOR counter GOES FROM 1 TO numberOfCakes
        8.1.  Get (Barbara, REFERENCE: weight ) ;
        8.2.  totalWeight ← totalWeight + weight ;
    ENDFOR
9.  averageWeight ← totalWeight ÷ numberOfCakes ;
10. Display ( averageWeight ) ;
```

Program 12.1

Calculating cake weights

Think Spot

In Program 12.1 Bob needs to engage in dialogue with Barbara each time he wants a cake weight. In addition, after calculating the average weight Bob has no record of the weights of individual cakes as they are not stored anywhere. We could get round this by declaring nine weight variables (weight1...weight9) one for each cake. Can you see a problem with this? What if we wanted to deal with 50 or even 100 cakes? We would not want to declare 50 or 100 cake weight variables. Of course, we could store the cake weights in a file and read them in each time we need them using the above algorithm, but if you think about it, a file is just a data structure held on disc rather than in the computer's memory. What would be useful is to have a data structure to hold all the cake weights but which allows easy access. This is where the array comes in. Imagine now that each time Barbara bakes a cake she weighs it and writes its weight on a blackboard (see Figure 12.7).

The board in Figure 12.7 shows the weights in kilos of nine large chocolate cakes. In effect, we have an array of weights. The array is called 'Large chocolate cake weights' and it has nine elements (numbered from 1 to 9), where each element is a value corresponding to the weight of an individual cake. With the data so arranged we could now calculate the average weight of a large chocolate cake which is, of course:

$$\frac{2 + 1.8 + 2.1 + 1.9 + 2 + 2 + 1.7 + 2 + 1.9}{9} = 1.9$$

The advantage of storing the data in an array is that the individual values can be easily accessed through the array's identifier 'Large chocolate cake weights'. The weight of the first element in the array *Large chocolate cake weights* is 2 kg, the weight of the ninth is 1.9 kg. The entire set of weights can be carried around by

FIGURE 12.7   **The weights (in kilos) of 9 large chocolate cakes**

Large chocolate cake weights

1	2	3	4	5	6	7	8	9
2	1.8	2.1	1.9	2	2	1.7	2	1.9

picking up the blackboard and moving it. The array is a static data structure because it has a maximum capacity (in this case nine cakes). The array would take up the same physical space regardless of whether there were nine cake weights chalked on it or none. What the blackboard array does is to allocate a storage space for nine related data items. It is then up to Bob and Barbara to add and remove weights as they see fit knowing that they can never store more than nine cake weights. What we have done is to replace the need for nine separate storage areas each with its own name with a single data structure with a single name 'Large chocolate cake weights' that can store nine data items.

Declaring an Array

Figure 12.8 illustrates how a simple array variable is declared with the *HTTLAP* pseudo-code. The name of the variable is `weights`. The keyword ARRAY tells us that this variable holds an array of values rather than a single value. The number in square brackets is the size of the array, that is, the number of elements it can store. Finally, the type of the array elements is given. So, Figure 12.8 declares a new variable, `weights`, that is a nine-element array of **real** values. (Notice how all the elements have to be of the same type. If you want to mix data types then you will need to define a record structure and then declare an array of records.) This means that `weights` can store anything from zero to nine real numbers.

FIGURE 12.8   **How to declare an array variable**

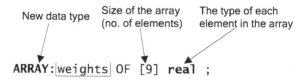

It cannot store more than nine values, however, so you need to be careful when declaring an array that you have thought through the size it should be. Make it too large and you are using up extra storage and making your algorithms less efficient. Make it too small and you may run out of room. Normally, you would only use an array when you have a pretty good idea of the number of values you are going to store and are confident that the number will not fluctuate very much. If you are in a position of having a data structure that stores a few then a lot of records repeatedly, or which may need to grow, then you should consider a dynamic structure (see Chapter 13).

Why can't an array store values of different types? This seems like a needless restriction.

It's to do with the way memory is allocated. When an integer variable is declared, say, an amount of memory necessary to hold an integer value is reserved. Suppose an integer requires four bytes of storage, then a 100-element array of integers would use 100 × 4 bytes = 400 bytes plus a few bytes extra overhead for the array identifier. Because an array is a static structure, its memory allocation must be worked out when it is declared. If we were to allow an array to store values of any and all types in its different elements, then we could not know how much storage space needs to be set aside: a real number requires more bytes than an integer, for example. There are ways that this limitation could be overcome by the language designers, but one of the principal advantages of arrays is that they are very quick to access and efficient to store because of their data type restrictions. If a more flexible scheme were needed, then an untyped collection would be required. Object-oriented languages tend to offer just such a data structure, but it is beyond the scope of this book to cover this.

Zero-based Indexing

Figure 12.9 is a visualization of the array following its declaration. `weights` has a memory location (`$1DA0`) which is used as the entry point to the array. Its nine elements are shown as empty compartments each with its respective index in square brackets below.

FIGURE 12.9 **Picturing the `weights` array**

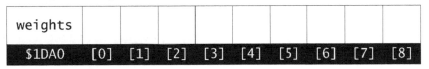

Notice that the array elements are numbered from 0 to 8 rather than 1 to 9. This is because programming languages tend to use *zero-based indexing* when dealing with array-type structures. This means that the first element of an array has an index value of zero. The ninth element in `weights` would thus be accessed by `weights [8]`.[7]

---

[7] Not all languages use zero-based indexing. BASIC, for example, uses 1 as the index for an array's first element, whilst Visual BASIC, Fortran, and Pascal let the programmer decide what base to use for each array.

Zero-based indexing is not as silly as it might first appear. In the binary numbering system we know that a byte (8 bits) can store 256 values, but that those values are zero (00000000) to 255 (11111111). That is, the *first* value that can be stored in a byte is zero and the 256th value is 255. It may take you a little bit of time to get used to zero-based array indices, but it is worth learning it now rather than learning 1-based indexing now and then having to unlearn it when you write programs in Processing or Java. That said, zero-based indexing remains the cause of bugs in many novice programmers' code as in the beginning it is natural to read weights [2] as meaning the second element in the weights array (wrong) rather than the third element (correct).

Accessing an Array

Accessing the individual elements of an array is straightforward requiring the use of an index number after the array variable name. For example, the following statement would assign the value 2.0 to the first element in the weights array.

weights [0] ← 2.0 ;

Read the above statement as "assign the real value 2.0 to the element with an index of zero in the array called weights." This is like writing the value 2.0 in the first column of the blackboard, or writing "2.0" on the piece of paper in the first compartment in the box called weights. Note that we write weights [0] rather than weights [1] to refer to the first element of the array because of zero-based indexing. Figure 12.10 shows the state of the array after the above assignment statement has been executed.

FIGURE 12.10   **The array after the assignment statement**

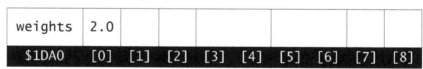

Let's use the array of cake weights we declared earlier to see how arrays can be accessed and manipulated. As we have seen, the most straightforward way to assign a value to an array element is to use the element's index explicitly in an assignment statement:

weights [0] ← 2.0 ;

which assigns the real value 2.0 to the first element in weights. The value in brackets does not have to be an integer literal, it can be any expression that evaluates to an integer. We could write

weights [0 + 1] ← 3.0 ;

or

weights [index] ← 4.5 ;

or even

weights [index + 3] ← 7.0 ;

where `index` is an `integer` variable. We could also use the value of one element in the assignment of another:

weights [0] ← weights [8] ;

This last statement assigns the value of the ninth element to the first element.

To check you have grasped array indexing, assume the integer variable **index** has the value 5 and write the results of the five assignment statements above in the array pictured below:

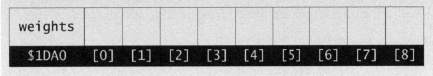

What do you think would be the result of the following assignment?

weights [index + 4] ← 2.0 ;

Once an array element has a value we can use it in other program statements, for example:

```
Display (weights [0]) ;
Display ('Two of the first cake would weigh', weights [0] × 2.0,
         ' kilos.') ;
```

Index Warning

Be careful never to supply an index value that is less than zero or that is greater than the capacity of the array. A statement such as

weights [10] ← 2.0 ;

Index bounds ▶
error

does not make sense because weights does not have 11 elements. This error would likely be spotted by a language compiler as it is clearly an attempt to access an array element that does not exist. This is called an *index-out-of-bounds* error for the obvious reason. Whilst this blatant type of indexing error is easy enough to spot (though you would be surprised at how many times you will make this mistake), the more subtle version is

weights [index + 1] ← 2.0 ;

The above statement may or may not cause an error. As long as `index` is between −1 and 7, then there is no problem. But if `index` has a value of less than −1 or more than 7 then `index + 1` will yield a value that is outside the permitted index range for the weights array (0–8). A compiler would not pick up this manifestation of the index-out-of-bounds error because it is not always going to be an error. The bug will only manifest itself during the program run-time and then only if index is less than −1 or more than 7. This type of bug is harder to spot as the cause may lie far away from the problem (for example, index may be assigned the errant value in a procedure in another part of the program).

Initializing an Array

In some languages arrays are initialized to some starting value upon declaration, whilst in others no initialization takes place. When designing programs it is, perhaps, better to assume that no initialization takes place and to design specific initialization code. If the language you are using does support automatic initialization then you can just leave out the extra code. So, in our example weights has been declared and its nine elements have undefined values. We could, of course, initialize the array by setting each element in turn to zero:

```
weights [0] ← 0.0 ;
...
weights [8] ← 0.0 ;
```

This is cumbersome but manageable for a small array, but it is not very workable for larger arrays. What if the array had 100 elements? The answer is to use a loop. Because the size of an array is already known (it had to be specified in its declaration) we should use a FOR loop. With a loop we can set each element in turn to zero, thus:

```
1.   integer: counter ;
2.   FOR counter GOES FROM 0 TO 8
         2.1.   weights [counter] ← 0.0 ;
     ENDFOR
```

The FOR loop uses counter as the loop counter which is then used as the index to the array in statement #2.1. The first time round the loop counter will be 0 so weights [counter] refers to weights [0]. On the ninth iteration counter will have the value 8 so this time the ninth element of the array will be set to 0.0. If our programming language has a function that tells us the size of the array, we could use that in the FOR loop to make the code easier to change in the event that we redefine the capacity of the array in a later version of the program. Some languages have a function called Length (or similar) that returns the capacity of an array expressed as the maximum number of its elements. We could rewrite the above as:

```
1.   integer: counter ;
2.   FOR counter GOES FROM 0 TO Length (weights) − 1
         2.1.   weights [counter] ← 0.0 ;
     ENDFOR
```

Note, you only need to initialize an array if you require all its elements to have a defined value prior to assigning any values. For example, you might have an array to store the statistics of different players in an online game. Each time a player wins a match its score is added to the element corresponding to that player. At any time you might inspect the array to see which player is performing best and calculate the average. In this case you should initialize each element of the array to zero so that if no scores are entered for a particular player their element will have the defined value of zero. If initialization is not done then you might try to calculate the average based on an array element whose value is undefined. This would crash the program at best, or give incorrect results at worst.[8]

Huh?

Why did you write:

FOR counter GOES FROM 0 TO Length (weights) – 1

What is the −1 for?

We said the function **Length** returns the size of an array expressed as the number of its elements. The array **weights** has nine elements, so **Length (weights)** returns the value 9. Remember though that arrays use zero-based indexing, so to access the ninth element of weights we need to refer to **weights [8]**. Thus the subtraction of 1 is needed to ensure the **FOR** loop goes from 0–8 rather than 0–9 which would cause an index-out-of-bounds error.

Shorthand Array Initialization

Above we saw how to initialize an array within a loop. Modern languages like Processing and Java offer a way of initializing an array at the time it is declared. For example, let's say we have an array of three integers and we want to put the values 25, 8, 90 into the three elements. Here is the *HTTLAP* shorthand way of declaring and initializing the array in one go:

ARRAY: numbers OF [3] **integer** ← {25, 8, 90} ;

The list of values to go into the array is placed inside a pair of {} braces; the first value in the list is placed in the first array element, the second value in the second element, and so on. If, when declaring an array you know what initial values you want it to have, then you can consider using this shorthand notation. Be warned, though, you will need to provide a value for every element. So, if your array is 1000 elements long, you might not want to use this technique as a loop will be much easier to write.

In the case of Bob's bakery, we could say that initialization takes place when Barbara enters the nine cake weights. An outline algorithm could be:

```
1.  FOR each element in cake weights array
        1.1  Prompt for and get cake weight ;
    ENDFOR
```

---

[8] A program crash is preferable here because you know there is a problem. If the results are merely incorrect you might not realize the program has a bug.

In more formal pseudo-code this becomes:

```
1.    integer: counter  ;
2.    FOR  counter  GOES FROM 0 TO Length ( weights ) − 1
          2.1.   Display ('Enter a cake weight : ') ;
          2.2.   Get (Barbara, REFERENCE: weights  [ counter ]) ;
      ENDFOR
```

Notice how statement #2.2 works. The Get procedure takes as its first parameter the name of the stream that provides the data (in this case Barbara) and as its second parameter a reference to the array element to be filled, so whatever is given by Barbara gets put directly into the array. (We may decide that it would be better to specify the keyboard as the input stream rather than Barbara as the keyboard is how Barbara will enter the weights.) Now that the cake weights are in the array Bob can find the heaviest one, work out the average weight, display the weights in a formatted table, and so on, as in Solution 12.2.

Solution 12.2 Using the cakes array

```
1.    PROGRAM cakeweights
2.    ARRAY: weights  OF [9] real ;
3.    integer: counter  ;
4.    FOR  counter  GOES FROM 0 TO Length ( weights ) − 1
          4.1.   Display ('Enter a cake weight : ') ;
          4.2.   Get (Barbara, REFERENCE: weights  [ counter ]) ;
      ENDFOR
//Calculate heaviest cake and average weight
5.    real: average ,
6.          totalWeight ,
7.          heaviestCake  ;
8.    average  ← 0.0 ;
9.    totalWeight  ← 0.0 ;
10.   heaviestCake  ← 0.0 ;
11.   FOR  counter  GOES FROM 0 TO Length ( weights )− 1
          11.1.   totalWeight  ←  totalWeight  +  weights  [ counter ] ;
          11.2.   IF ( weights  [ counter ] >  heaviestCake )
                      11.2.1.   heaviestCake  ←  weights  [ counter ] ;
                  ENDIF
      ENDFOR
12.   IF ( total  > 0.0)
          12.1.   average  ←  total  ÷ Length ( weights ) ;
      ENDIF
13.   Display ('Average cake weight is ',  average ) ;
14.   Display ('Heaviest cake weight is ',  heaviestCake ,
      'kilos');
// Display cake weights as table
15.   Display ('Cake no. Weight') ;
```

Think Spot

```
16.  Display ('~~~~~~~~ ~~~~~~') ;
17.  FOR counter GOES FROM 0 TO Length (weights )- 1
         17.1.  Display (counter:8, weights [counter]:6:2) ;
     ENDFOR
// End program
```

Why does statement #12.1 in Solution 12.2 not say **Length** (weights) – 1 ?

Table Lookup: Looking up Values in an Array

Solution 12.2 above shows two operations that can be performed on an array: iterating through it to display its contents and iterating through it to find the largest value. Another common task is to search an array for a particular value. Imagine Bob is concerned about cakes that weigh too little, specifically, he wants to know if there are any cakes that weigh less than 1.8 kg. Assuming the weights array has been populated with the values shown in Figure 12.11: then the

FIGURE 12.11   **The populated weights array**

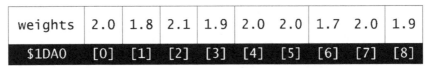

weights	2.0	1.8	2.1	1.9	2.0	2.0	1.7	2.0	1.9
$1DA0	[0]	[1]	[2]	[3]	[4]	[5]	[6]	[7]	[8]

pseudo-code in Solution 12.3 would determine whether there is at least one cake that weighs less than 1.8 kg.

Solution 12.3 Searching the array for a particular value

```
1.  boolean: found ;
2.  integer: counter ;
3.  found ← False ;
4.  counter ← 0 ;
5.  WHILE (counter ≤ 8) AND (NOT found)
        5.1.  found ← weights [counter] < 1.8 ;
        5.2.  counter ← counter + 1 ;
    ENDWHILE
6.  IF (found)
        6.1.  Display ('A low weight cake was found at element no.',
              counter) ;
    ENDIF
```

Examine the above pseudo-code to make sure you understand what it does. The heart of the algorithm is the WHILE loop in statement #5. The purpose of statements #5.1 and #5.2 should be fairly clear. Statement #5.1 sets the value of **found** according to whether the current list element is less than 1.8 or not. Statement #5.2

increments the loop counter. The WHILE loop terminates either when the end of the array is reached or a value of less than 1.8 is found. If the array in Figure 12.11 were used then the loop would terminate with a value of True in **found** and a value of 6 in **counter**. You may have recognized that this solution uses a WHILE as a count-controlled loop. Why, then, did I not use a FOR statement which is purpose-built for count-controlled loops? The main answer lies in the compound condition that is used to terminate the WHILE. Notice how the WHILE does not necessarily visit each element of the array? If the first element contained a value of less than 1.8 the loop would terminate after the first iteration. The loop is, indeed, count-controlled, but the counter has been supplemented with the test that checks whether the current element is the value we are looking for. To see how a FOR loop leads to a less efficient and less concise version of the algorithm consider Solution 12.4.

Solution 12.4 Search the array with a FOR loop – not recommended

1. **boolean:** found ;
2. **integer:** counter ,
3.   location ;
4. found ← false ;
5. counter ← 0 ;
6. FOR counter GOES FROM 0 TO Length (weights) – 1
    6.1. IF (weights [counter] < 1.8)
        6.1.1. found ← true ;
        6.1.2. location ← counter ;
    ENDIF
  ENDFOR
7. IF (found)
    7.1. Display ('A low weight cake was found at element no.', counter) ;
  ENDIF

Notice two things about this FOR loop solution. First, every element of the array is visited because the FOR is a strict count-controlled loop: it will always step through each of its iterations.[9] This means that even if the first element contains the target value the loop will still iterate through the whole array. Secondly, because each array element is visited we cannot use the Boolean assignment technique from statement #5.1 in Solution 12.3; although **found** would be set to True at element 7 it would be reset to False at element 8. Therefore, **found** must be initialized to False

---

[9] There are mechanisms in most programming languages for leaving a block early. For example, the **goto** keyword in C, C++ , C# allows control to move to a defined area of code. However, using **goto** type keywords can be very dangerous in the hands of the inexpert programmer and can lead to very badly structured and difficult to debug code. So, for our purposes it is best ignored. You can also use the **break** keyword in C-based languages to leave a block early. **goto** and **break** allow you build loop-and-a-half iterations. I think it is safer for us to stick with the zero-or-more or at-least-once iterations. When you have mastered these then you can look at the refinements offered by **break** and **goto**. Note that Java does not have a **goto** keyword precisely because it is so easy to misuse.

before the loop and then an IF construct employed to set it to True when the target value is found. Finally, and again because the loop steps through each element, an extra variable, location, is needed to store the value of an element that contains the target. You might also notice that this algorithm finds the *last* occurrence of the target whereas Solution 12.3 finds the *first* occurrence.

If the array is sorted, that is, ordered according to the values of its contents, then search algorithms can be further refined. Also, there are many algorithms available for sorting arrays (or other lists) into ascending or descending order. It is beyond the scope of this introductory text to explore those algorithms, though we will look at algorithms for manipulating lists that are already sorted in Chapter 13.

Random Access in Arrays

Our array processing up till now has been sequential. That is, we have worked through the arrays element-by-element starting with the first and ending with the last. Actually, arrays do not have to be processed in this way. Consider Bob and Barbara again. Every time Barbara bakes cakes she will tell Bob who will add the information to the tally he is keeping. Bob wants to keep track of the cake types, so Barbara will say things like "Another large chocolate", or "Two more lemon drizzles". Bob will then add the quantity to the respective cake totals (see Figure 12.12).

FIGURE 12.12 **Bob's cake tally**

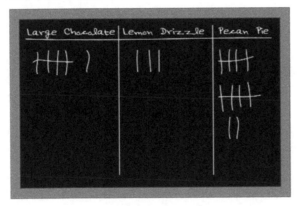

We could declare an array to hold the cake tallies:

1. ARRAY: cakeTally OF [3] **integer** ;

where index zero holds the large chocolate cake tally, index 1 the lemon drizzles and index 2 the pecan pie numbers. We can initialize the array so that we start off with a zero count for each cake type.

2. **integer**: counter ;
3. FOR counter GOES FROM 0 TO Length (cakeTally) – 1
    3.1. cakeTally [counter] ← 0 ;
   ENDFOR

When Barbara bakes a cake we do not know in advance what type it is going to be. Therefore, we cannot simply step through the array sequentially reading in cake values. Instead we need to be able to repeatedly read in pairs of data representing the cake type and the quantity baked and then increment the corresponding array element. The following pseudo-code shows how we could do this. The user types in a cake type (a value between 0 and 2) and a quantity. A `cakeType` value greater than 2 will indicate there are no more cake quantities to enter.

```
4.    integer: cakeType  ,
5.             quantity  ;
6.    Get (keyboard, REFERENCE: cakeType , REFERENCE: quantity ) ;
7.    WHILE ( cakeType  ≤ Length ( cakeTally )) – 1)
      7.1.   cakeTally  [ cakeType ] ←  cakeTally  [ cakeType ] +
             quantity  ;
      7.2.   Get (keyboard, REFERENCE: cakeType , REFERENCE:
             quantity ) ;
      ENDWHILE
```

The body of the WHILE loop adds the quantity entered to the array element indexed by the cake type entered and then reads the next data pair. This means that the user could enter the cake quantities in any order because the quantity is accompanied by the cake type it should be added to. This is another common way of processing arrays and is called *random access*. It is not a random process; the term means that the array elements are accessed in a non-sequential manner.

Huh?

What does WHILE (cakeType ≤ Length (cakeTally) – 1) mean in the above example? How does it check that the type is between 0 and 2? How does the loop terminate?

Barbara is going to enter an unspecified number of cake quantities. Each time she bakes anything she will enter its type (0, 1, 2) and the quantity she baked. She might bake a lemon drizzle followed by two pecan pies, then another lemon drizzle and then three large chocolate cakes. The ordering of the cake types cannot be known in advance. Therefore, the loop needs to continue until Barbara enters a cake type greater than 2. I could have written:

```
WHILE ( cakeType  ≤ 2)
```

which is more straightforward. However, what if Bob added another two cake types to his range? Not only would the array declaration need to be changed to:

```
ARRAY: cakeTally  OF 5 integer ;
```

But the loop would also have to be changed to:

```
WHILE ( cakeType  ≤ 4)
```

This is bad programming practice because it would be easy to forget to change the WHILE condition when the array size changes which would lead to errors. What I have done is to link the WHILE to the size of the array. The line

```
WHILE ( cakeType  ≤ Length ( cakeTally )) – 1)
```

checks the size of the **cakeTally** array (which is 3) and subtracts to put the value back into the zero-based indexing range needed for array access. Thus, the condition does in fact check to see whether **cakeType** is less than or equal to 2. However, if Bob added two more cake types, we would only need to modify the array's declaration as the **WHILE** loop would still work. **Length (cakeTally)** would now give 5, and subtracting 1 would give 4 and thus the loop would continue while **cakeType** is in the range 0 to 4.

An Array of Records

When looking at records in Section 12.2 I asked how we could store several patient records and said we could use an array or a linked list (section 13.1). The following pseudo-code statement declares an array variable that can store ten patient records.

ARRAY: patientArray OF [10] **PatientRecord** ;

We could then display the given name field of the seventh patient thus:

Display (patientArray [6]. givenName) ;

Notice that we simply use the dot selector after the index value. The above statement reads "Display the **givenName** field of the record stored in the seventh element of the array **patientArray**."

Write statements to assign the values **'Professor'**, **'Higgins'**, **'Henry'** to the **title**, **familyName** and **givenName** fields of the patient record held in the second element of the **patientArray** array.

Take-home Lesson

The main lesson to learn about arrays is that they are really quite straightforward data structures to set up and use, and yet they can cause the beginning programmer such misery that one would think they were some kind of advanced quantum calculus. In my experience the main stumbling block with beginners is using the array index correctly. This is especially true with zero-based indexing (where the first element of the array has an index number of zero). Say we have a ten-element array of integers called **numbers**. A common mistake is to write code equivalent to the following to initialize the array:

```
1.   FOR  counter  GOES FROM 1 TO 10
        1.1.   numbers [ counter ] ← 0 ;
     ENDFOR
```

Because zero-based indexing is used, the first element of the array will not be initialized and then the program will generate an error when it tries to access an 11th element that does not even exist! A corrected solution is:

```
1.   FOR  counter  GOES FROM 0 TO 9 DO
        1.1.   numbers [ counter ] ← 0 ;
     ENDFOR
```

However, as we saw above, if the size of the numbers array is ever changed, the FOR loop would also need to be amended. A more future-proof and maintainable solution then is:

1.   FOR counter GOES FROM 0 TO Length (numbers)-1 DO
        1.1.   numbers [counter] ← 0 ;
      ENDFOR

To recap: an array is a variable that stores many values rather than a single value. You might like to use the metaphor of a lot of boxes tied together to understand how the array is stored in the computer's memory. The boxes have a collective identity which is the name of the array variable. Each box can be individually accessed by specifying the array name and the *index* value of the box, where zero is the index value of the first element and *n*-1 is the index value of the *n*th element.

12.5   Arrays as Tables

Simple arrays are useful structures for storing lists of values or records. Often we need to work with tabular data rather than simple lists. A table has rows and columns. For instance, consider Table 12.2 which shows cake sales by month in Bob's bakery.

Table 12.2   **Bob's bakery: sales of cake by month**

Cake Type	J	F	M	A	M	J	J	A	S	O	N	D
Large chocolate	30	25	12	5	8	10	11	5	9	10	20	40
Lemon drizzle	15	12	16	12	18	11	49	40	29	13	12	30
Pecan pie	39	20	25	25	33	32	24	20	23	60	52	75

To hold the sales data in a program we could declare three arrays of 12 elements, one for each of the three cake types:

1.   **integer:** arraySize IS 12 ;
2.   **ARRAY:** largeChocolate OF [arraySize] **integer** ;
3.   **ARRAY:** lemonDrizzle OF [arraySize] **integer** ;
4.   **ARRAY:** pecanPie OF [arraySize] **integer** ;

Then we could perform operations on each of the three arrays and, with some careful logic, we could work out averages and totals for each cake type and all of the cakes combined. But what if Bob had not three but 30 cake types? We would not want 30 array variables. It seems like we are back where we started when we needed to store multiple values in one variable.

What is needed is an array of arrays, that is, an array where each element is itself an array, in effect, defining a table. The rows of the table will be used for the cake types and the columns for the months. And this is just what programming languages allow us to do. Consider the following declaration:

ARRAY: salesTable OF [3,12] **integer** ;

The size part of the declaration has been extended to [3,12]. This means, declare an array called salesTable that has two dimensions: the first dimension has three elements and each of those elements itself has 12 elements. The easiest way to visualize this is as a table. The first dimension tells us the number of rows and the second dimension the number of columns. So, salesTable has three rows of 12 columns. An alternative way of declaring this table (which is closer to the way you would do it in Processing and Java) is:

ARRAY: salesTable [3] [12] OF **integer** ;

All we have done is place the size of each dimension in its own set of square brackets. The above declaration says salesTable is an array of three elements each of which has 12 elements. You can use either notation for the purposes of this book as they mean the same thing. We can visualize salesTable as Figure 12.13.

FIGURE 12.13   Visualization of the salesTable array

| $2F3C |
| salesTable |

	[0]	[1]	[2]	[3]	[4]	[5]	[6]	[7]	[8]	[9]	[10]	[11]
[0]												
[1]												
[2]												

Figure 12.13 shows the array salesTable with three rows of 12 cells. In effect, salesTable is an array of arrays – each element in the rows array is itself an array of 12 columns. We could use the salesTable array for holding Bob's cake sales figures. If weights [0] provides access to the first element of the one-dimensional weights array we looked at earlier, how do you think we can get access to an individual cell in the salesTable array? Think about how you specify a grid square on a map or road atlas.

Think Spot

There are two ways we can address an array element in a two-dimensional array. The following two statements both assign the value 25 to the second column in the first row:

salesTable [0, 1] ← 25 ;

salesTable [0] [1] ← 25 ;

The two statements have the same function and result in the table now looking like Figure 12.14.

FIGURE 12.4   **The salesTable array with one value**

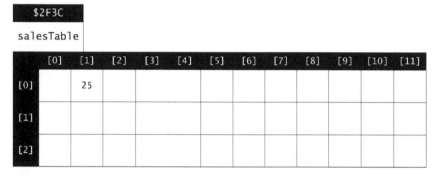

Access to elements in a two-dimensional array like salesTable is given by specifying the index value of both dimensions. In a two-dimensional table we can think of these two dimensions as being rows and columns, so we provide the row index followed by the column index.

Initializing a Two-dimensional Array

You have seen how to initialize a one-dimensional array. Have a go now at sketching an outline algorithm for initializing all the cells in the salesTable array to zero. Using the *HTTLAP* strategy will help you to clarify your thoughts. Remember the main parts of the strategy: understanding the problem, devising a plan to solve the problem, carrying out the plan, assessing the result, describing what you have learned, and documenting the solution.

Understanding the Problem

Q. What are you being asked to do? What is required? Can the problem be better expressed by drawing a diagram or picture?

A. We need to fill the salesTable array with zeros. That is, at the end of the algorithm every cell in the array should have the value 0. The diagram in Figure 12.14 gives a useful visual representation of the problem. If I had a real table to fill in with zeros what would I do?

Q. What are the principal parts of the problem?

A. There is the array `salesTable`. The array has three rows in it and each row has 12 columns which gives a total of 36 individual cells or elements. Each cell needs to be assigned a value of zero. Thus, I can possibly treat the array as a series of rows within which is a series of individual cells.

Devising a Plan to Solve the Problem

Q. Have you solved this problem before? Is this problem similar to one you have solved before? If so, can you use any knowledge from that problem here?

A. It looks like an extension to the problem of initializing a one-dimensional array. It is still an array only this time it has two dimensions rather than one. Therefore, I can probably use the previous array initialization algorithm and adapt it for this problem. Looking at the diagram I can see how I would solve the problem with a real table, or set of pigeon holes. I would simply work through the table row by row filling each cell in turn. At the end of a row I would move to the start of the next row, as in Figure 12.15.

FIGURE 12.15   **Stepping through a table**

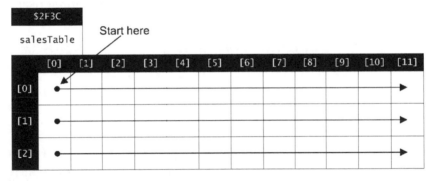

Carrying Out the Plan

Solution 12.5 shows the basic sequence of actions to work through the table:

Solution 12.5 Outline sequence for filling in the table

```
1.  Fill in each cell in the first row
2.  Fill in each cell in the second row
3.  Fill in each cell in the third row
```

There appears to be an implicit iteration here: each row has the same processing, that is, fill in all the cells. I could rewrite the steps using the technique from the one-dimensional array as in Solution 12.6.

Solution 12.6 Reusing the array fill technique

```
1.  FOR each row in the table
        1.1.  Fill in each cell in the row
    ENDFOR
```

Looking at statement #1.1 I can also see an implicit iteration. There are twelve cells in each row so there is a repeated action here. I know I want to insert the same value into all the cells, so I can use another FOR loop within the first one to accomplish this, giving Solution 12.7.

Solution 12.7 Using nested loops to work through the table

```
1.   FOR each row in the table
        1.1.   FOR each column in the row
                    1.1.1.   Set current cell to zero ;
                ENDFOR
    ENDFOR
```

Assessing the Result

Q. Use your solution to meet the requirements of the problem. Did you get the right answer or the correct outcome?

A. The above solution seems to mimic what I did by hand with the table. I need to turn it into more formal pseudo-code so that I can trace it through with the actual array variable.

Solution 12.8 Turning the algorithm into more formal pseudo-code

```
1.   integer: rows  IS 3 ;
2.   integer: columns  IS 12 ;
3.   ARRAY:salesTable OF [ rows ,  columns ] integer ;
4.   integer: thisRow ,
5.            thisColumn  ;
6.   FOR  thisRow  GOES FROM 0 TO ( rows  - 1)
        6.1.   FOR  thisColumn  GOES FROM 0 TO (columns - 1)
                    6.1.1.   salesTable  [ thisRow , thisColumn ] ← 0 ;
                ENDFOR
    ENDFOR
```

In Solution 12.8 I have introduced two variables, thisRow and thisColumn which are used as the loop counters for the two FOR loops. There are also two constants, rows and columns which specify the size of the arrays. Notice also that by using constants in the array declarations my FOR loops are also simpler as we do not have to use the Length function to find the size of the arrays.

Statement #6.1.1 assigns the value 0 to the element in salesTable indexed by thisRow and thisColumn. If you trace through this algorithm you will find that it does, indeed, do what we want. The first FOR loop starts with thisRow having a value of 0. The second loop then iterates 12 times with thisColumn going from 0 to 11. During each of these 12 iterations thisRow will still be 0. When the second FOR loop has finished the first FOR loop will iterate again this time with thisRow having the value 1. So, you can see that the outer loop deals with the three rows and the inner loop deals with the 12 columns within each row. This is a very common technique for processing two-dimensional arrays. We could use the same nested loop structure as the basis for an algorithm that displays the contents of the array, or for one that calculates averages and totals of the data in the array.

Why did you put (`rows` − 1) and (`columns` − 1)? Why did not you just write 0 TO 2 and 0 TO 11?

Go back to page 334 and review the section on array initialization again.

Random Access in a Two-dimensional Array

We can also use a random-access technique with a two-dimensional array. We can let Bob enter his monthly sales data in any order (perhaps his filing system is not very orderly). To enable random access all we need is for Bob to type in three pieces of data for each sales total: the cake type, the month, and the actual sales value. The algorithm in Solution 12.9 continues and extends Solution 12.8 (which is why the statement numbers start at #7) to allow Bob to enter his sales data. Bob can enter as many or as few sales values as he wants. Entering a duplicate value (that is, two values for the same cake and month) will cause any existing value to be overwritten. To stop entering data Bob just needs to type in a set of values where the cake type is greater than 2.

Solution 12.9 A random-access loop to populate the array

```
 7.  integer: cakeType ,
 8.           month ,
 9.           salesValue ;
10.  Display ('Enter cake type, month, and sales value. ') ;
11.  Display ('Enter type of >2 to exit') ;
12.  Get (keyboard, REFERENCE: cakeType , REFERENCE: month ,
     REFERENCE: salesValue ) ;
13.  WHILE ( cakeType  ≤  rows  − 1)
        13.1.    salesValue [ cakeType ,  month ] ←  salesValue  ;
        13.2.  Get (keyboard, REFERENCE: cakeType , REFERENCE: month ,
                     REFERENCE: salesValue ) ;
     ENDWHILE
```

Finally, Solution 12.10 shows an algorithm based upon Solution 12.9 to display the contents of the `salesTable` array with row and column totals. It continues on from Solution 12.9 above (which is why the statements start at #14).

Solution 12.10 Displaying the table with row and column totals

```
14.  integer: rowTotal  ;
15.  ARRAY: columnTotal  OF [ columns ] integer ;
16.  integer: currentValue ;
17.  FOR thisColumn  GOES FROM 0 TO  columns  − 1
        17.1.    columnTotal [ thisColumn ] ← 0 ;
     ENDFOR
```

```
18. FOR  thisRow  GOES FROM 0 TO  rows  − 1
    18.1.    rowTotal  ← 0 ;
    18.2.    FOR  thisColumn  GOES FROM 0 TO  columns  −1
             18.2.1.   currentValue  ←  salesTable  [ thisRow ,
                        thisColumn ] ;
             18.2.2.  Display ( currentValue ) ;
             18.2.3.   rowTotal  ←  rowTotal  +  currentValue  ;
             18.2.4.  columnTotal [ thisRow ] ←  columnTotal
                        [ thisRow ] +  currentValue  ;
             ENDFOR
    18.3.   Display ( rowTotal , ⏎) ;
    ENDFOR
19. FOR  thisColumn  GOES FROM 0 TO  columns  − 1 DO
    19.1.   Display ( columnTotal  [ thisColumn ]) ;
    ENDFOR
```

You should be able to recognize the nested FOR loop structure in Solution 12.10 which processes the rows and columns as being based upon Solution 12.9. There are a few features that may need explanation. First of all, I have introduced a variable currentValue which stores the value of the current array element. This is simply because three statements use that value (#18.2.2, #18.2.3, and #18.2.4) and referring to currentValue is less cluttered than referring to salesTable [thisRow, thisColumn]. The new variable rowTotal (statement #14) should be self-explanatory: it is used to hold the total sales value for each row. It is initialized to zero at the start of a row and then has each of the 12 sales values for that row added to it in the second FOR loop (see statement #18.2.3). rowTotal is then displayed at the end of a row in statement #18.3. (Recall that the ⏎ symbol in statement #18.3 makes the next Display invocation to write to the next line on the screen.) We can show the outline algorithm for dealing with row totals as in Solution 12.11.

Solution 12.11 Outline algorithm for producing row totals

```
1.  FOR each row in turn
    1.1.   Initialize row total to zero ;
    1.2.   FOR each column in turn
               1.2.1.   Add current cell to row total ;
           ENDFOR
    1.3.   Display row total ;
    ENDFOR
```

As rowTotal is reset to zero at the start of each row we only need a simple integer variable for the purpose. Column totals, however, are a bit more complicated. You will have seen that Solution 12.11 uses an array to store the column totals and then waits until the entire salesTable array has been displayed before displaying the column totals. If this is confusing to you, consider what a column total is: it is a total of all the values in a column. The problem is that the algorithm is not processing the table column-by column but row-by-row. We cannot use a

Think Spot

simple `columnTotal` variable because each cell processed is in a different column. Therefore, we use an array to store all 12 column totals. The outline algorithm in Solution 12.12 should make this clearer.

Solution 12.12 Outline algorithm for processing column totals

```
1.  Initialize column totals to zero
2.  FOR each row in turn
        2.1.  FOR each column in turn
                  2.1.1.  Add current cell to column total for cur-
                          rent column ;
              ENDFOR // End of inner FOR loop
    ENDFOR // End of outer FOR loop
3.  FOR each column in turn
        3.1.  Display column total for current column ;
    ENDFOR
```

Remember that the inner FOR loop (statement #2.1) works through the 12 columns for a given row. We cannot, therefore, have a complete column total for any column until we have processed all the rows which will not happen until the outer FOR loop (statement #2) has finished. Thus we can use an array to keep track of the running column totals. This array can then be displayed after the main table has been displayed (statement #3). Putting the algorithms in Solution 12.11 and Solution 12.12 together results in the complete algorithm in Solution 12.10.

Displaying a Transposed Table

The last table array technique I want to look at is *transposition*. The `salesTable` array is arranged in rows and columns to correspond to Table 12.2. Sometimes we might want to look at a transposed table so that the columns are displayed horizontally and the rows vertically.[10] We can display a table in transposed layout *without* physically changing the array.

Think about how this might be accomplished. Hint: if the table can be displayed normally by processing the columns within the rows, what does this suggest for a transposed output?

The solution to the transposition problem is really very straightforward except for one aspect that tends to catch the unwary programmer out. We know how to display a two-dimensional array in its normal form. We just use the following basic algorithm:

```
1.  FOR each row in turn
        1.1.  FOR each column in turn
                  1.1.1.  Display current cell ;
              ENDFOR
    ENDFOR
```

---

[10] You might have come across transposed tables already if you have ever used the *pivot table* feature in spreadsheet programs.

All we have to do to display the array the other way around is to process the columns in the outer loop and the rows in the inner loop. Solution 12.13 shows how this could be done with the salesTable array.

Solution 12.13 Displaying an array in transposed form

Think Spot

    1.   FOR column GOES FROM 0 TO columns −1
            1.1.   FOR row GOES FROM 0 TO rows −1
                    1.1.1.   Display (salesTable [row , column]) ;
                  ENDFOR
            1.2.   Display (↵) ;
          ENDFOR

What is different in Solution 12.13? The loops have been reversed so that the outer one goes through the 12 columns whilst the inner one processes the three rows. So, when column is 0 the contents of the three cells in rows 0, 1, and 2 are displayed. Then column becomes 1 and rows 0, 1, and 2 are again processed. And so it goes on until the outer loop has finished with the 12th column. The output would thus look like Figure 12.16. You should convince yourself that Figure 12.16 is, indeed, the transposed form of Table 12.2.

FIGURE 12.16   **Transposed array output**

30	15	39
25	12	20
12	16	25
5	12	25
8	18	33
10	11	32
11	49	24
5	40	20
9	29	23
10	13	60
20	12	52
40	30	75

I mentioned that array transposition has a trap for the unwary. It lies in statement #1.1.1 of Solution 12.13. Notice that although we have transposed the two loops so that the outer one processes columns whilst the inner one processes the rows, the array indices remain in the **same order as before**, that is salesTable [row, column]. A common mistake is to transpose the indices too:

    salesTable [column , row].

This is a fatal mistake as the first index **always** refers to first dimension of the array. In this case the first dimension only has a size of 3, that is, there are only three rows. But `column` will take 12 values (0–11) meaning that the first index will go out of bounds causing an error. When doing array transpositions **always transpose the loops and not the indices**!

12.6 Arrays of More than Two Dimensions

Whilst one-dimensional arrays (lists) and two-dimensional arrays (tables) are, perhaps, the most common arrays in use, you can actually declare arrays of more than two dimensions. For instance, you might have a three-dimensional array to represent coordinates in a space war game. For example, the following declaration could be used to store the number of spaceships in each sector of a region of space in a space combat game:

ARRAY: shipDensity OF [5, 5, 5] **integer** ;

The array has three dimensions – let's call them x, y, and z, and represents a volume of space divided into five units along each axis. We may visualize a three-dimensional array as Figure 12.17.

FIGURE 12.17 **Visualization of a 3D array**

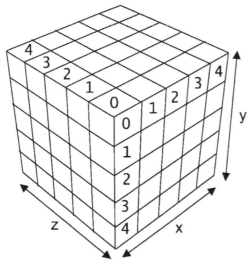

There is nothing to stop you using arrays of four, five, six, or even more dimensions, though my drawing skills are not sufficient to produce diagrams that could visualize them! Just include as many dimensions as you need in the array declaration. Here is a four-dimensional array (perhaps the fourth dimension could be for time):

ARRAY: spaceTime OF [10, 20, 5, 15] **real** ;

There is no need for all the dimensions to have the same size, as the `spaceTime` example above shows. Whilst you can have arrays of many dimensions, you must be careful to get your indices in the correct order when accessing the array otherwise you will get severe problems. It is bad enough getting the rows and columns the wrong way round in a two-dimensional array, so you can imagine how difficult to debug a program might be if the indices of a four- or five-dimensional array were written in the wrong order.

Jagged Arrays

Some programming languages have the concept of a *jagged array*. A jagged array is a multi-dimensional array where the rows do not necessarily have the same number of columns (it also works for higher dimension arrays too). You could declare a jagged table thus:

ARRAY: salesTable OF [3,] **integer** ;

where the second dimension is unspecified. If you find that confusing, do not worry as we are not going any further with the idea. Just be aware that such a thing exists in some languages so that it is not a complete shock should you encounter jagged arrays.

Arrays as Types

Before we leave the subject of arrays, it is worth noting that we can also declare new types based on arrays. Consider the following:

NEWTYPE **Year** IS **ARRAY** OF [12] **integer** ;
Year: yearlyRainfall ;

In this example, the variable yearlyRainfall is of type Year which is the new type we have just defined which holds a single 12-element array of integers. If we want to do the job thoroughly, we can reuse the MonthType we defined earlier (Section 12.2) in the definition of Year as follows:

NEWTYPE **Year** is ARRAY OF [12] **MonthType** ;

We can now use this new type. Say we wanted to compare book sales for March 2008 with March 2007 where all monthly book sales are held in arrays, one for each year:

```
MonthType: sales2008 ,

           sales2007 ;
...
// Statements for populating the arrays with their values...
...
// Test to see if sales are down
IF ( sales2008 [2] < sales2007 [2])
    Display ('Sales for March are down on the year before') ;
ENDIF
```

12.7 Chapter Summary

In this chapter you learned how to build and manipulate the two common static data structures, the *record* and the *array*.

12.8 **Exercises**

1. Given the following declaration:

    ARRAY:⌈numbers⌉ OF [7] **integer** ;

    And assuming the array has been populated with the values 2, 4, 6, 8, 10, 12, 14, what would the following Display statements output?

    Display (⌈numbers⌉ [4]) ;

    Display (⌈numbers⌉ [1]) ;

    Display (⌈numbers⌉ [6]) ;

    Display (⌈numbers⌉ [0]) ;

    Display (⌈numbers⌉ [7]) ;

2. Given the following declaration:

    ARRAY:⌈salesData⌉ OF [25] [12] **real** ;

    How many rows does the array salesData have? How many columns does it have?

3. Using the array declaration from exercise 2 above, state which of the six statements below, a, b, c, d, e, or f correctly places the value 100 into the array at row 10 column 6:

    a. ⌈salesData⌉ [10] [6] ← 100 ;

    b. ⌈salesData⌉ [6] [10] ← 100 ;

    c. ⌈salesData⌉ [11] [7] ← 100 ;

    d. ⌈salesData⌉ [7] [11] ← 100 ;

    e. ⌈salesData⌉ [9] [5] ← 100 ;

    f. ⌈salesData⌉ [5] [9] ← 100 ;

4. Earlier we introduced the function Length which returns the size of an array expressed as the maximum number of its elements. A problem with this function is that it can cause the algorithm designer to inadvertently introduce a bug into their program because of zero-based array indexing. If an array has 10 elements Length will return the value 10, but because of zero-based indexing, the 10th element of the array is accessed by an index value of 9, i.e. Length (array) − 1. Using the *HTTLAP* strategy design a new function MaxIndex that returns the index value of an array's final element rather than the array's length. That is, MaxIndex would return 9 for an array with a maximum of 10 elements, 99 for a 100-element array, and so on. Your solution can make use of the Length function.

5. Design a program that solves the problem of allowing a user to create a shopping basket for an online store. The program should allow the user to enter products (up to a maximum of 50 items) which will be added to the basket (stored as an array). Do not worry about deletion at this time. Items will always be added to the end of the array.

6. Extend your solution to Exercise 5 to allow items to be deleted from the basket. You need to consider what happens to gaps: should items be moved up the array to close gaps left by deletion? Start by solving the simpler problem of deleting a value without considering the gaps. Once you are happy with that solution, then tackle the problem of the gaps. For example, if the second array element is deleted all the elements from the third downwards should be moved up one position.

7. The algorithm for randomly accessing the cakeTally array (see page 333) could be written at least two other ways by using a continuation flag instead of a cakeType value greater than 2 being entered. Using the *HTTLAP* strategy design two alternative algorithms for this problem. One should use a WHILE loop and the other a DO ... WHILE loop.

8. Look at the patient record structure in Section 12.1. As it stands, it has fields to hold various address and date items. It might be more natural to think of an address as a record structure in its own right, and similarly a date. Amend the record type by creating two new types: AddressRecord and DateRecord. The address record structure will have the following fields: streetAddressLine1, streetAddressLine2, postalTown, and postCode each of which should be a string. A DateRecord will have three integer fields: day, month, and year. Using these two new types, amend the PatientRecord type by removing the address and date fields and replacing them by four new fields: address (of type AddressRecord), birthDate, checkupDate and joinDate (which should be of type DateRecord).

9. Change Solution 12.13 so that it displays the table in transposed form where the rows appear in *reverse order.*

10. An input file, numbers.txt, contains 10 real numbers. Design an algorithm to calculate the average value of the 10 numbers and to display all the numbers that are greater than the average together with their position in the file. For example, if numbers.txt contained:

        1.3 21.0 7.8 4.5 5.7 8.9 3.5 1.4 4.1 9.0

then the algorithm would display the following:

        Average is 6.72
        Greater than average & position:
        21.0, position 2
        7.8, position 3
        8.9, position 6
        9.0, position 10

12.9 Projects

StockSnackz Vending Machine

Extend your algorithms to remove the multiple stock level variables and replace them by a single array. Each element of the array should correspond to one of the snack items and the element's value will hold the stock level of that item.

Stocksfield Fire Service

Extend your EAC program to use an array as a lookup table for the fire-fighting method codes. What is an advantage of storing the strings like this? To assist you in this task you may assume that an *HTTLAP* function called Ord already exists. Here is the function header for Ord:

```
FUNCTION Ord (character:aCharacter) RETURNS integer
```

Ord accepts a single character value in its parameter and returns the ordinal value (ASCII code) of that character. Make use of function Ord (character). You can remind yourself of the ASCII codes associated with each character by looking at Table 9.5.[11,12,13]

Puzzle World: Roman Numerals and Chronograms

No exercise for this case study.

Pangrams: Holoalphabetic Sentences

An isogrammatic pangram is one that not only uses each letter of the alphabet but one in which each letter is used only once. Thus, an isogrammatic pangram uses only 26 letters. Amend your pangram function so that it returns an integer value indicating whether the sentence is not a pangram (0), is a simple pangram (1), or is an isogrammatic pangram (2). A one-dimensional array should be used to keep track of the number of occurrences of each letter (do not count spaces and punctuation).

Online Bookstore: ISBNs

Amend your program from Chapter 11 so that a batch of ISBNs is read in from a text file (one ISBN per line, an ISBN of 'XXXXXXXXXX' is used as an end marker). The program should validate each ISBN read in. If the ISBN is valid, a hyphenated version is to be stored in an array of valid ISBNs. If the ISBN is invalid, the non-hyphenated version is added to an array of invalid ISBNs. After all the ISBNs have been processed, the contents of each array (one ISBN per line) are to be displayed beneath appropriate headings (e.g. 'Valid ISBNs' and 'Invalid ISBNs').

---

[11] Hint: If you store the EAC fire-fighting method strings in an array you need a simple way of getting them back out. Each method is associated with a single digit code from 1 to 4. Arrays are indexed by integer values. What relationship is there between the ordinal value of the characters '1', '2', '3', '4' and the integer index values of the array elements?

[12] A further hint: You can convert a character digit to its corresponding integer value by taking the ordinal value of the character and subtracting 48. The ordinal value of character digit "0" is 48. 48 − 48 = 0 = the integer equivalent of character digit '0'. (See Table 9.5 to see how this works.) Now you have the integer equivalent you can use this in the array lookup.

[13] Another hint: Don't forget about the zero-based indexing though.

13 Dynamic Data Structures

Learning Objectives

- Understand how to build dynamic data structures that grow and shrink as needed
- Understand the differences between the list, the stack, and the queue data structures
- Learn a repertoire of algorithms for solving problems requiring the use of dynamic data structures
- Recognize the difference between pointer and value variables and understand how to use both in data structures

In this chapter you will learn how to build *dynamic* data structures that can grow or shrink in size as needed. We will cover three of the basic dynamic structures: the *list*, the *stack*, and the *queue* (Section 13.1). The remaining sections develop algorithms for manipulating these data structures and so provide you with a foundation for building your own more complex structures.

13.1 Lists, Stacks, and Queues

The array is a very useful data structure and can be used in the solution of many programming problems. It does have a limitation in that its size is usually fixed when the program is compiled. Also, to put an item into an array we must explicitly specify the position (its element index) at which this will take place. Just as arrays are good data structures for storing vectors, matrices, and tables of data, other structures can be used for other situations. Three common data structures are the stack, the queue, and the list and each can brought to bear on many programming problems.

The List

We saw in the last chapter that the single-value variables are arguably the simplest data structures as they contain only one value. It is more common to think of a data structure as being a collection of related values. The list is an ABSTRACT DATA TYPE (ADT)[1] which can be modified to form most of the data structures we will encounter. In formal terms, the list is ". . . a finite, ordered sequence of data items known as elements" Shaffer (1998, p.77). When I go to the supermarket I take with me a shopping list which, to save time, is set out according to the order the products are laid out in the aisles.

FIGURE 13.1   **My ordered shopping list**

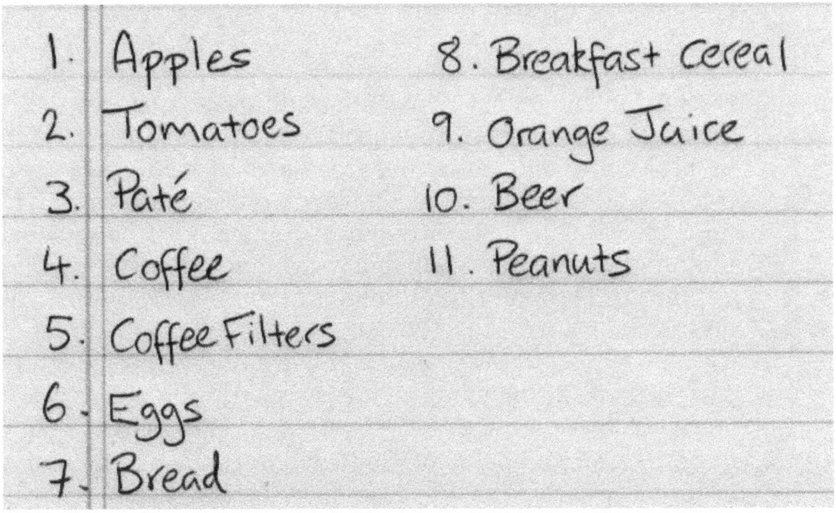

---

[1] Recall from Chapter 6 that an abstract data type is a definition of a data type without any reference to how it is implemented in the computer. An ADT simply defines the set of values an item of the type can take together with permissible operations. The ADT does not specify how the data are to be stored or the operations implemented. The mathematical definition of the integer is really an ADT because programming languages generally implement a restricted, or constrained, version. For example, whilst the range of integer values is, theoretically, infinite, computer memories cannot store infinitely large values, so integer types in programming languages restrict the type to a maximum value (generally using 32 or 64 bits). Thus, the Java type `int` is an implementation of the integer ADT.

Lists have certain properties. First, they can be *empty*, that is, they can have no elements in them (e.g. a blank shopping list). A list has a length which is equal to the number of elements in it. So, the shopping list in Figure 13.1 has a length of 11. A list also has a *head* and an *end*. The head points to the first item in the list and the end to the last. Thus, the head of my shopping list is 'Apples' and the end is 'Peanuts'. Lists can be sorted or unsorted. Sorting might be in ascending order of value, descending order of value, or some other ordering (e.g. aisle position of products in the supermarket). The most basic operations that can be performed on a list are adding (*inserting*) and removing elements. Depending on how the list is implemented, insertion may take place at the head, at the end, or at some position between the head and the end. The list is such a fundamental data structure that it has many forms and implementations in different programming languages with a variety of supporting operations.

If we think back to the arrays we encountered in Chapter 12, we see that an array can be viewed as an implementation of the list ADT. Like a list, an array has a finite number of elements, it has a head and an end, and elements can be added and removed. For simple problems where the maximum number of elements to be stored is known in advance and where the speed of the program's execution is not too important, the array is a convenient, easy-to-manage way of implementing list data structures.

Define an array for the shopping list in Figure 13.1.

Arrays are not always suitable ways of implementing lists. The primary reason for this is that arrays are *static* data structures which means that their maximum size is specified when the program is compiled. The size of an array is absolutely fixed and cannot grow beyond the bounds given in its definition – trying to add an element to a full array will generally result in some kind of run-time error.[2] Often, the maximum number of items to be stored in a list is unknown at the time a program is written. For example, a list might be required to hold customer details for Bob's bakery. How many customers might Bob have on his mailing list? 10? 100? 10 000? It might start out as a small number, but if Bob's business grows such that extra outlets are added then the number of customers could rapidly increase. As programmers we might take an educated guess (or make an ASSUMPTION) that Bob will never have more than, say, 2000 customers on his books and could define a 2000- element array accordingly. But if Bob only deals with 200 customers then we are needlessly using up memory allocated to the array that is too large for our needs. Conversely, if Bob acquired 2001 customers then the array is no longer big enough. In these situations where the magnitude of the list size cannot be reasonably determined in advance we need something other than the static array – we need a *dynamic* data structure that can grow and shrink as needed taking up just the amount of memory needed.

Dynamic data ▶
structure

---

[2] Java does provide special array types that can grow, but they are not generally very efficient.

The Linked List

The dynamic version of the list is commonly called the *linked list*. Conceptually, linked lists are very simple. However, many beginning programmers encounter a great deal of trouble when it comes to implementing them. This is because extra variables are needed to keep track of the head and end, and these variables are usually pointers (references in Processing and Java) which can be difficult to understand at first. Before we look at what a linked list is and how to build and maintain one, let us go back to the basics and consider identifiers and memory locations once more. Please do not skip this section; while the details may seem to be laboring a point and going over old ground, in my experience of teaching beginning programmers, it is often necessary to plough a furrow more than once. At one university I taught at we had a rule of thumb when it came to teaching linked lists: teach them in the first year and then teach them again in the second year after which point most students understand them. I hope that going over the basics again removes the need to have another chapter on lists later on. However, if you find at the end of this chapter that you cannot do the exercises, then go through it again and make sure you understand the following section on list basics before you go any further.

Linked List Basics: Identifiers and Memory Revisited

Chapter 5 introduced the idea of working storage and Chapter 9 showed that variables occupy parts of the computer's memory. Each variable is known in a program by its *identifier* which is a name given to the data by the programmer which describes the nature and purpose of the variable. In Chapter 10, when looking at sub-program parameters we dealt with *references* to variables. Recall that a reference parameter is one that contains the address of another variable rather than a data value. The address specifies the location in memory where the sub-program may find the data item in question. This indirect way of accessing data is what allows a sub-program to modify the values of its parameters.

When a variable is declared its identifier and type are specified. The type tells the computer how much memory to set aside (e.g. a 32-bit integer would need four bytes of memory). The identifier is the name given to stand for that value. Whilst identifiers are convenient for programmers, the computer does not use them in the way we do. When a program is compiled, all the identifiers are put by the compiler into a *symbol table*. Each identifier is then assigned a memory address which is the location in memory where that identifier's data will be held. Rather than dealing with identifier names, the running program actually only deals with memory locations. We can say that a variable's identifier is just a convenient label given by the programmer to a memory address. Normally the memory addresses are assigned by the computer and the programmer does not need to know where they are. Every time an identifier appears in a program instruction it is converted by the computer into the corresponding memory address.

Symbol table ▶

This is not a totally alien concept as we use something akin to this in the real world. When a political journalist talks about "Downing Street sources", the name "Downing Street" is really just convenient shorthand for the UK prime minister's residence, the full postal address of which is "10 Downing Street, London, SW1A 2AA, United Kingdom" Likewise, "The White House" is shorthand for "The White House, 1600 Pennsylvania Avenue NW, Washington, DC 20500, USA". An identifier, then, is just a programmer-friendly label given to a location in the computer's memory. Notice that the address does not tell you anything about the characteristics of the building that exists there. If you want to know what colour the carpet is at 10 Downing Street you would have to visit the address, open the front door, and look in.

Figure 13.2 shows the familiar box but with one difference. Now, the label that has the variable's identifier also shows the memory address (in hexadecimal format, that is, base 16 rather than the decimal base 10) that the variable occupies. In this case the integer variable with the identifier barbarasSalary resides in memory location $F020 (the $ prefix is commonly used to denote hexadecimal numbers).

FIGURE 13.2   **An integer variable with identifier and memory address**

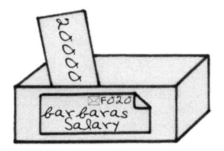

That is, every time the identifier barbarasSalary appears in the program, the computer refers to memory location $F020. Most of the time, the programmer never needs to know the memory location occupied by a variable. However, it is important that programmers understand that a variable can be accessed either through its identifier, or directly via its address. Many programming languages provide facilities for getting at the memory addresses of identifiers. The reason for this will become clearer when we look at how to build a linked list. For the time being, consider the following pseudo-code which declares and assigns a value to the variable shown in Figure 13.2.

1.   **integer**: barbarasSalary ;
2.   barbarasSalary ← 20000 ;

The memory address occupied by the variable barbarasSalary is allocated by the computer when the program is compiled and run, so the programmer does not need to specify this aspect. This also means that unless we specifically ask, we will not know where in the computer's memory our variable resides. From the above, let us examine instruction #2. Up till now, our understanding of instruction #2 is that the value 20000 is assigned to the variable barbarasSalary. But we now know that barbarasSalary is just a programmer-friendly name for a memory address. When the program is compiled, the actual memory address occupied by the variable is substituted for the identifier barbarasSalary. Assuming that barbarasSalary lives at memory location $F020 (Figure 13.2) then statement #2 is really just placing the value 20 000 into the memory location $F020. We could add an instruction to display the value of barbarasSalary:

```
3.   Display ( barbarasSalary ) ;
```

Again, this would cause the value stored in the memory location represented by the identifier barbarasSalary to be displayed on the screen. Let us consider what happens when two variables are involved by looking at Program 13.1. Hypothetical memory addresses that the computer might allocate to the variables are shown in comments after the declarations in statements #1 and #2.

```
1.   integer: a ; // Allocated to location F030
2.   integer: b ; // Allocated to location F032
3.   a ← 256 ;
4.   b ← a ;
5.   Display ( b ) ;
```

Program 13.1
Two identifiers

Below is a table showing the contents of the memory locations occupied by the two integer variables a and b from Program 13.1. The number in the first column of the table corresponds to the statements in Program 13.1. The first two rows have been completed. Note, very often programming languages do not initialize variables to a particular value after they have been declared. Therefore, unless you know that initialization takes place it is better to assume that when a variable is declared its value is undefined until an assignment operation takes place.

Complete the rows for statements #3 and #4.

| | Memory contents for Program 13.1 | |
Statement	$F030	$F032
1	Undefined	–
2	Undefined	Undefined
3		
4		

If you are stuck, perhaps it is because we are talking about memory addresses rather than the more familiar identifiers. If variable a resides at memory location $F030 and statement #3 assigns a value to variable a, what will be the value stored in location $F030 after statement #3 has taken place? The answers, then, to this small problem are thus:

| | Memory contents for Program 13.1 | |
Statement	$F030	$F032
1	Undefined	–
2	Undefined	Undefined
3	256	Undefined
4	256	256

Statement #3 assigns the value 256 to a; a resides at memory address $F030, so the location $F030 will hold the value 256. The variable b has not yet been assigned a value, so its memory address still has an undefined value. Statement #4 assigns the value of variable a to variable b. So, the value in the memory location occupied by a (256 at $F030) is copied to the memory occupied by b ($F032). After statement #4 location $F032 will also contain the value 256. From this example, you should now be able to see that a variable's identifier is synonymous with its memory address: the programmer knows the variable by its identifier whilst the computer refers to it by its address. When we encounter a statement such as

```
Display (b) ;
```

the computer looks up the value in the memory location occupied by b and displays it on the screen. Whenever you use an identifier you are really talking about an address. This concept of identifiers and addresses is important for the understanding of linked lists and other dynamic data structures.

Pointer and Reference Variables

If you are still at all unsure about the relationship between a variable and its address then please go back and review the sections above as this section extends that idea. This section deals with variables whose values are themselves addresses of other variables. Understanding such pointer or reference variables is key to understanding how dynamic data structures can be built using linked lists.[3] It may be necessary to go over this section and the ones above two or three times until you are confident you understand the concepts. If you can do the in-text exercises without looking ahead to the answers then that is a good measure of your comprehension.

The Linked List Game

Merely talking about computer memory and addresses can lead to poor comprehension as the subject becomes too theoretical and far removed from our real-world frame of reference. With practice you will be able to start

---

[3] For the sake of simplicity at this point we shall treat pointers and references as synonyms; indeed, a pointer is an implementation of a more general reference type. However, there are some subtle but important differences between the two terms the meanings of which are also affected by individual programming languages. The interested reader can learn about this by looking at POINTERS VS REFERENCES in the Reflections chapter.

visualizing the computer memory and understand how data and pointers move around. In fact, this skill is vital to being able to debug faulty programs.[4] To try and give you a real-world anchor you can use as a help to visualizing the list and its pointers, I offer you *The Linked List Game*. In the Linked List Game your house (or other convenient building) becomes the computer's memory, and each room becomes a memory location. You need two rooms to serve as the head and end reference variables and then as many other rooms as possible to act as the list elements. If you do not have enough rooms at your disposal, then divide up the room you are in. Each corner can be a memory location, as can items of furniture. Pick two locations for the head and end variables respectively and the remaining locations to serve as homes for list elements. Now take a piece of paper and write the word "head" at the top of it. In the centre, put a sticky note, or draw a box. Take another piece of paper and sticky note, and write "end" at the top. You should have something that looks like Figure 13.3.

FIGURE 13.3   **Head and End variables**

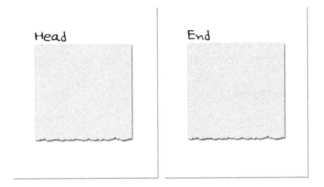

You now have two *pointers*, one to point to the head of the list and one to point to the end. Now make up a list record. In this game the list will hold titles of books. Each record needs two fields: one to store the book title and a pointer to say where the next record can be found (that is, which room of the house it is in). Take another piece of paper, draw a line horizontally across the middle and put two sticky notes in each half. Above the first sticky note write "bookTitle" and above the second write "next" (see Figure 13.4). Make one such record sheet for each room or location.

---

[4] Correcting errors will become a familiar chore when you start doing serious work with linked lists, so the better you understand the fundamentals the less problematic this will be. When I was a beginning programmer I found this aspect particularly troublesome and was never comfortable working with linked lists until I really understood the difference between value and reference variables. It is worth persisting with this topic as understanding now will make the following sections much easier to deal with (especially when it comes to trying out the exercises).

FIGURE 13.4   **Record variable**

The rules for the game are simple. New book records are added to the end of the list. The head pointer will always point to the first record and the end pointer to the last one in the list. Each time a book record is added, the "next" field of the record that was at the end of the list prior to the new record's insertion must be changed to show where the new record is. The end pointer must also be updated to point to the new record. The list is built by visiting rooms and updating the records and pointers. Taking my house as an example, we will build a short list. I shall choose my study as the first room to hold a book record, so I go into the study, and complete a book record sheet (see Figure 13.5). Because this is the first record, I have set the "next" field to NULL, or "nowhere". This means that there is no next book in the list. At this moment the head and end pointers also point to nowhere.

FIGURE 13.5   **The first record in my list**

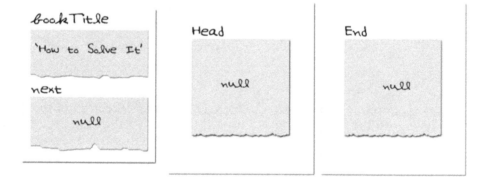

I need to update the head pointer to show that there is now a book in the list and direct the end pointer to the study too as this is also currently the last book in the list. My head pointer is located in the hallway, and the end pointer in the guest room. The complete list with one element and properly directed pointers is shown as Figure 13.6. Before proceeding with the next record it may be wise to recap at this point. In my hallway I now have a sheet of paper labelled "head" with a sticky note that says "Study". This means that the first record in my list can be found in the study. If I want to know where the last record is, I can inspect the end pointer which is located in the guest room. So, a visit to the guest room reveals a piece of paper labelled "end" whose sticky note also says "Study". So, the record at the head of the list is currently at the end also. A quick trip to the study reveals a book record sheet with a book title "How to Solve It" and a "next" field of NULL (i.e., pointing to nowhere).

FIGURE 13.6   **The list with one element**

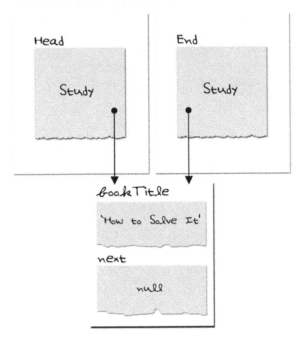

Now make your own list with one book record using your own chosen rooms or locations. Remember to put the head and end pointers in locations of their own. After you have done this, you might also like to draw a map of your house with the various locations indicated on it and arrows joining the rooms that are currently part of the list. A floor plan showing the list I created above is given in Figure 13.7.[5]

FIGURE 13.7   **Linked list map**

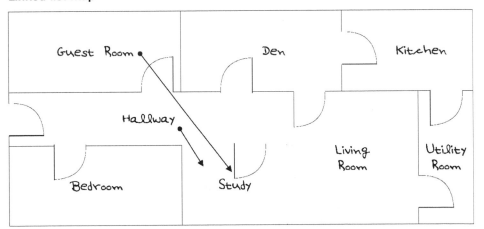

---

[5] The ground floor of my house is not actually like that. Some of the rooms have been removed, others added, and staircases taken out!

You said the **head** pointer is in the hallway and the **end** pointer is in the guest room. Why aren't these room addresses shown in Figure 13.6? You need to remember that **head** and **end** are pointer/reference variables rather than value variables. The value of a pointer variable is the address of some other variable, record, data structure, etc. If we are interested in knowing the address of **head** or **end** we could look them up, but it is unlikely we need to know their addresses directly. Figure 13.7 shows the locations of **head** and **end** in relation to the rest of the list.

Now I want to add another book to my list. The next location in my house is the den. What I need to do is go to the den, add a new book record and then update the end and the "next" field of the study record to reflect this. The new book record in the den would thus look like Figure 13.8. Notice that its "next" field should be set to NULL as it must not point anywhere yet.

FIGURE 13.8   **New book record for the den**

Next, I need to change the "next" field of the study record to point to the one in the den, and then change the end to point to the den also. The new list would thus look like Figure 13.9. Notice how the head still points to the study, but the end now points to the den as does the "next" field in the study record. I have also updated the map as Figure 13.10.

FIGURE 13.9   **Two records in the list**

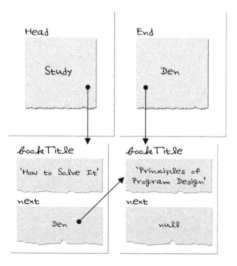

FIGURE 13.10   **Map for list with two records**

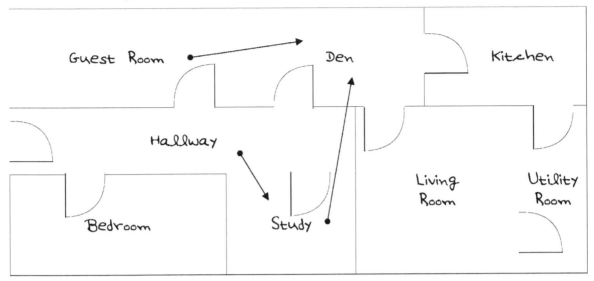

Now add another record to your list. Once you have done that go back to the location that holds the head pointer and walk your way through the list by following the pointers. The head tells you where to find the first record. When you go to the location where your first record is stored you can find the next record by looking at the location written in the "**next**" field. Go to the location indicated and you should find the second record you added. You can tell that you have arrived at the last record in the list because its "**next**" field should say "NULL".

Figure 13.11 shows my completed list with two more rooms populated with book records. I have two rooms free which means my list can grow by two more records if desired.[6] Notice how each record always points to the next one in the list except for the last record which points to nowhere. The head always points to the first record and the end to the last. The complete map is shown in Figure 13.12.

---

[6] You might be thinking at this point that because the list can only store two more records that it has a fixed size, just like an array which has some spare elements. The difference is that the size of an array is fixed at the time the program is written, whereas a linked list can grow to occupy as much memory as the computer has available. Thus, an array of five elements could only store five values regardless of whether the house it is in has five rooms or 20 rooms. A linked list, on the other hand, could occupy as few as zero rooms (empty list) or as many rooms as the house has available – moving from a smaller house to a larger house allows the list to grow bigger. The only constraint on list size, then, is the amount of memory the computer can offer.

FIGURE 13.11   **The complete list**

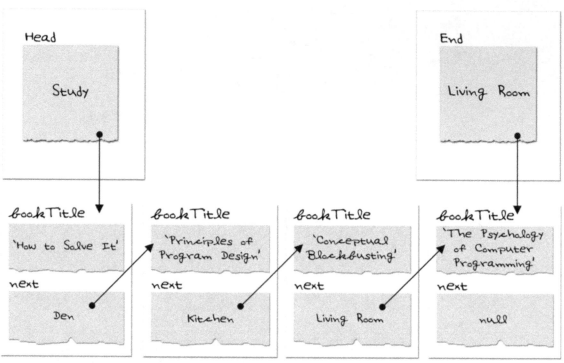

FIGURE 13.12   **The map of the complete list**

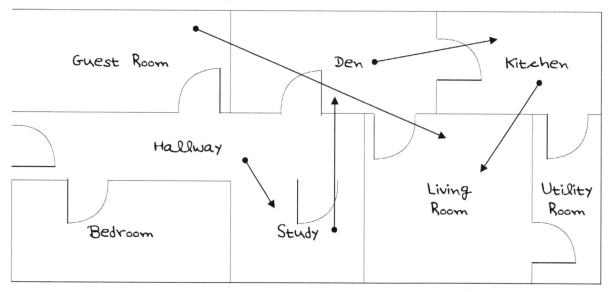

Complete your list and its map. After that, take a walk through the list starting at the head. You should be getting a feel for how the list elements are joined. There is no physical link between elements. Rather, each record stores the address of the next item in the list.

Below are three more exercises for you. Be careful to think through the answers carefully as it is easy to rush to an incorrect solution. The answers are given below, but do not look at them until you have had a good stab at answering the questions as getting these right means you have gained a good grasp of the concepts so far.

1. In my linked list, how can I find out the book title held in the third record? Be careful here: the answer is not as simple as going straight to the kitchen and having a look.
2. If I am standing in the kitchen looking at the third item, how do I find the second item? A related question (but with a different answer) is: given any list item how do I get access to the previous element?
3. There are two rooms left in the house shown in Figure 13.12. If we add another record to the list, in which of the remaining rooms should it go?

Question 1

The answer to the first question does, of course, involve a visit to the kitchen. However, the real question is how do we know we have to visit the kitchen? Think about what these records actually are. They are not variables in the usual sense because they do not have their own identifiers. If there is no identifier how do we find the data? We need something to tell us where the data is. That is, we need a pointer. What is it that points to the third record? In the example above, the only thing that is pointing to the third record is the "**next**" field of the second record. And what points to the second record? – the "**next**" field of the first record. The first record is, as we know, pointed to by the **head** variable. So, we access the third record by starting at the head and working our way through the list until we get to the third record. We have to work through the list element by element because there is no direct access to any of the list elements. Of course, we can look at the map that we drew, and go to the kitchen, but that involves the same process. Consider the following map (Figure 13.13). The floor plan is the same but I have put records in different rooms and in a different order. The hallway and the guest room contain the **head** and **end** pointers respectively as before.

Now where is the third element? It is actually still in the kitchen, but I imagine you had to start in the hallway and follow the arrows. Now imagine the list had not four elements but 400. Where is the 356th element?

FIGURE 13.13 **An alternative layout**

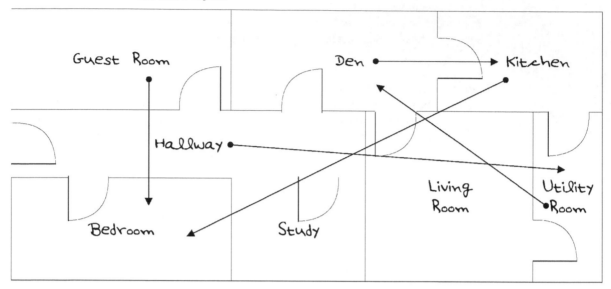

You can illustrate the process well by explaining to a friend that in the hallway (or wherever your **head** pointer is) is a piece of paper with the name of the room in which they can find a book record. The book record will have a book title and the room address of the next record. Ask them to follow the trail until they have found the third book record which they are to write down and bring back to you. You will find that the only way they can tell which record is the third one is by following the trail. Simply visiting rooms at random and reading off the third title they find will not necessarily give the right answer as the records do not indicate their position in the list.

Question 2

The second question poses a more difficult problem. Using the list shown in Figure 13.11 and Figure 13.12, we are currently standing in the kitchen and want to find the title of the second book in the list. We remember from having built the list that the second record is in the den. But if you put your friend in the kitchen and asked them to find the second record what would they do? The fact that we are currently looking at the third item is a red herring as there is nothing in the record to say it is the third item and that the second item is next door in the den. The solution is exactly the same as for the first question: we must go back to the **head** and trace our way through the list again until we get the second item.

Given that we were at the third element and we wanted to find the value of the second one, is there no way that we could have stepped back through the list by one item? This leads us to the solution to the second part to the question which asked how can we access the previous item in the list. We know how to access the next item in the list– we look at the "next" field. To get the previous item we need to extend the book record to include a third field which points back to the record's

 Think Spot

Doubly linked ▶
list

predecessor. Having a **predecessor** pointer field would allow us to walk backwards as well as forwards through the list. Such a list is called a *doubly linked list* because each element has links forwards and backwards.

Question 3

Which of the remaining two rooms should be used when a fifth element is added? It does not matter. Because the first four records were placed in rooms in the order you would walk through them in the house you might have assumed that the fifth book should go into the utility room. But it really does not matter which rooms the records go in as long as each record has the address of the next one in the list in its "next" field.[7] As you can see from the alternative arrangement in Figure 13.13 a record can be in a non-adjacent room to its list neighbors.

Here is a further question to consider. What would happen if you deleted the address stored in the **head** variable? Unless you had kept a copy of the **head** somewhere, then if you lose it you have effectively lost the list because you no longer know where the first element is in memory. My home computer has 1 GB of RAM which is enough memory to store more than 1,000,000,000 8-bit values. If you lost your **head**, as it were, then you would have several hundred million memory locations to search to find the first record in the list. Even if you found what appeared to be a list element, how would you know if it was the first one or not (assuming there is no predecessor pointer)? As you can see, the linked list is quite different in implementation terms from an array.

Creating Pointer Variables

Having studied the principles of a linked list in the comfort of our own home, we need to introduce some new pseudo-code to deal with pointers. Consider these two declarations:

PatientRecord: patient ;

→**PatientRecord:** patientReference ;

The first variable declaration is familiar enough as it declares a variable **patient** that is of type **PatientRecord**. **PatientRecord** is a type we defined earlier (in Chapter 12) for holding the various data items related to a patient. So, **patient** is a record variable that can be visualized as Figure 12.3. The second declaration looks the same except for the arrow immediately preceding the data type. The arrow indicates that this is a reference, or pointer variable. So, **patientReference**, rather than being of type **PatientRecord**, is instead a variable that *points to* a **PatientRecord** variable. That is, rather than holding a record value **patientReference** holds a *reference* to a **PatientRecord** structure. Figure 13.14 shows how **patientReference** is related to a **PatientRecord** structure.

---

[7] In extreme cases there might be questions of efficiency to consider in which case it would be wise to ensure that the records are placed in contiguous (adjacent) memory locations. However, it is beyond the scope of this book to go into algorithm efficiency. There are plenty of good specialist books on efficient algorithm design that will clue you in on this important topic, but after you have got the hang of the basics.

FIGURE 13.14   **A reference variable and its referent (the record to which it points)**

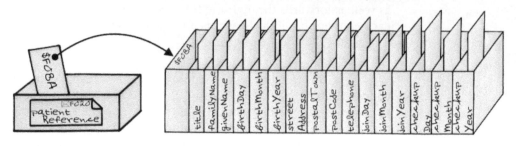

Creating a List Element

In Figure 13.14 the first variable `patientReference` is the reference variable. `patientReference` is located in memory address $F020 (the address is written above the identifier on the box's label). Notice its value is also an address. This address $F08A is the location at which a `PatientRecord` structure can be found. The second box in the diagram is the record to which `patientReference` points. This record has no identifier – it is accessed via the reference variable. If the record has no identifier, how then is it created? Up till now we have created variables by declaring them explicitly with an identifier. The point about linked lists is that they are dynamic data structures which means new records are created as they are needed. All we need to create a list element is a reference variable, and it would be done in the *HTTLAP* pseudo-code with the following assignment statement:

Think Spot

patientReference ← New (**PatientRecord**) ;

We have introduced the special function New which takes as its parameter the name of a data type. New allocates a chunk of memory large enough to hold one variable of the type given in its parameter and it gives back (returns) the address of that chunk. In this example New causes a `PatientRecord` structure to be set up somewhere in memory (a room in the house is chosen by the computer). It then assigns the *address* of that location to the reference variable `patientReference`. Thus, assuming that New caused address $F08A to be allocated (as in Figure 13.14) then the statement

Display (patientReference) ;

would cause the value $F08A to be displayed on the screen. Remember that the value of a reference variable is the *address* of another other record structure or variable. Having created a record structure in memory which is pointed to by `patientReference` we can now assign values to the record's fields thus:

patientReference →.familyName ← 'Higgins' ;

Do not be put off by the strange-looking notation. First of all, the above statement is just an assignment statement. Remember how assignments work: the value of the expression on the right hand side of the assignment operator '←' is assigned to the operand on the left. The right hand expression is a string literal with the value 'Higgins'. But what is 'Higgins' assigned to? The dot selector indicates that `familyName` is a record field, but of what record? The '→' symbol means the identifier or expression on its left *references* or *points to* the item on its right.

The → symbol's left-hand operand is the reference variable `patientReference` and its right-hand operand is the record field `familyName`. Putting it all together, and reading from right to left, we can read the statement as: "the string literal 'Higgins' is assigned to the `familyName` field of the record referenced (or pointed to) by `patientReference`." Having given the `familyName` field a value we could display it on the screen:

Display ([patientReference]→.[familyName]) ;

This will display the value of the field `familyName` in the record pointed to by `patientReference`. Please note that `patientReference` is **not** itself a record and it does not have fields. `patientReference` has a single value which is an address and it is only at that address that a record can be found. This is why when we want to access the record pointed to by `patientReference` we use the → operator after the reference variable's identifier. To recap:

Display ([patientReference]) ;

would display the *value* of `patientReference` which is simply a memory address.

Display ([patientReference]→) ;

displays the value of the thing *pointed to* by `patientReference`. That is, instead of displaying `patientReference`'s value (an address), the → operator causes the `Display` procedure to go to the address stored in `patientReference` and display what it finds there. This is like going to an address on an envelope (10 Downing Street, say) and opening the door and looking at what's inside. Returning to the list built in the linked list game (see Figure 13.11) try answering the following questions.

What would the following statements produce as output?

Display ([head]) ;

Display ([head]→.[bookTitle]) ;

Before we proceed to looking at algorithms for processing lists, here are a few more short exercises designed to see whether you have grasped the main concepts.

Consider the following declarations and assignments:

```
integer:x ;
→integer:a  ;
→integer:b  ;
x ← 7 ;
a ← New (integer) ; // Assume the new integer is located
                    // at memory location $30FF
b ← a ;
```

1. What would the following statements display on the screen?

   Display ([x]) ;
   Display ([a]) ;
   Display ([b]) ;

2. What does the following assignment do?

   [a]→ ← [x] ;

3. What is the effect of this assignment?

   [a]→ ← [a]→ + 3 ;

4. What would the following statements display on the screen?

   Display ([x]) ;
   Display ([a]) ;
   Display ([b]) ;
   Display ([a]→) ;
   Display ([b]→) ;

5. What is the effect of this assignment?

   [a]← ← [x] ;

13.2 Linked List Algorithms

It is now time to present some of the most common algorithms for building and maintaining sorted and unsorted linked lists. Below you will find algorithms for adding an item to a list, removing an item, and finding an item. We will cover both sorted and unsorted lists to provide you with a good selection of model algorithms that you can adapt to fit the various list problems you will undoubtedly come across in the future. Mastering the basic algorithms now will pay dividends later as you will not need to reinvent new algorithms but adapt ones you already know. Recall that one of the principles of the *HTTLAP* strategy is to identify problems you have solved in the past that are similar to the one you are solving now to see if that solution can be brought to bear in some way on the present one. Over time you will come to see that a great many programming problems are composed of variations of themes you have seen before.

The following algorithms will all use the same record types so that you can compare them more easily. We will use the book records from the linked list game as they are small and easy to understand. Here are the declarations and initializations needed for the linked list algorithms.

```
1.   NEWTYPE BookRecord IS
2.       RECORD
             string:[bookTitle] ;
             →BookRecord:[next] ;
         ENDRECORD
```

```
3.    →BookRecord:[head],
4.                 [end],
5.                 [current],
6.                 [book]  ;
7.    [head]  ← NULL  ;
8.    [end]  ← NULL  ;
```

BookRecord is the type for our book records. Each record has two fields: a string bookTitle to hold the title of a book and a reference next which will be used to point to the next element or node of the list. There are then four reference variables: head, end, current, and book. head and end we have seen before. They are pointers to a BookRecord and will therefore be used to point to the start and end of the list. current and book also reference a BookRecord. current will be used in the following algorithms to keep track of the current record in the list. book will be used for creating new book records. There are four basic algorithms we will design for the linked lists:

1. Add a node (an element)
2. Delete a node
3. Find a node
4. Display the list

These algorithms can then be used in programs to build and maintain a list. For example, building a list would require repeatedly invoking the add-a-node algorithm.

Unsorted Lists

An unsorted list is one in which records are not stored in any particular order. New nodes are added to the end of the list in the order of arrival. If you created a list of the names of people you randomly stopped in the street then this would be unsorted.[8] A head pointer is used to indicate the start of the list and an end pointer can be used to show where the end of the list is.

Adding a Node to an Unsorted List

Rather than just giving the algorithm for adding a node to an unsorted list we will build it from scratch using the *HTTLAP* strategy. This will be an interactive process as you will need to try and solve the sub-problems yourself before I present a solution.

The basic requirement is to solve the problem (construct an algorithm) of how to add a node to an unsorted linked list. Each new record will be added as a new node at the end of the list. You can assume for now that there will always be sufficient memory, though a robust solution should be able to deal with the situation in which a new node cannot be created because of a lack of memory.

---

[8] Unless, of course, you also wrote down the time at which you stopped the person, in which case the list would be sorted by stop time. Certainly, the list would not be sorted by name though.

To begin, think about the circumstances in which a node can be added to the list; how should **head** and **end** be updated and when? We are in the "understanding the problem" phase of *HTTLAP* here.

Understanding the Problem

Q. What are you being asked to do?

A. I need to add a node to an unsorted linked list.

Q. What is required?

A. Each time a node is needed I need to create a new record and add it to the list.

Q. Is that all that is required? What is the unknown?

A. A node always needs to go at the end. This is fine for a list that already has nodes, but if it is the first node then the **end** does not point anywhere. For that matter, neither does the **head**. We need to differentiate between adding a node to an empty list and adding one to a list with one or more nodes. Here is a diagram that makes it clearer:

FIGURE 13.15   **An empty and a non-empty list**

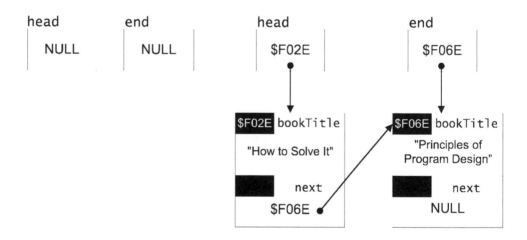

In an empty list both **head** and **end** will be NULL, so adding a node will affect both **head** and **end**. In the list with one or more nodes the new record must go at the end which will affect **end** and the **next** pointer of the current last record.

Q. What are the principal parts of the problem?

A. The new node, the node at the end (if the list is not empty), the end pointer, and the head pointer.

Q. Have you made any assumptions?

A. Only the given one that there will always be enough memory to add any new node.

Devising a Plan to Solve the Problem

Q. Have you solved this problem before? Is it similar to one you have solved before?

A. I think this is a new problem, though we have seen how to create a list node before.

Q. Are some parts of the problem more easily solved than others?

A. Creating the new node is easier than deciding where it should go.

Q. Does restating the problem help?

A. The diagram was something of a restatement and helped to clarify matters.

Q. Did you make use of all the information in the problem statement?

A. Yes.

Q. Can you satisfy all the conditions of the problem?

A. Yes, because I think I have identified all the different cases that affect where a new node is to be added. Therefore, I should be able to add a node to any list, empty or not.

Q. Have you left anything out?

A. Not that I can see.

Carrying Out the Plan

To write down the basic sequence of actions necessary to solve the problem I will begin by creating a new node. I'll use the declarations we gave earlier, so the node creation solution starts at statement #9 in Solution 13.1.

Solution 13.1 Creating a node for the add-a-node algorithm

```
1.   NEWTYPE BookRecord IS
2.        RECORD
          string: bookTitle   ;
          →BookRecord: next    ;
          ENDRECORD
3.   →BookRecord: head ,
4.                end ,
5.                current ,
6.                book  ;
7.   head  ← NULL ;
8.   end  ← NULL ;
```

```
// Create a new book record and assign its address to a pointer
// variable.
9.    book ← New (BookRecord) ; // Assigns address of a
                                 // new BookRecord to book
// Assign values to the new record's fields
10.   book ⊢→.bookTitle ← '';
11.   book ⊢→.next ← NULL ;
```

Statement #9 creates the new record and assigns its address to book. Statement #10 sets the bookTitle field of the new record to an empty string whilst statement #11 sets its next field to NULL as any new node will be at the end of the list and therefore has no other book record to point to. Next we need to tackle the problem of where to add the node.

What can we do to determine whether the list is empty?

An empty list has no nodes in it, so head will be NULL. Therefore, we can test for an empty list by looking at the value of head. If head is NULL the list is empty and we must point both head and end to the new node, otherwise we should put the new record at the end of the list. We can add this selection structure to our solution:

```
12.   IF (head = NULL)
            12.1. Update head and end pointers to point to new record ;
13.   ELSE
            13.1. Add node to end ;
      ENDIF
```

Now it remains to solve the problems in statements #12.1 and #13.1. For adding a node to an empty list all we have to do is point both head and end to the new record. If neither head nor end currently points to a record, what can we use to access the new record we have just created? When we created the record in statement #9 its address was assigned to the pointer variable book which is what we need to use to access the record until we have linked it into the list. We can simply add the node to the empty list with the two statements:

```
head ← book ;
end ← book ;
```

The first of the two statements above assigns the value of book to head. Because both book and head are reference variables their values are addresses. The value of book is the address of the new record and it is this address that is assigned to head making head now point to the new record as well. As the record is the only one in the list then end should also point to it, hence the second statement. We can show this diagrammatically as Figure 13.16:

Think Spot

FIGURE 13.16   **Inserting a node at the list head**

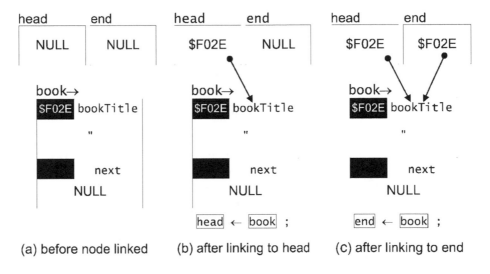

In Figure 13.16 why do you show book→ to represent the bookrecord, but not head→ and end→ to represent the head and end? Also, why are **head** and **end** small boxes yet **book** (which is of the same type) is a whole record?

This question arises from confusion typical when meeting pointers for the first time. The first thing to remember is that **head**, **end**, and **book** are all the same type of variable – they are all pointers to a **BookRecord**. That is, **head**, **end**, and **book** are not **BookRecords** themselves (they don't have all the fields associated with a **BookRecord**), rather they are simple single value variables in which the value is the *address* of a **BookRecord**. Figure 13.16, then, shows **head** and **end** as they really are: their values are addresses which point to the location at which a **BookRecord** can be found. If you look carefully at Figure 13.16 you will see that it does not show **book** but **book→**. The value of **book** is the address of the **BookRecord** that was created with the statement

    book ← New (BookRecord) ;

Figure 13.16 shows that this new **BookRecord** was placed in memory location $F02E, therefore the value of **book** is also $F02E. **book→** is a different animal. The → means that we are de-referencing book, that is, we are dealing with the variable that is pointed to by book. So, **book→** is referencing the new **BookRecord**. In effect, we are using **book→** as the identifier of the new **BookRecord**. Thus **book→.bookTitle** refers to the book title field of the **BookRecord** that is pointed to by **book**. To recap:

- **book** is the address of a **BookRecord**
- **book→** is the Book Record itself.

Now we need to solve the problem of adding a node to the end of a non-empty list. Look back at Figure 13.15. The non-empty list there has two nodes. If the new record is to go at the end of the list then it must come after the "Principles of Program Design" record.

Having created the record in statements #9–#11, how do we link it to the end of the list? What pointers need to be changed?

The new record is going to be the last one in the list so **end** needs to point to it. But we must also remember to point the **next** field of the current last node to the new one. The following two statements do just that:

$$\boxed{\text{end}} \rightarrow.\boxed{\text{next}} \leftarrow \boxed{\text{book}} \; ;$$
$$\boxed{\text{end}} \leftarrow \boxed{\text{book}} \; ;$$

The first statement changes the **next** field of the current last node to point to the new record. Check that you understand just what this statement is doing. **end** currently points to the last record in the list. So, **end→.next** is the **next** field of the last record in the list. Assigning the value of **book** (an address) to this field will add the new record to the end of the list. The second statement simply updates **end** so that it now points to the new node rather than the previous one. Again, we can show this diagrammatically as in Figure 13.17.

FIGURE 13.17   **Adding a node to the end of the list**

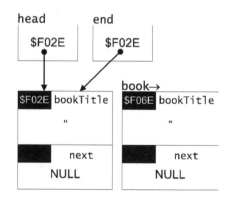

(a) before node linked

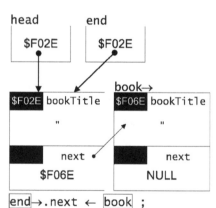

(b) after linking to last item

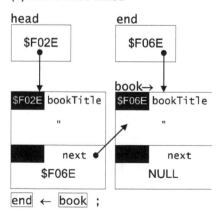

(c) after linking to tail

Note that none of the book records has a book title. This is because we have never assigned a title. We will return shortly to this aspect to show one way we could go about this. Now let's see the complete algorithm for adding one node to an unsorted list (Solution 13.2).

Solution 13.2 Algorithm to add a node to an unsorted list

```
1.   NEWTYPE BookRecord IS
2.      RECORD
           string: bookTitle  ;
           →BookRecord: next    ;
        ENDRECORD
3.   →BookRecord: head  ,
4.                end  ,
5.                book  ;
6.   head  ← NULL ;
7.   end  ← NULL ;
// Create a new book record and assign its address to a pointer
   variable.
8.   book  ← New (BookRecord) ;
9.   book  →. bookTitle  ← '';
10.  book  →. next   ← NULL ;
11.  IF ( head  = NULL) //An empty list
        11.1.   head  ← book  ; //Link new record to head
        11.2.   end  ← book  ; //Link new record to end
12.  ELSE //Not an empty list
        12.1.   end  →. next  ← book  ; //Link new record to
                                           //current end node
        12.2.   end  ← book  ; //Link new record to end
     ENDIF
```

Because statements #11.2 and #12.2 are the same, that is, we always need to update the end pointer, we could alter statements #11 and #12 thus:

```
11.  IF ( head  = NULL) //An empty list - add to head
        11.1.   head  ← book  ; //Link new record to head
12.  ELSE //Not an empty list - add to end
        12.1.   end →. next  ← book  ; //Link new record to current
                                          //end node
     ENDIF
13.  end  ← book  ; //Link new record to end
```

This alternative solution is functionally the same but removes the action common to both parts of the selection and places it in sequence after the selection as statement #13.

We still need to add a book title to a node. The reason we have not addressed this yet is because we have been concerned with the general problem of adding a node to a list. You can use this general algorithm in many programs where an unsorted list is required. The normal way you would do this is to change the algorithm into a sub-program which would then be invoked each time it is needed. The sub-program could take parameters containing the values of the various data fields of the record. Here is a procedurized version of the add-a-node algorithm. From now on to save space we will not repeat the declarations.

Solution 13.3 Add a node procedure

```
1.  PROCEDURE AddNode (string: theTitle )
    1.1.   book  ← New (BookRecord) ;
    1.2.   book →.bookTitle  ← theTitle ;
    1.3.   book →.next  ← NULL ;
    1.4.   IF ( head  = NULL) //An empty list
             1.4.1.   head  ← book  ; //Link new record to head
    1.5.   ELSE //Not an empty list
             1.5.1.   end →.next  ← book   ; //Link new record
                                              //to end node
           ENDIF
    1.6.   end  ← book  ; //Link new record to end
    ENDPROCEDURE
```

Notice how we have taken the algorithm and wrapped it up in a procedure declaration. There is one formal parameter, theTitle, which is a string. The value of this parameter is assigned to the bookTitle field of the new record in statement #1.2. There is a word of warning about this procedure. Notice that the procedure refers directly to head and end. This solution assumes that head and end have been declared as global variables that can be accessed by this sub-program wherever it is situated. A better and safer solution would be to pass head and end as reference parameters to the procedure as well. This would allow the procedure to alter the list head and end pointers as well as allowing it to be used in different programs, or even to add nodes to more than one list within the same program. Here is the fully parameterized solution.

Solution 13.4 Fully parameterized AddNode procedure

```
1.  PROCEDURE AddNode (string: theTitle ,
                       REFERENCE:→BookRecord: listHead ,
                       REFERENCE:→BookRecord: listEnd )
    1.1.   book   ← New (BookRecord) ;
    1.2.   book →.bookTitle  ← theTitle ;
    1.3.   book →.next  ← NULL ;
    1.4.   IF ( listHead  = NULL) //An empty list
             1.4.1.   listHead  ← book  ; //Link new record to
                                           //head
    1.5.   ELSE //Not an empty list
             1.5.1.   listEnd →.next  ← book  ; //Link record to
                                                 //end node
           ENDIF
    1.6.   listEnd  ← book  ; //Link new record to end
    ENDPROCEDURE
```

To show how this procedure could be invoked Solution 13.5 shows a program that repeatedly prompts the user to type in book titles. Each time a book title is entered AddNode will be invoked to create a BookRecord structure and insert it into the list. For this example I have included all the declarations so you can see more easily how it all fits together.

Solution 13.5 A complete program to build a list using the AddNode procedure

```
1.    PROGRAM BuildList
2.    NEWTYPE BookRecord IS
3.    RECORD
      string:│bookTitle│ ;
      →BookRecord:│next│ ;
      ENDRECORD
4.    PROCEDURE AddNode (string:│theTitle│,
                         REFERENCE:→BookRecord:│listHead│,
                         REFERENCE:→BookRecord:│listEnd│)
        4.1.   →BookRecord:│book│; // variable to store new book
        4.2.   │book│ ← New (BookRecord) ;
        4.3.   │book│↦.│bookTitle│ ← │theTitle│;
        4.4.   │book│↦.│next│ ← NULL ;
        4.5.   IF (│listHead│ = NULL) //An empty list
            4.5.1.  │listHead│ ← │book│ ; //Link new record
                                          // to head
        4.6.   ELSE //Not an empty list
            4.6.1.  │listEnd│↦.│next│ ← │book│ ; //Link record to
                                                 //end node
               ENDIF
        4.7.   │listEnd│ ← │book│ ; //Link new record to end
      ENDPROCEDURE
5.    →BookRecord:│head│,
6.                │end│,
7.                │book│ ;
8.    string:│title│ ;
 // Main statement block
9.    │head│ ← NULL ;
10.   │end│ ← NULL ;
11.   DO
        11.1.  Display ('Please enter a book title ('ZZZ'
                                             to exit)') ;
        11.2.  Get (keyboard, REFERENCE:│title│) ;
        11.3.  AddNode (│title│, │head│, │end│) ;
      WHILE (│title│ ≠ 'ZZZ') ;
 // End of program
```

Having developed the AddNode algorithm as a procedure we shall develop the remaining algorithms as sub-programs too.

Displaying the Contents of a List

Once the list is built we need to be able to access the data it holds. A common task is to save the list to a file before the program ends so that the data are retained. To that end we will now develop a procedure that, starting at the head and finishing at the end, displays the contents of the list on the screen. Adapting the procedure to save the list to a file is fairly straightforward requiring some additional statements to set up and open the file, and replacing the `Display` statements with file output operations. As before we will structure our thinking with the *HTTLAP* strategy.

Understanding the Problem

Q. What are you being asked to do?

A. Design a procedure to display the contents of the list on the screen

Q. What is required?

A. The details of each node in the list to be displayed on the screen. We must start at the head and end at the end.

Q. What is the unknown?

A. The size of the list. In fact, the list could even be empty. Figure 13.18 is a diagram of an empty list and a populated list.

FIGURE 13.18 **An empty and a populated list**

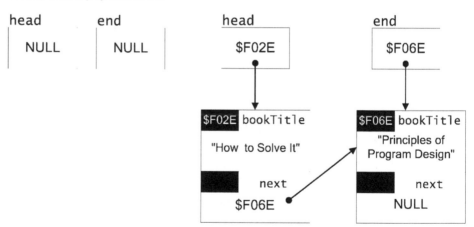

Q. What are the principal parts of the problem?

A. The list head, the end, the nodes, and the fields within the nodes. There should be a traversal of the list from head to end and a display of each record.

Devising a Plan to Solve the Problem

Q. Have you solved a problem similar to this?

A. It is related to the `AddNode` algorithm I think because that had to deal with both empty and populated lists.

Q. Are some parts of the problem more easily solved than others?

A. Yes – displaying a node is straightforward.

Q. Did you use all of the information in the problem statement?

A. I think so.

Q. Can you satisfy all the conditions of the problem?

A. Yes. We managed it with the AddNode algorithm, and this is using the same principal parts.

Carrying Out the Plan

We need to write down the sequence of actions necessary to solve the problem. For each node we must display it and then move to the next one in the list. This needs two actions:

```
Display (current→.bookTitle) ;
current ← current→.next ;
```

The first action is straightforward enough: if current points to the current node then displaying current→.bookTitle will display the bookTitle field of the node pointed to by current. Let's say that current points to the first record in the list in Figure 13.18 above, in which case its value would be $F02E. The display action would print the bookTitle field of the record that resides at location $F02E ('How to Solve It'). The next action assigns the value of the next field of the record pointed to by current to current itself. The next field of the record pointed to by current is $F032, so this action would assign $F032 to current. As $F032 is where the second record is located, current now points to the second record ('Principles of Program Design'). This technique can be repeated for each record in the list.

Traversing the list requires starting at the head and then for each record displaying its title and moving to the next one until we run out of records. This is an iterative process – we are repeatedly executing the display and move-to-next actions. The algorithm must be able to deal with an empty list, so it is possible for this iteration to execute zero times. This means that the WHILE loop is the ideal iteration structure for this problem.

What is the terminating condition for the WHILE? When will we know that we have processed the last record and have reached the end of the list? Look at Figure 13.18 and see if you can answer this question.

There are two solutions to this sub-problem. First, we can tell that we have reached the end of the list when the next field of the current record is NULL. Alternatively, we can make use of the end pointer. end always points to the last record, so when the value of current equals the value of end (that is, both reference variables point to the same record) we know we have arrived at the last node in the list. For the purposes of building a WHILE loop it is easier to test whether the next field of the record pointed to by current is NULL than to compare current with end. Using this knowledge we can build a WHILE loop to traverse the list (Solution 13.6).

Solution 13.6 **WHILE** loop to traverse and display a list

```
1.   current  ←  head  ;
2.   WHILE ( current  ≠ NULL)
         2.1.  Display ( current →. bookTitle ) ;
         2.2.  current  ←  current →. next  ;
     ENDWHILE
```

Think Spot

Statement #1 assigns the value of head to current which makes current point to the first item in the list. The WHILE loop in statement #2 then iterates through the list as long as current is not NULL. As soon as current is NULL we know we have reached the end of the list. Convince yourself that this WHILE loop deals with the empty list condition as well as processing a populated list. If you need a diagram to help, then refer back to Figure 13.18 which has both an empty and a non-empty list. Statement #2.1 displays the book title of the node pointed to by current, and statement #2.2 points current to the next item in the list.

> Try rewriting the loop, this time comparing **current** to **end** to check for the end of the list. You should find that the solution is not quite as straightforward as it first sounds.

Looking at Solution 13.6 we can see that it is sufficient to solve the problem of traversing through the list. Now we just have to turn the algorithm into a procedure. As before, we shall parameterize it.

Solution 13.7 The parameterized DisplayList procedure

```
1.   PROCEDURE DisplayList (→BookRecord: listHead )
         1.1.  →BookRecord: current  ;
         1.2.  current  ←  listHead  ;
         1.3.  WHILE ( current  ≠ NULL)
                  1.3.1.  Display ( current →. bookTitle ) ;
                  1.3.2.  current  ←  current →. next  ;
               ENDWHILE
     ENDPROCEDURE
```

There are a few observations to make about the procedure. First, the single parameter listHead is a value parameter. In AddNode listHead was a reference parameter because we needed to update its value. In DisplayList we do not need to alter the value of the head pointer, so it should be passed as a value parameter. Secondly, we have declared current as a local variable inside the procedure as the pointer to keep track of the current position in the list. We can now use this procedure in a list processing program. For instance, we could add the following statement to the program in Solution 13.5:

```
12. DisplayList ( head ) ;
```

This would pass the list head as a value parameter to the DisplayList procedure which would then traverse the list displaying each book record in turn.

Finding a Node in an Unsorted List

Once data are stored in a list we will need to access individual records, perhaps to update them, to display their contents, or to delete them. It is useful, therefore, to have an algorithm that can find any node in a given list. The algorithm needs to be able to search through the list looking for a record that matches a given search criterion. If it finds the record it should return its address, otherwise it should return a NULL value.

Understanding the Problem

Q. What are you being asked to do?

A. We are being asked to design a search facility that will locate any record in a list or will return a NULL value if the record is not found.

Q. What is required?

A. A pointer to the found record or else a NULL pointer.

Q. What is the unknown?

A. Whether the record we are looking for exists in the list. Also, we do not know if the list is empty or not.

Q. What are the principal parts of the problem?

A. We need a way of working through each record in the list to see if it is the one we are looking for. We need a search criterion then as well. In our list the records only have one data field, bookTitle, so the search will be on a book title string. We need something to indicate that the record has been found. We need a pointer to hold the address of the found record (or NULL if the record is not found).

Devising a Plan to Solve the Problem

Q. Have you solved this problem before or is it similar to one you have solved before?

A. I think the list traversal loop in the DisplayList algorithm might be useful here too.

Q. Are some parts of the problem more easily solved than others?

A. Traversing the list should be easy as we have done that before.

Q. Can you satisfy all the requirements of the problem?

A. I think so.

Q. Have you left anything out?

A. Not as far as I can see.

Carrying Out the Plan

Finding a record will involve working through the list checking each record in turn, so the DisplayList algorithm can be adapted for this problem. We can remove the statement that displays the contents of the record and replace it by actions that check whether the record is the one we are looking for. If the book title we are looking for is stored in a string variable called, say, searchTitle, we can simply compare the bookTitle field of the current record with the searchTitle string. If the two strings match then we have found the right record. We can write down the algorithm we have so far. For now, we will use a fixed search string, though in the final version it should be a parameter supplied to the sub-program.

Solution 13.8 First draft of search algorithm

```
1.    string: searchTitle  ;
2.    searchTitle  ←  'Principles of Program Design'  ;
3.    current  ←  listHead  ;
4.    WHILE ( current  ≠ NULL)
          4.1.   IF ( searchTitle  =  current →. bookTitle )
                      // Record found
                 ENDIF
          4.2.   current  ←  current →. next  ;
      ENDWHILE
```

Think Spot

In Solution 13.8 we have reused the list traversal loop from the DisplayList procedure. Statement #4.1 is the selection to test whether the current record is the target of the search. Now we have a sub-problem to solve: what should happen if the record is found? It would be a good idea to stop the search as it is pointless to work through the rest of the list when the target has already been found. In addition, the address of the target needs to be stored. How should the search be stopped? What determines whether the search continues? The WHILE loop's controlling condition is the heart of the search. Currently the loop only terminates when the end of the list is reached. We need to extend this condition so that the loop terminates when the end of the list is reached *or* the target is found. We know the target has been found when the condition in statement #4.1 is true. So, if we use a Boolean variable found to store the value of the condition in statement #4.1 we can use this variable in the WHILE loop. Here is the body of the IF statement filled in:

```
4.1.   IF ( searchTitle  =  current →. bookTitle )
           4.1.1.   found  ← true ;
           4.1.2.   target  ←  current  ;
       ENDIF
```

Statement #4.1.1 sets found to true, and statement #4.1.2 stores the address of the current record (the one we are searching for) in a reference variable called target. The declarations for these variables would be:

```
boolean: found  ;
→BookRecord: target  ;
```

Now we just have to extend the WHILE loop so that it also terminates when the target record is found. Have a go yourself at writing the new loop condition.

There are two ways we can write the compound WHILE loop condition. We can either think about the condition that will be true at the point the loop terminates and then write the condition so that the loop iterates while that terminating condition *is not* true. Or, we can think about the condition that must be true for the loop to continue iterating and write the condition so that the loop iterates while that continuation condition *is* true. Let's start with the condition that will be true when the loop should terminate.

There are two parts to the condition that will be true when the loop terminates: the end of the list is reached or the target record has been found. So, we have:

(current = NULL) OR (found)

This is the condition that is true when the list terminates, so we need to write the condition so that the loop iterates until this terminating condition is not true. We can do this very simply by using the logical operator NOT and applying it to the whole condition:

NOT ((current = NULL) OR (found))

When we put this into the WHILE loop it looks like this:

WHILE NOT ((current = NULL) OR (found))

Read this as "WHILE the terminating condition is not met".

The other way of writing the WHILE loop is to write the continuation condition, that is, the condition that is true each time the loop iterates. This requires neither the end of the list to be reached nor the target to be found, hence:

WHILE (current ≠ NULL) AND (NOT found) DO

We see that

NOT ((current = NULL) OR (found))

and

(current ≠ NULL) AND (NOT found)

are logically equivalent. You can prove this by using De Morgan's laws to transform one into the other.

Now that we have completed the WHILE loop and the selection within it, it remains to put it all together and, as before, wrap it up in a sub-program. This time we need to use a function rather than a procedure as the sub-program is required to give back the address of the target record. The complete function is given below as Solution 13.9.

Solution 13.9 The complete FindNode function

```
1.   FUNCTION FindNode (→BookRecord:listHead,
                         string:searchTitle) RETURNS →BookRecord

   1.1.    →BookRecord:current,
   1.2.              target ;
```

```
1.3.    boolean: found  ;
1.4.    found  ← false ;
1.5.    target  ← NULL ;
1.6.    current  ← listHead  ;
1.7.    WHILE ( current  ≠ NULL) AND (NOT found )
            1.7.1.  IF ( searchTitle  = current ↦. bookTitle )
                        1.7.1.1.   found  ← true ;
                        1.7.1.2.   target  ← current  ;
                    ENDIF
            1.7.2.   current  ← current ↦. next  ;
        ENDWHILE
1.8.    RETURN target  ;
ENDFUNCTION
```

Notice that the function has three local variables (**current**, **target**, and **found**) and two parameters (**listHead** and **searchTitle**). Also, as it is a function it returns a pointer to a **BookRecord**. Statement #1.8 is the action that returns the result. If the string held in the parameter **searchTitle** is found in a record in the list then **target** will contain its address (see statement #1.7.1.2), otherwise it will contain the value NULL (the value it was initialized to in statement #1.5). Read through Solution 13.9 to make sure you can understand how it works.

Deleting a Node from an Unsorted List

The final common list-processing routine is one to delete an element from the list. The node to be deleted will be identified through its book title. Deleting nodes can be confusing to the beginner as pointers need to be redirected. Consider the list in Figure 13.19 which has four nodes.

Say we wished to delete the third record (**'Conceptual Blockbusting'**). What pointers must be redirected to accomplish this?

FIGURE 13.19   **A list from which we want to delete the third node**

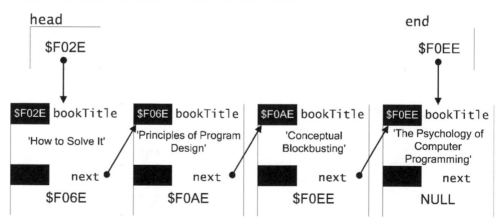

Deleting a node is like removing a link from a chain: the link is removed and the two adjacent links are joined together. To remove 'Conceptual Blockbusting' from the list we just need to join its two adjacent nodes to each other, as in Figure 13.20.

FIGURE 13.20   **The third node unlinked**

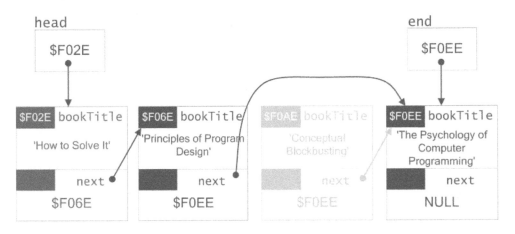

Notice how the **next** field of the predecessor to 'Conceptual Blockbusting' has been changed to point to the node that comes after 'Conceptual Blockbusting'. This means that a list traversal would now skip 'Conceptual Blockbusting' and jump straight from 'Principles of Program Design' to 'The Psychology of Computer Programming'. However, there is some unfinished business. The record has not actually been deleted, it has just been unlinked from the list. To get rid of the record from the computer's memory we would need to do something akin to **New** in reverse. Most languages have functions and procedures for de-allocating memory resources (indeed, Java even handles *garbage collection* automatically and removes objects when there is no longer anything pointing to them). The *HTTLAP* pseudo-code uses the procedure **Delete**. We will use the **Delete** procedure because thinking about clearing up memory after you when processing lists is a good habit to get into as not all languages offer automatic garbage collection.

The pointer updates for deleting a node from the middle of the list are reasonably straightforward. What about deleting the node at the head or the end? Looking at Figure 13.19 again, you should be able to see what pointer changes need to be made to remove the first item in the list.

To unlink the item at the head of the list simply requires redirecting **head** to point to the second node (that is, **head→.next**) as shown in Figure 13.21. When we build the actual procedure we will see how to use the **Delete** procedure to remove the node from memory.

Deleting the node at the tail requires two pointer changes, as shown in Figure 13.22. First, the **next** field of the node before the final record must be set to **NULL**. Secondly, the **end** pointer must be changed to point to the node adjacent to the last one in the list.

FIGURE 13.21   **Deleting the first item in the list**

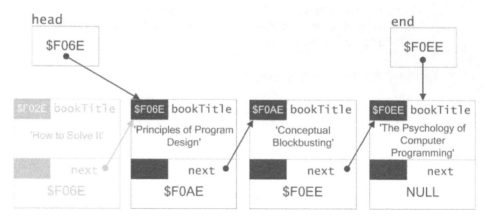

FIGURE 13.22   **Deleting the end node**

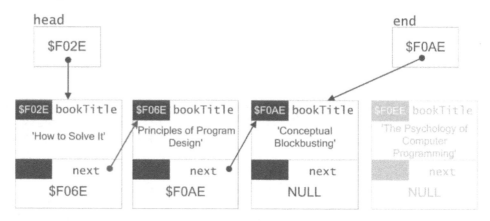

The requirements of the `DeleteNode` function are that it should look for a record whose book title matches a given string. If the node is found then it should be deleted and the Boolean value `true` should be returned to indicate a successful deletion. If the node could not be found (that is, the search string does not exist in the list) then no deletions should take place and the function should return the Boolean value `false` to indicate failure. The function must be able to delete nodes from the head, middle, and end of the list.

Understanding the Problem

Q. What are you being asked to do?

A. We are being asked to design a delete facility that will delete any record in a list.

Q. What is required?

A. A function that accepts the list head and a search string as parameters and which deletes the record that matches the search string. The function should return Boolean `true` if it could find the record and perform the deletion otherwise it should return `false`.

Q. What is the unknown?

A. Whether the record we are looking for exists in the list. Also, we do not know if the list is empty or not.

Q. What are the principal parts of the problem?

A. We need to search the list for the specified record. Ideally I would like to use the `FindNode` function for this part, but we will have to see whether it is suitable. The required record could be at the head, in the middle, or at the end of the list which affects the way we handle it. The nodes adjacent to the target node are also important as they need to be linked together.

Devising a Plan to Solve the Problem

Q. Have you solved this problem before or is it similar to one you have solved before?

A. It is a bit like `AddNode` in reverse. It also needs to search the list to find the node in question. Either we can simply invoke the `FindNode` function or if that turns out not to work the way we need we can adapt it and create a purpose-built search routine.

Q. Are some parts of the problem more easily solved than others?

A. I suspect deleting the node at the head is easier than deleting from the middle or the end.

Q. Can you satisfy all the requirements of the problem?

A. I think so.

Q. Have you left anything out?

A. Not as far as I can see.

Carrying Out the Plan

A function is required, so here is the header with all its parameters:

```
1.   FUNCTION DeleteNode (→BookRecord:listHead,
                          string:searchTitle) RETURNS boolean
     ENDFUNCTION
```

Before the node can be deleted we must first establish whether it exists in the list. We had hoped to use the `FindNode` function, so let's see whether that is possible.

Solution 13.10 First attempt at `DeleteNode` function, a partial solution

```
1.   FUNCTION DeleteNode (→BookRecord:listHead,
                          string:searchTitle) RETURNS boolean
   1.1.   →BookRecord:current ;
   1.2.   current ← FindNode (listHead, searchTitle) ;
   1.3.   IF (current = NULL) //Record not found
        1.3.1.   RETURN false ;
```

```
            1.4.   ELSE //Record found
                       1.4.1.   // Delete the record
                       1.4.2.   RETURN true ;
                   ENDIF
        ENDFUNCTION
```

Think Spot

So far it looks fine, so let's see if we can use the pointer returned by FindNode to delete the node. There are three different deletion problems to solve: deleting from the head, from the middle, and from the end. Putting this knowledge into the solution gives us Solution 13.11.

Solution 13.11 Second draft of DeleteNode, a partial solution

```
    1.    FUNCTION DeleteNode (→BookRecord:⎡listHead⎤,
                                string:⎡searchTitle⎤) RETURNS boolean
            1.1.   →BookRecord:⎡current⎤ ;
            1.2.   ⎡current⎤ ← FindNode (⎡listHead⎤, ⎡searchTitle⎤) ;
            1.3.   IF (⎡current⎤ = NULL) //Record not found
                       1.3.1.   RETURN false ;
            1.4.   ELSE //Record found, so delete it
                       1.4.1.   IF (⎡current⎤ = listHead) //Node at head
                                    1.4.1.1.   ⎡listHead⎤ ← ⎡current⎤→.⎡next⎤ ;
                                               //Unlink
                                    1.4.1.2.   Delete (⎡current⎤) ;
                                               //Remove node
                       1.4.2.   ELSE IF (⎡current⎤→.⎡next⎤ ≠ NULL)
                                       // Node in middle
                                    1.4.2.1.   //Delete node
                       1.4.3.   ELSE //Node at end
                                    1.4.3.1.   //Delete node
                                ENDIF
                       1.4.4.   RETURN true ;
                   ENDIF
        ENDFUNCTION
```

In Solution 13.11 I have put in a three-way selection to deal with the three positions from which a node can be deleted. Also, in statements #1.4.1.1 and #1.4.1.2, I have put in the actions to delete the node from the head of the list. Statement #1.4.1.1 redirects listHead to point at the second node in the list. Statement #1.4.1.2 uses the Delete procedure we talked about earlier to remove the first node from the computer's memory. The redirection of listHead raises an issue. listHead is one of DeleteNode's parameters, so changing its value will have no effect on the actual list head pointer unless we make it a reference parameter. This also means that we need to include the list end as a reference parameter because we will change its value too.

Now we need to write the actions to remove a node from the middle of the list (statement #1.4.2.1). Figure 13.20 showed diagrammatically what needs to be done. The node immediately prior to the target (its predecessor) needs to have its next field redirected to the node immediately after the target (its successor).

Looking at the information returned by the **FindNode** function in statement #1.8 in Solution 13.9 can you see the difficulty we face in removing the selected node from the list?

FindNode gives us the address of the node we want to delete and from this we can get the address of its successor by looking in its next field. But we have no pointer to the node's predecessor. If we had implemented a doubly linked list with predecessor as well as next pointers then this problem would not exist. But we do not have a doubly linked list so we need to find a way round the problem.

Work through this problem and suggest two or three ways of solving it.

There are at least three ways we can work round this problem. First, we could rewrite the FindNode function so that it returns a pointer to the target's predecessor. You could either return the predecessor instead of the target pointer, or as an additional reference parameter. A difficulty with this approach is that you would need to change everything that uses FindNode. This could potentially be a huge task if the function is widely used. A second solution is to write a special find function that is only used by the DeleteNode function (in fact, it could be incorporated into DeleteNode directly). This new find function could give a pointer to the target's predecessor. A third solution would be, after locating the node we want to delete, to traverse the list again until we reach the target's predecessor. This solution is quite inefficient as it involves two list traversals: one to find the target and one to find its predecessor. We will adopt the second approach for this problem but will use the first approach when we come to designing the FindNode function for an ordered linked list later on.

You can see how, with hindsight, we could have designed a more generalized FindNode function that would have wider applications than our solution. Whilst you cannot envisage every possible use to which you may want to put an algorithm, experience will teach you that there are certain features and tricks that are easy to build in and which make your routines much more useful. In this case, adding a parameter to hold the target's predecessor would have made the function more useful as the parameter could just be ignored when not needed.

We will create a new function called FindPred which we will adapt from the FindNode algorithm. Like FindNode, FindPred will return a pointer, but this time to the target's predecessor rather than the target itself. There is one difficulty with finding the predecessor to the target. When the target is at head of the list it has no predecessor. In this case we can set the predecessor to NULL. So, if the returned pointer is NULL then the target was found at the head of the list. If the next field of the returned pointer is NULL then we know the search string was not found as predecessor is pointing to the last record in the list. Here is the FindPred function, adapted from FindNode.

Solution 13.12 The FindPred function

```
1.    FUNCTION FindPred (→BookRecord: listHead ,
                         string: searchTitle ) RETURNS →BookRecord ;
  1.1.    →BookRecord: current ,
```

1.2.   predecessor ;
1.3.   **boolean:** found ;
1.4.   found ← false ;
1.5.   current ← listHead ;
// Find the target's predecessor.
1.6.   predecessor ← NULL ;
1.7.   current ← listHead ;
1.8.   found ← false ;
1.9.   WHILE (current ≠ NULL) AND (NOT found)
      1.9.1.   IF (searchTitle = current→.bookTitle)
          1.9.1.1.   found ← true ;
      1.9.2.   ELSE
          1.9.2.1.   predecessor ← current ;
      ENDIF
      1.9.3.   current ← current→.next ;
    ENDWHILE
1.10. RETURN predecessor ;
ENDFUNCTION

The changes to the original algorithm are shown as bold statements. We have introduced a new pointer variable called **predecessor**. This is initialized to NULL at the start. Then, as the list is traversed **predecessor** is updated to point to the current record and **current** is then pointed to the next record in the list. However, notice in statement #1.9.1.1 **predecessor** is only updated if the current record does not match the search string. This is so that **predecessor** does not point to the record that matches the search string but to the one before it. Because we do not need to know the address of the record that contains the search string I have removed all references to **target** from FindPred. If you are having trouble following how the algorithm works, trace through it by hand using Figure 13.19 as an example list.

Now that we have a pointer to the predecessor of the record that matches the search string we can continue with deleting the record from the list. We need to adjust DeleteNode so that it uses FindPred instead of FindNode. We also need to add listHead and listEnd as reference parameters.

Solution 13.13 Finished DeleteNode function

1. FUNCTION DeleteNode (**REFERENCE:→BookRecord:** listHead,
                   REFERENCE:→BookRecord: listEnd,
                string: searchTitle) RETURNS **boolean**
1.1.   **→BookRecord:** current ,
1.2.   predecessor;
1.3.   predecessor ← FindPred (listHead, searchTitle) ;
1.4.   IF (predecessor→.next) = NULL) //Record not found
    1.4.1.   RETURN false ;

```
1.5.    ELSE //Record found, so delete it
        1.5.1.  IF (predecessor = NULL) //Node at head
                1.5.1.1.  current ← listHead ;
                1.5.1.2.  listHead ← listHead→.next ;
                          //Unlink
                1.5.1.3.  Delete (current) ;
                          //Remove node
        1.5.2.  ELSE IF (predecessor→.next ≠ NULL)
                //Middle
                1.5.2.1.  current ← predecessor
                          →.next ;
                1.5.2.2.  predecessor→.next ← current
                          →.next;
                1.5.2.3.  Delete (current) ;
        1.5.3.  ELSE //Node at end
                1.5.3.1.  current ← predecessor→.next ;
                1.5.3.2.  predecessor→.next ← NULL ;
                1.5.3.3.  listEnd ← predecessor ;
                1.5.3.4.  Delete (current) ;
                ENDIF
        1.5.4.  RETURN true ;
        ENDIF
ENDFUNCTION
```

Solution 13.13 first assigns the result of FindPred to the variable predecessor (statement #1.3). Then comes the deletion selection in statement #1.4. First predecessor is inspected to see if its next field is NULL. If it is this means the search string was not found in the list as predecessor is pointing to the last node in the list. In this case the function returns false to show that it did not manage to delete anything. If predecessor is not pointing to the end then the record was found and can be deleted. Statement 1.5.1 deals with deleting the node at the head of the list, statement 1.5.2 from the middle of the list and 1.5.3 from the end. Changing the list head to point to the next node in the list is simple (see statement #1.5.1.2). But we also want to delete the record from memory. Statement #1.5.1.1 sets a pointer to listHead so that when listHead is updated we still have a copy of its previous value in current. Once listHead is redirected then the memory pointed to by current can be cleared with the Delete procedure.

Deleting a node from the middle of the list requires the next field of the target's predecessor to be redirected to the target's successor, hence the instruction

```
predecessor→.next ← current→.next ;
```

in statement 1.5.2.2 where current is the node to be deleted; statement #1.5.2.1 gave current its value. Once the node has been unlinked then Delete can again be used to remove it from memory.

To remove the node at the end, current is again used to store the location of the node to be deleted. The next field of its predecessor is then redirected to NULL in statement #1.5.3.2 as it will become the last link in the list and the last node should always point to NULL.[9] Next listEnd is updated to point to the new end record, and finally the target record (pointed to by current) is removed from memory.

You will find it instructive to work through this algorithm with the list in Figure 13.19 seeing what happens when the predecessor points to NULL, to the head, to a record in the middle, and to the record at the end.

Sorted Lists

Now that we have examined manipulating an unsorted list we can consider the sorted list. In a sorted list all the nodes are stored in ascending or descending order of some key value. A telephone directory is a sorted list of telephone subscribers where the key value is the customer's name. With the unsorted list we always added new nodes to the end. In a sorted list each new node must be added at the correct position that maintains the sort order. For example, we could sort our book list by ascending order of book title which would give us: 'Conceptual Blockbusting', 'How to Solve It', 'Principles of Program Design', and 'The Psychology of Computer Programming'. This is a very literal alphabetic ordering where the strings are compared to each other character for character until a difference is found. In a book catalog we might expect 'The Psychology of Computer Programming' to come under P for psychology rather than T for 'the'. Also, unless we explicitly deal with it, the word 'POET' would come before 'Petal'. Even though 'O' comes after 'e' in the alphabet, the character 'O' has a lower ASCII value than 'e' (all the upper-case characters come before the lower-case ones in the character set) which results in 'POET' being judged to be *lexically* less than 'Petal'. This can be quite easily worked around by temporarily converting each string to upper-case and then doing the comparison. For now we will just work with the default ordering to show how the ordered list algorithms can be built. You can try implementing true alphabetic ordering as one of the exercises at the end of the chapter.

Our sorted list will have add, delete, find, and display routines. We can use the unsorted list routines as the starting point.

Displaying the Contents of a Sorted List

Displaying the contents of an unsorted list requires starting at the head and working through the list record by record until the end was reached displaying the contents of each node along the way. The requirements for the sorted list are exactly the same, so we can use the DisplayList procedure in Solution 13.7 without any amendments.

Finding a Node in a Sorted List

The process of finding a node in a sorted list is similar to that for finding a node in an unsorted list but we refine the algorithm to optimize it for a sorted list. In an unsorted list, looking for a specific record involves searching each node until either

---

[9] This is not always true. Sometimes you may want to implement a circular list in which the tail node points back to the head.

the target is found or the end of the list is reached. We can use the ordering of a sorted list to our advantage. Take our four-node book list sorted by book title in Figure 13.23 below.

FIGURE 13.23   **A sorted book list**

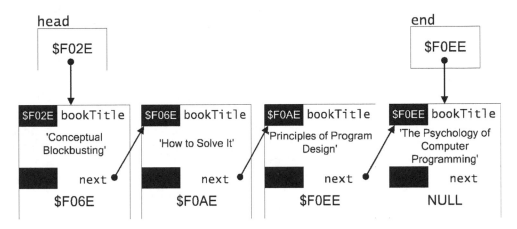

If we wanted to search for 'How to Solve It', rather than search every node until it is found or the end is reached we can stop when it is found **or** when a node is reached whose book title comes alphabetically after 'How to Solve It'. This is because the list is sorted by book title, so as soon as we find a title that comes alphabetically after the target we know the target is not in the list. In Solution 13.14 I have adapted the earlier FindNode function to take account of the list ordering. I have made a few other changes too. First, the function returns a Boolean value to indicate whether the target book was found. Second, rather than return a pointer to the target node the function gives back (via a reference parameter) the predecessor to the target. As before, the predecessor will be NULL if the target is at the head of the list. One big difference though is that even if the target is not found the predecessor will still have a value as it indicates where the target *would have been* had it been in the list (that is, it finds the alphabetic position where such a book title would be located). In Table 13.1 are some examples that use the list in Figure 13.23 to show the various permutations.

If the search string is 'Conceptual Blockbusting', then the function will return Boolean **true** as this book is in the list. Because it is at the head the **predecessor** is set to NULL. When the search string is 'How to Solve It', its **predecessor** will be

Table 13.1   **Finding the Predecessor in a Sorted List**

Search title	Predecessor	Target found?
Conceptual Blockbusting	NULL	True
How to Solve It	Conceptual Blockbusting	True
A Book on C	NULL	False
System Design	Principles of Program Design	False
Z for Software Engineers	The Psychology of Computer Programming	False

Think Spot

'Conceptual Blockbusting' and the function again returns *True*. The remaining three search strings all cause the function to return *False* because none of them is in the list, yet the function still gives a value to predecessor. Take the search string 'System Design'. This book is not in the list yet predecessor points to 'Principles of Program Design' which is the book that would immediately precede 'System Design' if it were in the list. This will come in very useful when we want to insert records into the list because predecessor will always point to the record that should come immediately before the new record.

Here is the general algorithm in outline pseudo-code:

1. FindSortedNode
    1.1.   WHILE not at end of list AND search title greater than the current one ;
            1.1.1.   Store current record as predecessor ;
            1.1.2.   Point current to the next record in the list ;
        ENDWHILE
    1.2.   IF the current title matches the one we are looking for
            1.2.1.   We found it ;
    1.3.   ELSE
            1.3.1.   We did not find it ;
        ENDIF
    1.4.   Return found/not found result ;

Solution 13.14 below shows this algorithm written as an *HTTLAP* function.

Solution 13.14 The FindSortedNode function

1. FUNCTION FindSortedNode (→**BookRecord**:`listHead`,
                                    string:`searchTitle`,
                                    REFERENCE:→**BookRecord**:`predecessor`)
                                    RETURNS **boolean**
    1.1.   →**BookRecord**:`current` ;
    1.2.   **boolean**:`found`;
    1.3.   `predecessor` ← NULL ;
    1.4.   `current` ← `listHead` ;
    1.5.   WHILE (`current` ≠ NULL) AND
                     (`searchTitle` > `current`→.`bookTitle`)
            1.5.1.   `predecessor` ← `current` ;
            1.5.2.   `current` ← `current`→.`next` ;
        ENDWHILE
    1.6.   IF (`current` ≠ NULL)
            1.6.1.   `found` ← `searchTitle` = `current`→.`bookTitle` ;
    1.7.   ELSE
            1.7.1.   `found` ← false ;
        ENDIF
    1.8.   RETURN `found` ;
ENDFUNCTION

Notice how the WHILE condition has changed from the unsorted FindNode function? Because the list is sorted we can stop searching as soon as we reach a record that has a title that is greater than (comes alphabetically after) the one we are looking for, or if we reach the end of the list. So, if the search string were 'A Book on C' we could stop as soon as we reached 'Conceptual Blockbusting' as 'A Book on C' comes before 'Conceptual Blockbusting'. Inside the loop predecessor is pointed to the current record and current is updated to point to the next one. This means that when the loop exits predecessor will point to the node with the book title that comes before the one we are looking for. Thus if the search string were 'System Design' predecessor would be pointing to 'Principles of Program Design'. Likewise, if the search string were 'The Psychology of Computer Programming' predecessor would also point to 'Principles of Program Design'.

After the WHILE loop comes a selection to determine whether the search string was found or not. If the book title of the record pointed to by current matches the search string then statement #1.6.1 will set found to true otherwise it will assign it the value false. The reason for the selection in statement #1.6 is that current could be NULL. It can cause a program to crash if an attempt is made to follow (de-reference) a NULL pointer. So, if current is NULL then found is set to false as the search string cannot have been found. If it is not NULL then statement #1.6.1 determines whether the book was found or not. Some programming languages allow NULL pointers to be de-referenced without crashing the program, but others are more strict, hence the selection in statement #1.6.

Adding a Node to a Sorted List

Adding a node to a sorted list is similar to adding to an unsorted list except that rather than always adding to the end, a new record must be inserted into the correct position to maintain the ordering. This means that we will need to use the FindSortedNode function to locate the insertion point. Also, some sorted lists allow duplicate records and others do not – it depends on the problem the list is required to solve. In our case we will assume that book titles are unique and that we will not allow a title to appear more than once in the list.[10] We can use the return value of FindSortedNode to determine whether it is possible to insert the new record (that is, whether the book already exists in the list). If it is possible, FindSortedNode will also have given us the predecessor of the record's insertion point. Once the correct insertion point has been found we still need to be aware of whether the insertion point is at the head of the list or not. This time though, when we insert at the head, the list is not necessarily empty. Below is a version of the AddNode procedure adapted to work with a sorted list. Notice I have removed any reference to the list end. This is because insertion can take place anywhere in the list. We needed the end pointer with the unsorted list as new nodes were always inserted at the end. With the sorted list we do not need to

---

[10] There is an assumption here that book titles are unique. But, as this book demonstrates, this assumption does not always hold. This book's title is "How To Think Like A Programmer" with the subtitle "Program Design Solutions For The Bewildered". However, there is a smaller version of this book (the first eight chapters only) with the same main title but the sub-title "Problem Solving For The Bewildered". If we only dealt with books' main titles then the two versions of this book would be a problem.

keep track of the end. By leaving the end pointer out of the `AddSortedNode` algorithm we are keeping the function concise and uncluttered.[11]

1. `AddSortedNode`
    1.1.   `Search for record ;`
    1.2.   `IF Record found`
           1.2.1.   `Return failure result ;` **`//No duplicates`**
                                     `//allowed`
    1.3.   `ELSE`
           1.3.1.   `Create new record and set its fields ;`
           1.3.2.   `IF insertion point at head of list`
                   1.3.2.1.   `Make next field of new record`
                               `point to first record in list ;`
                   1.3.2.1.   `Point listHead to new record ;`
           1.3.3.   `ELSE` **`//inserting at middle or end`**
                   1.3.3.1.   `Make new record point to its`
                               `successor ;`
                   1.3.3.2.   `Point predececessor to new`
                               `record ;`
                 `ENDIF`
           1.3.4.   `Return a success result ;`
         `ENDIF`

Solution 13.15 shows the algorithm written as an *HTTLAP* function. Although the original **AddNode** was a procedure I have made **AddSortedNode** into a function as the no-duplicates rule means that the algorithm may fail to insert a new record. Thus **AddSortedNode** returns True if the insertion was successful, otherwise it returns False. Of course, you could keep the algorithm as a procedure and use a Boolean reference parameter to pass back the insertion status instead.

Solution 13.15 An AddSortedNode function

1.   `FUNCTION AddSortedNode` (**REFERENCE:→BookRecord:**`listHead`,
                                     string:`theTitle`)
                                 `RETURNS` **boolean**
    1.1.   **→BookRecord:**`predecessor`,
    1.2.   `book`;
    1.3.   `IF (FindSortedNode (`listHead`, `theTitle`, `predecessor`))`
                            `//Title found in list`
           1.3.1.   `RETURN false ;`
    1.4.   `ELSE`
           1.4.1.   `book` ← `New (`**BookRecord**`) ;`
           1.4.2.   `book`→.`bookTitle` ← `theTitle`;
           1.4.3.   `book`→.`next` ← `NULL ;`

---

[11] Of course, that means we no longer have a reference dedicated to pointing to the end. If this was really necessary (though it's unlikely with a sorted list) we would have to add the end-processing statements into the algorithm.

```
            1.4.4.  IF ([predecessor] = NULL) //Head of list
                    1.4.4.1.  [book]→.[next] ← [listHead] ;
                    1.4.4.2.  [listHead] ← [book] ; //Link new
                                                 //record to head
            1.4.5.  ELSE //In middle or at end
                    1.4.5.1.  [book]→.[next] ←
                              [predecessor]→.[next];
                    1.4.5.2.  [predecessor]→.[next] ← [book] ;
                    ENDIF
            1.4.6.  RETURN true ;
        ENDIF
    ENDFUNCTION
```

It is worth working through the **AddSortedNode** function to get a good grasp of how it works. With the list in Figure 13.23 as a starting point use **AddSortedNode** to try to add the following six book titles. For each title start with a fresh copy of the list from Figure 13.23.

1. Communicating with Sequential Processes
2. Conceptual Blockbusting
3. How to Solve It
4. A Book on C
5. System Design
6. Z for Software Engineers

You can do this exercise either by drawing a copy of the list and using pencil to update the pointers, or you can cut out pieces of paper for each node and use bits of string or paper arrows as the pointer links (this is what I did). You should also draw up a trace table that allows you to follow the values of the variables and parameters, statement by statement, and which shows the return value from the function.

Table 13.2 shows a trace table and it is followed by a series of diagrams showing the first title, "Communicating with Sequential Processes" being added to the list. A value of "?" means the identifier has been declared but not assigned a value. A blank cell means the identifier has not yet been declared.

Notice in statement #1.4.1 in Solution 13.15 when book is allocated memory, I have just made up a memory address. For the purposes of this exercise it does not matter what the address is as long as it is different from the other book records. I hope that you can follow what is happening just from the trace table, but if not, the following series of diagrams illustrates the process. In the figures below I have used cut-out cards for the nodes and pointer arrows rather than the computer-drawn figures used above. All the addresses are written onto the cards in pencil so that they can be updated. It may seem like a lot of trouble, but I think manipulating physical objects while tracing through an algorithm will help you to get a more complete grasp of what is going on than if you try it more as a thought experiment. On the

Table 13.2 **Trace table for AddSortedNode with "Communicating Sequential Processes"**

Statement	listHead	predecessor	predecessor→.next	book	book→.next	book→.bookTitle
1	$F02E					
1.1	$F02E	?	?			
1.2	$F02E	?	?	?	?	?
1.3	$F02E	NULL	NULL	?	?	?
1.4.1	$F02E	NULL	NULL	$F12E	?	?
1.4.2	$F02E	NULL	NULL	$F12E	?	Communicating with Sequential Processes
1.4.3	$F02E	NULL	NULL	$F12E	NULL	Communicating with Sequential Processes
1.4.4	$F02E	NULL	NULL	$F12E	NULL	Communicating with Sequential Processes
1.4.4.1	$F02E	NULL	NULL	$F12E	$F02E	Communicating with Sequential Processes
1.4.4.2	$F12E	NULL	NULL	$F12E	$F02E	Communicating with Sequential Processes

FIGURE 13.24 **List status at invocation of AddSortedNode**

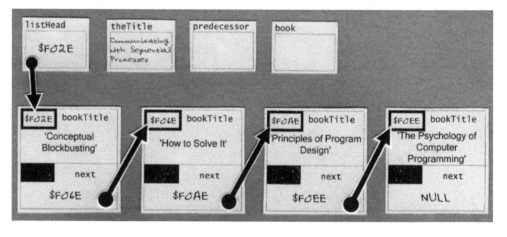

book's website at http://www.cengage.co.uk/vickers you will find blank templates which you can download and print out to make your own physical linked lists.

Figure 13.24 shows the state of the list when the AddSortedNode function is invoked in statement #1. listHead and theTitle are parameters so their values as passed in the function call. predecessor and book are variables that are declared inside the function so they do not have any values yet.

Figure 13.25 shows the state of play after executing statements #1.1 to #1.3. Statements #1.1 and #1.2 declare the identifiers predecessor and book. Statement #1.3 calls the FindSortedNode function which looks for 'Communicating with Sequential Processes' in the list. The book is not found in the list so the function returns **false** and a value of NULL in predecessor. predecessor contains NULL indicating that 'Communicating with Sequential Processes' should be inserted at the head before 'Conceptual Blockbusting' – by definition the record at the head cannot have a predecessor, hence the value of NULL. If this is confusing, go and look back at the FindSortedNode function. book is undefined because it has been declared but not assigned a value yet.

FIGURE 13.25   **After executing statements #1.1 to #1.3**

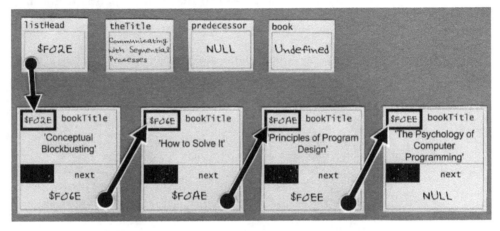

Because FindSortedNode returned false the function will execute the block belonging to the ELSE path in statement #1.4. Figure 13.26 shows the new record

FIGURE 13.26   **After executing statements #1.4.1 to #1.4.3**

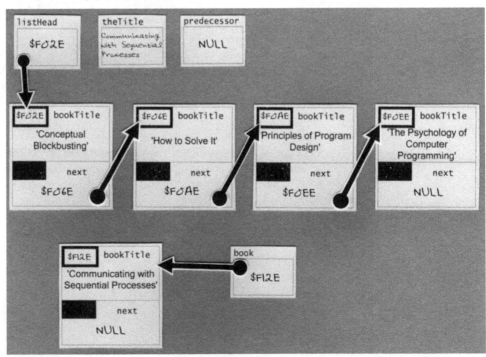

structure that was created in statement #1.4.1. Not only does this statement create the new record, but it points **book** to it so that it can be accessed. Statement #1.4.2 sets the **bookTitle** field of the new record and statement #1.4.3 sets its next field to **NULL**. So, the record exists, and is pointed to by **book** and now it remains to link it in to the list at the head position.

Statement #1.4.4.1 is executed next because **predecessor** is **NULL**. This statement points the **next** field of the new record pointed to by **book** (i.e. book→.next) to **listHead** so that it now points to the first record in the list. This is shown in Figure 13.27.

FIGURE 13.27 **After executing statement #1.4.4.1**

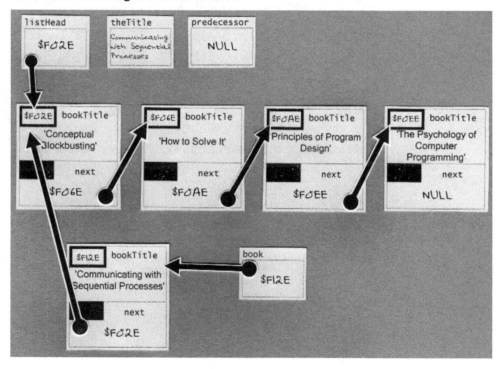

Now it remains to point **listHead** to the new record (statement #1.4.4.2) and then exit the function returning a value of **true** to denote success (statement #1.4.6). The state of the list at the end of the function, then, is shown below in Figure 13.28.

We can see from Figure 13.28 that the new book has been successfully linked into the list. The list head pointer now points to the new node and the new node's **next** field points to **'Conceptual Blockbusting'** which used to be at the head of the list.

Try using the card-and-arrows approach now to trace through the **AddSortedNode** function with the remaining five book titles. Why does the function not need to deal explicitly with the case of adding a record to the end?

FIGURE 13.28   **After the node has been fully linked**

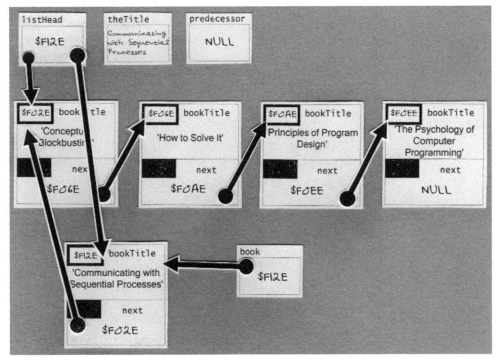

Deleting a Node from a Sorted List

The last algorithm to develop is the `DeleteSortedNode` function. Like `AddSortedNode` this will be a function so that it can return a Boolean value to denote success or failure. Think for a minute about the steps you think should be taken to delete a node from a sorted list. If you need a hint see the footnote.[12]

The process for deleting a node from a sorted is similar to adding one. First we must search the list to see if the node exists. If it does we ascertain its position and update the pointers of its adjacent nodes, after which we can remove the record from memory. Like adding a node, removing a node from the head of the list requires slightly different actions from deleting one in the middle or from the end. We can describe the general algorithm as Solution 13.16.

Solution 13.16 General algorithm for deleting a node from a sorted list

```
1.  DeleteSortedNode
        1.1.  Search for record ;
        1.2.  IF record does not exist
                  1.2.1.  Return a failure result ;
        1.3.  ELSE
                  1.3.1.  Create a temporary pointer to the record ;
                  1.3.2.  IF record at head of list
```

---

[12] What does deleting a node have in common with adding a node?

```
                              1.3.2.1.   Point list head to the one
                                         after the record ;
            1.3.3.   ELSE //Record in middle or end
                              1.3.3.1.   Point record's predecessor to
                                         the record's successor ;
                     ENDIF
            1.3.4.   Remove the record from memory
            1.3.5.   Return a success result ;
         ENDIF
```

The outline algorithm is extremely similar to that for adding a node, and can be expressed as an *HTTLAP* function as in Solution 13.17.

Solution 13.17 DeleteSortedNode function

```
1.   FUNCTION DeleteSortedNode (REFERENCE:→BookRecord: listHead ,
                                  string: theTitle ) RETURNS boolean
     1.1.   →BookRecord: current ,
     1.2.                predecessor ;
     1.3.   IF NOT(FindSortedNode ( listHead , theTitle ,
            predecessor ))
            1.3.1.   RETURN false ;
     1.4.   ELSE //Record found, so delete it
            1.4.1.   IF ( predecessor = NULL) //Node at head
                              1.4.1.1.   current ← listHead ;
                              1.4.1.2.   listHead ← listHead →. next ;
                                         //Unlink
            1.4.2.   ELSE //Middle or end
                              1.4.2.1.   current ← predecessor →
                                         . next ;
                              1.4.2.2.   predecessor →. next ←
                                                    current →. next ;
                     ENDIF
            1.4.3.   Delete ( current ) ;
            1.4.4.   RETURN true ;
         ENDIF
   ENDFUNCTION
```

Using the list from Figure 13.23 again, trace through the **DeleteSortedNode** function trying to delete the following books and in each case state the value of the return result.

1.   C# Concisely
2.   Conceptual Blockbusting
3.   Principles of Program Design
4.   The Psychology of Computer Programming
5.   Z for Software Engineers

13.3 The Stack

As you may have picked up by now, many programming terms take their names from real-world objects or phenomena and the stack is no exception. The stack is a very simple data structure that is widely used in programming language compiler programs, and which has some useful applications. First of all, what is a stack?

Take a coin and put it on the table. Then take another coin and put it on top of the first. Do this with a few more coins and soon you will have a *stack* of coins (see Figure 13.29).

FIGURE 13.29 **Building a stack of coins**

The second coin is placed on top of the first one. Subsequent additions are always made to the top of the stack. Items are removed from the stack in reverse to the order they were placed there, that is, the top item was the last item put onto the stack but is the first to be removed from it.

Only the item at the top of the stack is accessible. Of course, with a stack of coins on the table you could push a coin out of the middle of the stack with a pin, so imagine that a stack data structure is held inside a tube that is sealed at the bottom and open at the top. If you put a coin in the tube, and then put another on top of it, the only way to get the first coin out is to take the top coin off first.[13]

A stack data structure has only two operations that can be performed upon it: adding an item to the stack and removing an item from the stack. Adding an item is known as *pushing* onto the stack and removing an item is called *popping* from the stack. Because only the last item added is accessible, the stack is known as a LIFO structure. LIFO is not the name of a pet poodle but stands for last-in-first-out – the last item added is the first one that can be removed.

Pushing and ▶
popping

LIFO ▶

Stacks are commonly implemented as linked lists, though you can use arrays if you have a fixed-size stack of a reasonable size. Because a stack only supports the push and pop operations there are only two algorithms to design.

Pushing onto a Stack

Items are always pushed onto the top of the stack, so we will need a pointer to the stack's head. Each node in the stack only needs a pointer to the next item down

---

[13] A more violent example is an ammunition clip for an automatic weapon. There is usually a spring-loaded magazine into which bullets are inserted one at a time from the top. The last bullet put into the magazine is the first one to be fired.

so that when an item is removed the head pointer can be redirected to the next item. We need a reference variable, say, stackTop that will keep track of the top item on the stack. Each item in the stack needs fields for its data and a reference field to point to the next item down.

Draw an outline algorithm for the **push** procedure. You can use the informal pseudo-code to begin. Use the *HTTLAP* strategy to structure your thinking. You may be able to reuse some of the ideas from the earlier linked list routines. My outline algorithm is given below but please do not look at it until you have come up with your own solution.

Solution 13.18 Outline algorithm for stack push

1. Push
    1.1. Create new record ;
    1.2. Set record's data fields ;
    1.3. Point record's next field to stackTop ;
    1.4. Point stackTop to new record ;

Think Spot

Did you get anything like Solution 13.18? Perhaps you had a selection to deal with whether the stack is empty or not. If you think about it carefully it does not matter if the stack is empty or not. Statement #1.3 says to make the new record point to the record that is pointed to by the stack top pointer. If the stack is empty then stackTop will be NULL, and so the new record's next field will also be NULL which is what we want to happen. If the stack is not empty then the new record's next field will point to whatever record stackTop is pointing to. Statement #1.4 then updates stackTop to point to the new record. We do not need to worry about duplicates because they are allowed in stacks. We can now turn this algorithm into a more formal *HTTLAP* procedure. We will make a stack of our book records to keep things familiar.

Solution 13.19 Stack push procedure

1. PROCEDURE Push (**REFERENCE:**→**BookRecord:**`stackTop`,
                    string:`theTitle`) ;
    1.1. →**BookRecord:**`book` ;
    1.2. `book` ← New (**BookRecord**) ;
    1.3. `book`→.`bookTitle` ← `theTitle` ;
    1.4. `book`→.`next` ← `stackTop` ;
    1.5. `stackTop` ← `book` ;
ENDPROCEDURE

The procedure could be invoked thus:
Push (**REFERENCE:**`stackTop`,
'Communicating with Sequential Processes') ;

Popping an Item from the Stack

Popping an item is also straightforward. We simply need to dispose of the record at the top. There is no searching to be done as popping can only be done on the top item.

Having seen how simple pushing an item is, you should not need long to come up with an outline **pop** algorithm. Have a go now. My solution is given below.

Solution 13.20 Outline algorithm for stack pop

1. Pop
    1.1.   Set a pointer to the top item ;
    1.2.   Make stackTop point to the next item down ;
    1.3.   Delete the record ;

And here is the algorithm as an *HTTLAP* procedure.

Solution 13.21 Stack pop procedure

1. PROCEDURE Pop (**REFERENCE:**→**BookRecord:** stackTop) ;
    1.1.   →**BookRecord:** current ;
    1.2.   current ← stackTop ;
    1.3.   stackTop ← stackTop →. next ;
    1.4.   Delete (current) ;
    ENDPROCEDURE

Using a stack

The stack is a data structure with such simple operations you may wonder what it could be used for. Stacks are very important in computing, and especially in programming language compilers. You may have heard the term *stack dump* which refers to a listing of every item in the computer's main stack which is used to keep track of all its running processes. Knowing what was on the stack when a program crashed is very useful to software developers for debugging. Because stacks are simple to implement (and quite an efficient use of the computer's resources) they are often used when only a very basic dynamic data structure is required. With a stack there are no search algorithms and only one pointer (the stackTop) to keep track of. Because the stack is a LIFO structure it is very useful for reversing the order of some input stream. Imagine we wanted to see whether a given word was a palindrome (it reads the same forwards as backwards). We could enter a string and store it one character at a time on a stack. We could then build a second string by repeatedly popping the stack. The two strings could then be compared for equality. Take the following palindrome: "Cigar? Toss it in a can. It is so tragic".[14] To simplify matters we will assume for now that the user will enter the palindrome without spaces or punctuation marks. We can use our push and pop algorithms to help solve this problem. Solution 13.22 is an outline solution:

---

[14] You can find this and many other palindromes at http://www.palindromelist.com.

Solution 13.22 Outline algorithm for palindrome test

```
1.   Palindrome test
       1.1.   initialize stack ;
       1.2.   initialize first and second strings ;
       1.3.   Get first character from keyboard ;
       1.4.   WHILE letters to type
                 1.4.1.   Add character to first string ;
                 1.4.2.   Push character onto stack ;
                 1.4.3.   Get next character
              ENDWHILE
       1.5.   WHILE stack not empty
                 1.5.1.   Add stack item to second string ;
                 1.5.2.   Pop stack ;
              ENDWHILE
       1.6.   IF strings are the same
                 1.6.1.   'Display It is a palindrome!' ;
       1.7.   ELSE
                 1.7.1.   'Display It is not a palindrome!' ;
              ENDIF
```

The algorithm is in four parts: initialization of variables, pushing characters onto the stack and building the first string, popping the stack to build the second string, and comparing the two strings. Solution 13.23 shows the algorithm written out as an *HTTLAP* program. I have adapted the push and pop procedures to work with the record structure used in this example.

Solution 13.23 Complete palindrome test program

```
1.   PROGRAM Palindrome test ;
2.   NEWTYPE CharRecord IS
       RECORD
         2.1.   character: letter ;
         2.2.   →CharRecord: next ;
       ENDRECORD
3.   PROCEDURE Push (REFERENCE:→CharRecord: stackTop ,
                     character: theCharacter ) ;
       3.1.   →CharRecord: charRec ;
       3.2.   charRec ← New (CharRecord) ;
       3.3.   charRec →. letter ← theCharacter ;
       3.4.   charRec →. next ← stackTop ;
       3.5.   stackTop ← charRec ;
     ENDPROCEDURE
4.   PROCEDURE Pop (REFERENCE:→CharRecord: stackTop ) ;
       4.1.   →CharRecord: current ;
       4.2.   current ← stackTop ;
       4.3.   stackTop ← stackTop →. next ;
```

```
            4.4.  Delete ([current]) ;
        ENDPROCEDURE
  5.    →CharRecord:[stackTop] ;
  6.    string:[string1],
  7.           [string2] ;
  8.    character:[aCharacter] ;
  9.    [stackTop] ← NULL ;
 10.    [string1] ← '' ;
 11.    [string2] ← '' ;
 12.    Display ('Enter a string. The / character terminates') ;
 13.    Get (keyboard, REFERENCE:[aCharacter]) ;
 14.    Display ([aCharacter]) ;
 15.    WHILE ([aCharacter] ≠ '/')
            15.1.    [string1] ← [string1] + [aCharacter] ;
            15.2.    Push (REFERENCE:[stackTop], [aCharacter]) ;
            15.3.    Get (keyboard, REFERENCE:[aCharacter]) ;
        ENDWHILE
 16.    WHILE ([stackTop] ≠ NULL)
            16.1.    [string2] ← [string2] + [stackTop]→.[letter] ;
            16.2.    Pop (REFERENCE:[stackTop]) ;
        ENDWHILE
 17.    IF ([string1] = [string2])
            17.1.    Display ([string1], ' is a palindrome!') ;
 18.    ELSE
            18.1.    Display ([string2], ' is not a palindrome! ');
        ENDIF
ENDPROGRAM
```

We will leave the stack there. If you need to do more with stacks then any book on data structures will deal with them, but not necessarily in very much detail because they are such simple structures.

13.4 The Queue

The last kind of data structure we will look at is the queue. Like the stack a queue can be implemented as an array or a list. As with the stack we will focus on the linked list implementation. A queue is a special case of the unsorted linked list. Items are always added to the end of a queue but are consumed from the head. The queue is very much like what you find in a bank or outside the cinema. People wait in line and get served in the order in which they arrived (assuming queue jumping is strictly prevented). The queue is thus a FIFO (first-in-first-out) structure. Because elements are added to the end but removed from the front we need two pointers to maintain a queue: one for the front and one for the end. Queues are not sorted because new

FIFO ▶

items always go to the end of the queue. Duplicates are also normally allowed in queues, so no search algorithms are needed. The two standard queue operations are *enqueue* (add an item to the rear of the queue) and *dequeue* (remove an item from the front). In addition, you might want to include a display routine to print the contents of the queue, but you will find that this is exactly the same as the unsorted list display procedure so we do not need to concern ourselves with it here.

Enqueuing: Adding an Item to the Rear of the Queue

Enqueuing an item is straightforward as all items are added to the rear of the queue which simply involves linking the new item to the last one in the queue and updating the end pointer.

> But are there any special cases we must take into account? Under what circumstances will an item be added to the queue?

Of course, the queue can be empty or not empty when adding an item. When empty then both the front and end pointers will be NULL, so we need to treat this as a special case. Here, then, is the general algorithm for adding an item to a queue.

Solution 13.24 Enqueue algorithm for adding an item to a queue

```
1.    Enqueue
        1.1.    Create new record ;
        1.2.    Set record's data fields ;
        1.3.    Set record's next field to NULL ;
        1.4.    IF queue is empty
                  1.4.1.   Make front point to new record ;
        1.5.    ELSE
                  1.5.1.   Make next field of last item in queue
                           point to the new record ;
                ENDIF
        1.6.    Make end point to the new record ;
```

The new record is created in statements #1.1 to #1.3. The selection in statement #1.4 tests to see whether the queue is empty. If it is then the new item will be at both the front and the end of the queue so the front pointer needs to point to it (statement #1.4.1). If the queue is not empty then the next field of the current last record will be pointed to the new item (statement #1.5.1). Finally, the end is updated to point to the new arrival in statement #1.6. We could implement Enqueue for a queue of book records as shown in Solution 13.25.

Solution 13.25 Enqueue procedure

```
1.    PROCEDURE Enqueue (REFERENCE:→BookRecord: front ,
                         REFERENCE:→BookRecord: rear , string: theTitle ) ;
        1.1.    →BookRecord:book ;
        1.2.    book  ← New (BookRecord) ;
```

```
  1.3.    book →. bookTitle  ←  theTitle  ;
  1.4.    book →. next  ← NULL ;
  1.5.    IF ( front  = NULL)
               1.5.1.    front  ←  book  ;
  1.6.    ELSE
               1.6.1.    rear →. next  ←  book  ;
          ENDIF
  1.7.    rear  ←  book  ;
ENDPROCEDURE
```

Dequeuing: Removing the Item at the Front of the Queue

Removing the front item of the queue mainly involves changing the front pointer to point to the next item in the queue and then deleting the dequeued item. Of course, when the queue only has one item in it then the end pointer also needs to be updated as removal will leave the queue empty.

You can probably guess how the algorithm should look by now, so try writing it yourself. The solution is below, but do it yourself before peeping.

Solution 13.26 Dequeue algorithm for removing an item from a queue

```
  1.   Dequeue
          1.1.    Set a pointer to the top item ;
          1.2.    Make head point to the next item down ;
          1.3.    IF item at end of list
                     1.3.1.   Make end NULL
                  ENDIF
          1.4.    Delete the item ;
```

Because dequeuing works from the front of the queue the algorithm is almost identical to the stack **pop** algorithm. The only difference is that the queue also has an end pointer which needs to be updated if the item being dequeued is the last item in the queue and hence at both the front and the rear. This algorithm can be easily turned into an *HTTLAP* procedure.

Solution 13.27 Dequeue procedure

```
  1.   PROCEDURE Dequeue (REFERENCE:→BookRecord: front ,
                          REFERENCE:→BookRecord: rear ) ;
          1.1.    →BookRecord: current  ;
          1.2.    current  ←  front  ;
          1.3.    front  ←  front →. next  ;
          1.4.    IF ( current  =  rear )
```

> 1.4.1.   rear ← NULL ;
> ENDIF
> 1.5.   Delete (current) ;
> ENDPROCEDURE

Think Spot

If the rear pointer needs to be set to NULL when the last item in the queue is removed (statement #1.4.1) why does the procedure not appear to do the same for the front pointer? Actually, it does. It is all taken care of by statement #1.3. Remember that front points to the item in question so front→.next is the value of the next field of the record at the front of the queue. When the item is also the last one in the queue, then its next field will be NULL (and thus so is front→.next) and so front will be set to NULL in statement #1.3. If the item is not the last one, then its next field will not be NULL, so front→.next is the address of the next item in the queue.

You can have lots more fun with queues (such as implementing fixed-size circular queues using lists or arrays) as you will discover on any data structures course. But we have covered the basics which was the goal of this chapter, so the more advanced details you can get from a specialist book or course.

There is much more fun to be had with data structures, especially the dynamic ones. We have looked at the fundamentals of dynamic list manipulation with the unsorted list, the stack, and the queue. We have touched upon some refinements by considering the ordered list. These are all in a class that is sometimes called *simple dynamic data structures*. There is a world of more elaborate structures out there known as *recursive dynamic data stuctures*. If you are on a degree-level computing course you are likely to come across some of these in later semesters (such as binary trees, B-trees, balanced multi-way trees, and so on). What I hope this chapter has given you is a good understanding of the principles that underpin the implementation of program data structures. If you feel confident with the basic list-handling algorithms presented above then you have achieved a great deal for I have seen many second- and even third-year college students struggling to master these basics let alone the more advanced techniques needed for the really interesting recursive data structures. If you cannot master the basics then the more intricate and advanced structures will be a source of pain rather than a source of joy. And that is a shame, because once you really understand how to implement data structures great satisfaction can be gained from implementing algorithms to manipulate recursive structures that let you solve the really interesting and fun programming problems.

13.5 Chapter Summary

In this chapter you learned about dynamic data structures and how they can be built using records that point to (or reference) other records. You learned about the three most common dynamic structures: the list, the stack, and the queue and you saw how to develop algorithms to build and maintain them. The chapter also introduced you to pointer/reference variables and showed how pointers are necessary in the implementation of dynamic data structures.

13.6   **Exercises**

1. Explain why a stack is a LIFO (Last In, First Out) data structure.

2. In addition to the head pointer, what other pointers are needed to maintain a queue data structure?

3. What would happen if the pointer to the head of a linked list were accidentally deleted in a program?

4. Given the added complexity involved in building a maintaining a linked list, why can't we just use arrays for storing lists of data?

5. What changes would be necessary to the `FindSortedNode` function (Solution 13.14) if our list of books were required to be sorted by descending order of book title?

6. In the section on creating pointer variables we created a linked list element of type `PatientRecord` which was referenced by the variable `patientReference`. State what is wrong with the following statement and provide a correct version:

    `patientReference` . `givenName` ← 'Henry' ;

7. Using the sub-programs given, write a new function AmendNode which will change the title of a specified book record in an unsorted list. The function will have three formal value parameters: `listHead`, `searchString`, and `replaceString`. `searchString` will hold the title of the book whose title we want to change. `replaceString` holds the new title of the book. The function will return a Boolean value true if the replacement was successful or false if a record matching `searchString` could not be found.

8. Repeat the above exercise but this time for the sorted list.

9. When comparing one string to another to test for alphabetic ordering, we would want `'e'` to be judged to come before `'F'`. The default would be for `'e' < 'F'` to be false as `'e'` comes *after* `'F'` in the character set. The AddSortedNode procedure for an ordered linked list uses the `FindSortedNode` function (Solution 13.14). Amend `FindSortedNode` to ensure that `'Paul'` would come before `'POET'` in the list.

13.7   **Projects**

StockSnackz Vending Machine

No exercises for this project.

Stocksfield Fire Service

Take your EAC program and make one linked list for the fire-fighting method codes and another for the precaution codes. The first list will need four nodes (one for each code). Each node should have three fields: a character to store the fire-fighting method code ('1', '2', '3', '4'), a string to hold the corresponding method instruction ('Coarse spray', 'Foam', etc), and a pointer to link to the next node in the list. The second list will have a node for each of the precaution codes ('P', 'R', 'S', etc.). Each node will have a character field to store the code, a string to store the explosion risk (either blank or 'Risk of violent or explosive reaction'), a string to store the fire-fighters' precaution instruction (e.g. 'LTS(CPC)'), another string to store the spillage management string ('Dilute spillage' or 'Contain spillage'), and a pointer field to link to the next record.

Amend your program and the EAC-processing function to make use of these linked lists.

There is an ineffiency in the way we are storing the strings in the second list because strings such as 'LTS(CPC)', 'Dilute spillage', and 'Risk of violent or explosive reaction' are repeated in several nodes. How might you go about removing this inefficiency?

Hint: Think about lookup tables.

Another hint: Use Boolean flags for explosion risk, LTS/BA and dilute/contain spillage instructions.

Puzzle World: Roman Numerals and Chronograms

Extend your program from Chapter 9 so that each time the user enters a Roman number it is also added to a queue. After the user chooses the 'quit' option the program should display the contents of the queue (one Roman number per line) on the screen.

Pangrams: Holoalphabetic Sentences

Not content with pangrams, some people like to construct palindromic pangrams. A palindrome is a string that reads the same backwards as forwards (e.g. words like "boob", or sentences like "A man, a plan, a canal: Panama!" (ignore punctuation). Extend your program from Chapter 9 to test whether the input sentence is palindromic or not. You can choose whether to do separate tests for pangrams and palindromes, or whether to test for palindromes only when the sentence is also a pangram. Use a stack for your palindrome test.

Hint: Push each character of the sentence onto the stack and then pop them off again. What does that give you?

Online Bookstore: ISBNs

Replace the arrays from your solution to Chapter 10 with two linked lists: one for valid ISBNs and one for invalid ISBNs. When displaying the valid ISBNs, you should additionally display the 13-digit equivalent of each ISBN. You do this by prefixing the 10-digit ISBN with the digits 978 and then computing a new check digit. The ISBN-13 check digits use a modulus 10 scheme as follows.

Each of the first 12 digits is multiplied by the weighting factors shown in Table 13.3 below. The results are summed, the sum is divided by 10 and the remainder is taken. The remainder is then subtracted from 10 to give the check digit.

For example, using the ISBN 0-14-012499-3 we remove the check digit (3) and add the prefix 978 giving 978014012499. We multiply each digit by the weights in Table 13.3 giving a sum of 104. The remainder after dividing by 10 is 4 which, when subtracted from 10, gives us a new check digit of 6. So, the ISBN 0-14-012499-3 becomes 978-0-14-012499-6.

ISBN-10 to ISBN-13 Conversion

ISBN digits

ISBN	9	7	8	0	1	4	0	1	2	4	9	9
	×	×	×	×	×	×	×	×	×	×	×	×
Weights	1	3	1	3	1	3	1	3	1	3	1	3
Values	9+	21+	8+	0+	1+	12+	0+	3+	2+	12+	9+	27+

Total = 104

For a final challenge, consider the problem of hyphenating any 10-digit ISBN. Table 13.4 shows the lengths of all possible group identifiers.

ISBN Group Identifiers

ISBN Group Identifier Code Ranges
0–7
80–94
950–993
9940–9989
99900–99999

That is, the single-digit group codes take the digits 0..7, the two-digit codes the values 80..94 and so forth. So, an ISBN with a single-digit group code will have a hyphen after the first character, one with a four-digit code will have a hyphen after the fourth character, and so on. Also, we know that there is always a hyphen before the check digit. The only unknown is the lengths of the different publisher codes. In fact, as you can see just from the group 0 and group 1 problems, there is quite a lot of variation around the publisher code lengths. How might you go about solving this problem? Where will you get the information required to enable you to correctly separate the publisher code from the book title code?

14

Object Orientation Revisited

Learning Objectives

- Understand in more detail the basic object-oriented concepts of encapsulation, polymorphism, and inheritance
- Learn how encapsulation allows the internal workings and data of an object to be hidden
- Understand how the two main types of polymorphism (overloading and overriding) are used in inheritance relationships to provide new, modified, or more flexible object behaviour
- Understand how inheritance allows descendant object classes to specialize behaviour for specific needs

In Chapter 7 we began to look at the object-oriented programming (OOP) paradigm and saw how problems can be solved by thinking in terms of object classes. We saw how a class describes a set of data items (properties) together with the algorithms (methods) needed to manipulate those items. In this chapter you will extend your knowledge and understanding of object-oriented programming as we consider the concepts of *encapsulation*, *inheritance*, and *polymorphism* which are key to fully understanding OOP.

14.1   A Little History

Although touted as the modern way of programming, object-oriented programming languages have been around for more than 40 years. SIMULA 1 (1962–65) and Simula 67 (1967) were the first object-oriented programming languages, though it was not until Bjarne Stroustrup developed C++ in the 1980s by adding object-oriented extensions to C (Stroustrup, 1986) that the principles of object orientation became more widespread. Since the release of Java in the mid 1990s object-oriented programming has become a very popular tool. For web-based enterprise-level applications Sun Microsystems' Java and Microsoft's C#.NET platforms are the market leaders for new system developments today.

14.2   Key Terms

We learned in Chapter 7 that where procedural programs focus upon operations that are applied to data, an object-oriented program focuses on the notion of an *object* and that objects belong to *classes*. An object is a mechanism for gathering together into a single package a set of related data items and operations that manipulate those data. This bringing together the data and its operations is called *encapsulation*. Objects of the same class share characteristics with one another. A class can *inherit* characteristics from another *ancestor* class and a class can share its properties with one or more *descendant* classes. Classes can override the `behaviour of` ancestor classes by redefining inherited data items and operations through a technique known as *polymorphism*. Any language that claims to be object-oriented must provide support for the four object-oriented fundamentals: *objects and classes*, *encapsulation*, *inheritance*, and *polymorphism*. The key concepts underlying object-oriented programming then, are:

Encapsulation ▶

Inheritance ▶

Polymorphism ▶

- **Encapsulation**: the bringing together of data and operations into a single unit, or package, which is called an **object**. Encapsulation allows access to an object's data items to be restricted – this is known as **data hiding**.
- **Classes** define the characteristics of sets of objects.
- **Inheritance** is the passing of characteristics from one class to another (a bit like the way humans and dolphins share mammalian characteristics yet are distinct and different species).
- Through **polymorphism** shared characteristics can be modified between and within ancestor and descendant classes.

In the sections that follow we will examine these terms in more detail.

14.3   Encapsulation: Objects and Classes Revisited

We know that, in object-oriented programming, programs are built around objects and classes and that, in simple terms, an object is a collection of related data items and the operations required to manipulate those items packaged into a single unit. There are a number of advantages to this, the chief one being that data and its associated operations are kept together separate from other data and operations. Access to the data is tightly controlled which, in theory, makes it much harder for one part of a program to cause problems in another part. Also, there is an element of common sense in all this. Let's say I have a legitimate need to find out how much money several people are carrying on them (perhaps we need to chip in for a restaurant meal). If I want to know how much money a person has I could look through their pockets to count the change. If they kept their money in a wallet I would have to find that first and then look inside. What if they don't have pockets and they keep their wallet in a bag? Rather than worrying about searching people and finding all the money (notes and coins) and counting it myself, in the real world I would simply ask a person to tell me how much money they are carrying. It is then up to the person to know where they keep their money and to report back the total; I no longer need to know where their money is or how they count it, I just need to ask them the question and wait for the answer. This is what an object is like. The object knows all about its own data and we send the object requests to reveal information about that data, or to change the data in some way. In all cases, the object handles the requests and it is the object which manipulates its data (a bit like me giving you money and you putting it in your own wallet yourself).

A simple example would be an integer class that has operations to assign and retrieve the value of integer objects. Requests to change the value of the integer must be passed to the individual object which can determine whether or not to allow the value to be changed. Similarly, nothing outside the object can read the integer's value directly; instead a request must be made to the object to return the integer's value. This practice is called *data hiding* and in this way very tight control is kept over how data are manipulated. Because nothing outside the object can see how its properties are stored we can actually change the details of the properties as long as the way data are passed out of the object (its interface) remains the same. For example, we might, for some reason choose to store the numeric value of integer objects in a string form. The method that retrieves the numeric value would do the conversion from string to integer and then pass the integer value out. Also, all the operations associated with a particular data item are located with that item, which, in theory, means that object-oriented programs support greater *reusability*: as objects are self-contained, they can be shared between different programs. Thus, a bank account object (which would contain all the variables associated with a bank account and all the operations that are allowed on an account) could be used in several different financial programs. Of course, procedural code can be reused, but the gathering together of data and operations into a single object makes this simpler.[1]

We saw how to declare simple classes in Chapter 7. For example Figure 14.1 gives a definition for a `Person`.

▶ Data hiding

---

[1] Of course, life is rarely so simple, and recent studies have suggested that object-oriented programming does not support reusability as well as early proponents have claimed.

FIGURE 14.1   **Class definition for a Person**

class **Person**	
Properties	awake: yes, no ; inBed: yes, no ; needsShower: yes, no ; isDressed: yes, no ;
Methods	WakeUp ; GoToSleep ; GetUp ; GoToBed ; GetWashed ; GetDressed ; GetUndressed ;

What we did not do in Chapter 7 was look at how to write the object methods. This is because a method is a type of sub-program and these were not introduced until Chapter 10. To show how a class can be specified more fully, consider the case of a player in an online multiplayer computer game. In the game a player can belong to a clan (groups of people who play together) or can be an individual gamer. We might define a Player class that has properties for the player's name, the number of games played, the number of games won, the number of games lost, and the name of the clan (if any) that the player belongs to. The class should also have the following methods: Player (the class constructor – see below for explanation of constructors), Name (a function to return the name of the Player object), GamesPlayed (a function to return the number of games played), GamesWon (a function to return the number of games won), GamesLost (a function to return the number of games lost), and Clan (a function to return the name of the clan the player belongs to). Notice how these methods closely resemble the identifiers of the class properties? This is because it is these methods which other objects call in order to obtain the values of a Player object's properties.[2] We might also decide that a player can join and leave a clan at any time, so we need two more methods to deal with this: LeaveClan (a procedure to set the player's clan name to empty) and JoinClan (a procedure that supplies the name of a player's new clan). JoinClan should only allow a clan to be joined if the current value of the clan property is empty (that is, the player

[2] Methods that pass out the value of an object's properties are called *accessor* methods because they provide a controlled form of access to the object's private data. Whilst this goes a long way to supporting the idea of encapsulation (also known as data hiding) it is not a complete solution. There is a lot of debate in the OOP community about when accessor methods should be used (if at all). It is quite beyond the scope of this book to delve into that very subtle debate. For the purposes of getting the main points across, the examples in this chapter use accessor methods liberally.

has left their previous clan before joining a new one). Figure 14.2 shows the definition for the Player class complete with the methods.

FIGURE 14.2   **Class definition for Player**

```
CLASS:Player
    // Properties
    string:[name] ;
    integer:[numberGamesPlayed],
             [numberGamesWon],
             [numberGamesLost] ;
    string:[clan] ;
    // Constructor
    METHOD Player (string:[aName], string:[aClan])
        [name] ← [aName] ;
        [clan] ← [aClan] ;
        [numberGamesPlayed] ← 0 ;
        [numberGamesWon] ← 0 ;
        [numberGamesLost] ← 0 ;
    ENDMETHOD
    // Methods
    METHOD GamesPlayed RETURNS integer
        RETURN [numberGamesPlayed] ;
    ENDMETHOD
    METHOD GamesWon RETURNS integer
        RETURN [numberGamesWon] ;
    ENDMETHOD
    METHOD GamesLost RETURNS integer
        RETURN [numberGamesLost] ;
    ENDMETHOD
    METHOD Clan RETURNS string
        RETURN [clan] ;
    ENDMETHOD
    METHOD LeaveClan
        [clan] ← '' ;
    ENDMETHOD
    METHOD JoinClan (string:[newClan]) RETURNS boolean
        boolean:[success] ;
        IF ([clan] ≠ '')
            [clan] ← [newClan] ;
            [success] ← true ;
        ELSE
            [success] ← false ;
        ENDIF
        RETURN [success] ;
ENDCLASS
```

To create an object belonging to a class you will recall from Chapter 7 that we have to create an *instance* of the class. We saw how to do this using the keyword new. For example, we created a new Person object like this:

$\boxed{\text{brian}}$ ← new Person ;

Constructor ▶

? Think Spot

It is now time to see what happens when an object is instantiated. A statement such as the one above to create a new Person object automatically calls the constructor belonging to the class in question. A constructor is a special kind of method that exists solely to deal with the initialization of an object's properties when that object instance is created. In object-Oriented programming languages, constructors typically have the same name as the class. In Figure 14.2 we see that the Player class has a method with the same name as the class (Player), and this is the constructor. If we create a new Player object it is the constructor Player that is invoked (called) by the keyword new. Notice that the Player constructor has two parameters, aName and aClan. What does this suggest needs to be supplied when a Player object is created? How would we go about creating a Player object?

> Try writing a pseudo-code statement to create a Player object variable brian with a name of 'Brian Wildebeest' and a clan of '[XX] Black Label'.[3]

To create a Player object, we need to use the keyword new and provide the Player constructor with two arguments: the name of the Player object and their clan. This is because Player's constructor which is invoked automatically requires two parameters so these must be provided. The following statement would do what we need:

Player: $\boxed{\text{brian}}$ ← new Player ('Brian Wildebeest', '[XX] Black Label') ;

The above statement declares an identifier brian of type Player and then initializes brian by instantiating a new Player object with a name of 'Brian Wildebeest' and a clan name of '[XX] Black Label'. Perhaps you can see more clearly why constructors have the same name as their class? The statement above looks like we are calling a procedure called Player with two arguments. Well, this is precisely what we are doing, albeit indirectly: we are asking to create a new Player object and are giving it two arguments which are automatically passed to the constructor of the same name.

Huh?

> I am really puzzled by this constructor idea. How can a constructor have the same name as a class? Don't the names clash?
>
> The constructor is not a method in the usual sense. It exists in order to allow an instance of the class to be created. Because the constructor is invoked automatically when an instance of the class is created it is, necessarily, strongly associated with the class. If you like, the constructor is the birthing method for a class and so it has the same name. Another point is that it is easy to see in any class what the constructor is as it always has the same name as the class. We also do not need to worry about calling the constructor because it happens automatically when we create an object using the keyword new.

---

[3] Black Label is the clan I belong to when I play "Resistance: Fall of Man" online. [XX] is the clan's shorthand name, or "tag", which appears against players' names during online games.

Having created the `brian` object we can now invoke its methods. The following statement would display the number of games `brian` has won:

```
Display ([brian].GamesWon) ;
```

Remember `GamesWon` is a function method and so returns a value. It is this value that will be displayed. We could try and make `brian` join a new clan:

```
IF ([brian].JoinClan('[BS!] Bearded Squirrels')
    Display ('Success! New clan joined') ;
ELSE
    Display ('Failed. You have to leave a clan before joining a new
    one') ;
ENDIF
```

How does the condition in the above **IF** statement work?

In the above `IF` statement there is a call to `brian`'s `JoinClan` method. `JoinClan` is a function which returns the Boolean value **true** if the new clan could be joined and **false** if `brian` is already a member of a clan. Because `JoinClan` returns a Boolean value, the IF statement is simply testing `JoinClan`'s return value. If it returns **true**, then we can display a success message otherwise a failure message is displayed. The IF statement above is logically equivalent to:

```
IF ([brian].JoinClan('[BS!] Bearded Squirrels' = true)
```

but if you recall from Chapter 9, there is no need to write the "= **true**" as this is already implied.

Notice how the methods are called? First, we specify the name of the object to which the method belongs, then we add a dot (just like when we access fields in a record), and finally we specify the name of the method to invoke together with a full list of parameters. Perhaps from this example you can begin to see even more clearly why it is called object-oriented programming – every action is done in terms of an object. To display how many games a `Player` object has won we ask the object representing the player to invoke the appropriate method to give us the value of its `numberGamesWon` property.[4]

Looking at Figure 14.2 it is clear that the `Player` class needs more methods to allow `numberGamesPlayed`, `numberGamesWon`, and `numberGamesLost` to be updated as `brian` takes part in online games. However, it is sufficient to get us going.

A class, then, is a specification for the data and behaviour of a set of individual objects that share those data and behaviours. This is like car models. In object-oriented parlance, we could have a class called "Aston Martin DB5", and objects which are the individual cars, that is, all the Aston Martin DB5s that

---

[4] In the accessor/no accessor debate those who argue that accessors break the principle of encapsulation would suggest that the `Player` class should contain methods for displaying its properties in all the contexts in which such a display might be needed (such as via an HTTP web request, on a form on a screen, etc.

were ever made.[5] This is a bit like types and variables in procedural programming. The type defines a range of values, and a variable is an instance of that type. The difference is that a class defines a number of behaviours, or capabilities which are derived from its properties (or data items) and the associated methods (functions and procedures) to access and manipulate those properties. If you like, you can think of a class as a record type with functions and procedures needed to manipulate the record's fields attached to it, and an object as a variable of that record type. This is rather an over-simplification but it is a useful starting point. In the example above notice how we have extended the *HTTLAP* pseudo-code with the word METHOD. This is to reinforce the fact that these functions and procedures (for in all other respects METHODs are declared just like the functions and procedures we have seen before) are part of an object class: remember, in object oriented programming, we talk of methods.[6]

This practice of bundling an object's data with the operations to manipulate that data is called *encapsulation*. Encapsulation is one of the cornerstone features of object orientation and is one of the ways in which object-oriented languages support software reuse.

Polymorphism Part 1: Overloading

One of the key terms listed in Section 14.2 above was polymorphism. Polymorphism comes from two Greek words meaning "many forms" and in OOP it refers to the phenomenon of multiple methods with the same name existing across related classes. There are two main types of polymorphism to consider and in this section we will look at how it may be used to bring about a technique known as method overloading which allows a class to have multiple constructors all with the same name.

▶ Overloading

Figure 14.2 presents us with a Player class that requires two string arguments each time a Player object is created. But what if we wanted to create a Player object for someone who does not belong to a clan? We could, of course write:

```
Player: eliza  ← new Player ('Eliza Dolittle', '') ;
```

but having to specify an empty string to represent the absence of clan membership seems clumsy. The principle of polymorphism enables us to get round this problem by writing multiple versions of the constructor, each one taking a different number of parameters. Figure 14.3 shows a new version of the Player class in which two versions of the constructor exist: one with two parameters and one with a single parameter.

---

[5] In case you are interested, the Aston Martin DB5 that Sean Connery drove as James Bond in *Goldfinger* (1964) had the chassis number DP/216/1, the engine number 400/P/4, and the registration (license plate) number "BMT 216 A". Actually, the car had a revolving number plate with an assortment of different registration numbers (one of them was "4711-EA-62"). How would you deal with that in a class definition?

[6] The purists talk only of methods, yet in many textbooks on Java, C#, C++, etc, you will still see talk of functions and procedures.

FIGURE 14.3 **Polymorphic Player class**

```
CLASS: Player
    // Properties
    string: name ;
    integer: numberGamesPlayed ,
             numberGamesWon ,
             numberGamesLost ;
    string: clan ;
    // Constructors
    METHOD Player (string: aName )
        name ← aName ;
        clan ← '' ;
        numberGamesPlayed ← 0 ;
        numberGamesWon ← 0 ;
        numberGamesLost ← 0 ;
    ENDMETHOD
    METHOD Player (string: aName , string: aClan )
        name ← aName ;
        clan ← aClan ;
        numberGamesPlayed ← 0 ;
        numberGamesWon ← 0 ;
        numberGamesLost ← 0 ;
    ENDMETHOD
    // rest of the methods, as before
    . . .
ENDCLASS
```

This idea of having multiple constructors with the same name might seem strange, but in practice it allows us to use classes much more naturally. What happens is that when a Player object is created if two arguments are supplied then the second constructor will be called. If only one argument is provided then the first constructor, the one that only has one parameter, will be called instead. If no arguments are provided then an error would arise as there is no constructor specified which has zero parameters. Thus both of the following object instantiations would be allowable:

```
Player: brian ← new Player ('Brian Wildebeest', '[XX] Black Label') ;
Player: eliza ← new Player ('Eliza Dolittle') ;
```

The first statement would invoke the second constructor that takes two parameters, so the brian object would have a player name and a clan name set. The second statement only provides one argument so the first constructor would be called instead. Therefore, the eliza object would have a player name but the clan name would remain empty. Notice how each constructor has a very similar set of statements; the only difference is the statement assigning a value to clan – in the first constructor it assigns an empty string, in the second it assigns the value passed in the `aClan` parameter. You may be thinking that this is an inefficient and possibly error-prone thing to do as it results in duplicate code. If so, you are right, and there alternative ways to deal with CONSTRUCTOR INVOCATION and a discussion is presented in the Reflections chapter. For the purposes of keeping matters as straightforward as possible, and also with the next example in mind in which optimizing the constructs becomes a trickier problem we will stick with this present approach.

Having multiple copies of a method or a constructor is known as *overloading* and can be really useful. It allows us to define classes from which objects can be created with the bare minimum of information needed or with a much fuller set of data. In our simple example above, `Player` objects can now be created so that they just have a name (allowing a clan to be joined later on) or they can be created with a clan name already specified. This gives us much more flexibility. Such polymorphism is extremely common in OOP and so it is worth spending some time now going over the above section to make sure you grasp the basic concept.

14.4 Inheritance

The striped ground cricket, or to give him his scientific name, *nemobius fasciatus fasciatus*, is an interesting fellow – the speed of his chirping is proportional to the ambient air temperature. A rate of 20-chirps-per-minute means the air temperature is 31.4°C (88.6°F); when it is 27°C (80.6°F) he only makes around 16 chirps a minute. What has the striped ground cricket got to do with object-oriented programming? Nothing, except that his scientific name leads us into the next aspect of OOP: inheritance.

Inheritance is less to do with legacies left by rich uncles and more to do with the kinds of categorizations used by biologists and botanists to classify living organisms. In biology, living organisms are classified in a set of ordered relationships known as a *taxonomy*. Every organism is a member of a species (and sometimes a sub-species). Members of a species breed to produce new members of that same species. Thus, male and female striped ground crickets breed and produce the next generation of striped ground crickets. Every striped ground cricket is like every other member of that species: it has wings, it is an insect, it chirps, and does striped-ground-crickety-types of things. This is because a baby cricket inherits genetic material from its parents ensuring that it resembles them. Biologists have long observed that there are different families of species. For instance, there are different kinds of cricket, such as the striped ground cricket and the black field cricket. These two kinds of cricket are different from each other but they are both crickets; that is, while they are different species, they have common characteristics which are shared by every other insect that belongs to the cricket family. We can go higher still and observe that crickets are winged insects and have characteristics in common with other winged insects. Winged insects have something in common with non-winged insects: they all have six legs, so at this level all insects are related, and so on. This sharing of characteristics is known as *inheritance*. The striped ground cricket inherits the characteristics common to all types of cricket; crickets inherit characteristics that belong to all winged insects; winged insects inherit from the insect category; all insects are hexapods (six legs – not everything with six legs is an insect), and all hexapods are arthropods. Arthropods have tough exoskeletons and a segmented body to which appendages (such as legs) are joined in pairs. Spiders are not insects (eight legs) but they are arthropods. Finally, all arthropods are animals, so like it or not, you and the striped ground cricket have something in common!

This hierarchic classification of living things was first worked out by the Swedish botanist Karl Linné (1707–78). In this Linnaeus system every *species* belongs to a *genus*, each genus to a *family*, each family to an *order*, each order to a *subclass*, each subclass to a *class*, each class to a *subphylum*, each subphylum to a *phylum*, each phylum to a *subkingdom* and each subkingdom to a *kingdom*; also, sometimes a species will have one or more sub-species. Table 14.1 lists the full scientific classification of the striped ground cricket.[7]

Table 14.1 **Taxonomic Classification for the Striped Ground Cricket**

Taxonomic Category	Latin Name	English Meaning
Kingdom	Animalia	Animal, animals
Phylum	Arthropoda	Arthropods
Subphylum	Hexapoda	Hexapods
Class	Insecta	Insects
Subclass	Pterygota	Winged insects
Order	Orthoptera	Crickets, grasshoppers, grilo, katydids, locusts
Family	Trigonidiidae	
Genus	Nemobius	
Species	Nemobius fasciatus	Striped ground cricket
Subspecies	Nemobius fasciatus fasciatus	

At the bottom level of the taxonomy we find the actual organisms (crickets, whales, people, trees, etc.). The organism inherits attributes from the next category up in the taxonomy. Or, each level down is a specialization or variation. So, spiders and insects are both specializations of arthropods: they both have exoskeletons and segmented bodies with legs arranged in pairs, but the spider has eight legs whilst the insect has six. We can think of each taxonomic category as a general class to which one or more variations, or subclasses, can belong. To bring this back to the programming domain, Figure 14.4 shows a taxonomy for the constructs in the *HTTLAP* pseudo-code.

[7] Source: the Integrated Taxonomic Information System at http://www.itis.usda.gov/index.html

FIGURE 14.4   **A taxonomy for the *HTTLAP* pseudo-code**

The simple IF statement is the species from the genus IFs from the family Selection from the order Construct type. Construct type itself belongs to sub-class Syntax Part (not shown). The WHILE statement can thus be classified as Construct type Iteration Indeterminate WHILE.

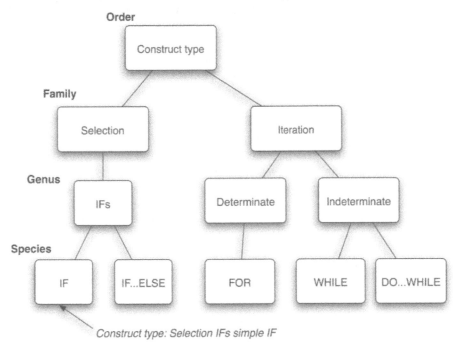

Construct type: Selection IFs simple IF

The hierarchy of the set of *HTTLAP* constructs is shown clearly in Figure 14.4 where the top box is the general category "Construct type". Below Construct type are two variant categories: "Selection" and "Iteration". These two categories represent two different kinds of construct – those which choose between alternative courses of action and those that repeatedly execute blocks of code. Selections and iterations are different from each other but they are both constructs so they inherit features common to all constructs (such as some kind of control statement and an executable block). Going down the taxonomy we see that selections (IF statements) are divided into the simple form and those with an ELSE path. The bottom level of the taxonomy shows the actual constructs (organisms) that are used to write programs. But the taxonomy also shows how the constructs are related to each other. The IF and the IF...ELSE, are selections, but they are slightly different from each other (just as the striped ground cricket and the black field cricket are different and do not interbreed, but are both types of cricket nevertheless). This idea of inheritance is fundamental to object-oriented programming. In an object-oriented program we can define an object class with certain properties and methods. We then define a new class which inherits the features of the previous class but which adds some new features of its own or modifies existing features.

Typically, every object-oriented programming language has at the top of its class hierarchy a class called Object. The Object class will specify a basic set of properties and methods that all objects in a program will have (such as a method to return the identity of an object, or a method to test for equality with another object).

For example, consider our previous `Person` class. This class currently defines some basic properties and behaviours, to which we could reasonably add a few more such as date of birth, family name, given name, sex, and so forth. Now consider our `Player` class. In reality, `Player` just defines some special properties and behaviours that people who play online games would have. It would be useful if a `Player` object, given that it represents a real person, could also make use of the properties and behaviours common to all people as defined in the `Person` class. What we have identified is that a `Player` *is a* `Person` too. Inheritance provides us with the mechanism for implementing such "is a" relationships. What we need to do is amend our `Player` class to indicate that it is descended from the `Person` class thereby inheriting all the features of a `Person` object in addition to its own more specialist aspects (such as clan name, number of games played, etc.). First, let's define a simple `Person` class to replace the earlier one which was very much based around the problem of getting up in the morning from Chapter 7. Let's give a `Person` some basic properties: `givenName`, `familyName`, `birthDay`, `birthMonth`, `birthYear`, and `sex`, with appropriate constructors and methods. The only mandatory data for a `Person` shall be `givenName` and `familyName`. If no sex is specified then a default value of "X" (to mean "not-specified") should be used. To specify a date of birth we need either all three of day, month, and year to be provided in which case the object properties will be assigned accordingly, otherwise no date information at all should be given in which case a default date of birth of 1 January, 1970 should be set. Also if a date of birth is specified then the person's sex is also to be verified.

Try writing a class specification for our new **Person** class as outlined above.

Figure 14.5 shows my interpretation of the above requirements.

FIGURE 14.5   **Redesigned Person class**

CLASS: **Person**

    // **Properties**

    string: givenName ,

            familyName ;

    char: sex ;

    integer: birthDay ,

            birthMonth ,

            birthYear ;

    // **Constructors**

    METHOD Person (**string:** gName , **string:** fName)

        givenName ← gName ;

        familyName ← fName ;

        sex ← 'X' ;

        birthday ← 1 ;

```
            birthMonth ← 1 ;
            birthYear ← 1970 ;
        ENDMETHOD
        METHOD Person (string: gName , string: fName , char: theSex )
            givenName ← gName ;
            familyName ← fName ;
            sex ← theSex ;
            birthday ← 1 ;
            birthMonth ← 1 ;
            birthYear ← 1970 ;
        ENDMETHOD
        METHOD Person (string: gName , string: fName , char: theSex ,
                    integer: dd , integer: mm , integer: yy )
            givenName ← gName ;
            familyName ← fName ;
            sex ← theSex ;
            birthday ← dd ;
            birthMonth ← mm ;
            birthYear ← yy ;
        ENDMETHOD
        // Methods
        METHOD GivenName RETURNS string
            RETURN givenName ;
        ENDMETHOD
        METHOD FamilyName RETURNS string
            RETURN familyName ;
        ENDMETHOD
        METHOD BirthDay RETURNS integer
            RETURN birthDay ;
        ENDMETHOD
        METHOD BirthMonth RETURNS integer
            RETURN birthMonth ;
        ENDMETHOD
        METHOD BirthYear RETURNS integer
            RETURN birthYear ;
        ENDMETHOD
        METHOD Sex RETURNS char
            RETURN sex ;
        ENDMETHOD
ENDCLASS
```

Figure 14.6 shows the `Player` class definition from Figure 14.3 updated to show it as a descendant of the `Person` class.

FIGURE 14.6   **First attempt at a `Player` class demonstrating inheritance**

```
CLASS:Player EXTENDS Person
    // Properties
    string: Name  ;
    integer: numberGamesPlayed ,
             numberGamesWon ,
             numberGamesLost  ;
    string: clan  ;
    // Constructors
    METHOD Player (string: aName )
        Super() ;
        Name  ←  aName  ;
        clan  ←  '' ;
        numberGamesPlayed  ←  0 ;
        numberGamesWon  ←  0 ;
        numberGamesLost  ←  0 ;
    ENDMETHOD
    METHOD Player (string: aName , string: aClan )
        Super() ;
        Name  ←  aName  ;
        clan  ←  aClan  ;
        numberGamesPlayed  ←  0 ;
        numberGamesWon  ←  0 ;
        numberGamesLost  ←  0 ;
    ENDMETHOD
    // rest of the methods, as before
    . . .
ENDCLASS
```

Looking at Figure 14.6 we see that the first line of the new `Player` class definition has a new keyword EXTENDS. This is the mechanism by which we show `Player` to be descended from `Person`. In OOP terms, `Player` is now a *subclass* of `Person` and `Person` is `Player`'s *superclass*. What this means in practice is that a `Player` object, in addition to the data items and methods defined in the `Player` class, also has data items called `givenName`, `familyName`, `sex`, `birthDay`, `birthMonth`, and `birthYear`, and all the methods belonging to the `Person` class. The EXTENDS `Person` part of the `Player` class definition causes `Player` to *inherit* all the properties and behaviours of `Person`, just like in the biological classification system discussed earlier spiders and insects have both inherited all the features common to arthropods (their superclass) in addition to their own specific features.

Subclass and superclass ▶

Instantiating a Descendant Object

When a class inherits from another class we need to do some additional work when an object of the subclass is instantiated (created). Up till now, we have been content that when an object is created its constructor is called to give initial values to all its properties. But how do those properties inherited from the superclass get their initial values? There are no statements in the `Player` constructors that assign values to these additional data items. Actually, a more careful look at Figure 14.6 shows how this initialization of inherited properties is done.

> Examine Figure 14.6 closely and try to identify what part of the pseudo-code appears to play a role in the initialization of the inherited properties.

When an object is created its properties are initialized by its constructor. If we create an object that inherits properties from a superclass, then what we must do is ensure that when the object's constructor is called it first calls the constructor of its own superclass. In Figure 14.6 the first statement in the constructor with two parameters is an attempt to do just that:

    Super() ;

`Super` is the name by which an object knows the ancestor class from which it inherits properties and methods. Thus, a call to a method called `Super` is actually a call to the superclass's constructor, hence the name `Super`. But something is missing. Now that a `Player` inherits from `Person`, we need also to supply a `Player` object with at least a given name and a family name which we can then pass on up the chain to the `Person` class's constructor. What is needed, then, is to amend the constructors in the `Player` class so that they also receive parameters which can be sent to the `Person` class constructor. Recall from Figure 14.5 that the `Person` class offers three constructors: one that takes just the given and family names, one that takes the names and the person's sex, and one that takes the names, the sex, and the three date values. Clearly, we want to be able to create new `Player` objects with the same flexibility, so as the first attempt at the inheritance-based `Player` class (Figure 14.6) itself had two constructors, that gives us six valid combinations of arguments which means the `Player` class needs six constructors. Figure 14.7 shows the updated `Player` class with these six constructors.

FIGURE 14.7 **The redesigned Player class with a full constructor set**

```
CLASS:Player EXTENDS Person
    // Properties
    string: name  ;
    integer: numberGamesPlayed ,
             numberGamesWon ,
             numberGamesLost  ;
    string: clan  ;
```

```
// Constructor 1
METHOD Player (string: aName , string: gName , string: fName )
    Super ( gName , fName ) ;
    name  ←  aName  ;
    clan  ←  '' ;
    numberGamesPlayed  ←  0 ;
    numberGamesWon  ←  0 ;
    numberGamesLost  ←  0 ;
ENDMETHOD
// Constructor 2
METHOD Player (string: aName , string: gName , string: fName ,
               char: theSex )
    Super ( gName , fName , theSex ) ;
    name  ←  aName  ;
    clan  ←  '' ;
    numberGamesPlayed  ←  0 ;
    numberGamesWon  ←  0 ;
    numberGamesLost  ←  0 ;
ENDMETHOD
// Constructor 3
METHOD Player (string: aName , string: gName , string: fName ,
               char: theSex , integer: dd , integer: mm ,
               integer: yy )
    Super ( gName , fName , theSex , dd , mm , yy ) ;
    name  ←  aName  ;
    clan  ←  '' ;
    numberGamesPlayed  ←  0 ;
    numberGamesWon  ←  0 ;
    numberGamesLost  ←  0 ;
ENDMETHOD
// Constructor 4
METHOD Player (string: aName , string: aClan , string: gName ,
               string: fName )
    Super ( gName , fName ) ;
    name  ←  aName  ;
    clan  ←  aClan  ;
    numberGamesPlayed  ←  0 ;
    numberGamesWon  ←  0 ;
    numberGamesLost  ←  0 ;
ENDMETHOD
// Constructor 5
METHOD Player (string: aName , string: aClan , string: gName ,
               string: fName , char: theSex )
```

```
        Super (gName , fName , theSex ) ;
        name  ←  aName  ;
        clan  ←  aClan  ;
        numberGamesPlayed  ← 0 ;
        numberGamesWon  ← 0 ;
        numberGamesLost  ← 0 ;
ENDMETHOD
// Constructor 6
METHOD Player (string: aName , string: aClan , string: gName ,
               string: fName , char: theSex  , integer: dd ,
               integer: mm , integer: yy )
        Super (gName , fName , theSex , dd , mm , yy ) ;
        name  ←  aName  ;
        clan  ←  aClan  ;
        numberGamesPlayed  ← 0 ;
        numberGamesWon  ← 0 ;
        numberGamesLost  ← 0 ;
ENDMETHOD
    // rest of the methods, as before
    . . .
ENDCLASS
```

Spend some time now looking over Figure 14.7 and convince yourself that the six constructors handle all the valid combinations of arguments needed by the **Player** and **Person** classes. Notice where the **Person** constructor is actually invoked.

The following statements all successfully create instances of the **Player** class. Notice the different numbers of arguments in each of the statements. The first statement would cause **Player**'s first constructor to be called, the second would call the second constructor, and so on.

```
1.  Player: jack  ← new Player ('CapnJack', 'Jack', 'Sparrow') ;
2.  Player: jack  ← new Player ('CapnJack', 'Jack', 'Sparrow',
                                'M') ;
3.  Player: jack  ← new Player ('CapnJack', 'Jack', 'Sparrow',
                                'M', 9, 6, 1963);
4.  Player: eliza  ← new Player ('elizagirl', '[XX] Black Label',
                                 'Eliza', 'Dolittle') ;
5.  Player: eliza  ← new Player ('elizagirl', '[XX] Black Label',
                                 'Eliza', 'Dolittle', 'F') ;
6.  Player: eliza  ← new Player ('elizagirl', '[XX] Black Label',
                                 'Eliza', 'Dolittle', 'F', 21, 1, 1965) ;
```

Look at the six assignment statements above. How many properties (data items) would the object **jack** have following statement #1? How many properties or data items would the object **eliza** have following statement #6?

The answer to both questions is 11. Statement #1 creates the object **jack** with three arguments, but jack is a **Player** object. **Player** objects have five properties directly listed in the **Player** class: name, numberGamesPlayed, numberGamesWon, numberGamesLost, and **clan**. But because **Player** is descended from **Person**, it also inherits the six **Person** properties: givenName, familyName, sex, birthDay, birthMonth, and birthYear. The number of arguments provided in the object instantiation simply determines which properties get specified values and which ones get assigned default values.

Assume that the **Player** object **eliza** has been created using statement #4 above. Answer the following questions:

1.   What is the value of **eliza's yearOfBirth** property?
2.   What is **eliza's** sex?

Because a year of birth value was not included in the constructor call, **eliza's yearOfBirth** has the default value of 1970 given by the constructor in the superclass **Person**. Similarly, as no sex was specified, it too will have the default value, in this case 'X'.

Just to cement your understanding, do the following exercise.

What is wrong with the following statements?

1.   **Player:** aPlayer   ← new Player ('CapnJack', 'Jack', 'Sparrow', '[XX] Black Label') ;

2.   **Player:** aPlayer   ← new Player ('CapnJack', '[XX] Black Label', 'Jack', 'Sparrow', 3, 4, 1987) ;

In the above exercise Statement #1 is trying to pass four arguments to the **Player's** constructor. However, we can see from Figure 14.7 that the constructor that takes four string parameters (Constructor #4) expects the first parameter to be the **Player's** name, the second to be a clan name, the third to be a given name (a property inherited from **Person**), and the fourth to be a family name (also inherited from **Person**). In Statement #1 above, the fourth argument is a string holding a clan name. This would not cause an error per se, but would result in the aPlayer object having a name of 'CapnJack', a clan of 'Jack', a given name of 'Sparrow', and a family name of '[XX] Black Label'. Remember that arguments are matched one for one with the parameters in the order in which they appear. To create a **Player** object with name, clan, given name, and family name we must do this:

Player; aPlayer ← new Player ('CapnJack', '[XX] Black Label',
                                  'Jack', 'Sparrow') ;

In Statement #2 there is no constructor to match its arguments of string, string, string, string, integer, integer, integer. The statement has neglected to specify a**Player**'s sex which would come between the family name and the day of birth in the argument list.

Polymorphism Part 2: Overriding

Inheritance lets us explore a second aspect of polymorphism. We have already seen how polymorphism allows us to specify multiple copies of an object class constructor each taking a different number of parameters. In classes that inherit from a superclass (as **Player** does from **Person**) we are able to redefine methods that belong to the superclass by creating a method of the same name in the subclass but which behaves differently. This is polymorphism because across the class hierarchy we see multiple versions of the same method name. It is also known as *overriding* because the subclass overrides the implementation of a superclass method. By way of example, consider Figure 14.8 which shows a revised **Player** class, with a polymorphic, or overridden, GivenName method.

FIGURE 14.8   **Player class with overridden GivenName method**

```
CLASS:Player EXTENDS Person
    // Properties
    string: Name  ;
    integer: numberGamesPlayed ,
             numberGamesWon ,
             numberGamesLost  ;
    string: clan  ;
    // Constructors as before
    . . .
    // Overridden GivenName method
    METHOD GivenName RETURNS string
        RETURN '[' +  givenName  + ']';
    ENDMETHOD
    // rest of the methods, as before
    . . .
ENDCLASS
```

To see how the overriding works, compare the GivenName method in the **Player** class in Figure 14.8 with the GivenName method of the **Person** class in Figure 14.5. The headers of the two GivenName methods are the same, that is, they both receive no parameters and return a **string** value. The difference is that the **Person**'s GivenName method simply returns the value of the givenName property whilst **Player**'s GivenName method encloses the name in square brackets. Notice that the overridden method in `Player` has exactly the same signature (return type and parameter list) as the method in the `Person` class. This is very important: a subclass must not change the signature of an overridden inherited method. If you need a version of an inherited method in a subclass that differs in its return type or parameter list then you must define an *overloaded* method. We saw in the previous section how overloading lets us write multiple versions of a constructor method where each version has a different parameter list. We can do the same with regular methods. For example, consider the `BirthMonth` method in the `Person` class in Figure 14.5. This method receives no parameters and returns an integer (the value of the `birthMonth` property). We can envisage a situation in which we want a method to return the month name as a three-character abbreviation (e.g. Jan, Feb, Mar) rather than the number of the month. We can define an overloaded version of `BirthMonth` in the `Player` class which returns a string rather than an integer value. As a first attempt we might try to write a version of the method inside the `Player` class as given in Figure 14.9.

FIGURE 14.9   **First attempt at an overloaded `BirthMonth` method**

```
METHOD BirthMonth RETURNS string
     ARRAY: months  OF [12] string ← {'Jan', 'Feb', 'Mar', 'Apr',
                                       'May', 'Jun', 'Jul', 'Aug',
                                       'Sep', 'Oct', 'Nov', 'Dec'} ;
     RETURN  months  [ birthMonth  - 1] ;
ENDMETHOD
```

Why can't an overridden method change its parameters or return types?

Because to override a method effectively means to replace it. Any other object that asks a `Person` object to run its `GivenName` method would expect a `Player` object's `GivenName` method to return the same type of value for the same arguments, as a `Player` is a descendant of a `Person`. As the overridden method is a replacement for the one in the superclass it must look the same and be able to be invoked in the same way.

The body of the overloaded method in Figure 14.9 creates an array of strings each element of which is the three-letter abbreviation of a month name. The method then returns the array element indexed by `birthMonth` − 1. Remember that arrays are zero indexed which means the string 'Jan' for month 1 is held in array element 0; thus we need to subtract 1 from `birthMonth` to get the corresponding array element. However, there is a problem with the overloaded `BirthMonth` method as it stands.

Examine the method in Figure 14.9 and try to work out what the problem is with it.

The problem is simply that the new `BirthMonth` method which we have attempted to put in the `Player` class has the same number of parameters as the one in the `Person` class but has a different return type. This means that when a call is made to a `Player` object's `BirthMonth` method it is not possible to determine which version to invoke: the one that returns an integer or the one that returns a string. Overloading requires the different versions of a method to have different parameter lists. Then the version corresponding to the arguments passed in the method call would be the one that is executed. So, if we want an overloaded `BirthMonth` method in the `Player` class that returns a string rather than an integer, we must give it a different parameter list. Figure 14.10 shows a corrected version of the overloaded method, this one taking a single integer parameter.

FIGURE 14.10   **A corrected overloaded** `BirthMonth` **method**

```
METHOD BirthMonth (integer: number ) RETURNS string
    ARRAY: months  OF [12] string ← {'Jan', 'Feb', 'Mar', 'Apr',
                                      'May', 'Jun', 'Jul', 'Aug',
                                      'Sep', 'Oct', 'Nov', 'Dec'} ;
    RETURN  months  [ birthMonth  + 1] ;
ENDMETHOD
```

Think Spot

The new version of `BirthMonth` takes a parameter but this parameter is never used inside the method. All we have to do to get back a month name rather than a month number is to call the `BirthMonth` method with *any* integer as an argument, for example:

```
Display ( eliza .BirthMonth(9999)) ;
```

You may think that this is inelegant, and I think you'd be right. As no parameter is needed in order to calculate what string to pass back, what is needed is a new method with a different name, say `BirthMonthName` which takes no parameters, as in Figure 14.11.

FIGURE 14.11   **A** `BirthMonthName` **method**

```
METHOD BirthMonthName RETURNS string
    ARRAY: months  OF [12] string ← {'Jan', 'Feb', 'Mar', 'Apr',
                                      'May', 'Jun', 'Jul', 'Aug',
                                      'Sep', 'Oct', 'Nov', 'Dec'} ;
    RETURN  months  [ birthMonth  + 1] ;
ENDMETHOD
```

The take home lesson here is that if you want to override an inherited method, it *must* have the same signature (return type and parameter list) as the original version in the ancestor class. If you want a method of the same name but which returns a different type or takes different parameters then you are dealing with an **overloading** situation (as we saw how to do with class constructors earlier). If what you want to do is simply change the return type of an inherited method whilst leaving the parameter list alone, then you need to declare a new method with a new name that reflects the difference in operation between it and the original method.

14.5 Getting into the Detail

There is quite a lot more detail to OOP that you will need to study if you are going to learn to build systems in an object-oriented language. In the sections above we have done little more than to scratch the surface of the subject, but I hope you at least have begun to grasp some of the main concepts. Any good book on OOP will provide you with much more information and will deal with the many subtleties that I have (necessarily) glossed over. Some would say that the OOP languages are totally different from the procedural languages, but I do not believe this to be the case. The main OOP languages have a great many procedural concepts built into them: indeed, one could write a program in Java or C# that makes minimal use of object classes (other than the in-built system ones that cannot be escaped). Similarly, with careful use of records and strict adherence to information hiding practices one could write an OOPish program in C.[8]

14.6 Chapter Summary

This optional chapter took the basic notions of classes and methods discussed in Chapter 7 and introduced you to some of the remaining foundational principles of object-oriented programming, namely encapsulation (data hiding), inheritance, and polymorphism. We saw how polymorphism a) allows methods inherited by a subclass to be overridden and b) lets us define multiple versions of a method each of which takes a different set of parameters.

14.7 Exercises

As this is a largely optional chapter there are only a few exercises.

1. Add a method to the Player class (Figure 14.2) called WinLoseRatio which has no parameters but which returns a real value which is the ratio of the number of wins to losses (i.e. numberGamesWon ÷ numberGamesLost).

2. Assume the Player object rxforwar has already been instantiated and the real player has played a number of online games. Write an IF. . .ELSE statement which calls rxforwar's WinLoseRatio method (see exercise 1 above) and displays 'Congratulations, you have a good Win:Lose ratio' if the ratio is greater than 1.0, otherwise 'Sorry, your Win:Lose ratio is low and you need more practice'.

---

[8] It is easier to write a procedural program in Java than it is to write an object-oriented program in a procedural language as the imperative languages do not necessarily support the mechanisms needed to achieve true polymorphism.

3. Say we learn that the game has been modified so that there are now two classes of player: normal and league. The Win:Lose ratio for normal players is the same as before, but for league players (those who have signed up for a premium content game with competitions and prizes) the Win:Lose ratio is only based on the number of league games lost and won. League players may join "normal" players in a game but such games will not count towards their ratio. Declare a new class `LeaguePlayer` which inherits from `Player` but overrides the `WinLoseRatio` class to conform to the new system.

14.8   Projects

Choose any of your projects and investigate how your solution could be redesigned using the OOP principles covered in this chapter.

Getting It to Run in Processing: Putting your Programs into a Real Programming Language

Learning Objectives

- Learn how to begin translating pseudo-code into programming language code
- Appreciate that programming languages add their own set of problems to the task
- Understand that a particular programming language will change the shape and structure of the algorithm

This chapter explores how the pseudo-code algorithms from the earlier chapters may be translated into real programming language code and run on a computer. A new language called Processing, which is a simplified version of Java, is used but the principles apply to other languages too.

15.1   Introduction

One aspect of this book I have been very conscious of is that because all the algorithms are developed in pseudo-code it has not been possible to get any of them to actually run on a computer. As I said in the preface and the introduction there are very good reasons for this. However, by now you should be at the point where you have grasped the basics of algorithmic problem solving and so are ready to take the next step of entering the weird world of programming language syntax, compilers, errors, and working programs.

This chapter, then, provides something of a bridge between the *HTTLAP* pseudo-code and real programming languages. To achieve this I have chosen the language called "Processing" as the vehicle for showing how pseudo-code may be translated into programming language syntax. There are a few good reasons for this choice:

▪ Processing is a new, open-source (read "free"), multi-platform (Windows, Linux and Mac OS X), and very accessible programming environment with a very simple user interface.

▪ Processing is based on Java (in fact all Processing programs end up as Java code after the compiler has done its thing) but it removes much of the complexity that can so easily get in the way of the beginning programmer.

▪ Processing grows with you. Because Processing has three different modes of operation, it allows programs to be written in a procedural style (the approach adopted in this book), in a simplified Java-like object-oriented style, or as full-blown Java with its very rich and comprehensive library of resources.

What this means is that we can take many of the algorithms in this book and without too much bother translate them into Processing statements and then run them on the computer. Because it will also support object-oriented code we can also start experimenting with implementing objects and calling their methods. In fact, the only way to implement some of the techniques explored in previous chapters is to use objects and classes, so you should ideally make sure you have read Chapter 14 before going too much further with this chapter.

What this Chapter Is Not

This chapter is not a guide to programming in Processing or Java. There are already many comprehensive texts dealing with that subject (see http://www.processing. org). Neither is this chapter an instructional manual showing how every algorithm in this book can be translated into Processing. Rather, the aim here is to give you a flavour of the basics. Appendix A provides a translation table showing each element of the *HTTLAP* pseudo-code and its equivalent in Processing (as well as a few other popular languages).

15.2   Processing: It's like Java but Really Cool and Fun

Processing is an open source project developed by Ben Fry and Casey Reas at the MIT Media Lab. It was designed as a friendly and accessible language which could be picked up quickly by new programmers. Its aim is to help teach the basics of computer programming but also to be useful as a tool for the professional production of multimedia systems. Because it is open source it is completely free to download. There are downloads available for Mac OS X, Linux, and Windows.

The Processing Environment

The Processing environment is very simple and uncluttered as Figure 15.1 shows.

FIGURE 15.1   **The Processing environment**

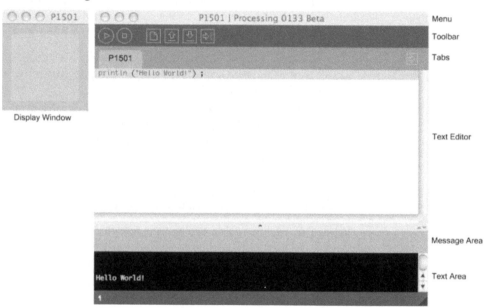

The program code appears in the Text Editor window. The dark area below the code pane is the Text Area where the program can display basic output. The Display Window is a separate window where Processing programs display their main graphical output – none of the programs in this chapter make use of that part. As you can see from the Toolbar there are very few controls to master. The round button with the triangle is the Play button which is used to compile and run a program that has been typed into the Text Editor area. More information on the Processing environment can be found at http://www.processing.org/reference/environment/index.html.

Hello World!

For some absurd reason, just about every programming book has as its first example a program to display "Hello World!" on the screen. So as not to disappoint, Program 15.1 shows the Hello World program in Processing syntax. Because

Processing is designed to get you going very quickly you will notice how short the program is (unlike its equivalent in pure Java).

Program 15.1

The Hello World program in processing

```
println ("Hello World!") ;
```

Figure 15.1 shows the Hello World program in the Processing editing window. Pressing the Run button generates the output in the text area of the Processing window.

Declaring and Assigning Variables

All variables in Processing need to be declared before they can be used and have to belong to a type. For example, we could declare an integer variable `number` in Processing thus:

```
int number ; // declare number as an integer variable
```

The assignment operator is the '=' character, so we can assign the value 7 to `number` like this:

```
number = 7 ; // number becomes equal to 7
```

Notice that statements are terminated by a semicolon. Because Processing is really just Java with a simplified and highly abstracted front-end, it allows you, like Java, to assign a value to a variable at the same time it is declared. So, we could combine the above two statements into one like this:

```
int number = 7 ;
```

However, note that all subsequent references to `number` should not include the type label as they are only used when identifiers are declared. So:

```
int number = 7 ;
int number = number + 2 ;
```

would be invalid as it attempts to declare `number` twice, and should instead be:

```
int number = 7 ;
number = number + 2 ;
```

Data Types

Table 15.1 shows the *HTTLAP* data types and their nearest equivalent in Processing, so you should now be able to declare variables of all these basic types.

Declare the following variables in Processing syntax: i (integer), b (byte), si (short integer), li (long integer), f (a floating point value), d (a double float), c (character), s (a string), flag (Boolean).

Table 15.1   **Processing Equivalents of *HTTLP* Data Types**

HTTLAP Type	Processing Type	Representation	Range of Values/Comment
byte	byte	Signed 8-bit	−128 . . .127
shortint	short	Signed 16-bit	−32,768 . . .32,767
integer	int	Signed 32-bit	−2,147,483,648 . . . 2,147,483,647
longint	long	Signed 64-bit	−9,223,372,036,854,775,808 . . . +9,223,372,036,854,775,807
real	float	32-bit	± 1.40239846E-45 . . . ± 3.40282347E + 38 with 7−8 significant digits
doublereal	double	64-bit	± 4.94065645841246544E-324 . . . 1.79769313486231570E + 308 with 15−16 significant digits
character	char	8-bit	
string	String	variable length	Processing uses the Java **String** class which has a helpful set of methods
boolean	boolean		true, false

Here are the answers to the exercises above:

```
int i ;
byte b ;
short si ;
long li ;
float f ;
double d ;
char c ;
String s ;
boolean flag ;
```

Notice how the `String` type has an uppercase first letter? This is deliberate as `String` is a Java class rather than a simple data type. Because it is a class it has a set of methods that can be used to manipulate and provide information about the string value it holds. Table 15.2 lists `String`'s methods.

We could declare and initialize a string thus:

```
String name = "Brian B. Wildebeest" ;
```

Then we could use the methods in a short program (see Program 15.2). Figure 15.2 shows Program 15.2 in the text editor part of the Processing environment with its output shown in the text area at the bottom of the window. The program itself (along with all the others in this chapter) can be downloaded from the book's website.

```
String name = "Brian B. Wildebeest" ;
println (name.charAt(0)) ;
if (name.equals("Paul Vickers")
```

```
      println ("The names are the same") ;
   else
      println ("The names are not the same") ;
   println (name.indexOf("Wildebeest")) ;
   println (name.length()) ;
   println (name.substring(9)) ;
   println (name.substring(9, 13)) ;
   println (name.toLowerCase()) ;
   println (name.toUpperCase()) ;
```

Program 15.2

Using the String
class's methods

Table 15.2 **Methods of the Processing/Java String Class**

Method Name	Description
charAt()	Gives you back the character at the position in the string indicated by its parameter. So, charAt(0) would give you back the first character of the string.
equals()	Compares current string with another string (the identifier of which is passed as the parameter). If the strings match it returns Boolean true otherwise false.
indexOf()	This method takes a character (or a string) as its argument and gives back the position of the first occurrence of that character/string in the string. If the character or substring can be found in the string, then its position in the string is returned otherwise -1 is returned.
length()	Takes no arguments and gives back the number of characters in the string (i.e. its length).
substring()	This method can take one or two parameters: substring (startposition) ; substring (startposition, endposition) ; In the first case it gives back the portion of the string between startposition and the end of the string. In the second case it gives back the substring between startposition and endposition − 1.
toLowerCase()	This method converts all the characters in the string to lower case.
toUpperCase()	This method converts all the characters in the string to upper case.

Constants

Processing also allows you to declare constants. To declare a constant in *HTTLAP* we do this:

type: constIdentifier IS value ;

FIGURE 15.2   **String methods in action**

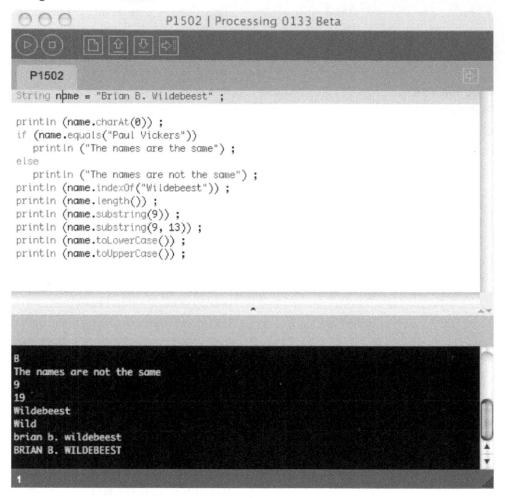

So, for example we can declare a constant to hold the number of weeks in a year:

byte: ⊡weeksPerYear⊡ IS 52 ;

Processing uses the keyword `final` to denote constant identifiers (that is, the value specified is the final value the identifier can take):

```
final byte weeksPerYear = 52 ;
```

Operators

Table 15.3 shows the Processing "spelling" of the *HTTLAP* operators.
Processing has a shorthand way of adding a value to an identifier. Instead of writing

```
number = number + 2 ;
```

Table 15.3   **The Processing Equivalents of the *HTTLAP* Operators**

HTTLAP pseudo-code	Processing
Assignment	
$\boxed{\text{varIdentifier}}$ ← expression ;	varidentifier = expression ;
Arithmetic operators	
+	+
−	−
×	*
÷	/
MOD	%
Relational operators	
=	==
≠	!=
<	<
≤	<=
>	>
≥	>=
Logical connectives	
AND	&&
OR	||
NOT	!

we can write

```
number += 2 ;
```

although I would counsel beginners to use the longhand notation until they are comfortable with what they are doing. There are special operators for subtraction, multiplication, division, and modulus too:

```
number −= 2 ; // subtract 2 from number
number *= 2 ; // multiply number by 2
number /= 2 ; // divide number by 2
number %= 2 ; // assign to number the remainder after
              // dividing it by 2
```

There are two more operators which are in very common usage by Processing/Java programmers. Often we will want to add or subtract 1 to or from an integer variable. In *HTTLAP* we have done this by writing:

$\boxed{\text{number}}$ ← $\boxed{\text{number}}$ + 1 ;

We have seen above that you can also do this in Processing with:

```
number += 1 ;
```

But there is an even shorter way of doing it:

```
number++  ; // adds 1 to number
number-- ; // subtracts 1 from number
```

You will see the ++ operator used a lot in for loops in Processing and Java programs (see below). Both ++ and -- are handy so you should become familiar with their use. In the example above we have used ++ as a postfix operator. It can also be used as a prefix operator, as in:

```
++number ;
```

For a discussion on the difference see the PREFIX AND POSTFIX OPERATORS section in the Reflections chapter.

Control Abstractions

Processing comes equipped with a full set of control abstractions. Table 15.4 shows how the *HTTLAP* constructs can be translated into Processing code.

15.3 Examples

In this section we will see how the above information can be used to translate a few programs from earlier chapters into Processing code. Once translated they can be typed into Processing and then executed by pressing the Run button (see Figure 15.1).

Calculating a Grade – Solution 6.3

In Solution 6.3 in Chapter 6 we built an algorithm for assigning a grade to a piece of work which looked like this:

```
IF (mark ≥ 80)
    grade ← 'A' ;
ELSE IF (mark ≥ 70)
    grade ← 'B' ;
ELSE IF (mark ≥ 60)
    grade ← 'C' ;
ELSE IF (mark ≥ 50)
    grade ← 'D' ;
ELSE IF (mark ≥ 40)
    grade ← 'E' ;
ELSE
    grade ← 'F' ;
ENDIF
```

Table 15.4 **Processing Equivalents of the *HTTLAP* Control Abstractions**

HTTLAP pseudo-code	Processing
IF statements	`if (condition)`
`IF (condition)`	`{`
`  Statement block ;`	`  Statement block ;`
`ENDIF`	`}`
`IF (condition)`	`if (condition)`
`  Statement block ;`	`{`
`ELSE`	`  Statement block ;`
`  Statement block ;`	`}`
`ENDIF`	`  Statement block ;`
	`}`
Zero or more iterations	
`WHILE (condition)`	`while (condition)`
`  Statement block ;`	`{`
`ENDWHILE`	`  Statement block ;`
	`}`
At-least-once iteration	
`DO`	`do`
`  Statement block ;`	`{`
`WHILE (condition)`	`  Statement block ;`
	`}`
	`while (condition) ;`
Count-controlled iteration	
`FOR counter GOES FROM start`	`for (counter = start;`
`  TO finish`	`     counter <= finish;`
	`     counter++ )`
`  Statement block`	`{`
`ENDFOR`	`  Statement block ;`
	`}`

Program 15.3 shows this algorithm implemented in Processing.

```
char grade ;
int mark = 50 ; //change value of mark for different grades
if (mark >= 80)
   grade = 'A' ;
else if (mark >= 70)
   grade = 'B' ;
else if (mark >= 60)
   grade = 'C' ;
else if (mark >= 50)
```

```
        grade = 'D' ;
    else if (mark >= 40)
        grade = 'E' ;
    else
        grade = 'F' ;
    println (mark + "gets grade" + grade + ".") ;
```

Program 15.3
Grade calculation
in Processing

You can play around with getting different grades by changing the value of mark in the second line. Program 15.3 looks very like Solution 6.3, the differences being the need to declare the two variables mark and grade, the fact that if and else are written in lower case, and the way the operators are written.

A Simple FOR Loop

Chapter 6 had the following pseudo-code to show how a FOR loop works:

```
FOR letter GOES FROM 'A' TO 'Z'
    Display letter ;
ENDFOR
```

This can be easily translated into Processing as shown in Program 15.4.

```
for (char letter = 'A'; letter <= 'Z'; letter++)
    {
    print (letter) ;
    }
```

Program 15.4
A for loop in
Processing

The output when this program is run is:

ABCDEFGHIJKLMNOPQRSTUVWXYZ

The structure of the for loop in Processing is exactly the same as Java, C, C++, and C#. The keyword for is followed by three expressions inside the parentheses. The first expression sets up the starting condition, the second states the terminating condition, and the third states what should happen after each iteration of the loop (in this case we add 1 to letter which, in effect, makes it move to the next character in the set). The statements enclosed by the braces (curly brackets) are obeyed each time the loop iterates.

Simple Command Procedures

Program 10.1 from Chapter 10 showed how to design some simple command procedures in pseudo-code. Program 15.5 below shows how this can be rewritten in Processing code. The Processing version closely follows Program 10.1. The main difference is that when using sub-programs Processing requires that program statements be placed in a special sub-program called setup. setup is called automatically when the program is run which is why Program 15.5 has no explicit invocation of it. There is another special sub-program in Processing called draw. setup is called when the program is launched, whilst draw is called repeatedly after setup has finished until the program is terminated. draw is used to hold

statements that manipulate and update the screen (such as animations) and we
do not need to know any more about it just yet.

```
// PROGRAM Simple Command Procedures
// Here are the procedure definitions
void Hello ()
    {
    println ("****************") ;
    println (" Welcome !!!! *") ;
    println ("****************") ;
    }
void Goodbye ()
    {
println ("****************") ;
println (" So long, and *") ;
println (" come again   *") ;
println ("****************") ;
    }
// Here is the main program block
// If any functions are declared then the main program
// block also has to be in a function. In Processing, the
// function setup() is automatically called when the program
// is run
void setup()
    {
    int number,
        square ;
    Hello () ; // Call the Hello procedure
    number = 13 ;
    square = number * number ;
    println (square) ;
    Goodbye() ; // Call the Goodbye procedure
    // End of program
    }
```

Program 15.5

Command
procedures in
Processing

Notice how the procedures Hello and Goodbye are defined. They each begin
with the keyword void. This is because, like Java, all sub-programs in Processing
are actually defined as functions. A command procedure is simply a function
that returns no value, so the return type of the function is specified as void, that
is, empty. In Processing, sub-programs are declared as follows:

```
returnType Identifier (parameter list)
    {
    Statements . . .
    }
```

The braces enclose the statement block. To show how functions that return
values can be used, Program 15.6 below is an implementation of the Cube
function from Program 10.6.

```
// PROGRAM Cubing a number
// Function definitions
int Cube (int number)
   {
   return number * number * number ;
   }
// Here is the main program block
void setup()
   {
   int myNumber,
       myNumberCubed ;
   myNumber = 3 ;
   myNumberCubed = Cube (myNumber) ; // Call the function
   println (myNumberCubed) ;
   }
//End of program
```

Program 15.6
The Cube
function in
Processing

You should be able to follow what is happening as it very closely resembles the pseudo-code original.

Call by Reference

Chapter 10 showed how to design functions and procedures that have their parameters passed by value or by reference. Because Processing is derived from the Java language which only allows call by value, it is not possible to directly pass a parameter by reference. In a sense this makes your life easier as the call-by-reference model can be confusing for beginners. However, it also means that you will have to find work arounds for those situations where you want a function to alter its parameters. Depending on the circumstances this may or may not be possible! Here is a technique that can be adapted to suit. Let's say we want to implement a Swap procedure (see Chapter 10 exercise 7) which swaps the values of its two integer parameters. We could write this in pseudo-code like this:

```
PROCEDURE Swap (REFERENCE:integer:a, REFERENCE:integer:b)
    integer:temp ;
    temp ← a ;
    a ← b ;
    b ← temp ;
ENDPROCEDURE
```

Then we could declare two integer variables x and y and swap them like this:

```
integer:x,
        y ;
x ← 3 ;
y ← 4 ;
Display (x, y) ;
Swap (REFERENCE:x, REFERENCE:y) ;
Display (x, y) ;
```

The first Display would show 3 followed by 4 while the second would show 4 followed by 3. To do this in Processing we need some way of passing a reference parameter which, as we have just learned, is not supported. When a parameter is passed in Processing (which is just Java under the lid) only its value is sent. However, like the pointers we saw in Chapter 13, a Java object identifier holds a reference to that object's address in memory rather than a normal value. What we can do, then, is create a wrapper object class with a single property which will hold the value we want to manipulate. If we then pass the address (reference) of this object to a function, that function can manipulate the object's properties. Program 15.7 shows the Swap function implemented in Processing code.

```
// Simulated call-by-reference to implement a Swap
function
class myInt
  {
  int value ;
  myInt (int n)
    {
    value = n ;
    }
  }
void Swap (myInt a, myInt b)
  {
  int temp = a.value ;
  a.value = b.value ;
  b.value = temp ;
  }
void setup ()
  {
  myInt x = new myInt (3) ;
  myInt y = new myInt (4) ;
  println ("x: " + x.value + ", y: " + y.value) ;
  swap (x, y) ;
  println ("x: " + x.value + ", y: " + y.value) ;
  }
```

Program 15.7

A Swap procedure using a call-by-reference workaround

There is a simple class called myInt which wraps up an integer value into an object. It has a single constructor which sets the value of the class's integer value property when it is instantiated. The Swap function in Program 15.7 now takes two myInt objects as parameters. Or rather, it takes two myInt object identifiers. The identifiers only hold the address of a myInt object, they don't hold the object itself. So, when the body of the Swap procedure is executed, the objects *referenced* by a and b inside the procedure have their values changed. As these are the same objects referenced by x and y in the main setup function we can see that the procedure behaves just as we want by swapping the values of the value property of the two objects. You can prove this to yourself by downloading Program 15.7 from the book's website, running it for yourself, and observing the output from the two println statements. While we have managed to simulate a call-by-reference mechanism, the solution is a little bit clunky inasmuch as the two integers we wish to swap now have to first be assigned to integer properties of two myInt objects.

Input File for Van Loading – Solution 5.18

In Chapter 5 we looked at how to load a van. The final version of the algorithm was given as Solution 5.18. Program 15.8 is a listing of this algorithm translated into Processing code with a file (Chapter 11) substituted for the conveyor belt. The overall structure of Solution 5.18 is maintained in Program 15.8 but you will also notice a few differences. This is because, as I indicated in Chapter 2 (Section 2.3) sometimes translating an algorithm into programming language syntax is a problem in its own right requiring further problem solving to be done. First let's look at Program 15.8.

```
// Solution 5.18 Instructions for loading vans with parcels
// Translated into Processing 11 January, 2008
final int capacity = 750 ; // constant
int numberOfVans = 0,
    heaviestVan = 0,
    parcelWeight,
    payload ;
String fileName = dataPath("weights.txt") ; // tells Processing to
                                             //   look in the Data
                                             //     folder
try
    {
    BufferedReader file = new BufferedReader (new FileReader
                                              (fileName)) ;
    parcelWeight = Integer.parseInt(file.readLine()) ;
    while (parcelWeight > 0)
        {
        payload = 0 ;
        while ((payload + parcelWeight <= capacity) &&
        (parcelWeight > 0))
            {
            payload += parcelWeight ;
            parcelWeight = Integer.parseInt(file.readLine()) ;
            }
        numberOfVans++ ;
        println ("Van " + numberOfVans + " has payload of " +
                                         payload + " kg.") ;
        if (payload > heaviestVan)
            heaviestVan = payload ;
        }
    println ("Number of vans used was " + numberOfVans + ".") ;
    println ("Heaviest van was " + heaviestVan + " kg." ) ;
    }
catch (Exception e)
    {
    println ("Error" + e) ;
    }
```

Program 15.8
Van loading in
Processing

The first few lines should be easy enough to understand as they declare the variables and constants needed by the program. The line:

```
String fileName = dataPath("weights.txt") ;
```

puts the name and location (path) of the input file "weights.txt" into the string variable fileName. The variable dataPath is already defined by the Processing environment and it will contain the full path of a folder called Data which should be in the same folder as the current program. So, if the program were in the folder "C:\My Documents\P1508", then dataPath would hold "C:\My Documents\P1508\Data", and fileName would hold "C:\My Documents\ P1508\Data\weights.txt".

The next part of the program is arranged in a

```
try
    {
     . . .
    }
catch (Exception e)
    {
    println ("Error" + e) ;
    }
```

structure. Where did this come from – it's not in the original algorithm? This part of the program is an example of one of those sub-problems that arise when translating algorithms into programming language code. Because Processing is built upon Java, every time a Java input–output operation is used (such as the readLine method) we are required by Java to deal with any errors that can occur. For example, trying to read data from a file that does not exist would result in an error. Java calls such errors "exceptions" and forces us to deal with the possibility of them happening. This is done with the try/catch structure. The try block simply contains all the code that would be executed in the normal run of events. The catch block contains code to handle any exceptions that occur. So, if the readLine operation in the try block failed for any reason, the program would automatically jump to the catch block which "catches" the exception and displays its identity on the screen. This is one of the reasons why the majority of this book has focused on algorithmic problem solving rather than an actual programming language: it is quite enough for the beginning/bewildered programmer to learn how to think algorithmically without being burdened with the extra complexities imposed by programming languages. Also, the complexity faced will depend very much upon the chosen programming language. It is unfortunate that the older languages offered greater simplicity for the beginner whilst the newer Java-style languages, whilst being very powerful, also bring extra layers of complexity.

Inside the try block we can see the main double while loop from Solution 5.18. The first line in the try block takes fileName and uses it to open the actual file "weights.txt" on the hard drive. The variable that is used to access this file is named, imaginatively, file. Again, the statement looks a bit complicated because opening a file in Processing requires use of the Java file-reader classes. Suffice it to say that this statement opens the "weights.txt" file and uses the variable file to point to it.

The next line reads an integer from file. Again, there is some Java magic going on here. The BufferedReader method readLine fetches a string from the given input file. We need to convert this string into an integer so we pass the string to the `parseInt` method of the `Integer` class. `Integer.parseInt` is a function that takes a string as its argument and returns the integer equivalent. So, the string "123" gets translated into the integer value 123. This integer is then assigned to the variable `parcelWeight`.

The outer while loop has as its condition (`parcelWeight > 0`) compared with Solution 5.18 which has (`conveyor not empty`). This is another example of translation requiring some more problem solving. Testing whether a file is empty or not is very programming language dependent. Some languages will tell you a file is empty after the last value has been read from it. Others will let you read the last value but will not say the file is empty until the invisible end-of-file marker (present in all files) is explicitly read. Java has a `ready()` method which tells us if the file has any data left in it to read. This means we could have written:

```
while (file.ready())
```

However, the `file.ready()` method will return False as soon as the last data item from the file has been read. The upshot of this would be that the very last parcel weight in the file would be ignored and not loaded onto a van. To get round this problem I have introduced an end-marker which is a parcel weight of zero. This is a bit like placing a "no more parcels" sign on the conveyor belt. So, the outer `while` loop will continue until this end marker has been read. In fact, there is a way of avoiding the use of the dummy zero record at the end of the file, and it is discussed in the DETECTING EOF section of the Reflections chapter.

The rest of the program should be understandable as it closely follows Solution 5.18. I have added a few extra `println` statements to give a bit more information about what the program is doing while running. If `weights.txt` contained the following data (from Table 5.3):

```
50
90
120
110
40
30
85
85
110
100
100
100
100
120
90
50
85
120
40
0
```

The output from Program 15.8 would be:

```
Van 1 has payload of 720 kg.
Van 2 has payload of 745 kg.
Van 3 has payload of 160 kg.
Number of vans used was 3.
Heaviest van was 745 kg.
```

The program and its data file can be downloaded from the book's website so you can experiment with it yourself.

Arrays and Records

We can define simple data structures such as arrays and records quite easily in Processing.

Arrays

Program 15.9 declares and initializes two one-dimensional arrays of integers and then displays the value of each element in a `for` loop.

```
// PROGRAM to show arrays
// The following statement declares a 10-element array and
// specifies the values of each element
int [] myArray = {1, 1, 2, 3, 5, 8, 13, 21, 34, 45} ;
// Display each element of the array
for (int counter = 0; counter < myArray.length; counter++)
   {
   println (counter + ":" + myArray [counter]) ;
   }
// Now declare a 5-element array. Values unspecified, so default
// to zero
int [] myOtherArray = new int[5] ;
// Display each element of the array
for (int counter = 0; counter < myOtherArray.length; counter++)
   {
   println (counter + ":" + myOtherArray[counter]) ;
   }
```

Program 15.9

Simple arrays in Processing

Notice the use of the `length` property in the `for` loops. Arrays in Processing are actually objects and one of their properties is an integer called `length` which contains the number of elements in the array. Just as in the *HTTLAP* pseudo-code, array indexing in Processing is zero-based. A two-dimensional array could be declared thus:

```
int [][] twoDArray = new int [3][3] ;
```

Records

Like Java, Processing has no explicit mechanism for defining record structures. Instead, an object class is declared in which the record fields are defined as properties, and no methods are included. Chapter 12 showed how to declare a patient record using the pseudo-code thus:

```
NEWTYPE PatientRecord IS
    RECORD
    string: title,
            familyName,
            givenName ;
    integer: birthDay,
             birthMonth,
             birthYear ;
    string: streetAddress,
            postalTown,
            postCode,
            telephone ;
    integer: joinDay,
             joinMonth,
             joinYear,
             checkupDay,
             checkupMonth,
             checkupYear ;
    ENDRECORD
    PatientRecord: patient ;
```

Program 15.10 shows how this could be achieved in Processing. Because the record has to be declared as a class, any variables of that type must be declared and instantiated as objects, hence the line in which the patient variable is declared:

```
PatientRecord patient = new PatientRecord () ;
```

As records are object classes we can do a lot more than Program 15.10 shows, such as providing a full range of methods and a set of constructors that can be called when a variable is instantiated to set initial values for the record's fields. Again, that is beyond the very introductory nature of this chapter.

```
// A *very* simple record structure
class PatientRecord
    {
    String title,
            familyName,
            givenName ;
    int     birthDay,
            birthMonth,
            birthYear ;
    String streetAddress,
            postalTown,
```

```
                  postCode,
                  telephone ;
         int      joinDay,
                  joinMonth,
                  joinYear,
                  checkupDay,
                  checkupMonth,
                  checkupYear ;
         }
     PatientRecord patient = new PatientRecord () ;
     patient.title = "Prof." ;
     patient.familyName = "Higgins" ;
     patient.givenName = "Henry" ;
     println (patient.title + " " + patient.givenName + " " +
                                        patient.familyName);
```

Program 15.10

A record structure in Processing

Dynamic Data Structures

Chapter 13 gave a comprehensive set of algorithms for manipulating stacks, queues, and linked lists. Although Processing provides some Java classes that do all the difficult bits for us which makes building dynamic data structures (and especially lists) much easier, the purpose of this chapter is not to teach Java programming but how to translate *HTTLAP* pseudo-code into Processing/Java. Although the solutions that follow are somewhat unnecessary given the facilities Processing/Java offer for handling lists, they provide a good bridge between a set of procedural algorithms and their implementation in an OOP language. Program 15.11 below shows how the sorted linked list algorithms from Chapter 13 can be implemented in a (mostly) procedural way in Processing.

```
// Program to implement the sorted linked list routines from
// Chapter 13. 12 February, 2008.
// A class implemented as a RECORD structure
class BookRecord
    {
    String bookTitle ;
    BookRecord next ;
    // Constructor just to make setting the title easy
    BookRecord (String t)
        {
        bookTitle = t ;
        }
    }

// BookPointer class. Java doesn't allow call by reference, so we
// pass a BookPointer object instead and update its theBook property
// which points to a BookRecord object
class BookPointer // Used to simulate a reference parameter
```

```
        {
        BookRecord theBook ;
        }
// DisplayList procedure
void DisplayList (BookRecord listHead)
        {
        BookRecord current = listHead ;
        while (current != null)
            {
            println (current.bookTitle) ;
            current = current.next ;
            }
        }
// FindSortedNode function for a sorted list
boolean FindSortedNode(BookRecord listHead, String searchTitle,
                       BookPointer predecessor)
        {
        BookRecord current = listHead ;
        boolean found = false ;
        predecessor.theBook = null ;
        while (current != null && searchTitle.compareTo
        (current.bookTitle) > 0)
            {
            predecessor.theBook = current ;
            current = current.next ;
            }
        if (current != null)
            found = searchTitle == current.bookTitle ;
        else
            found = false ;
        return found ;
        }
// AddSortedNode function: for a sorted list
boolean AddSortedNode (BookPointer listHead, String theTitle)
        {
        BookPointer predecessor = new BookPointer() ;
        BookRecord book ;
        if (FindSortedNode (listHead.theBook, theTitle, predecessor))
            return false ;
        else
            {
            book = new BookRecord (theTitle) ;
            book.next = null ;
            if (predecessor.theBook == null) // head of list
                {
                book.next = listHead.theBook ;
                listHead.theBook = book ;
                }
```

```
                else // in middle or at end
                   {
                   book.next = predecessor.theBook.next ;
                   predecessor.theBook.next = book ;
                   }
                return true ;
                }
         }
   // DeleteSortedNode function: for a sorted list
   boolean DeleteSortedNode (BookPointer listHead,
                                String theTitle)
      {
      BookRecord current ;
      BookPointer predecessor = new BookPointer() ;
      if (!FindSortedNode (listHead.theBook, theTitle, predecessor))
         return false ;
      else // record found, so delete it
         {
         if (predecessor.theBook == null) // node at head
            {
            current = listHead.theBook ;
            listHead.theBook = listHead.theBook.next ;
            }
         else // middle or end
            {
            current = predecessor.theBook.next ;
            predecessor.theBook.next = current.next ;
            }
         // No need to explicitly delete - Java's garbage
         // collection will do that automatically
         return true ;
         }
      }
   // Main function
   void setup()
      {
      BookPointer head = new BookPointer() ;
      AddSortedNode (head, "How to think like a programmer") ;
      AddSortedNode (head, "How to solve it") ;
      AddSortedNode (head, "Understanding Java") ;
      AddSortedNode (head, "Eats, shoots and leaves") ;
      DisplayList(head.theBook) ;
      DeleteSortedNode (head, "How to solve it") ;
      println ();
      println ("After the deletion:") ;
      DisplayList(head.theBook) ;
      }
```

Program 15.11
A sorted linked list

The main things to note in Program 15.11 are that we have defined a Java class BookRecord as a record structure to hold book details. There is a second class called BookPointer. Because Java (and thus, Processing) does not allow a call-by-reference model in sub-programs, the BookPointer class is a workaround for this using the same technique we employed earlier for the Swap procedure. The class is very simple: it has a single property which is a BookRecord object. If we pass a BookPointer object to a function (e.g. FindSortedNode) we can then get direct access from the function to a BookRecord object through the theBook property of the BookPointer parameter. That is, the theBook property of the BookPointer object points to the actual BookRecord object we are interested in. You should now compare the functions in Program 15.11 with the equivalent pseudo-code algorithms from Chapter 13.

There is one word of caution to make here and that is, the practice of directly accessing an object's properties is considered bad object-oriented programming style (see Chapter 14). I have done it here in order to make the simplest possible translation of the procedural linked list algorithms from Chapter 13 into Processing code. Ideally, we would either create a new OrderedLinkedList object class and make all the functions from Program 15.11 into methods inside that class, or we would use the existing Java list classes which are actually optimized for good performance. You can read more about the special Java list and stack classes in most Java textbooks.

Chapter 13 also shows algorithms for implementing stacks and queues, but as they are just specializations of a list, you should be able to use Program 15.11 as a basis for translating the remaining algorithms into Processing code.

Objects and Classes

Chapter 14 showed how to build classes featuring polymorphism and inheritance. To show how these class definitions may be implemented consider Program 15.12 which implements the Person and Player classes from the examples in Chapter 14 (Figures 14.5 and 14.7).

```
// Implementation of the Person
// and Player classes. 12 February, 2008
class Person
    {
    // Properties
    String givenName,
           familyName ;
    char sex ;
    int birthDay,
        birthMonth,
        birthYear ;
    // Constructors
    Person (String gName, String fName)
        {
        givenName = gName ;
        familyName = fName ;
        sex = 'X' ;
```

```
        birthDay = 1 ;
        birthMonth = 1 ;
        birthYear = 1970 ;
        }
Person (String gName, String fName, char theSex)
        {
        givenName = gName ;
        familyName = fName ;
        sex = theSex ;
        birthDay = 1 ;
        birthMonth = 1 ;
        birthYear = 1970 ;
        }
Person (String gName, String fName, char theSex, int dd,
                int mm, int yy)
        {
        givenName = gName ;
        familyName = fName ;
        sex = theSex ;
        birthDay = dd ;
        birthMonth = mm ;
        birthYear = yy ;
        }
// Methods
String GivenName ()
        {
        return givenName ;
        }
String FamilyName ()
        {
        return familyName ;
        }
int BirthDay ()
        {
        return birthDay ;
        }
int BirthMonth ()
        {
        return birthMonth ;
        }
int BirthYear ()
        {
        return birthYear ;
        }
char Sex ()
        {
        return sex ;
        }
}
```

```
class Player extends Person
  {
  // Properties
  String name ;
  int numberGamesPlayed, numberGamesWon, numberGamesLost ;
  String clan ;
  // Constructor 1
  Player (String aName, String gName, String fName)
    {
    super (gName, fName) ;
    name = aName ;
    clan = "" ;
    numberGamesPlayed = 0 ;
    numberGamesWon = 0 ;
    numberGamesLost = 0 ;
    }
  // Constructor 2
  Player (String aName, String gName, String fName, char theSex)
    {
    super (gName, fName, theSex) ;
    name = aName ;
    clan = "" ;
    numberGamesPlayed = 0 ;
    numberGamesWon = 0 ;
    numberGamesLost = 0 ;
    }
  // Constructor 3
  Player (String aName, String gName, String fName, char theSex,
            int dd, int mm, int yy)
    {
    super (gName, fName, theSex, dd, mm, yy) ;
    name = aName ;
    clan = "" ;
    numberGamesPlayed = 0 ;
    numberGamesWon = 0 ;
    numberGamesLost = 0 ;
    }
  // Constructor 4
  Player (String aName, String aClan, String gName, String fName)
    {
    super (gName, fName) ;
    name = aName ;
    clan = aClan ;
    numberGamesPlayed = 0 ;
    numberGamesWon = 0 ;
    numberGamesLost = 0 ;
    }
```

```
// Constructor 5
Player (String aName, String aClan, String gName, String fName,
            char theSex)
   {
   super (gName, fName, theSex) ;
   name = aName ;
   clan = aClan ;
   numberGamesPlayed = 0 ;
   numberGamesWon = 0 ;
   numberGamesLost = 0 ;
   }
// Constructor 6
Player (String aName, String aClan, String gName, String fName,
            char theSex, int dd, int mm, int yy)
   {
   super (gName, fName, theSex, dd, mm, yy) ;
   name = aName ;
   clan = aClan ;
   numberGamesPlayed = 0 ;
   numberGamesWon = 0 ;
   numberGamesLost = 0 ;
   }
// Overridden GivenName method
String GivenName ()
   {
   return "[" + givenName + "]";
   }
// rest of the methods, as before
int GamesPlayed ()
   {
   return numberGamesPlayed ;
   }
int GamesWon ()
   {
   return numberGamesWon ;
   }
int GamesLost ()
   {
   return numberGamesLost ;
   }
String Clan ()
   {
   return clan ;
   }
void LeaveClan ()
   {
   clan = "" ;
   }
```

```
boolean JoinClan (String newClan)
  {
  boolean success ;
  if (clan != "")
    {
    clan = newClan ;
    success = true ;
    }
  else
    success = false ;
  return success ;
  }
}
void setup()
  {
  Player p1 = new Player ("CapnJack", "Jack", "Sparrow") ;
  Player p2 = new Player ("CapnJack", "Jack", "Sparrow", 'M') ;
  Player p3 = new Player ("CapnJack", "Jack", "Sparrow", 'M', 9,
                          6, 1963);
  Player p4 = new Player ("elizagirl", "[XX] Black Label",
                          "Eliza", "Dolittle") ;
  Player p5 = new Player ("elizagirl", "[XX] Black Label",
                          "Eliza", "Dolittle", 'F') ;
  Player p6 = new Player ("elizagirl", "[XX] Black Label",
                          "Eliza", "Dolittle", 'F', 21, 1, 1965) ;
  println (p1.birthDay) ;
  println (p6.GivenName()) ;
  }
```

Program 15.12

Implementation of
the person and
player classes

The code in Program 15.12 is very similar to the original algorithms because Processing is really an OOP and so there is a much closer fit between the language and the pseudo-code.

15.4 Chapter Summary

This chapter has given a taste of how some of the algorithms in this book may be translated into a real programming language. It has shown that while some aspects of translation are trivial and very easy, others are much harder to accomplish, and this serves to highlight the fact that programming languages themselves introduce their own problems in addition to those provided by the problem situation for which the algorithm is a solution. You will also find the different programming languages make certain aspects of the coding process easier or harder. For example, getting input from the keyboard is not very easy in Processing because the language was not designed to handle such interaction. However, in Java it is easier and in older languages like C it is even easier. What this all goes to show is that the core discipline needed by programmers is the ability to solve problems. Having solved the problem in as precise a manner as possible with a semi-formal pseudo-code notation, it then remains for the programmer to acquaint himself or herself with

the particular programming language to be used and make sure that the best features of that language are used. This might result in the algorithm being changed
quite drastically in order to take advantage of (or meet the constraints of) the programming language. This is one of the reasons why this book has focused so much
on algorithm design and very little on programming language code: the lessons
learned in this book can be applied across a range of languages.

15.5　Exercises

There are no specific exercises for this chapter.

15.6　Projects

StockSnackz Vending Machine

Try and implement some of your algorithms for this project in Processing code.

Stocksfield Fire Service: Hazchem Signs

Try and implement some of your algorithms for this project in Processing code.

Puzzle World: Roman Numerals and Chronograms

Try and implement some of your algorithms for this project in Processing code.

Pangrams: Holoalphabetic Sentences

Try and implement some of your algorithms for this project in Processing code.

Online Bookstore: ISBNs

Try and implement some of your algorithms for this project in Processing code.

16 Testing, Debugging, and Documentation

Program testing can be a very effective way to show the presence of bugs, but it is hopelessly inadequate for showing their absence.

(Edsger W. Dijkstra, 1972, p. 864)

Learning Objectives

- Learn how testing can reveal errors (bugs) in a program or algorithm and how the process of removing those errors (debugging) can be tackled in a structured way
- Understand how different testing strategies (particularly black-box, white-box, and acceptance testing) can be used to reveal different kinds of error
- Appreciate how to write good documentation and understand how this can help to make a program more maintainable

In this chapter we will look at the basics of testing our programs, removing defects, and writing the documentation. You will learn about different types of testing such as design testing (Section 16.4) and black-box, white-box, and acceptance testing (Section 16.5). In Section 16.7 you will learn what debugging is and will be presented with an outline strategy for successful debugging. Section 16.8 teaches you about the importance of documentation – actually, you have been learning about this aspect all the way through the book but it is set out more formally here. The chapter is rounded off with a worked documentation example in Section 16.9 and some suggestions for further reading in Section 16.10.

16.1 Introduction

Because this chapter comes towards the end of the book you might be tempted to view it as an optional extra. After all, if it was so important, why did it not come earlier on? That is a good question, but the answer is quite simple: I wanted to cover the basics of programming first so that when it came to testing and debugging you would have some reasonably difficult testing and debugging problems to solve. In this chapter we are looking specifically at software bugs – those defects that exist in the compiled program. When coding programs we also encounter syntax errors that prevent the program from being compiled (e.g. missing off the semi-colon at the end of a statement). As a program cannot be compiled if it contains a syntax error, neither can it execute. The compiler issues error messages that help us to locate and identify syntax errors; so, while syntax error removal can be time-consuming, it is not the focus of this chapter. In this chapter we are going to look at bugs – the errors that cause our programs to fail or to operate incorrectly. Once testing has revealed a bug we then use debugging techniques to identify, locate, and remove the bug.

16.2 Testing

Automobile manufacturers spend large sums of money crash-testing their new designs to ensure that the cars meet (or exceed) legal safety standards. If a car does not perform to specification the cause must be identified and the problem rectified before the car can proceed to market. Testing is a vital and central task in manufacturing and engineering organizations: apart from the moral case of not selling faulty goods, it is much cheaper to identify defects before thousands of units have been sold at which point an expensive product recall is needed. It is the same with software. After a program has been written it should be tested to make sure it performs as expected. The reputation of a software company can suffer if it is known to sell software that does not work properly.

Testing is the process by which software is inspected to find defects (bugs). In a small program we can be fairly confident that if it has been tested thoroughly then it will not have any bugs. In large programs and systems (the majority of real-world software) it is very difficult (if not impossible) to guarantee that testing will find all the bugs. Today's software systems are the most complex artifacts ever built by people; their complexity of construction far exceeds that of even the most high-tech aeroplane, nuclear power plant, or space craft. In the real world software testing deals in probabilities rather than certainties: if the software has passed the testing procedure then it *probably* is bug-free (or has very few bugs left in it). If a testing procedure does not find any bugs, it does not mean there are no bugs in the software. It often means that our tests just weren't sufficient to find them. This point illustrates two main types of software testing: validation and defect detection. A validation test runs the software through a number of test cases to ensure that it meets its specification. A successful validation test is one in which the software did what was expected of it. A successful defect detection test, on the other hand, is one that causes the program to behave incorrectly; that is, its purpose is to make the software fail in order to expose defects.

There are many testing techniques and strategies used to verify software. Some are very simple and quick, others are very involved and require mathematical calculation and proof of the various test cases to be used. The amount and type of testing we do should be proportional to the risk associated with a software failure. If a word processor program fails to paginate a document properly, that is unlikely to be catastrophic – annoying, certainly, but not life-threatening. On the other hand, if the software controlling a nuclear power station fails the consequences are dire.

Of course, if software is well-written in the first place the testing is easier to do and the debugging is less time-consuming. In recent years there has been increased effort in improving the process of writing software. While many of the newer processes are aimed at the company and software-team level, there have been notable contributions designed to help the individual programmer improve his or her programming practice. A book that deals with this subject is Watts Humphrey's *Introduction to the Personal Software Process* (Humphrey, 1997). Humphrey's first-rate book shows the individual programmer how to become a reflective learner who aims to continually improve his or her practice.

16.3   Strategies for Testing

Testing is sometimes viewed lazily as a short activity that is done at the end of a software project to find any last bugs. Good testing takes place throughout the entire programming cycle. If you look at step 4 of the *HTTLAP* strategy you can see that testing (including reflection and evaluation) has always been part of the approach taken in this book. Assessing the result is a reflective practice in which you (and others) test your solution looking for mistakes.[1] Humphrey (1997, p.161) has asserted that, on average, the cost of locating and correcting a defect increases ten-fold with each phase of the development process, which makes it especially important to locate defects as early as possible. It has been estimated that testing consumes as much as 50 percent of the time spent on commercial software development projects. A good programmer will not only test the running program but will also test the program's design *before* writing any code. Of course, if you have been following the *HTTLAP* strategy fully you have already begun to develop this habit. We can separate testing into two stages: design testing and implementation testing. Testing the implementation (the actual program) typically falls into three broad categories:

- **Unit testing** – the testing of an individual program component (e.g. a procedure, function, method, or object) or a small program to check that it meets its individual specification (e.g. testing a function that returns the cube root of its parameter).
- **Integration/system testing** – here we test the program or system as a whole; that is we test the many hundreds or thousands of components that make up a whole system to see whether they work together and not just in isolation.
- **Acceptance testing** – the system is tested with the client or users present to check that it does what they expected it to do and in the way they want.

---

[1] Recently, a new way of working has emerged that has at its core continuous testing. It is called Extreme Programming and appears to be a very effective way for small teams to write software. Kent Beck's book *Extreme Programming Explained* (Beck, 1999) will give you a good idea of what it is all about.

16.4 Design Testing

There are two principal causes of software defects: either the program design itself is incorrect, or the design has been incorrectly translated into programming language code. Before writing any code it is good practice to test, as far as possible, the program design. An error found during the design stage is cheaper and easier to correct than if it is found after the code has been written for the simple reason that there is not yet any code to change. Errors in the design reveal our own misunderstanding or mistranslation of the program requirements for it is the design that expresses what we want the program to do. If the design is at fault there is little point in translating it into program code. Testing the design also helps to separate the detection of two different kinds of error: errors in the algorithm and errors that arise when expressing the algorithm as program code. We shall call these two classes *errors of design* and *errors of expression*. An error of design means that the algorithm itself is at fault and any resultant program will not function correctly even if the translation into programming language code has been carried out properly. A common and useful technique for testing the design is known as *desk checking*. Desk checking is so-called because you sit at a desk with pencil and paper and build *trace tables* which are used to help you walk through the algorithm by hand with some sample test data looking for errors; the only computer involved is that marvelous one inside your skull.

▶ Errors of design and errors of expression

Example Design Test

To show you how you can approach design testing consider the following problem. A function is required for an online CD seller that adds up the value of a customer's shopping basket. The individual basket items are provided one at a time on a stream by a shopping-basket-manager program. Each item comprises a catalog number (string), price (integer), and quantity ordered (integer). The function should fetch items from the basket stream until it is empty and then return the total value of all the items in the basket. Having worked through the *HTTLAP* strategy we have arrived at the algorithm shown in Example 16.1.

Example 16.1 Outline design for shopping basket function

```
1.  FUNCTION BasketTotal RETURNS integer
    2.   Initialize total to zero ;
    3.   Initialize catalog number to blank
    4.   Initialize price and quantity to zero ;
    5.   WHILE stream not empty
         5.1.  Display catalog number, quantity, price ;
         5.2.  total ← total + (quantity × price) ;
         ENDWHILE
    6.   RETURN total ;
    ENDFUNCTION
```

I have used the more informal *HTTLAP* notation rather than the one with identifiers and explicit conditions just to illustrate the point. Now we need some sample input data to run through the design; as we are checking by hand we do not want too much data. In addition, we need to write down what output the program, when implemented, should produce for the given input data.[2] Table 16.1 shows a sample basket with four items in the first column and the output that should be produced by the function together with its return value in the second column.

Table 16.1 **Input and Expected Output for Basket Function**

Input	Expected Output
CDRELX06 899 2	CDRELX06 899 2
SSR-8084 999 1	SSR-8084 999 1
5218950 1099 1	5218950 1099 1
602498568279 799 2	602498568279 799 2
	Returns total of 5494

Trace table ▶   Next we should construct a *trace table* that shows for each statement and condition in the algorithm the effect on the different variables and the corresponding output. A trace table enables us to test the design a bit more rigorously than simply reading through the algorithm. It is even better if we can get someone else to do the trace for us because we may make assumptions about the design that an impartial third party would not. For example, we might have written a condition incorrectly but which we assume to be correct; unless we are very meticulous in our checking it is possible that the error would remain undetected by our manual dry run. Somebody else would be less likely to make the same assumptions. Table 16.2 shows the first few rows of a trace table to check the design in Example 16.1.

Table 16.2 **Trace Table for Basket Algorithm**

Statements and Conditions	Cat no.	Price	Quantity	Total	Output
1	–	–	–	–	
2	–	–	–	0	
3	"	–	–	0	
4	"	0	0	0	
5 (true)	"	0	0	0	
. . .	. . .	. . .	. . .	. . .	. . .

Write out the table yourself and complete the trace of the algorithm. So far the table shows that we have got as far as carrying out statement #5 which is the condition in the WHILE loop that checks the stream is not empty. Carry on from statement #5.1 filling in the boxes as appropriate. If there is a problem with the algorithm you should find it eventually with the test data given in Table 16.1.

---

[2] Note, we will see in subsequent sections how to derive good test data.

Did you find any errors? You should have. Table 16.3 is my own trace table. If you did find an error in the algorithm, inspect my trace table to see if you found it at the same place. If you did not find an error, then examine my trace table carefully to see where you missed it.

Table 16.3   **Completed Trace Table for Basket Algorithm**

Statements and Conditions	Cat no.	Price	Quantity	Total	Output
1	–	–	–	–	
2	–	–	–	0	
3	"	–	–	0	
4	"	0	0	0	
5 (true)	"	0	0	0	
5.1 (true)	"	0	0	0	" 0 0
5.2 (true)	"	0	0	0	
5 (true)	"	0	0	0	
5.1 (true)	"	0	0	0	" 0 0
5.2 (true)	"	0	0	0	
5 (true)	"	0	0	0	
5.1 (true)	"	0	0	0	" 0 0
5.2 (true)	"	0	0	0	
. . .	. . .	. . .	. . .	. . .	. . .

I hope that you spotted quite quickly that something was wrong. The trace shows that the program repeatedly writes out a blank catalog number and zero price to the screen and never terminates. Why is this? Statement #5 keeps evaluating to true which means the WHILE loop never terminates. This is caused by forgetting to include a statement inside the loop to read a record from the stream. Example 16.2 shows the corrected algorithm with the read statement in place (new statement #5.1).

Example 16.2. Corrected design for shopping basket function

```
1.   FUNCTION BasketTotal RETURNS integer
        2.   Initialize total to zero ;
        3.   Initialize catalog number to blank
        4.   Initialize price and quantity to zero ;
        5.   WHILE stream not empty
                5.1.   Read basket item from stream ;
                5.2.   Display catalog number, quantity, price ;
                5.3.   total ← total + (quantity × price) ;
             ENDWHILE
        6.   RETURN total ;
     ENDFUNCTION
```

? Think Spot

We should check this corrected design to ensure that we have not overlooked some other error. Table 16.4 shows a trace of the corrected function and, as we can see from the trace, the algorithm appears to produce the results we want.

Table 16.4   **Trace Table for Corrected Basket Algorithm**

Statements and Conditions	Cat no.	Price	Quantity	Total	Output
1	–	–	–	–	
2	–	–	–	0	
3	"	–	–	0	
4	"	0	0	0	
5 (true)	"	0	0	0	
5.1	CDRELX06	899	2	0	
5.2	CDRELX06	899	2	0	CDRELX06 899 2
5.3	CDRELX06	899	2	1798	
5 (true)	CDRELX06	899	2	1798	
5.1	SSR-8084	999	1	1798	
5.2	SSR-8084	999	1	1798	SSR-8084 999 1
5.3	SSR-8084	999	1	2797	
5 (true)	SSR-8084	999	1	2797	
5.1	5218950	1099	1	2797	
5.2	5218950	1099	1	2797	5218950 1099 1
5.3	5218950	1099	1	3896	
5 (true)	5218950	1099	1	3896	
5.1	602498568279	799	2	3896	
5.2	602498568279	799	2	3896	602498568279 799 2
5.3	602498568279	799	2	5494	
5 (false)	602498568279	799	2	5494	
6	602498568279	799	2	5494	Returns 5494

With the read statement in place we see that the WHILE loop terminates when the end marker is reached and that the algorithm then proceeds to execute statement #6 and then stop. Being reasonably confident that our design is correct we can proceed to translating it into programming language code after which we move into implementation testing.

16.5   Implementation Testing: Finding Errors of Expression

If design testing lets us find errors of design, implementation testing sets out (amongst other things) to find errors of expression: those places where the program code does not correctly implement the design. Of course, design testing may not find all the design flaws so implementation testing may also reveal design errors that have thus far remained hidden.

For detecting errors in the code we need to conduct unit testing and integration testing. Recall that unit testing is the testing of an individual program component (e.g. a procedure, function, method, or object) or a small program to check that it meets its individual specification (e.g. testing a function that returns the cube root of its parameter). Integration testing is where we test the program or system as a whole; that is we test the many hundreds or thousands of components that make up a whole system to see whether they work together and not just in isolation.

There are several techniques available to the programmer for unit and integration testing and it is beyond the scope of this book to give an in-depth coverage. Instead we shall look at two common unit testing strategies: black-box testing and white-box testing. The kinds of programs written by the beginning programmer are unlikely to be large enough to need true integration testing. For coverage of other unit testing methods and techniques for integration and acceptance testing I would refer you to a good book on Software Engineering such as Pressman (2004) or Sommerville (2001).

Black-box Testing

Just as it is infeasible for market researchers conducting a survey on food purchasing habits to interview every person in the country, so exhaustive testing of every possible combination of permissible data values for even a single component (let alone an entire program) is, to all intents and purposes, impossible. Consider a function that takes three parameters containing integers and returns their sum if the parameters are all in the range 0, . . .,10,000, or returns -1 if any parameter is out of range:

```
1.    FUNCTION Sum (integer:first, integer:second, integer:third)
                  RETURNS integer ;
      1.1.    IF (first ≥ 0) AND (first ≤ 10000) AND
                 (second ≥ 0) AND (second ≤ 10000) AND
                 (third ≥ 0) AND (third ≤ 10000)
              1.1.1.   RETURN first + second + third ;
      1.2.    ELSE
              1.2.1.   RETURN -1 ;
              ENDIF
      ENDFUNCTION
```

The function Sum takes three integer parameters. The range of valid values for each integer is 0, . . .,10 000 giving 1,000,000,000,000 possible combinations of values. Assuming a computer could test 1,000,000 pairs of values each second, it would still take around $11^1/_2$ days to test all possible value combinations, and that is without testing to see what happens with values outside the valid range! Market researchers get round the problem of not being able to interview every person in the population by finding a smaller sample of people (usually in the low thousands) that is *representative* of the entire population. Likewise, we can devise sample data that are representative of the possible data that a component or program could encounter. Of course, because we are not doing exhaustive testing, there remains the possibility that our sample will still not be sufficient to test the component thoroughly. Therefore, the best we can do is estimate a probability, or likelihood, that the sample test data is representative of the entire set of possible values: when the component passes the test using the sample data, we say that there is a probability that there are no defects in it – we cannot say that there are definitely no bugs in it. (Calculating the exact probability requires recourse to statistical methods which are beyond the scope of this book.)

Black-box testing is so-called because it is done without any specific knowledge of how the component being tested works. All we concern ourselves with in a black-box test is the range of possible inputs and the corresponding output.[3] The processing that goes on in-between is viewed as a black box. With a black box test we typically generate three kinds of test data:

- Representative valid data – values that are representative of valid data that should lead to correct results, e.g. 4 and 1000 in the case of our Sum function.
- Data that lies at the boundaries of the acceptable range – e.g. 0, 1, 9999, and 10,000
- Invalid data – values that should be rejected, e.g. −1 and 10,000

This categorization of data is known as *equivalence partitioning* as it divides the set of possible input values into partitions of equivalent data. That is, the values 4 and 1000 are "equivalent" in the sense that they are examples of valid data, and so they belong to the valid-data partition. The values 0 and 10,000 lie on the boundaries of valid data and are in the boundary-data partition. Numbers less than 0 and greater than 10,000 lie in the invalid-data partition. Equivalence partitioning is useful because it allows us to specify test data that are designed to uncover specific classes of error. Pressman (2004) offers four guidelines for determining equivalence classes:

1. If input data are specified by a range (e.g. 0, . . .,10,001), then there is one valid equivalence partition (all the valid data) and two invalid equivalence classes (all the values less than the range and all the values greater than the range).
2. When a specific data value is required (e.g. send a birthday card to anyone who is 18 years old today) then there are one valid and two invalid equivalence classes: the specific value itself (18), all the values less than 18, and all values greater than 18.
3. If the input data belong to a set then there are two equivalence classes: a valid partition for all values that are in the set and an invalid partition for all values not in the set. For example, a function might require a parameter to be an even number. The valid partition is the set of all the even numbers and the invalid partition is the set of odd numbers.
4. When an input condition is Boolean there is one valid partition and one invalid partition. For example, a procedure that processes postal addresses might have a postcode parameter; if the parameter is empty then it is ignored otherwise

---

[3] Black-box testing is also called *behavioural testing*.

some processing is done on the postcode. This is a Boolean condition because the postcode is either present or absent. This gives us two equivalence partitions: a parameter containing a postcode and a parameter that is empty (or blank).

The principal strength of defining equivalence classes is that because testing with one member of a partition is logically equivalent to testing with another member of the same partition we are able to test a program component with a minimum number of test cases; that is, we get broad coverage with a small amount of data. Using *HTTLAP* as our method for working, here is an example of how we could go about selecting representative data samples for our Sum function.

Understanding the Problem

Q. What are you being asked to do? What is required?

A. We need to check that Sum correctly adds up three valid numbers and that it returns a -1 if any of the parameters is out of the range 0, . . .,10,000.

Devising a Plan to Solve the Problem

Q. Start thinking about the information you have and what the solution is required to do.

A. We need to find representative data to test the Sum function. To check that it adds up three valid numbers we need to give it three valid numbers, say, 4, 5, 6, and 9990, 9995, 9996. We also need to make sure it rejects invalid numbers, e.g. -10 and '11,000. It is also important to check values at the boundaries: 0 and 10,000 should work but $-11,000$ and '10,001 should generate errors. The reason for this is that the function contains relational expressions which we might have written incorrectly – e.g. writing `first > 0` rather than `first ≥ 0`.

Carrying Out the Plan

Having identified the kinds of data values needed to test Sum we should write a formal test plan. Table 16.5 shows a test plan for Sum. Each row is a test case and shows the input data and the expected result. If any of the test cases leads to a result that is different from the expected result then we have found a possible error in the program (we must first be careful to check that the expected result is, in fact, correct!). The partition to which the test data belong is shown in the second column. The last column of Table 16.5 is blank and is where we write down the results obtained from the test.

Assessing the result

From a possible 1,000,000,000,000 combinations of valid values for the three parameters we were able to construct just 14 test cases which would find errors in the Sum function. By checking the actual results against the expected results it is possible to assess whether the function is likely to give the right answers for any combination of integer parameters. If any of the test cases led to a difference between the expected and the actual output then we would go back to the function to see where the bug is. Also, because we have used equivalence partitioning

Table 16.5   **Test plan for** Sum

Test No.	Partition	Data	Expected Result	Actual Result
1	Normal	4, 5, 6	15	
2	Normal	9900, 9990, 9995	29885	
3	Boundary	0, 4, 5	9	
4	Boundary	4, 0, 5	9	
5	Boundary	4, 5, 0	9	
6	Boundary	10000, 9900, 9900	29800	
7	Boundary	9900, 10000, 9900	29800	
8	Boundary	9900, 9900, 10000	29800	
9	Invalid	−1, 4, 5	−1	
10	Invalid	4, −1, 5	−1	
11	Invalid	4, 5, −1	−1	
12	Invalid	10001, 9900, 9900	−1	
13	Invalid	9900, 10001, 9900	−1	
14	Invalid	9900, 9900, 10001	−1	

we have some additional clues as to what caused the error: we know whether the function failed to process valid data, whether it failed on one of its boundary cases, or whether it failed to deal with invalid data. Furthermore, because each of the boundary and invalid-data cases only tests a single parameter at a time, we can narrow the hunt for the bug down further. For example, if tests 1 to 6 gave the expected results but test 7 gave a result of −1 instead of the expected 29800 we would hypothesize that there is a bug with the section of the IF statement that tests the value of the parameter **second** (**second** has a boundary value in test 7).

The black-box approach is well suited to unit testing because it is reasonably straightforward to derive a representative set of test data. It is also known as *functional testing* because it is used to find errors in the functioning of a unit.

White-box Testing

Black-box testing simply shows that for a given set of inputs the program (or component) under test either behaves correctly or it does not. In white-box testing we use knowledge of how the program works to inform test case design. In theory we can devise a test plan that executes every program path at least once comparing the results with the expected output. But, there is a problem: if a program contains even a couple of loops (especially nested loops) then the number of unique paths that the program can take can become enormous. As Pressman (2004) observed, even a simple program with two nested loops and a few IF ... ELSE statements inside the inner loop might have as many as 10^{14} (i.e. 100,000,000,000,000) distinct paths or routes through it. If our computer could test 1,000,000 paths a second (a tall order I might add) then it would take over three years to follow every path.

We can use knowledge of the program's structure to define a set of paths that will ensure every branch and statement of the program is executed at least once. Although this is not as thorough as checking to see that every combination of statements is tested, it is at least a realistic proposition.[4] A white-box test, then, is one where the test cases are generated by taking account of the program structure in order to ensure that every statement in the program is executed. For this reason it is sometimes called *structural testing*. White-box methods generally use a Boolean algebra to define a set of directed- or flow-graphs of the program to be tested. Each directed graph specifies a path through the program and the set of directed graphs ensures all individual statements are executed. Some of the paths are combined using the Booleam algebra to derive the minimum set of test paths to achieve complete coverage of the program statements. There are several techniques used to calculate white-box test cases. Pressman (2004) gives a helpful discussion of a common method based on McCabe's Cyclomatic Complexity measure. King and Pardoe (1992) provide a useful tutorial for Structured Testing Method (STM) which can be used with programs that have been written using the Jackson Structured Programming method.

Whilst white-box testing is commonly used for system-level tests because it focuses on the structure rather than detailed function it can equally well be applied to unit testing; likewise black-box techniques can be applied at the system-testing level.

Acceptance Testing

Having completed the design and implementation tests it is time to test the system with the client or users present to check that it does what they expected it to do and in the way they want. For college assignments there is often no need for this aspect as the client is the professor who set the assignment!

16.6 Other Testing Strategies

In addition to these basic types of testing, sometimes more specialist strategies will be adopted. Systems that have high security requirements (e.g. banking and e-commerce systems) will usually undergo a phase of *security testing.* Security testing aims to expose vulnerabilities in the system that could be exploited by

---

[4] You may have wondered why some popular software gets released with bugs in it. If you consider that Microsoft Windows XP is compiled from around 40 million lines of code, it is not difficult to appreciate that the theoretical number of discrete paths through the system is ineffably large (kind of on the same order as saying that the universe is very big). It is impossible to test every combination of input data and statement ordering, so developers have to settle for a compromise. However good the compromise, it is still not exhaustive and so some bugs will always get through. Consider this. An organization that meets CMMI-5 (the highest level of the Software Engineering Institute's Capability Maturity Model for quality, (see `http://www.sei.cmu.edu/cmmi/`) should have an average bug rate of 0.001 percent, that is, 1 bug per thousand lines of code (Jones, 2000). The latest Windows Vista release is estimated to comprise around 50 million lines of code which means that if Microsoft were a CMMI-5 rated company even at this accepted high level of software quality, upon release Vista could contain 50,000 bugs! (see `http://blogs.borland.com/davidi/archive/2005/10/09/21652.aspx`).

people looking to compromise its security. Just as you can never completely secure your house against burglary, so computer systems are not totally invulnerable to attack. But, just like the house with good locks and other security systems, a well-secured software system will take longer to penetrate than is viable for the potential hacker who will look elsewhere for an easier target.

Performance testing is used to ensure that a system operates within its specified performance requirements. For example, an engine control system might need to check the temperature of the engine every 50 milliseconds to maintain safety: performance testing would check to see that this requirement is met.

Whilst it is unlikely to be critical if a simple calculator program crashes and loses your last few calculation steps, it is absolutely vital that a bank's accounting system does not lose any data should it fail for any reason. *Recovery testing* is the process of causing software to crash or fail in order to check that when it is restarted it has not lost any data and can continue its work where it left off. Recovery testing is closely related to *stress testing*. In the world of physical engineering, components are stress tested to find out at what point they will fail so that safe load and usage limits can be established. For example, if stress testing reveals that a new car engine tends to burn out if it exceeds 7000 RPM, limiters can be put in place to ensure the driver can never cause it to reach this point. Likewise, stress testing of software reveals under what loading and processing conditions a piece of software is likely to fail: we can find out just how many concurrent users a web server can support before it fails. If we know our web server system crashes if more than 10,000 people try to access it at once then we know it will need reinforcement if it is to be deployed in an online bookshop that can expect anything up to 15,000 simultaneous users.

16.7   Debugging or Defect Removal

There is some debate about whether debugging skill is innate or learned. It is possible that some people will always be better at debugging than others because they have an intuitive mind that just seems to be good at sniffing out clues. However, there is a great deal the programmer can do to improve his debugging skill. The presence of a bug can cause waves of terror in beginning programmers because they do not have a repertoire of typical error messages, error types, causes, and symptoms upon which they can draw to investigate the bug. But this is true of many jobs and professions: the car mechanic learns to diagnose faults through listening to the engine and observing the car's `behaviour`; a doctor gets taught a great many symptoms and disease indications at medical school but continually refines his skill by building up a repertoire of case histories. Experienced mechanics and doctors have learned to analyze symptoms and behaviour that direct them to likely candidate causes of failure or disease. The programmer similarly builds up a knowledge base of programming errors which he uses to track down bugs.

Hypothesis testing

Debugging is a hypothesis-testing exercise: the program demonstrates errant behaviour and the programmer uses knowledge of the program and past experience to hypothesize what and where the bug is. He then focuses on the section of code in question and employs a range of probing, inspection, and testing techniques to see if the bug is there: if it is he fixes it; if not he forms a new hypothesis. For example, consider a program that will read in a set of mobile telephone account balances and display on the screen the highest bill that has been run up and the number of accounts processed. The phone charges are held in an input file with one account record per line. Each line contains the telephone number (a 10-digit character string) and the outstanding balance in pence/cents (an integer). An end-of-data marker (a line that contains a phone number of ten 9s ("9999999999") and a balance of zero) terminates the file. An informal pseudo-code design for the body of the program is given as below as Example 16.3.

Example 16.3 Outline design for accounts program

```
Open input file ;
Initialize highest balance to -1 ;
Initialize counter to zero ;
Read first phone number and balance from file ;
WHILE end marker not reached
    IF balance is the highest so far
        Set highest balance to balance ;
    ENDIF
    Add 1 to counter ;
    Read next number and balance from file ;
ENDWHILE
Display highest balance ;
Display number of accounts processed ;
Close input file ;
```

Program 16.1 shows the algorithm implemented in Processing except that it contains one error. Note, Chapter 15 gave a basic tutorial on how to implement the algorithms and programs in this book in the Processing language which will allow you to experiment with getting programs to actually run on a computer. Table 16.6 shows the contents of the input file, the expected output that a correct version of the program would produce and the actual output generated by Program 16.1.

Study the outline design in Example 16.3 to get a feel for the intended logic of the program. You might like to step through the algorithm using the input data shown in column 1 of Table 16.6 to check that the outline design is correct. Once you are happy that the outline design is correct and you understand the relationship between the input data and the expected output (column 2 of Table 16.6) move on to studying the actual output (column 3 of Table 16.6) produced by the implementation in Program 16.1. What are the principal differences between the expected output and the actual output? What might be the cause? Look at the implementation (Program 16.1): Do you still have the same hypothesis about the error?

```
int balance,
    highest = -1,
    counter = 0;
String phoneNumber,
    temp ;
String line [] ;
String accountsFile = dataPath("accounts.txt") ;
try
    {
    BufferedReader file = new BufferedReader (new FileReader
                          (accountsFile)) ;
    line = split (file.readLine(), " ") ; // read a line from the
                                           file and split into 2
                                        // strings in line [0]
                                           // and line [1]

    phoneNumber = line [0] ;
    balance = Integer.parseInt(line [1]) ;
    while ((phoneNumber.compareTo("9999999999")!=0) && (balance !
        = 0))
        {
        if (balance > highest)
            highest = balance ;
        counter ++ ;
        println (phoneNumber + " " + balance) ;
        line = split (file.readLine(), " ") ;
        phoneNumber = line [0] ;
        balance = Integer.parseInt(line [1]) ;
        }
    println ("Highest charge is " + highest) ;
    println (counter + " accounts processed" ) ;
    file.close() ;
    }
catch (Exception e)
    {
    println ("Error" + e) ;
    }
```

Program 16.1
Account calcula-
tion written
in processing

The program appears only to be processing four of the accounts in the input file – at least, that is what the actual output indicates. In addition, and possibly as a consequence of this, the program is also incorrectly reporting the highest account balance to be 9300 instead of 9900.

What part of the program controls how many accounts are processed? Why is the program failing to process more than four accounts? Why does it seem to stop at the record containing the phone number "1912437614" and an account balance of 0? See if you can determine where and what the bug is. If you can, suggest a correction for it. The solution to this problem is given in section 16.9.

Table 16.6   **Finding the Bug in the Accounts Program**

Input File	Expected Output	Actual Output
5551234567 9300	5551234567 9300	5551234567 9300
2120009999 2199	2120009999 2199	2120009999 2199
3035554394 6750	3035554394 6750	3035554394 6750
1512312283 2200	0512312283 2200	0512312283 2200
1912437614 0	1912437614 0	Highest charge is 9300
1512274804 9900	1512274804 9900	4 accounts processed
1462527470 8721	1462527470 8721	
2024561414 0	2024561414 0	
2079250918 6850	2079250918 6850	
4959100766 2183	4959100766 2183	
1818118055 9875	1818118055 9875	
6955750089 7800	6955750089 7800	
4658752398 8200	4658752398 8200	
1117658894 6500	1117658894 6500	
9999999999 0	Highest charge is 9900	
	14 accounts processed	

Some have suggested that debugging is an innate skill which means that some people will always be better at it than others. However, this does not mean that if you are not one of the lucky few born debuggers that you cannot successfully debug programs. I have seen over quite a few years of teaching beginning programmers that once even a small bug repertoire has been built up and a methodical approach to debugging is adopted most programming students can achieve a good level of success in this area.

I said in Chapters 2 and 3 that ASSUMPTIONS are dangerous as they can lead to incorrectly-specified programs that do not do what the customer wanted. Likewise, the assumption is the enemy of good debugging: assuming you know what is causing a bug before you have carried out proper inspection and probing of the faulty program can lead you down a time-wasting dead-end at best, and to "fixing" the wrong piece of code at worst (thereby probably introducing even more bugs). In fact, debugging is often so badly done, that some have cynically called SOFTWARE MAINTENANCE the art of replacing one bug by another (or even two). Some programming 'experts' (beware the smug expert) suggest that debugging is so hard that it is more of an arcane art form that can only be properly carried out by the lucky few possessed of enough insight and intelligence to probe the mysteries of the gossamer web that is programming logic. Utter rubbish! Whilst debugging large systems can be mind-numbingly tedious and hair-tearingly frustrating, there are strategies you can use that, if followed, will give you a fighting chance of locating and repairing your bugs.

Tell it to the Teddy Bear

There is not room in this book to cover debugging strategies exhaustively. A good starting point though (which is also often an ending point when done properly) is to carry out a desk trace of the suspect code. For small sections of code with loops that iterate only a few times, desk tracing is a very effective way to inspect code for errors. There is a danger though that because you wrote the program you may be letting the same assumptions that led to you introduce a defect in the first place cause you to misinterpret the way your code actually behaves, thereby still not spotting the defect. This is why it can be a good idea to have somebody else do your desk traces for you – they did not write the code and so may not be blind to its defects. In fact, the simple act of showing the code to someone else can reveal a defect without the need to do a trace. I have often witnessed a bewildered student call me over for help with a program only to watch them discover the error for themselves while explaining the problem to me. Explaining the problem to someone else is a very effective debugging tool. Brian Kernighan (one of the inventors of C) and Rob Pike described a university programming course in which the computer lab had a teddy bear in one corner (Kernighan and Pike, 1999). Students were forbidden from approaching any of the teaching assistants for help until they had first described their problem to the teddy bear. Apparently, the tactic was very effective. There is something about articulating a difficulty to someone else that causes us to think more precisely about the problem (we have to be precise and clear in our language or the other person will not understand) which, in turn, can give us the insight we were looking for. Actually, all this does is take us back to step 1 of the *HTTLAP* strategy: explaining a problem out loud often gives us greater understanding of it.

Expect the Unexpected and Insert a Probe

Looking carefully at the output of a program can give clues to the nature and location of a defect. Sometimes a variable will take an unexpectedly large (or small) value.

Consider the Processing code in Program 16.2. The program reads in sales values from a file "sales.dat" which contains the four integer values 1000, 15,000, 16,000, 12,000. An integer variable **totalSales** is used to maintain a running total of the sales values read in from the file. The **while** loop keeps accumulating the total and reading new sales figures until the end of the file is reached (**ready()** is a Java method that returns False when the file has no more data left to read). After all the values in the file have been processed, the total sales value is displayed on the screen. Read through Program 16.2 and write down the value of **totalSales** that the **println** statement should write to the screen.

```
String fileName = dataPath('list.txt') ;
short salesValue, // short data type stores values between -32,768
                  // and +32,767
       totalSales = 0 ;
```

```
try
  {
    BufferedReader file = new BufferedReader(new
                          FileReader(fileName)) ;
    while (file.ready()) // file.ready() effectively means
                         // 'not-end-of-file'
      {
      // readLine returns a String object. We can turn this into a
      // short by sending it to the parseShort method of the Short
      // class which will take a String object and return a short
         value
      salesValue = Short.parseShort(file.readLine());
      totalSales += salesValue ;
      println (salesValue) ;
      }
    println ("The total sales were " + totalSales) ;
    }
catch (Exception e)
    {
    println ("Error" + e) ;
    }
```

Program 16.2

Sales figures

Given that the program reads four values (1000, 15,000, 16,000, and 12,000) we would expect total Sales to have the value 44,000 (1000 + 15,000 + 16,000 + 12,000). However, when I compiled and ran the program it gave the following output:

The total sales were −21536.

What went wrong? The answer −21536 is quite unexpected as adding four positive numbers should not give a negative result. What is causing this problem?

Try a desk trace of the program. Did you get −21,536 or 44,000? It is likely you got 44,000 because the error in this program is more subtle than an incorrect arithmetic statement.

Where are we now? We have checked the program with a desk trace which appears to produce the expected results, so we do not believe the algorithm logic is wrong. Yet when it executes the program produces the wrong answer. Let's see if we can narrow it down to a particular statement. We shall use an older debugging trick called a *probe*. Probes are statements that are inserted into the program to inspect variables as the program is running. I shall put in a display probe that writes the value of total Sales to the screen every time it is updated after its initialization. The probe statement is shown in bold type in Program 16.3 below.

```
String fileName = DataPath dataPath("list.txt");
short salesValue, // short data type stores values between -32,768
                  // and +32,767
      totalSales = 0 ;
```

```
try
    {
    BufferedReader file = new BufferedReader(new
                           FileReader(fileName)) ;
    while (file.ready()) // file.ready() effectively means
                         // 'not-end-of-file'
        {
        // readLine returns a String object. We can turn this into a
        // short by sending it to the parseShort method of the Short
        // class which will take a String object and return a short
           value
        salesValue = Short.parseShort(file.readLine());
        totalSales += salesValue ;
        println (salesValue) ;
        println ("totalSales is " + totalSales) ;
        }
    println ("The total sales were " + totalSales) ;
    }
catch (Exception e)
    {
    println ("Error" + e) ;
    }
```

Program 16.3
Sales figures
with debugging
probe

When run, the amended program produces the output shown in Figure 16.1.

FIGURE 16.1   **Output from debugging probe**

```
1000
totalSales is 1000
15000
totalSales is 16000
16000
totalSales is 32000
12000
totalSales is -21536
The total sales were -21536
```

? Think Spot

Everything is fine until the fourth value of 12,000 is added to totalSales at which point instead of going from 32,000 to 44,000 totalSales changes from 32,000 to −21,536. What can cause an integer variable to suddenly change from a large positive value to a large negative value? In Processing/Java, the short data type stores 16-bit signed integer values between −32,768 and +32,767. The reason I chose to use short is that none of the individual sales values was larger than 32,767. Thus when the program adds 12,000 to totalSales its value exceeds 32,767 and so wraps around into the negative range giving an overflow error. To correct is simple: I just change the program so that totalSales is the larger 32-bit int integer type (which can store values between −2,147,483 648 and +2,147,483,647,32). The revised program with changes shown in bold is given below as Program 16.4.

```
// Program SalesFigures
// Paul Vickers, December 21, 2007
String fileName = dataPath("list.txt") ;
short salesValue ; // short data type stores values between
                   //  -32,768 and +32,767
long totalSales = 0 ;
try
   {
   BufferedReader file = new BufferedReader(new
                          FileReader(fileName)) ;
   while (file.ready()) // file.ready() effectively means
                        // "not-end-of-file"
      {
      // readLine returns a String object. We can turn this into a
      // short by sending it to the parseShort method of
         the Short
      // class which will take a String object and return
                 a short value
      salesValue = Short.parseShort(file.readLine());
      totalSales += salesValue ;
      println ("totalSales is " + totalSales) ;
      println (salesValue) ;
      }
   println ("The total sales were " + totalSales) ;
   }
catch (Exception e)
   {
   println ("Error" + e) ;
   }
```

Program 16.4
Corrected
sales figure
program?

The use of probes is very common and is a useful debugging aid. An alternative, if you are using a compiler environment that supports it, is to use step-and-trace techniques, variable "watches" and breakpoints. A step-and-trace facility enables the programmer to execute the program a line (or sub-program) at a time and to inspect the state of the program's data (a "watch") without having to insert probes. A breakpoint is marker that is inserted into the program that causes the development environment to stop execution of the program when the breakpoint is reached – the program can then be inspected and traced through as desired. Breakpoints are very useful for skipping over sections of code that we know (or believe) to be correct. If you have a compiler environment that offers step-and-trace and breakpoint facilities, then I strongly suggest that you experiment with them because they are extremely helpful tools.

One Step at a Time

When looking for defects, it is tempting to try to correct more than one problem at a time, or to correct a single problem by amending several possible suspect lines of code. The danger with this approach is that because you are changing more than one thing at a time, how will you know which change solved the problem? A good programmer will change only one thing at a time and will carefully note the changes in behaviour after each amendment. This way you can be more confident that when the defect finally goes away it was for the right reason. Changing more than one thing may mean that although the defect you were looking for is fixed, another bug is inadvertently dropped in. Take your debugging one step at a time. You need more patience for this approach but it is a much safer way and leads to higher quality programs.

More Debugging Strategies

In addition to the desk traces, probes, and checking one thing at a time, there are other techniques that programmers can use to help locate and fix defects. In his very readable little book *Debugging: The 9 Indispensable Rules for Finding Even the Most Elusive Software and Hardware Problems*, David Agans (2002) offers some simple but very useful guidance on debugging. His nine rules are really just applied common sense, but applied within a coherent and well-grounded framework. Common sense is much under-used and it is surprising how easy it is for common sense to fly out of the window when we are engaged in a vexing bug detection and fixing exercise. Here are Agans' nine rules of debugging:

1. Understand the system.
2. Make it fail.
3. Quit thinking and look.
4. Divide and conquer.
5. Change one thing at a time.
6. Keep an audit trail.
7. Check the plug.
8. Get a fresh view.
9. If you did not fix it, it ain't fixed.

You can see that we have already been using some of these rules: we have worked for understanding (rule 1), we have suggested showing the program to someone else (rule 8) and we have suggested changing only one thing at a time (rule 5). Not all the rules will have to be followed in all cases. Take #7, *check the plug*: if your TV stops working then after having ensured that it is not due to a power cut, you would not take the back off straight away and starting poking around inside. The first thing I would do is check the plug – perhaps the fuse has blown, or one of the wires has come loose. If the plug is at fault no manner of circuit testing inside the TV would have got the TV working. Sometimes, though, "checking the plug" is much more complicated when it comes to software. Agans recounts the story of a colleague who spent weeks trying to locate an error in the code when, in fact, it was the compiler that had the bug. Remember, ASSUMPTIONS are dangerous: just because the compiler was produced by Mega Software Wizard Compilers Inc., does not mean it is bug free. I once had a colleague who was smart and *did* remember to check the plug and actually found a bug in a compiler produced by one of the biggest computer manufacturers of the time. Of course, I would not expect beginning programmers to be able to track down bugs in the compiler!

Whilst some problems are solved by applying just one or two of Agans' rules, others will require starting at #1 and working through the list until the defect is located and removed. You might be able to see some similarity between the nine rules and our own *HTTLAP* strategy for programming: they both begin with gaining understanding. It is surprising how many times even experienced programmers neglect to do this when looking for bugs (often they assume the system works in a particular way). Working for understanding does not just apply when writing the program but when debugging it. If it is not working, make sure you understand how all the bits of the program fit together and how they relate back to the design and how the design relates back to the original problem statement.

There is not room in this book to go into Agans' nine rules in detail, especially as Agans has done it rather well himself in his own book. So, at this point I would refer you to his book which is an excellent way to continue your introduction to debugging.

16.8 Documentation for the Bewildered

If Oscar Wilde had been a programmer he might have observed that there is only one thing worse than not doing documentation and that is doing documentation badly. Documentation is something of a Cinderella in the software world. Programmers hate to write it, users hate to read it, and maintenance programmers curse it because it is non-existent, too superficial to be of any use, or inaccurate. In the mid 1980s Donald Knuth proposed that writing programs should be like writing a piece of literature because literature is aimed at human readers. It is humans that debug and maintain programs, so Knuth argued that programs should be made as easy to read as possible. He proposed a method called *Literate Programming* which combined programming language syntax with a documentation language. The result, he argued, was programs that are "more robust, more portable, more easily maintained, and arguably more fun to write than programs that are written only in a high-level language".[5] Knuth's original article appeared in *The Computer Journal* in 1984, but you can find a reprint of the article in his 1992 book *Literate Programming* (Knuth, 1992).

The thing about documentation is that many programmers do not really know why they write it. Some appreciate its importance for assisting with debugging and maintenance, but do not know what good documentation comprises. Beginning programmers on university courses tend to be working to very tight assignment deadlines and when faced with the choice between getting their program to work and writing good documentation usually choose the former.

I could go on at length about the importance and value of good documentation, the professional imperative for producing it, and the benefit to those who consume it, but this book is targeted at the bewildered programmer. Once you are competent at understanding and solving problems and expressing those solutions in programming language syntax then I think you will benefit from learning about the different kinds of software documentation. Until then, I believe we should concentrate on writing the kinds of documentation that will help *you*, the beginning programmer. The following sections will not cover the more traditional aspects of software documentation but will focus on those features that will help you to understand the

---

[5] http:// www-cs-faculty.stanford.edu/~knuth/lp.html.

problems you are trying to solve and to better understand the solutions you have written. One aim of documentation for the bewildered is to make sure that when you pick up a program you wrote a month, six months, or even a year ago, you will still be able to understand what it does and how it works. It is no good coming up with an inventive way of solving a particular type of problem if the next time you encounter this type of problem you have to start over because you cannot understand the earlier solution and so are unable to adapt it to the current situation. We will write documentation for us: Assume that any program you write you will file away as part of your programming repertoire to be retrieved at a later date and brought to bear on a new problem. If you are unable to learn from your earlier programs because you can no longer understand them or why you wrote them a certain way then your future programming efforts will take longer than they ought.

We will focus on two aspects of documentation. Steps 5 and 6 of the *HTTLAP* strategy deal specifically with documentation. Step 5, "describing what you have learned", is concerned with reflecting upon the problem solving process noting the main achievements and the difficulties faced. In Step 6, "documenting the solution", we aim to add explanatory text to the solution to make it as easy to understand as possible. In the following sections we will explore these two steps and see how documentation can help us both understand our solutions better now, and ensure that those solutions will be a learning resource for us in the future. Both types of documentation will help to build your repertoire of programming and debugging knowledge and skill. If you write down the lessons you learned today you can draw upon those lessons tomorrow. First we will discuss the *HTTLAP* documentation requirements and then I will present a complete set of documentation for a problem.

Describing What You Have Learned

Step 5 of *HTTLAP* is principally a reflective exercise. By thinking about what you have learned during a programming task you are helping to consolidate and organize that learning in your own mind as well as providing a permanent resource that you can draw upon in the future. Writing down your achievements and difficulties will draw out aspects of the task that are still unclear to you; it is only when writing something down that we know whether we really understand it. The first pair of questions in step 5 is:

Q. What did you learn from this exercise? What do you know now that you did not know before you started?

> This is an important question as it addresses programming repertoire. Each new programming problem will either consolidate and reinforce existing knowledge or teach you some new skill; either way, learning takes place. It is good for your morale to document your progress. Too often, because programming remains a struggle over the weeks of a course, the bewildered programmer thinks he or she has not learned anything and becomes discouraged. When you write down every little thing that you have learned you may be surprised at just how much knowledge you have picked up along the way. For instance, you may have learned how and when to construct a FOR loop; knowing the difference between the various iteration constructs is a major step forward for the beginning programmer, and so it is important to document each achievement no matter how insignificant it seems at the time.

A programming problem may shed new light on something you thought you already understood quite well. Take, for example, the overflow problem we dealt with earlier on. After fixing the defect by changing the type of the `totalSales` variable you could write down that you have learned about overflow errors and how to fix them.

In the future, you can look back at this documentation to refresh your memory about the problems you faced and how you solved them. Eventually, this knowledge will become incorporated into your long-term memory adding to your programming repertoire. In the meantime, while acquiring the experience needed to form these long-term memories, the documentation serves to ensure that the lessons learned are not forgotten.

Q. What particular difficulties did you encounter? Were there any aspects of the problem that caused you especial difficulty? If so, do you think you would know how to tackle them if you met something similar in the future?

This group of questions is not wholly different from the last and is intended to tease out the remaining lessons. The first question was explicitly concerned with the positive lessons learned, whilst this group focuses on the negative aspects of the learning experience, that is, what was difficult about the problem. Here you should aim to describe the difficulties as precisely as you can. Ideally, you should describe any particular error symptoms you encountered together with your diagnosis and solution. In this way you are building up your debugging repertoire that will help you fix defects in future programs.

Finally, step 5 asks us to:

Q. Compare your finished solution with your first attempt. What do the differences teach you?

It can be instructive to see how your finished solution differs from your initial attempt. If you have had trouble answering the first two groups of questions in step 5 this group will help. If the finished solution is different in any way from your first attempt then that indicates some learning or critical analysis has taken place along the way. Was the finished version different because the first attempt was incorrect? If so, how was it incorrect and how did you discover that? Did the deficiencies of the first version highlight misunderstandings you had about the problem or the use of the programming syntax? What you are aiming for in this task is to identify what you have learned – these lessons then become part of your programming and debugging repertoire.

Documenting the Solution

Where step 5 of *HTTLAP* deals with what you have learned, step 6 focuses on making sure your problem solution is clear and well explained. The first group of questions is:

Q. Are there any aspects of your solution that are hard to understand? Is this because they are badly written, or simply because the solution is just complicated?

To answer these questions you need to critically analyze your own work. If part of the solution is hard for you to understand (bearing in mind that you wrote it), could that be because you have expressed the solution in an unclear way?

Sometimes, we deliberately write code that is not transparent for efficiency or other reasons. In that case we must ensure that the difficult-to-follow code is really well explained so that six months down the line you will still be able to amend the program if needed. Here is an example. A few years back I wrote a system that incorporated the control of a MIDI music synthesizer on the computer's sound card.[6] To play musical sequences a procedure was needed that would wait for a period of time specified as a musical length (e.g. a crotchet or quarter note, a half-note or semibreve, etc.). The musical length had to be converted into a period in milliseconds the length of which depended on the tempo (speed) of the music. Program 16.5 shows the Wait function I wrote to solve the problem. Note, the original was written in Turbo Pascal but Program 16.5 presents the code in Processing to make it more current.

Program 16.5

A Processing
wait function

```
void Wait (int length, int bpm)
{
/*
   Delay for 'duration' milliseconds.
   Parameter 'length' = duration of musical event in terms of
   clicks.
*/
int duration ;
duration = length * 625 % bpm ;
delay (duration) ;
}
```

You can see that there are only three lines of code in the function. The first declares the variable duration. The second is an assignment statement that calculates the period to wait and the third passes this duration to the library function delay which causes the program to halt for the required number of milliseconds. Look at the assignment statement that calculates the duration. It is written that way because I wanted to keep all the calculations in the integer domain to save rounding errors caused by converting to real numbers and back again. As a result it is not at all clear how this statement relates to the problem. To make certain that I could still understand in the future how this function worked (in case I needed to change it), I elaborated the function with some documentation. The documented version is shown in Program 16.6. Note that the lines between the function's header line and the declaration of duration are all commentary (the /* and */ delimit multi-line comments in Processing).

```
void Wait (int length, int bpm)
{
/*
   Delay for 'duration' milliseconds.
   Parameter 'length'  = duration of musical event in terms of
                   clicks.
```

---

[6] MIDI, or Musical Instrument Digital Interface, is a set of software and hardware protocols to enable different sound-generating devices (e.g. musical keyboards, computer sound cards, musical software programs, and so on) to communicate with each other. You can get detailed information about the latest MIDI standard at http:// www.midi.org.

```
    Parameter 'bpm' = the tempo expressed as beats-per-minute
    The resolution chosen is such that a crotchet takes 96 clicks
    or time units.
    A quaver is hence 48 clicks and a minim 192.
    The actual duration of an event depends on 3 factors:
        1) The chosen tempo of the music, given as bpm (beats per
            minute) which is, in effect, the number of crotchets per
            minute.
        2) The relative length of the event (e.g. a quaver, crotchet
            triplet).
        3) The number of resolution pulses per crotchet (given as 96).
    Given that there are 60,000 msecs in a minute, the real-time
    duration of an event can be given by:

    duration = (event_length / pulses_per_crotchet) * (60000 /
                beats_per_minute)

    event_length / pulses_per_crotchet gives the relative duration
    in terms of beats of the event.

    60000 / beats_per_minute gives the number of msecs per crotchet.
    Multiplying the two expressions gives the actual event duration
    in msecs.

    The expression can be rearranged to give:-

    duration = length * 60000 / pulses / bpm

    Because the processing is to be done in real time, an efficiency
    gain can be made from the serendipitous fact that 600000 / 96 =
    625. Hence the expression now reads:-

    duration = length * 625 / bpm.
*/

int duration ;

duration = length * 625 % bpm ;
delay (duration) ;
}
```

Program 16.6
Documented
version of
wait

Three lines of executable code are supported by 30 lines of documentation. However, if I need to make changes to the function I can read the documentation to find out how it works and thus how to change it. Other times the solution might just be needlessly complex in which case it is better to recognize it and see if the offending code can be rewritten in a clearer or simpler way.

The final question in step 6 is:

Q. **If you were to pick up your solution in five years' time do you think any bits would be hard to understand?**

This question follows on from the previous one and is reinforcing the point that we *must* address hard-to-understand programs. If you think any aspects of the program would be hard to understand in the future then you should identify those aspects and make sure they are clearly documented.

Documentation for the bewildered, then, is not traditional program documentation as taught on computer science courses and in text books. Rather, it aims to document the programs so that you, the learner, can understand your own work better, take stock of the lessons learned during the programming process, and build up a repertoire of knowledge and skill that you can draw upon in future problem-solving exercises.

16.9   Solution to Telephone Accounts Processing Problem

Before we move on, it remains to fix the defect in the telephone account processing program from Section 16.7. The bug in the program is caused by a common novice programmer error. Many beginning programmers tend to use their natural language understanding of a program when solving a problem (Bonar and Soloway, 1985) as they have not yet learned the difference between natural language and the more precise logic of programming languages. This is especially so when trying to write code involving compound Boolean expressions. The way that words like "and" and "or" are used in natural language, to the novice, can make their precise use in programming languages appear counterintuitive. The accounts processing program contains a bug I have seen many times in learners' programs. The WHILE loop was required to process telephone records as long as the phone number was not "9999999999" and the account balance was not zero. This requirement was expressed in Processing (Program 16.1) as

```
while (phoneNumber != '9999999999' && balance != 0)
```

In the *HTTLAP* pseudo-code this would be:

```
WHILE (phoneNumber ≠ '9999999999') AND (balance ≠ 0)
```

The program requirement was expressed in natural language as "the WHILE loop was required to process phone records as long as the phone number was not "9999999999" and the balance was not zero'. Notice how the requirement description uses the word 'and' to link the two conditions. After all, this sounds very natural: process the file while the phone number is not equal to "9999999999" and the balance is not zero. Unfortunately, we have carried this natural language use of "and" over to the implementation where it causes the program to stop processing phone records as soon as a balance of zero is encountered. The truth table in Table 16.7 shows this clearly.

From Table 16.7 we see that a record with a phone number that is not "9999999999" and a balance that is not 0 (e.g. "5551234567", 9300) causes the WHILE condition to be True and the loop to continue. However, notice how all three of the remaining combinations cause the loop to terminate, including the case where a real phone number ("1912437614") has a legitimate balance of zero (perhaps no phone calls were made). Although the WHILE condition sounds right

Table 16.7 **Truth Table for '(**phoneNumber **≠ ZZZZZZZZZ') AND (balance ≠ 0)'**

phoneNumber	balance	p	q	P AND q	Comments
5551234567	9300	True	True	True	Loop continues
9999999999	0	False	False	False	Loop terminates
9999999999	9900	False	True	False	Loop terminates
1912437614	0	True	False	False	Loop terminates!

q = phoneNumber ≠ 'ZZZZZZZZZ'
p = balance ≠ 0

in English, it terminates when *either* the phone number is "9999999999" *or* the balance is zero rather than when *both* the phone number is "9999999999" and the balance is zero. So, what should the correct condition be? Start by writing down the condition that is true when the terminating record is read:

(phoneNumber = '9999999999') AND (balance = 0)

That is, we know we have reached the end of the input data because the phone number is '9999999999' and the balance is zero. We want the loop to continue while this condition is not met (i.e. we have not reached the terminating record) which gives us the following WHILE statement:

WHILE NOT ((phoneNumber = '9999999999') AND (balance = 0))

Alternatively, we could apply De Morgan's laws to transform

(phoneNumber = '9999999999') AND (balance = 0)

into

(phoneNumber ≠ '9999999999') OR (balance ≠ 0)

which gives us the WHILE statement:

WHILE (phoneNumber ≠ '9999999999') OR (balance ≠ 0)

The conditions "NOT ((phoneNumber = '9999999999') AND (balance = 0))" and "(phoneNumber ≠ '9999999999') OR (balance ≠ 0)" are logically equivalent and either could be used.

Trace through the program again but this time substituting either of these conditions for the incorrect one in the program; convince yourself (using a truth table) that the bug has been fixed.

Retesting is vital: if you do not retest a program after correcting a bug, how will you be sure you have corrected it, or that you have not inadvertently introduced another bug? It is very important not to skip this stage.

16.10   Further Reading

Testing and Debugging

1. There used to be a nice little book about tracking down errors in software. It was called *The Software Sleuth* by Martin and Burton Kaliski (Kaliski and Kaliski, 1991). It appears to be out-of-print now, but if you come across a copy it is well worth a look. It has sample bugs in programs written in a variety of programming languages and so gives you insight into some of the pitfalls of different languages.

2. A more recent book in the same vein is Adam Barr's *Find The Bug: A Book of Incorrect Programs* (Barr, 2004).

3. I have already talked about David Agans' entertaining book *Debugging: The 9 Indispensable Rules for Finding Even the Most Elusive Software and Hardware Problems* (Agans, 2002) which I heartily recommend to experienced and inexperienced programmers alike.

4. If you want a very structured approach to writing programs that aims to get the programmer to continually improve his practice, then Watts Humphrey's *Introduction to the Personal Software Process* (Humphrey, 1997) is a strongly recommended read. Humphrey sets out some very practical steps and techniques which, if followed, have been shown to improve a programmer's skill and expertise. The Personal Software Process is independent of any programming language and is generally applicable. Heartily recommended.

Documentation

5. Documentation often gets overlooked during the programming process and it likewise suffers in the publishing world. Browse through any publisher's software development catalog and you will find very few titles dedicated to this important aspect. At the start of this section I mentioned Donald Knuth's literate programming approach. His book (Knuth, 1992) is a good place to start in appreciating an alternative view of software development and documentation. Sylvio Levy and Donald Knuth's *The CWEB System of Structured Documentation* (Knuth and Levy, 1994) describes a system for writing literate programs in C.

6. Watts Humphrey's *Introduction to the Personal Software Process* (Humphrey, 1997) is also a very effective documentation-oriented method for writing software. Humphrey's approach is designed specifically to aid the programmer in improving his or her performance and skill. This is a good book to read once you have moved from the bewildered phase into the competent beginner's stage.

16.11   Chapter Summary

In this chapter you learned about testing, debugging, and documentation. Specifically, you learned about the importance of testing the programs you write and how to go about it using a combination of design testing and implementation testing (black-box and white-box). Testing reveals errors (bugs) so you also learned how to go about locating and removing bugs from your programs. Finally, you learned how to document your work so that other programmers could pick it up and carry on working with it.

16.12 Exercises

1. In the solution to the accounts processing bug problem above we stated that the conditions "NOT ((phoneNumber = '9999999999') AND (balance = 0))" and "(phoneNumber ≠ '9999999999') OR (balance ≠ 0)" are logically equivalent and either could be used to form the WHILE statement. Show that they are equivalent by drawing truth tables.

2. Take one of your solutions to an exercise from three or four earlier chapters and produce documentation using the guidelines outlined in this chapter.

3. Humphrey (1997) suggested that reading through your design before you code it and through your code before you compile it is a more efficient method for finding defects than testing the program once it has been compiled. Give some reasons for why this might be so. Why should reading your code be more effective than employing one of the many software testing strategies?

16.13 Projects

For all five projects you should now:

1. Fully document your completed solutions.
2. Devise test plans to ensure the algorithms are correct. Remember to include details of the test data to be used together with the expected results.
3. Carry out your test plans noting down the results.
4. If any tests resulted in incorrect or unexpected values employ the debugging techniques to a) ensure unexpected results were not as a result of your expectations being faulty! and b) debug the programs. Then repeat the testing.

This chapter is entirely optional. It contains my own observations and opinions about some current programming practices (e.g. variable initialization, functional decomposition, and others). I have also included more-detailed explanations of some concepts that I felt would have broken up the flow of the main body. All sections in this chapter are referred to at various points in the main text by words in SMALL CAPITAL LETTERS. Feel free to dip into this chapter whenever you like (or even not at all).

Abstract Data Type

The abstract data type, or ADT, is a mathematical specification of a set of data and the operations that can be performed upon that data. The important feature of an ADT is that it is specified *independent* of any particular implementation. Here is an example. We could define a stack (think of a stack of plates), X onto which a value, n, can be pushed or from which a value, n, can be popped. We can define operations to create a new stack, push an item onto the stack, and pop an item off the top of the stack. The data items belonging to an ADT can only be accessed by the defined operations which means that the internal workings (the implementation) of the ADT can be changed without affecting anything outside it (as long as the changes do not cause it to stop working). ADTs are foundational in the construction of object-oriented programs.

Abstraction

There are two principal kinds of abstraction in programming: data abstractions and control abstractions. Data abstractions are concerned with the properties of data: what values can be stored and what operations can be performed upon those values. Control abstractions are to do with how the flow of control (the execution) of the program is controlled. Sequences, selections, and iterations are all control abstractions. Each programming language implements data and control abstractions in a particular way. When understanding problems we work at quite a high level of abstraction: we think of loops and numbers. When designing algorithms we work at a lower level of abstraction: in this book we dealt with ranges of numbers and three different ways of expressing a loop. When translating algorithms into programming language code we work at an even lower level of abstraction: we differentiate between whole and fractional numbers, letters, strings of letters, and other kinds of data item. We even distinguish between different sizes of whole numbers. What you must learn to do to think like a programmer is manage different abstraction levels, and often *at the same time*.

Acronym

Computing is full of acronyms. BASIC is an acronym as are COBOL and FORTRAN. An acronym is a new word made up from or based upon the initial letters or syllables of a compound word or phrase. Thus *laser* is an acronym of **l**ight **a**mplification by **st**imulated **e**mission of **r**adiation and *radar* of **ra**dio **d**etection **a**nd **r**anging. Many people confuse acronyms with abbreviations which are also rife in computing. CPU is a three-letter abbreviation of central processing unit. There are so many three-letter abbreviations in computing that they are known as TLAs. People mistakenly think this stands for "three-letter acronym", but it does not, as it does not form a word (well, maybe it is a word in Klingon, but not in English). If TLA is an abbreviation of three-letter abbreviation, is acronym itself an acronym? Lawrence Hannay who worked in the IBM Labs at Hursley Park, England once told me that acronym stands for **a**lphabetically **c**onsistent **r**epresentation of **n**eologically **y**clept **m**agniloquence. That is so good it just deserves to be true, and yes, they are all real words – look them up if you do not believe me.

The point of this reflection? Only that there are many acronyms and abbreviations to learn. Knowing the difference between an acronym and an abbreviation shows an eye for detail worthy of a programmer.

Assumptions

We make assumptions every day. We assume that we will get to work or to college safely. We assume our home will still be there when we get back. Life would unbearable if we couldn't take things for granted. But this can be disastrous for software developers. Manny Lehman estimated that, on average, in every ten lines of program code there lies buried one programmer-made assumption. Assumptions are made when the programmer fails to fully understand the problem, its requirements, and the real world in which it is situated. Software development methods that lead you to question your decisions are more helpful in reducing assumptions than those that do not. See DYSFUNCTIONAL DECOMPOSITION.

The Ariane 5 was the famously explosive successor to the Ariane 4, and cost more than $7 billion to develop. Much of the navigation control software was reused from the earlier Ariane 4 system (see REUSABILITY). The failure happened when the guidance computer received a horizontal bias value much larger than it had been programmed to deal with. The problem lay in a piece of code that translated a 64-bit floating-point value into a 16-bit integer. The designers of the Ariane 4 calculated that the horizontal bias could never be so large as to require more than 16 bits to store it. Consequently, no *exception handler* to trap values larger than the 16-bit limit was included in the software as no such error could ever occur. (An exception handler is a special section of code that is executed when unexpected values (exceptions) occur – it will trap the rogue value and cause remedial action to take place, for example by either correcting the value or safely shutting the system down.) This guidance software was copied unmodified into the Ariane 5. It was assumed it would work as it had worked fine in the Ariane 4. The trouble was, the Ariane 5 was a more powerful and faster rocket than its predecessor and *could* generate horizontal bias values larger than could fit in a 16-bit signed integer. The result was that the bias value overflowed its storage, the software routine failed, the computers crashed, and the rocket self-destructed destroying $500 million worth of uninsured satellites in the process (Quinn, 2004). Ouch. If you are interested, you can read the whole story in the European Space Agency's enquiry board report (Lions, 1996).

Bag

An easier way of carrying the character tiles around (Chapter 9) would be to put them into a paper bag. So why do we need a string? Because a paper bag enforces no ordering on the characters. In set theory terms, a bag is an unordered collection of items that permits duplicate values. A mathematical set is also unordered, but does not permit duplicates. For example, inserting the character tiles 'D', 'o', 'd', 'o' into an empty set would give the set {'D', 'd', 'o'}.[1] Inserting the same characters into an empty bag would give {'D', 'd', 'o', 'o'}. We can think of a bag as being like a paper bag: you can put things in, in any order, even duplicates, but cannot say anything about the order in which they may come out. If you have played Scrabble you will be familiar with this idea – the cloth bag holds all the tiles. Shaking it up means that when you reach in you do not know which tiles are going to come out. There are also duplicates letters in Scrabble. If we were writing a Scrabble game program we might choose to use a bag data structure to hold all the available tiles.

Computer Error

There is no such thing as computer error, only programming error. One phrase I hate hearing when something goes wrong is that the fault is due to computer error. There is really no such thing. Computers only produce wrong results because their programs are in error. The only real computer error is if the electronic components breakdown, the hard disc crashes, etc. The rest are all defects introduced by programmers.

Constructor Invocation

Think Spot

The constructor with one parameter invokes the `Player` constructor with two parameters passing on the single argument it received and adding an empty string for the second argument. The second constructor with two parameters then gets called and does its thing. Why do this instead of simply writing the assignments inside the first constructor? The reason is that when you have multiple constructors, they are all likely to be doing similar things. So, the actions that are common are only put in the constructor with the largest number of parameters and

---

[1] In mathematics, sets are shown as lists of values separated by commas within a pair of braces {}. The values are also normally shown in their ordinal sequence. We say the set is unordered inasmuch as it does not matter what order things are placed into the set, it will still look the same. Thus, inserting 1, 2, 3 into an empty set gives {1, 2, 3}, and inserting 3, 1, 2 into an empty set also gives the set {1, 2, 3}. So, our set of characters is shown as {'D', 'd', 'o'} because in computing the upper-case letters come before the lower-case ones in the character set. Notice the use of the word "set" here – it is called the *character set* because it shows *all* the allowable characters once only (no duplicates).

this is called by the other constructors which substitute default values as appropriate for the missing parameters. This simplifies the code and avoids the problem of, say, correctly assigning a Player's name in the second constructor but writing the assignment statement incorrectly in the first constructor.

Coupling and Cohesion

Coupling is a term that defines the level to which functions, procedures, methods, units, modules, and programs are interconnected and mutually dependent. It is said that modules (and by that I mean all forms of sub-program) should be functionally independent and should perform only a single function. Coupling allows modules to share data and reduces functional independence. Programmers strive for the lowest coupling possible, but that does not mean we can aim for zero coupling. There are several ways modules can be coupled, but in terms of this book, consideration of the following three will suffice:

- Allowing modules to share values by providing direct access to their internal data. This is known as *pathological coupling* (yes, really!).
- Allowing modules to share values by giving them access to global data, that is, data defined and stored outside the modules and to which they have full access. This technique is known as *global-data coupling.*
- Allowing modules to share values through parameter passing. That is, values are transferred from one module to another, but it up to the receiving module how it allows these values to affect its own internal data. This is known as *data coupling* and is the preferred mechanism for coupling modules. If you have read Chapters 7 and 14 on object-oriented programming then you will see that defining methods to update and return an object's internal data is a way of enforcing data coupling.

A term often discussed alongside coupling is *cohesion.* If a programmer strives to achieve low coupling (or rather, maximum use of data coupling where coupling is necessary), he also aims to achieve *high* cohesion. Cohesion is a measure of the functional independence of a module, that is, the degree to which the parts of a module are associated with each other in terms of the function the module carries out. It also applies to the way in which each *module* is related to the other modules in a system. High cohesion is where each part of a module is functionally related, and low cohesion is where its parts are arbitrarily grouped together. The highest form of cohesion, known as *functional cohesion*, means that all the parts of a module (and all modules within a unit, and so on) contribute to the single goal of that module; that is, they all work together towards carrying out a single task. At the lowest end of the cohesion scale is *coincidental cohesion* where parts of a module do not have any functional relationship to each other. For example, you might have a few useful functions that you use a lot in your programs, say a currency converter function and a Celsius to Fahrenheit converter. If you grouped these together in a module (or package) called, say, UsefulUtilities, this module would have low cohesion for its two functions have no relationship to each other. In a system with high cohesion you would have all your currency-related functions in one package, temperature functions in another, and so on. You might have seen this already in programming languages you have used. For example, in the C language, common mathematical functions are collected in a library file called `math.h`, whilst functions for dealing with keyboard, monitor, and text file input and output are grouped together in `stdio.h` (Standard Input Output). Programs with high cohesion often exhibit low coupling, and vice versa.

Detecting EOF

Detecting the end of a file (EOF) is a common programming task. Unfortunately, how exactly it is accomplished is *so* dependent on how individual programming languages deal with stream input that it can become a real minefield. When I first learned programming in the 1980s using the Pascal language, dealing with EOF was very simple. The Pascal EOF function returned True after the last line in a file was read. When I picked up C later on it was slightly different but not too much of an adjustment; the C `feof` function returned False after the last line was read and didn't return True until another read was attempted. The way I dealt with it in Chapter 15 was to introduce a dummy `parcelWeight` record at the end of the file. However, if you really want to avoid this technique, below is another version of Program 15.7 that does away with the end marker and tests directly for EOF.

```
Solution 5.18 Instructions for loading vans with parcels using EOF test
// Translated into Processing 8 February, 2008
final int capacity = 750 ; // constant
int numberOfVans = 0,
heaviestVan = 0,
parcelWeight,
payload ;
String fileName = dataPath("weights.txt") ; // tells Processing to
                                            // look in the Data
                                            // folder

String input ;
try
    {
    BufferedReader file = new BufferedReader (new FileReader
    (fileName)) ;
    input = file.readLine() ;
while (input ! = null)
    {
    payload = 0 ;
    parcelWeight = Integer.parseInt(input) ;
    while ((payload + parcelWeight <= capacity) && (input!=null))
        {
        payload += parcelWeight ;
        input = file.readLine() ;
        if (input != null)
        parcelWeight = Integer.parseInt(input) ;
        }
    numberOfVans++ ;
```

Program 15.7

A Swap procedure using a call-by-reference workaround

```
        println ("Van " + numberOfVans + " has payload of " + payload +
        " kg.") ;
        if (payload > heaviestVan)
            heaviestVan = payload ;
        }
    println ("Number of vans used was " + numberOfVans + ".") ;
    println ("Heaviest van was " + heaviestVan + " kg." ) ;
    }
catch (Exception e)
    {
    println ("Error" + e) ;
    }
```

Documentation

Too little and too late. Documentation is the Cinderella of the programming world, for it often gets little attention and, if it does, it is left until the last minute to write it at which point only lip service is paid. There are several reasons for this. First, programmers are busy people who like to write programs, not document them. They are often pressed for time because their project is behind schedule (perhaps because the design and specification documents weren't very good) and so do not have time to bother documenting what they have done. Secondly, the documentation that programmers write may never be looked at again (at least, not by the programmers who wrote it) so why bother? Unfortunately, when a poor maintenance programmer is asked to fix a defect or add some new features the documentation he finds does not help him to do his job.

One of the best cases made for documentation that I have seen is in *Introduction to the Personal Software Process* (Humphrey, 1997). In that excellent book, Watts Humphrey shows how a diligent approach to documenting everything we do when writing programs actually leads to improvements in the way we, as individual programmers, write programs – a reflective approach makes us better programmers.

Dysfunctional Decomposition

In 1975 Michael Jackson described an iconoclastic program design technique which turned the received wisdom of structured programming on its head (Jackson, 1975). Up until that point the accepted way of doing *structured programming* (as opposed to *unstructured* programming, clearly a bad thing) was to use the principles of TOP-DOWN design as espoused by Niklaus Wirth in his classic article *Program Development by Stepwise Refinement* (Wirth, 1971). The central idea of TOP-DOWN design has a very common-sense feel about it. The program being developed is treated as a hierarchy and the first step of development is to describe the top level of this hierarchy. For example, the coffee making problem might be described in the first step as: "Make and pour coffee for the guests". Clearly, this description is not detailed enough to build the algorithm yet, so we *decompose* the description into the next level. Wirth describes the process thus:

In each step, one or several instructions of the given program are decomposed into more detailed instructions. This successive decomposition or refinement of specifications terminates when all instructions are expressed in terms of an underlying computer or programming language, and must therefore be guided by the facilities available on that computer or language. (Wirth, 1971, p. 221)

That is, we keep decomposing each successive level of the hierarchy until the descriptions can be written in programming language code. This is the guiding principle behind the use of data-flow diagrams (see Section 8.3) in methods such as SSADM and Yourdon Structured Method. One of the difficulties is that TOP-DOWN techniques offer no guidance as to exactly how the problem should be decomposed: should the hierarchy be organized this way or that? Jackson says:

Top-down is a reasonable way of describing things which are already fully under-stood. It is usually possible to impose a hierarchical structure for the purposes of description, and it seems reasonable to start a description with the larger, and work towards the smaller aspects of what is to be described. (Jackson, 1983, p. 370)

Thus, we might quite easily use a TOP-DOWN approach to describing the structure of the coffee making problem; we already understand the overall problem quite well and we merely have to finesse some of the details. But, as Jackson points out, this is to confuse the method of *description* with the method of *development*. Using some unwritten scheme we have solved the problem of coffee making in our head and are simply using TOP-DOWN notation to describe the solution. What happens when we turn to a problem that we do not understand clearly? In such a case TOP-DOWN does not help much because it offers no guidance other than the general instruction that we should keep decomposing hierarchic levels until "all instructions are expressed in terms of an underlying computer or programming language" (Wirth, 1971, p. 221). Thus, we proceed decomposing the problem into a functional hierarchy that may, or may not, be an appropriate algorithm for the solution. It is only at the end, when we have a thorough understanding of the problem, that we can see whether the chosen hierarchy is a good fit. Alas, it is at the start of the process, when we understand the problem the least, that we make the most crucial and far-reaching decomposition decisions as we define the overall shape of the hierarchy. Surely it is better to make these important decisions when we more fully understand the problem?

Actually, around the same time that this idea of TOP-DOWN "design", or *functional decomposition* was being promoted in the literature, some of its proponents were also, albeit unwittingly, acknowledging its central weakness. In his classic book of essays on software engineering problems, *The Mythical Man Month*, Frederick Brooks offered the following insight:

In most projects, the first system built is barely usable. . . . There is no alternative but to start again . . . and build a redesigned version. . . . Hence, plan to throw one away; you will, anyhow. (Brooks, 1974, p. 226)

When he gave this advice Brooks believed the first version of a system was unusable because of some inherent difficulty in building software. Personally, I am persuaded that it is the use of functional decomposition that leads to this awful state of affairs. It is because TOP-DOWN methods make you take the most risky design decisions when you understand least about the problem and often lead to having to redesign the system that I call it *dys*functional decomposition.

Is there an alternative? After all, even today the majority of programming courses espouse TOP-DOWN as the way to go. Jackson has written a number of excellent books on software engineering that will steer you towards looking at the discipline in a different way. For an easy, light-hearted, and insightful read, have a look at his book *Software Requirements and Specifications: A Lexicon of Practice, Principles and Prejudices* (Jackson, 1995). *Problem Frames* (Jackson, 2001) describes a way of decomposing problems, rather than functions, in a non-TOP-DOWN way that, it is claimed, leads to better problem definition and understanding.

Fourth-Generation Languages

If there is one thing the software profession has been good at, it is inventing silver bullets to kill the werewolf of software project development and maintenance problems. Except, as Frederick Brooks wrote in 1987, there *is* no silver bullet (Brooks, 1987).[2] In the 1970s the solution to software development ills was *structured programming* (see DYSFUNCTIONAL DECOMPOSITION). In the 1980s it was so-called *fourth generation languages* or 4GLs. With machine code being the first generation of languages, assembly language the second, and the compiled and interpreted languages such as C and BASIC being the third, the fourth-generation languages (4GLs) of the 1980s took abstraction a level higher and provided programmers with the means to write software in a kind of specification language. In the 1950s and 1960s it was claimed that languages like COBOL would solve the software maintenance problem as one page of COBOL code could replace many pages of assembly language thus shortening the length of listings and so, it was claimed, making programs easier to understand and modify. However, two factors invalidated this: first, computing power grew and so did programs and soon the COBOL listings became many times longer than the simpler assembly programs they replaced. Secondly, as one line of a third-generation language like COBOL was functionally equivalent to many lines of assembly language, the potential for unwanted side effects in each line of COBOL (i.e. defects) was that much greater. Changing even one line of code led to greater problems. In the 1980s 4GLs were going to solve the *software crisis* as it had become known, by giving shorter and more powerful programs (we have heard this argument before). Alas, the same problems occurred as when COBOL replaced assembly language for mainstream commercial software development projects: the programs became even longer and more complex and harder to understand. In the early 1990s I was at a software maintenance conference where I got talking to a project manager from a large UK life assurance company. He told

---

[2] Brooks's famous "No silver bullet" article first appeared in IEEE Computer magazine (Brooks, 1987) and was later reprinted in the special anniversary edition of his classic book *The Mythical Man Month* in 1995.

me that they had just thrown out all their recent systems that built using 4GLs and had rewritten them in COBOL 2 (an object-oriented dialect of COBOL) because the 4GL systems were simply un-maintainable. As the French say, *plus ça change, plus c'est la même chose*.[3]

Heuristic

Heuristic investigation can be thought of as a process of guided trial and error. The word comes from the Greek word ευρισκω (*heuriskein*) which means "to find out". You may recall the story of Archimedes in the bath. When he discovered the principle of displacement and buoyancy he leapt out of the bath (so the story goes) and ran through the streets of Syracuse yelling "Eureka!", meaning "I have found it!". Pólya's *How to Solve It* (Pólya, 1990) was all about using heuristics to solve mathematical problems. Heuristic investigation is sometimes called "trial and error" though this implies a lack of logic. Heuristic investigation is a rational way to approach problems and search for solutions – it is much more than fumbling around in the dark. A set of common sense rules aim to increase the likelihood of solving some problem. Heuristic methods typically constitute a process of exploration, investigation, and discovery and may require selecting a solution from several possible alternatives I hope that this book, which draws upon heuristic method, has helped you by turning the light on, as it were. Once you can see the problem from a number of different view points you have a better chance of finding a way to solve it.

Initialization of Variables

Some programmers (and teachers) think it is a good idea to initialize every variable upon declaration. The argument goes that if you initialize everything then you cannot get caught out later on by wrongly assuming a variable has a value of zero (or whatever it was initialized to) the first time you use it. Others think you should only initialize variables that need to have a particular value upon their first use. I belong to the latter camp. I can see the logic in the "initialize everything" argument as it offers a degree of safety. However, it is not strictly needed. Consider the following example given in both C and Pascal:

In C	In Pascal
`int counter = 0 ;`	`VAR`
`int numberSugars = 0 ;`	`    counter,`
`scanf ("%d", &numberSugars) ;`	`    numberSugars : Integer ;`
`while (counter <= numberSugars)`	`BEGIN`
`    {`	`counter := 0 ;`
`    counter ++ ;`	`numberSugars := 0 ;`
`    }`	`Readln (numberSugars) ;`

---

[3] The more that something changes, the more it stays the same (the more it is the same thing). Or, as the writer of Ecclesiastes put it, *there is nothing new under the sun* (Ecclesiastes 1:9).

```
WHILE (counter <= numberSugars) DO
   BEGIN
   counter := counter + 1
   END ;
END.
```

Note that C allows variables to be initialized upon declaration whilst standard Pascal does not, so the Pascal program needs two assignment statements to initialize the two variables. counter certainly needs to be initialized at some point as the WHILE loop depends on it having a starting value of zero. However, numberSugars does not need to be initialized as its first value is provided by the scanf/Readln statements. The initialization of numberSugars is, therefore, redundant. So what? Well, blanket initialization can actually get you into trouble. What if the program had two WHILE loops both of which relied on counter having a starting value of zero? The first one would be OK, as counter has been initialized. However, the second loop may not work properly as we cannot say what the value of counter will be. So really variables should be initialized to a starting value at the point at which that value is needed. Furthermore, when you consider how the program has to be coded in standard Pascal, which does not allow initialization of variables at declaration, you can see that needless initialization introduces redundant statements. Apart from cluttering up the program, these initialization statements could, themselves be written incorrectly thus introducing more scope for defects. Yuk.

Logical Operators and Connectives

The Boolean operators found in programming languages (AND, OR, NOT, etc.) are derived from the logical operators used in the branch of mathematics known as *propositional logic*. Aristotle coined the word "logic" and developed it as a precise method for reasoning about knowledge. Gottfried Leibniz (1646–1716) developed the first system of binary arithmetic and George Boole (1815–64) took this a stage further and used arithmetic as a basis for logical operations. Instead of working with numbers, Boole's system used the *truth values* True and False (which can be represented by the numbers 0 for False and 1 for True). Where Leibniz only used multiplication in his system, Boole added the addition and subtraction operators which in his system stood for disjunction and negation respectively. In Boole's scheme multiplication is a *conjunction*. Thus, Boole gives us the tools to define two predicates p and q which stand for two statements that represent truth values. For example, we might say that p stands for the expression "I am cold" and q for "I am hungry". Using Boole's conjunction, disjunction, and negation operators we can construct logical arithmetic statements such as:

- $p \times q$ which means "I am cold and I am hungry."
- $p + q$ which means "I am cold or I am hungry."
- $-p$ which means "I am not cold."

In Boole's system the $\times$ behaves like arithmetic multiplication but is restricted to only two values, 0 and 1. Thus $0 \times 0 = 0$, $0 \times 1 = 0$, $1 \times 0 = 0$, and $1 \times 1 = 1$. If we think of 0 and 1 as standing for False and True, and read $\times$ as "AND" then we can see that 0×0 means False AND False is False, False and True is False, True and False is False, and True AND True is True. In Boolean arithmetic for the conjunction operator to give a True result, both its operands must be True. So, in the above example, the statement "I am cold AND I am hungry" is only True when both of the predicates *conjoined* by the AND ($\times$) are true; that is p must be true and q must be true. If I am actually not cold then the statement "I am cold AND I am hungry" will be False.

The disjunction operator ($+$) works like the arithmetic addition operator on the two values 0 and 1. $0 + 0 = 0$, $0 + 1 = 1$, $1 + 0 = 1$, and $1 + 1 = 1$ (discarding the carry). Actually, to avoid this problem of carry where an arithmetic $1 + 1$ gives a result greater than 1, Boole used a special case of disjunction which is known today as the *exclusive or*, or XOR. The XOR operator only gives a True result when either, *but not both*, of its operands are True. So, Boole's disjunction gives the following results: $0 + 0 = 0$, $0 + 1 = 1$, $1 + 0 = 1$, $1 + 1 = 0$. Boole also modified the normal meaning of negation to avoid values of less than 0. In normal arithmetic, $0 - 1$ would give -1. As Boole's values 0 and 1 stand for truth values, we cannot allow any other values (things are either true or false). So, in Boole's scheme the following definitions apply: $-1 = 0$ and $-0 = 1$. If you think about this in logical terms it makes perfect sense. Boole's negation operator ($-$) is read as NOT which has the effect of returning the opposite value of its operand. Something that is NOT True is False and that which is NOT False is True. As -0 is read as NOT False, the definition $-0 = 1$ makes sense. The logical operators AND, OR, and NOT and Boolean logic lie at the heart of programming. The ability to test expressions for truth or falsehood means we can write statements such as:

```
IF (salary is greater than 20000) then pay some tax.
```

Either the salary *is* greater than 20,000 (the expression is True) or it is not (the expression is False). Since Leibniz and Boole, various schemes have arisen that make use of the truth values and the conjunction, disjunction, and negation operators. To muddy the waters further, different notations have been adopted to represent the operators. The table below shows these logical operators and some of the common symbols used to represent them together with their equivalents in some popular programming languages.

Logical Operators and their Symbolic Representations

	Mathematics		How they Appear in Programming Languages			
Operator	Name	Symbol	Pseudo-code	C/C++/Java	Pascal	BASIC
AND	Conjunction	$\cap$ or $\wedge$	AND	&&	AND	AND
OR	Disjunction	$\cup$ or $\vee$	OR	||	OR	OR
NOT	Negation	$\neg$	NOT	!	NOT	NOT
XOR	Exclusive disjunction	$\oplus$	XOR	$\wedge$	XOR	XOR
if	Implication	$\rightarrow$ or $\Rightarrow$	N/A	N/A	N/A	N/A
iff	Mutual implication	$\leftrightarrow$ or $\Leftrightarrow$	N/A	N/A	N/A	N/A

Implication

The first three rows of the table deal with the basic operators AND, OR, and NOT. The remaining rows show Boole's exclusive OR, and the two *implication* operators *if* and *iff*. The operator *if* is represented by the symbol → or ⇒. The statement

$$p \rightarrow q$$

means "*p*" implies "*q*" which can be read as "if *p* is true then *q* is true". In logic terms the statement $p \rightarrow q$ is true if either *p* is false or *q* is true. In other words, if *p* is true *q* is true, but not vice versa. This means that when *p* is true so will *q* be, but *q* being true does not necessarily make *p* true. Thus, the only case that causes $p \rightarrow q$ to be false is when *p* is true and *q* is false. *p* is said to be a *sufficient condition* for *q* and *q* is a *necessary condition* for *p*. That is, *q* will be true whenever *p* is true (sufficient condition) and *p* cannot be true without *q* being true (necessary condition – though that does not mean that when *q* is true so will *p* be true!).

There is an extended implication called *iff* (meaning *if-and-only-if*) that is represented by the symbols ↔ and ⇔. The statement

$$p \leftrightarrow q$$

means "if, and only if, *p* is true then *q* is true". *p* is now said to be both necessary and sufficient for *q*: *q* cannot be true unless *p* is true (*p* is sufficient for *q*) and *q* cannot be true without *p* being true (*p* is necessary for *q*). This relationship is also known as mutual implication because if *p* is necessary and sufficient for *q* then *q* is also necessary and sufficient for *p* – the implication relationship is mutual.

The difference between *if* and *iff* is easy to see with a simple example. Let's define *p* as *I am soaked through* and *q* as *I am cold*. The *if* relation

$$p \rightarrow q$$

can be read as "if *I am soaked through* then *I am cold*". Note that the corollary does not apply, that is, being cold does not make me wet. However, the mutual implication relationship $p \leftrightarrow q$ means exactly that: "if, **and only if**, *I am soaked through* then *I am cold*". That is, I cannot be cold without being soaked through and I cannot be soaked through without being cold.

A truth table for the logical operators NOT, AND, OR, XOR, *if*, and *iff* is given in the table below. Pay particularly close attention to the entries for *if* and *iff* and try to convince yourself that they are correct: they can seem counter-intuitive at first.

Truth table for common logical operators

		NOT	AND	OR	XOR	*if*	*iff*
P	Q	¬P	P ∧ Q	P ∨ Q	P ⊕ Q	P → Q	P ↔ Q
T	T	F	T	T	F	T	T
T	F	F	F	T	T	F	F
F	T	T	F	T	T	T	F
F	F	T	F	F	F	T	T

Note that operators like NAND (¬AND) and NOR (¬OR) are also in common use, especially in electronic engineering where they are used as logic gates in circuit design.

If you would like to read more about propositional logic and predicate calculus the classic book in the field is W.V. Quine's *Methods of Logic* (Quine, 1982). Originally published in 1950 but now in its fourth edition Quine's book is regarded as essential reading for all students of logic and computer science.

A Final Twist

We have looked at AND, OR, NOT, XOR, if, and iff, but it does not stop there. If you fancy engaging your brain just a little bit further, then search out the *modal logic* operators □ and ◊. □ means *necessarily true* and ◊ means *possibly true*. Something is necessarily true if and only if it is not possibly false:

$\Box p \equiv \neg\Diamond\neg p$ (where ≡ means *is logically equivalent to*)

And something is possibly true if and only if it is not necessarily false:

$\Diamond p \equiv \neg\Box\neg p$

You can have great fun with this and write statements such as:

$\Box p \rightarrow \Box\Box p$

which reads "if p is necessary then p is necessarily necessary"![4]

Natural Numbers

In programming we talk of integers, whereas mathematicians talk more of natural numbers. A natural number is either a positive integer {1, 2, 3, . . ., ∞} (the definition used in *number theory*) or a non-negative integer {0, 1, 2, 3, . . ., ∞} (the definition used in computer science). The set of all natural numbers is called ℕ. The integers are all the natural numbers ℕ and their negatives {−1, −2, −3, . . ., −∞}, and zero. The name given to the set of all integers is ℤ. Natural numbers (and by extension the integers) are used for two purposes:

- Counting things – "There are 30 bedrooms in the hotel" (cardinality).
- Ordering things – "He graduated second in his class" (ordinality).

A cardinal number, then, is a measure of the size of something, whilst an ordinal number is a measure of the position of something. In programming we use the ordinal set of integers both to count things:

```
vansDespatched  ←  vansDespatched + 1 ; // Add 1 to vansDespatched,
                                        // i.e. increase cardinality
                                              by 1
```

and to order things:

```
Display (employeeArray [2]) ; // Display element of employeeArray
                              // held in ordinal position 2
```

---

[4] This example was taken from Sowa (2000, p. 27).

Pointers versus References

We have talked in this book of pointer variables and reference variables as if they were the same thing. Actually, they're not, but the difference is subtle and I thought it best to leave a treatment of those differences to this Reflections chapter rather than cluttering up the main text and, possibly, adding to the bewilderment.

In languages that have *pointers* it is usually possible to access the pointer variable itself as well as the item it points to. However, in languages that use *references* rather than pointers (e.g. Java and C#) reference variables always refer to the item being referenced: the value of the reference variable itself is not accessible. This has the knock-on effect that whilst pointers can be involved in type casts (see optional section after the exercises in Chapter 9) references cannot be cast to another type. All that can be done to a reference is to copy its binding (the address of the item it references to) into another reference variable.

Depending on the language there may be other restrictions on reference usage. For example, in C++ references cannot be changed to reference a different item and nor can they take **NULL** values.

If you would like a bit of fun, watch Nick Parlante's *Binky Pointer Fun Video* at Stanford University's Computer Science Education Library website.[5] There are instructional videos explaining pointers/references for C, C++, Java, Pascal, and Ada.

George Pólya

Strangely, I did not discover Pólya until relatively recently. I guess it is because I did not formally study mathematics beyond age 16. It is a shame because I think I would have benefited from his insights when I was a student. Pólya died in Palo Alto on 7 September, 1985. This was the same day that I received an offer of a place to study for a computing degree. Later, whilst studying for my PhD, Palo Alto was the setting for the first conference paper I presented that came out of my PhD research. As I said, I like to look for the small details.

Prefix and Postfix Operators

We saw in Chapter 15 how the languages based on the original C syntax (C, C++, C#, Processing, Java, etc.) have shorthand operators for performing simple arithmetic on identifiers. Specifically we saw how to add or subtract 1 to a variable in Processing thus:

```
int a = 3 ;
a++ ; // Adds 1 to a
a-- ; // Subtracts 1 from a
```

It was then said that ++ and -- can come both before (prefix) and after (postfix) the identifier. There is a very subtle but important difference in

---

[5] See http://cslibrary.stanford.edu/104/.

the way prefix and postfix operators behave. The net result is eventually the same:

```
a++ ;
```

And

```
++a ;
```

both result in a being increased by 1. The difference is *when* the addition takes place. Consider the following code:

```
int a = 3 ;
println (a) ;
int b = a++ ;
println (b) ;
int c = ++a ;
println (c) ;
```

The first statement assigns the value 3 to a. The second statement displays its value (3) on the screen. The third statement does two things. It adds 1 to a and it assigns the value of a to b. It may surprise you to find that the fourth statement (`println (b) ;`) displays a value of 3 on the screen. The reason for this is that in its postfix form, the ++ operator is carried out *after* the assignment operator. So, first the current value of a (3) is assigned to b and *then* a is increased by 1. The fifth statement uses ++ in its prefix form which means that first 1 is added to a and then this value is assigned to c; this is why the output from the sixth statement is 5. This is another example of how expressing a solution in programming language code is a separate problem from coming up with the algorithmic solution in the first place.

Reusability

If, in the 1980s, developers hoped the fourth-generation languages would be the salvation of the software crisis, in the 1990s as object-oriented languages gained the ascendancy, the focus switched to software reuse. Ivar Jacobson was one of the main proponents and the argument goes that with object-oriented languages the programmer does not need to write the same functions for each project he works on, but can reuse functions over and over again. In principle this is a neat idea: the OOP principles of encapsulation, inheritance, and polymorphism, mean that we can build self-contained objects that can be plugged into a variety of different programs. As objects use information hiding to protect their internal data, it is unlikely that any other object can corrupt their data, thus promoting software reuse which, in turn leads to increasing reliability, speeding up development, facilitating compliance with standards, and reducing defects. That is the theory, anyway.

Let's wind the clock back 20 years and consider the software reuse horror story that was the Therac-25 linear accelerator. The Therac-25 used high-energy electron beams and X-ray beams to treat tumors. The Therac-25 was an attempt to build on the success of the earlier Therac-6 and Therac-20 models. To reduce costs some of the safety features were implemented in software on the computer rather than using the hardware solutions of the earlier models. Also, because the model 6 and model 20 machines were so reliable, much of their software was reused in the Therac-25. So far, so good. Unfortunately, the machine was prone to crashing many times each day, and in the case of six patients administered overdoses of radiation (in some cases over 100 times the required dose); three of these patients later died.

The reasons for the Therac-25's failures are complex, but stem mainly from the removal of the hardware overdose-protection features which allowed previously undetected defects in the reused software code to manifest themselves. The Therac-6 and Therac-20 had the same software errors but they simply were not revealed because when the software caused a condition that would lead to an overdose, the hardware fail-safe systems kicked in and prevented the error.

You can read a full account of the problems in Leveson and Turner's (1993) article in the IEEE's *Computer* magazine. Less dramatically, Ian Sommerville (2001) enumerates some of the other potential problems that arise from reusing software. As systems that reuse components are changed over time it is possible that the reused components themselves need updating to maintain compatibility. This is fine if the source code is available, but if not, the maintenance costs are dramatically increased as these reused components will need to be rewritten from scratch. Even if reliable components are available for reuse, finding them in the many available libraries can be time consuming and difficult; some programmers may simply prefer to write new components themselves.

What's the moral of this reflection? Simply that reuse is a great idea in principle, but you have to be really careful to do it properly otherwise you can literally end up killing people. The ethics of software development is an interesting area of study that all software professionals should consider. *Ethics for the Information Age* (Quinn, 2004) is a very readable primer and heartily recommended. Quinn discusses the ethical issues that arise from several high-profile software failures, including the Therac-25, the Patriot Missile System, and the Ariane 5 rocket.

Small Capital Letters

OK, so it was only an example of the typesetting that identifies entries in the Reflections chapter. But programmers need to be consistent and not leave anything undone. So what is there to say about small capital letters? Not much except that they provide a useful alternative to hyperlinks in printed books.

Software Maintenance

Software maintenance can be loosely defined as anything that happens to a piece of code after it has been completed or delivered. You might assume that this only involves removing defects, but there are four accepted classes of maintenance activity. First, there is *corrective maintenance* or removing known defects from the program (also known as debugging, and cynically known as the art of replacing one bug by another). It is estimated that corrective maintenance accounts for 17 percent of all maintenance activity. Secondly, there is *adaptive maintenance*, or modifying a program so that it fits in with a changing environment (such as new hardware, or an updated version of the operating system). This task is reckoned

to consume about 18 percent of the total maintenance activity. Adaptive maintenance is known by cynics as the art of replacing good working code by bugs. Next
comes *perfective maintenance.* This is actually the most common type of maintenance encompassing enhancements to both the function and the efficiency of the
code. It is carried out when extra features are added to the software or when
existing aspects are rewritten to make them faster. Finally comes the lesser
known fourth category of *preventive maintenance.* This is the process of changing
software to improve its future maintainability or to provide a better basis for
future enhancements.

Top Down

One of the more popular approaches advocated in programming methods and
books is TOP-DOWN design, also known as "functional decomposition" or "stepwise
refinement" (see DYSFUNCTIONAL DECOMPOSITION). It is popular because it is general
and because it makes an appeal to common sense. The premise of TOP-DOWN
design is simple: starting with an overall problem statement you decompose it
into a set of smaller sub-problems. Each sub-problem in turn is decomposed into
its own smaller sub-problems. This process is continued until at the bottom level
the sub-problems are so small that they can be easily expressed in programming
language code. The result is a hierarchy of sub-problems:

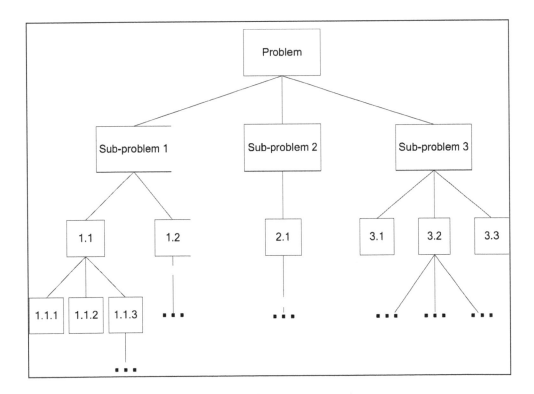

This process of stepwise refinement has psychological appeal as we are led to
believe that we are gaining understanding of a problem through breaking it up into

simpler sub-problems in a kind of divide-and-conquer approach. Indeed, is not this just what *HTTLAP* recommends? Actually, no. In *HTTLAP*, whilst we are trying to solve the big problem by solving simpler related problems, there was no indication that the set of simpler problems is in any way hierarchically related. TOP-DOWN design does not give any advice on *how* to decompose the hierarchy; it merely says that we should keep on decomposing the problems until we arrive at some easily understood level. This division of a problem into separate sub-problems requires that we make the biggest decision (deciding what the first level of decomposition will be) at the start of the process just when we know the least about the problem. To be able to do an effective functional decomposition we must first have already solved the problem in our heads. The TOP-DOWN design then becomes a description of a problem already solved rather than something that helps to actually solve the problem.

Barry Cornelius hints at this in *Understanding Java* (Cornelius, 2001, p. 6) when he says that a drawback of TOP-DOWN design is that it does not scale well. That is, it does not work very well for large problems that are difficult to understand. Of course, even very small problems can be hard to understand and the TOP-DOWN approach still does not offer any help on how to understand and solve the problem. Consider the "small" problem of finding the next prime number from a given starting point. There is a single requirement and no awkward decisions about milk, sugar, whether the machine is plugged in or not, and so on. Yet this is an intellectually demanding problem and I do not see how a top-down approach will help you to solve it. Cornelius also points out that because each sub-problem is intimately related to its parent then very little of a solution described in a TOP-DOWN manner can be used in another programming task. Code reusability is a driving force behind object-oriented programming as it means that code that has been built and tested can be used in other projects thus reducing development effort and increasing reliability. This is, of course, a gross oversimplification on my part because there are many reasons why software development projects fail and many reasons why even "reusable" code is not reusable and has to be rewritten. But that is for another time and another book.

Another criticism of TOP-DOWN design made by Jackson (1995, p. 199) is that it imposes a neatly segmented and partitioned hierarchical structure, yet the real world (in which our problems are situated) is usually made up of overlapping problems. For example, consider a book club. Members buy books at a discount

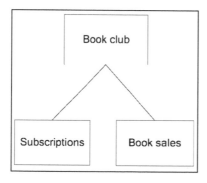

and pay an annual membership fee. The size of their annual fee is dependent on the number of books purchased in the previous year: the more books they buy the lower their subscription becomes. Using a TOP-DOWN approach you may reasonably come up with this functional decomposition.

We have decided that there are two main processes needed to carry out the business of the book club: one to deal with members' subscriptions and another to deal with book sales. We could set about decomposing these two processes. The issue here is that the hierarchical decomposition into a subscriptions function and book sales function does not reflect the complexities of the real world of the book club. We know there is a relationship between the number of books purchased and the size of the subscription due, so which process deals with that? In fact, the problem of dealing with book sales overlaps with the problem of dealing with calculating subscriptions. Both sub-problems have some unique features yet share some other characteristics. Constraining designs to a functional decomposition description stores up dangers. One of the claimed benefits of TOP-DOWN is that the sub-process separation means that each task (or box on the diagram) can be modified without affecting the other sub-processes. But, as we have just seen, this claim is spurious as it does not reflect the complexities of the real world and instead leads to simplistic abstractions.

For these reasons I like to call the technique DYSFUNCTIONAL DECOMPOSITION as it does not work as well as it claims on the tin. *HTTLAP*, though advocating looking for simpler problems in an attempt to understand the overall problem does not suggest a TOP-DOWN approach. *HTTLAP* is more of an HEURISTIC approach to problem solving than a function decomposition technique.

John von Neumann

John von Neumann (1903–57) is credited with developing a workable architecture for a universal computer. He studied under Pólya in Zurich. Pólya said of von Neumann: "Johnny was the only student I was ever afraid of. If in the course of a lecture I stated an unsolved problem, the chances were he'd come to me as soon as the lecture was over, with the complete solution in a few scribbles on a slip of paper. I was never afraid of my students, but after that, I was afraid of von Neumann." And, unfortunately (albeit unwittingly), so are many students of computer programming. The third-generation languages like C, BASIC, and Pascal were designed to allow programs to be written that would run on a von Neumann machine. Newer computer architectures have given us new programming paradigms (such as parallel programming) and new languages to support them, but behind it all, in the dawn of computing history, lies the good old von Neumann architecture.

Do not be afraid. Use the principles of *HTTLAP* and conquer your fear. Hooray!

References

Adams, J. L. (2001). *Conceptual Blockbusting: A Guide to Better Ideas*. Cambridge, MA: Perseus Publishing.

Agans, D. J. (2002) *Debugging: The 9 Indispensable Rules for Finding Even the Most Elusive Software and Hardware Problems*. New York: Amacom.

Ashworth, C. and Goodland, M. (1989). *SSADM: A Practical Approach*. Maidenhead, UK: McGraw-Hill.

Avison, D. E. and Fitzgerald, G. (1995). *Information Systems Development: Methodologies, Techniques, and Tools*. Maidenhead, UK: McGraw-Hill.

Barr, A. (2004) *Find the Bug: A Book of Incorrect Programs*. London: Addison-Wesley.

Beck, K. (1999). *Extreme Programming Explained: Embracing Change*. London: Addison-Wesley.

Bonar, J. and Soloway, E. (1985). Preprogramming Knowledge: A Major Source of Misconception in Novice Programmers. *Human-Computer Interaction*, 1 (2), pp. 133–161.

Brooks, F. P. (1987). No silver bullet: essence and accidents of software engineering. *IEEE Computer*, 20 (4), pp. 10–19, .

Brooks, F. P. (1995). The *Mythical Man Month and Other Essays on Software Engineering*. London: Addison-Wesley.

Checkland, P. and Holwell, S. (1997). *Information, Systems and Information Systems: Making Sense of the Field*. Chichester: John Wiley and Sons.

Cornelius, B. (2001). *Understanding Java*. London: Addison-Wesley.

Dijkstra, Edsger W. (1972). The humble programmer. *Communications of the ACM*, 15 (10), pp. 859–66.

Dromey, R. G. (1982). *How to Solve It by Computer*. London: Prentice-Hall International.

Humphrey, W. S. (1997). *Introduction to the Personal Software Process*. Harlow: Addison-Wesley.

Jackson, M. (1995). *Software Requirements & Specifications: A Lexicon of Practice, Principles and Prejudices*. Wokingham: ACM Press/Addison-Wesley.

Jackson, M. (2001). *Problem Frames: Analyzing and Structuring Software Development Problems*. London: ACM Press/Addison-Wesley.

Jackson, M. A. (1975). *Principles of Program Design*. London: Academic Press.

Jackson, M. A. (1983). *System Development*. London: Prentice-Hall International.

Jones, C. (2000). *Software Assessments, Benchmarks, and Best Practices*. London: Addison-Wesley Professional.

Kaliski, M. E. and Kaliski, B. S. Jr. (1991). *The Software Sleuth*. West.

Kernighan, B. and Pike, R. (1999). *The Practice of Programming*. Reading, MA: Addison-Wesley.

King, M. J. and Pardoe, J. P. P. (1992). *Program Design Using JSP: A Practical Introduction*. MacMillan.

Knuth, D. E. (1984). Literate Programming. *The Computer Journal*, 27: 97–111.

Knuth, D. E. (1992). *Literate Programming*. Stanford, CA: Center for the Study of Language and Information.

Knuth, D. and Levy, S. (1994). *The CWEB System of Structured Documentation*. Reading, MA: Addison-Wesley.

Ledgard, H. F. (1975). *Programming Proverbs*. Rochell Park, NJ: Hayden.

Leveson, N. G. and Turner, C. S. (1993). An investigation of the Therac-25 accidents. *Computer*, 26 (7), pp.18–41.

Lions, J. L. (1996). ARIANE 5: Flight 501 Failure, Report by the Enquiry Board, European Space Agency.

Pólya, G. (1990). *How to Solve It*. London: Penguin Books.

Pressman, R. (2004). *Software Engineering: A Practitioner's Approach*. London: McGraw-Hill.

Quine, W. V. (1982). *Methods of Logic*. Cambridge, MA: Harvard University Press.

Quinn, M. J. (2004). *Ethics for the Information Age*. London: Addison Wesley.

Shaffer, C. A. (1998). *A Practical Introduction to Data Structures and Algorithm Analysis, Java Edition*. London: Prentice-Hall.

Shalloway, A. and Trott, J. J. (2001). *Design Patterns Explained: A New Perspective on Object-oriented Design*. London: Addison-Wesley.

Sommerville, I., *Software Engineering*. Addison-Wesley, London, 2001.

Sowa, J. F. (2000). *Knowledge Representation: Logical, Philosophical, and Computational Foundations*. London: Thomson Brooks/Cole.

Stroustroup, B. (1986). *The C++ Programming Language*. Wokingham: Addison-Wesley.

Tennent, R. D. (1981). *Principles of Programming Languages*. London: Prentice-Hall International.

Thompson, S. (1997). Where do I begin? A problem-solving approach to teaching functional programming. *First International Conference on Declarative Programming Languages in Education*. K. Apt, P. Hartel and P. Klint (Eds), Springer Verlag.

Weinberg, G. M. (1971). *Psychology of Computer Programming*. New York: Van Nostrand Reinhold Company.

Wirth, N. (1971). Program development by stepwise refinement. *Communications of the ACM* 14 (4), pp. 221–227.

Yourdon, E. (1988). *Modern Structured Analysis*. London: Prentice Hall International.

Pseudo-code

This appendix has two sections. The first summarizes the syntax, meaning, and usage of the *HTTLAP* pseudo-code. The second gives translations of the *HTTLAP* pseudo-code in a number of modern programming languages.

HTTLAP Pseudo-code Elements and Their Meanings

Element	Meaning	Example
;	End of instruction. A bit like a stop in English, the semi-colon terminates an instruction or *statement*. It separates instructions to show distinct sequences of actions.	Pour coffee ; Add cream ; Add sugar ;
←	Assign a value. Give a value to something. The value on the right of the ← is given to the thing on the left.	numberSugars ← 2 ;
→	Dereference a pointer. The → is placed after a reference variable to access the memory *pointed to* by that variable rather than the value of the reference variable itself. The first Display command opposite would display the value of intRef which would be the address of the variable **a**, whilst the second Display would characters (either display the value held in the location pointedt to by intRef, that is, the value of **a** which is 3.	integer: a ; → integer: intRef ; a ← 3 ; intRef ← AddressOf(a) ; Display (intref) ; Display (intref →) ;

Element	Meaning	Example
↵	Newline marker. Move the cursor to the next line on the output.	Display ('Hello World!'↵) ;
☐	Denotes a variable. The identifier gives a name to the item. The box is used to show that this is a variable rather than just another word We visualize a variable as a box into can. which a value is placed. The name of the variable, its *identifier* is written on the lid of the box.	integer:sugars ;
☐	Denotes constant data. Constants can not have their value changed within the program.	real:pi IS 3.14159 ;
integer	Type label for variable declaration. integer variables can only store whole numbers.	integer:sugars ; sugars ← 2 ;
real	Type label for variable declaration. real variables can store real (fractional) numbers, such as 3.14159.	real:temperature ; temperature ← 98.6 ;
character	Type label for variable declaration. character variables can store single characters (either ASCII or Unicode).	character:intial ; initial ← 'Q' ;
string	Type label for variable declaration. string variables can store sequences of ASCII or Unicode).	string:name ; name ← 'John Doe' ;
NULL	The value used when you want to make a reference variable point to no where.	intRef ← NULL ;

NEWTYPE	Used for defining new data types. New data types can be specialisms of existing ones (e.g. integer sub-ranges) or complex data structures (such as records).	NEWTYPE **MonthType** IS 1..12; NEWTYPE **Person** IS
		   RECORD
		     string:name ;
		     integer:age ;
		   ENDRECORD
		 MonthType:month ;
		 Person:employee ;

RECORD	Used to define record-type data structures – see examples in NEWTYPE above.	

Element	Meaning	Example
REFERENCE	Used to pass the reference of a variable rather than its value in a sub-program call.	PROCEDURE Tax (**REFERENCE:real**:salary) salary ← salary × 0.8 ; ENDPROCEDURE
ARRAY	Used to define one- and multi-dimensional array data structures.	**ARRAY**:myTable OF [10] **integer** ; **ARRAY**:my2DTable OF [3, 4] **integer** ;

Arithmetic operators

+	Addition operator	sum ← 3 + 4 ;
−	Subtraction operator	difference ← 4 − 3 ;
×	Multiplication operator	product ← 4 × 3 ;
÷	Division operator	quotient ← 12 ÷ 3 ;
MOD	Modulus, returns the remainder after integer division	leftOver ← 13 MOD 3 ;

Relational operators

=	Test for equality	IF (a = b)
		  Display ('Equal') ;
		ENDIF

≠	Test for inequality	IF (a ≠ b)
		  Display ('Unequal') ;
		ENDIF

<	Less than	IF (a < b)
		  Display ('Less') ;
		ENDIF

≤	Less than or equal to	IF (3 ≤ 4)
		  Display ('Yes!') ;
		ENDIF

>	Greater than	IF (a > b)
		  Display ('Bigger') ;
		ENDIF

≥	Greater than or equal to	IF (5 ≥ 4)
		  Display ('Yes') ;
		ENDIF

Logical connectives

AND	Logical **AND**. Returns True if both operands are True.	IF (4 > 3) AND (2 < 4)
		  ...
		ENDIF

Element	Meaning	Example

OR	Logical OR. Returns True if either or both operands is True.	IF (4 > 3) OR (2 < 4)
		...
		ENDIF

NOT	Logical NOT. Returns opposite truth value of its single operand.	IF NOT (4 > 3) ... ENDIF
Constructs		

IF (condition)
   Action ;
ENDIF
	The basic conditional. IF asks a question the answer to which can be true or false. If the answer is true then the instruction following the IF is obeyed otherwise it is not. Parentheses () are used to enclose the question which is called the condition. The action, or sequence of actions to be obeyed when the condition is satisfied (true) is written below the IF and indented by three spaces and is terminated by the keyword ENDIF. The IF..ENDIF brackets are helpful as they distinguish between the following two cases:
	Case 1
	IF (condition)
	  Action 1 ;
	  Action 2 ;
	ENDIF
	Case 2
	IF (condition)
	  Action 1 ;
	
	Action 2 ;
	In Case 1 the square brackets indicate that both
		IF (sugar required)
		  Add sugar ;
		ENDIF
		
		IF (sugar required)
		  Add sugar ;
		ENDIF
		IF (white coffee required)

Element	Meaning	Example

	Action 1 and Action 2 are carried out when the condition is met. In Case 2 only Action 1 is only obeyed when the condition is met, whilst Action 2 comes after the IF and so is obeyed regardless of the condition. In the example, coffee will always be poured whilst milk and sugar will only be added if their conditions are met.	```Add milk ;```
		```ENDIF```
		```Pour coffee ;,```

```IF (condition)```
```   Action ;```
```ELSE```
```   Action ;```
```ENDIF```
	An extension of the IF construct. If the condition is True then the action block is executed as in the normal IF. However, when the condition is False, the first action block is ignored and instead the one following the ELSE is executed.	```IF (a > 10)```
		``` Display ('High') ;```
		```ELSE```
		``` Display ('Low') ;```
		```ENDIF```

```//```	A comment. Used to put in explanatory notes that aren't instructions to be coded or carried out.	```// Get the input```

```WHILE (condition)```
```   Action block ;```
```ENDWHILE```
	WHILE is an indeterminate iteration whose action block is executed zero or more times. The condition is tested and if *true* then the action block is executed. The iteration continues until the condition becomes *false.* The action block must provide a mechanism for making the condition *false* otherwise theloop will never terminate.	```Get record ;```
		```WHILE (not end of```
		``` records)```
		``` Process record ;```
		``` Get next record;```
		```ENDWHILE```

Element	Meaning	Example

DO	Indeterminate one-or-more iteration.	DO
		    Display (⒜) ;
		    ⒜ ← ⒜ + 1 ;
		WHILE (a ≤ 12) ;

FOR	A count-controlled loop.	FOR ⒜ GOES FROM 1 TO 10 Display (⒜) ; ENDFOR

Sub-programs

Element	Meaning	Example

PROCEDURE	A command sub program. Procedures do not return results but, if using the call-by-reference model, can change the values of reference parameters.	PROCEDURE
		Blanks(**integer**:ⓧ)
		    integer:ⓘ ;
		    FOR ⓘ GOES FROM 1 TO ⓩ
		        Display (' ') ;
		    ENDFOR
		ENDPROCEDURE

FUNCTION	A function is an expression procedure that normally takes one or more parameters (though it may have zero parameters) and which returns a single value. Optionally, using the call-by-reference model, a function can change the values of arguments.	FUNCTION Cube (**integer**:ⓧ) RETURNS **integer** ; RETURN ⓧ × ⓧ × ⓧ ; ENDFUNCTION

Built-in commands

Element	Meaning	Example
Display	Used to indicate that when the program is rewritten in a real programming language it should display some parameters on the screen.	Display ('Hello World!') ;

Get	Used to indicate that when the program is rewritten in a real programming language it should get some input from the indicated stream.	Get (keyboard,
		    REFERENCE:ⓨ) ;
		Get (⟦infile⟧,
		    REFERENCE:⟦age⟧) ;

Open	Open the indicated file.	Open (⟦infile⟧) ;
Close	Close the indicated file.	Close (⟦infile⟧) ;
Write	Write the parameters to the specified file.	Write (⟦outfile⟧, 'Hello World!') ;

Programming Language Equivalents of *HTTLAP* Pseudo-code

HTTLAP Pseudo-code to Visual Basic

HTTLAP	VB, VBA
Data types	
`integer, shortint, longint, byte`	`Integer, Long`
`real, doublereal`	`Single, Double`
`boolean`	`Boolean`
`character`	`Char (VB.NET)`
`string`	`string`
Constant declaration	
`type:`|`constIdentifier`|`IS value ;`	`CONST constIdentifier AS type = value`
Variable declaration	
`type:`|`varIdentifier`|`, … ;`	`DIM varIdentifier AS type`
Assignment	
`varIdentifier ← expression ;`	`varidentifier = expression`
Relational operators	
`=`	`=`
`≠`	`<>`
`<`	`<`
`≤`	`<=`
`>`	`>`
`≥`	`>=`
Logical connectives	
`AND`	`AND`
`OR`	`OR`
`NOT`	`NOT`
IF statements	

`IF (condition)`
`    Statement block ;`
`ENDIF`
	`IF (condition) THEN`
	`    Statement block`
	`ENDIF`

`IF (condition)`
`    Statement block ;`
`ELSE`
`    Statement block ;`
`ENDIF`
	`IF (condition) THEN`
	`    Statement block`
	`ELSE`
	`    Statement block`
	`ENDIF`

HTTLAP	VB, VBA

Zero-or-more iteration

```
WHILE (condition)
    Statement block ;
ENDWHILE
```

```
DO WHILE (condition)
    Statement block
LOOP
Or
WHILE (condition)
    Statement block
WEND
```

Once-or-more iteration

```
DO
    Statement block ;
WHILE (condition)
```

```
DO
    Statement block
LOOP WHILE (condition)
```

Count-controlled iteration

```
FOR counter GOES FROM start TO
finish
    Statement block
ENDFOR
```

```
FOR counter = start TO finish
    Statement block
NEXT counter
```

Record structures

```
NEWTYPE recordTypeName IS
    RECORD
    type: fieldIdentifier ;
    type: fieldIdentifier2 ;
    ...
    ENDRECORD
```

```
TYPE recordTypeName
    fieldIdentifier AS type
    fieldIdentifier2 AS type
    ...
END TYPE
```

Reading from text files

```
file: inFile ;
inFile ← 'file path' ;
Open (inFile) ;
Get (inFile, REFERENCE: varIdent, ...) ;
Close (inFile) ;
```

```
OPEN 'file path' FOR
    INPUT AS inFile
INPUT #inFile, varIdent...
CLOSE #inFile
```

Writing to text files

```
file: outFile ;
outFile ← 'file path' ;
Open (outFile) ;
Write (outFile, varIdent, ...) ;
Close (outFile) ;
```

```
OPEN 'file path' FOR
    OUTPUT AS outFile
OUTPUT #outFile, varIdent...
CLOSE #outFile
```

HTTLAP	VB, VBA

Arrays

HTTLAP	VB, VBA
ARRAY: arrayName OF [size] **type** ;	DIM arrayName (1 TO size) AS type

ARRAY: arrayName2D OF [size,size]
type;
arrayName [index] ← expression ;
varIdentifier ← arrayName [index] ;
	DIM array Name2D (start TO
	    maxrow, start TO maxcolumn)
	    AS type arrayName (index)
	  = expression varIdentifier
	  = arrayName (index)

Sub-programs

HTTLAP	VB, VBA

FUNCTION FuncIdentifier
 	
(**type:** parameter1, …,)RETURNS **type**
    Statements ;
    RETURN expression ;
ENDFUNCTION
PROCEDURE ProcIdentifier
(**type:** parameter1, …,)
    Statements ;
ENDPROCEDURE
	FUNCTION FuncIdentifier
	(params)
	        AS type
	    Statements
	    FuncIdentifier = return value
	END FUNCTION
	SUB SubIdentifier (params)
	    Statements ;
	END SUB

HTTLAP Pseudo-code to C/C++

HTTLAP	C/C++

Data types

HTTLAP	C/C++
integer, shortint, longint, byte **real, doublereal** **boolean** **character** **string**	int, long float, double bool // C++ char string // C++ char [] // C

Constant declaration

HTTLAP	C/C++
type: constIdentifier IS value ;	const type constIdentifier = value;

Variable declaration

HTTLAP	C/C++
type: varIdentifier , … ;	type varIdentifier ; type varIdentifier = value ;

Assignment

HTTLAP	C/C++
varIdentifier ← expression ;	varidentifier = expression ;

HTTLAP	C/C++
Relational operators	

HTTLAP	C/C++
=	==
≠	!=
<	<
≤	<=
>	>
≥	>=

Logical connectives

HTTLAP	C/C++
AND	&&
OR	||
NOT	!

IF statements

```
IF (condition)              if (condition)
    Statement block ;           {
ENDIF                           Statement block ;
IF (condition)                  }
    Statement block ;       else
ELSE                            {
    Statement block ;           Statement block ;
ENDIF                           }
```

Zero-or-more iteration

```
WHILE (condition)           while (condition)
  Statement block ;             {
ENDWHILE                        Statement block ;
                                }
```

Once-or-more iteration

```
DO                          do
  Statement block ;             {
WHILE (condition)               Statement block ;
                                }
                            while (condition) ;
```

Count-controlled iteration

```
FOR counter GOES FROM start TO finish   for (counter=start; counter
  Statement block                           <=finish; counter++)
ENDFOR                                      {
                                            Statement block ;
                                            }
```

HTTLAP	C/C++

Record structures

```
NEWTYPE recordTypeName IS
    RECORD
    type: fieldIdentifier ;
    type: fieldIdentifier2 ;
    ...
    ENDRECORD
```

```
struct recordType Name
    {
    type fieldIdentifier ;
    type fieldIdentifier2 ;
    ...
    }
```

Reading from text files

```
file:inFile ;
inFile ; 'file path' ;
Open (inFile) ;
Get (inFile, REFERENCE: varIdent, …) ;
Close (inFile) ;
```

```
In C++
#include <fstream.h>
ifstream inFile ;
inFile.open("file path") ;
inFile >> varIdent ;
inFile.close() ;
In C
FILE *inFile =
    fopen ("file path", "r") ;
fscanf(inFile,
"format_specifier",
&varIdent, …) ;
fclose (inFile) ;
```

Writing to text files

```
file:outFile ;
outFile ; 'file path' ;
Open (outFile) ;
Write (outFile,varIdent, …) ;
Close (outFile) ;
```

```
In C++
#include <fstream.h>
ofstream outFile ;
outFile.open("file path") ;
outFile<< varIdent<<" " ;
outFile.close() ;
In C
FILE *outFile =
    fopen ("file path", "w") ;
fprintf(outFile,"format_
    specifier",
varIdent, …) ;
fclose (outFile) ;
```

Arrays

```
ARRAY:arrayName OF [size] type ;
ARRAY:arrayName2D OF [size,size] type ;

arrayName [index] ← expression ;
```

```
type arrayName [size] ;
type arrayName2D
    [size][size] ;

arrayName [index]
```

HTTLAP	C/C++
	= expression ;
varIdentifier ← arrayName [index] ;	varIdentifier = arrayName [index] ;

Sub-programs

HTTLAP	C/C++
FUNCTION FuncIdentifier (**type:**parameter1, …,)RETURNS **type**	type FuncIdentifier (type parameter1, …) {
Statements ;	Statements ;
RETURN expression ;	return expression ;
ENDFUNCTION	}
PROCEDURE ProcIdentifier (**type:**parameter1, …,)	void FuncIdentifier (type parameter1, …) {
Statements ;	Statements ;
ENDPROCEDURE	}

HTTLAP Pseudo-code to Java

HTTLAP	Java

Data types

HTTLAP	Java
integer, shortint, longint, byte	int, long
real, doublereal	float, double
boolean	boolean
character	char
string	String // in java.lang.String

Constant declaration

HTTLAP	Java
type:constIdentifier IS value ;	final type constIdentifier = value ;

Variable declaration

HTTLAP	Java
type:varIdentifier, … ;	type varIdentifier ; type varIdentifier = value ;

Assignment

HTTLAP	Java
varIdentifier ← expression ;	varidentifier = expression ;

Relational operators

HTTLAP	Java
=	==
≠	!=
<	<
≤	<=
>	>
≥	>=

HTTLAP	Java

Logical connectives

```
AND                                       &&
OR                                        ||
NOT                                       !
```

IF statements

```
IF (condition)                  if (condition)
    Statement block ;               {
ENDIF                               Statement block ;
IF (condition)                      }
    Statement block ;           else
ELSE                                {
    Statement block ;               Statement block ;
ENDIF                               }
```

Zero-or-more iteration

```
WHILE (condition)               while (condition)
    Statement block ;               {
ENDWHILE                            Statement block ;
                                    }
```

Once-or-more iteration

```
DO                              do
    Statement block ;               {
WHILE (condition)                   Statement block ;
                                    }
                                while (condition) ;
```

Count-controlled iteration

```
FOR counter GOES FROM start TO finish    for (counter=start ;
                                             counter<=finish;
                                             counter++)
    Statement block;                     {
ENDFOR                                   Statement block ;
                                         }
```

Record structures

```
NEWTYPE recordTypeName IS        class recordTypeName
    RECORD                           {
    type: fieldIdentifier ;          type fieldIdentifier ;
    type: fieldIdentifier2 ;         typefieldIdentifier2 ;
    ...                              ...
    ENDRECORD                        }
```

HTTLAP	Java

Reading from text files

```
file: inFile ;
inFile ← 'file path' ;
Open (inFile) ;
Get (inFile, REFERENCE: varIdent, …) ;

Close (inFile) ;
```

```
final BufferedReader inFile =
    new BufferedReader (new
    FileReader("file path")) ;
// Reading from file depends
// on type of data to read
inFile.close() ;
```

Writing to text files

```
file: outFile ;
outFile ← 'file path' ;
Open (outFile) ;
Write (outFile,
varIdent, ...) ;
Close (outFile) ;
```

```
final PrintWriter outFile =
    new PrintWriter(new
    BufferedWriter (new
    FileWriter("file path")))
outFile.println(varIdent) ;
outFile.close() ;
```

Arrays

```
ARRAY: arrayName OF [size] type ;

ARRAY: arrayName2D OF
       [size,size] type;
arrayName [index] ← expression ;
varIdentifier ← arrayName


[index] ;
```

```
type [] arrayName
    = new type [size] ;
type [][]arrayName2D =

    new type[size][size] ;
arrayName [index] =
expression ;
varIdentifier = arrayName
[index] ;
```

Sub-programs

```
FUNCTION FuncIdentifier


(type: parameter1, …,)
RETURNS type
   Statements ;
   RETURN expression ;
ENDFUNCTION
PROCEDURE ProcIdentifier


(type: parameter1 , …,)
   Statements ;
ENDPROCEDURE
```

```
access_level type
FuncIdentifier
(type parameter1, …)
   {
   Statements ;
   return expression ;
   }
access_level void
   FuncIdentifier
(type parameter1, …)
   {
   Statements ;
   }
```

HTTLAP Pseudo-code to Pascal/Delphi

HTTLAP	Pascal/Delphi
Data types	

HTTLAP	Pascal/Delphi
integer, shortint, longint, byte	Integer
real, doublereal	Real, Single, Double
boolean	Boolean
character	Char
string	String

Constant declaration

HTTLAP	Pascal/Delphi
type: constIdentifier IS value ;	CONST constIdentifier = value;

Variable declaration

HTTLAP	Pascal/Delphi
type: varIdentifier , … ;	VAR varIdentifier, …:type ;

Assignment

HTTLAP	Pascal/Delphi
varIdentifier ← expression ;	varidentifier := expression ;

Relational operators

HTTLAP	Pascal/Delphi
=	=
≠	<>
<	<
≤	<=
>	>
≥	>=

Logical connectives

HTTLAP	Pascal/Delphi
AND	AND
OR	OR
NOT	NOT

IF statements

```
IF (condition)                  IF (condition) THEN
   Statement block ;               BEGIN
ENDIF                               Statement block ;
IF (condition)                      END ;
   Statement block ;            IF (condition) THEN
ELSE                                BEGIN
   Statement block ;                Statement block ;
ENDIF                               END ;
                                ELSE
                                    BEGIN
                                    Statement block ;
                                    END ;
```

HTTLAP	Pascal/Delphi

Zero-or-more iteration

```
WHILE (condition)
    Statement block ;
ENDWHILE
```

```
WHILE (condition) DO
    BEGIN
    Statement block ;
    END ;
```

Once-or-more iteration

```
DO
    Statement block ;
WHILE (condition)
```

```
REPEAT
    Statement block ;
UNTIL NOT (condition) ;
```

Count-controlled iteration

```
FOR counter GOES FROM start
TO finish
    Statement block
ENDFOR
```

```
FOR counter:=start TO finish DO
    BEGIN
    Statement block ;
    END ;
```

Record structures

```
NEWTYPE recordTypeName IS
    RECORD
    type:fieldIdentifier ;
    type:fieldIdentifier2 ;
    …
    ENDRECORD
```

```
TYPE
recordTypeName=RECORD
    fieldIdentifier:type ;
    fieldIdentifier2:type ;
    …
END ;
```

Reading from text files

```
file:inFile ;
inFile ← 'file path' ;
Open (inFile) ;
Get (inFile, REFERENCE:varIdent, …) ;

Close (inFile) ;
```

```
VAR
    inFile:Text ;
Assign (inFile, 'file path') ;
Reset (inFile) ;
Readln (inFile, varIdent) ;
Close (inFile) ;
```

Writing to text files

```
file:outFile ;
outFile ← 'file path' ;
Open (outFile) ;
Write (outFile,varIdent, …) ;
Close (outFile) ;
```

```
VAR
    outFile:text ;
Assign (outFile, 'file path') ;
Rewrite (outFile) ;
Writeln (outFile, varIdent) ;
Close (outFile);
```

HTTLAP	Pascal/Delphi

Arrays

```
ARRAY:arrayName OF [size] type ;    VAR
ARRAY:arrayName2D OF                    arrayName:ARRAY [start..finish]
   [size,size] type;                       OF type ; = new type
                                               [size] ;
                                        arrayName2D:ARRAY [start..finish,
arrayName [index] ← expression ;        start..finish] OF type ;
varIdentifier ← arrayName [index] ;  arrayName [index] = expression ;
                                        varIdentifier = arrayName [index] ;
```

Sub-programs

```
FUNCTION FuncIdentifier              FUNCTION FuncIdentifier
(type: parameter1 , …,)RETURNS type        (parameter1:type ;…): type ;
   Statements ;                          BEGIN
   RETURN expression ;                    Statements ;
ENDFUNCTION                               FuncIdentifier := expression ;
                                          END ;

PROCEDURE ProcIdentifier             PROCEDURE ProcIdentifier
(type: parameter1 , …,)                    (parameter1:type ; …) ;
   Statements ;                          BEGIN
ENDPROCEDURE                             Statements ;
                                          END ;
```

Glossary

abstract   The simplification of detail. "Car" is an abstraction for a very complex piece of machinery with many thousands of individual components. Abstraction is a key feature of computing for it allows the construction of data types and operations.

algorithm   A set of procedures or instructions for solving a problem or computing a result. The word is a derivation of Al-Khwarizmi (native of Khwarizm), the name given to the ninth century mathematician Abu Ja'far Mohammed ben Musa who came from Khwarizm (modern day Khiva in the south of Uzbekistan).

array   A collection of equally sized components. Each array element is accessed by its index (its position in the array). Analogous with the racks of pigeon holes used for storing mail in an office. In mathematics it would be known as a vector.

bit   A binary digit. The fundamental unit of storage. Can hold 2^0 values (0 . . .1).

Black Label   The best clan in the online mode of Insomniac Games' best selling Playstation 3 game *Resistance: Fall of Man*.

Boolean   After George Boole (1815–1864) who devised a system of algebra (Boolean algebra) whose elements have one of two possible values: True and False. Operations on the elements are logical (AND, OR, NOT, etc.) rather than arithmetic ($+$, $-$, $\div$, $\times$, etc.).

bug   The commonly used term for a software defect. Defects are errors in programming that cause programs to produce the wrong answers or even crash.

byte   8 bits. Can store 2^8 values (0 . . .255, or -128 . . .$+127$).

byte code   The machine code of the Java Virtual Machine. Byte code is produced by a Java compiler and is interpreted by the JVM.

C   A *programming* language. C is a *procedural language*. It has been around for a long time. Its syntax allows for very powerful coding techniques but its flexibility can trip up the unwary novice.

C#   C#, pronounced "C sharp" (or "C hash" if you are feeling mischievous) is Microsoft's answer to *Java*. It is a bit like *C++* and a bit like *Java*. You can look the rest up for yourself.

C++   C++ (pronounced "C plus plus") is an *object-oriented* programming language. It is regarded as a descendant of *C*. Its name is a pun. In *C* the *++ operator* adds 1 to a variable. Hence *C++* is *C* code for C-plus-one. Hah hah. *C++ is* very popular today, especially with games programmers.

code, source code   A set of statements or instructions written in a human-readable programming language (e.g., Java). The source code is compiled to produce the machine-executable program.

comments   Strings of text put into program source code that are ignored by the compiler. Comments are used to annotate source code to make it easier to read and understand.

compilation   The process of translating source code understood by humans into the binary form computers can read.

condition   A test of a Boolean relation against which certain processing is carried out depending on the relation's truth value. For example:

```
IF (salary > 20000)
    Display ('High salary') ;
ELSE
    Display ('Low salary') ;
ENDIF
```

constant   A data item whose value cannot be changed within a program. We would use a constant, say, to represent the value of pi in a program:

```
real:pi IS 3.14159 ;
```

data   The values passed into, around, and out of a program.

data structure   A collection of data items in some ordered way.

data types   See *type*.

debugging   The removal of bugs or defects from a program.

defect   Also known as a bug, a defect is something that causes a program to behave incorrectly or to produce erroneous results.

element   A member of a data structure. For example, a node in a list, or the data that occupies one index position in an array.

file   A place for storing data outside of a program. A company might have a file of employee records and another file that stores order details.

float   The *type* used to store *real* numbers in C, C++, Java, and other C-like languages.

flow   The path taken through a program; the progression from one program statement to the next.

flowchart   A diagrammatic representation of the set of possible paths through a program.

function   A sub-program that processes zero, one, or more parameters and returns a result. For example, we could write a function that takes a number as a parameter and returns the square root of that number.

identifier   The name given to a *variable*.

input   The values that go into a program or subprogram.

iteration   A technique for performing the repeated execution of one or more statements within a program.

Java   Another *object-oriented* language. It shares many syntactic features with C and C++ but is quite different in many aspects. It is very popular for programming Web-based applications. Unlike C, C++, Pascal, and other languages, Java is not compiled to machine code. Instead the Java compiler creates a higher-level *byte code* which is interpreted and executed by a Java virtual machine (JVM), JVMs exist for most of today's computing platforms such as Windows, UNIX, Linux, etc. This means that a programmer can write a Java program knowing that it will run successfully on all computers regardless of their *operating system*. This is unlike the traditional languages like C and Pascal which require a special compiler for each operating system on which the program is intended to be run. One of the drawbacks of Java though is that the byte code is slower to execute than the machine code produced by other language compilers.

JavaScript   Do not confuse JavaScript with *Java*. It has a few superficial similarities to Java but that is about it. It was developed by Netscape Corporation and the name is a property of Sun Microsystems. Microsoft has its own version of the language called JScript. JavaScript is a *scripting language* rather than a compiled language which means that programs written in it can only run within a dedicated environment (such as a web page). JavaScript is handy for putting clever features into web pages but is not used for mainstream software development.

Linux A popular operating system developed by Linus Torvalds and based on the well-established UNIX operating system.

loop See iteration.

memory The parts of a computer that retain data. The hard disc is a permanent memory that retains data even when powered down, while the RAM (random access memory) that the computer uses to store running programs is typically *volatile* memory that loses its data when power is removed.

method The name given to the subprograms of a class in an object-oriented program.

Object-oriented programming A style of programming that uses the principles of encapsulation, inheritance, polymorphism, and data hiding.

OOP See *objected-oriented programming.*

operand The data manipulated by an operator. The arithmetic expression $3 + 4$ has one operator, "+", and two operands, 3, and 4.

operating system The special piece of software that controls a computer's hardware and which manages the basic system operations (such as running programs, copying files, etc.). The most popular operating systems for today's personal computers are Apple's OS X, Linux, and Microsoft Windows (not in that order).

operator Something that performs an operation on one or more operands (see *operand* above).

output The data passed out of a program or sub-program.

Parameter A data item passed to a sub-program (function, procedure, or method). Parameters have three forms:

•. Input: used only to pass values into the sub-program.

•. Output: used by the sub-program for passing values out.

•. Input/Output: a data value passed into a sub-program which is subsequently modified by the sub-program.

problem What you will have if you do not study hard enough.

procedure A type of sub-program that performs a series of actions, which may receive zero or more parameters, and which (depending on the calling technique used) may change the values of zero or more of its parameters.

program A collection of statements representing an algorithm that carry out some specified purpose. Also known as software.

programming language A set of syntactic and semantic rules that allows a human to write a set of instructions in human-readable form that can be translated by a compiler into a form that is executable on a computer.

pseudo-code A bit like a programming language, but lacking the formal syntactic and semantic rules. It is used as a general way of writing algorithms without being tied down to any particular programming language.

RAM Random Access Memory – formally a type of computer storage whose contents can be accessed in any order. Normally we think of RAM as being the memory chips on a computer that store running programs and which, these days, is measured in the hundreds of megabytes. However, formats like DVD-RAM allow random access memory on optical discs. Though most RAM can be written to, strictly speaking the term refers to any memory whose contents can be accessed in any order.

recursion See page 553.

Resistance: Fall of Man The classic Playstation 3 first-person shooter game from Insomniac Games. Mayhem and laughter for all.

ROM Read-Only Memory. A form of computer memory that can be read from (usually in a random access manner) but which cannot be written to. CD-ROMs are of this form.

schematic logic   See *pseudo-code*.

selection   See *condition*.

sequence   An ordered set of instructions in a computer program.

source code   See *code*.

statement   An action or command in a computer program.

state-transition diagram   A diagrammatic representation of the different states a system can be in, and the transitions that can occur between states.

structure chart   An ill-defined term that covers a number of diagrammatic representations of the structure of programs and software systems. There are many different notational forms.

structure text   See *pseudo-code*.

structured English   See *pseudo-code*.

syntax   The set of allowable words and symbols and their permitted orderings in a programming language.

syntax error   An error in which a programming language's rules of syntax have been violated resulting in source code that will be rejected by a compiler.

type   A name for a set of values together with the various operations that can be performed on values of that type.

UML   Unified Modelling Language. A set of diagrammatic notations used to design and document object-oriented software.

UNIX   An operating system developed in the 1960s which is still widely used today owing to its renowned stability. Popular among middle-aged bearded types with pony tails. The BSD UNIX distribution is the underlying operating system beneath Apple's OS X.

variable   A place in memory (with an *identifier* as a name) where a value is stored. Its value can be changed by the program.

Visual Basic   One of a stable of Microsoft programming languages beginning with the word "visual." These are not *visual programming* languages in the true sense but are so named because they include sophisticated interface builders that allow the program's graphical user interface (its windows, menus, etc.) to be created by dragging and dropping objects on the screen. The dragging and dropping of graphical objects is the only similarity these languages have with true *visual programming* languages.

visual programming   A visual programming language uses a spatial arrangement of special symbols, graphics, and textual elements to define a program. Visual programming languages are typically very graphical and often show connections between components as arrows and lines. Do not confuse with Visual Basic which is not, despite what its name suggests, a visual programming language.

window   A central feature of the graphical user interface. Windows are typically rectangular and contain some interface components (buttons, text boxes, etc.), some graphics, or some text (e.g., a document window in a word processor). The window can be manipulated with a pointer controlled by a mouse or keyboard. Common operating systems that use windowing today are Apple OS, X Window System (on UNIX), and Microsoft Windows.

word   A grouping of one or more *bytes* used to store a *data* item. A computer that stores *integer* numbers in 2-byte (16 *bit*) words can, therefore, represent integers from 0 to 65,535 (or between −32,678 . . . 0 . . . 32,767 if negative numbers are required). A 1-byte word can only store 256 (i.e. 2^8) different values as 0 . . . 255 or −128 . . . 0 . . . 127. It is important when writing programs that you know what the word size is on the computer and compiler system that you are writing for as this will affect the maximum and minimum values that your variables can hold – see ASSUMPTIONS.

Solutions to Selected Exercises

Here are solutions to some of the exercises in the book. Some of the solutions are as full as I can make them, others are partial.

In-text Exercises (All Chapters)

In-text Exercise 01 (Chapter 4)

Before you leave home in the morning you check to see whether it is raining; if it is you take an umbrella with you. Write an IF...ENDIF *construct that shows this decision-making process.*

```
1.   IF (raining)
         1.1.   Take umbrella ;
     ENDIF
```

In-text Exercise 02 (Chapter 4)

Write an IF...ENDIF *construct that adds a 10% tip to a restaurant bill and compliments the chef if the service was of a high standard. After the* ENDIF *add a statement to pay the bill and convince yourself that the tip is only added when good service is received.*

```
1.   IF (high-standard service)
         1.1.   Add 10% tip to bill ;
         1.2.   Compliment the chef ;
     ENDIF
2.   Pay bill ;
```

In-text Exercise 03 (Chapter 4)

In the above WHILE *loop, why is there a statement to add 1 to the number of sugars added?*

If the statement were not there then the loop would never terminate. The algorithm would never update its own tally of how many sugars had been added and so the condition controlling the WHILE loop would always be true. The statement comes at the bottom of the loop because only after adding a sugar to the cup should we update the tally.

In-text Exercise 04 (Chapter 5)

Look at Solution 5.1 and identify these two aspects of the problem. State which group of actions deals with making the coffee and which group describes how to process a single cup.

Tasks #1 to #8 deal with making the coffee and Tasks #9 to #14 describe how to *process* a single cup.

In-text Exercise 05 (Chapter 5)

Why has the task "Make note of van's payload" been removed?

Because the new Tasks #1 and #3.2 mean that after despatching the van we already know its payload.

In-text Exercise 06 (Chapter 6)

Do not move on until you understand how the three conditions are mutually exclusive, that is, only one can be true at a time. You can show this by drawing a truth table:

parcelWeight	Condition		
	parcelWeight up to (and including) 5 kilos	parcelWeight more than 5 and less than 10 kilos	parcelWeight 10 kilos or over
4 kg	**True**	False	False
5 kg	**True**	False	False
9 kg	False	**True**	False
10 kg	False	False	**True**
11 kg	False	False	**True**

In-text Exercise 07 (Chapter 6)

Explain why this is a determinate loop.

We do not know until we ask our guest how many times the loop's action body should be executed, and the number would likely vary from guest to guest. But, once we have found out how many sugars are required we can calculate how many times to go through the loop. If two sugars are wanted then the loop must execute twice. If no sugar is required then the loop will iterate zero times, that is, the action block will not be carried out.

In-text Exercise 08 (Chapter 9)

Write down the ASCII codes for the following characters

Character	ASCII code	Character	ASCII code
B	**66**	TAB	**9**
V	**86**	{	**123**
3	**51**	Z	**90**
?	**63**	z	**122**

In-text Exercise 09 (Chapter 9)

What does the following statement assign to myLetter?

$$\boxed{myLetter} \leftarrow Chr\ (Ord\ ('B'))\ ;$$

A weird statement. It assigns 'B' to myLetter. Ord('B') is 66 and Chr (66) is 'B'!

In-text Exercise 10 (Chapter 9)

We said that strings are ordered collections of characters. Assume that each character's position in a string is given by an integer, where the first character occupies position 0 and the last character occupies position n-1 where n is the length of the string. Write down what characters occupy positions 0, 1, and 7 in the string shown in Figure 9.5.

Position	Character
0	'A'
1	' ' (a space)
7	'g'

What is the position of the last character in the string in Figure 9.5?

The position is 7: although it is the eighth character, the position numbering starts from zero, so the eighth character occupies position 7 in the string.

In Figure 9.5 the space follows the 'A' in the string. Does the space character come before or after the 'A' in the ASCII character set?

Before. The space is ASCII number 32, and the 'A' is ASCII code 65. 32 comes before 65, so the space comes before 'A' in the ASCII set.

In-text Exercise 11 (Chapter 9)

Using the HTTLAP pseudo-code declare two string *variables* firstName *and* lastName. *Then write two assignment statements to assign your first name to* firstName *and your family name to* lastName.

```
string: firstName ,
        lastName  ;
firstName  ← 'Paul' ;
lastName  ← 'Vickers' ;
```

In-text Exercise 12 (Chapter 9)

Declare a constant monthsInYear to hold the value 12.

```
integer: monthsInYear  IS 12 ;
```

In-text Exercise 13 (Chapter 11)

Write pseudo-code to declare an integer number, request the user to enter an integer, get the integer from the keyboard, and display that integer multiplied by 2 on the screen.

```
integer: number  ;
Display ('Please enter a number: ') ;
Get (keyboard, REFERENCE: number ) ;
Display ( number  × 2) ;
```

In-text exercise 14 (Chapter 11)

Write pseudo-code to declare a file to hold a set of class test marks, open the file, and then close it again.

```
file: marks  ;
marks  ← 'testMarks.txt' ;
Open ( marks ) ;
Close ( marks ) ;
```

In-text Exercise 15 (Chapter 12)

To check you have grasped array indexing, assume the integer variable index has the value 5 and write the results of the five assignment statements above in the array pictured below:

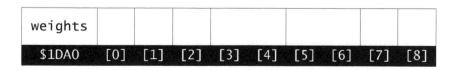

What do you think would be the result of the following assignment?

```
weights  [ index  + 4] ← 2.0 ;
```

Here are the first four assignment statements:

```
weights [0] ← 2.0 ;
weights [0 + 1] ← 3.0 ;
weights [index] ← 4.5 ;
weights [index + 3] ← 7.0 ;
```

And this is what the array would look like afterwards:

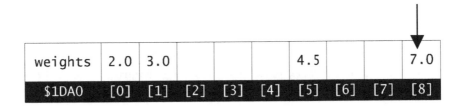

The first statement puts 2.0 into the first element (index [0]).

The second puts 3.0 into the second element index [1] (because the expression 0 + 1 is 1).

The third statement puts 4.5 into the sixth element (index [5]) because the variable index has the value 5.

The fourth statement puts 7.0 into the ninth element (index [8]) because index + 3 is 8.

The fifth statement

```
weights [0] ← weights [8] ;
```

causes the array to look like this:

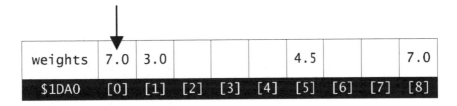

The first element has been overwritten with the value 7.0 because the statement assigns the value of array element [8] to array element [0].

Finally, the statement

```
weights [index + 4] ← 2.0 ;
```

is in error because index + 4 is 9 and the array does not have an element with an index of 9.

In-text Exercise 16 (Chapter 12)

Why does statement #12.1 in Solution 12.2 not say Length (weights) - 1 ?
Because statement #12.1 is calculating the average of all the array elements. To calculate an average you have to divide the sum of all the elements by the

number of elements. `weights` has nine elements, so the sum of all the elements needs to be divided by 9. If we used `Length (weights) - 1` we would be dividing by 8 and not 9. You need to be very careful when working with array sizes to check when you are using the array size as an index and when you are not. Index values have to start from zero.

In-text Exercise 17 (Chapter 12)

Write statements to assign the values `'Professor'`, `'Higgins'`, `'Henry'` *to the* `title`, `familyName` *and* `givenName` *fields of the patient record held in the second element of the* `patientArray` *array.*

```
patientArray[1].title ← 'Professor' ;
patientArray[1].familyName ← 'Higgins' ;
patientArray[1].givenName ← 'Henry' ;
```

In-text Exercise 18 (Chapter 13)

Define an array for the shopping list in Figure 13.1.

```
ARRAY:shoppingList [20] OF string ;
```

In-text Exercise 19 (Chapter 13)

What would the following statements produce as output?

```
Display (head) ;
```

would write `'Study'` to the screen as that is the room address held in `head`.

```
Display (head→.bookTitle) ;
```

would give us "How to Solve It" as that is the value of the `bookTitle` field in the record stored at the address held by `head`. `head` is not a record and it has no fields – `head` just points to a record (see Figure 13.11).

In-text Exercise 20 (Chapter 13)

Consider the following declarations and assignments:

```
integer:x ;
→integer:a ;
→integer:b ;
x ← 7 ;
a ← New (integer) ; // Assume the new integer is located
                    // at memory location $30FF
b ← a ;
```

1. *What would the following statements display on the screen?*

```
Display (x) ;
```

x is a regular integer variable, so its value (7) is displayed.

Display (a *) ;*

a is a *pointer* to an integer, so the address of the integer it points to is displayed. The comment following the assignment said to assume the new integer is created at location $30FF, so "30FF" would be displayed.

Display (b *) ;*

b is also a pointer. Recall how assignments work: the value of the expression on the right of the ← is assigned to the variable on the left. On the right of the ← is a whose *value* is $30FF (an address) so this address is *copied* into b. Thus the value "30FF" is again displayed on the screen by the `Display (` b `)` statement.

2. *What does the following assignment do?*

   a→ ← x *;*

   At first sight this looks horrific, but you can solve the puzzle by applying the assignment rules as normal. The expression on the right of the ← is a variable identifier x. Thus, the value to be assigned is the value of x which is 7. What is the 7 being assigned to? The variable on the left is *a* → which we know is read as "the thing *pointed to* by *a*" (that's what the → means). What is *pointed to* by *a*? The integer stored in memory location $30FF. So, the value 7 is assigned to the integer *pointed to* by *a* at memory location $30FF. Note that 7 is not being assigned to a directly but by the thing being pointed to by a. It is very important to remember to use → when assigning values to items referenced by pointer variables.

3. *What is the effect of this assignment?*

   a→ ← a→ + 3 *;*

   We now know that we are assigning the value on the right to the integer pointed to by *a*. The expression on the right says "the value of the integer pointed to by *a* + 3". The integer pointed to by a has the value 7 (from the assignment in question 2), which gives us the expression 7 + 3 which evaluates to 10. Putting it all together then, we are assigning the integer value 10 to the integer residing at address $30FF (the location pointed to by a).

4. *What would the following statements display on the screen?*

   Display (x *) ;*

   This displays 7 as before.

   Display (a *) ;*

   This displays 30FF because we are referencing the value of a (an address) rather than the integer pointed to by a.

   Display (b *) ;*

   This also displays 30FF because b also has the value $30FF.

   Display (a→ *) ;*

This statement, because it is referencing the integer pointed to by a , displays the value 10 on the screen.

Display ($\boxed{b}{\rightarrow}$) ;

As does this because a and b both point to the same memory location.

5. *What is the effect of this assignment?*

$\boxed{a} \leftarrow \boxed{x}$;

This assigns the integer value 7 to the pointer variable a, in effect replacing the address \$30FF previously held in a with the address \$0007. a now no longer points to the integer at \$30FF but to the memory location \$0007.

In-text Exercise 21 (Chapter 13)

Try rewriting the loop, this time comparing **current** *to* **end** *to check for the end of the list. You should find that the solution is not quite as straightforward as it first sounds.*

We might at first try the following solution which simply replaces NULL with end in the WHILE's condition:

```
current ← head ;
WHILE (current ≠ end)
   Display (current→.bookTitle) ;
   current ← current→.next ;
ENDWHILE
```

There's a problem with this though. Using the following list as an example, let's follow the algorithm through.

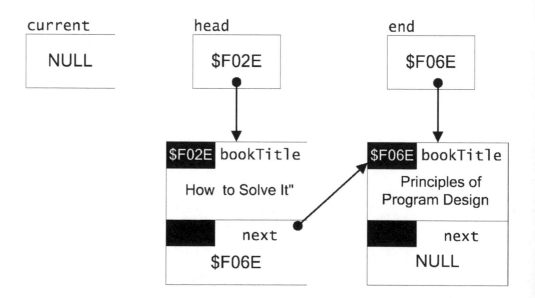

First, we assign the value of head to current giving:

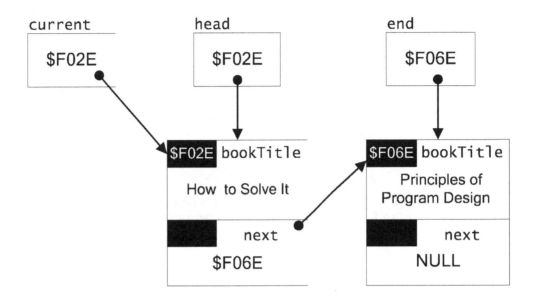

Then we test the WHILE loop. current does not equal end so the loop body is entered. The Display procedure is called writing "How to Solve It" on the screen and current is updated to current→.next giving us:

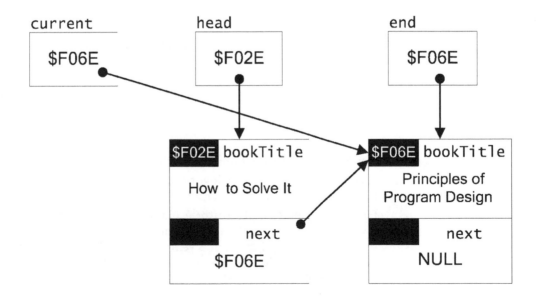

Now `current` points to the last record in the list. But when we test the WHILE condition again it is False because `current` *does* equal `end` (they're both $F06E – pointing to the last record). This time the loop body is not entered and so the title of the last book in the list is not displayed. Here is one way round the problem:

```
current  ←  head  ;
WHILE ( current  ≠  end )
    Display ( current →. bookTitle ) ;
    current  ←  current →. next  ;
ENDWHILE
Display ( current →. bookTitle ) ;
current  ←  current →. next  ;
```

It is not an elegant solution and offers more scope for programmer errors, and so I advise you to stick to testing for NULL rather than equivalence with the end pointer.

In-text Exercise 22 (Chapter 13)

Using the list from Figure 13.23 again, trace through the `DeleteSortedNode` function trying to delete the following books and in each case state the value of the return result.

1. *C# Concisely* — False: doesn't exist in the list.
2. *Conceptual Blockbusting* — True: first record.
3. *Principles of Program Design* — True: third record.
4. *The Psychology of Computer Programming* — True: last record.
5. *Z for Software Engineers* — False: book not in the list.

Chapter 1

End of Chapter Exercises

1. There are some quite formal definitions, but in layman's terms an algorithm is a set of clear instructions to carry out a defined task.
2. A computer program is an algorithm expressed in a programming language to be carried out by a computer.
3. **High**: black leather. **Medium**: A black leather billfold with a single fastening. Two main currency pockets plus slots for cards. **Low**: A black leather billfold with a single fastening about 5 years old, contains £25 in cash: a £20 note (the old design with Edward Elgar on the back) and a £5 note; 4 debit card receipts, 1 ATM receipt, 1 debit card, 1 credit card, and my Engineering Council registration card ...

6. Well, you might be a history student taking programming as a compulsory course! The answer "the assassination in Sarajevo of Archduke Ferdinand by Gavrilo Princip" is too simplistic and will not receive credit.

Chapter 1 Projects

StockSnackz Vending Machine

No solutions for this chapter.

Stocksfield Fire Service: Hazchem Signs

No solutions for this chapter.

Puzzle World: Roman Numerals and Chronograms

No solutions for this chapter.

Pangrams: Holoalphabetic Sentences

No solutions for this chapter.

Online Bookstore: ISBNs

No solutions for this chapter.

Chapter 2

End of Chapter Exercises

1. Car's range = 840 km (60 × 14). 2000 km ÷ 840 km = 2.38, therefore we must **fill the tank 3 times** (doing it only twice causes the car to stop at 1,680 km).

   How many miles can you travel on 10 gallons of fuel?

   Fuel consumption = 14 km/l = (14 ÷ 1.609344) = 8.699 miles/litre.

   8.699 miles/litre = 8.699 ÷ 0.219969157 = 39.55 miles/imperial gallon = 8.699 ÷ 0.264172051 = 32.93 miles/U.S. gallon.

   Therefore, 10 imperial gallons will get you 39.55 × 10 = 395.5 miles. 10 U.S. gallons will take you 32.93 × 10 = 329.3 miles.

2. Getting dressed in the morning:

   ```
   Put on underwear.
   Put on socks.
   Put on trousers.
   Put on shirt.
   Put on shoes.
   ```

4. Filling a car with fuel:

   ```
   Drive to petrol station.
   Unlock fuel cap.
   Get out of and lock car (remember to take wallet).
   ```

```
Select correct fuel (diesel or unleaded).
Put nozzle into filler cap.
Pump desired amount of fuel.
Replace nozzle.
Replace fuel cap and secure.
Pay for fuel.
Unlock car, get in, drive away.
```

Chapter 2 Projects

StockSnackz Vending Machine

1. Install the new machine.
2. Turn on power.
3. Load machine with snacks.
4. Dispense snacks.
5. Show dispensing report.

Stocksfield Fire Service: Hazchem Signs

1. Decode first character and give fire-fighting instructions.
2. Decode second character and give precaution instructions.
3. Decode third character and state whether public hazard exists.

Puzzle World: Roman Numerals and Chronograms

No solution provided.

Pangrams: Holoalphabetic Sentences

No solution provided.

Online Bookstore: ISBNs

No solution provided.

Chapter 3

End of Chapter Exercises

Note, for space reasons, documentation is not included.

1. A difficult question until you realize algebra is the way to go. n = Nick, l = Lynne, a = Alf, s = Shadi, c = Chris.

   Nick's computer has three times the memory of Lynne's and Alf's computers put together:

   (1) $n = 3(l + a)$

Shadi's PC has twice as much memory as Chris's:

(2) $s = 2c$

Nick's computer has one-and-a-half times the memory of Shadi's:

(3) $n = \dfrac{3}{2}s$

Between them, Alf and Shadi's computers have as much memory as Lynne's plus twice the memory of Chris's:

(4) $a + s = l + 2c$

Shadi, Chris, Nick, Alf, and Lynne's PCs have 2,800 megabytes of memory between them:

(5) $s + c + n + a + l = 2800$

We know from (1) that $l + a = \dfrac{n}{3}$, so we can rearrange (5) to give:

(6) $c + s + \dfrac{4}{3}n = 2800$

We also know from (2) that $c = \dfrac{s}{2}$, so we can substitute again to change (6) into:

(7) $\dfrac{3}{2}s + \dfrac{4}{3}n = 2800$

We also know from (3) that $n = \dfrac{3}{2}s$, so $\dfrac{4}{3}n = \dfrac{4}{3} \times \dfrac{3}{2}s = \dfrac{12}{6}s = \dfrac{4}{2}s$ which means we can substitute in (7) to give:

(8) $\dfrac{7}{2}s = 2800$

Therefore, $7s = 5600$, $s = 800$, so Shadi's computer has 800 MB. From (2) we can say that Chris's computer has 400 MB. Nick's PC has 1200 MB (from (3)). (4) tells us that Lynne and Alf's computers have the same amount of memory, and between them they have 400 MB from (1), therefore they must have 200 MB each. To double check, we can add these all up: 800 + 400 + 1200 + 200 + 200 = 2800.

Try doing this exercise with words alone!

2. Here is my solution:

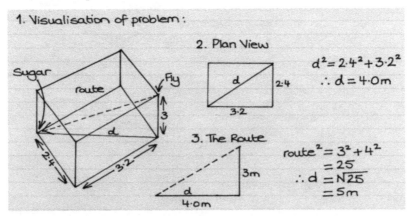

3. Look at the row and column numbers of the white squares. R1C1 is white, R2C2 is white, R1C3 is white, R2C3 is black. What's the pattern?
A square whose row and column numbers are either **both** odd or **both** even is white.

5. It's a problem of repeated division and amounts left over after division. To keep the solution short lets work with U.S. coins because there are fewer of them, but the principle is the same regardless of the number of different coin denominations:

```
// Note we need to do whole number division, so 76 ÷ 25 = 3,
remainder 1.
1.  No. of 25¢ coins needed is amount of change to give ÷ 25 ;
2.  Amount left over = remainder from step 1 ;
3.  No. of 10¢ coins = amount left over ÷ 10 ;
4.  Amount left over = remainder from step 3 ;
5.  No. of 5¢ coins = amount left over ÷ 5 ;
6.  No. of 1¢ coins = remainder from step 5 ;
```

Chapter 3 Projects

StockSnackz Vending Machine

Solution looks a lot like the one from Chapter 2:

```
1.  Install the new machine ;
2.  Turn on power ;
3.  Load machine with snacks ;
4.  Dispense snacks ;
5.  Show dispensing report ;
```

Stocksfield Fire Service: Hazchem Signs

```
1.  Decode first character ;
2.  Give fire-fighting instructions ;
3.  Decode second character ;
4.  Give precaution instructions ;
5.  Decode third character ;
6.  State whether public hazard exists ;
```

Puzzle World: Roman Numerals and Chronograms

See accompanying website.

Pangrams: Holoalphabetic Sentences

See accompanying website.

See accompanying website.

Chapter 4

End of Chapter Exercises

1. We use the IF when we want to choose whether or not to perform a single action (or sequence of actions). We use the WHILE when we want to repeatedly perform an action or sequence of actions. Both involve conditionally carrying out an action, but they differ in that the WHILE will repeatedly carry out its action block whereas the IF will only carry out its action block once.

2. When it is raining the hat and shoes are worn. When it is not raining (which could be sunny) then the hat, shoes, and sunglasses are worn. Sunglasses are worn conditionally dependent on the IF construct.

3. What items will be purchased a) on Thursday, b) on Saturday?
   Answer: a) milk and bread, b) milk, newspaper, peanuts, bread
   You might have thought that peanuts were bought on Thursday too, but this is because the buy peanuts action is wrongly indented. The thing which really matters is that the buy peanuts action comes inside the ENDIF keyword. All the actions between the IF and ENDIF keywords are carried out when the condition is true.

4. No stories will be read as the WHILE loop is conditional upon breakfast not being finished but we can see from steps 1 and 2 that breakfast has been eaten before the WHILE loop action is reached.

5. Adding cheese, lettuce and tomatoes:
```
Get cheese, lettuce, and tomatoes requirements ;
IF (cheese required)
   Add cheese ;
ENDIF
IF (lettuce required)
   Add lettuce ;
ENDIF
IF (tomatoes required)
   Add tomatoes ;
ENDIF
```

7. Potency calculator:
```
1.   Start potency at 100% ;
2.   WHILE (potency greater than or equal to 50%)
        2.1.   Display Month & potency message ;
        2.2.   Reduce potency by 6% ;
        2.3.   Move to next month ;
     ENDWHILE
```

10. *Earth's Next Top Professor*

First solution

```
1.   Ask judge for professor's name ;
2.   Get teaching ability score ;
3.   Get humor score ;
4.   Get knowledge score ;
5.   Get good looks score ;
6.   IF (teaching + humor + knowledge + looks is greater than 20)
          6.1.   Display 'scores too high' message ;
          6.2.   Set teaching ability score to 5 ;
          6.3.   Set humor score to 5 ;
          6.4.   Set knowledge score to 5 ;
          6.5.   Set good looks score to 5 ;
     ENDIF
```

Second solution

```
1.   WHILE (professors to judge)
          1.1.   Ask judge for professor's name ;
          1.2.   Get teaching ability score ;
          1.3.   Get humor score ;
          1.4.   Get knowledge score ;
          1.5.   Get good looks score ;
          1.6.   IF (total score is greater than 20)
                     1.6.1.   Display 'scores too high' ;
                     1.6.2.   Set teaching ability score to 5 ;
                     1.6.3.   Set humor score to 5 ;
                     1.6.4.   Set knowledge score to 5 ;
                     1.6.5.   Set good looks score to 5 ;
                 ENDIF
     ENDWHILE
```

Third solution

```
1.   WHILE judges to give scores
          1.1.   WHILE (professors to judge)
                     1.1.1.   Ask judge for professor's name ;
                     1.1.2.   Get teaching ability score ;
                     1.1.3.   Get humor score ;
                     1.1.4.   Get knowledge score ;
                     1.1.5.   Get good looks score ;
                     1.1.6.   IF (total score is greater than 20)
                                  1.1.6.1.   Display 'scores too high' ;
                                  1.1.6.2.   Set teaching ability score
                                             to 5 ;
                                  1.1.6.3.   Set humor score to 5 ;
                                  1.1.6.4.   Set knowledge score to 5 ;
                                  1.1.6.5.   Set good looks score to 5 ;
                              ENDIF
                 ENDWHILE
     ENDWHILE
```

11. Making an omelette.
```
Find out how many people to feed (up to 3) ;
Add (2 × no. people) eggs to bowl ;
Add (pinch × no. people) salt to bowl ;
Add (pinch × no. people) pepper to bowl ;
Add (100 ml × no. people) milk to bowl ;
Add (0.25 × no. people) onion to bowl ;
Add (60 gm × no. people) cheese to bowl ;
Add (knob × no. people) butter to bowl ;
Put pan on heat ;
Mix ingredients in bowl ;
Add mixture to pan ;
WHILE (surface not firming up)
   Cook omelette ;
ENDWHILE ;
Get garnish requirements ;
IF (parsley required)
   Sprinkle parsley ;
ENDIF
IF (parmesan required)
   Sprinkle parmesan ;
ENDIF
Divide omelette by no. people ;
WHILE (portions served not equal to no. required)
   Serve portion on plate ;
   Add 1 to number portions served ;
ENDWHILE
```

13. Constrained hamburger problem:
```
Get cheese requirements ;
IF (cheese required)
   Add cheese ;
ENDIF
IF (cheese NOT required)
   Add lettuce ;
   Add tomatoes ;
ENDIF
```

The IF appears to be missing the ability to automatically add lettuce and tomatoes when cheese is not required.

Chapter 4 Projects

StockSnackz Vending Machine

Pushing Button 1 dispenses a milk chocolate bar, Button 2 a muesli bar, Button 3 a pack of cheese puffs, Button 4 an apple, Button 5 a pack of popcorn, while pushing Button 6 displays on the machine's small screen a summary of how many of each item have been dispensed. Pushing the Buttons 0, 7, 8, or 9 has no effect.

Dispense a single snack:

```
IF (button 1 pressed)
   Dispense milk chocolate ;
ENDIF
IF (button 2 pressed)
   Dispense muesli bar ;
ENDIF
IF (button 3 pressed)
   Dispense cheese puffs ;
ENDIF
IF (button 4 pressed)
   Dispense apple ;
ENDIF
IF (button 5 pressed)
   Dispense popcorn ;
ENDIF
IF (button 6 pressed)
   Print sales summary ;
ENDIF
```

Do this repeatedly:

```
1.   Install machine ;
2.   Turn on power ;
3.   Fill machine ;
4.   WHILE (not the end of the day)
          4.1.   IF (button 1 pressed)
                     4.1.1.   Dispense milk chocolate ;
                 ENDIF
          4.2.   IF (button 2 pressed)
                     4.2.1.   Dispense muesli bar ;
                 ENDIF
          4.3.   IF (button 3 pressed)
                     4.3.1.   Dispense cheese puffs ;
                 ENDIF
          4.4.   IF (button 4 pressed)
                     4.4.1.   Dispense apple ;
                 ENDIF
          4.5.   IF (button 5 pressed)
                     4.5.1.   Dispense popcorn ;
                 ENDIF
          4.6.   IF (button 6 pressed)
                     4.6.1.   Print sales summary ;
                 ENDIF
     ENDWHILE
```

Stocksfield Fire Service: Hazchem Signs

```
// First character
IF character is 1
   Use coarse spray ;
ENDIF
```

```
IF character is 2
   Use fine spray ;
ENDIF
IF character is 3
   Use foam ;
ENDIF
IF character is 4
   Use dry agent ;
ENDIF
// Second character
IF character is P
   Use LTS ;
   Dilute spillage ;
   Risk of explosion ;
ENDIF
 ...
IF character is Z
   Use BA & Fire kit ;
   Contain spillage ;
ENDIF
// Third character
IF character is E
   Public hazard ;
ENDIF
```

Puzzle World: Roman Numerals & Chronograms

See accompanying website.

Pangrams: Holoalphabetic Sentences

See accompanying website.

Online Bookstore: ISBNs

See accompanying website.

Chapter 5

End of Chapter Exercises

1. a) 7 – the expression 3 + 4 gives 7.
   b) 14 – result was already 7 from the last assignment so adding another 7 takes it to 14
   c) 14 – we just assigned the value of result to itself.
   d) 7 – now we have just subtracted 7 from result.
2. Swapping variables. This algorithm will swap any two variables without the use of temporary storage. Try it out for yourself.
   1. a ← a + b ;
   2. b ← a - b ;
   3. a ← a - b ;

4. Division by subtraction.
   1. Get `firstNumber` ;
   2. Get `secondNumber` ;
   3. `counter` ← 0 ;
   4. `remainder` ← `firstNumber` ;
   5. WHILE (`remainder` ≥ `secondNumber`)
      5.1. `remainder` ← `remainder` - `secondNumber` ;
      5.2. `counter` ← `counter` + 1 ;
      ENDWHILE
   6. Display `firstNumber` divides `secondNumber` by `counter` times ;

   Note, this solution assumes both numbers are positive.

9. Calculating the lightest and average payload weight. Additions show in bold.
   ```
   // ****************************************
   // Instructions for loading vans
   // Written by Paul Vickers, June 2007
   // ****************************************
   // Initialize variables
   ```
   1.   `capacity` ← 750 ;
   2.   `numberOfVans` ← zero ;
   3.   `heaviestVan` ← zero ;
   4.   **`lightestPayload` ← 751 ;**
   5.   **`totalPayload` ← zero ;**
   6.   **`averagePayload` ;**
   7.   Get first `parcelWeight` ;
   8.   WHILE (conveyor not empty)
        // Process vans
        8.1. `payload` ← zero ;
        8.2. WHILE (`payload` + `parcelWeight` less than or equal to `capacity`) AND (conveyor NOT empty)
              // Load a single van
              8.2.1. Load parcel on van ;
              8.2.2. `payload` ← `payload` + `parcelWeight` ;
              8.2.3. Get next `parcelWeight` ;
              ENDWHILE
        8.3. Despatch van ;
        8.4. `numberOfVans` ← `numberOfVans` + 1 ;
              // Check whether this is the heaviest van
        8.5. IF (`payload` more than `heaviestVan`)
              8.5.1. `heaviestVan` ← `payload` ;
              ENDIF
              // Check if this is the lightest van
        8.6. **IF (`payload` less than `lightestPayload`)**
              8.6.1. **`lightestPayload` ← payload ;**
              ENDIF

```
                    //Add payload to total payload
        8.7.    totalPayload  ←  totalPayload  +  payload  ;
    ENDWHILE
// Calculate average payload ;
9.  IF (totalPayload NOT equal to zero) // Can't divide by zero
        9.1.  averagePayload  ←  totalPayload  ÷  numberOfVans  ;
    ENDIF
10. Report  numberOfVans  used ;
11. Report  heaviestVan  sent ;
12. Report  lightestPayload  sent out ;
13. Report  averagePayload  sent out ;
```

Chapter 5 Projects

StockSnackz Vending Machine

Identifier	Description	Range of Values
chocolateStock	Stock level for chocolate bars	{1..20}
muesliStock	Stock level for muesli bars	{1..20}
cheesePuffStock	Stock level for cheese puffs	{1..20}
appleStock	Stock level for apples	{1..20}
popcornStock	Stock level for popcorn	{1..20}

```
1.  Install machine ;
2.  Turn on power ;
3.  Fill machine ;
4.  chocolateStock  ← 5 ;
5.  muesliStock  ← 5 ;
6.  cheesePuffStock  ← 5 ;
7.  appleStock  ← 5 ;
8.  popcornStock  ← 5 ;
9.  WHILE (not the end of the day)
        9.1.  IF (button 1 pressed)
                IF (chocolateStock > 0)
                    Dispense milk chocolate ;
                    chocolateStock  ←  chocolateStock  - 1 ;
                ENDIF
                IF (chocolateStock = 0)
                    Display 'Sold out message' ;
                ENDIF
            ENDIF
        9.2.  IF (button 2 pressed)
                IF (muesliStock > 0)
                    Dispense muesli bar ;
                    muesliStock  ←  muesliStock  - 1 ;
                ENDIF
```

```
                              IF (muesliStock = 0)
                                  Display 'Sold out message' ;
                              ENDIF
                          ENDIF
             9.3.    IF (button 3 pressed)
                          IF (cheesePuffStock > 0)
                              Dispense cheese puffs ;
                              cheesePuffStock ← cheesePuffStock - 1 ;
                          ENDIF
                          IF (cheesePuffStock = 0)
                              Display 'Sold out message' ;
                          ENDIF
                      ENDIF
             9.4.    IF (button 4 pressed)
                          IF (appleStock > 0)
                              Dispense apple ;
                              appleStock ← appleStock - 1 ;
                          ENDIF
                          IF (appleStock = 0)
                              Display 'Sold out message' ;
                          ENDIF
                      ENDIF
             9.5.    IF (button 5 pressed)
                          IF (popcornStock > 0)
                              Dispense popcorn ;
                              popcornStock ← popcornStock - 1 ;
                          ENDIF
                          IF (popcornStock = 0)
                              Display 'Sold out message' ;
                          ENDIF
                      ENDIF
             9.6.    IF (button 6 pressed)
                          Print sales summary ;
                      ENDIF
             9.7.    IF (button 0, 7, 8, 9 pressed)
                          Display 'Invalid choice message' ;
                      ENDIF
             ENDWHILE
```

Stocksfield Fire Service: Hazchem Signs

Identifier	Description	Range of Values
fireFightingCode	Fire fighting code	{1,2,3,4}
precautionsCode	Fire fighters' precautions	{P,R,S,T,W,X,Y,Z}
publicHazardCode	Public hazard	{V,blank}

Puzzle World: Roman Numerals and Chronograms

See accompanying website.

Pangrams: Holoalphabetic Sentences

See accompanying website.

Online Bookstore: ISBNs

See accompanying website.

Chapter 6

End of Chapter Exercises

1. There are two things wrong with the following IF statement. What are they?

```
IF (mark ≥ 40)
    Display 'You have passed.' ;
ELSE IF (mark ≤ 40)
    Display 'You have failed.' ;
ENDIF
```

First it is ambiguous – what should happen when **mark** is 40 as 40 satisfies both conditions? Second, the ELSE doesn't need the IF: it should just be

```
IF (mark ≥ 40)
    Display 'You have passed.' ;
ELSE
    Display 'You have failed.' ;
ENDIF
```

2. FOR loop: when you want to implement a count-controlled loop and the number of repetitions is known in advance or can be determined prior to the start of the loop.
DO...WHILE: When you want to iteratate an undetermined number of times but at least once.
DO...WHILE is a 1-or-more loop, while the WHILE is a zero-or-more loop.

3. They allow a more precise control abstraction. WHILE offers a general control abstraction that can be used to implement any iteration, but if upon examination the nature of the loop reveals certain characteristics (such as those listed in question 2) then use the appropriate iteration construct. The principle here is use the control abstraction that most closely fits the problem.

5. Calculating grades.

```
IF (studentMark at least 4) // A Grade
    studentGrade ← A ;
ELSE IF (studentMark at least 3) // B Grade
    studentGrade ← B ;
ELSE IF (studentMark at least 2) // C Grade
    studentGrade ← C ;
ELSE //Anything under 2 is a fail
    studentMark ← F ;
ENDIF
```

6. Changed grade boundaries.

```
IF (studentMark at least 4) // A Grade
    studentGrade ← A ;
ELSE IF (studentMark at least 3.5) // B Grade
    studentGrade ← B ;
ELSE IF (studentMark at least 3) // C Grade
    studentGrade ← C ;
ELSE IF (studentMark at least 2) // D Grade
    studentGrade ← D ;
ELSE //Anything under 2 is a fail
    studentMark ← F ;
ENDIF
```

7. Without the **ELSE** paths:

```
IF (studentMark at least 4) // A Grade
    studentGrade ← A ;
ENDIF
IF (studentMark at least 3.5 but less than 4) // B Grade
    studentGrade ← B ;
ENDIF
IF (studentMark at least 3 but less than 3.5) // C Grade
    studentGrade ← C ;
ENDIF
IF (studentMark at least 2 but less than 3) // D Grade
    studentGrade ← D ;
ENDIF
IF (student mark less than 2) //Anything under 2 is a fail
    studentMark ← F ;
ENDIF
```

8. For twenty students:

```
numberGrades ← 0 ;
classSize ← 20 ;
FOR (numberGrades GOES FROM 1 to classSize)
    Get studentMark ;
    IF (studentMark at least 4) // A Grade
        studentGrade ← A ;
    ELSE IF (studentMark at least 3.5) // B Grade
        studentGrade ← B ;
    ELSE IF (studentMark at least 3) // C Grade
        studentGrade ← C ;
    ELSE IF (studentMark at least 2) // D Grade
        studentGrade ← D ;
    ELSE //Anything under 2 is a fail
        studentMark ← F ;
    ENDIF
ENDFOR
```

11. Beaufort scale.

```
Display 'Enter a wind speed' ;
windSpeed ← value typed by user ;
IF (windSpeed = 0)
    Display 'Beaufort scale:0, Calm' ;
ELSE IF (windSpeed ≤ 3)
    Display 'Beaufort scale:1, Light air' ;
ELSE IF (windSpeed ≤ 7)
    Display 'Beaufort scale:2, Light breeze' ;
ELSE IF (windSpeed ≤ 12)
    Display 'Beaufort scale:3, Gentle breeze' ;
ELSE IF (windSpeed ≤ 18)
    Display 'Beaufort scale:4, Moderate breeze' ;
ELSE IF (windSpeed ≤ 24)
    Display 'Beaufort scale:5, Fresh breeze' ;
ELSE IF (windSpeed ≤ 31)
    Display 'Beaufort scale:6, Strong breeze' ;
ELSE IF (windSpeed ≤ 39)
    Display 'Beaufort scale:7, Near gale' ;
ELSE IF (windSpeed ≤ 46)
    Display 'Beaufort scale:8, Gale' ;
ELSE IF (windSpeed ≤ 54)
    Display 'Beaufort scale:9, Strong Gales' ;
ELSE IF (windSpeed ≤ 63)
    Display 'Beaufort scale:10, Storm' ;
ELSE IF (windSpeed ≤ 72)
    Display 'Beaufort scale:11, Violent storm' ;
ELSE
    Display 'Beaufort scale:12, Hurricane' ;
ENDIF
```

Chapter 6 Projects

StockSnackz Vending Machine

Use IF...ELSE:

```
1.  Install machine ;
2.  Turn on power ;
3.  Fill machine ;
4.  chocolateStock ← 5 ;
5.  muesliStock ← 5 ;
6.  cheesePuffStock ← 5 ;
7.  appleStock ← 5 ;
8.  popcornStock ← 5 ;
9.  WHILE (not the end of the day)
        9.1.  IF (button 1 pressed)
                  IF (chocolateStock > 0)
                      Dispense milk chocolate ;
```

```
                                chocolateStock ← chocolateStock - 1 ;
                        ELSE
                            Display 'Sold out message' ;
                        ENDIF
         9.2.   ELSE IF (button 2 pressed)
                    IF (muesliStock > 0)
                        Dispense muesli bar ;
                        muesliStock ← muesliStock - 1 ;
                    ELSE
                        Display 'Sold out message' ;
                    ENDIF
         9.3.   ELSE IF (button 3 pressed)
                    IF (cheesePuffStock > 0)
                        Dispense cheese puffs ;
                        cheesePuffStock ← cheesePuffStock - 1 ;
                    ELSE
                        Display 'Sold out message' ;
                    ENDIF
         9.4.   ELSE IF (button 4 pressed)
                    IF (appleStock > 0)
                        Dispense apple ;
                        appleStock ← appleStock - 1 ;
                    ELSE
                        Display 'Sold out message' ;
                    ENDIF
         9.5.   ELSE IF (button 5 pressed)
                    IF (popcornStock > 0)
                        Dispense popcorn ;
                        popcornStock ← popcornStock - 1 ;
                    ELSE
                        Display 'Sold out message' ;
                    ENDIF
         9.6.   ELSE IF (button 6 pressed)
                    Print sales summary ;
         9.7.   ELSE // we know an invalid button was pushed, no
                need to test for it.
                    Display 'Invalid choice message' ;
                ENDIF
        ENDWHILE
```

Checking for sufficient money (only partial solution given for effect):

```
  9.   priceOfChocolateBar ← 10 ;
 10.   WHILE (not the end of the day)
          10.1.   IF (button 1 pressed)
                    IF (money > priceOfChocolateBar)
                        IF (chocolateStock > 0)
                            Dispense milk chocolate ;
                            chocolateStock ← chocolateStock - 1 ;
                        ELSE
```

```
                        Display 'Sold out message' ;
                    ENDIF
                ELSE
                    Display 'Insufficient funds' message ;
                ENDIF
        10.2.  ELSE IF (button 2 pressed)
                ...
                ...
                ...
```

Giving change

Algorithm for giving change:

```
    1.    leftover ← money – priceOfSnack ;
    2.    numberFifties ← leftover ÷ 50 ;
    3.    leftover ← change MOD 50 ;
    4.    numberTwenties ← leftover ÷ 20 ;
    5.    leftover ← leftover MOD 20 ;
    6.    numberTens ← leftover ÷ 10 ;
    7.    leftover ← leftover MOD 10 ;
    8.    numberFives ← leftover ÷ 5 ;
    9.    leftover ← leftover MOD 5 ;
    10.   numberTwos ← leftover ÷ 2 ;
    11.   numberOnes ← leftover MOD 2 ;
    12.   FOR count GOES FROM 1 TO numberFifties
            Dispense 50p coin ;
          ENDFOR
    13.   FOR count GOES FROM 1 TO numberTwenties
            Dispense 20p coin ;
          ENDFOR
    14.   FOR count GOES FROM 1 TO numberTens
            Dispense 10p coin ;
          ENDFOR
    15.   FOR count GOES FROM 1 TO numberFives
            Dispense 5p coin ;
          ENDFOR
    16.   FOR count GOES FROM 1 TO numberTwos
            Dispense 2p coin ;
          ENDFOR
    17.   FOR count GOES FROM 1 to numberOnes
            Dispense 1p coin ;
          ENDFOR
```

Using change algorithm:

```
    9.    priceOfChocolateBar ← 10 ;
    10.   WHILE (not the end of the day)
            10.1.  IF (button 1 pressed)
                    IF (money > priceOfChocolateBar)
                        IF (chocolateStock > 0)
                            Dispense milk chocolate ;
```

```
                                chocolateStock ← chocolateStock - 1 ;
                                Insert change algorithm here...
                        ELSE
                            Display 'Sold out message' ;
                        ENDIF
                ELSE
                    Display 'Insufficient funds' message ;
                ENDIF
        10.2.  ELSE IF (button 2 pressed)
                ...
                ...
                ...
```

Stocksfield Fire Service: Hazchem Signs

Using IF ELSE

```
// First character
IF fireFightingCode is 1
   Use coarse spray ;
ELSE IF fireFightingCode is 2
   Use fine spray ;
ELSE IF fireFightingCode is 3
   Use foam ;
ELSE
   Use dry agent ;
ENDIF
// Second character
IF precautionsCode is P
   Use LTS ;
   Dilute spillage ;
   Risk of explosion ;
ELSE IF...
...
ELSE
   Use BA & Fire kit ;
   Contain spillage ;
ENDIF
// Third character
IF character is E
   Public hazard ;
ENDIF
```

What about dealing with an invalid code letter?

```
// First character
IF fireFightingCode is 1
   Use coarse spray ;
ELSE IF fireFightingCode is 2
   Use fine spray ;
ELSE IF fireFightingCode is 3
   Use foam ;
```

```
ELSE IF fireFightingCode is 4
   Use dry agent ;
ELSE
   Invalid fire fighting code ;
ENDIF
// Second character
IF precautionsCode is P
   Use LTS ;
   Dilute spillage ;
   Risk of explosion ;
ELSE IF...
...
ELSE IF precautionsCode is Z
   Use BA & Fire kit ;
   Contain spillage ;
ELSE
   Invalid precautions code ;
ENDIF
// Third character
IF publicHazardCode is E
   Public hazard ;
ELSE IF publicHazardCode is blank
   No hazard ;
ELSE
   Invalid public hazard code ;
ENDIF
```

Puzzle World: Roman Numerals and Chronograms

See accompanying website.

Pangrams: Holoalphabetic Sentences

See accompanying website.

Online Bookstore: ISBNs

See accompanying website.

Chapter 7

End of Chapter Exercises

2. The Person class outline was like this:

class Person	
Properties	awake: yes, no ; inBed: yes, no ; needsShower: yes, no ; isDressed: yes, no ;

Methods	WakeUp ; GoToSleep ; GetUp ; GoToBed ; GetWashed ; GetDressed ; GetUndressed ;

Method Algorithms
WakeUp
1.   awake ← Yes ;
2.   needsShower ← Yes ;

GoToSleep
1.   awake ← No ;

GetUp
1.   inBed ← No ;

GoToBed
1.   inBed ← Yes ;

GetWashed
1.   needsShower ← No ;

GetDressed
1.   isDressed ← Yes ;

GetUndressed
1.   isDressed ← No ;

3. The Alarm class outline was like this:

class Alarm	
Properties	ringing: yes, no ; time: 00:00:00 to 23:59:00 ; alarmTime: 00:00:00 to 23:59:00 ; alarmIsSet: on, off ;
Methods	SetTime hh:mm:ss ; GetTime ; SetAlarmTime: hh:mm ; GetAlarmTime ; SetAlarm ; UnsetAlarm ; StartRinging ; SwitchOff ; (i.e. stop ringing)

Method algorithms
SetTime: hh:mm:ss
```
1.   time ← hh:mm:ss ;
```

GetTime
```
1.   Display time ;
```

SetAlarmTime: hh:mm
```
1.   alarmTime ← hh:mm ;
```

GetAlarmTime
```
1.   Display alarmTime ;
```

SetAlarm
```
1.   alarmIsSet ← on ;
```

UnsetAlarm
```
1.   alarmIsSet ← off ;
```

StartRinging
```
1.   ringing ← yes ;
```

SwitchOff
```
1.   ringing ← no ;
```

4. Algorithm for counting sleeping people.
```
1.   stillInBed ← 0 ;
2.   WHILE (Person objects to look at)
        2.1.  tell Person BedStatus: answer ;
        2.2.  IF (answer = 'yes')
                 2.2.1.  stillInBed ← stillInBed + 1 ;
              ENDIF
        2.3.  Move to next Person object ;
     ENDWHILE
4.   Display stillInBed ;
```

6. i) Clothing classes.

class Socks	
Properties	beingWorn: yes, no ; dirty: yes, no wholePair: yes, no // **one sock may be missing**
Operations	PutOn ; TakeOff ; Wash ; Dispose ; // **if one sock is missing!**

class Underwear	
Properties	beingWorn: yes, no ; dirty: yes, no ;
Operations	PutOn ; TakeOff ; Wash ;

class Trousers	
Properties	beingWorn: yes, no ; dirty: yes, no ; Belt ; (class)
Operations	PutOn ; TakeOff ; DryClean ; ThreadBelt ; RemoveBelt ;

class Shirt	
Properties	beingWorn: yes, no ; dirty: yes, no ; wrinkled: yes, no ;
Operations	PutOn ; TakeOff ; Wash ; Iron ;

class Shoes	
Properties	beingWorn: yes, no ; dirty: yes, no ; wholePair: yes, no Laces ; (class)
Operations	PutOn ; TakeOff ; Polish ; ThreadLaces ; RemoveLaces ; Dispose ;

ii) Instantiation of objects.

```
tanPleats ← new Trousers ;
whiteBoxers ← new Underwear ;
blackAnkles ← new Socks ;
brownBrogues ← new Shoes ;
whiteLongSleeve ← new Shirt ;
```

iii) Calling methods.

```
tell tanPleats PutOn ;
tell whiteBoxers PutOn ;
tell blackAnkles PutOn ;
tell brownBrogues PutOn ;
tell whiteLongSleeve PutOn ;
```

Chapter 7 Projects

No solutions for projects.

Chapter 8

End of Chapter Exercises

1. Flowchart for coffee making problem

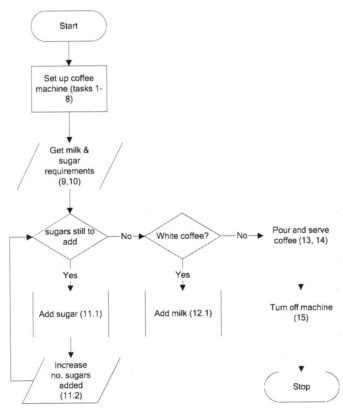

2. Tree diagram for coffee making problem

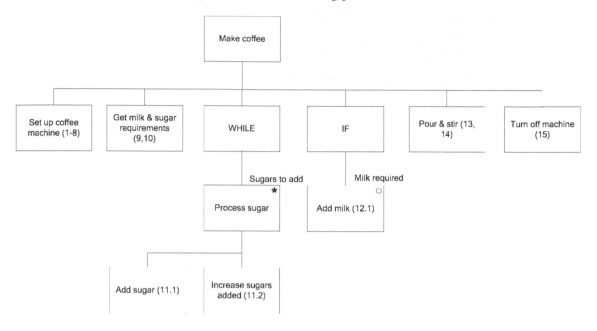

Chapter 8 Projects

No solutions provided as they are highly dependent on how you have structured your own solutions over the previous chapters.

Chapter 9
End of Chapter Exercises

1. A variable is an area of memory set aside to hold values. The value of the variable can be changed as the program runs. The value held in the variable is accessed via the variable's name, or identifier. A literal is simply a raw value which is not stored anywhere. For example, in the statement

   number ← 3 + number2 ;

   the variable number is assigned the value of the expression 3 + number2 where number2 is also a variable and 3 is a literal value.
2. No. They are real values and intNumber is an integer.
4. integer = 2,147,483,647, shortint = 32,767, byte = 127, longint = 9,223,372,036,854,775,807. See Table 9.2.
6. Storing individual occurrences of character symbols. For instance, you might want to keep a loop going every time the user presses the "Y" key on the keyboard in response to a prompt. The key pressed by the user could be stored in a character variable.
8. Simple, just remove the "= true" part:

```
IF ( onVacation )
  Display ('No milk today, thankyou') ;
ENDIF
```

10. 1: Multiplication comes before addition, so 3 + 28 = 31
    2: Multiplication comes before addition, so 28 + 3 = 31
    3: Expressions in parentheses evaluated first, so 28 + 3 = 31
    4: Expressions in parentheses evaluated first , so 4 times 10 = 40
    5: Multiplications done before the addition, so 28 + 24 = 52
    6: Parentheses, then multiplication, then addition, so 4 times 10 times 8 = 320
    7: All operators here of equal precedence so just work from left to right, so 28 divided by 2 = 14, then multiply by 3 = 42, then divide by 21 = 2
    8: Exponentiation comes first, so $3 \wedge 3$ = 27. Then work left to right: 28 divided by 2 = 14, multiply by 27 = 378, then divide by 21 = 18

12. The principal components of the problem are to do with whether the person is an adult, is a resident, is a Lord, is imprisoned, has a conviction, and is mentally incapable. We can declare Boolean variables to hold these values as well as the variable eligibleToVote:

    boolean: isAdult ,
    isResident ,
    isALord ,
    isImprisoned ,
    isMentallyIncapable ,
    hasConviction ,
    eligibleToVote ;

    Assuming the program has assigned values to the first six variables, we can assign eligibleToVote thus:

    eligibleToVote ← ((isResident) AND (isAdult)
                    AND NOT (isALord)
              AND NOT (isImprisoned) AND
              NOT (isMentallyIncapable) AND
              NOT (hasConviction)) ;

    With all the NOTs we could use parentheses and De Morgan to simplify the expression:

    eligibleToVote ← ((isResident) AND (isAdult) AND
                    NOT ((isALord) OR (isImprisoned) OR
                    (isMentallyIncapable) OR
                    (hasConviction)) ;

14. The first thing I would do if using a real programming language would be to look through the language's manual and see if it already has existing functions or procedures for doing this. Most languages have a ToUpper rou-

tine of some description. If this were the case then it would be a simple matter of:

```
theLetter ← ToUpper (theLetter) ;
```

job done! However, to do it from scratch we need to use what we know about character codes. All the lower case letters have ASCII codes between 97 ('a') and 122 ('z'). The upper case letters live in the range 65 ('A') to 90 ('Z'). The simple form of the problem is to assume that theLetter contains a lower case letter and we just need to set it to the character 32 places earlier in the character set. For example, 'a' = 97, subtract 32 gives 65 which is 'A'. The full problem requires us first to ascertain whether the character in theLetter is really a lower case letter. Put this all together using the Ord and Chr routines discussed in Section 9.1.5 and we get:

```
integer:newCharNumber ;
IF (theLetter ≥ 'a') AND (theLetter ≤ 'z')
    newCharNumber ← Ord (theLetter) - 32 ;
theLetter ← Chr (newCharNumber) ;
ENDIF
```

We could do it without the new variable newCharNumber like this:

```
IF (theLetter ≥ 'a') AND (theLetter ≤ 'z')
    theLetter ← Chr (Ord (theLetter) - 32) ;
ENDIF
```

Chapter 9 projects

StockSnackz Vending Machine

```
integer:chocolateStock,
        muesliStock,
        cheesePuffStock,
        appleStock,
        popcornStock ;
```

Stocksfield Fire Service: Hazchem Signs

```
character:fireFightingCode,
        precautionsCode,
        publicHazardCode ;
Get (keyboard, REFERENCE:fireFightingCode,
REFERENCE:precautionsCode, REFERENCE:publicHazardCode) ;
// First character
```

```
IF ([fireFightingCode] = '1')
   Display ('Use coarse spray⏎') ;
ELSE IF ([fireFightingCode] = '2' )
   Display ('Use fine spray⏎') ;
ELSE IF ([fireFightingCode] = '3')
   Display ('Use foam⏎') ;
ELSE IF ([fireFightingCode] = '4')
   Display ('Use dry agent⏎') ;
ELSE
   Display ('Invalid fire fighting code⏎') ;
ENDIF
// Second character
IF ([precautionsCode] = 'P')
   Display ('Use LTS⏎') ;
   Display (Dilute 'spillage⏎') ;
   Display ('Risk of explosion⏎') ;
ELSE IF...
...
ELSE IF ([precautionsCode] = 'Z')
   Display ('Use BA & Fire kit⏎') ;
   Display ('Contain spillage⏎') ;
ELSE
   Display ('Invalid precautions code⏎') ;
ENDIF
// Third character
IF ([publicHazardCode] = 'E')
   Display ('Public hazard⏎') ;
ELSE IF ([publicHazardCode] = ' ')
   Display ('No hazard') ;
ELSE
   Display ('Invalid public hazard code⏎') ;
ENDIF
```

Alternatively, we could access the EAC as a string:

```
string:[EAC] ;
Get (keyboard, REFERENCE:[EAC]) ;
IF ([EAC][0] = '1')
   Display...
```

Puzzle World: Roman Numerals and Chronograms

See accompanying website.

Pangrams: Holoalphabetic Sentences

See accompanying website.

Online Bookstore: ISBNs

See accompanying website.

Chapter 10

End of Chapter Exercises

1. In short, a procedure goes away and does something; a function goes away and does something and then gives you an answer back. Functions always return a value.

2. The RETURN statement is missing:

   ```
   FUNCTION FahrenheitToCelsius (real: fahrenheit )RETURNS real
       real: celsius  ;
       celsius  ← ( fahrenheit  − 32) ÷ 1.8 ;
       RETURN  celsius  ;
   ENDFUNCTION
   ```

   We don't need the extra variable celsius and could write instead:

   ```
   FUNCTION FahrenheitToCelsius (real: fahrenheit )RETURNS real
       RETURN ( fahrenheit  − 32) ÷ 1.8 ;
   ENDFUNCTION
   ```

4.
   ```
   FUNCTION Date (integer: day , integer: month , integer: year ,
                  boolean: UKFormat ) RETURNS string ;
       string: theDate  ;
       theDate  ← '' ;
       IF ( UKFormat )
           theDate  ←  theDate  +  day  + '/' +  month  + '/' +  year  ;
       ELSE
           theDate  ←  theDate  +  month  + '/' +  day  + '/' +  year  ;
       ENDIF
       RETURN  theDate  ;
   ENDFUNCTION
   ```

7.
   ```
   PROCEDURE Swap (REFERENCE:integer: a , REFERENCE:integer: b )
       integer: temp  ;
       temp  ←  a  ;
   ```

```
a ← b ;
b ← temp ;
ENDPROCEDURE
```

If you want to be really perverse and make it hard to understand, try this version which doesn't use a temporary variable:

```
PROCEDURE Swap (REFERENCE:integer:a, REFERENCE:integer:b)
    a ← a + b ;
    b ← a - b ;
    a ← a - b ;
ENDPROCEDURE
```

If you don't believe me, try it out with different values for a and b. It doesn't matter if a is greater than or less than b or if a or b is negative.

8.
```
FUNCTION IsEven (integer:number) RETURNS Boolean ;
IF (number MOD 2 = 0)
    RETURN True ;
ELSE
    RETURN False ;
ENDFUNCTION
```

Chapter 10 Projects

StockSnackz Vending Machine

The exercise was fairly open ended so no model solution is provided: there are several possible ways of meeting the aims.

Stocksfield Fire Service: Hazchem Signs

Turn it into a function that displays messages and returns True if no codes were invalid otherwise return False.

```
FUNCTION ProcessEAC (string:) RETURNS boolean
    boolean:valid ;
    valid ← True ;
    IF (EAC [0] = '1')
        Display ('Use coarse spray↵') ;
    ELSE IF (EAC [0] = '2')
        Display ('Use fine spray↵') ;
    ELSE IF (EAC [0] = '3')
        Display ('Use foam↵') ;
```

```
        ELSE IF ([EAC] [0] = '4')
            Display ('Use dry agent↲') ;
        ELSE
            Display ('Invalid fire fighting code↲') ;
            [valid] ← False ;
        ENDIF
```
// Process precautions
```
        IF ([EAC] [1] = 'P')
            Display ('Use LTS↲') ;
            Display (Dilute 'spillage↲') ;
            Display ('Risk of explosion↲') ;
            ...
        ELSE IF ([EAC] [1] = 'Z')
            Display ('Use BA & Fire kit↲') ;
            Display ('Contain spillage↲') ;
        ELSE
            Display ('Invalid precautions code↲') ;
            [valid] ← False ;
            ENDIF
```
// Process public hazard
```
        IF ([EAC] [2] = 'E')
            Display ('Public hazard↲') ;
        IF ([EAC] [2] = ' ')
            Display ('No hazard↲') ;
        ELSE
            Display ('Invalid public hazard code↲') ;
            [valid] ← False ;
        ENDIF
```

Puzzle World: Roman Numerals and Chronograms

See accompanying website.

Pangrams: Holoalphabetic Sentences

See accompanying website.

Online Bookstore: ISBNs

See accompanying website.

Chapter 11

End of Chapter Exercises

1. First solution to file writing section:

```
WHILE NOT (EndOfFile ([salaryFile]))
    Get ([salaryFile], REFERENCE:name, REFERENCE:[salary]) ;
    Display ([name], ':', [salary]↵) ;
    Write ([reportFile], [name], [salary]) ;
    IF ([salary] > 25000)
        Write ([reportFile], 'High'↵) ;
    ELSE
        Write ([reportFile], 'Normal'↵) ;
    ENDIF
ENDWHILE
```

Second solution to file writing section:

```
string:[salarySize] ;
WHILE NOT (EndOfFile ([salaryFile]))
    Get ([salaryFile], REFERENCE:[name], REFERENCE:[salary]) ;
    Display ([name], ':', [salary]↵) ;
    IF ([salary] > 25000)
        [salarySize] ← 'High' ;
    ELSE
        [salarySize] ← 'Normal' ;
    ENDIF
    Write ([reportFile], [name], [salary], [salarySize]↵) ;
ENDWHILE
```

2. Get needs to take a reference parameter:

```
Get (keyboard, REFERENCE:[myNumber]) ;
```

4. Errors in the distances algorithm. A new statement is needed before statement 9 to open the distances file. Statement 9.1 needs reference parameters. Statement 9.2 needs to divide by 1000 to convert from meters to km. Changes are shown below in bold with bold line number.

```
1.  integer:[metersPerNM] IS 1852 ;
2.  string:[city] ;
3.  real:[distance],
4.  [distanceInKM] ;
5.  file:[distancesFile] ;
6.  [distancesFile] ← distances.txt' ;
```

7. Display ('Distances of cities from Stocksfield (km)↵') ;
8. Display ('~~~~~~~~~~~~~~~~~~~~~~~~~~~~~~~~↵') ;
9. **Open** ([distancesFile]) ;
10. WHILE NOT EndOfFile ([distancesFile])
    10.1. Get ([distancesFile], **REFERENCE:**[city],
             REFERENCE:[distance]) ;
    10.2. [distanceInKM] ← [distance] × [metersPerNM] ÷ **1000** ;
    10.3. Display ([city], '=', [distanceinKM] ,'km'↵) ;
    ENDWHILE
11. Close ([distancesFile]) ;

Chapter 11 Projects

StockSnackz Vending Machine

See accompanying website.

Stocksfield Fire Service: Hazchem Signs

In the main program we can declare the file:

file:[logFile] ;
[logFile] ← 'log.txt' ;
Open ([logFile]) ;

Now we can add the file outputs to the function.

```
FUNCTION ProcessEAC (string:EAC) RETURNS boolean
    boolean:valid ;
    valid ← True ;
    IF (EAC [0] = '1')
        Display ('Use coarse spray↵') ;
        Write (logFile, 'Use coarse spray↵') ;
    ELSE IF (EAC [0] = '2')
        Display ('Use fine spray↵') ;
        Write (logFile, 'Use fine spray↵') ;
//...and so on.
ENDFUNCTION
```

More properly, we should really pass the log file as a parameter to the function.

Puzzle World: Roman Numerals and Chronograms

See accompanying website.

Pangrams: Holoalphabetic Sentences

See accompanying website.

Online Bookstore: ISBNs

See accompanying website.

Chapter 12

End of Chapter Exercises

1. 10 – index 4 is the fifth element.
   4 – index 1 is the second element.
   14 – index 6 is the seventh element.
   2 – index 0 is the first element.
   Error – index 7 doesn't exist; the array elements are numbered from 0 to 6.

2. The array `salesData` has 25 rows and 12 columns.

3. Arrays use zero-based indexing, so the tenth row will be index 9 and the sixth column will be index 5. The row index always comes before the column index, so statement (e) is the one we want.

4. FUNCTION MaxIndex (**ARRAY:**theArray) RETURNS **integer**
       RETURN Length (theArray) − 1 ;
   ENDFUNCTION

6. To delete one item without closing the gaps:

   PROCEDURE DeleteItem (**REFERENCE:ARRAY:**theBasket, **integer:**index)
       theBasket [index] ← 0 ;
   ENDPROCEDURE

   But to close the gaps:

   PROCEDURE DeleteItem (**REFERENCE:ARRAY:**theBasket, **integer:**index)
       integer:count ;
       FOR count GOES FROM index + 1 TO MaxIndex (theBasket)
           theBasket [index-1] ← theBasket [index] ;
           theBasket [index] ← 0 ;
       ENDFOR
   ENDPROCEDURE

   Note, the setting of each element to 0 after it has been copied could be avoided if we also keep track of the index of the current last item in the basket, with a variable called `lastIndex`, say. Then, we simply copy items back from index to `lastIndex` and then set the element at `lastIndex` to zero.

8. Patient records.

   NEWTYPE **AddressRecord** IS
       RECORD
       string:streetAddressLine1,
               streetAddressLine2,

```
                              postalTown ,
                              post Code  ;
              ENDRECORD
          NEWTYPE DateRecord IS
              RECORD
              integer: day ,
                       month ,
                       year  ;
              ENDRECORD
          NEWTYPE PatientRecord IS
              RECORD
              string:  title ,
                       familyName ,
                       givenName  ;
              AddressRecord: address  ;
              string: telephone  ;
              DateRecord: birthDate ,
                          joinDate  ,
                          checkup date ,
              ENDRECORD
```

Chapter 12 Projects

StockSnackz Vending Machine

See accompanying website.

Stocksfield Fire Service: Hazchem Signs

Make use of function Ord (character) RETURNS integer.

```
ARRAY: fireCodes  OF [4] string ← {'Use coarse spray↵', 'Use fine spray↵',
                                   'Use foam↵', 'Use dry agent↵'} ;
    Get (keyboard, REFERENCE: EAC ) ;
    Display ( fireCodes [Ord]( EAC [0])-49]) ;
    // Why -49? think about array indexing


    // How do we deal with invalid codes?
    IF (( EAC [0] ≥ '1') AND ( EAC [0] ≤ '4'))
        Display ( fireCodes [Ord( EAC [0])-49]) ;
    ELSE
        Display ('Invalid fire fighting code↵') ;
    ENDIF
```

Or, longhanded:

```
integer:ordinalCode,
        numericCode ;
character:code ;
code ← EAC [0] ;
ordinalCode ← Ord (code) ;
numericCode ← ordinalCode − 48 // ASCII code 48 = '0', so
                                // subtracting 48 turns character
                                // into numeric equivalent
Display (fireCodes [numericCode −1]) ; // subtract 1 because of
                                        // zero-based array indexing
```

Puzzle World: Roman Numerals and Chronograms

See accompanying website.

Pangrams: Holoalphabetic Sentences

See accompanying website.

Online Bookstore: ISBNs

See accompanying website.

Chapter 13

End of Chapter Exercises

1. Stacks are built by (metaphorically) placing data items one on top of the other. They are implemented using a list structure, but items are only added to the head and removed from the head. Therefore, the last item added is the first one that can be removed.

2. A queue end pointer is also needed as whilst records are removed from the head new records are added to the end (just like a real queue in a bank).

3. We would not be able to gain access to any records in the list because the entry point is the address held in the head pointer. Without the head pointer we cannot locate the first record in the list. In effect, the list would become lost.

5. Simply change the condition from

```
WHILE (current ≠ NULL) AND (searchTitle > current→.bookTitle)
to
WHILE (current ≠ NULL) AND (searchTitle < current→.bookTitle)
```

9. This is really quite straightforward. FindSortedNode uses the following WHILE condition to find the appropriate place in the list:

```
WHILE (current ≠ NULL) AND (searchTitle > current→.bookTitle)
```

All we need to do is compare the upper-case versions of the two titles. A small function ToUpperString (which uses the previous character function

ToUpper from Chapter 10) to return the upper-case version of a string would look thus:

```
FUNCTION ToUpperString(string:theString) RETURNS string
    integer:counter ;
    string:upper ;
    upper ← '' ;
    FOR counter GOES FROM 0 TO Length (theString)−1
        upper ← upper + ToUpper ( theString[ counter]) ;
    ENDFOR
    RETURN upper ;
ENDFUNCTION
```

All we then need to do is use this function in the WHILE loop:

```
WHILE (current ≠ NULL) AND (ToUpperString(searchTitle)>
                                ToUpperString(current→.bookTitle))
```

Chapter 13 Projects

StockSnackz Vending Machine

No exercises for this project.

Stocksfield Fire Service: Hazchem Signs

Make linked list of codes and strings.

```
NEWTYPE FireCodeRecord IS
    RECORD
    character:code ;
    string:fightingMethod ;
    →FireCodeRecord:next ;
    ENDRECORD
NEWTYPE PrecautionCodeRecord IS
    RECORD
    character:code ;
    string:explosionRisk ;
    string:precaution ;
    string:treatmentMethod ;
    →PrecautionCodeRecord:next ;
    ENDRECORD
    →FireCodeRecord:fcHead ;
    →PrecautionCodeRecord:pcHead ;
// Code for building lists
...
//
```

```
FUNCTION processEAC (string:EAC), →FireCodeRecord:fcListHead,
                          →PrecautionCodeRecord:pcListHead)
                     RETURNS Boolean
    →FireCodeRecord:fcCurrent ;
    →PrecautionCodeRecord:pcCurrent ;
    boolean:valid ;
    valid ← True ;
// Deal with fire fighting method
    fcCurrent ← fcListHead ;
    WHILE NOT ((EAC [0] = fcCurrent→.code) OR (fcCurrent =
NULL))
        fcCurrent ← fcCurrent→.next ;
    ENDWHILE
    IF fcCurrent ≠ NULL
        Display (fcCurrent→.fightingMethod) ;
    ELSE
        Display ('Invalid fire fighting code↵') ;
        valid ← false ;
    ENDIF
    // Deal with precautions
    pcCurrent ← pcListHead ;
    WHILE NOT ((EAC [1] = pcCurrent→.code) OR (pcCurrent =
NULL))
        fcCurrent ← fcCurrent→.next ;
    ENDWHILE
    IF pcCurrent ≠ NULL
        IF (pcCurrent→.explosionRisk) ≠ '')
            Display (pcCurrent→.explosionRisk) ;
        ENDIF
        Display (pcCurrent→.precaution) ;
        Display (pcCurrent→.treatmentMethod) ;
    ELSE
        Display ('Invalid precautions code↵') ;
        valid ← false ;
    ENDIF
    // Deal with public hazard
    IF(EAC [2] = 'E')
        Display ('Public hazard↵') ;
    ELSE IF EAC [2] = ' ')
        Display ('No hazard↵') ;
    ELSE
```

```
            Display ('Invalid public hazard code↵') ;
            valid ← False ;
        ENDIF
        RETURN valid ;
    ENDFUNCTION
```

Puzzle World: Roman Numerals and Chronograms

See accompanying website.

Pangrams: Holoalphabetic Sentences

See accompanying website.

Online Bookstore: ISBNs

See accompanying website.

Chapter 14

End of Chapter Exercises

1. METHOD WinLoseRatio RETURNS **real**
```
    IF (numberGamesLost > 0) AND (numberGamesWon > 0)
        RETURN numberGamesWon ÷ numberGamesLost ;
    ELSE
        RETURN numberGamesWon ;
    ENDIF
ENDMETHOD
```

2. IF rxforwar.WinLoseRatio > 1.0
```
    Display ('Congratulations, you have a good Win:Lose ratio') ;
ELSE
    Display (' Sorry, your Win:Lose ratio is low and you need more
    practice') ;
ENDIF
```

3. CLASS:**LeaguePlayer** EXTENDS **Player**
```
    // Properties
    string: name ;
    integer: numLeageGamesPlayed,
             numLeagueGamesWon,
             numLeagueGamesLost ;
    // Constructors
    METHOD Player (string: aName)
        Super (aName) ;
    ENDMETHOD
    ...
```

```
METHOD WinLoseRatio RETURNS real
    IF ([numLeagueGamesLost] > 0) AND ([numLeagueGamesWon] > 0)
        RETURN [numLeagueGamesWon] ÷ [numLeagueGamesLost] ;
    ELSE
        RETURN [numLeagueGamesWon] ;
    ENDIF
ENDMETHOD
// rest of the methods, as before
...
ENDCLASS
```

Chapter 14 Projects

No solutions provided as they will be highly dependent on how you have structured your own solutions over the previous chapters.

Chapter 15

End of Chapter Exercises

There are no specific exercises for this chapter.

Chapter 15 Projects

No solutions provided as they will be highly dependent on how you have structured your own solutions over the previous chapters.

Chapter 16

End of Chapter Exercises

No solutions as your answer will depend on what algorithms you have chosen to work with.

Chapter 16 Projects

No solutions for projects.

Table 2.2   How To Think Like A Programmer (HTTLAP)

1. Understanding the problem

You have to understand the problem. Do not go to the next stage until you have done this.

Sleep on the problem and come back to it fresh.

What are you being asked to do? What is required? Try restating the problem? Can the problem be better expressed by drawing a diagram or a picture? By using mathematical notation? By building a model out of wood, paper, or card?

What is the *unknown*? Is finding the unknown part of the problem statement? Write down what you **do know** about the problem.
Have you made any assumptions? If so, what can/should you do about it?
What are the principal parts of the problem? Are there several parts to the problem?

2. Devising a plan to solve the problem

Start thinking about the information you have and what the solution is required to do.

Stop bothering your brain and sleep on the problem.

Have you solved this problem before (perhaps with different values/quantities)? Is this problem *similar* to one you have met before? If so, can you use any knowledge from that problem here? Does the solution to that problem apply to this one in any way?

Are some parts of the problem more easily solved than others? If the problem is too hard, can you solve a simpler version of it, or a related problem?
Does restating the problem (perhaps telling it in your own words to someone else) help you to get a grip on it? Try describing the problem in a different *language* (e.g., diagrammatically, pictorially, using mathematics, building a physical model or representation).
Did you make use of all the information in the problem statement? Can you satisfy all the conditions of the problem? Have you left anything out?

3. Carrying out the plan

Write down your solution. Pay attention to things done in order (sequence), things done conditionally (selection) and things done repeatedly (iteration).

Sleep on it again.

Write down the basic sequence of actions necessary to solve the general problem. This may involve hiding some of the detail in order to get the overall sequence correct. Is your ordering of actions correct? Does the order rely on certain things to be true? If so, do you know these things from the problem statement? Or have you made any assumptions? If you have made assumptions then how will you verify that they are correct?
If you cannot see a way to solving the whole problem can you see any parts of the problem that you can solve? If the problem is too complicated, try removing some of the conditions/constraints and seeing if that gives you a way in.
Go back to your sequence of actions. Should all actions be carried out in *every* circumstance? Should some actions (or groups/blocks of actions) only be carried out when certain conditions are met?
Go back to your sequence of actions. Is carrying out each action once only sufficient to give the desired outcome? If not, do you have actions (or groups/blocks of actions) that must therefore be *repeated*?
Go back once more. Do any of your actions/blocks of actions belong *inside* others? For example, do you have a block of actions that must be repeated, but only when some condition is met?

4. Assessing the result

Examine the results obtained when using your solution.

Get someone else to use or follow your solution.

Use your solution to meet the requirements of the problem. Did you get the right answer or the correct outcome? If not, why not? Where did your solution go wrong? If you think you did get the right answer, how can you be sure? Did any parts of the solution seem cumbersome or not very sensible? Can you make those parts simpler, quicker, or clearer?
Give your solution to someone else and ask them to use it to complete the task. Were your instructions clear enough for them? Did they have to ask for help or clarification? Did they misinterpret your instructions? If so, why?
Did they get the same answer as when you did it? If not, whose answer was correct?

5. Describing what you have learned

Make a record of your achievements and the difficulties you encountered.

What did you learn from this exercise? What do you know now that you did not know before you started?

What particular difficulties did you encounter? Were there any aspects of the problem that caused you particular difficulty? If so, do you think you would know how to tackle them if you met something similar in the future?
Compare your finished solution with your first attempt. What do the differences teach you?

6. Documenting the solution

Explain your solution. Make sure that it can be understood.

Are there any aspects of your solution that are hard to understand? Is this because they are badly written, or simply because the solution is just complicated? If you were to pick up your solution in five years time do you think any bits would be hard to understand?